Lecture Notes in Business Information Processing 569

LNBIP reports state-of-the-art results in areas related to business information systems and industrial application software development – timely, at a high level, and in both printed and electronic form.

The type of material published includes

- Proceedings (published in time for the respective event)
- Postproceedings (consisting of thoroughly revised and/or extended final papers)
- Other edited monographs (such as, for example, project reports or invited volumes)
- Tutorials (coherently integrated collections of lectures given at advanced courses, seminars, schools, etc.)
- Award-winning or exceptional theses

LNBIP is abstracted/indexed in DBLP, EI and Scopus. LNBIP volumes are also submitted for the inclusion in ISI Proceedings.

Inge van de Weerd · Bedilia Estrada Torres ·
Han van der Aa
Editors

Business Process Management Workshops

BPM 2025 International Workshops
Seville, Spain, August 31–September 5, 2025
Revised Selected Papers

Editors
Inge van de Weerd
Utrecht University
Utrecht, Utrecht, The Netherlands

Bedilia Estrada Torres
Universidad de Sevilla
Seville, Sevilla, Spain

Han van der Aa
University of Vienna
Vienna, Austria

ISSN 1865-1348 ISSN 1865-1356 (electronic)
Lecture Notes in Business Information Processing
ISBN 978-3-032-13425-7 ISBN 978-3-032-13426-4 (eBook)
https://doi.org/10.1007/978-3-032-13426-4

This Springer imprint is published by the registered company Springer Nature Switzerland AG
The registered company address is: Gewerbestrasse 11, 6330 Cham, Switzerland

Preface

The International Conference on Business Process Management (BPM) has been organized since 2003 as a forum where academics and professionals exchange ideas and insights on the latest advances in business process management. In 2025, the conference was hosted in the vibrant city of Seville, Spain, from August 31 to September 5. As in previous years, the conference was complemented by a diverse workshop program, providing space for workshops on specialized topics, cross-disciplinary challenges, and novel trends and paradigms in BPM. This volume brings together the proceedings of the BPM 2025 workshops, which were held on September 1, 2025.

BPM 2025 invited proposals for one-day or half-day workshops. During the review and acceptance process, the goal was to curate a workshop program that covered the full spectrum of BPM research. Priority was given to workshops that not only addressed engaging topics but also promised innovative formats aimed at sparking active discussions and generating new ideas. From 16 submitted proposals, four were rejected and two were merged, resulting in a list of 11 selected workshops. These included several long-established workshops, as well as new initiatives on intelligent automation and distributed ledger technologies.

Below we present an overview of the 11 workshops.

- *The 9th International Workshop on Artificial Intelligence for Business Process Management (AI4BPM)* organized by Chiara Di Francescomarino, Fabrizio Maria Maggi, Andrea Marrella, Arik Senderovich, and Emilio Sulis. The AI4BPM workshop brought together researchers and professionals to discuss how AI is reshaping BPM, both by enhancing today's practices and by paving the way for entirely new process paradigms. The program kicked off with an inspiring keynote by Marlon Dumas, followed by two sessions of paper presentations.
- *The 1st International Workshop on Implementation and Management of Intelligent Process Automation Solutions (AUTOMATE)* organized by Simone Agostinelli, Tom Hohenadl, Antonio Martínez-Rojas, Ralf Plattfaut, Ronja Rieger, and Carolin Vollenberg. The AUTOMATE workshop explored how human expertise and intelligent technologies, from lightweight tools such as RPA and ChatGPT to advanced AI and LLM solutions, can be combined to drive hyper-automation in BPM. The program featured two sessions of paper presentations, followed by a closing session in which participants collaboratively developed a manifesto.
- *The 9th International Workshop on Business Processes Meet the Internet-of-Things (BP-Meet-IoT)* organized by Agnes Koschmider, Massimo Mecella, Francesco Leotta, Estefanía Serral, and Victoria Torres. The BP-Meet-IoT workshop explored how IoT-driven automation can enhance business processes and decision-making, and opened with a keynote by the BP-Meet-IoT workshop organizers on the past and future of BP-Meet-IoT, after which a session with paper presentations followed.
- *The 5th International Workshop on Change, Drift, and Dynamics of Organizational Processes (ProDy)* organized by Christian Bartelheimer, Iris Beerepoot, Daniel

Beverungen, and Bastian Wurm. This workshop brought together diverse perspectives and research streams on change, drift, and the dynamics of business processes. The program consisted of two sessions of paper presentations and concluded with a lively panel of young researchers.

- *The 1st International Workshop on Distributed Ledger Technologies in Business Process Management (DLT4BPM)* organized by Richard Hobeck, Simon Curty, and Andrea Morichetta. The DLT4BPM workshop, as the successor to the Blockchain Forum from previous BPM conference editions, served as a platform for presenting research and applications at the intersection of distributed ledger technologies and BPM, highlighting opportunities across a wide range of industries and domains. The program opened with a keynote by Julius Köpke, followed by two sessions combining paper presentations and lightning talks that fostered lively discussions with the audience.
- *The 3rd International Workshop on Formal Methods for Business Process Management (FM-BPM)* organized by Claudio Di Ciccio, Alessandro Gianola, and Andrey Rivkin. This workshop provided a platform to explore novel approaches and applications of formal methods in BPM, highlighting their role in constructing rigorous process models and supporting simulation, automated analysis, and repair. Although one paper was submitted, the workshop was organized as a fully discussion-oriented event, fostering interactive debate on the evolving role of Formal Methods in BPM and related technical challenges[1].
- *The 2nd International Workshop on Managing Process Innovation in the Era of Digital Transformation (Innov8BPM)* organized by Banu Aysolmaz, Amy Van Looy, Oktay Turetken, Marta Indulska, Flavia Santoro, and Panagiotis Keramidis. The workshop examined how the BPM discipline must evolve to address process innovation and create business value in an era of digital transformation. It began with a keynote by Jan vom Brocke and continued with two sessions of paper presentations, complemented by an interactive discussion where participants collaboratively identified future research opportunities.
- *The 4th International Workshop on Natural Language Processing for Business Process Management (NLP4BPM)* organized by Henrik Leopold, Jana-Rebecca Rehse, and Vinicius Stein Dani. The workshop provided a forum for researchers and practitioners to present and discuss advances in applying NLP and Large Language Models (LLMs) to BPM. The program opened with a keynote by Adrian Rebmann, continued with two sessions of paper presentations, and concluded with a round-table discussion on envisioning the next frontier for NLP in BPM.
- *The 3rd International Workshop on Object-Centric Processes from A to Z (OBJECTS)* organized by Marco Montali, Andrey Rivkin, and Jan Martijn van der Werf. This workshop addressed the growing interest in the interplay between processes and objects, providing a platform to discuss open challenges and future directions in object-centricity within BPM and process mining. The program featured two sessions of paper presentations and concluded with a presentation of the challenges identified at the BuzzOs workshop at ICPM 2024, followed by a panel discussion.

---

[1] The paper submitted to this workshop is not included in this volume.

- *The 2nd International Workshop on Processes, Laws, and Compliance (PLC)* organized by Laura Genga, Hugo A. López, Emilio Sulis, and Roberto Nai. The PLC workshop provided a forum for exchanging research and ideas on data-driven and process-oriented approaches in the legal domain, fostering collaboration between experts in IT and law. The program opened with a keynote by Karolin Winter followed by a paper presentation session.
- *The 2nd International Workshop on Visual Process Analytics (VIPRA)* organized by Jana-Rebecca Rehse, Francesca Zerbato, Luise Pufahl, Stef van den Elzen, and Alessio Arleo. The workshop brought together researchers from Visual Analytics and Process Mining to explore how interactive visualizations can support data-driven BPM and foster interdisciplinary collaboration. The program featured two sessions, opening with a keynote by Maria-Cruz Villa Uriol, followed by paper presentations, and concluding with a panel discussion on the present and future of visual analytics and BPM.

In total, the workshops received 79 submissions. Each workshop had an independent Program Committee that handled the selection process, with every paper undergoing at least three single-blind reviews. Altogether, 39 papers were accepted for presentation, corresponding to an acceptance rate of 49%. In addition, keynote speakers were invited to submit a contribution related to their presentation. This resulted in four invited short papers and two abstracts, reflecting the speakers' own preference for either writing a short paper or providing an abstract of their talk.

We warmly thank all workshop proposers, organizers, authors, reviewers, keynote speakers, presenters, and participants of the BPM 2025 workshops for their contributions to a successful workshop day. We are also grateful to the BPM 2025 General Chairs and local organizers in Seville for creating such a welcoming atmosphere and making the event truly enjoyable, and to the Proceedings Chairs for their support in producing this volume.

September 2025

Inge van de Weerd
Bedilia Estrada Torres
Han van der Aa

9th International Workshop on Artificial Intelligence for Business Process Management (AI4BPM 2025)

With the growing importance of Artificial Intelligence (AI), several novel methodologies and techniques are emerging and being applied across a wide range of domains. In particular, the application of AI methods to Business Process Management (BPM) has recently attracted the attention of both industry and academia. The use of AI in BPM is increasingly discussed as one of the emerging technologies that will impact almost all business process activities performed by humans. In some cases, AI will dramatically simplify human interaction with processes, while in others it will enable full automation of tasks that have traditionally required manual effort. We believe that, in the future, AI may have a significant impact across all phases of the BPM lifecycle: modeling, analysis, automation, implementation, and monitoring. Future AI-augmented BPM technologies will enable continuous improvement and adaptation through experiential learning, thereby supporting humans in tasks such as analysis and decision making.

The goal of the AI4BPM workshop is to establish a forum for researchers and professionals interested in understanding, envisioning, and discussing the challenges and opportunities of moving from current, largely programmatic approaches to BPM, toward emerging forms of AI-driven BPM.

This year, in his keynote speech, Marlon Dumas presented his vision for AI-Augmented Business Process Management Systems (ABPMS): process-aware systems that sense, reason, and act within human-defined boundaries to continuously adapt and improve processes in an explainable and conversational manner. In addition, the workshop attracted 14 submissions on a variety of topics, including Predictive Process Monitoring, the use of LLMs for process modeling, process discovery, and variant shift discovery. All submissions were reviewed by at least three program committee members (or their sub-reviewers), and seven papers were ultimately accepted.

Grigore et al. present an offline framework for detecting process changes through multi-dimensional profiling of trace variants, combining activity sequences, control-flow patterns, and temporal dynamics with discrete wavelet transforms. He et al. introduce I3SP, a novel encoder-decoder architecture for suffix prediction that integrates both intra-case behavior (trace prefixes) and inter-case dependencies (log prefixes), eliminating the need for handcrafted features. Parschew and Bala propose an approach for predicting task completion in software development processes by transforming low-level events from version control systems into meaningful process activities and analyzing them using time-series methods. Wang et al. present a dual-input framework for outcome-oriented Predictive Business Process Monitoring that models both event- and sequence-level attributes through a duration-aware pseudo-embedding strategy. Elhami et al. conduct a Systematic Literature Review (SLR) on Decision Mining (DM), identifying existing approaches, algorithms, datasets, and tools while highlighting the field's fragmented terminology and conceptual definitions. To this end, the authors developed the SLRO-DM ontology and instantiated it as a machine-readable Knowledge Graph (DM-KG). Brissard et al. systematically investigate Process Model Representations (PMRs) for Process Modeling with LLMs, comparing their structural properties, strengths, and limitations through both conceptual and empirical evaluation. Finally, Kalenkova et al. present an approach for discovering coordinated mis/disinformation processes in social networks by leveraging stochastic Petri nets to capture both the stochastic dynamics of information spread and the structural properties of online networks.

The presentation of each paper stimulated lively discussion and questions from the audience. The workshop reaffirmed its position as a key venue for researchers working on the application of AI techniques in the BPM field.

Organization

Organizing Committee

Chiara Di Francescomarino	University of Trento, Italy
Fabrizio Maria Maggi	Free University of Bozen-Bolzano, Italy
Andrea Marrella	Sapienza Università di Roma, Italy
Arik Senderovich	York University, Canada
Emilio Sulis	University of Turin, Italy

Program Committee

Simone Agostinelli	Mercatorum University of Rome, Italy
Anti Alman	University of Tartu, Estonia
Patrizio Bellan	FBK, Italy
Andrei Buliga	FBK, Italy
Marco Comuzzi	Ulsan Institute, South Korea
Francesco Corcoglioniti	Free University of Bozen-Bolzano, Italy
Claudio Di Ciccio	Utrecht University, The Netherlands
Sebastiano Dissegna	University of Trento, Italy
Ivan Donadello	Free University of Bozen-Bolzano, Italy
Joerg Evermann	Memorial University of Newfoundland, Canada
Stephan Fahrenkrog-Petersen	Humboldt University of Berlin, Germany
Peter Fettke	DFKI, Germany
Francesco Folino	CNR, Italy
Fabiana Fournier	IBM Research AI, Israel
Krzysztof Kluza	AGH University of Science and Technology, Poland
Henrik Leopold	Kühne Logistics University, Germany
Francesco Leotta	Sapienza University of Rome, Italy
Lior Limonad	IBM Research AI, Israel
Elisa Marengo	University of Turin, Italy
Francesca Meneghello	FBK and Sapienza University of Rome, Italy
Roberto Nai	University of Turin, Italy
Andrey Rivkin	Technical University of Denmark, Denmark
Massimiliano Ronzani	Fondazione Bruno Kessler, Italy
Giulia Ruffini	University of Turin, Italy
Tijs Slaats	University of Copenhagen, Denmark

Heiner Stuckenschmidt	University of Mannheim, Germany
Stefano Tedeschi	Università della Valle d'Aosta, Italy
Daniele Theseider Dupré	University of Eastern Piedmont, Italy
Matteo Zavatteri	University of Padua, Italy

1st International Workshop on Implementation and Management of Intelligent Process Automation Solutions (AUTOMATE 2025)

Process Automation technologies are rapidly transforming how organizations execute and manage business processes. Ranging from lightweight, low-code/no-code tools to advanced systems combining human expertise with Artificial Intelligence (AI), Machine Learning (ML), Natural Language Processing (NLP), and Large Language Models (LLMs) solutions, the spectrum of process automation offers both significant opportunities and complex challenges. This workshop aims to provide a holistic perspective on process automation, addressing both the managerial and engineering aspects from a Business Process Management (BPM) perspective.

In total, the workshop attracted 12 international submissions on a diverse range of topics around process automation. All submissions were reviewed by three Program Committee members, which led to the acceptance of six papers. These six show the full range of topics mentioned above.

Janiesch et al. propose 12 process patterns for human-machine interaction based on previously established levels of automation to enable the design of process-aware systems with varying degrees of independence. Authors have consolidated these levels using an integrative literature review and evaluated the results though an interview study.

Giaccio et al. adapt a methodology originally developed for evaluating Business Process Management Systems to assess RPA tools. It supports selection and ranking of key characteristics, enabling both exploratory analysis and theoretical/practical evaluation tailored to organizational needs. A real-world study demonstrates its effectiveness: from an initial set of 30 commercial RPA tools, two were identified as most suitable for the client, showing the methodology can quickly highlight the most promising RPA solutions.

Rodríguez-Ruiz et al. propose a hybrid approach that aims to integrate AI agents, more specifically, Graphical User Interface (GUI) agents, into the RPA lifecycle. More precisely, the paper proposes to integrate them within the monitoring stage — when the automation is already deployed — with the objective of handling UI-related exceptions by taking control of the process execution when needed. The findings of the paper show promising results for this approach to be integrated as a solution to UI-related exceptions during robot execution, thus, potentially reducing the need for manual intervention and preventing automation workflows from being blocked until robots are updated.

Kurowski et al. develop the UNstructured Document REtrieval SyStem (UNDRESS), a system that uses fuzzy regular expressions, techniques for natural language processing, and large language models to enable RPA platforms to effectively retrieve information from unstructured documents. The research involved the design and development of a prototype system, and its subsequent evaluation based on text extraction and information retrieval performance. The results demonstrate the effectiveness of UNDRESS in enhancing RPA capabilities for unstructured data, providing a significant advancement in the field. The findings suggest that this system could facilitate broader RPA adoption across processes traditionally hindered by unstructured data, thereby improving overall business process efficiency.

Jarijch et al. report on a pre-study to closely examine in what ways elements of automation affect knowledge worker skills. The paper also highlights two gaps in the literature regarding the context in which optimal automation effects occur and the lack of research regarding reskilling.

Finally, Skolik proposes the PM2RPA method, which allows process-driven development while focusing on systems integration and reporting, resulting in a structured and comprehensive method for developing RPA bots.

Together, these contributions illustrate the breadth of current research and the relevance of process automation for both academia and industry. They highlight the pressing need for methods, tools, and insights that can guide organizations in navigating the rapidly evolving automation landscape.

We would like to thank all authors who submitted their work to AUTOMATE 2025, the Program Committee for their careful reviews, and the BPM 2025 organizers for their support in hosting this workshop. We hope this event will serve as a catalyst for advancing process automation and inspire future collaborations at the intersection of research and practice. Encouraged by the strong reception of this first edition, we look forward to continuing this momentum and fostering the growth of AUTOMATE in the years to come.

Organization

Organizing Committee

Name	Affiliation
Simone Agostinelli	Mercatorum University of Rome, Italy
Tom Hohenadl	KU Eichstätt-Ingolstadt, Germany
Antonio Martínez-Rojas	University of Seville, Spain
Ralf Plattfaut	University of Duisburg-Essen, Germany
Ronja Rieger	University of Duisburg-Essen, Germany
Carolin Vollenberg	University of Duisburg-Essen, Germany

Program Committee

Name	Affiliation
Aleksandre Asatiani	University of Gothenburg, Sweden
Bernhard Axmann	Technische Hochschule Ingolstadt, Germany
Andreas Eckhardt	University of Innsbruck, Austria
Edona Elshan	University of St. Gallen, Switzerland
José González Enríquez	University of Seville, Spain
Mahendrawathi E. R.	Sepuluh Nopember Institute of Technology, Indonesia
Peter Fettke	German Research Center for Artificial Intelligence (DFKI) and Saarland University, Germany
Christian Janiesch	TU Dortmund University, Germany
Andrés Jiménez Ramírez	University of Seville, Spain
Marlon Kampmann	South Westphalia University of Applied Sciences, Germany
Damian Kedziora	LUT University, Finland
Kelly Kurowski	Utrecht University, The Netherlands
Andrea Marrella	Sapienza University of Rome, Italy
Artur Modlinski	University of Łódź, Poland
Manuel García Romero	University of Seville, Spain
Petr Průcha	Technical University of Liberec, Czech Republic
Jana-Rebecca Rehse	Universität Mannheim, Germany
José Luis Alonso Rocha	University of Seville, Spain
Rehan Syed	Queensland University of Technology, Australia
Alexander Skolik	University of Paderborn, Germany
Moe Wynn	Queensland University of Technology, Australia

9th International Workshop on Business Processes Meet Internet of Things (BP-Meet-IoT 2025)

The Internet of Things (IoT) has introduced a large network of connected devices equipped with sensors and actuators that are transforming how we manage business processes. IoT actuators enable task automation, while sensors provide real-time data that open new possibilities for process insights such as timely detection of bottlenecks, improved predictions, and efficient process automation. Integrating IoT into Business Process Management (BPM) makes processes more flexible, efficient, and responsive, helping organizations adapt to changing needs. Combining these two fields can also drive innovation beyond traditional business domains, reaching areas like smart cities, smart factories, smart homes, smart agriculture, and e-health. However, while the potential is significant, this integration also brings important challenges that must be addressed. The goal of BP-Meet-IoT is to attract novel research at the intersection of these two areas by bringing together practitioners and researchers from both communities who are interested in IoT-enhanced business processes.

The following main topics were welcomed in the workshop:

- Modeling IoT-aware business processes
- Dealing with context in IoT-aware business processes
- Privacy and security in IoT-aware business processes
- Connection of analytical processes with IoT
- Dealing with unstructured environments
- Specifying the autonomy level of IoT things
- Improving resource monitoring and quality of task execution
- IoT and ubiquitous technologies supporting BPM
- Sensor-based task management in BPM
- Business examples of IoT technologies applied to ubiquitous BPs
- IoT log preprocessing techniques

This workshop edition consisted of two sessions: a keynote and a presentation of the accepted research papers.

The keynote was given by Agnes Koschmider, Estefanía Serral, and Victoria Torres, who presented, respectively: the interesting story of how the workshop started; an overview of the workshop editions, summarizing the presented articles and the evolution of the state of the art across the different years; and, finally, the exciting future of the workshop, which was discussed with the audience. During the research papers session, the following three articles were presented:

- *The PM-EdgeMap: Towards Real -Time Process Mining on the Edge Cloud Continuum.* By Hendrik Reiter, Christian Imenkamp, Olaf Landsiedel, Andrea Maldonado, Patrick Rathje, Wilhelm Hasselbring.

This paper introduces PM-EdgeMap, a formalism that characterizes how process mining algorithms operate over distributed edge topologies and event streams, with explicit quality attributes such as processing time, resource utilization, load capacity, and scalability. A prototype edge-based conformance checking algorithm illustrates the approach and is evaluated across mobile cloud computing (MCC), multi-access edge computing (MEC), and cloudlet topologies, showing, for instance, lower per-event processing times and higher throughput on cloudlet setups. The work opens a research agenda for streaming process mining under edge constraints and heterogeneous compute environments.

– *IoT Miner – Intelligent Extraction of Event Logs from Sensor Data for Process Mining}*. By Edyta Brzychczy, Urszula Jessen, Krzysztof Kluza, Sridhar Sriram, Manuel Vargas Nettelnstroth

This paper introduces IoT Miner, a four-stage pipeline (preprocessing, unsupervised clustering, LLM-based labeling, and event log construction), that converts raw sensor streams into high-level, process minable logs. Evaluated on a Load Haul Dump (LHD) mining machine dataset, the approach introduces Similarity Weighted Accuracy to assess label quality and shows that richer, domain-informed prompts improve labeling consistency and correctness. The resulting logs (e.g., in XES) unlock process mining for scenarios where standard event data are unavailable.

– *Incorporating IoT Contexts into Business Processes: A Contextual Classification.* By Jia Wei, Chun Ouyang, Yannis Bertrand.

This paper addresses the gap between raw IoT data and process-level insights, and proposes a classification of process relevant IoT contexts developed via a rigorous taxonomy method. The classification integrates five process context levels (from IoT event to organizational context) with IoT context categories (e.g., physical object, spatial, temporal, human actor, environment), and adds an IoT device context capturing device characteristics. Its applicability and robustness are demonstrated through two real-world use cases, guiding which IoT data should be integrated into event logs to enable context-aware process analytics.

The workshop was held in the beautiful city of Seville, on 1 September 2025, and attracted around 20 participants who actively interacted during the workshop presentations and discussions. The organizers of this event would like to thank the authors of the submitted papers, as well as the active participants in the fruitful discussions. We would also like to thank the valuable input from the PC members and the conference organizers who supported and facilitated the workshop. We hope that the reader finds the final selection of papers interesting and useful for gaining better insights into the integration of IoT and BPM from both theoretical and practical points of view.

Organization

Organizing Committee

Agnes Koschmider	University of Bayreuth, Germany
Francesco Leotta	Sapienza Università di Roma, Italy
Massimo Mecella	Sapienza Università di Roma, Italy
Estefanía Serral	KU Leuven, Belgium
Victoria Torres	Universitat Politècnica de València, Spain

Program Committee

Ronny Seiger	University of St. Gallen, Switzerland
Yannis Bertrand	Ghent University, Belgium
Andrea Delgado	Universidad de la República, Uruguay
Jianwen Su	University of California, Santa Barbara, USA
Andreas Oberweis	Karlsruhe Institute of Technology, Germany
Pnina Soffer	University of Haifa, Israel
Vicente Pelechano	Universitat Politècnica de València, Spain
Zahra Ahmadi	KU Leuven, Belgium
Zakaria Maamar	University of Doha for Science and Technology, Qatar
Mathias Weske	HPI, University of Potsdam, Germany

5th International Workshop on Change, Drift, and Dynamics of Organizational Processes (ProDy 2025)

The workshop on Change, Drift, and Dynamics of Organizational Processes (Pro-Dy) brings together researchers who are interested in how socio-technical processes evolve in organizations. While intended to remain stable when implemented, business processes change over time. This change is caused by and connected to various fac-tors inside and outside the organization. Different descriptions of change phenomena have been discussed in the literature, such as incremental or seasonal drift, endoge-nous and exogenous change, along with roadblocks and enablers for process change. Recent research investigates, among others, how we can detect drift in processes, how we can use process mining to visualize change, how to theorize change in processes, and which methods can support the continuous (re-)design and adaptation of pro-cesses.

We organized and held ProDy 2025 in conjunction with the 23rd International Conference on Business Process Management in Seville, Spain. We received a total of ten submissions. Each submission underwent regular peer review by three members of the program committee. We accepted four papers for presentation at the work-shop and organized an additional panel discussion with one of the co-authors of each paper.

The workshop comprised four paper presentations and one panel discussion. First, Oukharijane presented a framework for Neuro-Symbolic Predictive Process Monitoring. Second, Skolik gave insight into the dynamics of a process mining implementation project based on log data. Third, Leribaux explained how actor behav-ior is related to process performance. Finally, van der Waal presented a resource-oriented workaround analysis. We concluded the workshop with a panel discussion about process dynamics and drift based on the presented papers.

We would like to thank everyone who contributed to making the workshop a success. We thank all authors, committee members, the workshop chairs, and all at-tendees for their contributions to the workshop.

Organization

Organizing Committee

Christian Bartelheimer	University of Göttingen, Germany
Bastian Wurm	LMU Munich School of Management, Germany
Iris Beerepoot	Utrecht University, The Netherlands
Daniel Beverungen	Paderborn University, Germany

Program Committee

Markus Becker	University of Southern Denmark, Denmark
Carl Corea	University of Koblenz, Germany
Sandro Franzoi	University of Münster, Germany
Thomas Grisold	Vienna University of Economics and Business, Austria
Bernd Löhr	Paderborn University, Germany
Jan Mendling	FU Berlin, Germany
Brian Pentland	Michigan State University, USA
Michael Rosemann	Queensland University of Technology, Australia
Flavia Santoro	Universidade do Estado do Rio de Janeiro, Brazil
Wouter van der Waal	Utrecht University, The Netherlands
Maxim Vidgof	Vienna University of Economics and Business, Austria
Anton Yeshchenko	University of Vienna, Austria
Sandra Zilker	Technische Hochschule Nürnberg Georg Simon Ohm, Germany

1st Workshop on Distributed Ledger Technologies in Business Process Management (DLT4BPM 2025)

The DLT4BPM Workshop provides a platform for presenting research on and applications of Distributed Ledger Technologies (DLTs), with a particular emphasis on their role in Business Process Management (BPM). By leveraging immutability, transparency, and decentralisation, DLT systems create new opportunities for transforming business processes across domains such as healthcare, logistics, finance, and education. At the same time, these opportunities are accompanied by challenges concerning security, privacy, scalability, and performance, which must be addressed to ensure successful integration into real-world applications.

Both academia and practitioners have approached these challenges from multiple perspectives: conceptual modelling for DLT and BPM; collaborative process execution on distributed ledgers; monitoring and auditing of process data; secrecy-preserving data sharing in multi-party settings; process mining for the validation of smart contracts; and, more recently, techniques involving large language models and machine learning. The workshop brought together researchers and practitioners to explore both the opportunities and the technical, organisational, and regulatory challenges of deploying DLTs for process management.

The program was designed to stimulate focused discussion. It opened with a keynote by Julius Köpke (University of Klagenfurt) entitled "Beyond the Hype: Blockchain meets BPM – Challenges on the Plains", followed by two research paper presentations and an interactive session with short lightning talks.

This proceedings volume comprises two accepted research papers presented at the workshop: "On LLM-Assisted Generation of Smart Contracts from Business Processes" by Fabian Stiehle, Hans Weytjens, and Ingo Weber, which investigates the use of large language models to derive executable smart contract code from business process descriptions and introduces an automated evaluation framework. "Gas Management Patterns in Blockchain-enabled Process Execution" by Hassan Atwi and Cesare Pautasso proposes and evaluates design patterns to model and optimise gas usage in blockchain-supported collaborative processes. In addition, the program featured two lightning talks—"A Methodology for Extracting and Decoding Smart Contracts Data" and "Compliance Checking for Decentralized Applications"—that enriched the on-site discussions.

We would like to thank the authors for their contributions and the members of the Program Committee for their careful reviews and constructive feedback, which ensured the quality of the program. Our gratitude also goes to the keynote speaker for opening the workshop with a forward-looking perspective, and to the BPM 2025 organisers for hosting DLT4BPM and providing the logistical support that enabled a productive event in Seville.

Organization

Organizing Committee

Simon Curty	University of Fribourg, Switzerland
Richard Hobeck	University of Berlin, Germany
Andrea Morichetta	University of Camerino, Italy

Program Committee

Marcel Bühlmann	University of Fribourg, Switzerland
Claudio Di Ciccio	Utrecht University, Netherlands
Walid Fdhila	University of Vienna, Austria
Hans-Georg Fill	University of Fribourg, Switzerland
Felix Härer	University of Fribourg, Switzerland
Tiphaine Henry	Université Paris-Saclay, CEA, List, France
Julius Köpke	University of Klagenfurt, Austria
Sidra Malik	CSIRO's Data61, Australia
Edoardo Marangone	Sapienza University of Rome, Italy
Alessandro Marcelletti	University of Camerino, Italy
Giovanni Meroni	Technical University of Denmark, Denmark
Mattia Salnitri	Politecnico di Milano, Italy
Fabian Stiehle	Technical University of Munich, Germany
Francesco Tiezzi	University of Florence, Italy
Ingo Weber	Technical University of Munich, Germany

2nd Workshop on Managing Process Innovation and Value Creation in the Era of Digital Transformation (Innov8BPM 2025)

Digital transformation continues to reshape the foundations of organizations, driving profound changes in how businesses operate, deliver value, and interact with their ecosystems. In this context, business process management (BPM) is no longer confined to its traditional role of structuring and optimizing operational processes. Instead, BPM must evolve into a discipline that enables continuous innovation, adaptability, and resilience in the face of uncertainty and rapid technological advancement.

Emerging technologies such as AI, process mining, IoT, and advanced analytics are not only automating tasks but also redefining the very nature of processes. These technologies introduce new opportunities for value creation, yet they also challenge established BPM practices. The shift from static, predefined processes to dynamic, data-driven, and sometimes ephemeral processes requires organizations to rethink governance, flexibility, and the role of human judgment in process execution. While many organizations embark on digital transformation journeys, realizing tangible business value remains a critical challenge. Success depends on more than technology adoption; it requires aligning strategy, processes, and organizational culture to foster innovation while maintaining control. This duality—balancing emergence and governance—is at the heart of current BPM research and practice.

Against this backdrop, the Innov8BPM workshop series serves as a platform for exploring how BPM can support process innovation and value creation in an era of continuous change. The workshop brings together scholars and practitioners to discuss conceptual foundations, practical approaches, and future directions for BPM in digitally enabled environments. This year, at the BPM 2025 Conference in Seville, the workshop focused on balancing emergence and control in BPM, reflecting the need to manage flexibility without losing governance in a world of ephemeral processes and digital ecosystems.

The workshop featured an inspiring keynote and four research paper presentations, followed by an interactive discussion session.

We were honored to host Jan vom Brocke, who delivered a keynote titled: "The BPM Sandwich Model – Balancing Emergence and Control in Times of Continuous Change." Organizations need to continuously adapt their business processes to keep pace with dynamic changes in their business environments. This implies that Business Process Management (BPM) needs to shift from static process models and governance structures to ephemeral process conceptualizations. The keynote introduced the concept of the BPM Sandwich Model, which emphasizes the need to combine top-down governance with bottom-up innovation. Vom Brocke highlighted how organizations can navigate the tension between stability and agility by adopting a layered approach that accommodates both structured processes and emergent practices.

The research contributions presented at the workshop reflected diverse perspectives on BPM innovation and value creation. The first paper, "The Increasing Importance of Knowledge with the Growth of BPM Maturity" by Marek Szelągowski and colleagues, explored how knowledge management becomes increasingly critical as organizations advance in BPM maturity. The authors emphasized the interplay between process governance and knowledge-driven innovation, highlighting the need for organizations to integrate knowledge practices into their BPM strategies.

The second paper, "Factors and Impacts of Gender Imbalance in Digital Transformation Projects: A Systematic Literature Review", also by Marek Szelągowski and co-authors, provided a systematic review of gender imbalance in digital transformation projects. The paper discussed the implications of gender diversity for inclusivity, collaboration, and project success, calling for greater attention to social dimensions in BPM research and practice.

Next, Ricardo M. F. Fernandes and his team presented the paper "Modeling Business Processes: From a BPMN Structured Process Flow to a Declarative Rule-Based ACM Method." This contribution proposed a transition from traditional BPMN-based modeling to a declarative, rule-based approach for Adaptive Case Management (ACM), enabling greater flexibility and adaptability in dynamic environments where rigid process models fall short.

The final paper, "Connecting the Digital Dots – Can Customer Journeys be Analyzed Purely from Event Logs?" by Kristoffer Alves Brekke and co-authors, investigated the feasibility of reconstructing customer journeys solely from event logs. The authors examined the opportunities and limitations of process mining for customer-centric analysis, raising important questions about data completeness and interpretability in digital journey mapping.

The workshop concluded with an engaging discussion session where we reflected on the most relevant topics to continue focusing on in the next editions of the Innov8BPM workshop. The preference lay on the business value of BPM, specifically related to process intelligence with AI and process mining, and governance and organizational capabilities for BPM in the digital era. We also reflected on the type of components to incorporate in the keynote. The participants favored keynotes above all others, regular paper presentations and brainstorming sessions being still valuable. New components such as paper development sessions were also suggested.

This year's Innov8BPM workshop made a significant contribution to advancing the BPM field by deepening the understanding of how organizations can navigate the tension between control and flexibility in an era of continuous change. Through the keynote insights, the presented research, and the interactive discussions, the workshop highlighted emerging themes such as knowledge-driven BPM maturity, inclusivity in digital transformation, adaptive modeling approaches, and customer-centric process analysis. These discussions not only reinforced the importance of BPM as a strategic enabler of digital transformation but also opened new avenues for research and practice focused on balancing governance with agility. We believe that the ideas exchanged during Innov8BPM 2025 will inspire future work and foster innovative solutions for managing processes in increasingly dynamic and technology-driven environments.

Organization

Organizing Committee

Banu Aysolmaz	Eindhoven University of Technology, the Netherlands
Amy Van Looy	Ghent University, Belgium
Oktay Turetken	Eindhoven University of Technology, the Netherlands
Marta Indulska	University of Queensland, Australia
Flavia Santoro	University of the State of Rio de Janeiro, Brazil
Panagiotis Keramidis	Copenhagen Business School, Denmark

Program Committee

Tahir Ahmad	Ghent University, Belgium
Marco Comuzzi	Ulsan National Institute of Science and Technology, South Korea
Sybren De Kinderen	Eindhoven University of Technology, The Netherlands
Mahendrawathi Er	Sepuluh Nopember Institute of Technology
Paul Grefen	Eindhoven University of Technology, The Netherlands
Joklan Imelda Camelia Goni	Ghent University, Belgium
Thomas Hildebrandt	University of Copenhagen, Denmark
Rob Kusters	Open University of the Netherlands/Eindhoven University of Technology, The Netherlands
Paola Lara Machado	Eindhoven University of Technology, The Netherlands
Henrik Leopold	Kühne Logistics University, Germany
Morten Marquard	DCR Solutions A/S, Denmark
Jan Mendling	Humboldt-Universität zu Berlin, Germany
Fredrik Milani	University of Tartu, Estonia
Kate Revoredo	Humboldt-Universität zu Berlin, Germany
Arisa Shollo	Copenhagen Business School, Denmark
Peter Trkman	University of Ljubljana, Slovenia
Montijn van de Ven	Eindhoven University of Technology, The Netherlands

4th International Workshop on Natural Language Processing for Business Process Management (NLP4BPM 2025)

Within the field of Business Process Management, Natural Language Processing continues to play a central role. It can be used to describe processes in a comprehensible manner, support modeling processes from available process descriptions, identify the meaning of events and activities, provide support for conducting process analysis, and more.

In this context, the goal of the NLP4BPM workshop is to bring together researchers and practitioners to present, discuss, and evaluate how Natural Language Processing (NLP) and Large Language Models (LLMs) can be used to establish new or improve existing methods, techniques, frameworks, tools, and systems that support the different phases of the BPM lifecycle. Furthermore, we aim to promote an exchange on the advances, challenges, and barriers researchers face, and establish an environment where collaborations can naturally emerge.

Between the third and fourth editions of NLP4BPM, the attention that LLMs received in the research community and public domain continued to be strong. Following recent advancements in generative AI and reasoning-focused model architectures, new opportunities for process modeling, analysis, and monitoring have emerged. In the context of these developments, the fourth edition of our workshop received a total of nine submissions, each of which was reviewed by three members of the Program Committee. From these, four papers papers were accepted and presented at the BPM Conference in Seville, Spain, attracting a large and engaged audience. The workshop started with a keynote by Adrian Rebmann and concluded with a lively discussion round on envisioning the next frontier in NLP for BPM, which highlighted opportunities and open challenges.

The four accepted papers cover a broad range of topics, from systematic literature reviews and domain-specific pipelines to reasoning benchmarks and practice overviews.

Wimmer, Costa, and Pufahl present a Systematic Literature Review on generating BPMN models from text using NLP and LLMs. By analyzing 17 studies, they classify methods, intermediate representations, supported BPMN elements, and evaluation strategies. Their study highlights strengths and limitations of current approaches (e.g., current solutions support only a limited set of BPMN elements, leading to oversimplified models), and calls for feedback loops, benchmarks, and open datasets to foster reproducibility and progress in the field.

Houshidari et al. introduce an LLM-based pipeline for the automatic extraction and evaluation of care pathways from clinical practice guidelines. Manually translating clinical practice guidelines into formal process models like BPMN is labor-intensive and prone to inconsistency. Their modular system supports BPMN generation, label alignment, and evaluation against reference models. A case study on stroke-related guidelines demonstrates that a multi-agent orchestration approach achieves higher fidelity than single-model frameworks, while a web-based UI and released open-source resources promote reproducibility.

Gonzalez Moyano et al. provide a structured review of how LLMs are applied in practice across all phases of the BPM lifecycle. Their review analyzes recent studies to understand current contributions, implementations, and evaluations per lifecycle phase. Key findings reveal that LLMs can integrate diverse process documents, generate models from text, support automation with executable outputs, and enable more accessible process analysis and monitoring. By synthesizing opportunities and limitations, their study bridges conceptual possibilities and practical applications, offering guidance for future research and system design. Common challenges, such as prompt sensitivity and scalability constraints, are also identified.

Berti et al. present PMLRM-Bench, a benchmark for configuring and evaluating Large Reasoning Models (LRMs) using process mining. Their framework classifies reasoning steps by type (e.g., deductive reasoning) and effect (Positive, Indifferent, or Negative), enabling detailed assessments of reasoning quality. A case study on the QwQ-32B LLM illustrates how tuning reasoning step distributions can improve task-specific outcomes. This contribution highlights the value of process mining for the structured evaluation and configuration of LRMs.

The organizers wish to thank all authors who submitted their work to the NLP4BPM 2025 workshop, the many participants who contributed to fruitful discussions, and the Program Committee members for their valuable reviews. We look forward to future editions of the NLP4BPM workshop and to future advancements in the field.

Organization

Organizing Committee

Henrik Leopold	Kühne Logistics University, Germany
Jana-Rebecca Rehse	University of Mannheim, Germany
Vinicius Stein Dani	Utrecht University, The Netherlands

Program Committee

Adrian Rebmann	University of Mannheim, Germany
Christoph Kecht	Technical University of Munich, Germany
Daniela Grigori	Paris Dauphine University - PSL, France
Fabrizio Maria Maggi	Free University of Bozen-Bolzano, Italy
Julius Köpke	University of Klagenfurt, Austria
Karolin Winter	Eindhoven University of Technology, The Netherlands
Lars Ackermann	Hof University of Applied Sciences, Germany
Patrizio Bellan	Fondazione Bruno Kessler, Italy
Sven Weinzierl	Friedrich-Alexander-Universitat Erlangen-Nürnberg, Germany
Wolfgang Kratsch	FIM Research Center for Information Management, Germany

3rd International Workshop on Object-centric Processes from A to Z (OBJECTS 2025)

The topic of object-centric processes has been gaining momentum in the last few years, with many works addressing foundational and practical problems on the interplay of processes and objects, where behaviour arises from the complex interplay among multiple business objects and their one-to-many/many-to-many relationships. Despite the surging number of results on the topic, many related problems have not yet been addressed. One such problem relates to correct modelling and analysis of such processes, where a suitable trade-off between expressiveness and feasibility of analytic techniques must be found. Another problem concerns how object-centric processes can be handled in Process Mining (PM), including novel, efficient PM techniques and suitable event data/log formats to operate over complex event data for such processes and fully unleash the insights hidden therein. The OBJECTS workshop provides a platform for researchers from the fields of Business Process Management and Process Mining who work on object-centric processes where they can share their ideas and current research addressing the aforementioned problems as well as discuss challenges and future directions of the field.

OBJECTS 2025 was the third edition of the workshop, and attracted 6 international submissions. Each paper was reviewed by at least three members of the Program Committee. Out of all submissions, three manuscripts were accepted and are published in these proceedings.

Chan, Ebert, Hillmann, Rubensson, Fahrenkrog-Petersen and Mendling studied how object-centric process mining can be applied in the context of team sports. Using football as a case study, they showed how to transform match data into object-centric logs and conduct relevant analyses of the football games.

Van Gansewinkel, Denisov and Fahland investigated how incorporating object information into queues can improve queue analysis. Specifically, they considered parallel queues involving multiple agents and teams, focusing on tasks such as inferring missing queue information and analyzing queue behavior and performance.

Schueler and Alpers reported on an automated approach to business process model generation based on the analysis of object instances from operational documents.

The workshop also featured two interactive sessions, where ongoing work on the conceptualization of object-centric BPM and challenges in the domain of object-centric processes were presented. The results were subsequently discussed in a plenary session.

We thank the authors for their interesting contributions and the members of the Program Committee for their invaluable help in the reviewing and discussion phase of the manuscripts. We hope that, by reading these papers, the reader will know more about the latest advances in research on object-centric processes.

Organization

Organizing Committee

Marco Montali	Free University of Bozen-Bolzano, Italy
Andrey Rivkin	Technical University of Denmark, Denmark
Jan Martijn van der Werf	Utrecht University, The Netherlands

Program Committee

Andrea Delgado	Universidad de la República, Uruguay
Dirk Fahland	Eindhoven University of Technology, The Netherlands
Amin Jalali	Stockholm University, Sweden
Ekkart Kindler	Technical University of Denmark, Denmark
Irina Lomazova	HSE University, Russia
Sander J. J. Leemans	RWTH Aachen University, Germany
Giovanni Meroni	Technical University of Denmark, Denmark
Andrea Morichetta	University of Camerino, Italy
Barbara Re	University of Camerino, Italy
Stefanie Rinderle-Ma	Technical University of Munich, Germany
Natalia Sidorova	Eindhoven University of Technology, The Netherlands
Pnina Soffer	University of Haifa, Israel
Dominique Sommers	Celonis, The Netherlands
Mathias Weske	Hasso Plattner Institute, Germany
Sarah Winkler	Free University of Bozen-Bolzano, Italy
Karolin Winter	Eindhoven University of Technology, The Netherlands

2nd International Workshop on Processes, Laws and Compliance (PLC 2025)

The PLC - Processes, Laws and Compliance workshop was held in conjunction with the 23rd International Conference on Business Process Management (BPM 2025) in Seville, Spain, on September 1, 2025.

The PLC workshop aims to provide a forum for exchanging research findings and ideas on data-driven and process-oriented techniques and practices in the legal domain, fostering collaboration among interdisciplinary experts, researchers, and practitioners working at the intersection of IT and law.

Research in legal informatics has grown significantly in recent decades, particularly with the increasing availability of information systems capable of recording legal processes (legal event logs), tender documents, and the temporal dimensions of legal procedures. Artificial Intelligence (AI) techniques now offer powerful means of analysing legal processes to extract insights that can support the work of public administrations as well as private organisations operating in the legal field.

Areas that particularly benefit from the application of AI methods - including Process Mining, Machine Learning, and Natural Language Processing - range from the automated discovery of legal procedures from historical data, to the formalisation of legal requirements through process discovery, the verification of regulatory compliance, and the prediction of the unfolding of ongoing legal cases.

The topics covered by the workshop include the intersection of automated process analysis and digital law, with a focus on innovative approaches to legal modelling and conceptualisation. Key topics include discovering process behaviour in legal artefacts such as laws, proceedings, and standards, as well as examining compliance between formal legal representations and their practical implementation. It also covers variant analysis of legal process executions, performance evaluation in the legal domain, and predictive analytics for legal cases. Further areas of interest include techniques for modelling and formalising laws, natural language processing (NLP) in the legal field, and methods for visualising and simplifying legal processes. Legal reasoning, information retrieval, multimedia search, and the "Rules as Code" (RaC) approach for developing compliant-by-design systems are also considered, alongside emerging applications in legal data and knowledge engineering.

The second edition of the PLC workshop started with an invited talk by Karolin Winter (Eindhoven University of Technology), titled "Towards Holistic Business Process Compliance: Leveraging Logs, Models and Textual Data". The keynote addresses topics at the intersection of the legal, compliance, and process domains, drafting a holistic approach to compliance, requiring the access and processing of heterogeneous sources, such as natural language texts, event logs, and process models, and discussing previous and ongoing work on these subjects. The keynote was followed by a session involving the oral presentation of two research papers, accepted at the end of a peer-review process: "From Text to Process: Leveraging LLMs to Unveil Italian Lawmaking", which showcases the use of LLMs to convert a dataset consisting of unstructured documents that reconstructs the Italian lawmaking process from 1985 to 2025 in a structured event log; and "Understanding Feature Contributions to Remaining Time Prediction in Judicial Processes", which applies machine learning methods to judicial data to analyze the predictive power of various feature sets for estimating the time-to-resolution of legal cases in Italian courts.

Finally, an interactive session was held with the participants to gather insights on future directions and open challenges of compliance management in BPM. Some of the key topics highlighted in the discussion were the role of human actors in successfully managing compliance, the need for involving legal experts, such as lawyers or judges, to design practically usable artefacts, as well as challenges due to the conflicting interests of different stakeholders involved in the compliance management process.

We thank all the contributing speakers, the members of our Program Committee for their timely reviews, and the BPM workshop chairs Han van der Aa, Bedilia Estrada Torres, and Inge van de Weerd for their support.

Organization

Organizing Committee

Laura Genga	Technical University of Eindhoven, The Netherlands
Hugo A. López	Technical University of Denmark, Denmark
Roberto Nai	University of Turin, Italy
Emilio Sulis	University of Turin, Italy

Program Committee

Han van der Aa	University of Vienna, Austria
Ilaria Amantea	University of Turin, Italy
Davide Audrito	University of Turin, Italy
Valerio Basile	University of Turin, Italy
Juanita Caballero Villalobos	Technical University of Denmark, Denmark
Luigi Di Caro	University of Turin, Italy
Chiara Di Francescomarino	University of Trento, Italy
Chiara Gallese	Technical University Eindhoven, The Netherlands
Thomas Hildebrandt	Copenhagen University, Denmark
Mieke Jans	Hasselt University, Belgium
Rohan Nanda	University of Maastricht, The Netherlands
Marinella Quaranta	University of Turin, Italy
Livio Robaldo	Swansea University, UK
Massimiliano Ronzani	FBK, Italy
Stefanie Rinderle-Ma	Technical University of Munich, Germany
David Restrepo Amariles	HEC Paris, France
Giulia Ruffini	University of Turin, Italy
Andrea Tagarelli	University of Calabria, Italy
Federico Torrielli	University of Turin, Italy
Andrea Vandin	Scuola Superiore Sant'Anna, Italy
Karolin Winter	Technical University Eindhoven, The Netherlands

2nd International Workshop on Visual Process Mining (VIPRA 2025)

Process Mining and Visual Analytics are two rapidly evolving fields that share the common objective of helping people make sense of complex event data. Process Mining focuses on extracting knowledge from event logs to discover, analyze, and improve business processes, whereas Visual Analytics leverages visualization, interactivity, and analytical methods to support exploration and decision-making. Although the two domains have developed largely in parallel, their integration offers unique opportunities to create powerful methods for understanding and optimizing processes. VIPRA aims to bridge this gap by creating a dialogue between the Process Mining and Visual Analytics communities.

The idea of initiating a workshop where both communities could meet emerged during the Dagstuhl Seminar *Human in the (Process) Mines*[2]. The participants expressed interest in having a workshop that alternates between Process Mining and Visual Analytics venues, thereby strengthening interdisciplinary exchange.

An international committee composed of both visualization and process mining experts set out to organize the first VIPRA workshop at the Eurographics Conference on Visualization[3] (EuroVis) 2024. This first successful experience led to the 2nd edition of VIPRA, held in conjunction with the International Conference on Business Process Management[4] (BPM) 2025 in Seville, Spain. The workshop attracted eight submissions, each of which was reviewed by three members of the Program Committee. Four papers were accepted and presented at the workshop, which was organized into two sessions that included a keynote speech, paper presentations, and a closing panel discussion. With a full room of participants, the workshop succeeded in establishing a lively and fruitful exchange between the two communities.

The program opened with a keynote delivered by Maria Cruz Villa Uriol *"What BPM Researchers Should Know About Visual Analytics"*. The talk provided a novel perspective on designing systems for exploring event sequence data and shared valuable strategies and lessons learned to avoid common pitfalls. The keynote was followed by the technical program, which included four presentations:

- Pnina Soffer presented *"Milana: Bridging process mining and visual analytics through task classification"*, a paper authored by Lisa Zimmermann, Katerina Vrotsou, Pnina Soffer, Philipp Koytek, Barbara Weber and Shazia Sadiq. Milana is a method that aims to link process mining tasks, operationalized as analysis questions, to requirements established in the visual analytics field.
- Andrea Burattin presented *"VESPA: Visual Event-Stream Progressive Analytics"*, authored by Andrea Burattin, Silvia Miksch, Shazia Sadiq, Hans-Jörg Schulz and

[2] https://www.dagstuhl.de/en/seminars/seminar-calendar/seminar-details/23271.

[3] https://www.eg.org/wp/eg-events/visualization-eurovis/.

[4] https://www.bpm2025seville.org/

Katerina Vrotsou. The paper introduces a framework for streaming event analysis that employs progressive visual analytics to support real-time decision making in contexts where data is incomplete, such as streaming environments.
- Luis Montana presented the paper *"Addressing Directly-Follows Graphs limitations with visualization of event sequences"* authored by Luis Montana, Manuel Resinas and Maria-Cruz Villa-Uriol. This contribution examines the limitations of directly-follows graphs and demonstrates how timeline-based visualizations can provide more interpretable, trace-level insights.
- To conclude the technical program, Lukas Liß presented the work *"Visualizing Object-Centric Petri Nets"* authored by Tobias Brachmann, István Koren, Lukas Liß, and Wil M. P. van der Aalst. In their work, the authors present a layout algorithm for Object-Centric Petri Nets implemented as an open-source visualizer.

The workshop concluded with a panel discussion moderated by Jana-Rebecca Rehse, involving the keynote speaker and the paper presenters. The discussion, enriched by active contributions from the audience, addressed topics such as how visualization design can be scoped around specific process mining tasks and user needs and how visualization methods should be evaluated in this interdisciplinary context. The debate underscored VIPRA's role as a unique venue for advancing research at the intersection of process mining and visual analytics.

The organizers are grateful to all the authors who submitted their work to the workshop, the participants who contributed to the stimulating discussions and lively atmosphere, and the Program Committee members for their valuable work in reviewing the submissions. We look forward to continuing this dialogue in future editions of the VIPRA workshop.

Organization

Organizing Committee

Jana-Rebecca Rehse	University of Mannheim, Germany
Francesca Zerbato	Eindhoven University of Technology, The Netherlands
Luise Pufahl	Technical University of Munich, Germany
Stef van den Elzen	Eindhoven University of Technology, The Netherlands
Alessio Arleo	Eindhoven University of Technology, The Netherlands

Program Committee

Alman, Anti	University of Tartu, Estonia
Beerepoot, Iris	Utrecht University, The Netherlands
Burattin, Andrea	Technical University of Denmark, Denmark
Di Ciccio, Claudio	Utrecht University, The Netherlands
Filipov, Velitchko	Vienna University of Technology (TU Wien), Austria
Mendling, Jan	Humboldt-Universität zu Berlin, Germany
Miksch, Silvia	Vienna University of Technology (TU Wien), Austria
Resinas, Manuel	University of Seville, Spain
Schuster, Daniel	RWTH Aachen University, Germany
Soffer, Pnina	University of Haifa, Israel
Tominski, Christian	University of Rostock, Germany
Villa-Uriol, Maria-Cruz	University of Sheffield, UK
Vrotsou, Katerina	Linköping University, Sweden
Weber, Barbara	University of St. Gallen, Switzerland
Yeshchenko, Anton	University of Vienna, Austria

Contents

9th International Workshop on Artificial Intelligence for Business Process Management (AI4BPM 2025)

Agentic Business Process Management Systems 3
Marlon Dumas, Fredrik Milani, and David Chapela-Campa

Revealing Trace Variant Shift via Multi-dimensional Profiling and Community-Aware Graph Modeling 15
Iuliana Malina Grigore, Gabriel Marques Tavares, Vincenzo Pasquadibisceglie, and Sylvio Barbon Junior

Predicting File Completion Using Time Series Models: Embracing the Life-Cycle Nature of Software Development 28
Nastasja Stephanie Parschew and Saimir Bala

Inter-case Informed Business Process Suffix Prediction Integrating Trace and Log Information 41
Xiaomeng He, Johannes De Smedt, Seppe vanden Broucke, and Jochen De Weerdt

What is the Best Process Model Representation? A Comparative Analysis for Process Modeling with Large Language Models 55
Alexis Brissard, Frédéric Cuppens, and Amal Zouaq

Discovering Coordinated Processes from Social Online Networks 69
Anna Kalenkova, Lewis Mitchell, and Ethan Johnson

Exploring Decision Mining Research: A Systematic Review Report and Knowledge Graph 82
Erfan Elhami, William Van Woensel, and Daniel Amyot

Leveraging Duration Pseudo-embeddings in Multilevel LSTM and GCN Hypermodels for Outcome-Oriented PPM 94
Fang Wang, Paolo Ceravolo, and Ernesto Damiani

1st International Workshop on Implementation and Management of Intelligent Process Automation Solutions (AUTOMATE 2025)

Levels of Automation Revisited: Standardizing Human-Machine Interaction with Process Patterns 109
Christian Janiesch and Seyyid A. Ciftci

Runtime-Recovery Agent: Solving UI-Related Exceptions in RPA Systems with GUI Agents 127
A. Rodríguez-Ruiz, J. G. Enríquez, and A. Jiménez-Ramírez

Structured Evaluation of Robotic Process Automation (RPA) Tools 139
Romina Giaccio, Emilio Gerolami, Daniel Calegari, and Andrea Delgado

From Chaos to Automation: Enabling the Use of Unstructured Data for Robotic Process Automation 155
Kelly Kurowski, Xixi Lu, and Hajo A. Reijers

Towards an Actionable Development Method for Robotic Process Automation Using Process Mining 171
Alexander Skolik

Process Automation and Skills in the Context of Knowledge Work (Short Paper) 187
Dries Jarijch, Mieke Jans, and Jan Mendling

9th International Workshop on Business Processes Meet the Internet-of-Things (BP-Meet-IoT 2025)

Incorporating IoT Contexts into Business Processes: A Contextual Classification 199
Jia Wei, Chun Ouyang, and Yannis Bertrand

The PM-EdgeMap: Towards Real-Time Process Mining on the Edge-Cloud Continuum 217
Hendrik Reiter, Christian Imenkamp, Olaf Landsiedel, Andrea Maldonado, Patrick Rathje, and Wilhelm Hasselbring

IoT Miner – Intelligent Extraction of Event Logs from Sensor Data for Process Mining 232
Edyta Brzychczy, Urszula Jessen, Krzysztof Kluza, Sridhar Sriram, and Manuel Vargas Nettelnstroth

5th International Workshop on Change, Drift, and Dynamics of Organizational Processes (ProDy 2025)

A General Framework for Neuro-Symbolic Predictive Process Monitoring 249
Jamila Oukharijane, Ivan Donadello, and Fabrizio Maria Maggi

Resource-Oriented Workaround Analysis: A Case Study 262
Wouter van der Waal and Hajo A. Reijers

Linking Actor Behavior to Process Performance over Time 274
Aurélie Leribaux, Rafael Oyamada, Johannes De Smedt, Zahra Dasht Bozorgi, Artem Polyvyanyy, and Jochen De Weerdt

Understanding the Dynamics of a Process Mining Project Analyzing Log Data of a Process Mining Platform 288
Alexander Skolik and Bernd Löhr

1st International Workshop on Distributed Ledger Technologies in Business Process Management (DLT4BPM 2025)

Beyond the Hype: Blockchain Meets BPM - Challenges on the Plains 303
Julius Köpke

Gas Management Patterns in Blockchain-Enabled Process Execution 311
Hassan Atwi and Cesare Pautasso

On LLM–Assisted Generation of Smart Contracts from Business Processes 327
Fabian Stiehle, Hans Weytjens, and Ingo Weber

2nd International Workshop on Managing Process Innovation in the Era of Digital Transformation (Innov8BPM 2025)

Modeling Business Processes: From a BPMN Structured Process Flow to a Declarative Rule-Based ACM Method 345
Ricardo M. F. Fernandes, Antonio M. Gutiérrez Fernández, Marek Szelągowski, and Christoph Ruhsam

The Increasing Importance of Knowledge with the Growth of BPM Maturity ... 360
Marek Szelągowski, Piotr Sliż, Marzena Grzesiak, Marek Moszyński, Karol Flisikowski, and Piotr Senkus

Connecting the Digital Dots - Can Customer Journeys Be Analyzed Purely from Event Logs? 374
Kristoffer Alves Brekke, Ragnhild Halvorsrud, Felix Mannhardt, Lasse Brurok, and Otas Meironas

Factors and Impacts of Gender Imbalance in Digital Transformation Projects: A Systematic Literature Review 387
Muhammad Febrilian Dwi Syahputra, Rinda Faiz Shabira, and E. R. Mahendrawathi

4th International Workshop on Natural Language Processing for Business Process Management (NLP4BPM 2025)

LLMs for BPM—From First-Wave Features to Process Understanding and Lasting Impact(?) 405
Adrian Rebmann

Configuring Large Reasoning Models Using Process Mining: A Benchmark and a Case Study 412
Alessandro Berti, Humam Kourani, Gyunam Park, and Wil M. P. van der Aalst

Natural Language Processing for BPMN Model Generation with LLMs: A Systematic Literature Review 425
Alena Wimmer, Ana Costa, and Luise Pufahl

Large Language Models for Business Process Management: A Practice Overview 438
Cielo González Moyano, Rachmadita Andreswari, Kristina Sahling, Jennifer Haase, Kate Revoredo, and Jan Mendling

An LLM Pipeline for Automatic Extraction and Evaluation of Care Pathways from Clinical Guidelines 451
Alireza Houshidari, William Van Woensel, Daniel Amyot, and El Mostafa Bouattane

3rd International Workshop on Object-centric Processes from A to Z (OBJECTS 2025)

Transforming Football Data into Object-Centric Event Logs with Spatial Context Information 467
Vito Chan, Lennart Ebert, Paul-Julius Hillmann, Christoffer Rubensson, Stephan A. Fahrenkrog-Petersen, and Jan Mendling

An Object-Centric Approach to Inferring and Analyzing Queues 479
Sander van Gansewinkel, Vadim Denisov, and Dirk Fahland

Object-Based Process Model Generation 492
Selina Schüler and Sascha Alpers

2nd International Workshop on Processes, Laws, and Compliance (PLC 2025)

Towards Holistic Business Process Compliance: Leveraging Logs, Models and Textual Data 507
Karolin Winter

From Text to Process: Leveraging LLMs to Unveil Italian Lawmaking 516
Matilde Contestabile, Chiara Ferrara, Alberto Giovannetti, Giovanni Parrillo, and Andrea Vandin

Understanding Feature Contributions to Remaining Time Prediction in Judicial Processes 531
Musa Salamov, Marlon Dumas, and Barbara Pernici

2nd International Workshop on Visual Process Analytics (VIPRA 2025)

VESPA: Visual Event-Stream Progressive Analytics 549
Andrea Burattin, Silvia Miksch, Shazia Sadiq, Hans-Jörg Schulz, and Katerina Vrotsou

Milana: Bridging Process Mining and Visual Analytics Through Task Classification 557
Lisa Zimmermann, Katerina Vrotsou, Pnina Soffer, Philipp Koytek, Barbara Weber, and Shazia Sadiq

Addressing Directly-Follows Graphs Limitations with Visualization of Event Sequences 573
Luis Montana, Manuel Resinas, and Maria-Cruz Villa-Uriol

Visualizing Object-Centric Petri Nets 582
Tobias Brachmann, István Koren, Lukas Liss, and Wil M. P. van der Aalst

What BPM Researchers Should Know About Visual Analytics 598
Maria-Cruz Villa-Uriol

BP-Meet-IoT: a Look Back at the Past, the Present, and the Future 603
Estefanía Serral, Agnes Koschmider, and Victoria Torres

Author Index 607

9th International Workshop on Artificial Intelligence for Business Process Management (AI4BPM 2025)

Agentic Business Process Management Systems

Marlon Dumas(✉), Fredrik Milani, and David Chapela-Campa

University of Tartu, Tartu, Estonia
{marlon.dumas,fredrik.milani,david.chapela}@ut.ee

Abstract. Since the early 90 s, the evolution of the Business Process Management (BPM) discipline has been punctuated by successive waves of automation technologies. Some of these technologies enable the automation of individual tasks, while others focus on orchestrating the execution of end-to-end processes. The rise of Generative and Agentic Artificial Intelligence (AI) is opening the way for another such wave. However, this wave is poised to be different because it shifts the focus from automation to autonomy and from design-driven management of business processes to data-driven management, leveraging process mining techniques. This position paper, based on a keynote talk at the 2025 Workshop on AI for BPM, outlines how process mining has laid the foundations on top of which agents can sense process states, reason about improvement opportunities, and act to maintain and optimize performance. The paper proposes an architectural vision for Agentic Business Process Management Systems (A-BPMS): a new class of platforms that integrate autonomy, reasoning, and learning into process management and execution. The paper contends that such systems must support a continuum of processes, spanning from human-driven to fully autonomous, thus redefining the boundaries of process automation and governance.

Keywords: Agentic Business Process Management · Automated Process Execution · Autonomous Process Execution

1 Introduction

Over the past five decades, process-aware information systems [1] have evolved from paper-driven systems supporting manual work and coordination into today's highly digitized and automated systems. Initially, workers relied on personal knowledge, paper documents, and individual judgment to complete tasks. Early business process automation waves introduced tools like standard operating procedures, checklists, and forms, followed by spreadsheets and collaborative software that organized work while still requiring human execution.

A leap occurred with the advent of case management and workflow management systems that could track work items and maintain digital records [2]. Soon

I. van de Weerd et al. (Eds.): BPM 2025 Workshops, LNBIP 569, pp. 3–14, 2026.
https://doi.org/10.1007/978-3-032-13426-4_1

after, Business Process Management Systems (BPMS) emerged, enabling organizations to design process models separately from their execution using notations like BPMN, while workflow engines automated routing between systems and people [3]. Parallel developments included business rules management systems that separated decision-making logic from applications, enabling automatic processing of routine decisions, and robotic process automation (RPA) that mimicked human interactions with software applications via their user interfaces [4]. Today's generation of process execution systems integrate real-time event processing, APIs, and machine learning to achieve higher levels of automation, combining execution with continuous monitoring and optimization [5].

The rise of Generative AI and Agentic AI are laying the ground for the next evolution in this field, by enabling the development of tools capable not only of executing predefined workflows, but also to dynamically generate new process variations, make contextualized decisions, and autonomously adapt workflows based on changing conditions and objectives [6]. Agentic AI differs from rule-based or script-based automation. Rule-based or script-based automation technology, such as RPA, are characterized by their deterministic nature. They follow a set of fixed, pre-defined rules. This capability makes them suitable for automating repetitive tasks, for which all possible scenarios can be anticipated and scripted. Agentic AI, on the other hand, can operate beyond a set of rules by sensing and reasoning about the current state of processes, and triggering next actions that align with performance objectives, within a set of constraints (also known as a frame [6]).

Agents are software entities that have the capability to sense (understand input), decide (analyse and determine what to do), and act (e.g. execute a task). Hence, agentic AI can emulate a human resource [7]. In the context of business process management and execution, agents can make use of process monitoring and process mining tools to sense the state of the process in real-time. Based on patterns extracted from historical executions, they can detect situations where certain actions need to be triggered, even if these actions deviate from predesigned execution flows. By leveraging rule-based or script-based automation tools, as well as automated planning techniques, AI agents can trigger actions to drive the execution of one or more processes in an adaptive manner.

Inspired by an earlier definition of AI-Augmented Business Process Management Systems [6], we define an Agentic Business Process Management System as a class of process-aware information systems that leverages agentic AI technology to enact business processes in such a way that: (1) the execution flows of a process are not (fully) pre-determined via predesigned rules, models or scripts; (2) adaptations to automated components of the process may not require explicit changes to the supporting software applications; and (3) improvement opportunities may be autonomously discovered, validated, and applied.

The rest of the paper outlines an architecture for an envisioned class of process management and execution systems, namely Agentic BPM system (A-BPMS). The paper argues that such systems need to support a range of processes, with different levels of autonomy embedded in them, all the way from largely manual or largely automated processes to almost-fully autonomous ones.

2 From Process Mining to Agentic BPM Systems

Underpinning an Agentic Business Process Management System (A-BPMS) is a collection of tools that allow for the transformation of data into insights and decisions. This collection of data-driven techniques can be conceptualized in the form of a pyramid of capabilities, depicted in Fig. 1. In this pyramid, each layer builds on top of the layers below and serves as the basis for the ones above, and comprises techniques pertaining to two use cases: *i) tactical*, aiming to inform managers in their business process change decisions, typically with timeframes of a few weeks to a few months between decision and change implementation; and *ii) operational*, aiming to issue recommendations or trigger actions in the context of running cases, to improve their performance on a day-to-day basis.

The first layer, *Descriptive Process Analytics*, comprises techniques focused on describing the current state of the process, generally addressing tactical use cases. Within this layer, we find four main capabilities: (1) *Automated process discovery*, aiming to discover process models from data, in order to exhibit the behavior happening in the process, identify unexpected exceptions, and highlight potential wastes. (2) *Conformance checking*, aiming to analyze the behavior recorded in the event log against the behavior modeled by the process model, enabling the identification of deviations in the process and the comparison between the designed and the real process. (3) *Performance mining*, aiming to analyze one or more processes in terms of performance measures, such as cycle time or cost per case. (4) *Variant analysis*, aiming to identify positive and negative deviance in a process by comparing how the process is performed for different subsets of cases – e.g., in different regions.

The second layer, *Predictive process analytics*, moves beyond describing the current state to estimating the future state of the process. The capabilities within this layer can be broadly classified into two categories: (1) *What-if digital process twins*, aiming to predict the impact of a (potential) process change at a macro-level. By applying process mining, statistical analysis, and machine learning techniques to historical event logs, we can construct a digital process twin (DPT) capable of replicating the behavior of the process. The DPT can then be used to estimate the impact that a change in the process might have on its performance metrics. (2) *Predictive process monitoring*, aiming to predict future states of a process. Typically implemented through machine learning or deep learning techniques, these approaches can operate both *i)* at the *case level*, making predictions about individual cases in a process; and *ii)* at the *process level*, predicting one or more process performance metrics across the entire process.

The third layer, *Prescriptive Process Optimization*, focuses on prescribing actions that, based on the current state and future predictions, might increase (or decrease) the probability of certain (un)desired events occurring – e.g., a loan offer being accepted by the customer. These capabilities can be sub-categorized

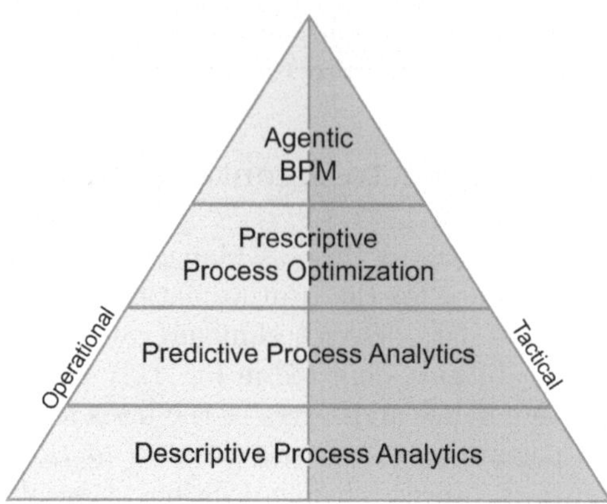

Fig. 1. The Agentic BPM Pyramid: a classification of data-driven BPM approaches (adapted from [8]).

as follows: (1) *Automated process optimization*, aiming to recommend changes to a process in order to strike a tradeoff between competing performance indicators – e.g., lowering cycle times while maintaining costs. (2) *Prescriptive process monitoring*, aiming to recommend actions in (near-)real-time to optimize the performance of a process. Existing techniques in this category are mainly designed to recommend actions to improve the performance at the *case level*.

Agentic BPM rests on top of the pyramid, illustrating the dependency of A-BPM systems on process intelligence. The aim of A-BPM systems is to autonomously manage and optimize processes to achieve the desired business outcomes, within the constraints and boundaries set by managers. This objective cannot be achieved without the insights and recommendations of the data-driven techniques from the layers below. Within this layer, we find two main categories of systems: (1) *Automated Systems* achieve the independence from human interaction through techniques that define, a priori, the entire set of decisions that can be made within the process – e.g., rule-based orchestration and execution. Although an automated system can theoretically function autonomously, the possibility of unforeseen situations with no predefined procedures to follow may force the system to either halt execution or depend on additional human input. (2) *Autonomous Systems* are composed of (AI) agents with the power to orchestrate and manage the process without human supervision. In an autonomous system, humans may act as supervisors, (proactively) intervening only in order to prevent undesired consequences.

3 Architecture of Agentic BPM Systems

We propose an architecture for an A-BPMS comprising five subsystems, as illustrated in Fig. 2: a data layer, a process intelligence layer, an action layer, an orchestration layer, and a conversational layer.

The *data layer* integrates both structured and unstructured data about business operations, including event logs that record the execution of past and ongoing business processes, repositories containing process models, records of past (improvement) decisions, as well as other relevant data and documentation about the processes managed by the system. This layer is fundamental for the A-BPMS to ground the management of the process on information about both the designed and the actual execution of the process. By doing so, it allows the A-BPMS to "perceive" the current state and evolution of the business process, as well as its surrounding environment [6].

On top of the data layer sits a *process intelligence layer*, which provides the collection of techniques introduced in Sect. 2. These techniques equip the A-BPMS with capabilities to "explain" the current and potential future states of the process, as well as to "improve" its performance and "adapt" to external changes through prescriptions or recommendations.

Next to the above layers, the *action layer* provides capabilities for triggering actions that affect the execution of the process. Such actions include, among others, *i)* creating or altering the state of a case in a business process, e.g., through a workflow management system; *ii)* interacting with external actors through collaboration tools, e.g., sending an e-mail to notify an applicant about a change in their application; *iii)* triggering a software bot to perform an automated activity; and *iv)* updating records in a CRM, ERP, or other Systems of Records. This layer enables the A-BPMS to handle the execution of the process ("enact").

The *orchestration layer* rests on top of these layers, coordinating the subsystems that manage the process and handling the decision-making to improve the process performance and adapt to external changes. Composed of agentic and/or rule-based process orchestration systems, this layer allows the A-BPMS to "reason" based on the analytics provided by the process intelligence layer, and to effectively perform the actions enabled by previous layers.

Finally, the *conversational layer* serves as an interface that exposes the capabilities of the system to various types of external agents and users. The interaction between users and the A-BPMS is channeled through conversational agents powered by generative AI techniques – e.g., Large Language Models. Meanwhile, the interaction with external agents is implemented through *Model Context Protocol* (MCP) [9] tools, which provide semantically rich descriptions for their consumption.

Within an A-BPM system, the data layer provides access to historical and current data for the techniques belonging to the process intelligence layer. These techniques, which establish an interface layer to access the process data for all other components, generate insights that are consumed by the action layer, the orchestration layer, and the conversational layer. The action layer utilizes these insights to make localized decisions – e.g., when executing the process or planning future allocations –, closing the cycle by producing process data that is fed back to the data layer. Meanwhile, the orchestration layer leverages the insights provided by process intelligence capabilities, as well as information from external agents and users, to coordinate the components of the action layer. Finally, the conversational layer constitutes an interface that channels the exchange of information between the system and the external agents and users.

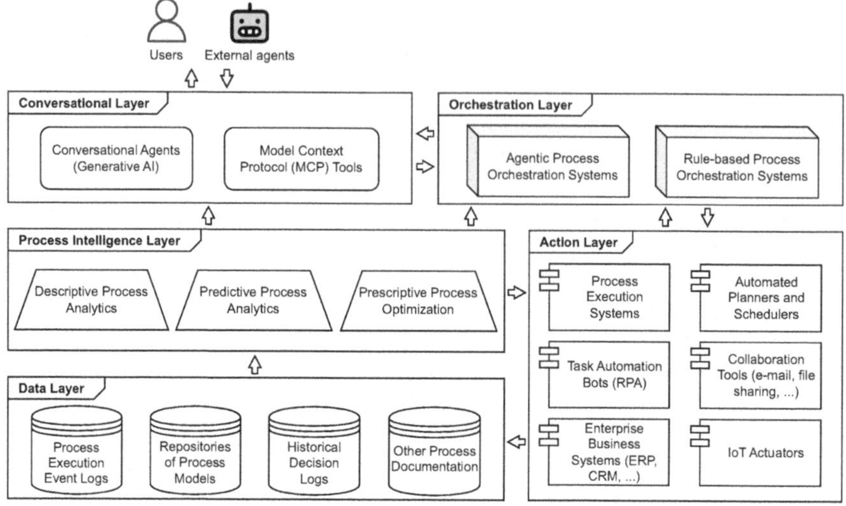

Fig. 2. Layered architecture of an Agentic BPM System.

4 Levels of Automation and Autonomy

Traditionally, the execution of processes has been viewed as a linear spectrum ranging from manual to automated [10,11]. The emergence of agentic AI presents a third and distinct mode: autonomous process execution [5,12]. In this section, we propose a conceptual model that extends the traditional human-to-automated spectrum with an autonomous dimension. This model classifies BPM systems depending on both the actor that executes an activity and the actor that orchestrates the process, i.e., a human (manual), a rule-based system (automated), or an agentic AI (autonomous).

4.1 The Process Execution Spectrum

Activities within a business process (either atomic, semi-atomic, or long-running) can be executed by either a human, a rule-based bot, or an agentic AI.

The execution of an activity is considered manual when the main actor is a human, even when supported by autonomous or automated systems. For instance, an employee registering an invoice in the system, even if assisted by a machine that automatically fills in the data, is considered a manual execution.

The automated execution of an activity is performed by rule-based bots that follow a fixed, pre-defined set of rules. Their value lies in automating repetitive tasks where all possible scenarios can be anticipated and scripted. For instance, a bot might be programmed to take an incoming invoice via email, extract the invoice data, and input the data into a system via an API [4]. In this context, no human interaction is needed.

The execution of an activity is considered autonomous when enabled by an agentic AI. In this context, we define agentic AI as a software that has the capability to *sense*, *decide*, and *act*. "Sense" refers to the ability to analyze its environment, process information from various sources – such as software APIs, databases, or physical sensors –, and extract relevant insights. "Decide" refers to the capabilities to evaluate multiple options, reason through scenarios, and determine the next course of action. "Act" is the capability to execute the chosen strategy by, for instance, interfacing with external systems, coordinating with other agents, or directly instructing other systems to achieve its specified objectives without requiring human support or supervision.[1] For instance, an agentic system may be designed to assess the potential fraudulence of a loan application by autonomously executing a set of machine learning algorithms and combining their outputs with domain-specific knowledge.

Similar to the execution of activities, a business process can be orchestrated by a human, a rule-based system, or an agentic AI. Here, the process orchestrator is the central entity responsible for guiding a business process from start to finish, defining the overall flow, managing dependencies, and ensuring the process achieves its objectives.

In human orchestration, a human is the central conductor of highly variable and knowledge-intensive processes. A rule-based orchestrator relies on predefined sets of rules or rigid workflow engines that execute deterministic processes automatically, a characteristic typical of traditional BPM suites, where the sequence of steps, decision points, and assignments are explicitly modeled upfront. An agentic orchestrator represents the most advanced form, where an agent autonomously determines and manages the entire process flow to achieve a high-level goal. We connect these foundational orchestrators into the (triangular) process execution spectrum depicted in Fig. 3, with three separated regions representing human, rule-based, and agentic orchestration of a business process.

At the bottom left region of the spectrum, we find processes orchestrated by human actors. The bottom left vertex corresponds to traditional BPM, where human employees are responsible for executing all activities of the process from start to finish. For instance, in criminal investigations [13], this manual process is exemplified by the investigative framework, where detectives assess each situation, make decisions about resource allocation, conduct face-to-face interviews with victims and witnesses, and physically attend crime scenes to gather evidence, among other tasks.

[1] Agentic AI is distinctly different from generative AI. While generative AI is capable of generating content once prompted, i.e., reactively, an agentic AI proactively performs actions and makes decisions in order to achieve a specific goal. Agents are, therefore, autonomous.

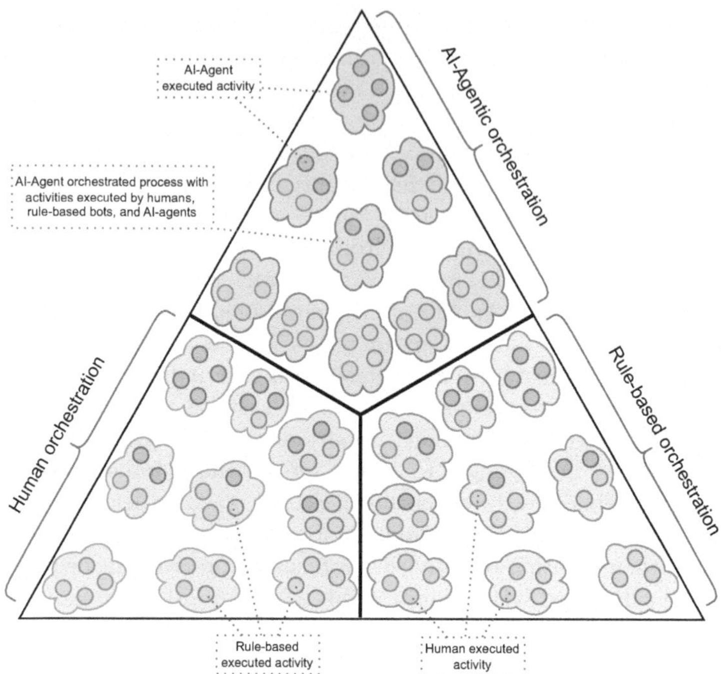

Fig. 3. Autonomy Spectrum of Business Process Execution.

At the bottom right region, we find processes orchestrated by rule-based systems. The bottom right vertex represents processes that are both managed and executed by a predetermined set of rules and procedures. This is the domain of traditional process automation. The orchestration is procedural and fixed. The system is designed to handle activities in a predictable and deterministic manner. While the rules were designed by humans, their execution is automated. For instance, in manufacturing companies, such as Tesla, this is exemplified by robots that perform welding, painting, and assembly operations according to exact specifications. Each robot executes its designated task in a predetermined sequence, following a program that dictates every movement, timing, and action [14].

Finally, at the top region of the triangle, we find agent-based orchestrated processes. The top vertex represents fully autonomous process execution, where (AI-)agents orchestrate the process – with the objective of achieving a defined high-level goal – and execute all its activities. For instance, in a procurement context, such AI agents autonomously conduct supplier negotiations. They analyze market conditions in real-time, assess supplier behavior patterns, dynamically adjust negotiation strategies, and have the authority to finalize deals [15].

4.2 Agentic Orchestration Patterns

Processes exist anywhere within this spectrum. For instance, the detective (human orchestrator) may maintain control and decision-making over the process, but delegate some activities to rule-based systems (e.g., database searches for criminal records) or to agentic systems (e.g., analysis of digital evidence patterns). As more automated or autonomous activity executions are included, the process position moves toward the bottom right (rule-based corner) or upward (agentic corner), but still within the human orchestration region of the triangle.

Within the boundaries of human, rule-based, or agentic orchestrator foundations, different types of agentic sub-orchestrators may emerge. Such patterns define how agents interact, delegate responsibilities, and manage workflows within a sub-process. These patterns vary in structure, adaptability, and communication style, allowing system designers to tailor agent behavior to specific use cases.

The most common and standard type would be *Sequential Orchestration*, where agents operate in a fixed pipeline. Sequential Orchestration involves arranging agents in a fixed linear pipeline where each agent performs a specific task and passes its output to the next agent in the sequence. For instance, in contract creation, the process might begin with a template selection agent, followed by a clause customization agent, then a compliance checker, and finally a risk assessment agent. Each agent adds value incrementally, ensuring a thorough and structured output.

A variation and slightly more complex type is the *Parallel Orchestration*, which enables multiple agents to operate concurrently, either on the same task or on different aspects of a task simultaneously. For instance, during product evaluation, technical, legal, and business agents can independently assess the product from their respective domains, providing a comprehensive and multi-faceted analysis that would be slower or less rich if done sequentially.

The next level of complexity requires some form of delegation where one agent acts as a supervisor or a manager. Here, the *Routing Pattern* features a central agent that routes tasks to specialized agents. This pattern would be more common in customer support systems, where a supervisor agent might route billing inquiries to a finance agent, technical issues to a support agent, and legal questions to a compliance agent. It ensures efficient handling of diverse queries while maintaining centralized oversight.

A variation is the *Managerial Orchestration*, where a master agent works with task delegation. Managerial Orchestration features a master agent that decomposes a complex task into subtasks and delegates them to specialized sub-agents. The master agent ensures that subtasks are executed in the correct order and that dependencies are respected. For instance, in a travel planning system, the master agent might assign hotel booking to one agent, flight search to another, and itinerary creation to a third, ensuring that all components align with the user's preferences and constraints.

When agents themselves decide when and to whom to transfer the work, we have *Adaptive Orchestration*, which allows agents to transfer control based on context. Adaptive Orchestration focuses on dynamic delegation, where agents transfer control to others based on the evolving context of a task. This pattern is useful in workflows that require adaptability and context-aware decision-making. An example could be a summarization agent that, after generating a summary, hands off the output to a visualization agent to create a graphical representation.

The next level of complexity is when agents can collaborate without direct supervision. For instance, *Mesh Orchestration* supports decentralized peer-to-peer coordination. In this model, agents communicate directly with one another, passing tasks off as needed without the need for a central controller. For instance, agents collaboratively resolving a support ticket might pass the issue from one to another based on expertise, availability, or context, adapting dynamically to the situation without relying on a central orchestrator.

Finally, the most advanced type is the *Self-orchestration*, where agents self-select tasks based on relevance. Self-orchestration introduces a mechanism where tasks emit signals that attract relevant agents. Agents evaluate these signals and self-select tasks based on their capabilities, availability, or interest. For instance, in a report analysis system, agents might self-assign to different sections of a document based on their domain expertise, ensuring that each part is handled by the most qualified agent.

Each pattern offers distinct advantages depending on the complexity, adaptability, and control requirements of the task at hand. The choice of pattern and implementation of Agentic AI should be determined from the nature of the business process that is to be supported or replaced. However, these patterns form a versatile toolkit for designing agentic AI systems that can support virtually all kinds of business processes.

4.3 Agentic Execution Patterns

In the execution of sub-processes and activities, different patterns emerge on how humans, rule-based systems, and agentic AI interact at various levels of granularity, including triage, human-assisted, agent-assisted, and verification patterns.

The *Triage Pattern* involves intelligent decision-making that dynamically routes cases or activities to the most appropriate executor – human, rule-based, or agent-based. This pattern optimizes resource allocation by ensuring that each activity is handled by the most suitable actor. For instance, in a customer service process, incoming inquiries are automatically assessed and routed. In this context, simple inquiries may be handled autonomously by AI; moderately complex issues that can be solved by executing predefined steps – e.g., billing disputes – may be processed by rule-based systems; and sensitive complaints may be escalated to human actors.

Human-Assisted Agent represents a pattern where an agent performs the primary activity, autonomously making decisions, while a human provides oversight, verification, or final approval to ensure quality, compliance, and accountability. This pattern is relevant, for instance, in high-stakes environments where human accountability remains non-negotiable. For instance, an AI agent might analyze market data, process complex algorithms, and generate investment recommendations for private banking customers. However, the client executive must review, validate, and approve these recommendations before they are executed.

Agent-Assisted Human, on the other hand, involves humans performing the primary activity or decision-making, while AI agents provide verification, quality assurance, additional insights, or real-time support to enhance human performance and reduce errors. For instance, in customer support operations, human representatives may handle complex customer calls that require empathy, problem-solving, and relationship management, while AI agents simultaneously analyze the conversation to assess factors such as tone, politeness, compliance with company policies, and customer satisfaction indicators.

The *Verification Pattern* establishes quality control mechanisms in which one type of performer systematically reviews, checks, or validates the output of another to ensure accuracy, compliance, and adherence to standards. An example of this pattern occurs in content creation workflows, where a human writer may produce initial content leveraging their creativity and domain expertise, while an AI agent conducts a comprehensive review for factual accuracy, tone consistency, and alignment with brand guidelines.

5 Implications for Research

The attention and traction of LLM models and Agentic AI might require revisiting traditional BPM, similar to how the maturation of client-server architectures impacted BPM. Earlier automation waves considered a spectrum of manual and rule-based execution. However, agentic performers introduce autonomous software that can sense, decide, and act beyond pre-programmed rules. This can open up the field for new research opportunities.

One area of research is in the process modelling stage. Today's activity-centric notations might prove inadequate once "agent" becomes a first-class performer. A purchase-to-pay model written in BPMN, for instance, lacks constructs for expressing an agent's planning capability or the constitutional frame that constrains it. Future formalisms should support, for instance, objective-based blocks, guard-rail annotations, and verification patterns.

The introduction of agentic AI systems, with their autonomous decision-making capabilities and complex human-AI interactions, necessitates the inclusion of verification-centric process design where quality control, accuracy validation, and compliance checking become part of the design phase. Research is needed to develop frameworks that identify where verification patterns should be embedded within processes, how to design multi-layered validation mechanisms that can operate across human, rule-based, and agentic components, and methods for ensuring that autonomous agents maintain accountability.

Organisations will gradually redesign existing processes to include LLM and agentic AI components. However, history has shown that technology substitution creates modest gains. Client-server platforms and the early Internet made broad automation possible, yet real value emerged only when firms redesigned work to exploit once-only data capture, automated rule checking, and web self-service. LLM and agentic AI follow the same pattern. By the same logic, it might be valid to consider what business process improvement opportunities LLM and agentic AI can enable. Hence, the existing catalogue of redesign heuristics (task elimination, parallelism, integral technology) might need an agentic extension.

References

1. Dumas, M., van der Aalst, W.M.P., ter Hofstede, A.H.M., eds.: Process-Aware Information Systems: Bridging People and Software Through Process Technology. Wiley (2005)
2. Davenport, T.H.: Process innovation: reengineering work through information technology. Harvard business press (1993)
3. Dumas, M., Rosa, L.M., Mendling, J., Reijers, A.H.: Fundamentals of business process management. Springer (2018)
4. Van der Aalst, W.M., Bichler, M., Heinzl, A.: Robotic process automation. Bus. & Inf. Syst. Eng. **60**(4), 269–272 (2018)
5. Janiesch, C., Kowalkiewicz, M., Rosemann, M.: Process autonomization: Rethinking business process management. In: International Conference on Business Process Management, pp. 361–377, Springer (2025). https://doi.org/10.1007/978-3-032-02929-4_21
6. Dumas, M., Fournier, F., Limonad, L., Marrella, A., Montali, M., Rehse, J.R., Accorsi, R., Calvanese, D., De Giacomo, G., Fahland, D., et al.: Ai-augmented business process management systems: a research manifesto. ACM Trans. Manag. Inf. Syst. **14**(1), 1–19 (2023)
7. Acharya, D.B., Kuppan, K., Divya, B.: Agentic ai: autonomous intelligence for complex goals-a comprehensive survey. IEEE Access (2025)
8. Chapela-Campa, D., Dumas, M.: From process mining to augmented process execution. Softw. Syst. Model. **22**(6), 1977–1986 (2023)
9. Hou, X., Zhao, Y., Wang, S., Wang, H.: Model context protocol (MCP): landscape, security threats, and future research directions. CoRR abs/2503.23278 (2025)
10. Zayas-Cabán, T., Haque, S.N., Kemper, N.: Identifying opportunities for workflow automation in health care: lessons learned from other industries. Appl. Clin. Inform. **12**(03), 686–697 (2021)
11. Mishra, S., Sree Devi, K., Badri Narayanan, M.: People & process dimensions of automation in business process management industry. Int. J. Eng. Adv. Technol. **8**(6), 2465–2472 (2019)
12. Vu, H., Klievtsova, N., Leopold, H., Rinderle-Ma, S., Kampik, T.: Agentic business process management: Practitioner perspectives on agent governance in business processes. In: Proceedings of the 23rd International Conference on Business Process Management, pp. 29–43. Springer, Cham (2025). https://doi.org/10.1007/978-3-032-02936-2_3
13. Innes, M.: The 'process structures' of police homicide investigations. Br. J. Criminol. **42**(4), 669–688 (2002)
14. Kaur, N., Sharma, A.: Robotics and automation in manufacturing processes. In: Intelligent Manufacturing, pp. 97–109. CRC Press (2025)
15. Herold, S., Heller, J., Rozemeijer, F., Mahr, D.: Brave new procurement deals: An experimental study of how generative artificial intelligence reshapes buyer-supplier negotiations. J. Purchasing Supply Manag. 101012 (2025)

Revealing Trace Variant Shift via Multi-dimensional Profiling and Community-Aware Graph Modeling

Iuliana Malina Grigore[1(✉)], Gabriel Marques Tavares[2,3], Vincenzo Pasquadibisceglie[4], and Sylvio Barbon Junior[1]

[1] Università degli Studi di Trieste, Trieste, Italy
iulianamalina.grigore@phd.units.it, sylvio.barbonjunior@units.it
[2] LMU Munich, Munich, Germany
tavares@dbs.ifi.lmu.de
[3] Munich Center for Machine Learning (MCML), Munich, Germany
[4] University of Bari Aldo Moro, Bari, Italy
vincenzo.pasquadibisceglie@uniba.it

Abstract. Tracking the evolution of trace variants over time is a challenging task in process mining, particularly in dynamic environments where process executions change independently. Existing approaches often fall short in detecting fine-grained, temporal changes at the variant level. In this paper, we present a novel technique that integrates multi-dimensional profiling with graph-based analysis to monitor variant-level shift. Each trace is represented through a comprehensive profile that combines control-flow and time-related information, including features extracted via discrete wavelet transform. These profiles are embedded into a similarity space and linked using a k-nearest neighbor graph to capture local structural patterns. By applying community detection, we identify clusters corresponding to distinct trace variants and analyze their evolution over time. This approach enables the detection of subtle, localized variant shifts, facilitating faster and more informed decision-making within organizations. Experiments on real-world event logs demonstrate the effectiveness of our method in revealing significant behavioral shifts from a variant-centric perspective.

Keywords: Process mining · Variant shift · Conformance checking · Clustering · Community detection · Change

1 Introduction

In today's dynamic business environment, processes are constantly evolving in response to external factors such as regulatory updates, market development, and changes in business rules. As processes evolve, new characteristics may be introduced and existing elements modified, leading to changes that make the process behavior more dynamic and less predictable [24]. The ability to quickly

I. van de Weerd et al. (Eds.): BPM 2025 Workshops, LNBIP 569, pp. 15–27, 2026.
https://doi.org/10.1007/978-3-032-13426-4_2

recognize and understand these changes has become a key competitive advantage for the company's management level. Organizations that can effectively manage process variability are better able to optimize workflows, reduce risk, and maintain efficiency.

Since variations in process execution often correspond to specific trace variants, recognizing concept drift, i.e., changes or shifts, at this level provides a deeper understanding of process evolution. Trace variants represent unique sequences of activities observed in an event log. Identifying changes in these variants allows organizations to monitor process deviations, diagnose the underlying causes, and update the process model accordingly. Traditionally, changes in process behavior have been studied through concept drift detection, especially in real-time online environments [3]. However, most approaches in the literature focus on identifying change at the process level without considering possible update strategies. Moreover, such approaches rely on partial data, typically based on small time windows, which makes them susceptible to noise and limits their ability to capture long-term or structural changes in processes. This limitation stems primarily from the focus of online process mining on enabling actionable decisions in real time [12].

Unlike online approaches to concept drift, our hypothesis is based on an offline strategy that analyzes complete event logs to provide a more comprehensive view of variant-level changes. We refer to these changes as **variant shifts** to emphasize our distinct perspective on process evolution. Rather than focusing on drift as a statistical deviance, we focus on how trace variants emerge and evolve. These changes may reflect structural adaptations that are not always captured by conventional drift detectors or subtle shifts that may be missed by real-time analysis.

Our method builds upon cluster-based shift detection techniques [22], extending them to the level of trace variants within a fully observable temporal context. The main goal is to achieve greater precision than traditional trace variant analysis by incorporating temporal information, which helps to avoid splitting behaviors that are the same. Additionally, our approach is more accurate than online methods, as it leverages the complete temporal information available in the entire event log.

For that, we represent each trace as a multi-dimensional profile that combines: (i) the sequence of activities to capture the execution order of tasks, (ii) transition patterns that reflect the structural flow of the process, and (iii) temporal dynamics extracted using the discrete wavelet transform (DWT) [8]. DWT offers the advantage of capturing both local and global timefrequency variations in execution, enabling the detection of subtle temporal shifts and patterns that traditional time features or statistical summaries might overlook. By creating a k-nearest neighbor (kNN) graph, we connect similar traces and apply community detection techniques to identify clusters of related trace variants, e.g., using unsupervised models. The most important contributions of this work are:

- A multi-dimensional trace profiling technique that integrates activity sequences, control-flow structures, and temporal dynamics using DWT.

- An offline framework that uncovers both behavioral shifts and stable trace variants by analyzing structural features from the kNN graph.

The paper is organized as follows: Sect. 2 gives an overview of related work on process change detection. Section 3 formulates the notion of trace variant shift. Section 4 presents our methodology. Section 5 discusses experimental results. Section 6 concludes the paper and points out directions for future work.

2 Related Work

Numerous efforts have focused on detecting deviations during process execution, particularly through online process mining, where event streams are analyzed in real time to detect and respond to changes [18–20, 22]. While these methods are effective for immediate adaptation, they deal with a different class of problems than the one studied here. Online process mining typically targets concept drift, where process behavior evolves dynamically over time and models must be adjusted during execution [19]. However, these methods often overlook the detailed evolution of trace variants and are not well-suited for retrospective analysis. Offline approaches, by contrast, leverage complete event logs to enable in-depth variant-level analysis. We illustrate the primary research areas relevant to offline process shift detection, as identified in [5]: (1) Time Window Analysis, (2) Clustering-based drift detection, (3) Graph-based analysis, and (4) Shift Detection.

Time Window Analysis. A common approach is to compare traces over time windows to detect significant changes [3]. One such method uses non-overlapping windows of fixed size for statistical analysis [2]. The effectiveness of this method strongly depends on the window size: a small window might under-detect drifts, whereas a large window might not capture more subtle variations. To solve this problem, adaptive window methods [11] dynamically adjust the window size, allowing more flexibility. Another approach uses sliding windows in combination with entropy-based methods and feature vector analysis [27]. This technique evaluates trace distributions in overlapping time windows and provides a more flexible and adaptive mechanism for drift detection. However, the sliding window approach requires careful tuning of parameters to balance sensitivity. In [17], the authors highlight the challenges in distinguishing different types of drift, especially when sudden and gradual drifts occur simultaneously. Conventional techniques often require extensive feature selection or high-dimensional representations to accurately detect both types of drift. More recently, drift detection methods based on embeddings have been introduced to overcome the limitations of window-based approaches [14]. These methods use encoded traces to capture the evolving process behavior and enable the detection of sudden shifts by identifying changes in the vector representations of traces.

Clustering Analysis. Clustering techniques are often used in offline environments to detect process behavior shifts by analyzing cluster structure changes over time. These methods typically abstract traces into feature vectors that capture control-flow and temporal features, allowing the identification of process variants and their evolution. Initial studies evaluated clustering strategies based on their ability to group similar traces without explicitly considering the temporal dimension [26]. Later work has extended this by combining clustering with concept drift detection mechanisms [21]. An agglomerative clustering approach proposed in [16] clusters traces based on features such as recursion metrics and initial timestamps. When a new cluster appears, indicating a behavioral change, a drift is inferred. Other studies use graph-based clustering [10] based on a behavior graph. This method reveals both common and uncommon behaviors by analyzing cluster density and size. Although effective, it requires extensive manual configuration and is sensitive to the choice of similarity metrics.

Graph Analysis. Graph-based approaches model process behavior as graphs, with nodes representing activities and edges representing control-flow transitions. Changes are detected by comparing structural properties across sub-protocols or time intervals. [23] uses statistical tests and graph metrics to quantify deviations. The method applies adaptive windows to isolate behavioral segments and compares the graph structures to assess the impact of changes. Although this approach effectively localizes changes, it relies on the heuristic miner, which is known to perform poorly in scenarios with long loops or high variability [23].

Grigore et al. [7] present a method for constructing k-NN graphs from multi-view trace variant representations. This method enhances anomaly detection through community analysis, showing improved modularity and clearer anomaly separation in experiments with object-centric event data compared to traditional clustering. However, it overlooks the temporal aspect of variants, which may affect the detection of time-related anomalies.

Shift Detection. Recent research has focused on the automatic detection of changes in process variants. Hmami et al. [9] propose a method based on a modified STAGGER algorithm to detect both abrupt and recurrent changes in configurable process models. However, their approach is limited to analysing the control-flow and does not consider other dimensions such as data or resource usage, nor does it explain the causes of the changes. Ghourchian et al. [6] combine clustering and control-flow analysis by segmenting event logs over time. While the method is effective in tracking how process behaviour evolves, it lacks explanatory power and does not address the underlying drivers of change. This limits its applicability for diagnostic or improvement-oriented tasks.

3 Variant Shift

Change mining deals with the identification of structural or behavioral process changes by analyzing historical event data. In contrast to drift detection, which often targets runtime adjustments, change mining attempts to understand long-term variability and supports retrospective optimization [15]. Managing process variability is critical to adapting processes to evolving requirements and ensuring robustness.

Given the novelty of the problem of **trace variant shift**, a proper definition is needed. Let $L = \{\sigma_1, \sigma_2, \ldots, \sigma_n\}$ be an event log, where each σ_i is a trace, defined as a finite sequence of activities over an alphabet $\mathcal{A}$, i.e., $\sigma_i \in \mathcal{A}^*$. A *trace variant* $v \subseteq \mathcal{A}^*$ is a unique control-flow sequence that represents a distinct ordering of activities. Let $\mathcal{V}_{t_i}$ denote the set of trace variants observed in a specific time window t_i and $\mathcal{D}_{\text{variant}}(t_i)$ represents the set of variant-level changes observed at time window t_i with respect to a reference set $\mathcal{V}_{\text{ref}}$ (e.g., computed from a stable historical baseline).

Variant Shift occurs when there is a significant change in control-flow behavior during t_i, as indicated by a shift in the set of observed variants relative to a reference variant set $\mathcal{V}_{\text{ref}}$, such that: $\mathcal{D}_{\text{variant}}(t_i) = \mathcal{V}_{t_i} \Delta \mathcal{V}_{\text{ref}} \neq \emptyset$, where Δ denotes the symmetric difference between the sets, capturing variants that have emerged or disappeared in t_i compared to the reference. A non-empty $\mathcal{D}_{\text{variant}}(t_i)$ indicates a deviation in control-flow execution patterns, signaling the presence of variant-level process shift.

Optionally, let $f : (\mathcal{V}_{\text{ref}}, \mathcal{V}_{t_i}) \to \{0, 1\}$ be a function that predicts the presence (1) or absence (0) of a structural shift between variant sets, where f can be defined explicitly through a control-flow distance function $d(v, v')$ with a tolerance threshold $\epsilon > 0$, or induced using a machine learning model trained to distinguish evolving behaviors. In this case, a shift is identified when there exists $v \in \mathcal{V}_{\text{ref}}$ and $v' \in \mathcal{V}_{t_i}$ such that $d(v, v') > \epsilon$ and $v \notin \mathcal{V}_{t_i}$, suggesting that variant v has evolved into v' through structural transformation.

4 Proposed Approach

This work introduces a modular framework for detecting variant shifts (i.e., behavioral changes) in event logs by leveraging multiview trace profiling and graph-based analysis. The overall pipeline, depicted in Fig. 1, consists of four main components: *Trace Profiling*, *Graph Modeling*, *Graph Analytics*, and *Shift Detection*. Each component was designed to detect trace-level changes and account for the specific characteristics of the proposed approach.

4.1 Trace Profiling

Given an event log, the first step is to extract and represent traces through multiple behavioral and structural perspectives. Specifically, we focus on the *Activity View*, *Transition View*, and *Resource View*, as well as the temporal behavior of each trace.

We encode each view using a combination of one-hot encoding and wavelet coefficients through DWT [8]. One-hot encoding transforms categorical information into a structured binary vectorial representation, enabling comparison across traces in terms of performed activities, control-flow structures, and resource involvement [25].

One of our main contributions is the usage of DWT to capture the temporal dynamics of execution. We extract time histograms from each trace (e.g., activity durations or inter-arrival times) and apply the Haar wavelet packet transform [4]. The transformation using the wavelet packet method with symmetric boundary

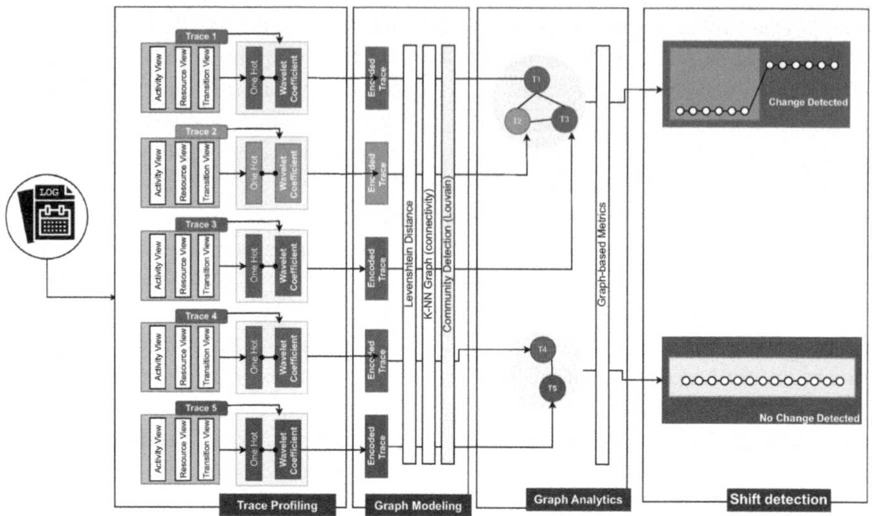

Fig. 1. Overview of the proposed approach: multiview trace profiling, graph construction, structural clustering, and behavioral shift detection.

handling and depth-limited decomposition (level 2) can represent subtle changes in the timefrequency structure of execution behavior between traces. Formally, each histogram is converted into a set of localized frequency components, capturing both coarse and fine temporal variations. The encoded feature vector is obtained by flattening the coefficients from all level-2 nodes in the wavelet packet tree, preserving both high-frequency (short-term fluctuations) and low-frequency (long-term trends) information.

Numerical Example. Consider a trace: $\tau = \langle(\mathit{Start}, r_1, 0), (\mathit{Approve}, r_2, 5), (\mathit{End}, r_2, 9)\rangle$, where each event is represented as a tuple (activity, resource, timestamp in minutes). Let the set of activities be $\mathcal{A} = \{\mathit{Start}, \mathit{Approve}, \mathit{Reject}, \mathit{End}\}$, the observed transitions $\mathcal{T}_A = \{(\mathit{Start}, \mathit{Approve}), (\mathit{Approve}, \mathit{End}), (\mathit{Start}, \mathit{Reject}), (\mathit{Reject}, \mathit{End})\}$, and the resources $\mathcal{R} = \{r_1, r_2\}$. The one-hot encoded nominal vector includes activity presence, transition occurrence, and resource usage: $v_{\text{nominal}} = (1,\ 1,\ 0,\ 1,\ 1,\ 1,\ 0,\ 0,\ 1,\ 1)$. From the timestamps, we compute inter-event durations (5 and 4 min), which are aggregated into a normalized histogram: $[0, 1, 0, 0, 1, 0, 0, 0]$. Applying a wavelet packet decomposition, in this example a Haar family, at level 2 to this histogram yields the temporal vector $v_{\text{wavelet}} = (0.5, -0.5, 0.5, -0.5)$. The trace representation is the concatenation of both components: $v_{\text{trace}} = (1, 1, 0, 1, 1, 1, 0, 0, 1, 1,\ \ 0.5, -0.5, 0.5, -0.5)$, capturing control-flow structure, resource involvement, and timefrequency behavior for downstream comparison and analysis.

4.2 Graph Modeling and Analytics

Once encoded, traces are modeled as nodes in a similarity graph to facilitate structural and topological analysis. The pairwise dissimilarity between traces is first computed using a configurable distance function, such as Levenshtein distance for sequence-based encodings or Euclidean distance for vector-based representations. Resulting in a distance matrix $D \in \mathbb{R}^{n \times n}$, where D_{ij} quantifies the dissimilarity between traces τ_i and τ_j.

To construct a graph that reflects the local neighborhood structure of the trace space, we generate a kNN graph using the precomputed distance matrix. Each node in the graph represents a trace, and an undirected edge is established between a trace and its k closest neighbors. This is implemented using a connectivity-based kNN approach, where an adjacency matrix is constructed such that: $A_{ij} = 1, \text{if } \tau_j \in \mathcal{N}_k(\tau_i) \text{ or } \tau_i \in \mathcal{N}_k(\tau_j), \text{ otherwise } A_{ij} = 0$, with $\mathcal{N}_k(\tau)$ denoting the set of k nearest neighbors of trace τ. The resulting sparse adjacency matrix is then converted into an undirected graph.

To support the structural analysis of trace variant behavior, we begin by extracting features from the kNN graph. This step ensures that subsequent graph-based operations include: community detection, centrality computation, and behavioral shift analysis.

Community detection is performed using the Louvain method [1], a widely used modularity optimization algorithm that partitions the graph into densely connected subgroups. Each resulting community corresponds to a subset of traces that exhibit similar structural and behavioral characteristics, such as recurrent control-flow motifs or similar timing profiles. To further characterize the role and influence of each trace within the graph, we compute a comprehensive set of node-level metrics derived from classical and spectral graph theory. These include degree-based metrics, such as degree, degree centrality, mean degree of neighbors (*degree_mean*), minimum neighbor degree (*degree_min*), and degree standard deviation (*degree_std*), which capture local connectivity patterns. In addition, we consider centrality measures including information centrality, load centrality, betweenness centrality, eigenvector centrality, closeness centrality, and approximate current flow betweenness, offering multiple perspectives on the structural importance and reachability of each node. Finally, we compute spectral descriptors such as subgraph centrality (using the exponential kernel) and the Estrada index, which reflects the node's participation in closed walks and its global communicability within the graph.

Each trace (node) is annotated with these descriptors, forming a structural profile that supports both global analysis (e.g., role distribution across communities) and local interpretation (e.g., identifying structurally anomalous or influential traces). These metrics are stored in a tabular format, facilitating their integration into downstream machine learning or interpretability pipelines. To better reflect real-life scenarios, we suggest the use of one-class classification models trained exclusively on non-shift behaviors, allowing the system to detect deviations without requiring labeled shifts.

4.3 Change Detection

To detect variant shifts over time, the proposed framework conducts change detection by analyzing structural variations in graph-based representations of the event log. We advocate for the use of one-class classification methods to identify deviations from a reference "safe" process variant, which can be either artificially modeled or derived from a controlled setting as proposed in [13]. The classifier learns patterns associated with structural features, capturing changes in community composition through variations in node centrality distributions or the emergence of high-centrality bridge nodes, both indicative of behavioral transitions.

5 Experiments

The proposed approach was evaluated using real event logs sourced from the 4TU Centre for Research Data repository[1], focusing on modeling process deviations through localized shifts in both control-flow and temporal dimensions. Wavelet coefficients and graph-based metrics were computed using Python, and a One-Class SVM model was employed to detect behavioral shifts. The full implementation, along with the event logs used, is publicly available as open-source software[2]. For the control flow perspective, we extracted all variants from each event log and manually analyzed their sequences. Variants with minor rearrangements or minor non-critical activities were classified as normal. In contrast, significant structural changes like new activities, removal of key steps, or major reordering were labelled as *control-flow shifted*. From the temporal perspective, we measured each variant's execution time, calculating the mean duration and standard deviation. A trace was considered *temporally normal* if it fell within one standard deviation of the mean; traces outside this were *temporally shifted*. We identified shifted behavior when a variant showed deviations in both control flow and time. We apply this analysis to four publicly available event logs to evaluate our approach. The Road Traffic Fine Management Process records the execution of an information system responsible for processing road traffic fines. The Hospital Billing log contains event data from the financial modules of the ERP system of a regional hospital. In addition, we used two logs from the BPI Challenge 2020: the International Declarations log, which records the customs declaration processes, and the Prepaid Travel Cost log, which documents the reimbursement process for business travel expenses.

Table 1 provides a concise overview of each event log, including the count of identified shifted traces. To introduce diversity in variant structure and activities, we selected varying numbers of variants for the event logs. For the Prepaid and International logs, we chose and analyzed the 10 most frequent variants. For the hospital and road traffic logs, which are much more extensive, we first selected specific time windows for the execution of each process. Then, we focused on the 16 most frequent variants for the hospital and 12 for the road traffic.

[1] https://data.4tu.nl/.

[2] https://github.com/grimali/04CL_changing.

Table 1. Description of the benchmark event logs.

Event log	#Events	#Traces	#Variants	#Activities	#Traces Shifted
Hospital	59606	10960	15	12	379
Road	45833	12427	12	11	572
Prepaid	12995	1548	10	16	65
International	37674	3554	10	19	251

5.1 Hyperparameter Definitions

Trace profiling is enriched with wavelet features, where each trace is transformed into a vector encoded using one-hot encoding for the trace, transitions, and resources, combined with wavelet coefficients computed across defined support levels. These `support` levels indicate the number of features used to represent temporal information. We investigate the values 4, 8, 16, and 32 as support levels. Graph representations are built using k-NN with `k` ranging from 2 to 24. Communities are detected via the Louvain algorithm with `resolution` values of 0.3, 0.5, 1.0, and 1.5.

For the One-Class SVM (OCSVM), we perform a grid search to identify optimal hyperparameters. The `nu` parameter is varied from 0.01 to 0.5 in increments of 0.05, while `gamma` is tested using both default settings (`auto` and `scale`) and numerical values ranging from 0.005 to 4.5.

5.2 Performance Results

We assess performance using the macro F1-score to address class imbalance, where stable variants are the dominant class. Table 2 summarizes the results of the OCSVM across datasets, with variations in `k`, `wavelet`, and `resolution`, as well as the optimized `nu` and `gamma` values selected to maximize macro F1.

Table 2. Macro F1-scores and settings (`k`, wavelet support, and `resolution`) for each dataset. The best configuration is highlighted in bold.

Event Log	k	wavelet	resolution	nu	gamma	F1-score	#Normal	#Shifts
Hospital	2	32	1.0	0.10	scale	0.49	417	14
	5	**8**	**0.5**	**0.05**	**1.25**	**0.71**	**164**	**13**
	24	16	1.5	0.15	scale	0	50	0
Road	5	4	1.5	0.05	scale	0.41	15	5
	24	**16**	**0.3**	**0.05**	**1.25**	**0.71**	**31**	**1**
	24	16	1.5	0.15	scale	0	31	0
Prepaid	10	8	0.5	0.20	scale	0.65	30	5
	15	**16**	**1.0**	**0.05**	**3.5**	**0.89**	**18**	**5**
	20	16	1.0	0.10	scale	0	12	0
International	10	16	0.5	0.05	scale	0.70	53	2
	20	**16**	**0.5**	**0.01**	**4**	**0.82**	**29**	**1**
	20	16	1.0	0.10	scale	0	26	0

The *Hospital* log is characterized by high process variability, with numerous optional and concurrent subprocesses leading to a large number of control-flow variants. This inherent complexity makes shift detection particularly challenging. The best-performing configuration achieves a macro F1-score of 0.71 with $k = 5$, wavelet support of 8, and resolution 0.5. This setting effectively balances local connectivity and temporal granularity, enabling the model to detect 13 out of 14 located shifts. In contrast, configurations with overly sparse ($k = 2$) or overly dense ($k = 24$) graphs perform significantly worse, with the latter failing to detect any shifts. Considering the *Road* log, which documents the handling of traffic fines, the control-flow structure is relatively simple, but there is considerable timing variability, particularly around incident reporting and resolution. The best result (F1-score of 0.71) is achieved with $k = 24$ and wavelet support of 16, suggesting that high temporal resolution is critical for detecting subtle delays or accelerations in subprocesses. The *Prepaid* log is derived from a structured reimbursement process with relatively few activities and tight execution constraints. In such environments, small deviations, like timing delays or out-of-sequence approvals, become more distinguishable. The method achieves its highest performance here (F1-score of 0.89) under $k = 15$, wavelet support of 16, and resolution 1.0. Finally, the *International* log captures cross-border declaration procedures with both structural variability and timing inconsistencies. These arise from interleaved subprocesses and varying approval workflows. The best configuration, with $k = 20$, wavelet support of 16, and resolution 0.5, yields an F1-score of 0.82 despite only one located shift.

5.3 Insights and Limitations

Across all datasets, high-performing configurations consistently rely on intermediate values of k (5–20) and wavelet supports of 8 or 16. These settings balance expressiveness and stability in the trace similarity graph and preserve both coarse and fine-grained temporal patterns. Interestingly, the resolution parameter exhibits less consistent impact on performance, suggesting that the model is relatively robust to community granularity within a moderate range.

Despite the limited number of shift instances, a realistic reflection of real-world process behavior, the method achieves high macro F1-scores, demonstrating its ability to detect shifts. The sharp performance degradation under non-optimal configurations further reinforces the importance of careful hyperparameter tuning or adaptive parameter selection mechanisms in practical applications.

6 Conclusion

By integrating control-flow, resource, and temporal features, particularly through DWT, into a unified trace representation, the approach enables robust detection of both structural and temporal shifts. The use of k-nearest neighbor graphs and Louvain community detection facilitates the identification of behavioral clusters and their evolution over time.

Experimental results across four real-world event logs demonstrate that the proposed method is effective in capturing subtle process changes, achieving high macro F1-scores. The analysis confirms that intermediate values for graph connectivity and wavelet support yield the best performance, emphasizing the importance of parameter tuning in practical deployments. Future work will focus on differentiating types of variant shifts and conducting multiple runs with the same hyperparameters to assess training stability.

Acknowledgments. This work has been supported by the European Union under the NextGenerationEU initiative, specifically through the NRRP (M4C2I1.1) and the REPA (aRtificial intElligence for Process Analytics) project. Additionally, it has received funding from the PORTRAIT project (Port to Rail Digital Twin in the Adriatic Region), which is funded by the PR FESR 20212027 under Action A1.1.2, DGR 784/2023 of the FVG Region in Italy. The work of Vincenzo Pasquadibisceglie was supported by PNRR project FAIR - Future AI Research (PE00000013), Spoke 6 - Symbiotic AI (CUP H97G22000210007) under the NRRP MUR program funded by the NextGenerationEU.

References

1. Blondel, V.D., Guillaume, J.L., Lambiotte, R., Lefebvre, E.: Fast unfolding of communities in large networks. J. Stat. Mech. Theory Exp. **2008**(10) (2008)
2. Bose, R.P.J.C., van der Aalst, W.M.P., Žliobaitė, I., Pechenizkiy, M.: Dealing with concept drifts in process mining. IEEE Trans. Neural Netw. Learn. Syst. **25**(1), 154–171 (2014)
3. Ceravolo, P., Tavares, G.M., Junior, S.B., Damiani, E.: Evaluation goals for online process mining: a concept drift perspective. IEEE Trans. Serv. Comput. **15**(4), 2473–2489 (2022)
4. Coifman, R.R., Wickerhauser, M.V.: Entropy-based algorithms for best basis selection. IEEE Trans. Inf. Theory **38**(2), 713–718 (1992)
5. Elkhawaga, G., Abuelkheir, M., Barakat, S.I., Riad, A.M., Reichert, M.: Conda-pm–a systematic review and framework for concept drift analysis in process mining. Algorithms **13**(7) (2020)
6. Ghourchian, N., Akhondzadeh Noughabi, E.: Concept drift and trace clustering: insights for managers from mining. Manag. Dec. (2025)
7. Grigore, I.M., Tavares, G.M., Junior, S.B.: Beyond flattening: detecting concurrency anomalies using k-nn graph-based modeling in object-centric event logs. In: Czekster, R.M., Milazzo, P. (eds.) From Data to Models and Back, vol. 15556. Springer, Cham (2025). https://doi.org/10.1007/978-3-031-87908-1_8
8. Guido, R.C.: Wavelets behind the scenes: practical aspects, insights, and perspectives. Phys. Rep. **985**, 1–23 (2022)
9. Hmami, A., Sbai, H., Fredj, M.: Handling sudden and recurrent changes in business process variability: change mining based approach. Int. J. Adv. Comput. Sci. Appl. **12**(4) (2021)
10. Hompes, B., Buijs, J., van der Aalst, W., Dixit, P., Buurman, J.: Detecting change in processes using comparative trace clustering. In: Ceravolo, P., Rinderle-Ma, S. (eds.) Proceedings of the 5th International Symposium on Data-driven Process Discovery and Analysis. pp. 95–108. CEUR Workshop Proceedings (2015)

11. Martjushev, J., Bose, R.P.J.C., van der Aalst, W.M.P.: Change point detection and dealing with gradual and multi-order dynamics in process mining. In: Matulevičius, R., Dumas, M. (eds.) Perspectives in Business Informatics Research, vol. 229. Springer, Cham (2015). https://doi.org/10.1007/978-3-319-21915-8_11
12. Junior, S.B., Tavares, G.M., Paolo Ceravolo, E.D.: A framework for trace clustering and concept-drift detection in event streams. CEUR Workshop Proceedings (2017)
13. Junior, S.B., Ceravolo, P., Damiani, E., Omori, N.J., Tavares, G.M.: Anomaly detection on event logs with a scarcity of labels. In: 2020 2nd International Conference on Process Mining (ICPM). pp. 161–168. IEEE (2020)
14. Khojasteh, F., Behkamal, B., Kahani, M., Khorasani, M.: Trace2vec-cdd: a framework for concept drift detection in business process logs using trace embedding. Comput. Knowl. Eng. **6**(1), 71–79 (2023)
15. Küster, J.M., Gerth, C., Förster, A., Engels, G.: Detecting and resolving process model differences in the absence of a change log. In: Dumas, M., Reichert, M., Shan, M.C. (eds.) Business Process Management. Springer, Berlin Heidelberg (2008)
16. Luengo, D., Sepúlveda, M.: Applying clustering in process mining to find different versions of a business process that changes over time. In: Daniel, F., Barkaoui, K., Dustdar, S. (eds.) Business Process Management Workshops. Springer, Berlin Heidelberg (2012)
17. Maaradji, A., Dumas, M., Rosa, M.L., Ostovar, A.: Detecting sudden and gradual drifts in business processes from execution traces. IEEE Trans. Knowl. Data Eng. **29**(10), 2140–2154 (2017)
18. Pasquadibisceglie, V., Appice, A., Castellano, G., Fiorentino, N., Malerba, D.: Stardust: a novel process mining approach to discover evolving models from trace streams. IEEE Trans. Serv. Comput. **16**(4), 2970–2984 (2023)
19. Pasquadibisceglie, V., Appice, A., Castellano, G., Malerba, D.: Darwin: An online deep learning approach to handle concept drifts in predictive process monitoring. Eng. Appl. Artif. Intell. **123**, 106461 (2023)
20. Pauwels, S., Calders, T.: Incremental predictive process monitoring: the next activity case. In: Polyvyanyy, A., Wynn, M.T., Van Looy, A., Reichert, M. (eds.) International Conference on Business Process Management, vol 12875, pp. 123–140. Springer, Cham (2021). https://doi.org/10.1007/978-3-030-85469-0_10
21. Prathama, F., Yahya, B.N., Danny Darmawan Harjono, M.E.: Trace clustering exploration for detecting sudden drift: a case study in logistic process. Procedia Comput. Sci. **161**, 1122–1130 (2019)
22. Sato, D.M.V., De Freitas, S.C., Barddal, J.P., Scalabrin, E.E.: A survey on concept drift in process mining. ACM Comput. Surv. **54**(9), 1–38 (2021)
23. Seeliger, A., Nolle, T., Mühlhäuser, M.: Detecting concept drift in processes using graph metrics on process graphs. In: Proceedings of the 9th Conference on Subject-Oriented Business Process Management. Association for Computing Machinery (2017)
24. Song, W., Jacobsen, H.A.: Static and dynamic process change. IEEE Trans. Serv. Comput. **11**(1), 215–231 (2018)
25. Tavares, G.M., Oyamada, R.S., Junior, S.B., Ceravolo, P.: Trace encoding in process mining: a survey and benchmarking. Eng. Appl. Artif. Intell. **126**, 107028 (2023)

26. Thaler, T., Ternis, S.F., Fettke, P., Loos, P.: A comparative analysis of process instance cluster techniques. In: Proceedings of the 12th International Conference on Wirtschaftsinformatik (WI-15) (2015)
27. Yaghoubi, M., Nazari, M.: An efficient drift detection approach using data entropy in business processes. In: 2021 5th National Conference on Advances in Enterprise Architecture (NCAEA), pp. 17–22 (2021)

Predicting File Completion Using Time Series Models: Embracing the Life-Cycle Nature of Software Development

Nastasja Stephanie Parschew[1(✉)] and Saimir Bala[1,2]

[1] Humboldt-Universität zu Berlin, Berlin, Germany
nastasja.parschew@student.hu-berlin.de, saimir.bala@hu-berlin.de
[2] SAP Signavio, Berlin, Germany

Abstract. In software development, predicting the completion time of tasks is crucial for effective project management. However, due to the complexity of identifying process activities and thereby creating event logs for further analysis, traditional process prediction techniques cannot be readily applied to software data. A key challenge is that development activities are recorded as fine-grained file changes, spanning over multiple artifacts and connected to various other entities, such as the users who made the changes, the module membership, or other related links. In this paper, we present an approach to extract and analyze information from artifacts present in software repositories, allowing us to identify completion patterns exhibited in projects. Subsequently, we leverage time-series analysis to understand the evolution of these artifacts and predict their completion times based on file-level activity. We evaluate this approach against real-world data, showing its effectiveness and usefulness in predicting file completion times. Our work provides project managers with actionable insights into critical development areas, highlighting regions of unpredictability or potential delays, and improving decision-making.

Keywords: Time series analysis · Software process prediction · Software process mining · File completion

1 Introduction

Software development processes are a category of processes that are complex and challenging to control. A key difficulty faced by managers in effectively managing a software development project is the ability to anticipate potential issues that can influence the time required to complete certain tasks. Therefore, data-driven approaches that focus on mining the traces of the development process are of vital importance. These approaches can assist managers in getting a more comprehensive understanding of how the project is evolving. To achieve the best insights, managers are interested in both the as-is and to-be processes concerning the development of the software for which they are responsible.

I. van de Weerd et al. (Eds.): BPM 2025 Workshops, LNBIP 569, pp. 28–40, 2026.
https://doi.org/10.1007/978-3-032-13426-4_3

Among the numerous data-driven techniques that help managers make decisions when dealing with highly complex and ambiguous data, process prediction methods stand out for their ability to provide a forecast about the completion times of activities. Unfortunately, these methods cannot readily be applied to *life-cycle* processes such as software development. When observing event logs from development, such as the ones extracted from version control systems (VCS), there are no explicit process activities that can be used to construct a traditional event log. Rather, activities must be inferred from low-level events that emerge from file changes of the artifacts recorded in the software repositories, such as GitHub, that are used by the VCS to track the software changes.

This paper proposes an approach to tackle the challenge of predicting task completion by leveraging time series analysis to help the manager understand the status of the process. We focus on the *case perspective* of the development, and our goal is to provide information on the quality and evolution of certain development cases, such as the development of a feature, the resolution of a bug, and so on. Our approach begins with identifying and extracting meaningful events from software repositories. We then introduce a method to map these events to specific process activities. By analyzing the time series data associated with these artifacts, we can predict task completion, offering valuable foresight into the software development life cycle. By doing so, our approach empowers project managers to detect areas of the software project that require attention, enhancing their ability to manage projects proactively.

The remainder of this paper is structured as follows. Section 2 describes the problem and discusses related work in the literature. Section 3 details our approach to the completion times of software development activities. Section 4 tests our approach against synthetic and real-world datasets. Section 5 discusses potential benefits and limitations. Section 6 highlights the key findings.

2 Background

2.1 Problem Description

Mining the Software Process. The problem described in this paper falls under the umbrella of mining software repositories to identify and predict process activities. These activities are normally known to the project managers and other stakeholders, but their traces are normally scattered across various repositories and tool logs. As well, these repositories and logs are rarely process-aware. This means that there is no notion of cases or activities associated with events in their logs. Therefore, standard process mining algorithms are not readily applicable [4,19].

One problem of traditional process mining algorithms is the assumption that cases are mono-dimensional (i.e., their activities follow a sequence). This assumption does not fit the case of software development, where changes happen in different dimensions at once. For example, to track the progress of a software process with standard process mining, one can assume, as *case*, the sequence of commits or the sequence of file changes, but not both. Object-centric process mining [1] overcomes this limitation by capturing related changes to each object. This allows for multi-dimensional process analysis techniques, which are more fit for analyzing software processes [11,16].

Yet, all these techniques still work with the assumption of an underlying process. That is, they all assume a so-called teleological process [23] to be in place. However, due to their ever-evolving nature [14], the software development process is rather a so-called life-cycle process [23]. As such, it is argued [12] that a suitable technique to analyze these processes is time-series analysis.

Analyzing the Progress. Let us now look at the specific problem tackled in this paper through the following exemplary scenario.

A software development manager oversees a project. Their goal is not only to monitor how work is progressing, but also to support the team effectively by reallocating resources when needed, identifying bottlenecks early, and ensuring timely delivery. To this end, the manager relies on various tools such as Jira for planning, shared calendars for scheduling, and regular stand-up meetings where team members discuss their progress. However, each of these sources has significant limitations. Jira and related planning tools describe what *should* happen, not what *is* happening. On the other hand, progress communicated in meetings is often subjective, influenced by individual perceptions or incomplete information. To make informed, proactive decisions, the manager needs a more objective, data-driven view of the actual development process.

Fortunately, the team uses a VCS (Git in combination with GitHub), which continuously records detailed event logs of code evolution. These logs offer a rich source of behavioral data about the development process. However, applying traditional process mining techniques to these logs proves ineffective, as discussed earlier in this section. The core problem is that software development is not a well-structured process with clearly repeatable activities and cases, but rather a fluid, life-cycle process that unfolds differently for each task.

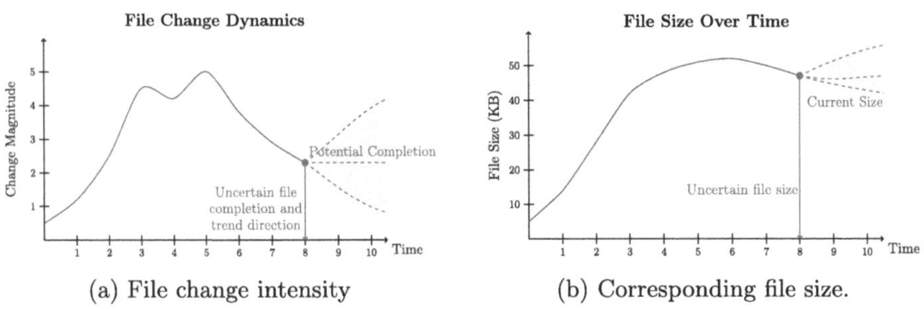

(a) File change intensity (b) Corresponding file size.

Fig. 1. (a): File change intensity during software development with uncertainty in future evolution. (b): Corresponding file size, which may grow, stabilize, or decrease depending on future changes.

To address this challenge, there is a need for techniques suited to life cycle processes. Therefore, we focus on analyzing development progress using time series extracted from version control data. Specifically, we consider the evolution of individual files that serve as meaningful indicators of a task's progression. As shown in Fig. 1, one plot (a) captures the intensity and direction of *file changes over time*, while the other plot (b) illustrates the corresponding *growth of file size*. These views help interpret whether a task is actively being worked on, undergoing refinement, or nearing completion. For instance, a sudden decrease in change magnitude accompanied by file size stabilization could indicate that a file, and potentially the associated task, is being finalized. Through such patterns, we aim to support managers with data-informed insights into development activity. This brings us to our central research question:

RQ: How can we analyze progress in software development using time series extracted from version control systems?.

2.2 Related Work

Previous work has extensively analyzed file-level metrics to assess software quality, change patterns, and defect susceptibility. Alshehri et al. [2] applied churn metrics in machine learning models to predict change-prone files, emphasizing their value for resource allocation. In related work, they also focused on identifying newly created files likely to change [3]. Bala et al. [5] introduced hidden co-evolution analysis to reveal non-hierarchical file dependencies, showing their impact on modularity and maintainability. Sas et al. [21] further linked frequent file co-changes to architectural flaws requiring refactoring. Additionally, Wang et al. [24] enhanced defect prediction by leveraging deep learning on semantic features extracted from file-level data.

While these studies contribute valuable insights, few integrate file evolution with process metrics or time-series analysis to support managerial decision-making. Bala et al. [5] used time-series methods to study development patterns but did not focus on predicting task progress. Choraś et al. [9,10] combined ARIMA models with process metrics to forecast Agile development indicators and built dashboards for managerial use, but did not focus on file-level granularity. Choetkiertikul et al. [7,8] offered predictive models for Agile sprints and story point estimation based on issue velocity and dependencies, remaining at a higher abstraction level. Similarly, Park and Song [17] and Rique et al. [20] addressed resource optimization through predictive analytics, yet did not consider the evolving dynamics of individual files. Most of these approaches rely on aggregated metrics, failing to capture granular trends at the file level.

Our work addresses this gap by combining file-specific time-series modeling with process metrics to predict the completion of individual files. This enables more fine-grained and actionable insights into development progress. As summarized in Table 1, our approach uniquely integrates file-level focus, time-series prediction, and practical managerial value, supporting improved task tracking.

Table 1. Comparison of Our Approach with Existing Work

Study	File-Level Focus	Time-Series Modeling	Completion Prediction	Managerial Use
Alshehri et al. [2,3]	✓	✗	✗	✗
Bala et al. [5]	✓	✓	✗	✗
Wang et al. [24]	✓	✗	✗(defects)	✗
Choetkiertikul et al. [7,8]	✗	✓	✓ (story points)	✓
Choraś et al. [9,10]	✗	✓	✓ (metrics)	✓
Park & Song [17], Rique et al. [20]	✗	✓	✗	✓
Our approach	✓	✓	✓	✓

3 Method

In this section, we outline our systematic approach to collecting, preprocessing, and analyzing data from multiple software repositories hosted on GitHub.

3.1 Overview of the Approach

Our approach is a structured, data-driven pipeline that transforms raw commit histories from GitHub repositories into predictive insights about file completion. The final output is a continuous target variable, *days until completion*, per file, enabling fine-grained tracking of development progress and informing managerial decision-making. The process unfolds in three major steps:

1. **Data Collection and Target Labeling**: We collect commit data at both the repository and file levels using the GitHub API. The data includes metadata, file changes, and commit histories. To ensure the robustness of our analysis, we select repositories based on the following criteria: *C1)* At least 2,000 commits, *C2)* Open-source and publicly accessible, *C3)* A minimum project age of one year. Based on these criteria, we curated a set of ten repositories for analysis.
2. **Feature Engineering and Model Input Construction**: From the collected commit data, we engineer a diverse set of features that describe temporal dynamics, file structure, and contributor behavior. These include rolling statistics, time intervals between commits, file size evolution, and categorical attributes such as file type and contributor identity. To build the predictive target, we define completion dates using three heuristics: stable line changes, file deletion, and prolonged inactivity. For each file with a completion date, we compute the number of days until completion for each commit.
3. **Model Training and Prediction**: We train supervised regression models including Random Forest [6], Gradient Boosting [15], and LightGBM [13] on the labeled dataset. Files without a valid completion label are excluded from training but can still be analyzed qualitatively. We evaluate model performance using Mean Absolute Error (MAE) on a hold-out evaluation set and

benchmark results against a linear regression model and a simple median baseline. To ensure generalization and avoid data leakage, we apply file-level splits and `GroupTimeSeries` cross-validation during model tuning.

3.2 Step 1: Data Preparation and Target Labeling

To model file-level completion within a software project, we begin by collecting and structuring the full commit history of each repository. Our goal is to transform raw, unstructured Git data into a clean, tabular dataset that can be used as input for machine learning models.

We use the GitHub REST API to extract: i) a complete list of commits in the repository (including SHA identifiers and timestamps), ii) detailed information for each commit (capturing added and deleted lines for each modified file), and iii) the full commit history of each file. For each commit, we record all affected file paths along with line-level changes and reconstruct the commit timeline for each file. This includes the file size after each commit, committer identity, and metadata such as commit intervals. The resulting structured dataset forms the foundation for feature engineering and model training.

To enable predictive modeling, we define the target variable as the number of days between a given commit and the moment a file is considered `complete`. Since Git data does not contain explicit labels for completion, we approximate completion using three strategies. First, if a file exhibits *minimal change* in at least three consecutive commits spanning over 14 days and then remains inactive for 30 or more days, we assign the last stable commit as the completion date. Second, if a file is *deleted* (indicated by its size dropping to zero), we label that commit as `complete` in the specific completion date and annotate the reason as `deleted`. Third, if a file has *not been modified* for a period that exceeds the 95th percentile of commit intervals in the repository (with thresholds clipped between 30 and 365 days), we assign its last commit as the completion point.

For files that meet any of these criteria, we compute the *days until completion* for each commit as the number of days until the identified completion date. Files that do not satisfy any of the conditions are considered incomplete and are excluded from supervised learning. The final dataset consists of one row per commit per file, including all derived features and possibly the target value. This dataset is now ready for the feature engineering and modeling steps that follow.

3.3 Step 2: Feature Engineering and Model Input Construction

With the structured commit data prepared, we construct a comprehensive set of features that capture both the temporal dynamics and structural characteristics of each file's evolution. The objective is to translate raw commit behavior into model-readable signals that can inform predictions about file completion.

For each commit in a file's history, we derive features based on commit activity, file size, and contributor behavior. These include rolling statistics over the most recent commits, such as moving averages of added and deleted lines, recent file size growth, and the frequency of changes. To capture trends without introducing excessive noise, we compute most rolling features over the latest seven commits, which balances short-term relevance with temporal stability. In addition, we incorporate temporal features such as the number of days since the previous commit, the density of activity over the last 30 and 90 days, and the variation in time intervals between commits. These features help to characterize development intensity and highlight periods of stability or inactivity.

We also extract structural attributes of each file, including its extension, depth in the directory hierarchy, and classification (e.g., source code, configuration, or script). These features are used to distinguish core implementation files from peripheral ones. To model developer contributions, we track the identity of the committer and group infrequent contributors, defined as those responsible for fewer than 1% of a project's commits, into a shared `other` category. This information is encoded as a categorical variable to reflect patterns in team activity. To ensure a consistent input space, we filter out files with fewer than five commits, as these provide insufficient data for modeling. We also limit the dataset to files residing within core implementation directories (e.g., `src/`), excluding test, documentation, or build files that are less relevant to predictive modeling of file-level completion.

At the end of this process, we obtain a machine-learning-ready dataset where each row corresponds to a file-level commit, each column encodes a structured feature, and the target variable represents the number of days until file completion.

3.4 Step 3: Model Training and Prediction

To predict file completion times, we train and evaluate machine learning models on our engineered dataset, focusing on files with assigned completion dates. This step allows us to validate our approach by comparing the predictive performance of multiple algorithms. To validate our approach, our pipeline includes the training of various models. This step enables us to evaluate the different models on their ability to predict a file's completion times.

We split the labeled dataset (files with a "days until completion" target) into a training and evaluation set using an 80:20 ratio. Furthermore, we ensure random sampling while preventing commits from the same file from appearing in both sets to avoid data leakage. Files without already assigned completion dates are excluded from supervised modeling but may be used for exploratory analysis. Numerical features (e.g., file size, rolling statistics) are scaled while categorical features (e.g., file type, committer group) are one-hot encoded if the machine learning model requires it.

We train three primary models: Random Forest [6], Gradient Boosting [15], and LightGBM [13]. We selected these models due to their strong performance on tabular datasets, ability to capture non-linear feature interactions, and widespread use in practical machine learning applications. Including all three enables a comparison between traditional ensemble methods and optimized gradient-based approaches.

We compare our results with two baseline models: a linear regression model and a median baseline. The median baseline is computed to store the median `days_until_completion` of the train set and return this value for all further entries of the evaluation set. We expect this to be of the lowest accuracy. We tune the hyperparameters through Grid Search [22] with a 5-fold cross-validation. Furthermore, we used a `GroupTimeSeriesSplit` [18] to ensure that no commit data from the same file would be found in the cross-validation splits. For Random Forest, we optimize parameters such as the number of trees (50–300) and the maximum depth (5–30). For Gradient Boosting, we tune parameters including the learning rate (0.01–0.1), the number of estimators (100–400), and maximum depth (3–7). Through this process, we ensure well-calibrated models.

During training, models learn to predict the continuous target "days until completion" from the engineered features. For evaluation, we withhold the target labels (days until completion) in the evaluation set. We then generate predictions for each commit. Afterwards, we compare the predictions with the actual values using MAE, which measures average prediction error in days.

4 Evaluation

To evaluate our approach, we tested our pipeline on real-world data, focusing on the accuracy of file completion time predictions. This section details the experimental setup, data collection, and results, emphasizing the generalizability and practical utility of our method.

4.1 Experimental Setup

To ensure reproducibility, we implemented a prototype[1] in Python. We conducted experiments on a system with an Intel Xeon CPU, 1TB of RAM, and Python 3.11. The core libraries include `pandas` (v2.2.3) for the dataset construction, `scikit-learn` (v1.6.1) for the implementation of the machine learning models, and `mlxtend` (v0.23.4) for grouped time series cross-validation using `GroupTimeSeriesSplit`. We evaluated our approach on 10 open-source GitHub repositories each, meeting criteria **C1** (>2,000 commits), **C2** (open-source), and **C3** (at least one year old), with files having assigned completion dates.

Our evaluation approach involves training models on the training set to predict the number of days until completion. For the evaluation set, we withheld completion labels, generated predictions, and compared those to the actual values. For each file in the evaluation set, the model predicts the number of days until completion. Predictions are then compared to actual values using Mean Absolute Error (MAE) as the primary evaluation metric.

[1] https://github.com/mornningstar/completiontimes.

4.2 Data Collection

We collected commit and file data from ten GitHub repositories that satisfy our selection criteria **C1** through **C3**. These repositories, summarized in Table 2, vary widely in terms of their commit history size, age, programming languages, and application domains. The primary programming languages include Python, TypeScript, HTML, and Java, reflecting a range of development environments such as natural language processing, web frameworks, UI components, and data serialization libraries. This diversity ensures that our evaluation of the predictive models is robust across different types of software projects and development practices.

Table 2. Characteristics of Evaluated GitHub Repositories

Repository	Commits	Age (Years)	Primary Language
flairNLP/fundus	2,890	2.6	Python
khoj-ai/khoj	4,797	3.8	Python
vuejs/core	6,671	7.0	TypeScript
mozilla/addons-server	61,092	11.3	Python
fastapi/fastapi	5,806	6.5	Python
pallets/flask	5,437	15.2	Python
keras-team/keras	11,554	10.2	Python
tabler/tabler	2,995	7.3	HTML
google/material-design-lite	2,872	10.3	HTML
google/gson	2,112	10.2	Java

The repositories range from relatively young projects with a few thousand commits to mature, long-standing codebases with tens of thousands of commits. The wide variation in repository age (2.6 to 15.2 years) and commit volume (2,112 to 61,092 commits) provides a comprehensive testing ground for our approach, demonstrating its applicability and effectiveness in varied real-world settings.

4.3 Prediction Results on Real-World Data

We report our prediction results in Table 3. It can be observed that LightGBM (LGBM) outperforms GradientBoosting (GBoost) and Random Forest (RForest) in 9 out of 10 projects. Furthermore, GradientBoosting outperformed Random Forest in most cases, although results vary depending on the project. The best performance was observed with the projects `flairNLP/fundus` (36.34 days with LightGBM) and `google/material-design-lite` (38.55 days with LightGBM), both having fewer than 3,000 commits, thus suggesting that smaller, younger projects are easier to predict. The most challenging projects to predict were `google/gson`, having an MAE over 200 days on average, and `fastapi/fastapi`, having an MAE of 266.36 days on average. The repository `google/gson` was one of the oldest (>10 years) and the only Java project in the set. The bad performance was likely due to complex commit patterns or language-specific characteristics. Surprisingly, `fastapi/fastapi` is the only project having better results with the Random Forest model and still being close to the worst LightGBM performance.

Table 3. Mean Absolute Error (MAE) in Days for Different Prediction Models Across Repositories. LinReg and Median are the baselines. Lower MAE means better predictive performance. Bold values highlight the best performance.

Repository	RForest	GBoost	LGBM	LinReg	Median
flairNLP/fundus	42.34	40.98	**36.34**	66.05	129.45
khoj-ai/khoj	124.20	115.69	**83.33**	131.55	128.92
vuejs/core	242.46	221.49	**139.25**	313.26	597.30
mozilla/addons-server	371.67	371.34	**347.14**	466.73	661.02
fastapi/fastapi	**266.36**	381.82	315.29	960.07	683.97
pallets/flask	221.03	304.21	**124.65**	668.95	417.32
keras-team/keras	208.47	187.82	**137.56**	249.73	383.85
tabler/tabler	250.18	287.49	**120.47**	307.22	518.79
google/material-design-lite	54.23	53.26	**38.55**	169.99	197.24
google/gson	294.45	296.07	**260.91**	1382.90	1541.89

To contextualize these results, we compared our approach to two baseline models: Linear Regression (LinReg) and Median Baseline (Median). There, we expected Linear Regression to perform better than the Median Baseline. Furthermore, we anticipated both to perform worse than our three main models (Random Forest, Gradient Boosting, and LightGBM). But this is not always the case. Only seven of the ten tried repositories validate the superiority of Linear Regression against a baseline algorithm, which predicts the training set's median days until completion. For the other three projects, the Median Baseline outperforms Linear Regression, which is unexpected. Nonetheless, throughout all ten repositories, the models depicted in Table 3 outperform any baseline algorithm. These results showcase the excellence of tree-based models concerning the variety of features and the possibility to learn from them.

5 Discussion

Unlike prior work that focused on aggregated metrics or issue-level, our approach works at the file level. This granularity allows project managers to identify specific files that are near or at completion, as well as those that are still under active development. By predicting days until a file's completion, project managers gain a forward-looking view into a project's state. This information supports them in evaluating timelines more precisely than commit count or higher-level project metrics alone allow.

Additionally, our approach combines temporal dynamics with structural properties, allowing a multi-faceted view of file evolution. By solely learning a project's patterns, it is not tailored to a single codebase or language, as demonstrated by our evaluation across ten open-source projects. As a result, the method is scalable and adaptable, requiring only minimal adjustments to be deployed in new development contexts.

Despite these strengths, limitations exist. Variability in commit practices, as seen with `google/gson`'s high MAE, may impact prediction accuracy. In such cases, large errors can signal ongoing refactoring, inconsistent development patterns, or frequent reopenings of seemingly finished files. These insights are still valuable for project managers. Extending file-level predictions to task-level outcomes also requires modeling task dependencies, a direction for future work.

Overall, our approach equips project managers with granular, interpretable, and adaptable insights, enhancing their ability to analyze the software process, anticipate bottlenecks, and drive project success.

6 Conclusion

In this paper, we presented a data-driven approach to predict file completion times using detailed commit histories. We implemented a prototype and analyzed data from multiple open-source repositories. By extracting meaningful features and applying machine learning models, especially LightGBM, our method consistently outperforms baseline models across diverse projects. These predictions provide valuable insights for project managers to monitor progress better and coordinate development efforts.

Future work can improve the approach by incorporating additional data sources such as issue trackers and communication logs, and by enabling real-time model updates. Furthermore, additional information on the task gathered from domain experts may be incorporated to best select the representative files, to which our time-series analysis applies. Enhancing the predictive accuracy and timeliness will further support proactive project management and improve software development workflows.

Acknowledgments. Supported by the Einstein Foundation Berlin EPP-2019-524.

References

1. Aalst, W.M.P.: Object-Centric Process Mining: Dealing with Divergence and Convergence in Event Data. In: Ölveczky, P.C., Salaün, G. (eds.) SEFM 2019. LNCS, vol. 11724, pp. 3–25. Springer, Cham (2019). https://doi.org/10.1007/978-3-030-30446-1_1
2. Alshehri, Y.A.: Predicting change in newly created files in a software product line project. Softw. Pract. Exp. **52**(12), 2499–2512 (2022)

3. Alshehri, Y.A., et al.: Can we predict the change in code in a software product line project? J. Softw. Eng. Appl. **13**(06), 91 (2020)
4. Bala, S., Mendling, J.: Monitoring the Software Development Process with Process Mining. In: Shishkov, B. (ed.) BMSD 2018. LNBIP, vol. 319, pp. 432–442. Springer, Cham (2018). https://doi.org/10.1007/978-3-319-94214-8_34
5. Bala, S., Revoredo, K., de A.R. Gonçalves, J.C., Baião, F., Mendling, J., Santoro, F.: Uncovering the Hidden Co-evolution in the Work History of Software Projects. In: Carmona, J., Engels, G., Kumar, A. (eds.) BPM 2017. LNCS, vol. 10445, pp. 164–180. Springer, Cham (2017). https://doi.org/10.1007/978-3-319-65000-5_10
6. Breiman, L.: Random forests. Mach. Learn. **45**, 5–32 (2001)
7. Choetkiertikul, M., Dam, H.K., Tran, T., Ghose, A., Grundy, J.: Predicting delivery capability in iterative software development. IEEE Trans. Software Eng. **44**(6), 551–573 (2018)
8. Choetkiertikul, M., Dam, H.K., Tran, T., Pham, T., Ghose, A., Menzies, T.: A deep learning model for estimating story points. IEEE Trans. Softw. Eng. **45**(7), 637–656 (2019)
9. Choraś, M., Kozik, R., Pawlicki, M., Hołubowicz, W., Franch, X.: Software Development Metrics Prediction Using Time Series Methods. In: Saeed, K., Chaki, R., Janev, V. (eds.) CISIM 2019. LNCS, vol. 11703, pp. 311–323. Springer, Cham (2019). https://doi.org/10.1007/978-3-030-28957-7_26
10. Choras, M., et al.: Measuring and improving agile processes in a small-size software development company. IEEE Access **8**, 78452–78466 (2020)
11. Fahland, D.: Multi-dimensional process analysis. In: Di Ciccio, C., Dijkman, R., del Río Ortega, A., Rinderle-Ma, S. (eds.) BPM. Lecture Notes in Computer Science, vol. 13420, pp. 27–33. Springer (2022). https://doi.org/10.1007/978-3-031-16103-2_3
12. Fahrenkrog-Petersen, S.A., Bala, S., Pufahl, L., Mendling, J.: Unraveling the never-ending story of lifecycles and vitalizing processes. In: Kaczmarek-Heß, M., Rosenthal, K., Suchánek, M., Da Silva, M.M., Proper, H.A., Schnellmann, M. (eds.) EDOC Workshops. Lecture Notes in Business Information Processing, vol. 537, pp. 68–81. Springer, Cham (2024). https://doi.org/10.1007/978-3-031-79059-1_5
13. Ke, G., et al.: Lightgbm: A highly efficient gradient boosting decision tree. Adv. Neural Inform. Process. Syst. **30** (2017)
14. Lehman, M.M., Ramil, J.F.: Software evolution and software evolution processes. Ann. Softw. Eng. **14**(1–4), 275–309 (2002)
15. Natekin, A., Knoll, A.: Gradient boosting machines, a tutorial. Front. Neurorobot. **7**, 21 (2013)
16. Nguyen, T., Bala, S., Mendling, J.: Multi-dimensional process analysis of software development projects. In: MODELSWARD. pp. 179–186. SCITEPRESS (2024)
17. Park, G., Song, M.: Optimizing resource allocation based on predictive process monitoring. IEEE Access **11**, 38309–38323 (2023)
18. Pedregosa, F., et al.: Scikit-learn: machine learning in python. J. Mach. Learn. Res. **12**, 2825–2830 (2011)
19. Poncin, W., Serebrenik, A., van den Brand, M.: Process mining software repositories. In: CSMR. pp. 5–14. IEEE Computer Society (2011)
20. Rique, T., Perkusich, M.B., Dantas, E., Albuquerque, D., Gorgônio, K.C., de Almeida, H.O., Perkusich, A.: On adopting software analytics for managerial decision-making: a practitioner's perspective. IEEE Access **11**, 73145–73163 (2023)
21. Sas, D., Avgeriou, P., Kruizinga, R., Scheedler, R.: Exploring the relation between co-changes and architectural smells. SN Comput. Sci. **2**(1), 13 (2021)

22. Sun, Y., Ding, S., Zhang, Z., Jia, W.: An improved grid search algorithm to optimize SVR for prediction. Soft. Comput. **25**(7), 5633–5644 (2021)
23. Van de Ven, A.H., Poole, M.S.: Explaining development and change in organizations. Acad. Manag. Rev. **20**(3), 510–540 (1995)
24. Wang, S., Liu, T., Nam, J., Tan, L.: Deep semantic feature learning for software defect prediction. IEEE Trans. Softw. Eng. **46**(12), 1267–1293 (2020)

Inter-case Informed Business Process Suffix Prediction Integrating Trace and Log Information

Xiaomeng He[1(✉)], Johannes De Smedt[1], Seppe vanden Broucke[2], and Jochen De Weerdt[1]

[1] Research Center for Information Systems Engineering (LIRIS), KU Leuven, Naamsestraat 69, 3000 Leuven, Belgium
{xiaomeng.he,johannes.desmedt,jochen.deweerdt}@kuleuven.be

[2] Department of Business Informatics and Operations Management, Ghent University, Tweekerkenstraat 2, 9000 Ghent, Belgium
seppe.vandenbroucke@ugent.be

Abstract. Predictive Process Monitoring aims to anticipate the future execution of business process instances, with suffix prediction focusing on forecasting the remaining sequence of events in an ongoing case. Most existing approaches assume that cases are executed in isolation, relying exclusively on intra-case information while neglecting inter-case dynamics. However, in real-world settings, cases often influence each other or share common system-wide constraints, such as resource availability. Current methods for incorporating inter-case information primarily focus on remaining time prediction by using manually engineered inter-case features. In this work, we propose `I3SP` (Integrated Inter-case Informed Suffix Prediction), a novel encoder-decoder architecture that integrates both trace and log prefixes for suffix prediction. Our approach directly learns inter-case dependencies from the log prefix, eliminating the need for selectively encoding inter-case features. Experimental results on real-life event logs demonstrate that `I3SP` effectively draws additional predictive power from the log prefix. Furthermore, an analysis of example predictions provides explanatory insights into the learned patterns that contribute to improved predictive performance.

Keywords: Predictive Process Monitoring · Suffix Prediction · Inter-Case Information · Deep Learning · Encoder-Decoder Architecture

1 Introduction

The widespread adoption of information systems across organizations has caused the underlying business processes to generate extensive digital footprints, which provide rich data for process mining. Unlike traditional descriptive analysis in process mining, Predictive Process Monitoring (PPM) takes a forward-looking approach by predicting the future execution of ongoing business process

I. van de Weerd et al. (Eds.): BPM 2025 Workshops, LNBIP 569, pp. 41–54, 2026.
https://doi.org/10.1007/978-3-032-13426-4_4

instances [2]. Among the various predictive tasks, suffix prediction focuses on predicting the remaining sequence of events and offers a comprehensive view of a process instance's future trajectory, thereby supporting other predictive analyses such as outcome prediction and remaining time estimation [11,16].

Despite its practical relevance, most existing suffix prediction methods rely exclusively on intra-case information, treating cases as independent entities. However, in real-world settings, process instances often exhibit inter-case dependencies, where the behavior of one case can be influenced by the patterns observed in other cases. Two primary mechanisms drive these dependencies. First, cases can directly interact with one another, meaning the execution of one case may depend on another. For instance, in production processes, the time at which an order enters production depends on the queue of existing orders. Similarly, in financial transactions, executing a stock sale may require the completion of prior stock purchases to ensure sufficient stocks are available for transfer. Second, temporally proximate cases may be influenced by shared system-wide conditions. Orders processed on a given day, for example, may follow an alternative workflow due to temporary resource changes, such as a substitute worker handling tasks differently from the regular staff. These external factors create similarities across cases that are not captured when analyzing cases in isolation.

Although prior research acknowledges these inter-case dependencies [3,16], existing approaches primarily focus on improving remaining time prediction by using handcrafted inter-case features [1,8,13], typically grounded in queuing theory or load-based assumptions. The potential of inter-case dynamics to enhance suffix prediction has received comparatively little attention [6]. Meanwhile, by selectively encoding predefined inter-case dependencies, the existing methods risk discarding valuable signals, such as control-flow patterns from concurrent cases.

In this work, we propose `I3SP`, a novel encoder-decoder architecture designed to enhance suffix prediction by incorporating both trace prefixes (capturing intra-case behavior) and log prefixes (capturing inter-case dependencies). Our approach eliminates the need for engineering inter-case features, enabling the model to learn inter-case relationships directly from event logs.

To validate our approach, we conduct empirical evaluations on four real-life event logs, comparing `I3SP` against conventional models that rely solely on trace prefixes. The results demonstrate that `I3SP` effectively leverages log prefixes to improve predictive accuracy. Additionally, a qualitative analysis of sample predictions reveals the inter-case patterns that contribute to improved predictive performance.

The remainder of this paper is structured as follows. Section 2 presents a real-life example to motivate this research, followed by discussing gaps in the existing literature. Section 3 introduces the encoder-decoder framework that integrates both trace and log prefixes. Section 4 describes the experimental setup for the empirical evaluation. Section 5 reports on the quantitative results and qualitative analysis. Section 6 concludes the paper, discusses limitations and points to elements for future work.

2 Motivation and Background

This section discusses the problem of inter-case information in suffix prediction and reviews related work.

2.1 Motivation

To illustrate the motivation behind this research, we consider a real-world purchase-to-pay process, recorded in the BPIC2019 event log[1]. Figure 1 presents two process instances, case 620 and case 478. Suppose we aim to predict the sequence of events following the event with activity label *Record Goods Receipt* in both cases. This target, known as the trace suffix (highlighted in green), is conventionally predicted based on all preceding events in the same case, referred to as the trace prefix (highlighted in yellow).

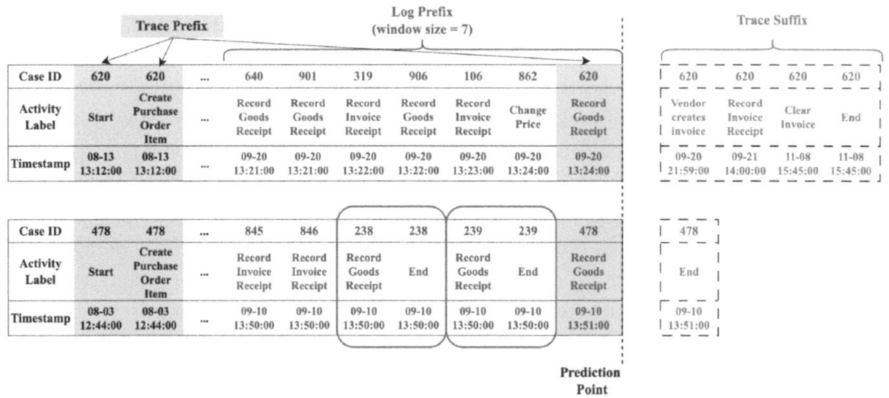

Fig. 1. Two process instances from the BPIC2019 dataset.

A closer inspection reveals that the trace prefixes of cases 620 and 478 are nearly identical—both containing three events with the same activity labels in the same order and highly similar time intervals. A predictive model relying solely on the trace prefix as input would likely be unable to distinguish between these cases, resulting in inaccurate predictions of their significantly different trace suffixes.

Nevertheless, the execution records of preceding cases, referred to as the log prefix (highlighted in blue), may provide the contextual information needed for effective discrimination. For case 478, the sequential pattern ⟨*Record Goods Receipt*, *End*⟩ appears multiple times in neighboring cases, suggesting that certain system-wide conditions may cause process instances to terminate after *Record Goods Receipt*. Leveraging this information may enable the model to

[1] https://doi.org/10.4121/uuid:d06aff4b-79f0-45e6-8ec8-e19730c248f1.

correctly predict *End* for case 478. In contrast, case 620 lacks this recurring sequential pattern, allowing the model to differentiate between the two cases.

This example demonstrates the importance of capturing system-wide patterns present in the log prefix. We therefore propose an approach that utilizes deep learning to extract such contextual signals from the log prefix, as detailed in the subsequent sections.

2.2 Related Work

Deep learning is a family of techniques that discover intricate patterns in data through deep neural networks. Various studies have employed deep learning techniques for suffix prediction. One paradigm, Single Event Prediction (SEP), trains a deep learning model to predict the next event and iteratively generates the suffix [4,15]. Consequently, any attribute used as input must also be set as a prediction target, which limits the utilization of attributes. Another more recent paradigm, Direct Suffix Prediction, trains a model to predict the entire trace suffix in a single step [5,18], instead of predicting one event at a time. While this approach partially addresses the limitation on feature utilization of SEP, it still relies solely on intra-case features, neglecting inter-case dependencies.

Although prior studies acknowledge the importance of inter-case dynamics in business process execution [3,16], relatively few studies have attempted to integrate inter-case information into predictive models. Most of them focus on improving remaining time prediction using manually engineered features, such as the number of related cases based on similarity metrics [13], features designed to capture batching behavior [8] or resource workload [1]. Only one recent work [6] has applied inter-case features to perform suffix prediction, encoding them as the number of active cases at key state points.

The narrow focus on remaining time prediction overlooks the broader potential of inter-case dynamics, especially their value for suffix prediction. More importantly, handcrafted approaches selectively preserve information based on predefined assumptions, which risks discarding valuable relationships. The approach proposed in this paper addresses these limitations by using deep learning techniques to directly learn inter-case dependencies from the log prefix, thereby enhancing suffix prediction performance.

3 `I3SP`: An Integrated Seq2Seq Model

This section defines the concept of the log prefix, which is used as an additional input, and introduces the architecture of the proposed model.

3.1 Preliminaries

In event logs, a case is a business process execution instance and an event captures a performed activity. Each event can be represented as a tuple $e = (a, t, c)$, where a is the activity label, t is the timestamp, and c is the case ID. For this study, we focus on the control-flow perspective and do not consider optional event or case attributes. However, our proposed technique can be extended to include such attributes if needed. Since capturing system-wide behavior requires tracking when cases start and end, we explicitly introduce Start-of-Case (SOC) and End-of-Case (EOC) events in our event logs.

Let all events from an event log L be sorted chronologically by their timestamps, with each event assigned a unique index i to denote its position in L. A trace σ_c is constructed by extracting all events with the case ID c from L and temporally ordering them. Each event is assigned an index j to denote its position in the trace. Therefore, an event can be represented as $e_{i,j}$, with i its index in the event log and j its index in the trace. For brevity, the index i or j of an event is omitted and replaced by a placeholder $\bullet$ when it is unknown, especially when discussing events relative to their positions. For example, the event preceding $e_{i,j}$ in the same trace is denoted as $e_{\bullet,j-1}$.

3.2 Model Input and Output

Conventional trace-based modeling approaches use trace prefixes as model input, while suffixes of activity labels [4,15,18], sometimes together with timestamps [18], serve as model output. This study similarly targets case-level prediction and simultaneously predicts suffixes of activity labels and timestamps, while incorporating an additional input—the log prefix.

Unlike the trace prefix, which consists of events from a single case, the log prefix is a temporally ordered sequence including consecutive events across multiple cases, capturing the global execution flow of the system and inherently containing inter-case information. It terminates at the last observed event but is constrained by a predefined window size to balance computational efficiency and information retention. To ensure clarity in terminology, we define the trace prefix, log prefix, and trace suffix as follows:

Definition 1 (Trace Prefix, Log Prefix and Trace Suffix). Consider an event log $L = \langle e_{1,\bullet}, \dots, e_{|L|,\bullet} \rangle$ and a specified log prefix window size w. For an event $e_{i,j} = (a, t, c)$ in L, let $\sigma_c = \langle e_{\bullet,1}, \dots, e_{\bullet,|\sigma_c|} \rangle$ represent the trace containing $e_{i,j}$. Treating $e_{i,j}$ as the last observed event, a corresponding tuple of trace prefix, log prefix and trace suffix can be generated by applying the following functions.

The function $hd_{trace}(\sigma_c, e_{i,j})$ extracts the **trace prefix** from σ_c, beginning at the first event $e_{\bullet,1}$ in σ_c and ending at $e_{i,j}$. Formally: $hd_{trace}(\sigma_c, e_{i,j}) = \langle e_{\bullet,1}, \dots, e_{i,j} \rangle$

The function $hd_{log}(L, e_{i,j}, w)$ extracts the **log prefix** from L. It starts at $e_{i-w,\bullet}$, the event occurring w steps prior to $e_{i,j}$ in L, and ends at $e_{i,j}$. Formally: $hd_{log}(L, e_{i,j}, w) = \langle e_{i-w,\bullet}, \dots, e_{i,j} \rangle$

The function $\tau(\sigma_c, e_{i,j})$ extracts the **trace suffix** from σ_c, beginning at $e_{\bullet,j+1}$ and ending at the last event $e_{\bullet,|\sigma_c|}$ in σ_c. Formally: $\tau(\sigma_c, e_{i,j}) = \langle e_{\bullet,j+1}, \dots, e_{\bullet,|\sigma_c|} \rangle$

Each event (except EOC) serves as the last observed event to generate a sample containing a trace prefix, a log prefix, and a trace suffix. Shorter prefixes and suffixes are padded to match the predefined lengths, which are one more than the longest case length in the event log for trace prefix and suffix, and the window size for the log prefix.

Model Input. Both trace and log prefixes are transformed into numerical feature vectors suitable for processing by deep learning algorithms. Each event in a prefix is encoded as an individual feature vector, and the entire prefix is represented as a sequence of feature vectors, preserving the order of events. An individual feature vector is the combination of the one-hot encoded activity label [12] and temporal feature(s).

For each event $e_{i,j}$, temporal features are derived from raw timestamps. Specifically, for the trace prefix, two temporal features commonly used in PPM [11] are included in the feature vector: (i) the time elapsed from the previous event $e_{\bullet,j-1}$ in the trace to $e_{i,j}$; (ii) the time elapsed from the start of the trace (i.e. the first event $e_{\bullet,1}$ in the trace) to $e_{i,j}$. For the log prefix, one temporal feature is included: the time elapsed from the previous event $e_{i-1,\bullet}$ in the event log to $e_{i,j}$, which gives information on system-wide event pacing.

Model Output. The model concurrently predicts the activity label suffix and the timestamp suffix. At each step, it estimates the time elapsed from the current event $e_{i,j}$ to the subsequent event $e_{\bullet,j+1}$, referred to as the Time Till Next Event (*TTNE*). Using this estimate, the timestamp of $e_{\bullet,j+1}$ is derived by adding the predicted TTNE value to the timestamp of $e_{i,j}$. Simultaneously, the model predicts the activity label of $e_{\bullet,j+1}$.

3.3 Model Architecture

Since both the model input and output comprise multiple sequences, we adopt an encoder-decoder architecture to handle this multi-sequence to multi-sequence mapping problem. This architecture has proven effective in sequence modeling tasks such as machine translation [14] and has been increasingly applied to predictive tasks involving multiple inputs and outputs [9].

The proposed model is implemented using an encoder-decoder architecture based on Long Short Term Memory networks (LSTMs) (in a *Seq2Seq* fashion) [14], as LSTMs have proven to be effective to PPM [11,12], and recent research [18] suggests that LSTM-based encoder-decoder models can perform comparably to Transformer models for suffix prediction tasks in non-data-aware settings.

Figure 2 illustrates the proposed model architecture. A standard Seq2Seq model consists of an encoder LSTM, which encodes the input sequence into a fixed-dimensional vector providing a context for decoding, and a decoder LSTM, which generates the output sequence step by step. To integrate both trace prefixes (capturing the case-specific context) and log prefixes (capturing the system-wide context), two separate LSTM encoders are employed. Their final hidden and cell states are concatenated to form a context vector, which serves as input for the decoding phase. The dual-decoder architecture then generates suffix predictions, with one decoder predicting activity labels via a softmax layer and the other predicting timestamps using a regression-based approach. Both decoders operate in an auto-regressive manner, ensuring that each predicted output conditions on previous outputs to maintain sequential consistency.

To improve the handling of long input sequences, we introduce an optional attention layer. At each decoding step, two context vectors are computed by attending to the two encoders' hidden states. These vectors are concatenated with the decoder's hidden state and projected to form an attention vector, which is then passed through a linear layer for prediction. For details on attention computation and vector fusion, we refer to [10,19].

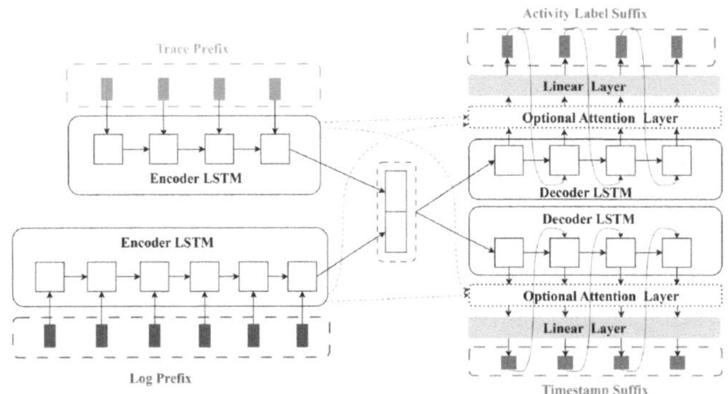

Fig. 2. Architecture of `I3SP`, the integrated Seq2Seq model.

4 Experimental Setup

This section outlines the datasets, preprocessing steps, and model configurations used for evaluation. The code is available at: https://github.com/Xiaomeng-He/I3SP.

4.1 Event Logs

For the empirical evaluation, we choose four real-life event logs with sufficient data volume for deep learning, while covering diverse process structures, case lengths, and execution durations. BPIC 2012[2] and BPIC2017[3] record loan applications from a Dutch financial institution in different years, with the latter being richer and cleaner. BPIC2019 tracks a purchase-to-pay process for a multinational coatings company, covering purchase orders submitted in 2018. BAC[4]

[2] https://doi.org/10.4121/uuid:3926db30-f712-4394-aebc-75976070e91f.

[3] https://doi.org/10.4121/uuid:5f3067df-f10b-45da-b98b-86ae4c7a310b.

[4] This dataset is not publicly available due to business confidentiality restrictions.

logs the luggage handling process of a major European airport in February 2018. Table 1 presents key statistics of the event logs after cleaning and debiasing (as described in Sect. 4.2). Case duration is recorded in days, except for BAC, where it is recorded in seconds.

Table 1. Summary statistics of event logs

Event log	Num. cases	Num. events	Num. activities	Num. variants	Max.case length	Avg.case length	Max.case duration	Avg.case duration
BPIC2012	9,430	168,349	24	775	78	17.85	32.24	7.29
BPIC2017	28,977	1,067,714	25	7992	87	36.85	47.80	20.57
BPIC2019	169,142	907,557	36	4162	13	5.37	143.33	72.55
BAC	362,506	1,964,221	57	7932	26	5.42	6728.00	731.36

4.2 Data Preprocessing

The data cleaning and debiasing procedure described in [17,18] is applied to remove duplicate records, chronological outliers, and cases with excessively long length or duration while addressing potential bias at the end of the dataset. Given the highly right-skewed distribution of the three temporal features, with most values being low and a few extremely high, a logarithmic transformation, defined as $ln(1 + x)$, is applied to each temporal feature, followed by max-min normalization.

For the train-test split, we adopt the strict temporal splitting method from [17]. Cases are ordered by start time, with the last 20% assigned to the test set and the rest to the training set. To prevent data leakage, cases that are still ongoing when the first test set case begins are excluded from training, as their log prefixes may contain future events. The last 20% of training cases serve as validation set for early stopping and hyperparameter tuning.

When using log prefixes as inputs, we adopt a default window size of 200 based on empirical evidence that LSTMs extract minimal contextual information beyond this length [7]. We additionally test the proposed model with reduced window sizes (20, 50, 100, 150) to evaluate the window size's influence on predictive accuracy.

4.3 Benchmark Models for Comparison

To assess the effectiveness of `I3SP`, we compare it against several benchmark models. The *integrated Seq2Seq model*, which incorporates both the trace prefix and log prefix as input, serves as the primary implementation of `I3SP`. To isolate the impact of the log prefix, we compare it with a *trace-based Seq2Seq model*, which has the same encoder-decoder architecture but only uses the trace prefix. All Seq2Seq models are implemented in two configurations: with and without attention mechanisms, where models with attention are denoted by the "-Attn" suffix.

For additional benchmarks, we include the *trace-based SEP models*, which predict the suffix recursively. These consist of a typical LSTM-based SEP model (*SEP-LSTM*) [4,15] and an XGBoost-based SEP model (*SEP-XGBoost*) as XGBoost offers a strong balance between predictive accuracy and computational efficiency [16]. The two trace-based SEP models serve as conventional baselines.

Configuration and training details vary across the Seq2Seq, SEP-LSTM, and SEP-XGBoost models, as specified below.

Seq2Seq Model. The Seq2Seq model is trained using a supervised learning approach, where parameters are optimized to minimize a loss function that measures the error between the predicted and observed outputs. Categorical cross-entropy loss is applied to the activity label suffix by comparing the predicted probability distribution with the true one-hot encoded label, while Mean Absolute Error (MAE) loss that measures the difference between predicted and actual TTNE is applied to the timestamp suffix. The final loss is the unweighted sum of both losses.

Hyperparameters related to model complexity and training are optimized separately for the trace-based and integrated Seq2Seq models, as well as for each dataset. Additionally, experiments indicate that assigning greater weight to End-of-Case (EOC) predictions in the cross-entropy loss enhances the model's ability to predict suffix endings and improves overall suffix prediction accuracy, especially on BPIC2012 and BPIC2017.

SEP-LSTM. The SEP-LSTM follows the architecture proposed in [15], consisting of a shared LSTM that processes the trace prefix, followed by two specialized linear layers for predicting the next activity label and next timestamp respectively. At each step, the LSTM receives a feature vector identical to that in the trace-based Seq2Seq model and training follows the same loss function with essential hyperparameters tuned accordingly.

SEP-XGBoost. The SEP-XGBoost follows the same suffix generation mechanism as the SEP-LSTM, but it differs in architecture and feature processing. The SEP-XGBoost consists of two independent XGBoost models to separately predict the next activity label and the next timestamp. Since XGBoost is not a sequence-ingesting model and requires a fixed-size input, the trace prefix is flattened into a single feature vector by concatenating all individual event-level representations. While this allows efficient parallel processing, XGBoost does not explicitly model temporal dependencies.

4.4 Evaluation Metrics

Activity label suffix prediction is evaluated using the normalized Damerau–Levenshtein (DL) distance, which quantifies the minimum number of insertions, deletions, substitutions, and transpositions required to transform the predicted suffix into the observed one, normalized by the length of the longer sequence. The predicted suffix ends when the EOC is generated or when the predefined suffix length is reached.

Timestamp suffix prediction is evaluated using both Mean Absolute Error (MAE) and Mean Squared Logarithmic Error (MSLE). While MAE is widely used in PPM for evaluating real-valued predictions, MSLE is included due to its reduced sensitivity to extreme outliers. They are defined as:

$$MAE = \frac{1}{\sum_{k=1}^{n} l_k} \sum_{k=1}^{n} \sum_{s=1}^{l_k} |y_{k,s} - \hat{y}_{k,s}| \tag{1}$$

$$MSLE = \frac{1}{\sum_{k=1}^{n} l_k} \sum_{k=1}^{n} \sum_{s=1}^{l_k} (ln(1 + y_{k,s}) - ln(1 + \hat{y}_{k,s}))^2 \tag{2}$$

where n is the number of samples, l_k is the length of the observed suffix in the k-th sample, $\hat{y}_{k,s}$ is the predicted TTNE and $y_{k,s}$ is the observed TTNE. The comparison is performed at each step until the observed suffix ends. While the decoder could continue generating predictions beyond this point, such predictions are excluded from evaluation since the case is already concluded in real-world settings.

For all three metrics, lower values indicate better predictive performance.

5 Results

This section presents the empirical findings, starting with a quantitative analysis of model performance, followed by an explanatory analysis to understand `I3SP`'s decision-making.

5.1 Quantitative Analysis

This section compares the performance of trace-based and integrated models and examines the effect of different log prefix window sizes on the integrated Seq2Seq model. The best results are bold and underlined, and the second-best are in bold. MAE values are reported in minutes, except for BAC, where they are reported in seconds.

Performance Comparison Across Models. Table 2 presents the performance of different models across all four datasets. For activity label suffix prediction, the integrated Seq2Seq model (`I3SP`) consistently outperforms trace-based models, confirming the predictive advantage of incorporating the log prefix. Between the two variants of `I3SP`, the non-attention version achieves the best performance across three datasets, suggesting that the attention mechanism offers limited benefit. Trace-based baselines perform comparably on BPIC2019 and BAC, whereas SEP-XGBoost struggles on BPIC2017 and SEP-LSTM underperforms on BPIC2012.

For timestamp suffix prediction, the integrated Seq2Seq models again perform best, except for BPIC2017. While its improvements over the trace-based Seq2Seq model are generally moderate, BPIC2019 shows a significant reduction in MSLE. The trace-based Seq2Seq model also performs notably better than the trace-based SEP baselines, particularly for BPIC2012 and BPIC2017, highlighting the effectiveness of the encoder-decoder architecture.

Table 2. Performance of different models for activity label suffix prediction (DL distance) and timestamp suffix prediction (MAE and MSLE)

Model	BPIC2012			BPIC2017			BPIC2019			BAC		
	DL distance	MAE	MSLE	DL distance	MAE	MSLE	DL distance	MAE	MSLE	DL distance	MAE	MSLE
Baseline: Trace-based Models												
SEP-XGBoost	0.6407	810	21.17	0.6545	971	19.26	0.1903	16548	27.12	0.2859	63.69	2.89
SEP-LSTM	0.7874	843	23.98	0.5873	936	21.51	0.1892	16272	25.48	0.2845	66.30	3.18
Seq2Seq	0.6075	652	13.39	0.5888	**908**	14.09	0.1880	15911	24.71	0.2905	62.34	**2.79**
Seq2Seq-Attn	0.6003	**651**	13.27	0.5819	**906**	**13.84**	0.1887	15899	24.81	0.2884	62.02	2.80
Integrated Seq2Seq Models												
I3SP	**0.5888**	652	**13.08**	**0.5713**	917	14.16	**0.1765**	**15735**	**21.77**	**0.2682**	**61.55**	**2.73**
I3SP-Attn	**0.5858**	**649**	**13.14**	**0.5721**	914	**13.99**	**0.1795**	**15831**	**22.14**	**0.2692**	**61.30**	**2.79**

Impact of Log Prefix Window Size. Table 3 evaluates the effect of different log prefix window sizes on I3SP (without attention). While a longer log prefix might be expected to enhance predictive performance, we do not observe a monotonic relationship between window sizes and performance metrics. Performance remains generally consistent across various window sizes, except for BPIC2017, where DL distance improves significantly at window sizes of 100 and 150. A window size of 150 appears to be optimal for activity label suffix prediction, achieving the best results on three datasets.

This stability may be due to the fact that short log prefixes already provide a reasonable amount of contextual information, and that even at a system-wide level the most relevant information may potentially be concentrated in recent events. Alternatively, this result may reflect the inherent limitations of LSTMs in capturing extended temporal dependencies.

Table 3. Performance of I3SP with different log prefix window sizes for activity label suffix prediction (DL distance) and timestamp suffix prediction (MAE and MSLE)

Log prefix window size	BPIC2012			BPIC2017			BPIC2019			BAC		
	DL distance	MAE	MSLE	DL distance	MAE	MSLE	DL distance	MAE	MSLE	DL distance	MAE	MSLE
20	**0.5877**	**650**	**12.98**	0.5813	**909**	**13.62**	0.1766	**15711**	22.37	0.2725	**61.29**	2.74
50	0.5914	656	13.22	0.5853	**906**	**13.63**	0.1768	15774	22.14	0.2704	61.47	**2.73**
100	**0.5877**	653	13.39	**0.5621**	919	14.04	**0.1764**	15779	22.03	0.2689	**61.27**	2.74
150	**0.5860**	**650**	13.11	**0.5564**	912	14.43	0.1789	**15708**	**22.02**	**0.2669**	61.96	2.74
200	0.5888	**652**	**13.08**	0.5713	917	14.16	**0.1765**	15735	**21.77**	**0.2682**	61.55	**2.73**

5.2 Explanatory Analysis

To better understand the predictive advantages of I3SP, we analyze several example predictions from the trace-based and integrated Seq2Seq models. This qualitative analysis intends to provide an intuitive understanding of the patterns contributing to the superior performance of the proposed model and influencing its decision-making process. For brevity, activity labels are represented by numbers[5].

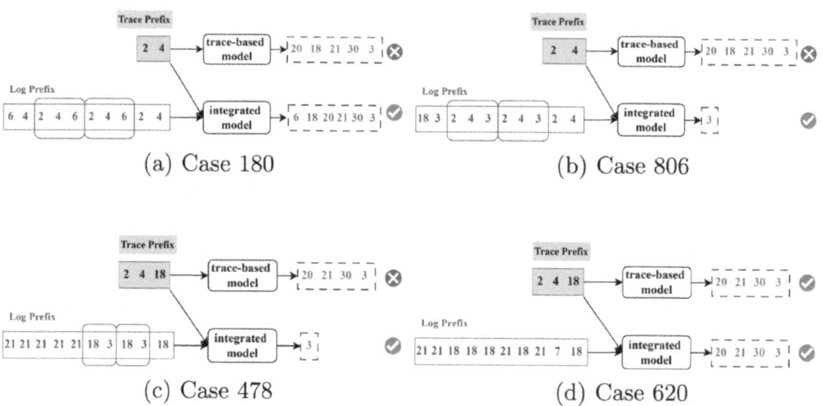

(a) Case 180 (b) Case 806

(c) Case 478 (d) Case 620

Fig. 3. Predictions generated by trace-based and integrated Seq2Seq models for specific cases.

Figure 3 presents four cases from BPIC2019, including cases 478 and 620 previously introduced in Sect. 2. These examples illustrate how the trace-based model tends to predict identical activity label suffixes when trace prefixes are identical, leading to incorrect predictions in cases 180, 806, and 478. In contrast, the integrated model correctly differentiates between these cases, leveraging system-wide behavior from the log prefix.

A key observation is that in cases where specific sequential patterns recur in the log prefix, the integrated model aligns its predictions accordingly. For example, in case 180, the sequence $\langle 2, 4, 6\rangle$ appears twice in the log prefix, and the integrated model correctly predicts 6 after $\langle 2, 4\rangle$. This suggests that I3SP effectively captures inter-case dependencies, adjusting its predictions based on observed system-wide behavior.

Moreover, case 620 demonstrates that when no obvious inter-case pattern is present, the integrated model does not over-rely on log-level information but still makes a correct prediction. This suggests that the integrated model not only

[5] The full activity labels corresponding to the numbers in Fig. 3 are as follows: 2—Start, 3—End, 4—Create Purchase Order Item, 6—Receive Order Confirmation, 7—Change Price, 18—Record Goods Receipt, 20—Vendor creates invoice, 21—Record Invoice Receipt, 30—Clear Invoice.

leverages inter-case patterns when they are present, but also adapts flexibly to cases where such patterns are absent, effectively distinguishing meaningful trends from noise.

6 Conclusion

In this work, we propose `I3SP`, an encoder-decoder architecture that leverages contextual information at both the trace level (past events within a trace) and log level (prior event sequences from the entire system) to predict a case's future trajectory. Unlike existing approaches that rely on manually engineered inter-case features, `I3SP` directly learns inter-case dependencies from the log prefix. While raw log prefixes may introduce noise, experimental results demonstrate that `I3SP` effectively extracts meaningful relationships, particularly improving activity label suffix prediction. Our explanatory analysis further highlights the model's ability to recognize unusual execution orders and align predictions with system-wide trends.

Despite these advantages, `I3SP` has certain limitations. The extent of performance improvement depends on the strength of inter-case dependencies in the event log, which varies across datasets. Due to the scarcity of public event logs suitable for deep learning, we were unable to evaluate the model on datasets with stronger inter-case dynamics, potentially limiting observed gains. Additionally, while longer log prefixes contain more context, they do not consistently improve performance, possibly reflecting LSTMs' limitations in capturing long-term dependencies.

In future work, we aim to enhance the model by utilizing additional attributes such as resource information, and explore potential performance improvements by experimenting with a Transformer-based encoder-decoder architecture, which may offer superior capabilities in capturing long-term dependencies and enable the incorporation of longer log prefixes.

Acknowledgments. This work was supported by the Research Foundation Flanders (FWO) under grant number G039923N, and Internal Funds KU Leuven under grant number C14/23/031.

References

1. Aalikhani, R., Fathian, M., Rasouli, M.R.: Enhancing remaining time prediction in business processes by considering system-level and resource-level inter-case features. Softw. Syst. Model (2025)
2. Ceravolo, P., Comuzzi, M., De Weerdt, J., Di Francescomarino, C., Maggi, F.M.: Predictive process monitoring: concepts, challenges, and future research directions. Process Sci. **1**(1), 2 (2024)
3. Di Francescomarino, C., Ghidini, C.: Predictive process monitoring. In: van der Aalst, W.M.P., Carmona, J. (eds.) Process Mining Handbook, LNBIP, vol. 448, pp. 320–346. Springer, Cham (2022)

4. Evermann, J., Rehse, J.R., Fettke, P.: Predicting process behaviour using deep learning. Decis. Support Syst. **100**, 129–140 (2017)
5. Gunnarsson, B.R., Broucke, S., De Weerdt, J.: A direct data aware LSTM neural network architecture for complete remaining trace and runtime prediction. IEEE Trans. Serv. Comput. **16**(4), 2330–2342 (2023)
6. Gunnarsson, B.R., vanden Broucke, S., De Weerdt, J.: LS-ICE: a load state inter-case encoding framework for improved predictive monitoring of business processes. Inf. Syst. **125**, 102432 (2024)
7. Khandelwal, U., He, H., Qi, P., Jurafsky, D.: Sharp nearby, fuzzy far away: How neural language models use context. In: Gurevych, I., Miyao, Y. (eds.) ACL 2018, pp. 284–294. ACL (2018)
8. Klijn, E.L., Fahland, D.: Identifying and reducing errors in remaining time prediction due to inter-case dynamics. In: ICPM, pp. 25–32. IEEE (2020)
9. Luong, M., Le, Q.V., Sutskever, I., Vinyals, O., Kaiser, L.: Multi-task sequence to sequence learning. In: ICLR 2016 (2016)
10. Luong, T., Pham, H., Manning, C.D.: Effective approaches to attention-based neural machine translation. In: Màrquez, L., Callison-Burch, C., Su, J. (eds.) EMNLP 2015, pp. 1412–1421. ACL (2015)
11. Rama-Maneiro, E., Vidal, J.C., Lama, M.: Deep learning for predictive business process monitoring: review and benchmark. IEEE Trans. Serv. Comput. **16**(1), 739–756 (2023)
12. Roider, J., Zanca, D., Eskofier, B.M.: Efficient training of recurrent neural networks for remaining time prediction in predictive process monitoring. In: Marrella, A., Resinas, M., Jans, M., Rosemann, M. (eds.) BPM 2024. LNCS, vol. 14940, pp. 238–255. Springer, Cham (2024)
13. Senderovich, A., Francescomarino, C.D., Maggi, F.M.: From knowledge-driven to data-driven inter-case feature encoding in predictive process monitoring. Inf. Syst. **84**, 255–264 (2019)
14. Sutskever, I., Vinyals, O., Le, Q.V.: Sequence to sequence learning with neural networks. In: Ghahramani, Z., Welling, M., Cortes, C., Lawrence, N., Weinberger, K.Q. (eds.) Advances in Neural Information Processing Systems, vol. 27, pp. 3104–3112. Curran Associates, Inc. (2014)
15. Tax, N., Verenich, I., La Rosa, M., Dumas, M.: Predictive Business Process Monitoring with LSTM Neural Networks. In: Dubois, E., Pohl, K. (eds.) CAiSE 2017. LNCS, vol. 10253, pp. 477–492. Springer, Cham (2017). https://doi.org/10.1007/978-3-319-59536-8_30
16. Teinemaa, I., Dumas, M., Rosa, M.L., Maggi, F.M.: Outcome-oriented predictive process monitoring: review and benchmark. ACM Trans. Knowl. Discov. Data **13**(2), 1–57 (2019)
17. Weytjens, H., De Weerdt, J.: Creating unbiased public benchmark datasets with data leakage prevention for predictive process monitoring. In: Marrella, A., Weber, B. (eds.) Business Process Management Workshops. BPM 2021. LNBIP, vol. 436, pp. 18–29. Springer, Cham (2021). https://doi.org/10.1007/978-3-030-94343-1_2
18. Wuyts, B., Vanden Broucke, S., De Weerdt, J.: SuTraN: an encoder-decoder transformer for full-context-aware suffix prediction of business processes. In: ICPM, pp. 17–24. IEEE (2024)
19. Zoph, B., Knight, K.: Multi-source neural translation. In: Knight, K., Nenkova, A., Rambow, O. (eds.) NAACL 2016. pp. 30–34. ACL (2016)

What is the Best Process Model Representation? A Comparative Analysis for Process Modeling with Large Language Models

Alexis Brissard[1,2,3(✉)], Frédéric Cuppens[1,2], and Amal Zouaq[1,3]

[1] Polytechnique Montréal, Montreal, Canada
{alexis.brissard,frederic.cuppens,amal.zouaq}@polymtl.ca
[2] LabCys, Montreal, Canada
[3] LAMA-WeST Lab, Montreal, Canada

Abstract. Large Language Models (LLMs) are increasingly applied for Process Modeling (PMo) tasks such as Process Model Generation (PMG). To support these tasks, researchers have introduced a variety of Process Model Representations (PMRs) that serve as model abstractions or generation targets. However, these PMRs differ widely in structure, complexity, and usability, and have never been systematically compared. Moreover, recent PMG approaches rely on distinct evaluation strategies and generation techniques, making comparison difficult.

This paper presents the first empirical study that evaluates multiple PMRs in the context of PMo with LLMs. We introduce the PMo Dataset, a new dataset containing 55 process descriptions paired with models in nine different PMRs. We evaluate PMRs along two dimensions: suitability for LLM-based PMo and performance on PMG. *Mermaid* achieves the highest overall score across six PMo criteria, whereas *BPMN text* delivers the best PMG results in terms of process element similarity.

Keywords: Business Process Modeling · Large Language Models · Process Model Generation · Process Model Representation

1 Introduction

1.1 Background

One of the most promising applications of LLMs in BPM is Process Modeling (PMo), where the goal is to assist or automate the construction of process models from textual process descriptions [6]. A central subtask in PMo is Process Model Generation (PMG), which involves generating a process model from a natural language input. To support this generation, researchers have introduced a variety of Process Model Representations (PMRs)—textual abstractions used to represent the output process model.

The initial motivation for using PMRs stemmed from the limitations of LLMs, which were unable to directly generate standard BPMN models due

I. van de Weerd et al. (Eds.): BPM 2025 Workshops, LNBIP 569, pp. 55–68, 2026.
https://doi.org/10.1007/978-3-032-13426-4_5

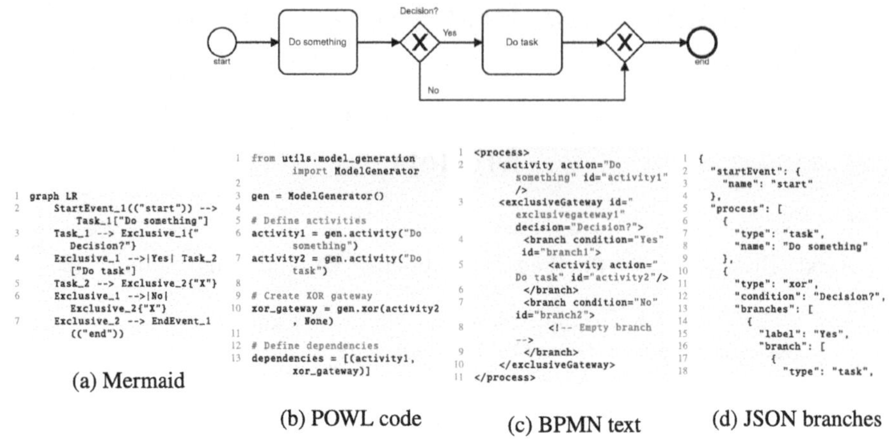

Fig. 1. Four Process Model Representations (PMRs) of the same process model.

to constraints in context length and suboptimal LLM performance [6,9]. To address these challenges, alternative representations such as simplified BPMN or existing diagram notations were introduced. Since then, more advanced PMG approaches have emerged, proposing new techniques such as constrained generation or multi-agents framework, often taking advantage of their own custom PMRs [10,14,16,19]. A subset of these PMRs are presented in Fig. 1.

Despite this progress, the evaluation of the generated process models remains a major challenge [4]. Each approach introduces its own evaluation methods, metrics, and benchmarks, preventing meaningful comparisons between them. Furthermore, the underlying PMRs differ significantly between approaches and have never been subject to a systematic comparative analysis. This fragmentation makes it difficult to assess which PMRs are most suitable for PMG and more broadly for PMo tasks.

1.2 Research Questions and Contributions

This work systematically investigates PMRs by assessing their respective strengths and limitations through conceptual and empirical evaluation. To clarify the current landscape and guide future research in the field, we address the following research questions:

RQ1: What are the key characteristics and features that distinguish different PMRs?

RQ2: Which PMRs are most suitable for PMo with LLMs?

RQ3: Which PMRs lead to the best performance on PMG?

To answer these research questions, we make the following contributions. First, we introduce the PMo Dataset, a new dataset comprising 55 process descriptions paired with process models in nine distinct PMRs. Second, we perform the first comprehensive review and intrinsic comparison of PMRs in the

Table 1. Main PMG approaches from the literature.

PMG approach	PMR	LLM	Evaluation set	Evaluation method
ConverMod [9]	Graphviz + Mermaid	GPT-4	Mangler + PET-7	Text similarity + Qualitative
PromoAI [14]	POWL code	GPT-4	2 descriptions	Qualitative
MAO [16]	BPMN text	GPT-4	BPMN for Research	BPMNDiff Viz
Multimodal [19]	PME	GPT-4V	SAP-SAM	PME similarity
BPMN-chatbot [10]	JSON branches	GPT-4o	PET-7	Qualitative

context of PMo with LLMs, analyzing their structural properties and representational characteristics using both qualitative and quantitative methods. Finally, we evaluate the effectiveness of each PMR as a target for PMG under standard prompting with LLMs, identifying which representations facilitate more accurate and faithful model generation.

The code of this project, containing all our data, prompts and results can be found at https://github.com/Lama-West/Process_Model_Representations.

2 Related Work

2.1 PMo with LLMs

LLMs have recently started to be used for Process Modeling (PMo) and show promising results [4,9,12]. [9] have framed their approach as *Conversational PMo*, we use the broader formulations *PMo with LLMs* or *LLM-based PMo*.

2.2 Main PMG Approaches

One of the most complete PMG studies is ConverMod [9], investigating the use of Graphviz and Mermaid as PMRs. They evaluate their approach on a subset of 7 documents from the PET dataset [2] for which they create business models (hereafter referred to as PET-7). Their main evaluation metric is the Jaccard index between the generated and gold sequence flows.

[13,14] introduce ProMoAI, a unique approach where Python code is generated and executed to obtain POWL process models. Designated as *POWL code*, this PMR requires extended prompts and multiple error correction rounds, which limits its practicality.

[10] proposes BPMN-chatbot, an enhancement of the ProMoAI framework that introduces a more structured and practical PMR. Labeled in this study as *JSON branches*, this PMR encodes the process branching structure in JSON format and leverages OpenAI's function calling to enforce schema adherence during generation. Using PET-7 as in Convermod, the authors conduct a qualitative evaluation and report improved performance over both previous approaches.

[16] uses a multi agent framework combined with a custom PMR (BPMN text) to improve the generation process. They evaluate their results on the

Table 2. PMR main features. PMRs are ordered by recency.

PMR	Language	Graph based	Branch based	Executable	Visualizable	Generation schema
BPMN	XML	✓	✗	✓	✓	✗
BPMN process	XML	✓	✗	✓	✗	✗
Graphviz	Graphviz	✓	✗	✗	✓	✗
Mermaid	Mermaid	✓	✗	✗	✓	✗
PME	JSON	✓	✗	✗	✗	✓
Simplified XML	XML	✓	✗	✗	✗	✗
POWL code	Python	✗	✗	✓	✗	✗
BPMN text	XML	✗	✓	✗	✗	✗
JSON branches	JSON	✗	✓	✗	✗	✓

BPMN for research dataset [3] using BPMNDiffViz [8], a tool to calculate the structural similarity between 2 processes. According to these metrics, their method outperform ProMoAI.

[19] evaluates the multimodal capabilities of LLMs by generating process models from process description and diagrams pairs. They introduce a PMR based on lists of process model elements (PME), used for both generation and evaluation.

Table 1 summarizes PMG approaches presented in this section. Despite recent progress, existing studies face several limitations: reliance on closed-source LLMs limits reproducibility, evaluation sets remain small, and performance is often assessed using non-standardized metrics. While some studies have begun to compare LLMs [12], the field still lacks a systematic and reproducible evaluation of PMG pipelines. In response, our study starts to address these gaps through a unified benchmark and a comparative framework, introduced in the following section.

3 Methodology

3.1 Initial Definitions

To ensure clarity throughout the paper, we distinguish between the following concepts:

Process model: An abstract model of a business process, independent of any specific formalism or notation. For brevity, we occasionally refer to it simply as a *model*.

Process Model Representation (PMR): A notation used to express a process model (e.g., BPMN, POWL, or Mermaid). A PMR defines the syntax and semantics by which a process model is described.

PMR model: A process model represented using a PMR (e.g., a BPMN model, a Mermaid model).

3.2 Process Model Representations

We choose to evaluate nine PMRs, presented in Table 2. Our selection is guided by two criteria. First, we include PMRs that are being used in existing PMG approaches, ensuring relevance to the current state of the art. Second, we ensure diversity in representation style, covering a range of structures and languages.

Our analysis focuses on a specific set of element types commonly found in process models. These include tasks, events, gateways (with optional labels referred to as *decisions*) and sequence flows (with optional labels referred to as *conditions*). Furthermore, we consider swimlanes, which feature lanes nested within pools, and message flows. We do not include data objects, textual annotations or other special elements due to their limited prevalence in the PMo Dataset.

Hereafter, we describe the main PMRs used in this study. **BPMN** is selected as our baseline given its status as a widely adopted standard. **BPMN process** is a BPMN model that only defines the process and does not include the BPMN diagram definition. Comparing BPMN and BPMN process allows us to directly measure the impact of specifying graphical elements. **Graphviz** is a graphical representation, meaning it can be directly visualized using the DOT engine. **Mermaid** is another graphical representation made for diagrams. **Process Model Elements** (PME) [19] consists of a JSON object containing 6 lists of elements: tasks, events, gateways, swimlanes, sequence flows and message flows. This flat structure enables easy counting of elements and comparison between models. **Simplified XML** is a simplification of XML originally proposed in [11]. Similarly to BPMN process, graphical and other non-essential elements are omitted. The XML structure is lightened, resulting in a more compact PMR. **POWL code**, introduced by [14], is Python code that can be executed to create a POWL model, itself translatable to BPMN. The main advantages of using code as a PMR is to leverage LLM's familiarity with coding tasks while enabling detailed feedback via execution of said code. POWL code lacks support for conditions, event labels, intermediate events, swimlanes and message flows, making it the least expressive PMR. **JSON branches** was developed by [10] specifically to reduce token count, be compact and provide schema following abilities for LLM generation. It only handles simple backward flows (represented as looping gateways) and cannot include multiple start and end events, message flows and swimlanes. **BPMN text** [16] is similar to JSON branches, but in XML format. It has the same limitations except that it supports role and object annotations in tasks.

3.3 PMo Dataset

To enable PMR comparison across a wide range of process models, we build the PMo dataset. It contains 55 process descriptions paired with process models represented in all PMRs from Sect. 3.2. The PMo dataset is constructed from five existing sources: 24 pairs from the Mangler dataset [17], 20 from the PMo

Benchmark [12], 6 from the PET-7 dataset [9][1], 4 from the BPMN for research dataset [3], and 1 from the CCC19 dataset [18].[2]

We chose these data sources because process models are handcrafted, or at least validated by domain experts. This explains why we did not include the much larger MaD dataset [15], which has been criticized for lack of variability of its models and their descriptions. Similarly, even though the descriptions are human-authored, the dataset in [1] also lacks diversity due to automatic process model generation (e.g., maximum 9 activities).

The PMo Dataset underwent extensive preprocessing to ensure optimal usability and applicability. For process descriptions, this involves cleaning special characters, correcting punctuation and spacing, sentence splitting, and removing irrelevant information such as modeling instructions. The ground truth BPMN models are also refined by sanitizing label texts, improving diagram layouts and positioning decisions and conditions optimally. The Mangler dataset received special attention due to having multiple models per description, each graded from 0 to 5. The model closest to the textual description (to our own judgment) is chosen among those with the best grade, with a preference for models including only common elements (e.g., no data objects or other special elements).

Following the preprocessing phase, we automatically convert all BPMN models into all the other representations to obtain our ground truth. We develop converters for each PMR and validate our conversions by transforming models from BPMN to PMRs and back. Some process models contain information that are not supported by every PMR. In this case, we ignore the additional information (e.g., conditions are not included in POWL code). In cases where the model cannot be represented by the PMR without significant loss of information, it is left out (e.g., models including swimlanes are not converted to JSON branches). For branching PMRs, two thirds of the BPMN models cannot be converted.

3.4 PMR for PMo with LLMs

Requirements. To guide our evaluation, we define six key requirements for an ideal PMR in the context of PMo with LLMs. A suitable PMR should be compact in terms of token count to fit within LLM context limits, reduce costs, generation time and energy consumption [10]. Strong expressiveness is essential, to ensure that a wide range of models can be represented. This is mainly measured by element coverage, i.e. how many elements from a model are representable by the PMR. The PMR should be human readable to support interpretability. More specifically, a non expert should be able to understand the general purpose and structure of the process by just looking at the PMR model itself [9]. Length in lines, words and characters are key metrics to consider for this requirement, as a longer model is often harder to understand. Beyond pure text, a PMR should should also support direct graphical visualization, ideally

[1] One pair is removed because its description is already included in the PMo Benchmark.

[2] The PMo Dataset is accessible at this url: https://doi.org/10.5281/zenodo.15857588.

without the need for additional conversions. The representation must be easily usable—parsable, editable, and generable by LLMs. This includes support for additional tooling such as JSON schema. Finally, it should be possible to extend it to fit specific modeling needs or add support for other process model elements.

In summary, our six requirements are Token compactness, Expressivity, Human readability, Visualization capabilities, Usability and Extensibility. These requirements are specific to the use case of PMo with LLMs and are designed to support the whole range of associated tasks (e.g., question answering, interactive modification). They represent our attempt to differentiate between PMRs using the PMo Dataset. Other criteria could also be included such as compositionality, but it would require a more advanced evaluation framework and dataset.

Evaluation. We perform a comparison of PMRs across six dimensions that reflect the previously defined requirements. This evaluation combines both quantitative and qualitative metrics. For quantitative analysis, we measure the length of each representation in terms of lines, tokens, words, and characters to assess their compactness and efficiency. We also compute the mean element coverage over the PMo Dataset by dividing the number of process elements representable in the PMR by the total number of ground truth elements. For qualitative analysis, we evaluate human readability, visualization capabilities, usability and extensibility.

3.5 PMR for PMG

We aim to measure the performance of each PMR for the specific task of PMG. To ensure a fair comparison, we perform all experiments under a standardized setting. Specifically, we restrict process elements to the following set: standard tasks, start and end events, exclusive and parallel gateways, and sequence flows. This simplified setting allows us to compare PMRs independently of their element coverage, while also limiting prompts length and complexity. Indeed, it would not be fair to compare a complex model generated in a PMR that supports swimlanes to a simpler model in a less expressive PMR.

Prompting. We design a PMG prompt that instructs the LLM to generate a process model-represented in a specific PMR based on a given process description. To ensure a fair evaluation across PMRs, we construct prompts with consistent size and structure. The LLM receives the same task description and general modeling instructions regardless of the PMR. For each representation, we provide specific formatting guidelines which include Markdown subsections and an example illustrating the expected output format.

LLM Choice and Generation Parameters. We perform our experiments with LLaMA-3.3-70b, which is a recent, open-source model with state of the art performance for its size. Our choice to use an open-source LLM is motivated by transparency, adaptability, and community support, which facilitate reproducibility and further research. While it could be interesting to evaluate additional LLMs, this is out of the scope of this paper. All experiments are performed using Google Vertex AI API. Generation parameters are set as follows: Top-K is left as default (i.e., –1), Top-P is 0.95 and Temperature is 0.2.

Evaluation. We evaluate the generated PMR models through comparison with the ground-truth PMR models along two dimensions: element counts, and PME similarity. Element counts capture the number of generated process elements for each type. To also take in account the semantic content of elements (i.e., task labels, decisions, conditions), we follow the evaluation methodology proposed by [19]. It consists of 2 steps: semantic matching and set similarity. Element pairs with semantic similarity higher than an experimentally defined threshold (0.7) are made identical using a 1-to-1 matching. To calculate this semantic similarity, we produce embeddings for each element using a sentence transformer trained for sentence similarity (`stsb-mpnet-base-v2`) and calculate their cosine similarity. Once the elements are semantically matched, the Dice–Sørensen coefficient is computed to assess similarity between the resulting sets, balancing precision and recall in a single score.

4 Results

4.1 PMR for PMo with LLMs

Length Comparison. Table 3 presents the length differences between ground-truth PMR models and our baseline, BPMN models. All PMRs lead to a significant reduction across all length metrics, successfully achieving their initial purpose. However, we observe substantial variation between PMRs: Mermaid is the most compact, achieving over 90% reduction in lines, tokens, words, and characters compared to BPMN. Looking at BPMN process, we can see that removing the BPMN diagram definition alone leads to a 70% decrease in token count. This highlights the importance of excluding non-essential elements such as graphical details.

POWL code, BPMN text, and JSON branches are reported in a separate section of the table as they do not cover all processes of the PMo Dataset, due to element coverage limitations. This explains the slight discrepancies between absolute and relative difference in the results. Nonetheless, they also achieve significant length reductions, comparable to Mermaid.

Evaluation Summary. Table 4 summarizes our evaluation of PMRs across the six requirements defined in Sect. 3.4. We graded each requirement from 1 to 5 based on specific quantitative and qualitative metrics detailed in the same section.

Token compactness reflects the results from Table 3, with Mermaid and POWL code achieving the highest scores.

Table 3. Mean length difference of ground-truth PMR models compared to BPMN models.

PMR	Line Count		Token Count		Word Count		Char Count	
	Rel	Abs	Rel	Abs	Rel	Abs	Rel	Abs
BPMN (Baseline)	384		4231		6531		19048	
BPMN process	-64%	-248	-70%	-2984	-69%	-4539	-63%	-11947
Graphviz	-87%	-336	-88%	-3734	-90%	-5888	-88%	-16803
Mermaid	**-91%**	**-350**	**-93%**	**-3934**	**-93%**	**-6095**	**-92%**	**-17524**
PME	-27%	-109	-65%	-2783	-73%	-4768	-62%	-11799
Simplified XML	-60%	-228	-83%	-3502	-79%	-5111	-70%	-13207
POWL code	-87%	-280	-93%	-3268	-94%	-5107	-91%	-14471
BPMN text	-89%	-284	-89%	-3119	-93%	-5032	-88%	-13900
JSON branches	-67%	-212	-88%	-3078	-92%	-4973	-80%	-12215

For expressiveness, we report the element coverage calculated on the PMo Dataset models. Branching PMRs such as POWL code and BPMN text score lower due to their limited element support (see Sect. 3.2).

Human readability scores are based on length results (Table 3) and ease of understanding of the process solely from the PMR model. Branching PMRs perform best in this regard due to their concise syntax and clearer structure. We also take in account the user study from [9], where participants preferred Mermaid to Graphviz representation.

BPMN, Mermaid and Graphviz have the best visualization capabilities as they can be directly represented graphically. BPMN process and POWL code can be visualized via standard libraries such as pm4py, while the remaining PMRs need to be converted. The PMRs that are not graph-based are harder to convert, hence their reduced grade.

Usability scores are based on 3 aspects: parsability, editability and support for external tooling. Parsability is highest for JSON and XML-based formats, which benefit from standardized parsers. Custom formats like Mermaid and Graphviz are less straightforward, while branching PMRs are penalized due to the need for recursive parsing. We remove one point to BPMN for editability due to the need to update the associated BPMN diagram when making a change to the process. We also account for LLM schema-following capabilities (see Table 2) by adding an additional point to JSON PMRs.

Extensibility grades are based on the inherent limitations of PMRs and effort needed to support additional element types (e.g., it is harder to update the POWL generation logic than the PME JSON schema).

Table 4. Evaluation summary of PMRs for LLM-based PMo. All grades are from 1 to 5.

PMR	Avg.	Token compact	Expressive	Human readable	Vizualisable	Usable	Extensible
BPMN	3.33	1	**5** ***(100%)***	1	**5**	3	**5**
BPMN process	3.50	2	**5** ***(100%)***	2	3	4	**5**
Graphviz	3.67	4	4 *(89%)*	3	**5**	3	3
Mermaid	**4.00**	**5**	4 *(89%)*	4	**5**	3	3
PME	3.20	2	**5** ***(100%)***	2	2	**5**	4
Simplified XML	3.50	3	**5** ***(100%)***	3	2	3	**5**
POWL code	2.83	**5**	1 *(71%)*	3	3	3	2
BPMN text	2.67	4	2 *(84%)*	**5**	1	2	2
JSON branches	3.00	4	3 *(87%)*	**5**	1	3	2

4.2 PMR for PMG

Element Counts. Table 5 presents the mean element counts of the generated process models for each PMR. On average, LLMs generate significantly smaller models, with roughly eight fewer nodes (tasks, events, or gateways) compared to the ground truth. Gateways are the most affected: the number of Exclusive gateways drops by 50%, and Parallel gateways by 65%. This indicates a tendency to simplify the model by retaining a single task sequence. Despite this general trend, differences between PMRs are notable. Branching PMRs (i.e., JSON branches and BPMN text) lead to substantially higher element counts than the other representations. This suggests that the branching structure can partially mitigate the LLMs' tendency to omit gateways. Interestingly, Graphviz stands out by producing more tasks and gateways than other graph-based PMRs. This may be attributed to its use of descriptive node names instead of identifiers, reducing generation complexity for the LLM.

PME Similarity. Table 6 reports PME similarity scores obtained for different element types. Branching PMRs-particularly BPMN text-consistently achieve higher similarity scores than graph-based ones. Graphviz also shows strong performance for gateway decisions, likely benefiting once again from its use of descriptive identifiers. POWL code scores are lowered by the high numbers of formatting errors (40% of generated models are invalid), reflecting the PMR shortcomings with a limited prompting budget.

Table 5. Mean element counts of generated PMR models compared to ground truth. Nodes include tasks, events and gateways. Sequence flows are reported separately as they directly depend on the number of nodes and would artificially increase the number of elements.

PMR	Nodes	Tasks	Events	Exclusive gateways	Parallel gateways	Sequence flows
Ground Truth	23.18	12.53	2	5.91	2.67	27.67
BPMN	-10.49	-4.62	+0.18	-4.09	-1.98	-13.93
BPMN process	-9.93	-4.35	+0.14	-3.96	-1.69	-13.21
Graphviz	-7.96	-2.71	+0.04	-3.82	**-1.40**	-10.29
Mermaid	-9.16	-3.87	+0.07	-3.75	-1.53	-11.80
PME	-9.56	-4.02	+0.09	-3.73	-1.82	-12.69
Simplified XML	-9.49	-4.36	+0.09	-3.51	-1.64	-12.38
POWL code	-9.36	-4.08	**0.00**	-3.91	-1.67	-12.94
BPMN text	**-3.86**	**-1.53**	**0.00**	-0.41	-1.85	**-6.01**
JSON branches	-4.29	-2.44	**0.00**	**+0.09**	-1.87	-6.07
Average	-8.23	-3.55	+0.07	-3.01	-1.72	-11.04

Table 6. Mean PME similarity scores of generated PMR models compared to ground truth for each PMR under standard PMG.

PMR	Overall	Tasks overall	Events overall	Gateways overall	Gateway decisions	Gateway types	Sequence flows
BPMN	0.43	0.48	0.55	0.38	0.16	0.45	0.36
BPMN process	0.44	0.48	0.55	0.4	0.15	0.5	0.38
Graphviz	0.47	0.5	0.74	0.49	**0.6**	0.54	0.38
Mermaid	0.48	0.49	0.74	0.45	0.18	0.54	0.42
PME	0.46	0.5	0.68	0.45	0.12	0.54	0.37
Simplified XML	0.45	0.48	0.57	0.46	0.07	0.58	0.4
POWL code	0.27	0.29	0.41	0.21	0.36	0.23	0.22
BPMN text	**0.54**	**0.52**	**0.75**	0.58	0.13	0.69	0.49
JSON branches	0.53	0.51	0.58	**0.61**	0.19	**0.7**	**0.5**

5 Discussion and Conclusion

This study offers a comprehensive analysis of PMRs in the context of PMo with LLMs, with a particular focus on the PMG task.

To support this investigation, we assemble the largest gold-standard dataset to date for PMo (55 pairs) coupled with various types of PMRs, enabling both qualitative and quantitative comparisons across nine PMRs drawn from the literature. Our analysis, guided by a set of functional requirements, identifies Mermaid as the most suitable PMR for PMo with LLMs, notably due to its token compactness and visualization capabilities.

We further examine the use of PMRs as generation targets for PMG. After generation based on standard prompting, we measure performance using process element counts and PME similarity. Results reveal a consistent tendency of LLMs to undergenerate process elements—particularly gateways—leading to simplified process models. However, PMRs that support explicit branching structures, such as BPMN text and JSON branches, mitigate this behavior. BPMN text, in particular, achieves the strongest similarity with ground truth elements for both raw numbers and semantic content.

Overall, our findings highlight the critical role of PMR design in enabling effective LLM-based process modeling and generation. While Mermaid appears to be the most versatile PMR, BPMN text yields better results for PMG. This suggests that using different PMRs at specific stages of the PMo pipeline may lead to more effective outcomes.

Several limitations must be acknowledged and provide avenues for future research.

First, our evaluation of PMRs for PMo with LLMs (Table 4), while incorporating quantitative metrics, remains primarily subjective, as it is based on the assessment of the authors. A more rigorous approach, such as combining the grades from multiple experts, would enhance the validity of our findings.

Second, the structure of PMRs is inherently flexible, and our evaluation relies on standardized representations (e.g., consistent identifier formats). Alternative formatting choices may influence LLM behavior and lead to different results. Moreover, several promising PMRs, such as BPMN Sketch [7] or JSON-Nets [5], were not included in this study and represent valuable directions for future exploration.

Third, another limitation is that PME similarity, although it captures semantic content, remains highly sensitive to the number of generated elements. While most generated elements match the ground truth, omissions significantly reduce the overall score. For this reason, we also report element counts. Moreover, it enables us to better understand the under-generation problem of LLMs.

Fourth, we do not manually evaluate the LLM-generated models, which could provide better insights of their quality and practical usability.

Finally, our PMG experiments, like most existing studies, focus on a reduced subset of process elements. As such, they do not capture the full expressive range of real-world models. Future research should investigate LLMs' ability to generate richer models that include more advanced elements such as swimlanes or data objects.

Acknowledgement. This study was funded by MITACS grant number IT32670.

Declarations of Interest. The authors have no competing interests to declare that are relevant to the content of this article.

References

1. Apaydin, K., Zisgen, Y.: Local Large Language Models for Business Process Modeling. In: Delgado, A., Slaats, T. (eds.) Process Mining Workshops. pp. 605–609. Springer, Cham (2025). https://doi.org/10.1007/978-3-031-82225-4_44
2. Bellan, P., van der Aa, H., Dragoni, M., Ghidini, C., Ponzetto, S.P.: PET: An Annotated Dataset for Process Extraction from Natural Language Text (2022). https://doi.org/10.48550/arXiv.2203.04860
3. Camunda: BPMN for Research Dataset (2015)
4. Fettke, P., Houy, C.: Evaluating the Process Modeling Abilities of Large Language Models – Preliminary Foundations and Results (2025). https://doi.org/10.48550/arXiv.2503.13520
5. Forell, M., Schüler, S.: Modeling meets large language models. In: Modellierung 2024 Satellite Events. p. 10.18420, modellierung2024. Gesellschaft für Informatik e.V. (2024)
6. Grohs, M., Abb, L., Elsayed, N., Rehse, J.R.: Large Language Models can accomplish Business Process Management Tasks (2023). https://doi.org/10.48550/arXiv.2307.09923
7. Ivanchikj, A., Serbout, S., Pautasso, C.: Live process modeling with the BPMN Sketch Miner. Softw. Syst. Model. **21**(5), 1877–1906 (2022). https://doi.org/10.1007/s10270-022-01009-w
8. Ivanov, S., Kalenkova, A., Aalst, van der, W.: BPMNDiffViz : A tool for BPMN models comparison. In: Daniel, F., Zugal, S. (eds.) Proceedings of the Demo Session of the 13th International Conference on Business Process Management (BPM 2015, Innsbruck, Austria, August 31–September 3, 2015). pp. 35–39. CEUR Workshop Proceedings (2015)
9. Klievtsova, N., Benzin, J.V., Kampik, T., Mangler, J., Rinderle-Ma, S.: Conversational Process Modeling: Can Generative AI Empower Domain Experts in Creating and Redesigning Process Models? (2024). https://doi.org/10.48550/arXiv.2304.11065
10. Kopke, J., Safan, A.: Efficient LLM-based conversational process modeling. In: BPM2024 (2024)
11. Kourani, H., et al.: Leveraging Large Language Models for Enhanced Process Model Comprehension (2024). https://doi.org/10.48550/arXiv.2408.08892
12. Kourani, H., Berti, A., Schuster, D., van der Aalst, W.M.P.: Evaluating Large Language Models on Business Process Modeling: Framework, Benchmark, and Self-Improvement Analysis (2024). https://doi.org/10.48550/arXiv.2412.00023
13. Kourani, H., Berti, A., Schuster, D., van der Aalst, W.M.P.: Process Modeling With Large Language Models (2024). https://doi.org/10.48550/arXiv.2403.07541
14. Kourani, H., Berti, A., Schuster, D., van der Aalst, W.M.P.: ProMoAI: Process Modeling with Generative AI (2024). https://doi.org/10.48550/arXiv.2403.04327
15. Li, X., Ni, L., Li, R., Liu, J., Zhang, M.: MaD: A Dataset for interview-based BPM in business process management. In: 2023 International Joint Conference on Neural Networks (IJCNN), pp. 1–8 (2023). https://doi.org/10.1109/IJCNN54540.2023.10191898
16. Lin, L., Jin, Y., Zhou, Y., Chen, W., Qian, C.: MAO: A Framework for Process Model Generation with Multi-Agent Orchestration (2024). https://doi.org/10.48550/arXiv.2408.01916
17. Mangler, J., Klievtsova, N.: Textual Process Descriptions and Corresponding BPMN Models (2023). https://doi.org/10.5281/zenodo.7783492

18. Munoz-Gama, J., de la Fuente, R.R., Sepúlveda, M.M., Fuentes, R.R.: Conformance Checking Challenge 2019 (CCC19) (2019). https://doi.org/10.4121/UUID:C923AF09-CE93-44C3-ACE0-C5508CF103AD
19. Voelter, M., Hadian, R., Kampik, T., Breitmayer, M., Reichert, M.: Leveraging Generative AI for Extracting Process Models from Multimodal Documents (2024). https://doi.org/10.48550/arXiv.2406.04959

Discovering Coordinated Processes from Social Online Networks

Anna Kalenkova[1(✉)], Lewis Mitchell[2], and Ethan Johnson[2]

[1] Adelaide Data Science Centre, School of Computer Science and Information Technology, College of Engineering and Information Technology, Adelaide University, Adelaide City Campus East, Adelaide, SA 5005, Australia
anna.kalenkova@adelaide.edu.au

[2] Adelaide Data Science Centre, School of Mathematical Sciences, College of Sciences, Adelaide University, Adelaide City Campus East, Adelaide, SA 5005, Australia
{lewis.mitchell,ethan.johnson}@adelaide.edu.au

Abstract. The rapid growth of social media presents a unique opportunity to study coordinated agent behavior in an unfiltered environment. Online processes often exhibit complex structures that reflect the nature of the user behavior, whether it is authentic and genuine, or part of a coordinated effort by malicious agents to spread misinformation and disinformation. Detection of AI-generated content can be extremely challenging due to the high quality of large language model-generated text. Therefore, approaches that use metadata like post timings are required to effectively detect coordinated AI-driven campaigns. Existing work that models the spread of information online is limited in its ability to represent different control flows that occur within the network in practice. Process mining offers techniques for the discovery of process models with different routing constructs and are yet to be applied to social networks. We propose to leverage process mining methods for the discovery of AI and human agent behavior within social networks. Applying process mining techniques to real-world Twitter (now X) event data, we demonstrate how the structural and behavioral properties of discovered process models can reveal coordinated AI and human behaviors online.

Keywords: Social network analysis · AI and human online agents · Process mining · (Stochastic) Petri nets · Process discovery

1 Introduction

The rise in popularity of social networks combined with the rapid advancement of artificial intelligence (AI) [14] has put the spread of misinformation and disinformation at an all-time high [18]. While both misinformation and disinformation pertain to incorrect information, the key difference is that misinformation can be a simple misunderstanding of facts passed as truth while disinformation is

We acknowledge support from the Australian Government through the Australian Research Council's Discovery Projects funding scheme (project DP210103700).

I. van de Weerd et al. (Eds.): BPM 2025 Workshops, LNBIP 569, pp. 69–81, 2026.
https://doi.org/10.1007/978-3-032-13426-4_6

deliberately deceptive in nature. Social networks are a perfect breeding ground for this mis/disinformation due to their accessibility and the ease of information spread by coordinated AI and human agents [27]. As such, the discovery of these coordinated processes is a significant issue.

The rise of AI tools like large language models (LLMs) increases the risk of rapid and coordinated mis/disinformation campaigns online, as they make it easier to generate large volumes of realistic text. A substantial body of research explores AI-generated text detection [11], and a variety of techniques exist [7]. However, numerous challenges remain when relying solely on text data to detect AI-driven coordinated mis/disinformation campaigns [31], and the trend of increasing realism in LLM-generated text means that purely content-based approaches are unlikely to be successful. Therefore, it is necessary to use metadata from social media posts to detect coordination, with post timings [6] being an attractive approach. Process mining thus emerges as a natural framework to detect AI-driven misinformation campaigns.

Several methods have been proposed for discovering coordinated AI behaviors online using metadata from social media posts [15]. Recent methods are focused on the discovery and analysis of *(online) social networks* [29], *coordinated networks* [4], *synchronized networks* [17], *information cascades* [5], and *threshold models* [3]. Online social, coordinated and synchronized networks can be modeled as directed or undirected graphs, where nodes represent accounts and edges denote communications. These models are static and do not capture the dynamic nature of social networks. In contrast, information cascades and threshold models represent the concurrent spread of information through a network, but do not account for alternative paths of information propagation.

Another approach to modeling online AI and human behavior is to leverage stochastic processes. Some techniques employ Hawkes processes [23] to model and categorize the user behavior. In these models, an event (such as a post or repost) can trigger new events (reposts) with an intensity that decreases over time. Although they represent the stochastic perspective, Hawkes processes do not capture the structure of the social network. Discrete-time Markov chains [20] and continuous Markov processes [2] have also been extensively used to discover and analyze user behaviors. While Markov chains and processes can be visualized, these models can be convoluted and challenging to comprehend. Moreover, we will demonstrate by an example that Petri nets are more suitable for modeling concurrent behaviors than Markov processes.

The main motivation for this research is to build models that capture both: (1) the stochastic dynamics of networks, such that the malicious AI behavior can be simulated and analyzed, and (2) the structure of the social network, including parallel and alternative pathways of information spread. Stochastic Petri nets are thus a promising tool for modeling these perspectives together. Although some methods for modeling social networks using Petri nets exist [8,28], the discovery and analysis of such models from social network data has not yet been studied.

Seminal work on discovering social networks within the domain of process mining is presented in [1]. The techniques in [16,25,26] focus on discovering agent behavior, while this paper introduces a method for learning process models that capture information flow. Other recent agent mining techniques [9,10] discover information flow and identify handovers between agents, but mainly analyze sequential interactions, while we propose an approach for discovering models in which information can be passed to multiple users.

The main contributions of this paper are as follows: (1) a novel concept of free-choice stochastic Petri nets; (2) a method for discovering free-choice stochastic Petri nets from event data; (3) methods for analyzing and categorizing AI and human agent behavior based on the discovered stochastic Petri net models; (4) an application of the proposed techniques to real-world social network data.

2 Motivating Examples

This section justifies the choice of stochastic Petri nets as a modeling tool for representing and analyzing user behavior online. First, we present an example demonstrating how Petri nets model concurrency in social networks and compare them to Markov processes. Second, we examine threshold models, which can represent concurrency but fail to capture patterns where only a specific group of users interacts with a post.

Consider user A and their followers, users B and C (see the social network presented in Fig. 1a).

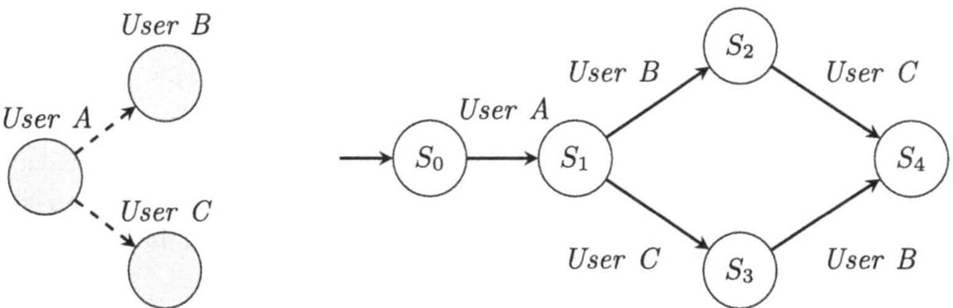

(a) A social network where users B and C follow user A.

(b) A Markov chain representation of the social network dynamics.

Fig. 1. A social network where users B and C follow user A and the dynamics of the social network.

Each time user A posts or reposts information, it is subsequently reposted by B and C. The event log generated by this model will contain traces in which activities initiated by users B and C alternate, i.e., $\langle \mathit{User\ A}, \mathit{User\ B}, \mathit{User\ C}\rangle$ and $\langle \mathit{User\ A}, \mathit{User\ C}, \mathit{User\ B}\rangle$.

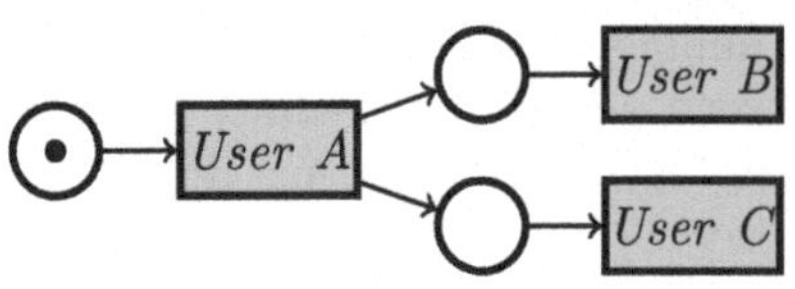

Fig. 2. A Petri net modeling the spread of information from user A to users B and C.

Figure 1b illustrates a Markov chain representing the dynamics of the social network, where states denote its configurations and transitions correspond to user activities. The Petri net, together with its initial marking, that models the spread of information from user A to users B and C is represented in Fig. 2. This Petri net models concurrency; however, the corresponding Markov chain (Fig. 1b) assumes that users make reposts sequentially[1]. As a result, the waiting times for the same dataset will be interpreted as shorter, because, in some cases, users B and C do not wait for A to submit the post but instead wait for each other.

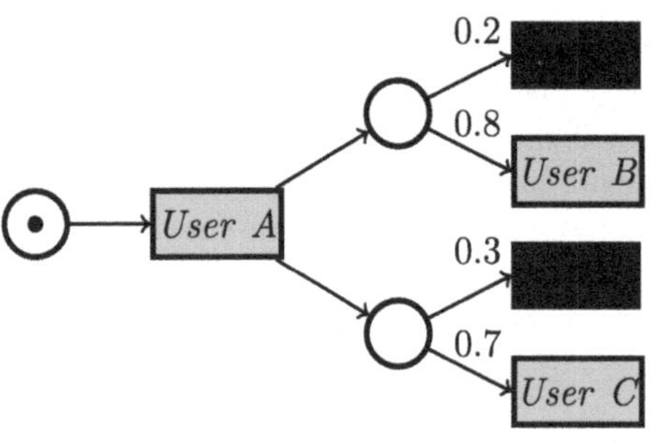

Fig. 3. A stochastic Petri net for the threshold model. "Black box" transitions indicate silent behavior when the post is not reposted by user B or user C.

Threshold models [3], in turn, are used to model concurrent processes within social networks. Consider the social network presented in Fig. 1a. In addition to the graph structure of the network, threshold models provide probabilities that a post will be reposted by followers. For example, user B reposts posts from user A with probability 0.8, and user C reposts posts from user A with probability 0.7. This can be modeled by a stochastic Petri net, as shown in Fig. 3, where "black box" transitions represent silent behavior when the post is not reposted. Although stochastic Petri nets can model behavior defined by threshold models, they also support choice constructs. This capability is particularly important when different groups of users are interested in specific topics.

The next section introduces the basic concepts, including free-choice stochastic Petri nets and related structural and behavioral measures, used in this paper.

3 Theoretical Background

In this section, we provide the basic definitions used to describe the proposed social network analysis approach. We first introduce stochastic process models and then define structural and behavioral characteristics of these models.

3.1 Process Models

Definition 1 (Petri net). *Let Λ be a set of labels. A Petri net is a 5-tuple $PN = (T, P, F, l, M_0)$, where T is a finite set of transitions, P is a finite set of*

[1] Real-world datasets typically include only the original tweet identifier, and concurrency needs to be discovered.

places, such that $P \cap T = \emptyset$, *F is a set of arcs, defined as* $F \subseteq (P \times T) \cup (T \times P)$, $l : T \to \Lambda \cup \{\tau\}$ *is a labeling function that assigns labels to transitions, symbol* $\tau \notin \Lambda$ *denotes silent transitions,* $M_0 : P \to \mathbb{N}$ *is the initial marking, which defines the initial number of tokens in each place. For a node* $n \in P \cup T$ *the set of* input *nodes and set of* output *nodes are defined as* $\bullet n = \{x|(x, n) \in F\}$ *and* $n\bullet = \{x|(n, x) \in F\}$, *respectively.*

Figure 2 illustrates an example of a Petri net. Places are depicted as circles, transitions as rectangles, and arcs as arrows. The initial marking of the Petri net is shown as a token in the leftmost place. Tokens move when a transition fires. The formal definition of transition firing is given below.

Definition 2 (Transition firing). *A transition* $t \in T$ *is* enabled *in a marking* $M : P \to \mathbb{N}$ *if, for all places* $p \in \bullet t$, *it holds that* $M(p) \geq 1$, *i.e., each input place contains at least one token. An enabled transition t can* fire, *consuming one token from each of its input places and producing one token to each of its output places. This results in a new marking* M', *defined as follows: 1)* $M'(p) = M(p) - 1$, *if* $p \in \bullet t$ *and* $p \notin t\bullet$, *2)* $M'(p) = M(p) + 1$, *if* $p \in t\bullet$ *and* $p \notin \bullet t$, *3)* $M'(p) = M(p)$, *in all other cases. We denote this firing as:* $M \xrightarrow{\Lambda(t)} M'$.

In this paper, we focus on free-choice Petri nets, which can be discovered using state-of-the-art process discovery techniques and model choice patterns.

Definition 3 (Free-choice Petri net). *A Petri net* $PN = (T, P, F, l, M_0)$ *is called free-choice iff* $\forall t_1, t_2 \in T$, $t_1 \neq t_2$ *if* $\exists p \in \bullet t_1, p \in \bullet t_2$, *then* $\nexists p' \in P$, *such that,* $p' \neq p, p' \in \bullet t_1$.

As stated in Definition 3, if two transitions share an input place, they must not have any additional input places. For example, the Petri nets shown in Fig. 2 and Fig. 3 are free-choice because their transitions either do not share input places or share the same single input place.

The behavior of a Petri net can be described by its reachability graph.

Definition 4 (Reachability graph). *Let* $PN = (T, P, F, l, M_0)$ *be a Petri net. We say that marking* M_n *is reachable from marking* M_1 *iff there exists a sequence of transitions* $t_1, t_2, \ldots, t_{n-1}$, *such that,* $M_1 \xrightarrow{t_1} M_2 \xrightarrow{t_2} \ldots \xrightarrow{t_{n-1}} M_n$. *By* $\mathcal{R}(M)$ *we will denote the set of all markings reachable from M. The reachability graph of PN is a directed graph* (G, E), $G = \mathcal{R}(M_0)$, $E \subseteq G \times (\Lambda \cup \{\tau\}) \times G$, *where* $e = (M_i, \lambda, M_j) \in E$ *iff* $M_i \xrightarrow{\lambda} M_j$.

We assume that all reachability graphs are finite, as this is typically the case for Petri nets discovered from event data by most process discovery algorithms.

We extend the concept of a Petri net by introducing arc probabilities and probabilistic delays for transitions, as arc probabilities and time delays will be used to categorize user behavior. Among all types of stochastic Petri nets, *generally distributed transition stochastic Petri nets* (GDT_SPNs) [24] and *labeled generalized stochastic Petri nets* (LGSPNs) [13] support silent transitions. However, these models impose a restriction that silent immediate transitions must fire first. Additionally, in LGSPNs, exponential distributions can be assigned to silent timed transitions. These limitations do not always apply to Petri nets discovered from event logs, where silent transitions are used to model loop and skip patterns, and therefore are not necessarily required to fire first or to represent additional time delays.

These limitations motivate us to propose a new definition of stochastic Petri nets suitable for discovery from event data. Since state-of-the-art process discovery algorithms used in practice, such as Inductive Miner [12], tend to discover free-choice Petri nets, which are easily interpretable and can be represented as flowchart process diagrams, we adopt a free-choice structure to provide clear semantics for conditions associated with the process branches. We refer to this class of models as *free-choice stochastic Petri nets.*

Definition 5 (Free-choice stochastic Petri net). *A 7-tuple* $FSPN = (T, P, F, l, M_0, Pr, D)$, *where* (T, P, F, l, M_0) *is a free-choice Petri net,* $Pr : F \cap (P \times T) \to [0, 1]$ *is the function that maps output arcs of places to probabilities, such that* $\forall p \in P$, *if* $\exists t \in p\bullet$, *then* $\sum_{t \in p\bullet} Pr(p, t) = 1$, $D : T \backslash \{t \in T : \Lambda(t) = \tau\} \to \mathcal{X}_{\mathcal{D}}$ *is the function that maps not silent transitions to independent random variables from the set* $\mathcal{X}_{\mathcal{D}}$ *that define random delays*[2].

Below, we define the semantics of free-choice stochastic Petri nets in a way analogous to the semantics of timed Petri nets as introduced in [32].

Definition 6 (Transition firing in free-choice stochastic Petri nets). *Consider a free-choice stochastic Petri net* $FSPN = (T, P, F, l, M_0, Pr, D)$ *in a marking* M. *In this marking, for all places* p, *such that* $M(p) > 0$, *if transitions from* $p\bullet = \{t_1, \cdots, t_k\}$ *are enabled (Definition 2), only one transition* $t_j \in p\bullet$ *is selected in respect to* $Pr(p, t_1), \cdots, Pr(p, t_k)$ *probabilities. This transition* t_j *consumes input tokens (Definition 2) and fires with a delay drawn from distribution* $D(t_j)$, *if it is not silent, and with 0 delay, if it is silent. Transitions with the same delay can fire in any order with no time delay between the firings.*

3.2 Structure Graph-Based Measures

Petri nets are graph-based models consisting of nodes and edges. We introduce graph-based measures for analyzing Petri nets, using a directed graph $G = (V, E)$, where $V = P \cup T$ is the set of nodes, $E = F$ is the set of edges.

Definition 7 (Graph density). *For a graph* $G = (V, E)$ *with* $|E|$ *number of edges and* $|V|$ *number of nodes, the graph density is:* $D(G) = \frac{|E|}{|V|(|V|-1)}$.

Definition 8 (Graph diameter). *The diameter of a graph* $G = (V, E)$ *is the longest shortest path between two nodes:* $d(G) = \max_{u,v \in V} \{\textit{min distance from } u \textit{ to } v\}$.

---

[2] Time distributions in social networks are not necessary exponential or gamma but can also be heavy-tailed.

3.3 Behavioral Process Measures

The first behavioral measure we apply is user waiting times. These times are calculated as the delays from the moment a transition is enabled to the moment it fires and releases tokens to its output places.

The other behavioral measure that we consider is Kolmogorov-Sinai entropy, and it is based on the underlying Markov chain. Due to the intrinsic behavior with arbitrary delays, free-choice stochastic Petri nets cannot be precisely represented as Markov chains with a finite or even countable number of states. However, stochastic Petri net behavior can be approximated and generalized by a discrete Markov chain built on top of the reachability graph and defined by a stochastic matrix $P = (P_{i,j})$, where each entry $P_{i,j}$ is the probability of transition from marking i to marking j.

Such a Markov chain can be obtained, for example, through the estimation of transition frequencies based on event data, and it will annotate the reachability graph with transition probabilities. Once the Markov chain is constructed, we can build its totally connected version by adding transitions that connect end states to start states and are labeled with probability 1 [21]. This will allow us to estimate the variability in model behavior by calculating Kolmogorov-Sinai entropy.

Definition 9 (Kolmogorov-Sinai entropy). *For a totally connected Markov chain with stochastic transition matrix $P = (P_{i,j})$, where P_{ij} is the transition probability from state i to state j, let $\mu_1, \mu_2, \ldots, \mu_n$ be stationary distributions of states satisfying: $\mu_j = \sum_{i \in V} \mu_i P_{ij}, \quad \forall j \in [1, .., n]$. The Kolmogorov-Sinai entropy is then given by: $h_{KS}(P) = -\sum_{i \in V} \mu_i \sum_{j \in V} P_{ij} \log P_{ij}$.*

4 Case Studies

In this section, we analyze Twitter datasets[3] collected for periods from January 2019 till March 2023 to identify coordinated efforts of individuals and groups in Honduras, United Arab Emirates [4], and Brazil [19] to manipulate public discourse[4]. Coordinated and uncoordinated online behavior is represented by different datasets in both Honduras and United Arab Emirates (UAE) data. For the Brazil 2018 election dataset, we split the event data according to the bot scores [30] provided. Specifically, posts and reposts made by users with bot scores above 0.9 were added to one dataset (Brazil 1), while those with scores below 0.1 were added to another (Brazil 2). Consequently, we built two datasets from the the Brazil 2018 election data.

The analyzed datasets contain the retweet information of users: the tweet they are sharing (trace identifier), the user that has retweeted the tweet (activity name), and the time at which they retweeted (timestamp). This dataset, like

[3] https://zenodo.org/records/10650967, http://zenodo.org/records/10669936.

[4] The code and the data are available at: https://github.com/ethanmjohnson/social_network_processes.git.

most social network datasets, does not contain information about which retweet was reposted. It only includes the original tweet number, meaning there is no information about which user influenced another. In such cases, process discovery algorithms, such as Inductive Miner [12], can be useful as they can identify concurrency and retweeting patterns. Based on the frequencies of directly-follows relations between the events, these algorithms can distinguish between the cases where two independent users followed the same predecessor and cases where they were following each other (see the example in Sect. 2).

We applied Inductive Miner with a noise threshold of 0.2 to all six event logs, corresponding to the three countries and different user behaviors. To make Inductive Miner applicable[5] to these large datasets, we limited each trace to its first 10 events. This adjustment was acceptable because fewer than 38% of the traces (except for the Brazil 2 event log) contained 10 or more events. As will be demonstrated later, even the beginning of a social network trace can indicate coordinated behavior and provide its early prediction. Additionally, we considered the first 300, 400, and 200 traces for the datasets of UAE, Honduras, and Brazil, respectively, because due to the nature of social network data, the event logs and the discovered Petri nets (Table 1) contained a large number of activities and nodes, even after filtering. As part of future work, we plan to enhance the current discovery technique by developing and applying a divide-and-conquer approach, in which the social network is discovered in parts and the resulting subnets are merged.

To further analyze the characteristics of social processes, we examine the structural and behavioral properties of Petri nets discovered from these datasets. Free-choice Petri nets discovered by the Inductive Miner were further enhanced with probabilities and time distributions based on the original event log data. The structural and behavioral characteristics of the discovered free-choice stochastic Petri nets are presented in Table 1. The number of nodes represents the total count of transitions and places. As observed in Table 1, these values are quite large compared to the number of nodes in typical business process models discovered from event logs, because they directly reflect the number of activities in the event data, which tends to be higher in social network processes.

The density of Petri nets representing uncoordinated behavior is 2 to 4 times lower than that of the corresponding Petri nets modeling coordinated behavior. The density parameter is independent of model size and can be considered an indicator of tighter communication and coordination between the users. A fragment of a Petri net discovered from the event data of coordinated user behavior in Honduras is presented in Fig. 4. This model, for example, contains a large "flower" pattern, when several users retweet in any order in a loop, and several parallel, sequential, and choice patterns inside this loop. These patterns represent coordinated groups of users.

Figure 5 shows a typical fragment of the Honduras dataset social network model representing uncoordinated behavior. While this model contains parallel and choice patterns, users are less interconnected, resulting in a sparser model.

[5] The experiments were run on an Intel Xeon w5-3435X × 32 with 512 GB of RAM.

Table 1. Characteristics, including number of nodes, density, diameter, mean user waiting times in seconds, and Kolmogorov-Sinai entropy (KS entropy), of free-choice stochastic Petri nets discovered from the social event data.

Event log	# Nodes	Density	Diameter	Mean waiting time	KS entropy
UAE coord.	1,349	0.0010	59	42,179	2.13
UAE uncoord.	3,385	0.0003	155	68,624	0.46
Honduras coord.	1,128	0.0012	111	16,697	1.19
Honduras uncoord.	3,993	0.0003	165	61,277	0.70
Brazil 1	1,138	0.0011	97	67,104	0.57
Brazil 2	2,628	0.0005	113	18,508	2.19

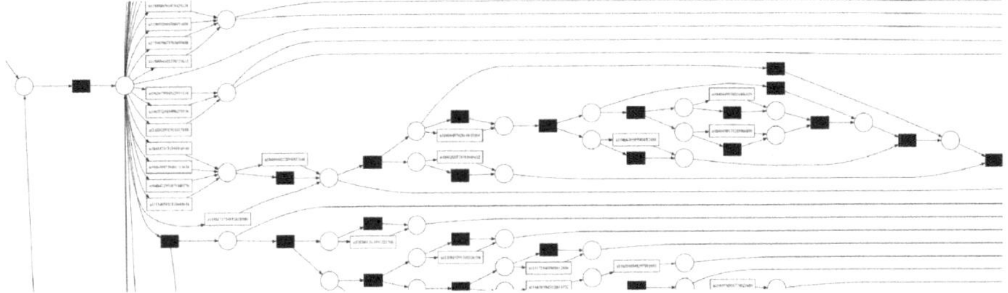

Fig. 4. A fragment of a Petri net discovered from the dataset representing coordinated user behavior in Honduras.

This is supported by the density and diameter parameters calculated for the coordinated and uncoordinated models. Overall, social process models representing coordinated behavior tend to be more compact (lower diameter) and denser.

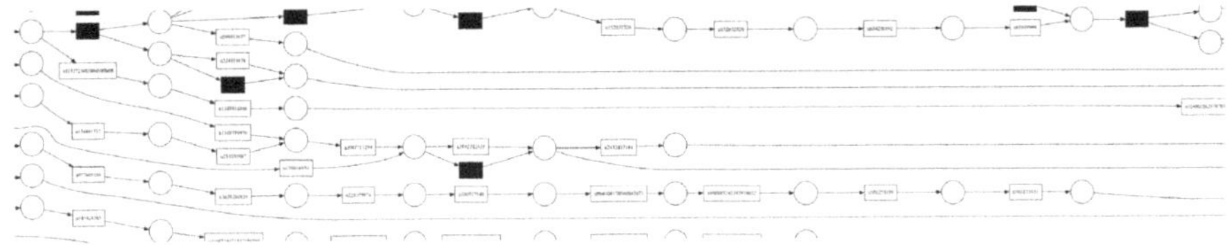

Fig. 5. A fragment of a Petri net discovered from the dateset containing uncoordinated user behavior in Honduras.

In addition to analyzing the structural parameters of the discovered models, we analyzed their behavioral characteristics. First, we assessed user waiting times, which can be calculated as the time gap between the moment a transition is enabled (see Definition 5) and the moment it fires, changing the marking. Table 1 contains mean of mean user retweet times (first, the mean waiting time is calculated for each user and then the mean value across all users is estimated). It shows that coordinated users retweet in mean faster than uncoordinated in the UAE and Honduras social process models. Figure 6a and Fig. 6b present mean user waiting time distributions for coordinated and uncoordinated behaviors in

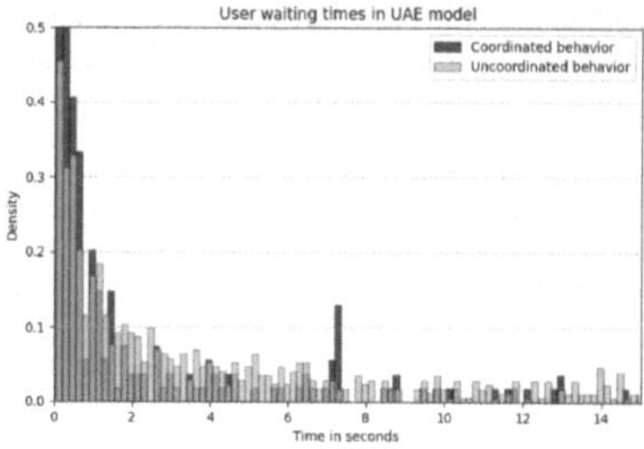

(a) User mean waiting times for UAE coordinated and uncoordinated models.

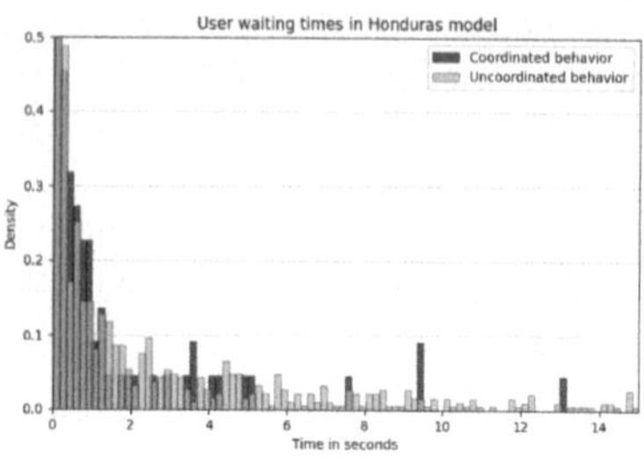

(b) User mean waiting times for Honduras coordinated and uncoordinated models.

Fig. 6. User mean waiting times for process models representing coordinated and uncoordinated behaviors.

UAE and Honduras models, respectively. The Kolmogorov-Smirnov test rejects the hypothesis that coordinated and uncoordinated behaviors are drawn from the same distribution with confidence 8.82×10^{-14} and 3.30×10^{-10}, for UAE and Honduras, respectively.

In contrast to the UAE and Honduras social process model results, mean user waiting times for the Brazil social network models exhibit different characteristics. The model discovered from the Brazil 1 dataset with users classified as bots has larger waiting times than the model discovered from the Brazil 2 dataset with users classified as not bots. More detailed analysis of the model discovered from the dataset Brazil 2 shows that this model contains a large "flower" loop pattern of more than 200 interconnected users. Additionally, a group of users from Barsil 2 dataset retweet in less than 1 min or even less than 1 s. According to the study in [22], which describes the original Brazil election dataset, Botometer [30] can assign false negative and false positive botscores and the results should also be checked manually. Therefore, the social network models discovered from Brazil 1 and Brazil 2 datasets should be analyzed with careful consideration as models with potentially mixed types of users.

We calculated Kolmogorov-Sinai entropy of the discovered models based on state frequencies and transition probabilities. As the results suggest, Kolmogorov-Sinai entropy is larger for models built from the UAE and Honduras datasets representing coordinated behavior. This can be attributed to groups of bots retweeting information in chaotic and unpredictable patterns, leading to increased entropy. However, regular users' behavior is more predictable with lower entropy values. For the Brazil social network models, results align with their time distribution characteristics, the Brazil 1 model exhibits smaller entropy values than the Brazil 2 model.

Overall, the structural and behavioral characteristics of discovered social process models consistently characterize bot behavior in UAE and Honduras datasets with established ground truth (i.e., thorough automated and manual analysis and labeling). However, these measures may exhibit inconsistencies, as observed in the case of the Brazil election dataset, where diverse user types may be present. Importantly, the proposed techniques can aid in identifying bot-like behavior within these mixed models by analyzing different sub-parts of the social processes. We consider this a promising direction for future research.

5 Conclusion

While various approaches exist for modeling and analyzing user behavior online, process models, including Petri nets, which capture advanced routing patterns such as choice and concurrency, have never been discovered from social network data before. In addition to representing complex routing patterns, these models have formal semantics and can be visualized, making them suitable for both qualitative and quantitative analysis.

This paper presents a new approach to analyze online user behavior based on process mining techniques that can discover models with advanced routing constructs from event data and distinguish between concurrent and sequential behavior. Our approach is effective in practice in categorizing user behavior online and can be applied to identify, visualize and simulate coordinated behavior. In future work, we aim to explore other process discovery algorithms and develop a modular divide-and-conquer technique for discovering Petri nets from large-scale social event data. We also plan to apply the approach to identify bot-like behavior in models with mixed user types.

References

1. van der Aalst, W.M.P., Song, M.: Mining Social Networks: Uncovering Interaction Patterns in Business Processes. In: Desel, J., Pernici, B., Weske, M. (eds.) BPM 2004. LNCS, vol. 3080, pp. 244–260. Springer, Heidelberg (2004). https://doi.org/10.1007/978-3-540-25970-1_16
2. Bolzern, P., Colaneri, P., De Nicolao, G.: Opinion influence and evolution in social networks: a Markovian agents model. Automatica **100**, 219–230 (2019)
3. Bozorgi, A., Samet, S., Kwisthout, J., Wareham, T.: Community-based influence maximization in social networks under a competitive linear threshold model. Knowl.-Based Syst. **134**, 149–158 (2017)
4. Cima, L., Mannocci, L., Avvenuti, M., Tesconi, M., Cresci, S.: Coordinated behavior in information operations on Twitter. IEEE Access **12**, 61568–61585 (2024)
5. Cinelli, M., Cresci, S., Quattrociocchi, W., Tesconi, M., Zola, P.: Coordinated inauthentic behavior and information spreading on Twitter. Decis. Support Syst. **160**, 113819 (2022)
6. Graham, T., Hames, S., Alpert, E.: The coordination network toolkit: a framework for detecting and analysing coordinated behaviour on social media. J. Comput. Soc. Sci. **7**(2), 1139–1160 (2024)
7. Hu, B., et al.: Bad actor, good advisor: Exploring the role of large language models in fake news detection. In: Proceedings of the AAAI Conference, vol. 38, pp. 22105–22113 (2024)

8. Karadoğan, A., Karcı, A.: Marked social networks: A new model of social networks based on dynamic behaviors. Eng. Sci. Technol. **35**, 100924 (2022)
9. Kirchdorfer, L., Blümel, R., Kampik, T., Van der Aa, H., Stuckenschmidt, H.: Agentsimulator: an agent-based approach for data-driven business process simulation. In: 2024 6th International Conference on Process Mining, pp. 97–104 (2024)
10. Klijn, E.L., Tentina, I., Fahland, D., Mannhardt, F.: Decomposing process performance based on actor behavior. In: ICPM 2024, pp. 129–136 (2024)
11. Kwon, S., Jang, B.: A comprehensive survey of fake text detection on misinformation and LM-generated texts. IEEE Access (2025)
12. Leemans, S.J.J., Fahland, D., van der Aalst, W.M.P.: Discovering block-structured process models from incomplete event logs. In: Ciardo, G., Kindler, E. (eds.) Application and Theory of Petri Nets and Concurrency, vol 8489, pp. 91–110. Springer, Cham (2014). https://doi.org/10.1007/978-3-319-07734-5_6
13. Leemans, S.J., Maggi, F.M., Montali, M.: Enjoy the silence: analysis of stochastic Petri nets with silent transitions. Inf. Syst. **124**, 102383 (2024)
14. Loth, A., Kappes, M., Pahl, M.: Blessing or curse? A survey on the impact of generative AI on fake news. CoRR **abs/2404.03021** (2024)
15. Mannocci, L., Mazza, M., Monreale, A., Tesconi, M., Cresci, S.: Detection and characterization of coord. online behavior: A survey. CoRR **abs/2408.01257** (2024)
16. Nesterov, R., Bernardinello, L., Lomazova, I.A., Pomello, L.: Discovering architecture-aware and sound process models of multi-agent systems: a compositional approach. Softw. Syst. Model. **22**(1), 351–375 (2023)
17. Ng, L., Carley, K.: A combined synchronization index for evaluating collective action social media. Appl. Netw. Sci. **8** (2023)
18. Olan, F., Jayawickrama, U., Arakpogun, E., Suklan, J., Liu, S.: Fake news on social media: the impact on society. Inf. Syst. Front. **26**(2), 443–458 (2024)
19. Pacheco, D.: Bots, elections, and controversies: twitter insights from Brazil's polarised elections. In: WWW '24. pp. 2651–2659 (2024)
20. Parmar, S., Rahul: Fake news detection via graph-based Markov chains. Int. J. Inf. Technol. **16**(3), 1333–1345 (2024)
21. Polyvyanyy, A., Solti, A., Weidlich, M., Di Ciccio, C., Mendling, J.: Monotone precision and recall measures for comparing executions and specifications of dynamic systems. ACM Trans. Softw. Eng. Methodol. **29**(3) (2020)
22. Rauchfleisch, A., Kaiser, J.: The false positive problem of automatic bot detection in social science research. PLoS ONE **15**(10), e0241045 (2020)
23. Rizoiu, M.A., Lee, Y., Mishra, S., Xie, L.: Hawkes processes for events in social media, pp. 191–218. ACM and Morgan & Claypool (2017)
24. Rogge-Solti, A., van der Aalst, W.M.P., Weske, M.: Discovering Stochastic Petri Nets with Arbitrary Delay Distributions from Event Logs. In: Lohmann, N., Song, M., Wohed, P. (eds.) BPM 2013. LNBIP, vol. 171, pp. 15–27. Springer, Cham (2014). https://doi.org/10.1007/978-3-319-06257-0_2
25. Tour, A., Polyvyanyy, A., Kalenkova, A.: Agent system mining: vision, benefits, and challenges. IEEE Access **9**, 99480–99494 (2021)
26. Tour, A., Polyvyanyy, A., Kalenkova, A., Senderovich, A.: Agent miner: an algorithm for discovering agent systems from event data. In: Di Francescomarino, C., Burattin, A., Janiesch, C., Sadiq, S. (eds.) Business Process Management. pp. 284–302. Springer, Cham (2023). https://doi.org/10.1007/978-3-031-41620-0_17
27. Wang, P., Angarita, R., Renna, I.: Is this the era of misinformation yet: combining social bots and fake news to deceive the masses. In: WWW'18, pp. 1557–1561 (2018)

28. Wang, Z., Wen, T., Wu, W.: Modeling and simulation of rumor propagation in social networks based on Petri net theory. In: 2015 IEEE 12th International Conference on Networking, Sensing and Control, pp. 492–497 (2015)
29. Weber, D., Nasim, M., Mitchell, L., Falzon, L.: Exploring the effect of streamed social media data variations on social network analysis. Soc. Netw. Anal. Min. **11**(1), 1–38 (2021). https://doi.org/10.1007/s13278-021-00770-y
30. Wojcik, S., Messing, S., Smith, A., Rainie, L., Hitlin, P.: Bots in the Twittersphere: an analysis of the links automated accounts share. Pew Research Center (2018)
31. Zeng, Z., et al.: Detecting AI-generated sentences in human-AI collaborative hybrid texts: Challenges, strategies, and insights. arXiv preprint arXiv:2403.03506 (2024)
32. Zuberek, W.: Timed Petri nets definitions, properties, and applications. Microelectron. Reliab. **31**(4), 627–644 (1991)

Exploring Decision Mining Research: A Systematic Review Report and Knowledge Graph

Erfan Elhami[1,2](✉), William Van Woensel[2], and Daniel Amyot[1]

[1] School of EECS, University of Ottawa, Ottawa, ON, Canada
[2] Telfer School of Management, University of Ottawa, Ottawa, ON, Canada
eelha081@uottawa.ca

Abstract. Process discovery is a data-driven method for discovering the control flow of processes – the *how* of a process. Complementary to this, Decision Mining (DM) uses machine learning techniques to discover the decisional criteria used in the process – the *why* of a process. Such decisional criteria, also known as guards, reflect the reasons why cases are routed along branches at a decision point. We performed a literature review on existing DM approaches and their utilized algorithms, datasets, and tools. We provide an interim report of our review in this paper. Additionally, to make our review results more accessible to DM practitioners and researchers, we present a structured, machine-readable, queryable and interactive representation of our review results. The Systematic Literature Review Ontology on DM (SLRO-DM) allows capturing work in DM as a Knowledge Graph (KG), from multiple perspectives, including research problems, proposed solutions, related works, and decision types. The SLRO part of the ontology is extendable and reusable, so it may be adapted for creating literature KG in other domains. The goal of the DM-KG is to support (a) practitioners in the practical application of DM, and (b) researchers in their exploration of the research landscape and identification of gaps. We evaluated our ontology using competency questions that target both these stakeholders.

Keywords: Decision Mining · Systematic Literature Review · Knowledge Graph · Ontology · Process Mining

1 Introduction

The growing need to manage increasingly complex business processes, together with the rising interest in artificial intelligence (AI) applications, provides opportunities to implement data-driven Business Process Management using *Process Mining* (PM) [1]. PM exists at the intersection of traditional BPM, data mining, and AI. It is centered on Process Discovery, i.e., the mining of a process's control flow in terms of activities and their temporal relations. Furthermore, PM offers a wide range of analytical capabilities based on discovered links between event

I. van de Weerd et al. (Eds.): BPM 2025 Workshops, LNBIP 569, pp. 82–93, 2026.
https://doi.org/10.1007/978-3-032-13426-4_7

logs and process models [2]. However, a salient aspect of real-world processes is missing from discovered control flows; i.e., decisional criteria that explain *why* a case was processed in a given way. An interesting subfield within PM is therefore *Decision Mining* (DM), which specifically focuses on discovering and analyzing decision making within business processes.

For this purpose, DM, also referred to as *Decision Point Analysis*, leverages techniques such as machine learning (ML) to mine decisional criteria (a.k.a. guards), which indicate why cases were routed along specific branches at a decision point. DM leverages the information embedded in event logs–assuming that event logs contain sufficient data about decision making—including relevant data attributes and prior events. In the healthcare domain, for instance, DM can support treatment processes by mining decisional criteria for patient cases, and then comparing these criteria with established clinical guidelines; knowledge on historical decisions may provide a more consistent and transparent service and enhance process outcomes [3]. DM shares clear similarities with *Predictive Process Mining* (PPM), since both apply ML to explore process routing. PPM applies ML on event logs to predict the future behaviour of ongoing cases, including their next event, remaining time, or outcome [4]. However, they differ in analytical objectives: PPM is concerned with prediction, whereas DM aims to explain decision-making behaviour.

Despite the existence of many systematic literature reviews (SLRs) on process mining, none exist that covers the DM field. Moreover, we found that DM studies often employ diverse terminologies and conceptual definitions, and present the same underlying problem differently in line with their distinct viewpoint. We thus conducted an SLR that identifies existing DM approaches and their utilized algorithms, datasets, and tools. We provide a summary report of the literature review here. To further make our review results more accessible, we developed an ontology of the identified DM concepts and relations, called SLRO-DM, as a shared DM vocabulary. We then used this ontology to capture the results of our review as a structured and machine-readable Knowledge Graph (KG). With this *DM-KG*, we support interested parties in their exploration of the DM field, albeit by visually navigating the KG and/or issuing targeted queries; helping (a) practitioners with finding DM tools and solving practical problems, and (b) researchers with identifying gaps in research and locating evaluation artifacts.

To the best of our knowledge, capturing the results of an SLR using a KG, while preserving traceability to the literature, has not yet been done. Hence, we started by developing a *Systematic Literature Review Ontology* (SLRO) [5], re-using parts of other ontologies (e.g., Fabio [6], PROV [7], DCMI [8]), to represent the results of SLR. Building on the SLRO, we developed the SLRO-DM to represent DM concepts and relations, and instantiated the latter as a KG to capture our review results. The DM-KG was evaluated using competency questions targeting DM practitioners and DM researchers to validate its relevance and completeness. Our contributions are thus as follows:

1. A summary report of our Systematic Literature Review on Decision Mining.
2. The SLRO-DM ontology that captures concepts from the DM field, and the DM-KG that captures concrete works from our SLR results.

Section 2 presents a background on DM. Section 3 discusses other DM literature reviews. Section 4 outlines the SLRO-DM and DM-KG, whereas Sect. 5 summarizes our SLR findings. Section 6 describes the evaluation of the ontology, and Sect. 7 offers Conclusions and Future Work.

2 Background: Decision Mining

In this section, we shortly summarize the core approach to DM [9]. In the first step (**1**), a control-flow model with Decision Points (DP) is identified using Process Discovery. For instance, in Petri nets, a DP is a place with multiple outgoing transitions. Figure 1 shows a Petri net for a simplified process to triage accident victims. The process includes four DPs (DP1 to DP4). Next (**2**), per DP and case, data is collected that may have contributed to the decision for that case: including data attributes of the case's events up until the DP (e.g., for DP1, `«Initial assessment»`), as well as outcomes of prior DP; e.g., an `«Immediate CPR»` decision at DP1 may influence a `«Transfer to the ICU»` decision at DP4.

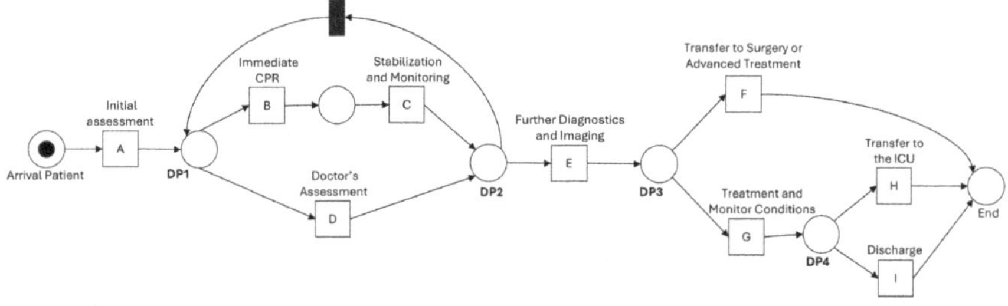

Fig. 1. Triage room process: CPR and critical care for accident victims

Next (**3**), per DP, cases are labeled with their associated decision, i.e., the DP's branch chosen for the case. After steps (**1**)–(**3**), per DP, we obtain a table where rows correspond to cases, and columns include data attributes, prior decisions, and the case's label (decision). In the last step (**4**), an interpretable classifier is trained per DP, on the labeled data, to predict an outgoing branch for a new case. Finally, the decisional criteria used internally by the classifier are extracted. These can then be attached to the process model as guards, represented using decision tables, or using the Decision Model and Notation (DMN) [10] standard. Most works use Decision Trees (DT) as interpretable classifiers: the path from the root to a leaf node represents the conjunctive criteria to classify instances (= cases) as the leaf node (= decision branch).

There are many considerations and potential complications here. Different types of process models can be used as input in step (1) (e.g., imperative vs. declarative), and step (4) may feature alternatives to decision trees or even classification (4). It is possible that some traces do not "fit" the discovered process model; these non-compliant traces will affect DM. We discuss these in Sect. 5.

3 Related Work

De Smedt et al. [11] categorized the DM literature in 2017 into (a) "decision-annotated PM", as it had been practiced up until that point and as described in Sect. 2; and (b) "decision-aware control flow discovery", which discovers a holistic decision model that captures all decisions for the entire process. All works until that point were put in category (a), and the author's work in category (b). In contrast, we present a multi-faceted perspective including the classification of research problems, solutions, algorithms, tools, and domains.

Leewis et al. [12] in 2020 examine DM in relation to business management methodologies, such as business intelligence, business process management, decision management, and decision support systems; and data analysis techniques, including data mining and PM. The authors consider DM, PM, and data mining as elements of Business Intelligence, as they generate information to support decision making, and present a conceptual framework that positions DM and PM as types of data mining. Hence, this literature review does not describe or categorize DM approaches, the problems involved and their solutions.

4 SLR-DM Ontology and DM Knowledge Graph

Figure 2 presents a conceptual overview of the SLRO-DM ontology. To represent bibliographic and publication metadata of SLR articles, the minimal SLRO incorporates concepts from Fabio [6], PROV [7], and DCMI [8] ontologies.

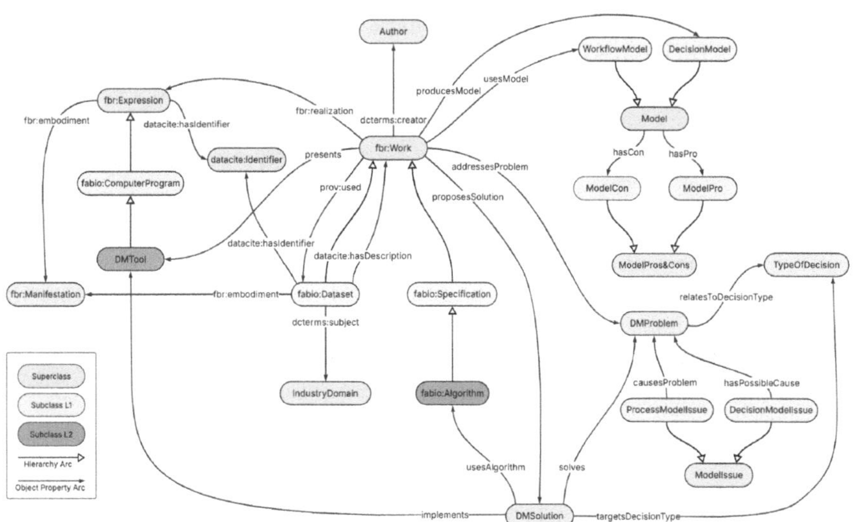

Fig. 2. Conceptual model of the SLRO-DM ontology (partial view)

The *Work* class is at the core of SLRO, representing the abstract conceptualisation of a research paper. An *Expression* is a concrete realization of a *Work*;

e.g., the preprint submitted to the publisher and its final published version are expressions of the same work. In turn, a *Manifestation* is a particular embodiment of an *Expression*, e.g., in electronic (HTML) or paper form (journal paper). The SLRO includes a selection of subclasses of *Work*, including (not all shown) *Dataset*, *Report*, *ScholarlyWork*, and *Specification* (which also covers algorithms); and *Expression* subclasses *Article*, *ComputerProgram* (covering tools used), and *ReportDocument*. The *Identifier* class represents unique identifiers of *Expressions* and *Datasets*. The *Author* class represents authors of works.

We developed *SLRO-DM* on top of SLRO using a combined bottom-up and top-down approach. Based on our literature review, in a bottom-up way, we established a set of common problems and their solutions, and industry domains, which were subsequently generalized into categories. The *DMProblem* class presents a hierarchical classification of the research problems addressed in the literature; the *DMSolution* class presents the hierarchy of proposed solutions.

Next, to improve the characterization of DM problems and solutions, we designed general classes that we subsequently specialized, in a top-down approach: (1) *TypeOfDecision*, which categorizes decisions based on decision dynamicity, temporality, and scope (local vs. global); (2) *Model*, which classifies input process models (*WorkflowModel* subclass) and the outputs of DM (*DecisionModel* subclass); (3) *ModelProsAndCons*, which represents strengths (e.g., easy to understand) and weaknesses (e.g., presence of invisible activities) models in the context of DM; and (4) *ModelIssue*, which includes quality-related metrics such as overfitting, underfitting, and low precision and recall of decision models. We then instantiated the *DM-KG* that captures the reviewed papers, their authors, problems, solutions, and their characterizations, using these concepts.

We expect that the SLRO can be extended in similar ways to model other research domains. The full ontology and KG can be found online [5].

5 Systematic Literature Review Report

This section summarizes the problems and solutions identified in our SLR (Sect. 5.1–5.4), as well as typical algorithms used (Sect. 5.5). All these concepts are modelled and instantiated in the SLRO-DM and DM-KG. We further discuss noteworthy links between certain problems and solutions. The SLR covers 25 papers from the past two decades, but it remains to be published. Details on the research method and SLR approach are publicly available as a Zenodo record [5].

5.1 Event Logs

Incomplete Log: this problem is characterised by the lack of events or data attributes necessary for DM, and is the most frequently addressed in the literature:

– *Missing Contextual Data*: PM only requires three essential data attributes: case identifiers, activity names, and timestamps [4]. Hence, additional data attributes, necessary for identifying decision criteria, are often absent from the event logs. A solution here is to *inject contextual data* required for DM. If the context data is available, it can be collated and injected into the event log, such as patient data that influences treatment decisions (e.g., [13,14]). Otherwise, the missing data can be obtained through qualitative research methods, such as questionnaires asking about past decisions and relevant data attributes [15]. Moreover, while the core approach to DM relies on data attributes measured at a single point in time, decisions can also be based on the evolution of data values; e.g., checking proteinuria if blood pressure is elevated over 4 days [16]. *Injecting temporal data* involves transforming external time series data, i.e., not found in the event log, into discrete features (e.g., min/max/mean, Taylor polynomial, identified trend), which are then injected into the event log (e.g., [16–18]).

– *Missing Decisions*: here, particular decisions were not captured in the mined control flow. For instance, in case activities H and I are missing from Fig. 1, the decision between ICU transfer or discharge will also be missing.

De Smedt et al. [19] propose the identification of missing decisions by analyzing their impact on variable values. If a variable's value changes often enough after an activity (shift ratio), the variable is considered the output of a decision occurring at that activity. Otherwise, it is considered an input variable. A Decision Requirement Diagram (DRD) is constructed where two decisions are linked if one generates an output that is used as input by the other. Winter et al. [20] focus on the discovery of decisions that span multiple process instances. For example, an order shipment process can be halted until other traces have reached that point, so multiple orders can be shipped together. This implies a DP routing cases to an invisible "wait" activity until the condition is met (e.g., Fig. 3(3)). Hence, there is a link between this problem and *instance-spanning decisions* discussed below.

Deviating Logs: unless there is perfect log fitness, some of the event log behaviours will deviate from the mined process model [21]. By default, however, data attributes of these non-compliant events will still influence DM. Leoni et al. [22] addresses this issue by first aligning the event log with the process model. Once aligned, the data-flow perspective of the process is discovered from the event log, including read/write operations. DM is then reduced to finding the best estimator of a function that maps written attribute values to a chosen DP branch.

5.2 Types of Decisions

Global Decisions: some decisions do not only rely on data at the current event (incl. the trace up to that point), but also require non-local, "global" information:

– *Temporal Decisions*: as mentioned, certain process decisions can be based on the temporal evolution of data values. The injection of time series data for DM occurs as follows: (1) collecting external time series data per case and taken as a whole, per fixed interval, or sliced as subsets per event; (2) transforming the time series data (subsets) into one or more discrete features; (3) injecting the discrete features into the event log (hence, there is a link with *injecting temporal data* above). DM then proceeds to discover decisional criteria that incorporate these time series features. Scheibel et al. [18] extract discrete features as trends (linear change in mean value), thresholds (sudden, non-sustained change in mean values), and other patterns. Banham et al. [17] define a linking function that identifies a time series per case, and a slicing function that identifies an event subset (e.g., values after the prior and before this event).

– *Instance-Spanning Decisions*: other process decisions can be based on data that spans multiple traces, or even different processes. For example, as mentioned, an order shipping decision may depend on the number and destination of other concurrent orders (running traces). A concurrent bill printing process may lead to a decision to halt another poster printing process, as the shared resource (printer) requires different paper for posters and bills. Winter et al. [23] focus on discovering such decisions, called *Instance-Spanning Constraints*. The authors hereby differentiate between (1) *Constrained activity execution*, i.e., related to quantitative aspects of the process (e.g., case execution time, # concurrent traces, or limitations on data attributes); and (2) *Constraints on control flow*, e.g., on parallelism or sequential execution across processes.

Dynamic Decision Rules: decisional criteria may evolve dynamically over time – for instance, seasonal price changes or updates in project requirements. Scheibel et al. [24] address this issue by maintaining a *decision rules history* to track patterns of rule variation over time. The performance of rules, i.e., decisional criteria, is periodically re-evaluated based on data from specific time windows. If a significant drop in the F1 score is observed, new rules are mined, and the updated versions will be added to the rules history.

Overlapping Decision Rules: here, different branches at a DP are associated with similar/overlapping decision criteria, meaning that the same case can be routed to different branches. This non-determinism is often due to the absence of salient context in the recorded event log [25]. Hence, there is a potential causal link between *incomplete event logs*, as described before, and this DM problem. For example, in a fine payment process, decisional criteria may not fully distinguish between directly paying or sending the fine, due to lack of a missing piece of context (e.g., legal need to pay the fine right away). A solution here is to incorporate relevant context data, i.e., *inject contextual data* (see before). Alternatively. Mannhardt et al. [25] train a separate decision tree on misclassified cases to purposefully mine overlapping decision rules. This method gives more flexibility in decision modeling and improves fitness at the cost of precision.

5.3 Evaluation

Conformance Checking: to evaluate DM output in terms of quality metrics, Banham et al. [26] introduce (1) *guard-recall*, which quantifies the extent to which guards (i.e., decisional criteria) permit behaviours from the event log, and (2) *guard-precision*, which measures the extent to which guards restrict behaviours to only those from the log. Moreover, the authors propose a set of fundamental characteristics for DM-related quality metrics.

Comparing DM Approaches: Jouck et al. [27] note that the objective comparison of DM methods is hampered by the small number of available event logs, and the lack of reference process and decision models. The authors propose the random generation of an artificial control-flow and decision model, and, subsequently, using these to simulate an artificial event log with decision-relevant data.

5.4 Type of Model

Alongside the event log, the process model typically serves as an input to DM to identify DP (step (1), Sect. 2). Hence, model characteristics and structural issues (e.g., invisible activities) can also influence DM.

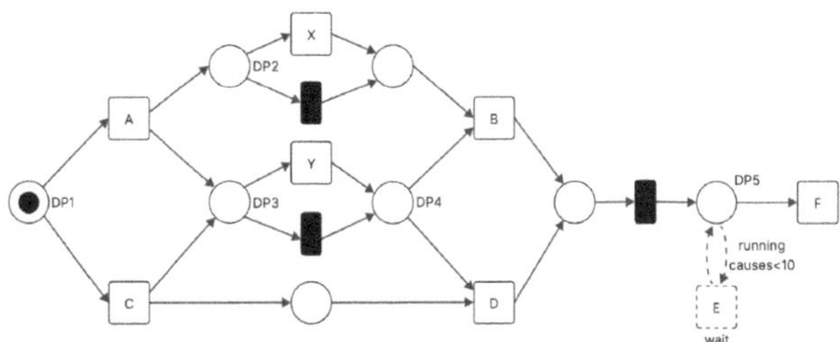

Fig. 3. Example: (1) trace ⟨A, B⟩ matching multiple execution paths, (2) non-free choice construct at DP4, (3) an instance-spanning decision at DP5.

Model Constructs: DM can be impacted in nuanced ways by certain elements.

– *Invisible Activities*: in a discovered process model, these serve for routing purposes and do not appear in the event log. They may complicate the determination of the chosen branch (step (3), Sect. 2). Moreover, it means that the same trace may correspond to multiple process model paths, as illustrated in Fig. 3(1). It is possible to choose only one of these paths by performing an alignment [22]. Alternatively, all relevant paths for the trace can be identified, allowing the trace to serve as training data for DP along all relevant paths [28].

– *Non-free Choice:* this refers to a mixture of choice and synchronization, such that a choice at one DP constrains the choice at another DP, as exemplified in Fig. 3(2). Sarno et al. [29] point out that, since the decision made at a prior

DP (e.g., DP1) will determine the decision at the subsequent DP (e.g., DP4), branches at these DPs should have similar decision criteria. Conversely, the discovery of similar decision rules across subsequent DP branches may indicate the presence of a non-free choice construct.

Model Suitability: so-called *declarative models* tend to be more suited for modeling highly variable processes, such as those in healthcare [3,30]. In contrast to *imperative models*, they do not exhaustively specify all allowed behavior, but instead assume an open world where anything that is not explicitly disallowed is allowed. Mertens et al. [3] propose an algorithm for mining *DeciClare* models, which integrate declarative control-flow constraints with decisional criteria.

5.5 DM Algorithms

The core DM approach, followed by the vast majority of papers, trains an interpretable classifier per DP (step (4), Sect. 2). However, Park et al. [31] note that an ML classifier should not only be interpretable, but also sufficiently predictive. The authors evaluate the use of Random Forests, XGBoost, Support Vector Machines (SVMs) and Neural Networks, combined with XAI methods (e.g., SHAP) for DM. Compared to decision trees, the authors found these algorithms to have a better (8 cases) or similar (2 cases) F1 score, but also note that SHAP explanations are less expressive. Finally, to the best of our knowledge, Mertens et al. [3] are the only ones that cast DM into an optimization instead of a classification problem, using genetic search to identify decisional criteria.

6 Evaluation

The ontology and KG were developed using Protégé [32]. The DM-KG, including the SLRO-DM ontology, is publicly available and maintained on GitHub [5].

A *competency question* is a formal inquiry for evaluating an ontology, i.e., whether it can accurately represent and reason about domain knowledge [33,34]. We evaluated the DM-KG using competency questions from two perspectives: *DM practitioners* and *DM researchers*. We re-engineered the ontology in several iterations based on its (in)ability to answer these questions. The list of questions, and their encoding in Description Logic or SPARQL, can be found online [5].

DM practitioner questions cover the application of DM for different types of decisions, solving observed problems, and finding tooling. For instance:

Solving Problems: "*I believe I am missing decisions in my process model. How can I identify them?*". This question is answered via the *addressesProblem* relation between *Work* and *DMProblem* (*i.e., MissingDecisions*). Then, using the *proposesSolution* relation between *Work* and *DMSolution* allows finding (the) solution(s) that propose to deal with missing decisions.

Types of decisions: "*I believe my case involves temporal decisions. How can I mine these?*". Answering this question relies on the *targetsDecisionType* relation between *DMSolution* and *TypeOfDecision* (i.e., *TemporalDecisions*). *Works* proposing these solutions can then be identified as above.

Causes of Issues: "*I'm observing poor recall (fitness with the event log) of mined decision rules in DM. What could cause this problem?*" This question is answered via the *hasPossibleCause* relation between *DecisionModelIssue* (*LowProcessModelRecall*) and *DMProblem*.

Tooling: "*What tooling is available for DM?*". This can simply be answered by checking for instances and subclasses of the *DMTool* class.

DM researcher questions target the research landscape, finding research gaps, and identifying artifacts for experiments. For instance:

Research landscape: "*What are the most well-studied problems in DM, ranked by their coverage in the literature?*", "*What are the problems tackled by papers with Rinderle-Ma as a co-author?*". Here, to answer the first question, we leverage the *addressesProblem* relation between *DMProblem* and *Work*. To answer the second question, the *creator* relation between *Work* and *Author*, and the aforementioned *addressesProblem* relation, are utilized.

Research gaps: "*Which existing works have applied neural networks for DM?*". To answer this question, we use the *proposesSolution* between *Work* and *DMSolution*, and the *usesAlgorithm* relation of the latter.

Finding artifacts: "*Are there datasets for evaluation in the healthcare domain?*". Here, we use the *subject* relation between *Dataset* and *IndustryDomain*.

7 Conclusions and Future Work

In this paper, we introduce SLRO-DM, an ontology that captures the concepts and relations from DM, and instantiated it as the DM-KG that captures concrete SLR results. This is novel work that models SLR outcomes from multiple perspectives, including research problems, proposed solutions, publications, datasets, domains, and decision types. The SLRO part of the ontology is also adaptable for representing SLR findings from other domains. To evaluate the ontology, we formulated two sets of competency questions: one from the perspective of DM practitioners, addressing practical queries, and another from the perspective of DM researchers, focused on exploratory and analytical queries. We further presented a narrative report from our SLR, which will be published in detail at a later point. As part of our future work, we plan to expand the ontology's coverage by updating studies and reviewing results. We also aim to explore the applicability of SLRO in modelling review outcomes across other research domains. Furthermore, we plan to improve the ontology reasoning and query abilities by considering more semantic constraints. Finally, we aim to look into the use of Large Language Models (LLM) to provide a conversational, natural language interface on top of the DM-KG.

Acknowledgement. This work is supported by NSERC's Discovery program and the University of Ottawa.

References

1. Czvetkó, T., Kummer, A., et al.: Data-driven business process management-based development of industry 4.0 solutions. CIRP J. Manufact. Sci. Technol. **36**, 117–132 (2022)
2. Aalst, W.: Data Science in Action. Presented at the (2016). https://doi.org/10.1007/978-3-662-49851-4_1
3. Mertens, S., Gailly, F., Poels, G.: Discovering health-care processes using DeciClareMiner. Health Syst. **7**(3), 195–211 (2018)
4. Van Der Aalst, W.M.P., Carmona, J.: Process Mining Handbook. Springer (2022). https://doi.org/10.1007/978-3-031-08848-3
5. Elhami, E., Van Woensel, W., Amyot, D.: Decision mining knowledge graph and slro-dm (2025). https://github.com/erfan-el/SLRO
6. Fabio, the frbr-aligned bibliographic ontology. http://purl.org/spar/fabio/
7. The prov namespace. http://www.w3.org/ns/prov#
8. Dcmi metadata terms. https://www.dublincore.org/specifications/dublin-core/dcmi-terms/
9. Rozinat, A., van der Aalst, W.M.P.: Decision mining in business processes. Technische Universiteit Eindhoven, Eindhoven (2006). https://research.tue.nl/files/1750830/609514.pdf
10. Object Management Group (OMG). Decision Model and Notation (DMN), v1.6 beta (2024). https://www.omg.org/dmn/
11. De Smedt, J., vanden Broucke, S.K.L.M., Obregon, J., Kim, A., Jung, J.-Y., Vanthienen, J.: Decision Mining in a Broader Context: An Overview of the Current Landscape and Future Directions. In: Dumas, M., Fantinato, M. (eds.) BPM 2016. LNBIP, vol. 281, pp. 197–207. Springer, Cham (2017). https://doi.org/10.1007/978-3-319-58457-7_15
12. Leewis, S., Smit, K., Zoet, M.: Putting decision mining into context: A literature study. Springer, In Digital Business Transformation (2020)
13. Martínez-Rojas, A., Jiménez-Ramírez, A., Enríquez, J.G., Reijers, H.A.: Analyzing variable human actions for robotic process automation. In: Business Process Management, vol. 13420, pp. 75–90. Springer, Cham (2022). https://doi.org/10.1007/978-3-031-16103-2_8
14. Jareevongpiboon, W., Janecek, P.: Enhancing decision patterns dicovered by process mining with semantic related data. In: ICEB 2011 Proceedings, pp. 12–19. AISeL (2011)
15. Lukassen, B., Genga, L., Zhang, Y.: Discovering Explicit Scale-Up Criteria in Crisis Response with Decision Mining. In: Sellmann, M., Tierney, K. (eds.) Learning and Intelligent Optimization, pages 459–474. Springer, Cham (2023). https://doi.org/10.1007/978-3-031-44505-7_31
16. Dunkl, R., Rinderle-Ma, S., Grossmann, W., Anton Fröschl, K.: A Method for Analyzing Time Series Data in Process Mining: Application and Extension of Decision Point Analysis. In: Nurcan, S., Pimenidis, E. (eds.) CAiSE 2014. LNBIP, vol. 204, pp. 68–84. Springer, Cham (2015). https://doi.org/10.1007/978-3-319-19270-3_5
17. Banham, A., Leemans, S.J.J., Wynn, M.T., Andrews, R.: xPM: a framework for process mining with exogenous data. In: Process Mining Workshops, pp. 85–97. Springer, Cham (2022)
18. Scheibel, B., Rinderle-Ma, S.: Decision mining with time series data based on automatic feature generation. In: Advanced Information Systems Engineering, pp. 3–18. Springer, Cham (2022a)

19. De Smedt, J., Hasić, F., vanden Broucke, S.K.L.M., Vanthienen, J.: Holistic discovery of decision models from process execution data. Knowl. Based Syst. **183**, 104866 (2019)
20. Winter, K., Rinderle-Ma, S.: Discovering instance-spanning constraints from process execution logs based on classification techniques. In: 2017 IEEE 21st International Enterprise Distributed Object Computing Conference (EDOC), pp. 79–88. IEEE CS (2017)
21. Buijs, J.C.A.M., van Dongen, B.F., van der Aalst, W.M.P.: Quality dimensions in process discovery: the importance of fitness, precision, generalization and simplicity. Int. J. Coop. Inform. Syst. **23**(01), 1440001 (2014)
22. de Leoni, M., van der Aalst, W.M.P.: Data-aware process mining: discovering decisions in processes using alignments. In: Proceedings of the 28th Annual ACM Symposium on Applied Computing, SAC '13, pp. 1454–1461. ACM (2013)
23. Winter, K., Stertz, Rinderle-Ma, S.: Discovering instance and process spanning constraints from process execution logs. Inf. Syst. **89**, 101484 (2020). ISSN 0306-4379
24. Scheibel, B., Rinderle-Ma, S.: Online decision mining and monitoring in process-aware information systems. In: Conceptual Modeling, pp. 271–280. Springer, Cham (2022b)
25. Mannhardt, F., de Leoni, M., Reijers, H.A., van der Aalst, W.M.P.: Decision Mining Revisited - Discovering Overlapping Rules. In: Nurcan, S., Soffer, P., Bajec, M., Eder, J. (eds.) CAiSE 2016. LNCS, vol. 9694, pp. 377–392. Springer, Cham (2016). https://doi.org/10.1007/978-3-319-39696-5_23
26. Banham, A., Hofstede, A.H.M.T., Leemans, S.J.J., et al.: Comparing conformance checking for decision mining: an axiomatic approach. IEEE Access **12**, 60276–60298 (2024)
27. Jouck, T., de Leoni, M., Depaire, B.: A framework to evaluate and compare decision-mining techniques. In: Business Process Management Workshops, pp. 482–493. Springer, Cham (2019)
28. Portolani, P., Savoia, D., Ballarino, A., Matteucci, M.: A novel decision mining method considering multiple model paths. Business-Process and Information Systems Modeling. Springer, Cham, In Enterprise (2023)
29. Sarno, R., Sari, P.L.I., Sunaryono, D., Amaliah, B., Mukhlash, I.: Mining decision to discover the relation of rules among decision points in a non-free choice construct. In: International Conference on Information, Communication Technology and System (ICTS) 2014. IEEE CS (2014)
30. Mertens, S., Gailly, F., Van Sassenbroeck, D., Poels, G.: Integrated declarative process and decision discovery of the emergency care process. Inf. Syst. Front. **24**(1), 305–327 (2022)
31. Park, G., Aaron Küsters, et al.: Explainable predictive decision mining for operational support. In: Service-Oriented Computing – ICSOC 2022 Workshops, pp. 66–79. Springer, Cham (2023). https://doi.org/10.1007/978-3-031-26507-5_6
32. Protégé, a plug-in architecture to build ontology-based applications. https://protege.stanford.edu/
33. Kendall, E.F., McGuinness, D.L.: Ontology engineering. Morgan & Claypool Publishers (2019)
34. Chari, S., Seneviratne, O., Gruen, D.M., Foreman, M.A., Das, A.K., McGuinness, D.L.: Explanation Ontology: A Model of Explanations for User-Centered AI. In: Pan, J.Z., Tamma, V., d'Amato, C., Janowicz, K., Fu, B., Polleres, A., Seneviratne, O., Kagal, L. (eds.) ISWC 2020. LNCS, vol. 12507, pp. 228–243. Springer, Cham (2020). https://doi.org/10.1007/978-3-030-62466-8_15

Leveraging Duration Pseudo-embeddings in Multilevel LSTM and GCN Hypermodels for Outcome-Oriented PPM

Fang Wang[1(✉)], Paolo Ceravolo[2], and Ernesto Damiani[1]

[1] College of Computing and Mathematical Sciences, Center for Cyber-Physical Systems, Khalifa University, Abu Dhabi, UAE
florence.wong@ku.ac.ae

[2] Computer Science Department, University of Milan, Milan, Italy

Abstract. Existing deep learning models for Predictive Process Monitoring (PPM) struggle with temporal irregularities, particularly stochastic event durations and overlapping timestamps, limiting their adaptability across heterogeneous datasets. We propose a dual input neural network strategy that separates event and sequence attributes, using a duration-aware pseudo-embedding matrix to transform temporal importance into compact, learnable representations. This design is implemented across two baseline families: B-LSTM and B-GCN, and their duration-aware variants D-LSTM and D-GCN. All models incorporate self-tuned hypermodels for adaptive architecture selection. Experiments on balanced and imbalanced outcome prediction tasks show that duration pseudo-embedding inputs consistently improve generalization, reduce model complexity, and enhance interpretability. Our results demonstrate the benefits of explicit temporal encoding and provide a flexible design for robust, real-world PPM applications. (The implementation code for LSTM hypermodels and pseudo-embedding matrix is available at https://github.com/skyocean/HyperLSTM-PPM).

Keywords: Outcome-oriented PPM · LSTM · GCN · HyperModels · Duration Pseudo-Embedding

1 Introduction

Outcome-oriented Predictive Process Monitoring (PPM) [1] is a key AI application in Business Process Management, aiming to forecast outcomes of ongoing cases using historical event logs [2]. Deep learning models, especially recurrent

This work has been partially supported by the European Union under the NextGenerationEU initiative through the REPA (aRtificial Intelligence for Process Analytics) project, Grant Assignment Decree No. 2022CJWPNA by the Italian Ministry of Ministry of University and Research (MUR).

I. van de Weerd et al. (Eds.): BPM 2025 Workshops, LNBIP 569, pp. 94–106, 2026.
https://doi.org/10.1007/978-3-032-13426-4_8

neural networks (RNNs) and Graph neural networks (GNNs) [3,4], have significantly improved PPM by capturing temporal and structural dependencies. Yet, existing methods face three core limitations.

First, they struggle with temporal irregularities, such as stochastic event durations and overlapping timestamps [2,5]. Second, fixed architectures and static hyperparameters hinder generalization across diverse datasets. Third, outcome-oriented PPM remains underexplored [1,6,7] with many approaches still relying on traditional machine learning models [8,9], lacking expressiveness and scalability. A key challenge lies in modelling temporal heterogeneity effectively without increasing complexity or overfitting. Many current models rely on hand-crafted features or flatten event traces, blurring event-level and case-level semantics.

To address these issues, we propose a dual-input framework that explicitly models event- and case-level attributes. At its core is a duration-aware pseudo-embedding matrix that encodes the relative importance of event durations into compact, learnable representations. This framework is instantiated in two baseline families, B-LSTM (recurrent) and B-GCN (graph-based), and extended to duration-aware variants, D-LSTM and D-GCN, by incorporating temporal pseudo-embeddings. Our contributions are threefold. First, we propose a duration-aware pseudo-embedding strategy that captures temporal irregularities directly from timestamps, thus eliminating the need for manual feature engineering. Secondly, we design self-tuned hypermodels for both LSTM and GCN variants, which enable automatic adaptation of the architecture to the characteristics of the dataset and the granularity of the input. Finally, we empirically demonstrate that our duration-aware models match or exceed baseline performance on balanced and imbalanced benchmark datasets while offering better interpretability and maintaining leaner architectures. This modular, temporal informed design advances adaptive PPM by providing a framework that considers the temporal aspects of the problem and incorporates modular components that can be adapted as necessary.

The rest of the paper is structured as follows: Sect. 2 introduces the architecture and pseudo-embedding strategy. Section 3 covers datasets and experiments. Section 4 presents results, and Sect. 5 concludes.

2 Model Architectures and Representations

In the PPM literature, a *case* is a sequence of events associated with a specific process instance, as recorded in an event log. When multiple cases exhibit identical sequences of events, these recurring patterns are referred to as *traces*.

This section introduces two families of predictive models that are commonly used for event sequence modelling: *Graph Convolutional Networks (GCNs)* and *Long Short-Term Memory Networks (LSTMs)*. For each family, we consider two variants: a baseline model and a duration-aware extension.

Both GCN and LSTM models adopt a multi-level input architecture that encodes information at two distinct levels: (i) **Event-level (node-level):** capturing attributes of individual events such as activity type, timestamp, and resource; (ii) **Case-level (graph-level):** capturing contextual or aggregated attributes of the entire case. We first outline each model's structure and data representation strategy, then introduce a shared duration-aware component: the *duration-aware pseudo-embedding.* This mechanism enriches event-level representations with temporal features, allowing the models to better capture process dynamics.

2.1 Graph Convolutional Network Models

Graph-Based Representation. Each case is represented as a directed, weighted graph $\mathcal{G}_{G_j}$, where nodes X_i represent individual events and edges capture temporal transitions. Node attributes include an activity label $\mathcal{A}_i$, universal attributes U_i, and conditional (specific) attributes B_i, collectively encoded into a composite vector $\mathbf{v}_{N_i} = [\mathcal{A}_i, B_i, U_i]$. Duration is computed from start and end timestamps of each event and treated as a universal attribute. Attributes are encoded using one-hot (categorical) or min-max scaling (numerical). Missing or irrelevant specific attributes are masked using median imputation (numerical) or a padding token (categorical, encoded as -1). At the graph level, each case G_j is associated with global attributes F_j, encoded as a vector $\mathbf{v}_{G_j}$. The resulting graph is defined by: *node matrix:* $\mathbb{V}_{N(G_j)} \in \mathbb{R}^{n \times d_N}$; *edge index tensor:* $\mathbb{E}_{G_j} \in \mathbb{R}^{2 \times (n-1)}$, connecting each $X_i \rightarrow X_{i+1}$; *edge weight vector:* $\mathbb{W}_{G_j} \in \mathbb{R}^{n-1}$. Edge weights $w_{(i \rightarrow i+1)} = T^s_{i+1} - T^s_i$ represent time gaps between consecutive event start times, normalized via min-max scaling. This captures temporal dependencies while accounting for simultaneous events (where $w = 0$). Unlike traditional end-time-ordered approaches, our method sequences events by start time to maintain temporal causality. This explicitly preserves cases where early-starting events with extended durations overlap subsequent events, with duration attributes encoded in node vectors to resolve scheduling ambiguities.

Baseline GCN Architecture(B-GCN). The baseline GCN (B-GCN) model processes graph structured event logs using edge weight aware graph convolutions. Each graph $\mathcal{G}_{G_j}$, containing node attributes $\mathbb{V}_{N(G_j)}$ and temporal edge weights $\mathbb{W}_{G_j}$, is fed through a stack of **GCNConv** layers. These layers aggregate information from local neighborhoods using weighted message passing, allowing the model to capture both structural and temporal dependencies.

We adopt the GCNConv variant that supports edge weights, extending the classical formulation by [10] to allow for time-sensitive propagation. The graph convolution layer updates node attributes using the normalized weighted adjacency matrix:

$$\mathbb{V}^{(l+1)} = \sigma\left(\tilde{D}^{-\frac{1}{2}}\tilde{A}_w\tilde{D}^{-\frac{1}{2}}\mathbb{V}^{(l)}W^{(l)}\right), \tag{1}$$

where $\tilde{A}_w = A_w + I$ includes edge weights and self-loops, and $\tilde{D}$ is its degree matrix. σ is a non-linear activation and $W^{(l)}$ is a learnable weight matrix. This normalization stabilizes learning across varying graph sizes and node degrees. After L convolutional layers, node embeddings $\mathbb{V}^L_{N(G_j)}$ are aggregated via global pooling into a graph-level vector $\mathbf{z}_{G_j}$. In parallel, the case-level attributes $\mathbf{v}_{G_j}$ are processed through dense layers to yield $\mathbf{v}^d_{G_j}$. The final trace representation is formed as: $\mathcal{Z}_{G_j} = Concatenate(\mathbf{z}_{G_j}, \mathbf{v}^d_{G_j})$. This representation is then passed through fully connected layers to produce the prediction $\hat{y}_{G_j}$.

2.2 LSTM Network Models

Sequential Representation Construction. For the LSTM models, each eventlog is modeled as an ordered sequence of event vectors. Each event X_i within a trace G_j is represented by a preprocessed feature vector $\mathbf{v}_{N_i} \in \mathbb{R}^{d_N}$, consistent with the node vector used in the GCN variant. These vectors are stacked in order of their event timestamps to form a matrix $\mathbb{S}_{G_j} \in \mathbb{R}^{n \times d_N}$, where n is the number of events in the trace. The ordered event sequence $\mathbb{S}_{G_j}$ serves as LSTM input, preserving temporal order. To support overlapping events, we augment each event vector with the time difference flag between consecutive start timestamps. Case-level attributes $\mathbf{v}_{G_j}$ are encoded separately and incorporated later during the output stage of the model. Padding and masking are applied to ensure uniform input shapes across variable-length sequences.

Baseline LSTM Architecture (B-LSTM). The baseline LSTM(B-LSTM) model consumes the event sequence matrix $\mathbb{S}_{G_j}$ and processes it through a multilayer LSTM network to capture temporal dynamics. The output of the final LSTM hidden state is taken as the trace-level representation $\mathbf{z}_{G_j}$. In parallel, the separately encoded case-level attributes $\mathbf{v}_{G_j}$ are passed through fully connected layers to obtain $\mathbf{v}^d_{G_j}$. Similar to GCNs, these two components are concatenated to form the combined representation: $\mathcal{Z}_{G_j}$, which is passed through dense prediction layers to produce the final output $\hat{y}_{G_j}$.

2.3 Duration-Aware Pseudo-embedding Augmentation

To enrich event level representations with duration-aware temporal context, we augment raw node/event inputs with a pseudo-embedding matrix derived from discretized duration attributes. These embeddings provide an auxiliary feature space that complements standard activity and attribute encodings. Following [11], we employ a hybrid binning strategy: durations below a fixed cut-off receive unique bins, while longer durations are grouped using quantile-based binning. This balances bin frequency while preserving granularity for short events.

Each event is then mapped to a (activity, duration-bin) pair, treated as a term in a TF-IDF-inspired scheme. Cases are treated as documents in a corpus, and we compute term relevance by weighing duration-bin frequency within a case against its global rarity. This yields a pseudo-embedding matrix encoding how distinctively each activity-duration combination characterizes a case. The full procedure is summarized in Algorithm 1. These embeddings are processed in parallel with raw inputs through separate GCN or LSTM layers and later fused to form a richer case representation.

Algorithm 1. Pseudo-Embedding Duration Bin Matrix

Require: Set of activities (nodes) $\{\mathcal{A}_i\}$; duration values $\{T_i^d\}$ for each $\mathcal{A}_i$; set of graphs $\{G_j\}$.
Ensure: Pseudo-embedding matrices where each $\mathcal{A}_i$ is represented as vector $\mathbf{v}_{bin_i}$ for all G_j.
Initialize cut-off value T_{cut} and number of quantile bins N_{quant}.
repeat
  for each event $\mathcal{A}_i$ **do**
    if $T_i^d < T_{\text{cut}}$ **then**
      Assign T_i^d to a unique bin b.
    else
      Calculate quantile bins $\{\bar{b}\}$ based on N_{quant}.
      Remove duplicates and adjust $\{\bar{b}\}$ to cover the full duration range.
      Assign T_i^d to the appropriate quantile bin $\bar{b}$.
    end if
    Assign final duration bin b_i' to $\mathcal{A}_i$.
  end for
  Calculate bin frequencies $\{f_b'\} = \{f_b, f_{\bar{b}}\}$.
  if bin frequencies $\{f_{\bar{b}}\}$ are balanced (within threshold) **then**
    break
  else
    Update T_{cut} and N_{quant} accordingly.
  end if
until stopping condition is met
Extract unique pairs $(\mathcal{A}_i, b_i')$.
Treat each pair $(\mathcal{A}_i, b_i')$ as a term in the corpus.
for each graph G_j **do**
  Treat G_j as a document.
  Construct a TF-IDF matrix with rows as $\mathcal{A}_i$ and columns as bins b_i':
  for each term $(\mathcal{A}_i, b_i')$ **do**
    Compute tf-idf$(\mathcal{A}_i, b_i')$.
  end for
end for
return Pseudo-embedding matrices $\mathbf{v}_{bin_i}$ for each $\mathcal{A}_i$ across all G_j.

This mechanism is integrated into both model families via a parallel encoding pathway, forming two new models- Pseudo-Embedding Duration LSTM (D-LSTM) and Pseudo-Embedding Duration GCN (D-GCN). Each case/graph has two input branches: one for the standard event/node attributes and another for the duration-based pseudo-embedding vectors. Both branches are processed independently through identical encoder layers (either GCN or LSTM). The resulting hidden representations are then concatenated and passed through additional GCN or LSTM layers, followed by pooling (in the GCN case), fusion with case level attributes, and final prediction layers. This design allows each input stream to be encoded in its own latent space before joint modeling, enabling the architecture to leverage both raw and duration-augmented perspectives.

2.4 HyperModel Configuration

We develop four hypermodels spanning GCN and LSTM architectures, each automatically tuned per dataset.**Common hyperparameters** across all models include: learning rate and schedule; optimizer type and configuration; batch size and loss function; Dropout and batch normalization options; dense layer size and activation function. **GCN-specific hyperparameters** include number of GCN layers and size and pooling operations. **LSTM-specific hyperparameters** include number of LSTM layers and hidden units and regularization strength. We handle masked feature values (encoded as -1) during preprocessing to prevent bias. Table 1 details all parameter types and ranges.[1]

Table 1. Hyperparameters and Their Tuning Ranges/Types

Hyperparameter	Range
Node/Event Level Layers	
Number of layers	GCN: 1–5; LSTM: 1–3
Hidden Units	16–512
Dropout	flag: Y/N; rates: 0.2–0.7
Batch norm	flag: Y/N; momentum: 0.1–0.999; eps:1e-5–1e-2
LSTM L2	1e-5–1e-2
GCN Activation	ReLU, Leaky_ReLU, ELU, Tanh, Softplus, GELU
GCN Skip Connection	Y/N
GCN Pooling	mean, add, max
Dense Layers	
Number of layers	1–3
Dense Units	GCN: 16–512; LSTM: 16–256
Dropout	flag: Y/N; rates: 0.2–0.7
Batch norm	flag: Y/N; momentum: 0.1–0.999; eps:1e-5–1e-2
Activation	ReLU, Leaky_ReLU, ELU, Tanh, Softplus, GELU(GCN)
LSTM L2	1e-5–1e-2
Optimizer and Learning Rate Scheduler	
Learning Rate	1e-5–1e-2 (log)
Weight Decay	0–1e-3
L1	0–1e-3
Optimizers	Adam, RMSprop, SGD
Schedulers	GCN: Step, Exponential, Reduce-on-Plateau, Polynomial, Cosine Annealing, Cyclic, One Cycle LSTM: Exponential, Inverse Time, Piecewise Constant, Polynomial
GCN Loss Function	CrossEntropy, MultiMargin
Batch Size	16, 32, 64, 128, 512

3 Experiments

3.1 Datasets and Processing

To evaluate model robustness and generalization under different data conditions, we use two representative datasets: one **highly imbalanced** and one **balanced**.

[1] Range and sub-parameters for each specific optimizer and learning rate scheduler are also tuned.

Specifically, we employ the synthetic **Patients** dataset to simulate extreme class imbalance, and the real-world **BPIC12** benchmark [12] to represent balanced classification tasks.

Patients (Synthetic Healthcare Data) dataset contains 2,140 cases representing patient interactions within a healthcare system. It includes 3 numerical and 1 categorical attribute at the case level, and 3 numerical plus up to 3 categorical attributes (including one universal) at the event level. Each case is labeled with one of five possible outcomes. The label distribution is highly skewed: the majority class accounts for 40.74% of cases, and the minority just 1.12%, yielding an imbalance ratio of approximately 36:1. This setup makes it ideal for testing model performance under class imbalance and attribute heterogeneity.

BPIC12 (Loan Application Event Log) captures real-world loan and overdraft application processes in a multinational financial institution. Each case ends with one of three outcomes: *accepted*, *declined*, or *canceled*. We use a curated version with balanced class sizes (2,224 cases per class). It includes one numerical attribute at the case level and two universal categorical attributes at the event level. BPIC12 introduces temporal modeling challenges due to frequent *timestamp collisions*—i.e., multiple events with identical start times[2]—which are well-suited for evaluating time-aware representations.

As summarized in Table 2, the datasets differ substantially in case length, attribute complexity, and temporal structure. *Patients* features shorter but more heterogeneous traces, while *BPIC12* has longer cases with simpler event attributes but denser temporal overlap. Case lengths range from 12 to 77 events, introducing varying degrees of temporal dynamics and representational demands.

All events are timestamped with start and completion times. Event durations are calculated as the difference between start and end times, rounded to the nearest minute. In *Patients*, durations under 5 min are assigned unique bins, while longer durations are grouped into 24 quantile-based bins. In *BPIC12*, durations are discretized into two bins: zero and non-zero duration. These bin labels feed into the pseudo-embedding module used for temporal augmentation.

Table 2. Statistics of the datasets used in the experiments

data	#Case	max-len	min-len	med-len	#Event Attr & Size			#Case Attr & Size			# O
BPI12	6672	77	12	18	(N)2	(C)0	-	(N)1	(C)0	-	3
Patients	2140	9	4	7	(N)3	(C)3	[10,3,3]	(N)3	(C)1	2	5

3.2 Hyperparameter Search

We employ two search strategies tailored to our model families and dataset characteristics. For LSTM-based HyperModels, we use the Hyperband algorithm,

[2] The start time and complete time of an activity is based on its transition status.

selected for its efficiency in large search spaces through early-stopping-based exploration. Search objectives differ by dataset type: for balanced datasets, validation accuracy is maximized; for imbalanced datasets, we optimize the weighted F1-score. Each run allows up to 300 training epochs, with a reduction factor of 3. An 80/20 train-validation split is used, and early stopping is applied to prevent overfitting. For GCN-based hypermodels, we use Optuna for more granular control over search and pruning. Each trial runs up to 300 epochs with a patience threshold of 30, and we perform 200 trials per model configuration. Search objectives again vary by dataset type, matching those used for LSTM models. The best hyperparameter set for both models is selected based on the top-performing trial, and final training proceeds for 300 full epochs to assess generalization beyond the peak epoch.

4 Results

4.1 Imbalanced Dataset (Patients)

Performance Evaluation. Table 3 reports class-wise and aggregate metrics for the baseline (B) and duration-aware (D) variants of both LSTM and GCN models. Weighted F1-score (WF1) is the main metric, capturing class imbalance more effectively than accuracy. Overall, D-LSTM outperforms B-LSTM on both WF1 (0.8706 vs. 0.8615) and accuracy (0.8808 vs. 0.8715), indicating that incorporating pseudo-duration embeddings enhances the model's ability to discriminate across temporally heterogeneous cases. In contrast, B-GCN marginally outperforms D-GCN on WF1 (0.8639 vs. 0.8595), with negligible difference in accuracy, suggesting that graph-based models may be less sensitive to temporal augmentation. Class-level analysis provides further insight: D-LSTM improves performance across nearly all classes. Notably, classes 2 and 3–both minority classes–see increased F1, showing that pseudo-embedding duration information stabilizes learning where raw data is sparse or noisy. For class 1 (majority),

Table 3. Classification Report of LSTM and GCN Models for Patients Dataset

Class	**B-LSTM**			**D-LSTM**			**B-GCN**			**D-GCN**			S
0	1	1	1	1	1	1	1	1	1	1	1	1	92
1	0.8095	0.9770	0.8854	0.8047	0.9943	0.8895	0.7838	1	0.8788	0.7793	0.9943	0.8737	174
2	0.7143	1	0.8333	1	1	1	1	1	1	1	1	1	5
3	1	0.9048	0.9500	1	1	1	1	0.9048	0.95	0.9091	0.9524	0.9302	21
4	0.7111	1	0.8312	0.7692	0.9375	0.8451	0.9143	1	0.9552	0.9091	0.9375	0.9231	32
5	1	0.5288	0.6918	1	0.5385	0.7000	0.9636	0.5096	0.6667	0.9815	0.5096	0.6709	104
Acc			**0.8715**			**0.8808**			**0.8762**			**0.8715**	428
MF1	0.8725	0.9018	0.8653	0.9290	0.9117	0.9058	0.9436	0.9024	0.9084	0.9298	0.899	0.8997	428
WF1	0.8976	0.8715	**0.8615**	0.9033	0.8808	**0.8706**	0.8969	0.8762	**0.8639**	0.8945	0.8715	**0.8595**	428

• S:Support; MF1: Macro Average F1; WF1: Weighted Average F1;

• For each model, columns are precision, recall and F1-score, respectively.

D-LSTM achieves higher recall without sacrificing precision, a critical property for reducing false negatives in outcome prediction. Class 5 remains challenging. Both duration-aware models show slightly higher F1 and little precision improvement over their baselines. Analysis of misclassifications reveals 3âĂŞ5 instances consistently mislabelled as class 4, pointing to possible overlap in feature space, label noise, or distribution shift. These challenges suggest that class 5's data is either inherently ambiguous or poorly represented, limiting all models' ability to generalize effectively.

Overall, duration-aware pseudo-embeddings clearly improve the performance of sequential models such as LSTMs, but offer limited benefits in GCNs. This is likely due to architectural constraints when it comes to leveraging dynamic features over static graph structures.

Hyperparameters Insights. Table 5 details the tuned hyperparameters for all models. B-LSTM uses a dual-layer structure with high dropout and L2 regularization to prevent overfitting from dense inputs. It employs the Adam optimizer with exponential decay, and a moderate dense output layer balancing expressiveness and generalization. D-LSTM extends this design with a dual-branch architecture: separate LSTM streams for event and duration aware pseudo-embedding inputs, merged via fusion layers. It uses RMSprop, which better handles non-stationary dynamics, and a piecewise constant learning rate schedule. A wider dense layer supports the richer fused representation, enabling better adaptation to underrepresented classes. For GCNs, tuning reveals key differences. D-GCN applies more GCN layers and wider hidden units, reflecting the need for deeper representations when fusing duration embeddings. It processes event and duration inputs via separate GCN pathways, integrating them later, implying that temporal signals require dedicated structural propagation. To manage overfitting, D-GCN uses higher dropout (up to 0.46), smaller learning rates, and lower L1 regularization. While both models use Adam, B-GCN adopts cosine decay, while D-GCN favors OneCycleLR, allowing for more dynamic training regimes. Pooling strategies also diverge: max-pooling in B-GCN vs. additive aggregation in D-GCN, possibly better preserving temporal signal accumulation. Despite this complexity, D-GCN's performance does not consistently exceed its baseline, reinforcing that static GCNs struggle to exploit temporal augmentations compared to their sequential counterparts.

4.2 Balanced Dataset (BPI12)

Performance Evaluation. Table 4 reports the classification accuracy of baseline (B) and duration-aware (D) variants of LSTM and GCN models on the balanced BPIC12 dataset. All models, regardless of architecture or temporal augmentation, achieve perfect accuracy (100%) across the three target classes: accept, decline, and cancel. Unlike prior approaches that decompose outcome prediction into multiple binary classifiers [13], our models use a single multiclass classifier per instance. This simplifies deployment while achieving comparable or

Table 4. Accuracy Scores of LSTM and GCN HyperModels and Previous Research Models on BPIC12 Dataset

	SVM [9]	LR [9]	RF [9]	XGB [9]	LSTM [13]	CNN [14]	DT [15]	**BGCN**	**DGCN**	**BLSTM**	**DLSTM**
accept	0.63	0.65	0.69	0.7	0.71	0.67	1	**1**	**1**	**1**	**1**
decline	0.55	0.59	0.6	0.62	0.64	0.61	1	**1**	**1**	**1**	**1**
cancel	0.70	0.69	0.7	0.7	0.73	0.7	1	**1**	**1**	**1**	**1**
avg	0.63	0.64	0.66	0.67	0.69	0.66	1	**1**	**1**	**1**	**1**

better performance than more complex pipelines, such as decision tree ensembles [15]. Duration-aware variants (D-LSTM, D-GCN) match baseline performance, showing that while temporal augmentation is supported, it is not necessary in settings where input traces are highly regular and easily separable.

This outcome is expected given the structural simplicity of BPIC12. Its low-variance, rigid traces enable even standard models to generalize effectively. While this supports model correctness, it provides limited evidence of robustness or temporal generalization. More challenging datasets with temporal irregularities are needed for stronger validation.

Hyperparameters Insights. All four models–B-LSTM, D-LSTM, B-GCN, and D-GCN–achieve perfect accuracy on the balanced BPIC12 dataset, yet their architectural responses to temporal signals differ significantly. B-LSTM, lacking explicit duration encoding, requires deeper recurrent layers to model variation, while D-LSTM benefits from dual stream inputs with pseudo-embeddings, achieving similar results with shallower configurations. Similarly, B-GCN depends on case-level graph encoding and lean activations, whereas D-GCN leverages separate GCN streams for duration and event semantics, employing deeper post GCN layers and stronger regularization. Optimization strategies also diverge, with B-models favoring simpler schedulers and D-models adapting to overfitting risk. These patterns highlight how duration-aware inputs not only enhance learning but also influence model efficiency and robustness.

5 Conclusion

This paper presents a systematic investigation of temporal representation strategies for outcome-oriented PPM, leveraging recurrent and graph-based neural architectures. We propose a dual-input model design that separately encodes event-level and case-level attributes and introduce a duration-aware pseudo-embedding mechanism to explicitly capture temporal irregularities across events.

To evaluate the effectiveness of this approach, two duration-augmented model variants are developed: D-LSTM and D-GCN, which enhance their respective baselines by incorporating time-aware representations. These models demonstrate improved handling of heterogeneous timestamp distributions by explicitly modelling temporal dynamics, particularly in event sequences with irregular or sparse timing patterns. To enable fair and robust comparisons across different input granularities and datasets, we implement self-tuned hypermodels. Empirical evaluations on balanced and imbalanced datasets demonstrate that the duration-aware variants consistently match or exceed the performance of their baseline counterparts while maintaining leaner model complexity and enhanced interpretability. Our findings reveal two key insights: (i) Augmenting event-level inputs with duration-informed features reduces reliance on deep or complex architectural designs by enabling more efficient learning of temporal dependencies. (ii) The dual-input architecture facilitates better generalisation across diverse process contexts by decoupling structural and temporal information.

By aligning the model architecture with the temporal characteristics inherent in event logs, this work provides a flexible and semantically grounded framework for predictive monitoring. Future research will extend this framework to accommodate noisy, multisource and streaming environments [16], critical steps toward scaling up learning-based techniques for real-world PPM applications.

A Appendix

Table 5. Hyperparameter Matrix for GCN and LSTM Models

Model	B	G(L)	G(U)	G(A)	SC	G(BM)	G(BE)	G(D)	P	D(L)	D(U)	D(A)	D(BM)	D(BE)	D(D)	Opt	LR	WD	Sch	Loss	L1
BG(I)	32	2	88	GELU	F				max	2(S)*	69	ReLU			0.1601	Adam	1.248e-3	7.736e-4	Cos	CE	3.424e-4
	(88)		151	l_rl	T	0.1764	2.471e-3				133	GELU	0.9650	9.671e-3	0.3444	(0.8837,			(3.037e-3,		
										1(C)*	188	GELU	0.2754	8.581e-3	0.3062	0.9405)			50)		
DG(I)	32	2(N)*	245	GELU					add	1(S)*	228	l_rl				Adam	1.361e-4	8.761e-4	OCL	CE	7.324e-5
	(61)		203	GELU		0.5817	9.520e-3			2(C)*	91	l_rl			0.1195	(0.9374)			(1.831e-2,		
		4(P)	38	GELU		0.5377	2.934e-3	0.1011			232	ELU	0.4174	9.586e-3	0.1100	0.9305)			0.1203,		
			194	ReLU															54000)		
			196	ELU																	
			159	sp		0.2075	6.602e-3	0.4605													
		1(C)*	32	ReLU	T																
BG(12)	32	2	151	tanh	F	0.2745	1.149e-3	0.469	max	1(S)*	111	tanh				RMS	7.234e-4	4.415e-3	Cy	MM	5.292e-4
	(25)		128	sp	F	0.4512	6.046e-3			1(C)*	169	l_rl			0.243	(0.9111,	0.7603,	8.523e-8)	(5.0392,	25,	0.0019)
DG(12)	64	2(N)*	48	l_rl					add	2(S)*	48	ELU			0.2663	Adam	2.459e-3	2.109e-3	RP	CE	3.930e-4
	(10)		218	GELU		0.8015	4.175e-3	0.2708			128	ELU				(0.9692,			(Max,		
		3(P)*	128	ReLU		0.2464	5.780e-3			1(C)*	83	ReLU			0.3718	0.9222)			0.8003,		
			156	ELU		0.3509	4.178e-4												25,		
			228	l_rl		0.2953	8.932e-3												7.531e-3,		
		1(C)*	128	ELU	T			0.2996											4.367e-3)		
M	B	L(L)	L(U)	L(L2)		L(BM)	L(BE)	L(D)		D(L)	D(U)	D(A)	D(L2)		D(D)	Opt	LR				
BL(I)	32	2	160	1.956e-4		0.81	3.345e-4	0.4914		1	144	ReLU	2.017e-4		0.4581	(Adam	Exp				
			48	4.433e-3				0.3156							0.93	0.992)	2.718E-03				
DL(I)	16	1(N)*	256	1.265e-3		0.61	6.736e-4	0.2088		2	192	(l_rl	2.857e-3		0.4401	rms	P-C				
		2(P)*	256	2.990e-3				0.4085			256	0.1997)	9.855e-5		0.2622		5.480e-4				
			64	9.411e-3		0.11	2.592e-5	0.3875				ReLU									
		2(C)*	128	1.121e-4				0.3635													
			96	1.140e-4		0.21	3.468e-4	0.4356													
BL(12)	16		160	1.351e-5		0.01	1.022e-5	0.3449		3	80	(l_rl	1.868e-3		0.1946	rms	Exp				
			224	1.011e-5				0.2			16	0.01)	1.001e-5		0.1		7.933e-3				
											16	ReLU	1.012e-4		0.1123						
DL(12)	128	1(N)*	224	1.410e-3				0.3647		1	224	tahn	1.098e-4		0.5757	(Adam	Poly				
		1(P)*	32	2.103e-5		0.81	2.403e-3	0.3106								0.91					
		1(C)*	160	1.567e-5		0.51	8.522e-5	0.3911								0.991)					

- Model: BG/BL/DG/DL: B-GCN/B-LSTM/D-GCN/D-LSTM; I: Patients Dataset; 12: BPI12 Dataset
- B: Batch size (Best Epoch); G(L)/L(L)/D(L): Number of hidden G(GCN)/L(LSTM)/D(Dense) layers; G(U)/L(U)/D(U): Units; G(A)/D(A): Activation; G(BE)/L(BE)/D(BE): Batch normalization epsilon; G(BM)/L(BM)/D(BM): Batch normalization momentum; G(D)/L(D)/D(D): Dropout rates; SC: Skip Connection flag; P: Pooling Method; Opt:Optimizer; LR: Learning Rate; WD: Weight Decay; Sch: Learning Rate Scheduler; Loss: Loss function; L1/L2: L1/L2 regularize; Empty cell in (BM)/(BE)/(D): No batch normalization or dropout applied.
- *:(N): Node/Event input (P):Pseudo-embedding input ; (S): Graph/case input; (C): Concatenation layer;
- l_rl: Leary_ReLU; sp:softplus; CE: CrossEntropy; MM: MultiMargin.
- Adam: Adam (β_1, β_2); SGD: SGD(momentum); rms:RMSprop(α, momentum, eps); Step: Step(step size, γ); Exp: Exponential(γ); RP: Reduce-on-Plateau(factor, patience, threshold, eps); Poly: Polynomial(total_iters, power); Cos: Cos(eta_min, T_max); OCL: One Cycle(max, pct_start, total_steps); Cy: Cyclic(base, max, step_size_up)

References

1. Ceravolo, P., Comuzzi, M., De Weerdt, J., Di Francescomarino, C., Maggi, F.M.: Predictive process monitoring: concepts, challenges, and future research directions. Process Sci. **1**(1), 2 (2024)
2. Ceravolo, P., Junior, S.B., Damiani, E., Van Der Aalst, W.: Tuning machine learning to address process mining requirements. IEEE Access **12**, 24583–24595 (2024)
3. Camargo, M., Dumas, M., González-Rojas, O.: Learning Accurate LSTM Models of Business Processes. In: Hildebrandt, T., van Dongen, B.F., Röglinger, M., Mendling, J. (eds.) BPM 2019. LNCS, vol. 11675, pp. 286–302. Springer, Cham (2019). https://doi.org/10.1007/978-3-030-26619-6_19
4. Wang, F., Ceravolo, P., Damiani, E.: Hgcn(o): a self-tuning gcn hypermodel toolkit for outcome prediction in event-sequence data. arXiv preprint arXiv:2507.22524 (2025)
5. Fracca, C., de Leoni, M., Asnicar, F., Turco, A.: Estimating activity start timestamps in the presence of waiting times via process simulation. In: Franch, X., Poels, G., Gailly, F., Snoeck, M. (eds.) International Conference on Advanced Information Systems Engineering. pp. 287–303. Springer, Cham (2022). https://doi.org/10.1007/978-3-031-07472-1_17
6. Bellandi, V., Ceravolo, P., Maghool, S., Pindaro, M., Siccardi, S.: Correlation and pattern detection in event networks. In: 2021 IEEE International Conference on Big Data (Big Data). pp. 4103–4112. IEEE (2021)
7. Weinzierl, S.: Exploring Gated Graph Sequence Neural Networks for Predicting Next Process Activities. In: Marrella, A., Weber, B. (eds.) BPM 2021. LNBIP, vol. 436, pp. 30–42. Springer, Cham (2022). https://doi.org/10.1007/978-3-030-94343-1_3
8. Aljebreen, A., Pang, A., de Kamps, M., Johnson, O.: Predicting unplanned hospital readmissions using outcome-oriented predictive process mining. In: Delgado, A., Slaats, T. (eds.) International Conference on Process Mining. pp. 421–433. Springer (2024). https://doi.org/10.1007/978-3-031-82225-4_31
9. Teinemaa, I., Dumas, M., Rosa, M.L., Maggi, F.M.: Outcome-oriented predictive process monitoring: review and benchmark. ACM Trans. Knowl. Discov. Data (TKDD) **13**(2), 1–57 (2019)
10. Kipf, T.N., Welling, M.: Semi-supervised classification with graph convolutional networks. arXiv preprint arXiv:1609.02907 (2016)
11. Wang, F., Ceravolo, P., Damiani, E.: Comprehensive attribute encoding and dynamic lstm hypermodels for outcome oriented predictive business process monitoring. arXiv preprint arXiv:2506.03696 (2025)
12. Van Dongen, B.: Bpi challenge 2012 (2012). https://data.4tu.nl
13. Wang, J., Yu, D., Liu, C., Sun, X.: Outcome-oriented predictive process monitoring with attention-based bidirectional lstm neural networks. In: 2019 IEEE International Conference on Web Services (ICWS). pp. 360–367. IEEE (2019)
14. Pasquadibisceglie, V., Appice, A., Castellano, G., Malerba, D., Modugno, G.: Orange: outcome-oriented predictive process monitoring based on image encoding and cnns. IEEE Access **8**, 184073–184086 (2020)
15. Donadello, I., Di Francescomarino, C., Maggi, F.M., Ricci, F., Shikhizada, A.: Outcome-oriented prescriptive process monitoring based on temporal logic patterns. Eng. Appl. Artif. Intell. **126**, 106899 (2023)
16. Wang, F., Damiani, E.: Time-aware and transition-semantic graph neural networks for interpretable predictive business process monitoring. arXiv preprint arXiv:2508.09527 (2025)

1st International Workshop on Implementation and Management of Intelligent Process Automation Solutions (AUTOMATE 2025)

Levels of Automation Revisited: Standardizing Human-Machine Interaction with Process Patterns

Christian Janiesch(✉) and Seyyid A. Ciftci

TU Dortmund University, Otto-Hahn-Str. 12, 44227 Dortmund, Germany
{christian.janiesch,seyyid.ciftci}@tu-dortmund.de

Abstract. Traditionally, business process management has automated work processes in a handcrafted and explicit manner through process models and decision tables. Robotic process automation has enabled agentic lightweight automation with software robots mimicking human users. Despite these technological advances, certain areas have remained off-limits for automation due to their complexity and required cognitive abilities. In this context, intelligent systems based on self-learned analytical models have become increasingly versatile to automate work previously not automatable. With this shift from deterministic to probabilistic automation, supervision and control of automated processes needs to be revisited. That is, a key issue in the development of intelligent automation is not only applying the appropriate level of automation, which ranges from human control to fully automated systems, but also determining how human-machine interaction should be designed in a reproducible and standardized manner. Process patterns provide a means to guide this interaction by ensuring balance between automation efficiency and retention of human control as well as – inversely – machine-in-the-loop safety. We propose 12 process patterns for human-machine interaction based on previously established levels of automation to enable the design of process-aware systems with varying degrees of independence. We have consolidated these levels using an integrative literature review and evaluated the results through an interview study.

Keywords: Human-machine interaction · levels of automation · process automation · process patterns

1 Introduction

The constant integration of novel, innovative technology into the toolbox of business process management (BPM) has been a transformative force, significantly enhancing efficiency, scalability, and innovation in organizational operations [16]. Historically, BPM employed manually crafted process models and decision rule tables for explicit task automation, reducing human error and streamlining operations [4]. The advent of robotic process automation (RPA) brought about a significant leap, introducing lightweight automation through software robots that mimic human interactions with digital interfaces. Such advancements have broadened the scope of automatable processes, pushing the boundaries of operational streamlining [37].

I. van de Weerd et al. (Eds.): BPM 2025 Workshops, LNBIP 569, pp. 109–126, 2026.
https://doi.org/10.1007/978-3-032-13426-4_9

The emergence of intelligent systems, underpinned by self-learning analytical models, is challenging the current limits of automation, offering new opportunities for automating previously manual tasks [19]. These systems have shown unprecedented versatility and capability of decision-making once thought to be the sole domain of humans [11]. This shift from deterministic to probabilistic automation introduced a degree of indetermination previously unknown to BPM and, hence, presents a new set of challenges and opportunities [18]. It highlights the importance of revisiting the classic concept of *levels of automation* [34].

Consequently, the dynamics of *human-machine interaction* demand careful consideration. It becomes ever more crucial to establish reproducible and standardized methods for human-machine interaction, balancing maximized automation efficiency with the retention of critical human oversight (and vice versa). Here, the concept of *process patterns* emerges as a promising vehicle to effectively orchestrate process automation and human control. Process (model) patterns are design patterns, general reusable solutions to common problems that occur within a given context in software design. Design patterns provide a template for how to solve a problem in a way that has been proven effective through experience and can be adapted to fit specific situations [15].

Patterns for process models have been a subject of BPM research since the 1990s and a current survey exists with Fellmann et al. [12]'s taxonomy and catalog at bpmpatterns.org. However, to date, no comprehensive list of process patterns for human-machine interaction exists for different levels of automation that go beyond Sheridan and Verplank [34]'s initial proposal for undersea teleoperation. Most existing patterns either deal with technical details of token routing or with domain patterns applicable to certain industries or business problems only.

As a response, in our research we have conducted a comprehensive integrative literature review and evaluated our findings through interviews with practitioners to consolidate said process patterns in two iterations of design science research cycles.

We contribute to the BPM body of knowledge by proposing 12 process patterns for human-machine interaction, based on a systematization of previously established levels of automation. These process patterns aim to standardize the permissible scope of machine automation in process-aware systems, fostering a blend of efficiency, control, and, thus, safety. We seek to provide a foundation for designing and implementing such systems to harness better the potential of intelligent automation, enabling standardized yet exchangeable human-machine interaction patterns. Thereby, we provide a new anchor for the integration of machine intelligence into business processes.

Our paper is organized as follows: In Sect. 2, we outline our research design. Section 3 comprises a consolidation of prior work on the systematization of control in human-machine interaction. Section 4 presents our process patterns, which are evaluated and discussed in Sect. 5 before we conclude in Sect. 6.

2 Research Design

Our methodology largely adheres to the iterative design science framework by Vaishnavi and Kuechler [35]. We structured our adapted methodology into four main phases: *awareness*, *data collection and suggestion*, *development*, and *evaluation and conclusion*.

We expanded the original design cycle to incorporate data collection and merged the final two phases.

Awareness. With the advent of evermore intelligent systems acting indeterministically as agents in complex human-machine relationships, we identified a lack of process-aware advice on how to structure these interactions through discourse with practice and research projects. We found a comprehensive and constantly refined body of knowledge on human-robot interaction and multi-agent systems also applied to the domain of information systems [17, 28, 34]. Yet, the work is not geared towards the definition of concrete interaction behavior documented as process patterns.

Data Collection and Suggestion. To review the state-of-the-art as well as to deliver our first contribution, we performed an integrative literature review considering the advice of Elsbach and van Knippenberg [7] and Boell and Cecez-Kecmanovic [1]. Based on a comprehensive review article, we refined and extended our own framework of levels of automation in the 1st iteration. During the 2nd iteration, we carried out semi-structured interviews to confirm and refine the initial version of the levels and patterns based on feedback received from the participants [6, 29].

Development. The initial configuration of the process patterns manifested from the results of the integrative literature analysis and the resulting levels of automation, which were later revised and extended by means of the expert interviews in the second iteration. We sought to exclude levels deemed inapplicable or irrelevant to our patterns in practice by experts. Conversely, we incorporated new levels suggested by the experts into our approach. Similarly, we refined the modeling of the concrete patterns.

Evaluation and Conclusion. Due to the nascent nature of our research, we decided to implement a naturalistic, summative evaluation based on a human risk and effectiveness strategy [36]. That is, we again demonstrated the levels and patterns to the interviewees and gathered their responses to evaluate the current state [30]. We used the results of the evaluation of the first iteration to finalize our results as outlined above.

All phases discussed above are sequential, but they have been iterated until consolidated levels and patterns manifested. In doing so, we conducted two major design iterations of data collection and suggestion, development, and evaluation and conclusion:

Iteration 1: Integrative literature review to improve theoretical sensitivity, consolidating prior work on levels of automation, and proposal of initial process patterns.

Iteration 2: Expert interview study, data coding, validated and consolidated levels and patterns, demonstration, and expert feedback.

3 Human-Machine Interaction in Levels of Automation

The interaction of human and machine requires careful design and execution. Establishing reproducible and standardized boundaries balancing maximized automation efficiency with the ability of critical human oversight has been a subject of prior research. When defining these boundaries for decision-making and assessing the need for certain decisions to undergo review by an assigned party, levels of automation can be employed [28]. These levels specify the degree of independence and oversight granted to each participant – varying from complete independence where machines operate without human involvement, to total reliance on humans without machine assistance. Using these levels improves our comprehension and fine-tuning of how interaction between humans and machines functions. They can serve as a baseline for process patterns to structure the cooperative mechanisms in action.

For our work, we used the levels proposed by Janiesch et al. [17] as a starting point of our investigation as the authors have integrated the state-of-the-art in a comprehensive multi-level framework. To ensure a current analysis, we conducted an additional integrative, hermeneutic review [1] of recent literature. The aim was not only to support the proposed levels but also to critically question, expand, or refine them where necessary. In doing so, we conducted one further hermeneutic cycle of each, search and acquisition as well as analysis and interpretation. The detailed analysis revealed that certain levels of automation can have multiple variants, which required a differentiated consideration and classification.

In particular, we reviewed the additional works of Draper [3], Proud et al. [31], Riley [32], Fereidunian et al. [13], and Milgram et al. [23] who have made a notable contribution to expanding and deepening our understanding of levels of automation. With their research, these authors have provided valuable insights and additions, which allowed us to expand and refine the original framework. Their findings led to a (re-) classification and evaluation of additional levels that consider both technological and organizational aspects. See Table 1 for an overview of our final 12 levels of automation for human-machine interaction. The table contains a level number, a description as well as the reference(s) of Janiesch et al. [17] as well as our own supporting references.

Independence and Notification. Level 1 "machine independence" is characterized by the absence of human involvement. In this level, the process of decision- making followed by executing a corresponding action is carried out independently by the machine [10, 13, 23, 31, 32]. Level 2 "notification" continues to emphasize machine independence but introduces an element of interaction through notifications. This level is segmented into three distinct aspects: (2a) whether the machine notifies the human at their discretion; (2b) whether the human must actively send a request; and (2c) a notification is sent for every action [3, 13, 23, 28, 31, 33, 34].

Ex-durante Interventions. Level 3 signifies the start of human oversight and intervention. The machine conducts decision-making and executes corresponding actions independently, while the human oversees (specific aspects of) the machine's operations and intervenes only when necessary [3, 8, 9, 20, 32]. It signifies "human-in-the-loop" behavior [25]. In level 4 "(re-)delegation" the machine is in principle responsible for decision-making and executing corresponding actions. Yet, it (re-)delegates cases to humans to ensure human situational awareness [3, 10, 27]. Level 5 "veto" enables machines to make independent decisions and execute actions based on those decisions until the human vetoes them. This level enables ex-durante interventions divided into a (5a) continuous veto opportunity against machine decisions at any time [27] and a (5b) veto for a limited time [10, 13, 28, 31, 33, 34].

Ex-ante Authorization. In contrast to the previous levels, level 6 "approval" signifies the boundary of permissioned machine automation and requires ex-ante authorization. It requires explicit human approval after the machine has completed the decision-making process. The machine can only execute the corresponding action if the approval is granted. [10, 13, 31] Level 7 introduces the concept of "action candidates", that is

Table 1. Consolidated view on levels of automation based on Janiesch et al. [17].

No	Description	References
1	M performs decision-making and corresponding actions independently; H is not involved	[8–10, 13, 23, 27, 28, 31–34]
2a	M performs decision-making and corresponding actions independently and notifies H at its own discretion	[3, 13, 23, 28, 31, 33, 34]
2b	M performs decision-making and corresponding actions independently and notifies upon H's request	[13, 28, 33, 34],
2c	M performs decision-making and corresponding actions independently and notifies H at all times	[28, 33, 34]
3	M performs decision-making and corresponding actions independently, while H monitors (certain aspects of) M and intervenes if necessary	[3, 8, 9, 20, 32]
4	M performs decision-making and corresponding actions independently and eventually delegates a case to H	[3, 10, 27]
5a	M performs decision-making and corresponding actions independently until H vetoes against them	[27]
5b	M performs decision-making independently and provides H with the opportunity to veto against it for a limited time	[10, 13, 28, 31, 33, 34]
6	M performs decision-making independently and executes the corresponding tasks only after H's approval	[8–10, 13, 21, 28, 31–34]
7a	M provides H with a single action candidate that H can refuse	[8, 13, 27, 28, 33, 34]
7b	M provides H with a selection of action candidates	[8–10, 13, 27, 28, 33, 34]
7c	M provides H with all action candidates	[10, 13, 21, 28, 32–34]
8	M and H collaboratively define action candidates and subsequently collaboratively perform decision-making as well as execute the corresponding actions	[2, 9, 14]
9a	H provides M with action candidates, while M performs decision-making and executes corresponding actions	[9]
9b	H performs decision-making and transfers corresponding tasks to M for execution	[8, 23, 32]

(continued)

Table 1. (*continued*)

No	Description	References
9c	H performs decision-making and corresponding actions until M takes over to execute the remaining tasks independently	[9, 34]
10	H performs decision-making and controls (certain aspects of) M	[20]
11	H performs decision-making and corresponding actions, and M monitors and intervenes in emergencies	[31]
12	H performs decision-making and corresponding actions, while M is not involved	[3, 9, 10, 13, 21, 23, 28, 31–34]

decision options a human can choose from: (7a) the machine sends the human a single action candidate, which the human can refuse; (7b) the machine provides the human with a selection of action candidates; and (7c) the machine provides the human with all (applicable) action candidates [10, 13, 21, 31, 32].

Hybrid Intelligence. Endsley and Kaber [9] describe level 8 as a level in which humans and machines collaboratively define action candidates and either (or both) the machine or the human can take over the decision-making process and execute the corresponding tasks. It signifies co-creation, collaboration (and ad hoc division) of decision and execution. It can be associated with the concept of "hybrid intelligence" [2].

Human Control. Level 9, represents another shift in the human-machine interaction paradigm and signifies the boundary of human control and machine-in-the-loop behavior [24]. It comprises three sub-levels of "delegation": (9a) The human provides the machine with a set of possible action candidates. The machine then performs the decision-making and executes the action independently [9]; (9b) delineates a division between decision-making and action. The human makes the decision and delegates the execution of corresponding actions to the machine [9, 23, 32]; and (9c) the machine is no longer directly involved in the process from the start. Instead, the human performs the decision-making and corresponding actions until the machine takes over to execute the remaining tasks automatically [9, 10, 34]. Closely related, levels 10 also signifies delegation of actions but also direct intervention and "control" by the human, who monitor the machine [20]. Level 11 constitutes the "machine-in-the-loop" behavior where the machine monitors the human, enabling it to intervene in emergencies [20, 31]. Conversely to level 1, level 12 delineates the "human control" scenario where the human is solely responsible for both decision-making and action execution, entirely excluding the machine from the process [3, 9, 10, 13, 21, 23, 28, 31–34].

Together these 12 levels comprise a framework from machine independence to human control that enables differentiated permissioned machine automation via ex-durante intervention and ex-ante authorization. It also includes co-creation and close collaboration within the concept of hybrid intelligence.

4 Process Patterns for Human-Machine Interaction

4.1 Machine Independence and Notification (Level 1 and 2)

All process patterns haven been modelled in BPMN [26] as abstract conceptual references that must be detailed for implementation. They represent the final design artifact after the second iteration of our design cycle.

Machine independence focuses on the intelligent system, which is responsible for both decision-making and performing the corresponding actions in its entirety. Human involvement is non-existent or minimized to being informed about the actions executed by the machine [2].

Level 1 is characterized by a state in which human involvement is absent, and the machine independently undertakes the task execution [8, 23, 31]. That is, there is no messaging across pools. In level 2, the human is depicted as an informed entity without any authorization. This level is differentiated into: (2a) a situational notification by the machine, triggered by a non-interrupting escalation boundary event to inform the human in cases where the machine deems this necessary, (2b) a notification upon the human's request, initiated by a message to the machine (see Fig. 1), and (2c) continuous information provided to the human about every step of the process (or a defined subset thereof) [28, 33, 34]. Note that other event types than escalation could be used.

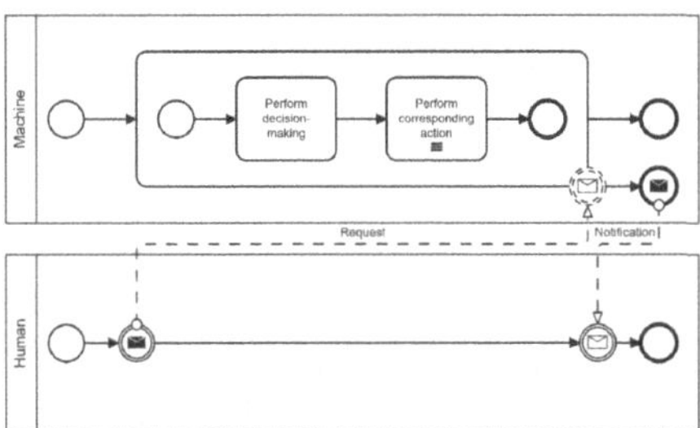

Fig. 1. Level 2b: Notification by request.

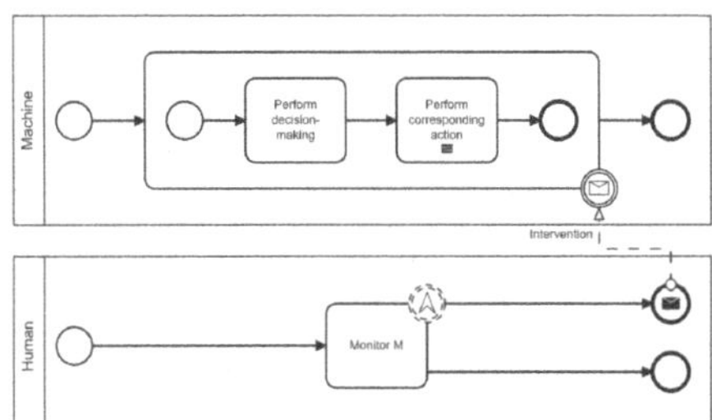

Fig. 2. Level 3: Human-in-the-loop.

4.2 Human Oversight and Ex-Durante Interventions (Level 3 to 5)

Whenever human oversight, that is the supervision of both decision-making and the execution of actions, is necessary, ex-durante interventions can be used that enable automated machine behavior until an exception requires human action.

In level 3, the human-in-the-loop monitors the machine until an intervention is necessary, modelled as an escalation boundary event sending a message to the machine (see Fig. 2). Again, other event types could be used. Level 4 represents the (re-)delegation of cases (see Fig. 3) to the human via message. This can happen for two reasons: the machine is not capable of performing the case/task by itself or it wants to ensure situational awareness of the human by involving them actively. Level 5 provides the human with an ability to veto. The pattern notifies the human about the machine's decision-making, waits for a defined time and, thus, gives them the ability to veto before and during further process execution. While (5a) enables a veto until the process is completed (see Fig. 4), (5b) offers only a limited timeframe to exercise this veto, modelled as an interrupting time boundary event (see Fig. 5).

4.3 Permissioned Machine Automation with Ex-Ante Authorization (Level 6 and 7)

In the context of permissioned machine automation, machines can assist humans not only with task automation but also with decision support. However, the decision-making results generated by machines are always reviewed and approved by humans before further actions take place [2, 28, 33].

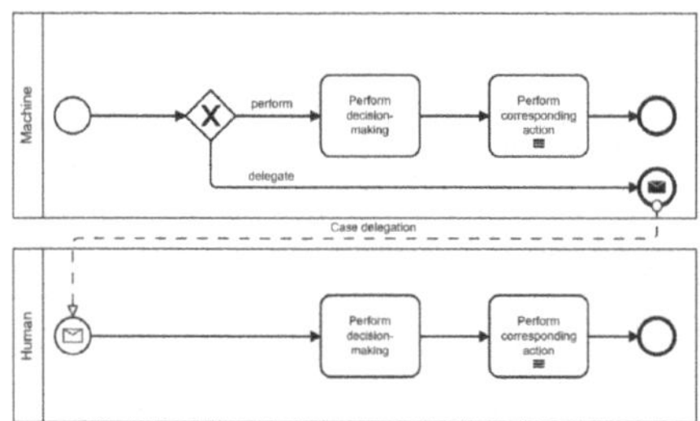

Fig. 3. Level 4: Case (re-)delegation.

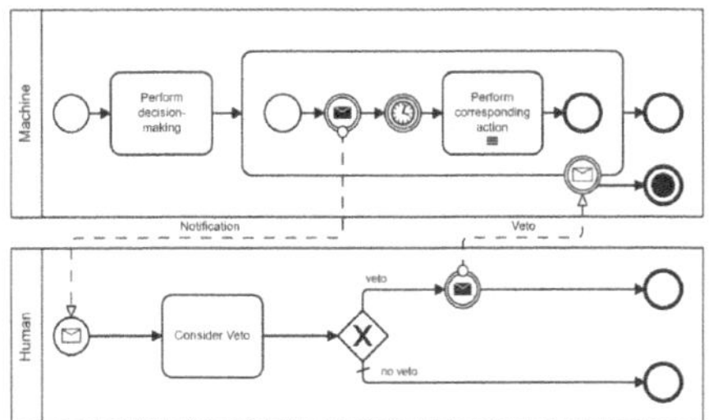

Fig. 4. Level 5a: Veto.

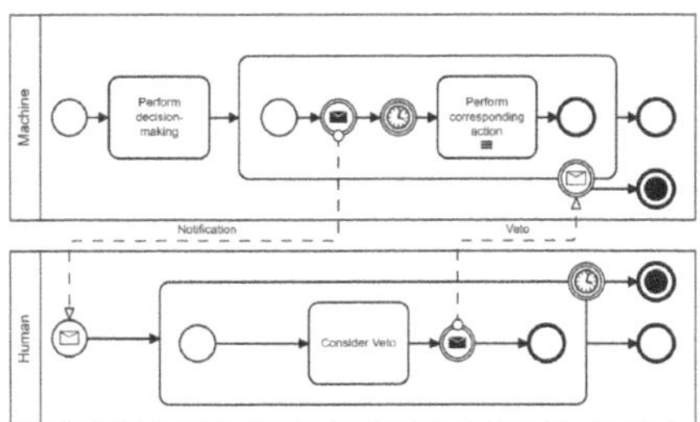

Fig. 5. Level 5b: Time-limited veto.

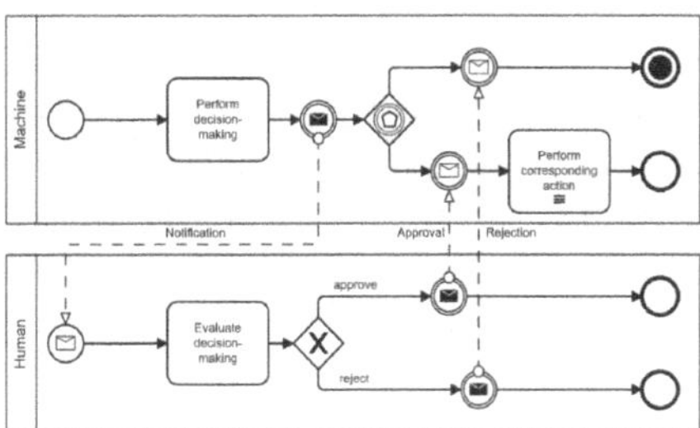

Fig. 6. Level 6: Approval.

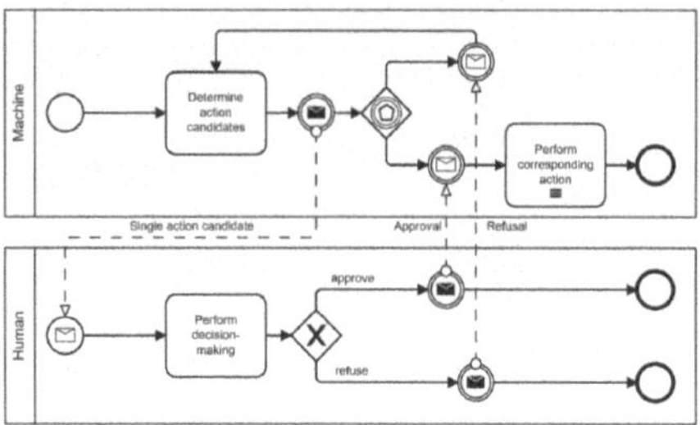

Fig. 7. Level 7a: Single action candidate.

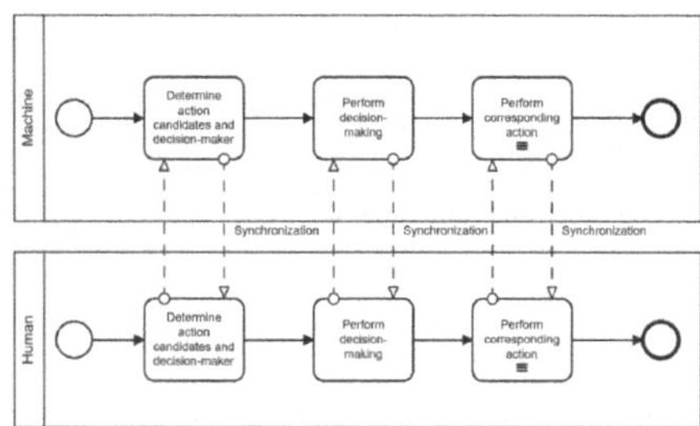

Fig. 8. Level 8: Hybrid intelligence.

Level 6 (see Fig. 6) requires explicit approval of machine decision-making with results being sent as a message to the human for review. The decision to approve or reject the authorization is made by the human. The machine can only carry out the corresponding action when it receives an approval message from the human otherwise the process is terminated. Level 7 differs from the previous level in that the machine does not make decisions, but instead determine action candidates that are then reviewed by the human. The human decision is then sent back to the machine via message and executed upon. Level 7a involves sending one action candidate, which can be refused – upon which a new action candidate is being sent by the machine (see Fig. 7). Levels 7b and 7c are almost identical in their modeling. In both cases, the machine sends the human a list of action candidates for decision-making, in one case a selection, in the other the full list. The human performs the decision-making and informs the machine via message about the outcome so that the corresponding actions can be performed. In all four scenarios, the machine is dependent on a human's ex-ante authorization and cannot proceed without it.

4.4 Hybrid Intelligence (Level 8)

Humans and machines, each have specific capabilities and limitations when working in isolation that limit their ability to complete certain tasks. Humans are constrained by their bounded rationality when it comes to aggregating information and drawing conclusions, while machines can be prone to judgmental errors, especially in areas with high cognitive requirements [2, 5]. To overcome these limitations, the concept of hybrid intelligence has been proposed, which uses the complementary strengths of human and machine, viz. Intelligent systems, to achieve superior results through collaboration. It signifies a process of co-creation rather than delegation.

Figure 8 depicts a basic process pattern for level 8 "hybrid intelligence". Humans and machines initially synchronize their information and knowledge through messages exchange. This alignment is crucial to agree on potential actions and the subsequent decision-making and continues through the pattern. During every task, human and machine synchronize their execution. At this stage, we have decided to avoid detailing this pattern into further sub-patterns as there is not yet sufficient consensus on archetypal modes of hybrid work modes in the literature. Naturally, these patterns can be nested to enable more interleaved decision-making and co-creation [14].

4.5 Human Control and Machine-In-The-Loop (Level 9 to 12)

The human control and machine-in-the-loop approach delineates a system wherein humans are the principal decision-makers and machines assume ancillary roles [2]. Operating from a position of observation [20], the machine performs only tasks delegated by human [9] or remains mostly inactive, allowing the process to be managed by human [3, 13, 23]. This concept represents the augmentation of human capabilities through technology, without compromising human autonomy.

Level 9 is characterized by the delegation of decisions (9a), actions (9b), or the remaining actions (9c) from human to machine. Depending on the specific sub-level, action candidates (see Fig. 9), decided actions (see Fig. 10), or residual actions are sent to the machine via message. Level 10 shows human decision-making and only the delegation of actions to the machine while continuous monitoring is in effect (see Fig. 11). Whenever the human deems it necessary, they can take control of task execution and control the machine signified via messages. Instead of an escalation boundary event to start control, other event types are conceivable. Level 11 represents independent human behavior with a supervisory machine-in-the-loop. The latter intervenes whenever deemed necessary, for example to ensure compliance. Again, non-interrupting escalation boundary events leading to messages could be exchanged for other event types (see Fig. 12). Lastly, level 12 represents complete human control, where machines are not involved in decision-making or task execution. While it represents full human autonomy, it also strictly entails manual labor as both pools are not connected.

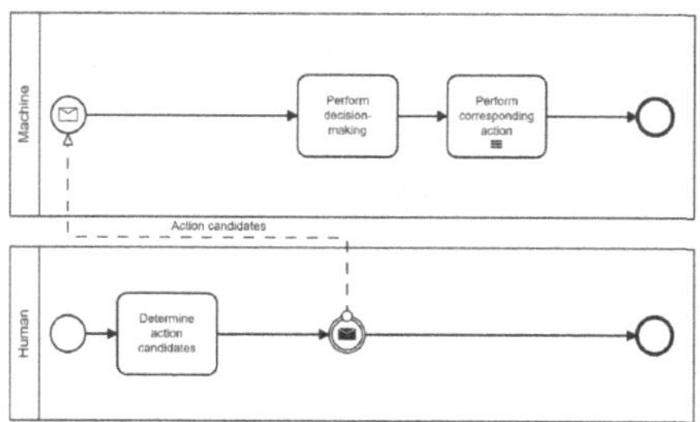

Fig. 9. Level 9a: Delegation of decision.

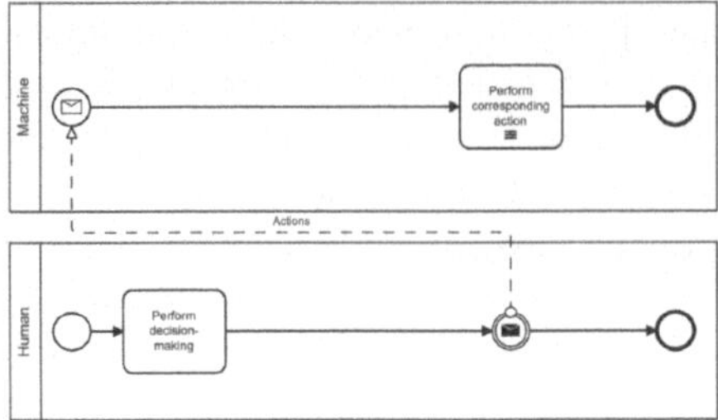

Fig. 10. Level 9b: Delegation of action.

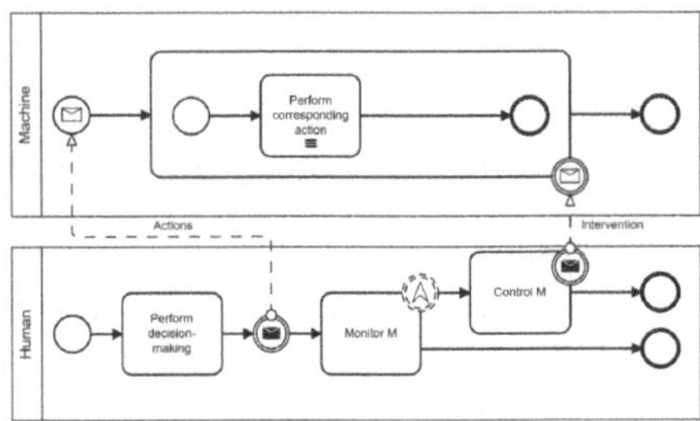

Fig. 11. Level 10: Delegation and control.

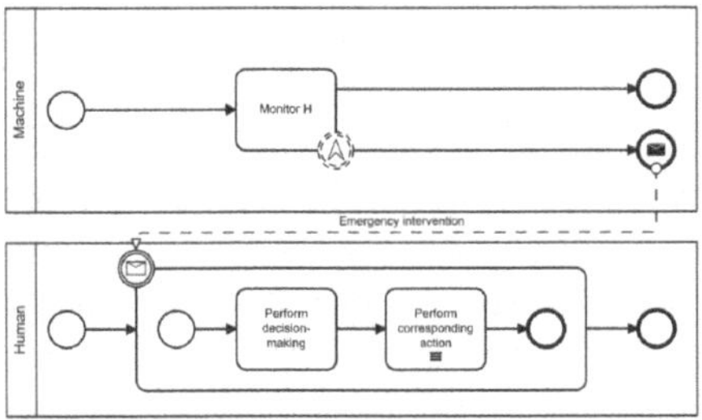

Fig. 12. Level 11: Machine-in-the-loop.

5 Evaluation and Discussion

In our evaluation, we conducted interviews with experts from practice to not only evaluate our first iteration of process patterns, but in doing so we also gathered further input for our design cycle. That is, this approach aimed not only to confirm the previously identified levels of automation but also to assess whether the identified process patterns adequately reflect these levels of automation. Furthermore, we analyzed to what extent these process patterns were modeled correctly and whether they would be applicable in practice.

By adopting this integrated approach, we were able to bridge the gap between theoretical conceptualization and practical applicability. The expert interviews allowed us to gather direct feedback from industry, which is essential for refining our artifacts to ensure their relevance in real-world application. This contributes to enhancing the validity and effectiveness of our developed solution and secures its practical viability.

We engaged with practitioners actively involved in the domain of process automation with BPM systems and RPA. A diverse cohort of five experts, varying in roles, industries, and organizational scales, consented to discuss their insights through semi-structured interviews. For the purposes of this study, we define an expert as an individual endowed with specialized knowledge, achievable only through direct involvement in at least one project encompassing BPM or RPA and intelligent system components. This definition extends to those with a profound comprehension of the varying levels of automation within the automated process. We provide the anonymized backgrounds of the interviewees in Table 2 for reference.

Table 2. Interviewees.

I	Role	Industry	Experience	Company size
I1	Product manager	Software	4 years	70 employees
I2	Senior consultant	Consulting	8 years	200 employees
I3	Chief technical officer	Software/Service	7 years	60 employees
I4	Consultant	Consulting	5 years	200 employees
I5	Project manager	Software	4 years	350 employees

We chose to conduct online interviews to facilitate real-time communication, allowing for immediate clarification and thorough exploration through follow-up questions without being limited by geographical constraints. We used a semi-structured interview guideline with three main sections: (A) exploring background information and participants expertise, (B) examining the alignment between theoretical and practical aspects, and (C) discussing our levels of automation and process patterns for human-machine interaction.

To bridge the gap between theory and practice, section (B) included questions about participants understanding of the subject matter and their experiences with human-machine automation processes in organizational settings. This approach enabled a detailed assessment of both theoretical concepts and practical implications that helped identify individual levels of automation. Subsequently, in section (C), we compared the identified levels of automation from literature with the corresponding process patterns. This part allowed participating experts to critically evaluate the applicability, order, and comprehensiveness of designated levels of automation alongside their corresponding process patterns. This discussion partially validated theoretically derived levels of automation while providing recommendation for changes as well.

The interview questions were intentionally open-ended to capture emergent insights effectively. All interviews were systematically recorded and transcribed. In total, the aggregate duration of our interview audio recordings amounts to 171 min. This corresponds to a transcription length of 107 pages. The interviews were analyzed using qualitative content analysis according to Mayring [22], with the aim of systematically extracting and interpreting information.

When analyzing the levels of automation, the experts generally confirmed, compressed, but also expanded on the findings derived from the literature review. The experts gave various arguments in favor of the levels of automation and confirmed the general ordering of the levels as suitable. All of them confirmed the comprehensibility of the description of the individual levels of automation.

However, our analysis revealed a specific high-level division of automation based on the characteristics of interaction across the examined levels. I3 describes it as: "*For me, there are actually only four standard cases: human completely alone; or machine completely alone; machine works and human can stop or influence in some way; or, as a human, I just give the go-ahead for the machine to do something. For me, these are actually the four basic types.*" We acknowledge this comment and have categorized the levels of automation into five groups to enable better oversight. We took into account I4's position as well as the unique position of level 8, which does not fit into any of these groups and serves as a sort of inflection point.

Further, none of the interviewees suggested an adjustment, extension, or reduction of the levels of automation. Even if not all levels were familiar or applicable in the field the interviewees, they confirmed that the levels would make sense in other industries and are, hence, justified. Yet, I2 commented: "*I think there tend to be more levels that deal with machine autonomy than with human autonomy. I wouldn't call it a bias, but I have seen a certain emphasis on the question of how autonomously machines can actually interact, perhaps because this is still rather unclear or there are more open questions than now with regard to the question of how autonomously humans can act.*" While we think there is some truth to the statement, we must highlight the fact that all patterns generally assume the human to be the principal who sets the goals so that there is no natural point of inflection at which roles invert within the levels of automation. Hence, it is only natural that the focus is on the autonomous behavior of the agent even though this situation may change in the future, when approaches such as algorithmic management and supervision through intelligent systems become more prevalent. This would entail that the machine takes supervisory role or even the role of the principal.

All interviewees showed a clear understanding of the process patterns presented and confirmed that they represent the levels of automation appropriately. The modelling of the patterns proved to be clear and comprehensible, which enabled problem-free understanding of the subject matter.

The interviewees found minor semantic errors, which we corrected in the figures above, and suggested a timer to be added to levels 5a and 5b to enable – in principle – veto before the start of task execution. Further, I2, I3, and I5 highlighted that not all events used are part of the common core of BPMN and more common (but more rigid) event types could be used. Further, I4 questioned whether the indetermination of "at their discretion" in pattern 2b was appropriate, as they preferred more deterministic notifications. This is possible with a subset of notifications in pattern 2c. We outlined this option in the narrative above, as "all" has to be further specified to be useful for humans.

Furthermore, I1, I2, I3, and I4 suggested further sub-levels of level 8 hybrid intelligence that had not previously emerged from the literature. I3 describes it as: "*What is now starting to happen in logistics, and what I have seen now, is that there are now collaborative robotic approaches, the machine does a basic unit of jobs, they are given by the system, and the human does the same jobs in parallel.* [...] *There is such a thing, that is that people and machines actually work in the same process without this interaction option, because it is usually made by the* [...] *system or something like that. This decision to work in parallel actually still exists in practice.*" However, rather than detailing sub-levels of level 8, we made the conscious decision to present an even more abstract model for the hybrid intelligence patterns than emergent from extant literature. This acknowledges the high variability and immediacy of co-creation interactions that should be explored in future research.

At the end of the second design cycle, we contacted the interviewees again to evaluate the final result of the levels of automation and process patterns and neither of the participants of the interview study raised grave concerns and generally agreed with the results.

6 Summary, Limitations, and Conclusion

In our research, we answered the question of how to design human-machine interactions in a standardized and reproducible manner using process patterns. To derive the process patterns, we have discussed and extended existing levels of automation, updated the body of knowledge, and re-structured and compressed the levels for the application to process design.

As a result, we introduce refined levels of automation relevant for the process design of human-machine interaction with automated systems. We presented 12 process patterns for human-machine interaction that structure the interaction between human and machine in the tradeoff between independence and permissioned or controlled behavior. The patterns are – for the most part – delegation patterns from the point of view of a human principal. The patterns are exchangeable against each other to provide a standardized means to ensure oversight but also independent and efficient automation.

Our work extends the body of knowledge of process patterns that has been started by compiling low-level workflow patterns for BPM system operations. Our patterns can be considered a type of orchestration and choreography pattern of Fellmann et al. [12]'s pattern taxonomy. As such, they resemble design patterns that enhance software development by promoting standardized human-machine interactions in workflows, and facilitating better communication of design intentions. This structured approach can lead to increased efficiency in the development process and reduce the arbitrariness in interaction decisions as well as the likelihood of errors resulting in a more consistent and maintainable business process. Furthermore, it serves as a catalog of design options to developers.

Naturally, our research comes with a few limitations. Our process patterns focus on 1:1 human-machine interactions, which is also signified by the activity multi-instance marker for sequential rather than parallel instances. It is not only conceivable but highly probable that many interactions may also be conducted in a 1:*n* or *n*:*n* fashion (with priorly known or unknown entities, some of which may only be "instantiated" at runtime) [38]. This may require adaptations to the patterns. Further, the interaction patterns focus mostly on human-machine delegation and execution tasks. All aspects of information acquisition [28] have not been considered and all aspects of ad-collaboration and co-creation has been summarized as the hybrid intelligence pattern (level 8) even though there may more fine-grained interactions as technology advances.

Lastly, we have adopted the classic terminology of levels of automation even though many practitioners and scholars speak of autonomy rather than automation when talking about intelligent systems. However, we believe the concept of artificial autonomy in this socio-technical context is still ill-defined and may – once properly understood – exhibit characteristics that require further levels or a different conceptualization altogether. We are confident that our research will start spawning more detailed discussions on process patterns and process automation as well as autonomy addressing some of our limitations in more detail and providing real-world evaluation to better understand the practical implications when dealing with independent machines.

Acknowledgments. This research and development project is funded by the German Federal Ministry of Research, Technology and Space (BMFTR) within the "Richtlinie zur Förderung von Projekten zur Erforschung oder Entwicklung praxisrelevanter Lösungsaspekte ("Bausteine") für Datentreuhandmodelle" (Funding No. 16DTM201B) and financed by the European Union – NextGenerationEU. The authors are responsible for the contents of this publication.

References

1. Boell, S.K., Cecez-Kecmanovic, D.: A hermeneutic approach for conducting literature reviews and literature searches. Commun. AIS **34**(1), 257–286 (2014)
2. Dellermann, D., Ebel, P., Söllner, M., Leimeister, J.M.: Hybrid intelligence. Bus. & Inf. Syst. Eng. **61**(5), 637–643 (2019)
3. Draper, J.V.: Teleoperators for advanced manufacturing: applications and human factors challenges. Int. J. Human Factors Manuf. **5**(1), 53–85 (1995)
4. Dumas, M., La Rosa, M., Mendling, J., Reijers, H.A.: Fundamentals of Business Process Management. Springer, Berlin (2018)
5. Ebel, P., Söllner, M., Leimeister, J.M., Crowston, K., de Vreede, G.-J.: Hybrid intelligence in business networks. Electr. Mark. **31**(2), 313–318 (2021)
6. Edwards, R., Holland, J.: What is qualitative interviewing? Bloomsbury, London (2013)
7. Elsbach, K.D., van Knippenberg, D.: Creating high-impact literature reviews: an argument for 'integrative reviews'. J. Manag. Stud. **57**(6) (2020)
8. Endsley, M.R.: The application of human factors to the development of expert systems for advanced cockpits. Proc. Human Factors Soc. Ann. Meet. **31**(12), 1388–1392 (1987)
9. Endsley, M.R., Kaber, D.B.: Level of automation effects on performance, situation awareness and workload in a dynamic control task. Ergonomics **42**(3), 462–492 (1999)
10. Endsley, M.R., Kiris, E.O.: The out-of-the-loop performance problem and level of control in automation. Human Factors **37**(2) (1995)
11. Engel, C., Ebel, P., Leimeister, J.M.: Cognitive automation. Electr. Mark. **32**(1) (2022)
12. Fellmann, M., Koschmider, A., Laue, R., Schoknecht, A., Vetter, A.: Business process model patterns: state-of-the-art, research classification and taxonomy. Bus. Process. Manag. J. **25**(5), 972–994 (2019)
13. Fereidunian, A., Lehtonen, M., Lesani, H., Lucas, C., Nordman, M.: Adaptive autonomy: Smart cooperative cybernetic systems for more humane automation solutions. In: IEEE International Conference on Systems, Man and Cybernetics, pp. 202–207 (2007)
14. Feuerriegel, S., Hartmann, J., Janiesch, C., Zschech, P.: Generative AI. Bus. & Inf. Syst. Eng. **66**(1), 111–126 (2024)
15. Gamma, E., Helm, R., Johnson, R., Vlissides, J.: Design Patterns: Elements of Reusable Object-Oriented Software. Addison-Wesley Longman Publishing, Boston, MA (1995)

16. Herm, L.-V., Janiesch, C., Reijers, H.A., Seubert, F.: From symbolic RPA to intelligent RPA: Challenges for developing and operating intelligent software robots. In: Polyvyanyy, A., Wynn, M.T., Van Looy, A., Reichert, M. (eds.) Business Process Management. Lecture Notes in Computer Science, vol. 12875, pp. 289–305. Springer, Cham (2021). https://doi.org/10.1007/978-3-030-85469-0_19
17. Janiesch, C., Fischer, M., Winkelmann, A., Nentwich, V.: Specifying autonomy in the Internet of Things: the autonomy model and notation. IseB **17**(1), 159–194 (2019)
18. Janiesch, C., Kowalkiewicz, M., Rosemann, M.: Process Autonomization: rethinking business process management. In: 23rd International Conference on Business Process Management Forum. Lecture Notes in Business Information Processing. Springer, Seville (2025)
19. Janiesch, C., Zschech, P., Heinrich, K.: Machine learning and deep learning. Electr. Mark. **31**(3), 685–695 (2021)
20. Jipp, M.: Levels of automation: effects of individual differences on wheelchair control performance and user acceptance. Theor. Issues Ergon. Sci. **15**(5), 479–504 (2014)
21. Lorenz, B., Di Nocera, F., Röttger, S., Parasuraman, R.: The effects of level of automation on the out-of-the-loop unfamiliarity in a complex dynamic fault-management task during simulated spaceflight operations. Proc. Human Factors Ergonomics Soc. Ann. Meet. **45**(2), 44–48 (2001)
22. Mayring, P.: Qualitative Content analysis: theoretical background and procedures. In: Bikner-Ahsbahs, A., Knipping, C., Presmeg, N. (eds.) Approaches to Qualitative Research in Mathematics Education: Examples of Methodology and Methods, pp. 365–380. Springer (2015)
23. Milgram, P., Rastogi, A., Grodski, J.: Telerobotic control using augmented reality. In: Proceedings 4th IEEE International Workshop on Robot and Human Communication (1995)
24. Mosqueira-Rey, E., Hernández-Pereira, E., Alonso-Ríos, D., Bobes-Bascarán, J., Fernández-Leal, Á.: Human-in-the-loop machine learning: a state of the art. Artif. Intell. Rev. **56**(4), 3005–3054 (2023)
25. Nunes, D.S., Zhang, P., Sá Silva, J.: A survey on human-in-the-loop applications towards an internet of All. IEEE Commun. Sur. & Tutorials **17**, 944–965 (2015)
26. Object Management Group®: Business Process Model and Notation. https://www.omg.org/spec/BPMN, Accessed 08 Mar 2024
27. Onnasch, L., Wickens, C.D., Li, H., Manzey, D.: Human performance consequences of stages and levels of automation: an integrated meta-analysis. J. Human Factors Ergonomics Soc. **56**(3), 476–488 (2014)
28. Parasuraman, R., Sheridan, T.B., Wickens, C.D.: A model for types and levels of human interaction with automation. IEEE Int. Conf. Syst., Man Cybern.- Part A: Syst. Humans 30(**3**) (2000)
29. Paré, G.: Investigating information systems with positivist case research. Commun. AIS **13**(1) (2004)
30. Peffers, K., Tuunanen, T., Rothenberger, M.A., Chatterjee, S.: A design science research methodology for information systems research. J. Manag. Inf. Syst. **24**(3), 45–77 (2007)
31. Proud, R.W., Hart, J.J., Mrozinski, R.B.: Methods for Determining the Level of Autonomy to Design into a Human Spaceflight Vehicle: A Function Specific Approach (2003)
32. Riley, V.: A general model of mixed-initiative human-machine systems. Proc. Human Factors Soc. Ann. Meet. **33**(2), 124–128 (1989)
33. Sheridan, T.B., Parasuraman, R.: Human-automation interaction. Rev. Human Factors Ergonomics **1**(1), 89–129 (2005)
34. Sheridan, T.B., Verplank, W.L.: Human and Computer Control of Undersea Teleoperators. MIT Technical report (1978)
35. Vaishnavi, V.K., Kuechler, W.: Design Science Research Methods and Patterns: Innovating Information and Communication Technology (2015)

36. Venable, J., Pries-Heje, J., Baskerville, R.: FEDS: a framework for evaluation in design science research. Eur. J. Inf. Syst. **25**(1), 77–89 (2016)
37. Willcocks, L.P., Lacity, M., Craig, A.: The IT function and robotic process automation. The Outsourcing Unit Working Research Paper Series (2015)
38. Yanco, H.A., Drury, J.L.: Classifying human-robot interaction: an updated taxonomy. IEEE Int. Conf. Syst., Man Cybern. **3** (2004)

Runtime-Recovery Agent: Solving UI-Related Exceptions in RPA Systems with GUI Agents

A. Rodríguez-Ruiz(✉), J. G. Enríquez, and A. Jiménez-Ramírez

Department of Computer Languages and Systems, University of Seville, Avenida Reina Mercedes, s/n, 41012 Sevilla, Spain
{arodriguez38,jgenriquez,ajimenez}@us.es

Abstract. Robotic Process Automation (RPA) has become a promising approach to automate repetitive processes by mimicking the way in which humans interact with user interfaces (UIs). However, RPA robots may fail to do so due to unexpected changes in the UIs, which alter the UI interaction flow and can result in exceptions being raised. This can create the need for human intervention, which can be time and resource costly. To these issues, existing work has identified the need for automatic exception handling and the addition of cognitive technologies within RPA processes. To address this problem, we propose a hybrid approach that aims to integrate AI agents —more specifically, Graphical User Interface (GUI) agents— in the RPA lifecycle. More precisely, we propose to integrate them within the monitoring stage —when the automation is already deployed— with the objective of handling UI-related exceptions by taking control of the process execution when needed. Our findings show promising results for this approach to be integrated as a solution to UI-related exceptions during robot execution; thus, potentially reducing the need for manual intervention and preventing automation workflows from being blocked until robots are updated.

Keywords: RPA · GUI Agent · Monitoring · Exception Handling

1 Introduction

In the last decade, *Robotic Process Automation* (RPA) has established itself in the industry as an efficient and reliable manner of automating repetitive processes by mimicking the way in which humans interact with user interfaces (UIs). Traditional RPA implies the analysis, design, and implementation of the processes to be automated, which typically requires manual work. Recently, new technologies have emerged as promising candidates for the next phase of automation, coined Agentic Process Automation (APA) [20]. This paradigm centers on large language models (LLMs) capable of handling complex and dynamic decision-making. The core of APA is the *Agent*, i.e., an LLM with access to systems and tools, and to which a task to complete is given. In the context

I. van de Weerd et al. (Eds.): BPM 2025 Workshops, LNBIP 569, pp. 127–138, 2026.
https://doi.org/10.1007/978-3-032-13426-4_10

of APA, Graphical User Interface (GUI) agents are the most closely related to RPA, which aim to automate tasks by interacting directly with user interfaces [3,4,19].

Although APA holds promise for robust and adaptable automation, agent-only solutions relying on LLMs are computationally expensive and difficult to operationalize at scale. In turn, RPA continues to suffer from a lack of runtime adaptability —a limitation closely related to its brittleness against UI changes. For instance, Syed et al. [18] emphasize the absence of cognitive capabilities in RPA systems, while Kurowski et al. [8] identify the lack of autonomous exception handling mechanisms as a key bottleneck preventing more resilient automation.

Despite the known limitations of RPA and rising interest in APA, no prior work has demonstrated a hybrid integration of GUI agents with traditional RPA robots specifically aimed at handling UI-related exceptions during runtime. This represents a critical research gap, as such a solution could combine the robustness of agentic decision-making with the cost-efficiency of conventional RPA systems. Furthermore, manual work to identify runtime exceptions, corrections, and redeployment of robots not only increases operational costs but also leads to service downtime and reduced trust in automation solutions, further supporting the need for automated recovery systems.

To address this gap, we investigate the following research question: *Can GUI agents be used to recover from UI-related exceptions from RPA robots?*

To answer this question, we propose a hybrid framework in which GUI agents are invoked only upon UI-related exceptions raised by RPA robots during execution. The goal of the GUI agent is to autonomously recover from the exception and return the automation flow to a state where the original robot can resume its operation. This integration aims to reduce manual intervention and increase system resilience without fully replacing the RPA layer with a resource-intensive agentic stack, as opposed to agent-only based GUI automation [20,21].

Furthermore, to test our approach, we designed and executed two scenarios with different levels of complexity in a controlled environment, where a GUI agent is tasked with recovering from the raised exception. The results indicate that the proposed solution is a promising approach to addressing the stated problem. It successfully identified correct strategies for both scenarios, fully executing one and partially executing the other, mostly due to current technical limitations.

Thus, the contribution of the paper is twofold: (1) the proposal of a novel hybrid framework that integrates GUI agents with RPA systems for runtime exception recovery in a resource- and cost-effective manner, and (2) the first empirical validation of GUI agents as a recovery mechanism in RPA.

The rest of the paper is structured as follows. Section 2 introduces the background concepts related to GUI agents, GUI grounding, and Language Models. Section 3 describes the related work regarding current approaches to agentic process automation and the use of LLMs within RPA. Section 4 explains the proposed framework. Section 5 evaluates the approach and analyzes the results obtained. Section 6 discusses the limitations of the approach and spells out future directions. Finally, Sect. 7 concludes the paper.

2 Background

This section covers key concepts necessary to understand this contribution, based on language models for interpreting visual and textual data, AI agents, GUI agents, GUI grounding , as well as the usage of AI within modern automation.

LLMs have emerged as powerful tools for natural language understanding and generation. A specific subtype of LLMs is vision-language models (VLMs), which combine the textual capabilities of LLMs while also accepting visual data as inputs. This allows VLMs to process and generate descriptions of images by combining visual and linguistic information. VLMs, such as CLIP [13] and BLIP [10], are designed to bridge the gap between visual and textual modalities. These models can generate detailed descriptions of images, making them suitable for applications such as image captioning and visual question answering.

In the context of modern automation approaches, contrary to rule-based automation such as RPA, technologies such as APA have emerged as a more flexible and capable automation approach, which puts at the center of its technology the figure of the AI agent, usually represened by an LLM [20]. APA has a set of characteristics which differentiate it from other automation approaches. More precisely, it is mostly based on the idea of *Intelligent Agents* [15]. An Intelligent Agent is an AI-based agent which interacts with an environment to achieve a given goal by iteratively perceiving, reasoning, and taking actions which leads it closer to the goal. Thus, APA relies on LLMs to transform their output into digital or physical actions [14]. These agents have been applied to many fields, including automation in computer use [19,20]. These specific implementations of AI agents, which aim to interact with a computer in a manner that resembles human-computer-like interaction, have been referred to in the literature with various different names, such as Web agents [9], Computer agents [3], or GUI agents [19]. These have slight differences; Web agents, for instance, are meant to only interact within a browser environment, while computer and GUI agents interact with the entire computer. The difference between the last two is that computer agents have access to system tools and external tools, while GUI agents directly interact with the graphical user interface, being the most similar to a human-computer interaction.

Furthermore, within GUI and Computer agents, the term *GUI grounding* is used to refer to the process of, given an action description (e.g. click on username input field) extracting the element and the coordinates on which the action must be executed. To that end, we find in the literature different approaches, some relying on fine-tuning VLM models, such as [19], while others rely on a combination of object detection, generating descriptions per UI element, and then using generalistic VLMs such as GPT4o to ground the target of the action, as in OmniParser [12].

3 Related Work

With the rise of LLMs and Agentic AI, APA has emerged as a novel approach to automate cognitive tasks as well as non-repetitive tasks, by leveraging the capabilities of LLMs to generate workflows [20,21], using code generated by these models as the main artifact of the automation. Other approaches mainly rely on the interaction between an LLM-based agent and a GUI to automate tasks, by receiving an instruction from the user, generating a plan, and executing it step by step. These systems can be divided into those that rely on structured UI information such as accessibility trees [5,9] and those which only rely on screenshots [4,19]. However, none of the aforementioned approaches consider existing automation technologies such as RPA as a complementary technology to APA.

Furthermore, while literature contains examples of leveraging LLMs within RPA systems to enhance their capabilities on document processing, classification, and information extraction [2,7,17], there is a lack of proposals to combine the rule-based nature of traditional RPA with the cognitive capabilities of agentic systems in a way that both can share the responsibility of executing the workflow.

Thus, to the best of our knowledge, our work presents the first hybrid proposal that leverages computer agents for executing part of the RPA process, i.e., the handling of UI-related exceptions.

4 Approach

To answer the research question, we propose integrating GUI Agents within RPA solutions by making them available to the orchestrator upon a UI-related exception that may occur. At a high level, our proposal is based on two main components. The first, and central point, would be GUI agent, responsible for analyzing the exception, planning the recovery steps, and finishing the activity in which the RPA robot has failed to do so. The second component would be the integration with a production-level RPA orchestrator (e.g., UIPath orchestrator). We propose to integrate the GUI agent as a fallback mechanism when the orchestrator detects that an RPA robot has failed due to UI-related interaction problems, rather than directly halting the execution. From a technical standpoint, while the GUI agent does not need to execute on the same machine as the automation, the integration component of our proposal would require it. In addition, it would require being able to input the actions provided by the GUI agent and taking screenshot after each action.

Figure 1 depicts in the form of a simplified sequence diagram the proposed integration of a GUI agent within an RPA system. More precisely, when a robot fails due to a UI-related exception (cf. Fig. 1 *M4*), the orchestrator must be responsible for triggering the recovery process by providing the GUI agent with: (1) a trace of the robot actions in the form of a UI log, (2) a short description of the task to perform, in terms of the currently ongoing process (e.g. user login), (3) a screenshot with the current state of the UI, (4) the error message given by the robot, (5) the currently focused window, and (6) a list of variables and values relevant to the process (e.g. clipboard content, username, password, etc.) (cf. Fig. 1 *M5*). The agent must then plan a series of steps to finish the provided task to later resume the robot execution (cf. Fig. 1 *M6*). After a plan is

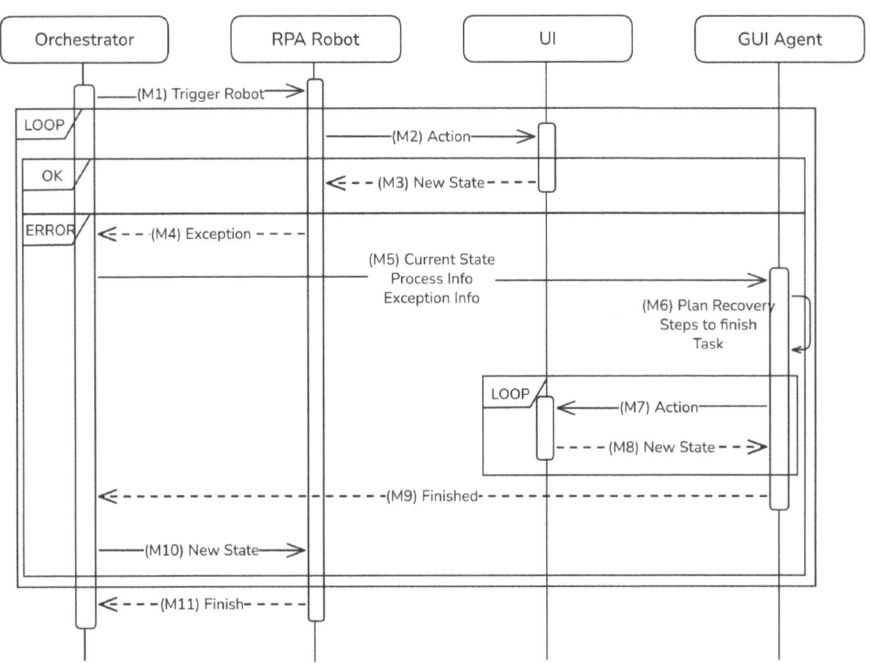

Fig. 1. Proposed integration of GUI agents within RPA systems.

proposed, the agent is provided the following information to ground the specific action, which is done for every step in the plan: (1) the task to perform, (2) full plan and plan reasoning, (3) the agent action history, alongside its result, (4) the current step in the plan (e.g. Focus the first name input), and (5) a screenshot corresponding to the current state of the UI. Then, similar to an RPA robot, the GUI agent executes actions and receives the new state of the UI for each step in the plan (cf. Fig. 1 *M7,8*). Finally, when the recovery plan is finished, a "Finish" message is sent to the orchestrator (cf. Fig. 1 M9), which must then continue the execution of the robot from the point corresponding to the next task, if any, or finish the execution.

5 Evaluation

Objective. The objective of this evaluation is to conduct a preliminary assessment of the proposed hybrid framework for runtime exception handling in RPA systems using GUI agents. Specifically, we aim to determine the feasibility and effectiveness of the agent in recovering from UI-related exceptions without explicit instructions from a human operator, thereby avoiding workflow interruption and human intervention.

Methodology. Given the early-stage nature of the artifact, a limited experimental evaluation approach is adopted. We simulate failure scenarios in a controlled environment, where the agent cannot directly interact with the UI, and assess the recovery capabilities of the agent via predefined inputs and expected outputs. Evaluation of plans is conducted by leveraging large language models (LLMs) to serve as judges [6], comparing them to ideal plans, while conversely, evaluation of actions is carried out by comparing expected click coordinates or written text to those given by the agent. Note that, for the purpose of evaluating each action individually, as well as overall accuracy, the agent is assumed to succeed in every action, thereby preventing error propagation between steps.

Response Variables. Therefore, to evaluate the quality of outputs by the agents, we leverage the following response variables:

- **Plan Completeness.** Indicates whether the agent-generated plan contains all necessary elements to resolve a problem, relative to a predefined ground-truth plan. It is measured as a percentage of the ground-truth plan steps indluded in the generated plan (e.g. A plan containing three out of five steps of the original plan would have a plan completeness of 60%).
- **Accuracy.** Percentage of actions correctly executed, which is measured relative to the executed action (e.g., coordinates falling within components on clicks, correct text typed within text inputs, etc.). It is measured as the percentage of actions which outcome is the expected one (e.g. The action click on username input must have its click coordinates within the username input field).

Evaluation Design. From the proposal described in Sect. 4, we designed a prototype available at[1]. For this implementation, we assume that the provided robot trace has been preprocessed to contain semantic descriptions of the actions performed, including elements interacted with during execution (e.g. click on username input field). Upon receiving the described information, we provide it to a planner, for which we used Qwen2.5 on its 32B-Instruct variant, alongside concrete instructions about how the plan must be constructed, and what constraints the generated steps must comply with (e.g. a *Type* step must be preceded by a *Click* step) and an example structured output. The planner must then respond with a set of steps to act upon on the screen to be able to finish the given task.

Then, for the action and element grounding of each of the steps in the plan, we leverage OmniParser [12], which returns the concrete action and action details, corresponding to one of the actions depicted in Table 1. We then evaluate according to a pre-established ground truth to calculate accuracy. In a real-world setting, these actions could then be executed via tools such as pyAutoGUI[2] or any alternative tool that supports performing actions via programmatic UI interaction.

[1] https://github.com/AntonioRodriguezRuiz/R2Agent-Prototype.

[2] https://github.com/asweigart/pyautogui.

Table 1. Agent allowed actions and evaluation method.

Action Type	Description	Evaluated Parameter
Mouse	RightClick	Click Coordinates
	LeftClick	Click Coordinates
	DoubleClick	Click Coordinates
	Scroll	Direction
Keyboard	Type	Typed text
	Press	Pressed key
Misc	Wait	–
	Finish	–

Test Scenarios. For the evaluation of the proposal, we designed two distinct synthetic scenarios in which a software robot has failed due to UI changes and dynamically rendered components, respectively. These failure conditions where chosen based on common UI failure points of RPA robots. Furthermore, each scenario is design with a different level of complexity in mind, meaning number of elements involved and number of interaction needed to recover from the failure. For each of these scenarios, we manually prepared the inputs defined in Sect. 4 for the proposed framework, as well as defined ground truth plans and action coordinates to verify the output of the agent. The designed scenarios, depicted in Fig. 2 with the corresponding UI changes highlighted, are as follows:

- **Failed Login.** We simulate a change in the UI flow that converts a login form into a 2 step form, by requiring the user to submit the username information before inputting the password, breaking the robot, which is not able to find the password input after typing the username. The objective of the agent in this scenario is to finish the user login process.
- **Client Registration.** Using the *RPA Challenge* platform[3], we simulate an scenario where the RPA robot fails registering a client due to the registration form being dinamically rendered, with inconsistant field order and positioning. The objective of the agent in this scenario is to finish the current user registation.

Evaluation Results. After conducting the evaluation, which involved running the two described scenarios through the implemented agentic system, we obtained the results depicted in Table 2, which shows, per scenario, the amount of ground-truth steps included in the plan, the accuracy of actions, and whether the recovery was successful or not.

We found that the GUI agent could identify, with the information provided, the correct path to solve both scenarios successfully, without being affected by the length of the solution. While in cases not optimal, introducing unnecessary

[3] https://rpachallenge.com/.

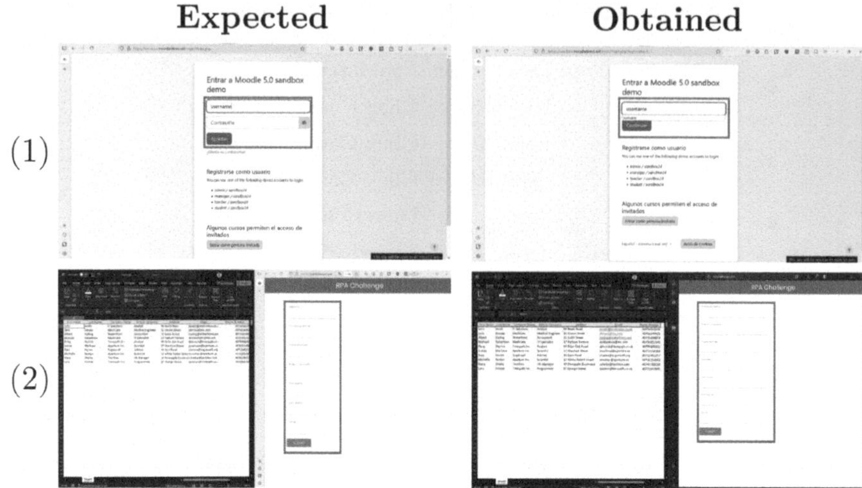

Fig. 2. Test Scenarios

Table 2. Evaluation Results.

Scenario	Plan Completeness (%)	Accuracy (%)	Succesful Recovery
User Login	100 (5/5)	100	✓
Client Registration	100 (15/15)	86.67	✗

Wait actions, or an additional *Click* to focus the browser window at the beginning of the plan, they were still valid to recover from the exception.

In contrast, only one of the scenarios was successfully resolved, due to found inaccuracies during the GUI grounding step with OmniParser [12]. These inaccuracies resulted in two of the eight click events in the executed plan targeting incorrect coordinates, not corresponding to the intended target UI element of the click action.

After analyzing the results, outputs and failure points during the evaluation, we found that AI agents can successfully be used for planning the recovery of a failed RPA robot after a raised UI-related exception. Conversely, while only one of the scenarios was successfully resolved, GUI grounding models and techniques were the primary source of failure during our evaluation, these are rapidly improving, with scores in ScreenSpot-Pro [11], the leading GUI benchmark, almost doubling in less than six months, going from roughly 20% [19] to almost 40% [12]. Thus, we argue that with future improvements, these systems will enable more precise GUI agents capable of solving more complex situations.

In response to the RQ: "*Can GUI agents be used to recover from UI-related exceptions from RPA robots?*", while technical challenges remain in the front of GUI grounding, we found that GUI agents can potentially be used to recover from UI-related exceptions from RPA robots by: (1) providing them with information about the current UI state, exception details, and task to complete, (2) generating a recovery plan, and (3) executing the actions in the plan.

6 Discussion, Limitations, and Future Work

6.1 Limitations

Although this work demonstrates the feasibility of agentic runtime recovery in RPA systems, several evaluation-related limitations must be acknowledged.

Only one agentic solution was implemented and tested (i.e., Omniparser [12]), chosen based on its open-source availability and sufficient capabilities for GUI grounding in our scenarios, achieving state-of-the-art performance according to the ScreenSpot-Pro benchmark [11]. Future work will design a solution-agnostic interface that allows easy integration of multiple agentic configurations through standardized connectors.

Evaluations were performed in a synthetic environment, which, while controlled, lacks real-world execution variabilities. However, all inputs provided (i.e., such as UI logs, screenshots, and process variables), are representative of real-world RPA execution data. Future work involves integrating the system into an operational RPA platform to evaluate recovery under real, forced exception conditions.

Moreover, only two synthetic test scenarios were used. Although they demonstrated the viability of the approach, this limits generalizability. Future evaluations should include a broader and more complex suite of failure cases to better assess the scalability and robustness of the system.

In addition, future work will aim to eliminate the possibility that the same UI-related exception occurs multiple times within a set timeframe, aiming to avoid the same exception to trigger a recovery plan twice. In this way, a mechanism will be designed to automatically apply corrections to robots after an exception has been correctly resolved, thus saving resources.

6.2 Open Challenges

While our results highlight the promise of GUI agents in runtime exception handling for RPA systems, several broader challenges must be addressed to enable real-world deployment.

A central technical challenge involves orchestrating execution control between RPA robots and GUI agents. Halting a robot mid-execution, safely handing over control to an agent, and resuming from a valid state introduces significant coordination complexities. Current RPA platforms are not designed inherently for third-party control during execution. Without robust control mechanisms, there is a risk of inconsistent states, duplicated actions, or workflow deadlocks. To mitigate these risks, future work should explore an execution checkpoint, transaction-safe interruption, and real-time verification of agent actions to ensure consistency with business logic.

Another critical challenge is managing the degree of freedom granted to GUI agents. Unlike rule-based automation, which follows scripted behavior within constrained environments [1], GUI agents operate dynamically and contextually [20]. This flexibility introduces the risk of interacting with unintended elements, triggering unrelated processes, or violating security policies –especially problematic in enterprise environments with strict compliance requirements. To ensure safe deployment, future research should define technical constraints on the agent's action space, balancing autonomy with safety and predictability.

Finally, beyond technical issues, social and organizational factors – particularly user trust– are crucial for adoption. Traditional RPA systems are transparent and deterministic, whereas agent-based recovery introduces autonomy and opacity. This can exacerbate concerns among users and stakeholders about control and reliability [16]. To address this, future systems should incorporate explainability mechanisms that present agent decision-making in a human-readable format, thereby fostering user trust and system acceptance.

7 Conclusions

In this paper, we presented a hybrid framework that proposes to integrate GUI agents [3,19] into the RPA lifecycle to address the issue of UI-related exceptions, by answering the research question (RQ): "*Can GUI agents be used to recover from UI-related exceptions from RPA robots?*". Through our approach, our goal is to bridge the gap between traditional RPA systems and emerging agentic approaches by proposing a runtime recovery mechanism that avoids automation disruptions caused by UI changes [8].

We propose a system in which the orchestrator activates a GUI agent upon an UI-related exception to realize this integration. The agent receives contextual data about the failed process, generates a recovery plan, grounds its actions using visual information, and executes those actions to restore the automation flow.

Our evaluation, based on two synthetic but representative scenarios, demonstrates the feasibility of the proposed approach. In both cases, the agent could construct recovery plans with full completeness. However, execution success varied due to limitations in GUI grounding accuracy [11], which affected one of the scenarios. These results support the viability of agentic recovery planning, while highlighting GUI grounding as the current bottleneck in achieving reliable end-to-end exception handling. Importantly, the evaluation demonstrates that agents can infer the intended process outcomes from contextual inputs and operate without human supervision, underscoring their potential to mitigating exceptions at runtime.

In conclusion, our framework illustrates a promising direction for augmenting RPA systems with cognitive capabilities using GUI agents. This hybrid approach maintains the efficiency of rule-based automation while improving flexibility and robustness. Future improvements in GUI grounding technologies are expected to further strengthen the reliability of agentic recovery systems, paving the way for intelligent self-healing automation pipelines in enterprise environments.

Acknowledgments. This research was supported by the EQUAVEL project PID2022-137646OB-C31, funded by MICIU/AEI/10.13039/501100011033 and by FEDER, UE.

Disclosure of Interests. The authors have no competing interests to declare that are relevant to the content of this article.

References

1. van der Aalst, W.M.P., Bichler, M., Heinzl, A.: Robotic process automation. Business Inf. Syst. Eng. **60**(4), 269–272 (2018). https://doi.org/10.1007/s12599-018-0542-4
2. Abdellaif, O.H., Hassan, A.N., Hamdi, A.: ERPA: efficient RPA model integrating OCR and LLMs for intelligent document processing. In: 2024 International Mobile, Intelligent, and Ubiquitous Computing Conference (MIUCC), pp. 295–300 (2024). https://doi.org/10.1109/MIUCC62295.2024.10783599
3. Agashe, S., Han, J., Gan, S., Yang, J., Li, A., Wang, X.E.: Agent s: an open agentic framework that uses computers like a human. In: NeurIPS 2024 Workshop on Open-World Agents (2024). https://openreview.net/forum?id=rnpjnH51Bz
4. Cheng, K., et al.: Seeclick: harnessing GUI grounding for advanced visual GUI agents. In: ICLR 2024 Workshop on Large Language Model (LLM) Agents (2024). https://openreview.net/forum?id=KZUH53BnIc
5. Deng, X., et al.: Mind2web: towards a generalist agent for the web. In: Advances in Neural Information Processing Systems (NeurIPS 2023). vol. 36, pp. 28091–28114. Curran Associates, Inc. (2023). https://proceedings.neurips.cc/paper_files/paper/2023/file/5950bf290a1570ea401bf98882128160-Paper-Datasets_and_Benchmarks.pdf
6. Gu, J., et al.: A survey on LLM-as-a-judge (2025). https://arxiv.org/abs/2411.15594
7. Ilagan, J.R., Ilagan, J.B., Basallo, C.L., Alabastro, Z.M.: Exploratory prompting of large language models to act as co-pilots for augmenting business process work in document classification. Procedia Comput. Sci. **237**, 420–425 (2024). https://doi.org/10.1016/j.procs.2024.05.123, international Conference on Industry Sciences and Computer Science Innovation
8. Kurowski, K., Martínez-Rojas, A., Reijers, H.A.: Control and monitoring of software robots: what can academia and industry learn from each other? In: Research Challenges in Information Science, pp. 56–64. Springer Nature Switzerland, Cham (2024). https://doi.org/10.1016/j.procs.2024.05.123
9. Lai, H., et al.: Autowebglm: a large language model-based web navigating agent. In: Proceedings of the 30th ACM SIGKDD Conference on Knowledge Discovery and Data Mining, pp. 5295–5306 (2024). https://doi.org/10.1145/3637528.3671620
10. Li, J., Li, D., Xiong, C., Hoi, S.: Blip: bootstrapping language-image pre-training for unified vision-language understanding and generation. In: Proceedings of the 39th International Conference on Machine Learning. Proceedings of Machine Learning Research, vol. 162, pp. 12888–12900. PMLR (2022). https://proceedings.mlr.press/v162/li22n.html
11. Li, K., et al.: Screenspot-pro: GUI grounding for professional high-resolution computer use. In: Workshop on Reasoning and Planning for Large Language Models (2025). https://openreview.net/forum?id=XaKNDIAHas

12. Lu, Y., Yang, J., Shen, Y., Awadallah, A.: Omniparser for pure vision based GUI agent (2024). https://arxiv.org/abs/2408.00203
13. Radford, A., et al.: Learning transferable visual models from natural language supervision. In: Proceedings of the 38th International Conference on Machine Learning. Proceedings of Machine Learning Research, vol. 139, pp. 8748–8763. PMLR (2021). https://proceedings.mlr.press/v139/radford21a.html
14. Reed, S., et al.: A generalist agent. Trans. Mach. Learn. Res. (2022). https://openreview.net/forum?id=1ikK0kHjvj
15. Russell, S.J., Norvig, P.: Artificial intelligence: a modern approach, Global Edn. 4e. Pearson (2021)
16. del Río Ortega, A., Marrella, A., Reijers, H.A., Wilde, A.G.: Improving trust between humans and software robots in robotic process automation: report from dagstuhl seminar 24292. Tech. rep. (2025). https://eprints.soton.ac.uk/498655/
17. Siderska, J., Aini, S.N.B.M., Kedziora, D.: Complementing robotic process automation with generative artificial intelligence (chatgpt), case of robocorp. In: Advances in Information and Communication, pp. 37–53. Springer Nature Switzerland, Cham (2024). https://doi.org/10.1007/978-3-031-53960-2_4
18. Syed, R., et al.: Robotic process automation: contemporary themes and challenges. Comput. Ind. **115**, 103162 (2020). https://doi.org/10.1016/j.compind.2019.103162
19. Wu, Z., et al.: Os-atlas: Foundation action model for generalist GUI agents. In: The Thirteenth International Conference on Learning Representations (2025). https://openreview.net/forum?id=n9PDaFNi8t
20. Ye, Y., et al.: Proagent: from robotic process automation to agentic process automation. arXiv preprint arXiv:2311.10751 (2023). https://doi.org/10.48550/arXiv.2311.10751
21. Zeng, Z., et al.: Flowmind: automatic workflow generation with LLMs. In: Proceedings of the Fourth ACM International Conference on AI in Finance, pp. 73–81. ICAIF '23, Association for Computing Machinery, New York (2023). https://doi.org/10.1145/3604237.3626908

Structured Evaluation of Robotic Process Automation (RPA) Tools

Romina Giaccio[1], Emilio Gerolami[1], Daniel Calegari[1](✉), and Andrea Delgado[2]

[1] Universidad ORT Uruguay, 11100 Montevideo, Uruguay
calegari@ort.edu.uy

[2] Instituto de Computación, Facultad de Ingeniería, Universidad de la República, Montevideo, Uruguay
adelgado@fing.edu.uy

Abstract. Robotic process automation (RPA) technologies enable the construction, execution, and management of "robots" that emulate human actions within an information system. Given the significant diversity of available RPA tools, selecting one can be a challenging task for organizations. A systematic approach and detailed evaluation, contextualized to the organizational environment in which the tool will be used, can significantly improve the selection process. In this paper, we adapt and apply an evaluation methodology for RPA tools derived from an existing methodology for evaluating Business Process Management Systems. The methodology proposes the selection and ranking of a set of characteristics of interest, supports exploratory screening, and facilitates both theoretical and practical assessment, thereby accommodating various evaluation strategies tailored to organizational needs. Its practical application is illustrated through a real-world study, in which we performed an exploratory analysis on an initial list of 30 commercial RPA tools, and then a theoretical evaluation of the two most suitable for the client's environment. Results demonstrate that the methodology can rapidly focus attention on the most promising RPA tools.

Keywords: robotic process automation · tool evaluation · methodology · software selection

1 Introduction

Hyperautomation is the application of advanced technologies, such as artificial intelligence, business process management, and low-code/no-code applications, to automate processes and significantly impact operational efficiency [10]. Its rise began with Robotic Process Automation (RPA), which allows the construction, execution, and management of "robots" that emulate human actions carried out in an information system [17]. They can automatically perform various actions, such as interpreting the content of a screen, interacting with it, and navigating

I. van de Weerd et al. (Eds.): BPM 2025 Workshops, LNBIP 569, pp. 139–154, 2026.
https://doi.org/10.1007/978-3-032-13426-4_11

complex logical actions through multiple systems. There is a significant diversity of RPA tools [8], with varying levels of functionality and support. Therefore, selecting one for use requires a detailed evaluation of its capabilities, contextualized within the organizational environment in which it will be used.

In previous works [4,6], we have defined a methodology for systematically evaluating Business Process Management Systems (BPMS) in consideration of the specific needs of each organization. Our approach involves identifying key features relevant to this type of system and a process that guides the evaluation of these features. Much of the evaluation process is tool-agnostic, and its inherent flexibility enables its application in other contexts. Thus, the methodology could be adapted to the specific characteristics of RPA tools.

In this paper, we present a methodology for evaluating RPA tools with an emphasis on organizational alignment. The methodology builds on the original BPMS evaluation methodology, systematically incorporating insights from diverse evaluation approaches to ensure both rigor and flexibility in the RPA context. It offers a straightforward process for prioritizing and filtering criteria, balancing exploratory, theoretical, and practical analyses, and includes reusable templates for test-case design and scoring. We illustrate its application through an exploratory study and theoretical evaluation of an initial set of 30 RPA tools.

The rest of this paper is organized as follows. In Sect. 2, we analyze existing evaluation methodologies. In Sect. 3, we propose an update to the former BPMS evaluation methodology. In Sect. 4, we present a survey of existing RPA tools and their main features for evaluation. Then, in Sect. 5, we present an example application of the methodology. In Sect. 6 we describe lessons learned, and in Sect. 7 we present some conclusions and future work.

2 Evaluation Methodologies

Several commercial off-the-shelf (COTS) selection methods were evaluated in [4]. DESMET decomposes decisions into hierarchical objectives and assigns weights through pairwise comparisons [13]; RCPEP begins with a market survey, applies a requirements-compliance matrix, and conducts scenario-based practical tests to score products [12]; OpenBQR, tailored to open-source software, uses rapid quality filters, data normalization, and visual dashboards to reveal strengths and weaknesses [16]; T-Check follows the scientific method by formulating hypotheses, defining criteria, running controlled experiments, and interpreting results to confirm suitability [15]; a systematic literature review catalogs and contrasts existing COTS selection methods [14]; and TAES-COTS proceeds through preparation, candidate identification, initial and detailed evaluations (including qualitative and quantitative proof-of-concept), and a selection phase to ensure alignment with organizational goals and non-functional requirements [3].

Table 1 summarizes the analysis performed on various evaluation proposals, based on several interests extracted from [4]. It indicates whether each proposal employs a generic or specific methodology and whether it defines a concrete evaluation process, assigns distinct roles to participants, and enumerates the characteristics being assessed. It also checks for inclusion of non-functional requirements, a filtering mechanism, and the development of case studies, as well as whether qualitative and quantitative evaluation methods are integrated. Additionally, it considers whether metrics are defined for each criterion, as well as whether user requirements and historical data are taken into account.

Table 1. Tool evaluation methodologies comparison (extended from [4])

Aspect	Desmet [13]	RCPEP [12]	O-BQR [16]	T-Check [15]	COTS [14]	T-COTS [3]	Eulerich et al. [7]	Kim et al. [11]	Cernat et al. [5]	Axmann et al. [1]	Calegari et al. [4]
Specific method	✗	✗	✗	✗	✗	✗	✓	✓	✓	✓	✓
Evaluation process	✓	✓	✓	✓	✓	✓	✗	✗	✗	✗	✓
Roles	✓	✓	✗	✓	✓	✓	✓	✓	✗	✗	✓
List of character.	✗	✗	✓	✓	✓	✓	✓	✓	✗	✓	✓
Non-fun aspects	✓	✓	✓	✓	✓	✓	✓	✓	✗	✓	✓
Filtering	✓	✓	✓	✓	✓	✓	✗	✗	✓	✓	✓
Case study	✓	✗	✗	✗	✓	✓	✗	✓	✓	✓	✓
Qualitative eval.	✓	✓	✓	✓	✓	✓	✓	✓	✗	✓	✓
Quantitive eval.	✓	✓	✓	✓	✓	✓	✓	✓	✓	✓	✓
Evaluation metrics	✗	✗	✓	✓	✓	✓	✓	✓	✓	✓	✓
User requirements	✓	✓	✓	✓	✓	✓	✓	✓	✗	✗	✓
Historical data	✓	✗	✗	✓	✓	✓	✗	✗	✗	✗	✗

Most evaluation methodologies are designed to be broadly applicable to various types of software rather than tailored to a specific domain, allowing them to be easily adapted to different organizational needs. Nearly all traditional approaches define a formal evaluation process and assign clear roles and responsibilities. Many of these methodologies explicitly list features to be assessed, incorporate non-functional criteria, and employ both filtering mechanisms and case studies to ensure contextual relevance. Additionally, most traditional methods combine qualitative and quantitative techniques, often defining specific metrics for each evaluation criterion, accounting for end-user requirements, and—where applicable—leveraging historical data to inform decision-making.

In [4], we extended the previously proposed methodology [6] for evaluating BPMS, partially considering the previously analyzed methodologies. The evaluation is driven by a concrete process depicted in Fig. 1, which begins by updating a hierarchical structure of functional and non-functional characteristics of interest for assessment and evaluation, and selecting the tools to be used for assessment. Key features are prioritized by organizational needs, and test cases and a case study are defined. Tools are evaluated using both theoretical (documentation-based) and practical (execution-based) methods, with support levels classified as complete, partial, or none, and implementation types as native, customized, or integrated. Based on this, a quantitative score is calculated, and a unified case study complements it with a qualitative view.

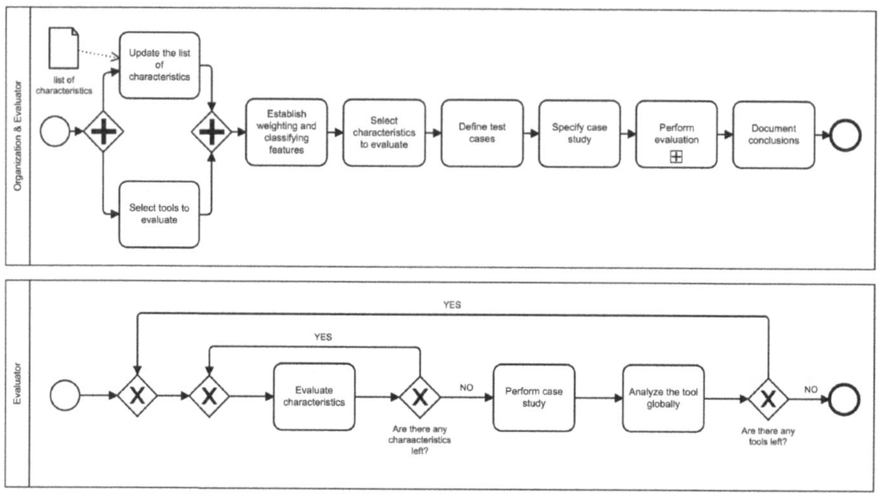

Fig. 1. BPMS evaluation methodology from [4]

There are also studies focused on evaluating RPA tools. One key contribution is the identification of inherent risks and challenges in RPA deployment [7]. The study highlights several critical weaknesses of RPA tools and hidden costs associated with maintenance and system updates, governance complexities that may hinder user productivity, and the loss of operational knowledge when manual procedures become overly reliant on automation without proper documentation. In [11], the authors approach RPA evaluation from the perspectives of adoption and selection. The study develops an evaluation breakdown structure using the Delphi method, engaging a panel of experts to refine evaluation criteria iteratively. Through statistical indicators, a stable and validated evaluation system emerges. The culmination of this process is a comprehensive table of selection criteria, serving as a structured guide for the successful implementation of RPA solutions. A related dimension explored in [5] involves the quality assurance of RPA tools through automated testing. It highlights the convergence between RPA and UI testing tools, with several RPA platforms. Finally, [1] presents a structured methodology for selecting RPA tools in three stages. First, it defines a set of selection criteria focusing on usability, programming requirements, price, integration capabilities, and reliability. These are tailored to favor tools that are accessible to non-programmers and offer scalable, secure automation. Next, a pairwise comparison method is used to assign weightings to the criteria, allowing organizations to prioritize factors according to project-specific needs. In the final step, each RPA tool is rated against these criteria, and a benefit-to-value is calculated to determine the most suitable option.

In summary, RPA-focused studies address specific aspects of tool evaluation but often overlook several key elements commonly found in traditional frameworks. While they acknowledge roles and include non-functional considerations, they frequently lack a fully articulated evaluation process, clear quantitative metrics, and integration of historical data. Moreover, some RPA methodologies do not consistently define case studies or user requirements, indicating that, although they offer valuable insights into RPA-specific challenges, they are less comprehensive in terms of structured, measurable evaluation compared to established COTS and generic software selection approaches. In contrast, the methodology proposed in [4] addresses these shortcomings by defining a detailed and reproducible evaluation process, structuring functional and non-functional characteristics hierarchically, incorporating both theoretical and practical assessments with weighted quantitative scores, and unified case studies. It allows for a more systematic, transparent, and adaptable evaluation framework that aligns with organizational priorities and supports informed decision-making. Nevertheless, certain elements, such as the characteristic hierarchy, must be extended and fine-tuned to capture RPA-specific concerns, ensuring the methodology remains equally effective beyond BPMS contexts.

3 Methodological Evaluation of RPA Tools

To develop a methodology for evaluating RPA tools, the BPMS evaluation methodology [4] was chosen as the starting point due to its flexibility and partial inclusion of previously analyzed methodologies. Through a comparative analysis, various aspects were reviewed to assess how the BPMS methodology could be adapted to the RPA context. Key findings indicated that while the BPMS process includes valuable components, such as a defined evaluation process, roles, characteristic lists, and case study integration, several adaptations are needed. For instance, functional and non-functional requirements should be reassessed for RPA, and the evaluation workflow must be clarified to accommodate multiple scenarios. Areas like quantitative metrics, filtering, and historical data reuse were also identified as needing refinement or integration.

As a result, we propose a focused adaptation to align the methodology with the specific needs of RPA tool evaluation. The revised approach retains the original proposal and introduces more precise and explicit definitions of several aspects that were formerly implicit. In particular, the process introduces stages for defining the evaluation strategy, exploratory analysis using cut-off criteria to narrow the tool universe, and optional steps, such as performing a case study, which should become optional or vendor-driven to avoid unnecessary evaluation overhead. While the base framework for qualitative and quantitative evaluations, metrics, and user requirement handling is preserved, further enhancements in these areas were left for future work.

Figure 2 depicts the complete refined RPA tool evaluation methodology. It is structured into three main stages: *Initialization*, *Analysis*, and *Documentation*.

Each stage involves specific activities and decision points that guide the evaluation process (including the sub-process of evaluating the tools) from preparation to documenting results, supporting multiple usage scenarios. Additionally, the analysis can be carried out with or without a predefined set of tools.

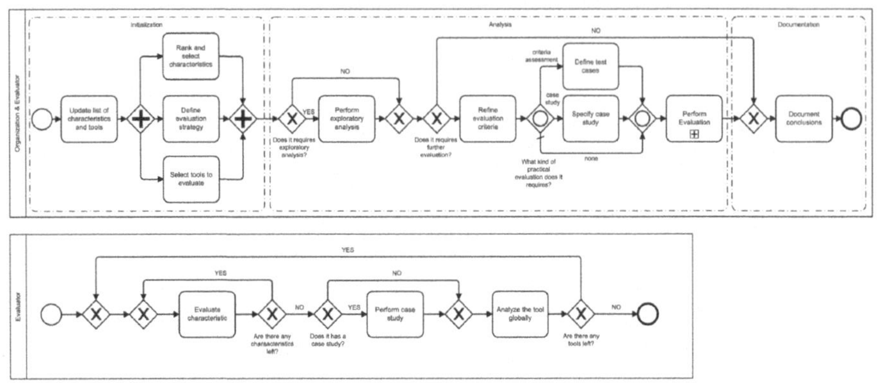

Fig. 2. RPA tool evaluation methodology

The process begins with **Update List of Characteristics and Tools**. This activity ensures that both the list of evaluation criteria and the inventory of available RPA tools are current and relevant. It is crucial when a significant amount of time has elapsed since the last evaluation or when new tools or technologies have emerged on the market. Next, the organization performs **Select Tools to Evaluate**. Here, a decision is made on whether to consider a specific subset of tools, already known or of interest, or to evaluate the complete set of available tools. Organizational priorities and the scope of the evaluation often guide this decision. In parallel, during the **Rank and Select Characteristics** activity, each evaluation criterion is assigned a priority level based on the organization's context and needs. These levels are: Mandatory, Medium Priority, Low Priority, and Not Considered. Special focus is placed on the definition of cut-off criteria, which represent essential, non-negotiable features a tool must support to remain in consideration. These criteria are usually related to the Priority-level criteria (or a subset of them) and can also be complemented with other criteria to inform. The organization also proceeds with the **Define Evaluation Strategy** activity. It outlines the evaluation scenario to be followed, establishes the method to be used for quantitative evaluation, and addresses how uncertainties, such as limited access to tools or incomplete information, will be handled.

Different evaluation scenarios are possible, ranging from quick exploratory analysis only, to detailed theoretical reviews, to hands-on theoretical – practical assessments with or without preliminary exploration, and optionally augmented by a case study for each tool. As an example, Fig. 3 depicts the activities performed during an exploratory analysis and theoretical assessment, as will be followed in the example evaluation of Sect. 5. These distinct scenarios add flexibility, aligning evaluation depth with organizational priorities and resource availability, ensuring a cost-effective yet comprehensive selection process. For instance, exploratory analysis enables rapid screening of a large tool set at minimal cost and effort, thereby focusing resources on the most promising candidates. Documentation-based theoretical analysis enables early risk and governance checks, eliminating the need for hands-on testing overhead. It also yields rigorous, repeatable metrics and qualitative insights when a deeper proof of concept is necessary. Finally, when a representative case study is included, it provides contextualized evidence of applicability in the organizational context, which can also involve vendors or third parties.

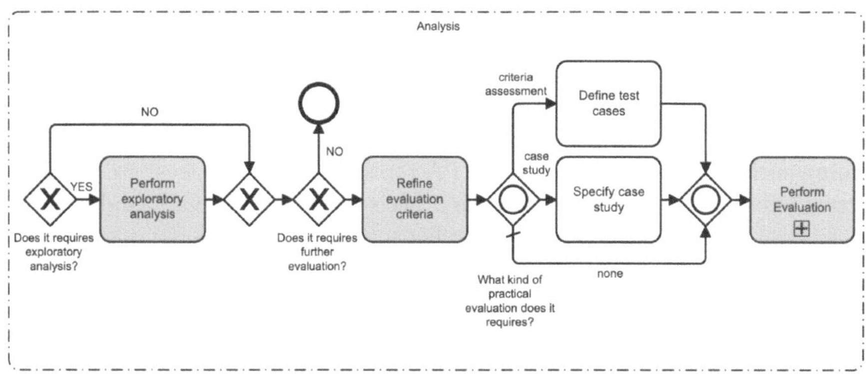

Fig. 3. RPA exploratory analysis and theoretical assessment activities

The next activity is to optionally **Perform Exploratory Analysis**. Tools are evaluated based on the defined cut-off criteria using the available data. This initial evaluation results in a classification of tools into levels of interest (from 0 to 3), which helps determine which tools are candidates for further analysis. The **Refine Evaluation Criteria** activity uses the results of the exploratory analysis or previous evaluations to fine-tune the evaluation criteria and the strategy for the theoretical – practical assessment. This customization allows the evaluation process to be more aligned with current project goals and constraints.

For practical evaluations, the organization must **Define Test Cases**. They are designed to evaluate whether specific tool features meet the required criteria. Cases from previous evaluations may be reused or adapted as necessary to save time and effort. When applicable, the **Specify Case Study** activity involves developing or adapting a real-world scenario relevant to the organization. It provides deeper insight into how each tool behaves in a realistic operational setting, serving as a complementary component to theoretical or practical evaluations.

The core activity of the process is **Perform Evaluation**. Each tool is evaluated either theoretically, based on documentation and secondary information, or practically, by running test cases. Functional characteristics are assessed using a support scale: Totally Supported, Partially Supported, or Not Supported. Additionally, the compliance level is recorded as Native (built-in), Particularization (custom development required), or Integration (a third-party component is needed). Non-functional criteria are evaluated separately using an appropriate method since the support scale does not apply. Each evaluated tool receives a weighted score based on the predefined importance of each criterion and the type of evaluation it undergoes. A unified case study may be used to complement the qualitative evaluation. As this activity is time-intensive, it is often outsourced to vendors or third parties, with findings presented in a workshop format.

Finally, in the **Document Conclusions** activity, the complete evaluation is formally documented. This documentation supports informed decision-making and serves as a reference for future evaluations of the tool.

4 RPA Tools and Evaluation Features

Our methodology is based on a comprehensive list of characteristics that assess the fulfillment of key technical and non-technical features in an RPA tool. For defining such a list, we searched for RPA tools in multiple stages, starting with Gartner's list of RPA tools[1], as well as other sources such as G2[2], and The Forrester Wave[3]. To ensure a more comprehensive list, an additional open internet search was performed. We found 70+ RPA tools. Moreover, to establish a realistic basis for comparison, a general assessment was conducted on the 16 most highly rated tools, including options such as Automation Anywhere, UiPath, Blue Prism, TrueBot, and Power Automate, among others. The analysis highlights a wide variety of RPA tools, each with distinct strengths and limitations. This superficial evaluation was conducted not to provide a comprehensive assessment of the tools, but rather as the basis for defining the evaluation criteria.

A comparison table was created based on the evaluation criteria identified in the RPA-focused studies mentioned in Sect. 2, the major assessment platforms, and insights from the highest-rated RPA tools. The evaluation criteria were progressively refined to form a comprehensive list. Its purpose is to guide organizations in selecting the most suitable RPA tool for their specific needs by allowing them to choose a relevant subset of criteria from the broader list. Complete information could be found in [9].

4.1 Key Features for RPA Tools

The final list of evaluation criteria is organized in four main categories according to the evaluation items proposed in [11]:

Customer Deployment Strategy. Includes technical and non-technical aspects, including economic feasibility, vendor capabilities, compliance with the organization's technology policy, and adherence to security policy.

[1] https://www.gartner.com/reviews/market/robotic-process-automation.

[2] https://www.g2.com/.

[3] https://www.forrester.com/research/.

Development and Operability. Includes elements such as robot management and operability, ease of automation development, and advanced technologies like AI, machine learning, and process mining.

Technical Architecture. Focuses on security and architectural standards, including local and cloud capabilities, as well as implementation standards.

Operation and Management Systems. Addresses the operation of automation processes, including operational models and monitoring support.

These categories are composed of evaluation criteria, some of which have been further refined into sub-criteria, as summarized in Table 2

Table 2. RPA Tool Evaluation Criteria (excerpt)

Category	Evaluation Item	Criteria
Customer Deployment Strategy	Economic Feasibility	Licensing and costs Pricing flexibility
		Return on investment
	Vendor Capabilities	Vendor maturity
		Product/service support
		Free/trial availability
		Tool documentation
		Supported languages
	Technology Policy Compliance	Hardware/software requirements
		System performance
		Product roadmap
		Automation methodology
	Security Policy Compliance	Data protection
		Identity/account management
Development and Operability	Robot Management and Operability	Scalability, reliability, customization Platform model, bot security
		Quality metrics and dashboard
		Robot orchestration and monitoring
		Availability and performance
		Multi-tenancy and maintainability
		Attended/unattended automation
	Automation Development and Convenience	API and integration support Command library
		Complex process automation
		GUI-based automation support
		Automation testing/debugging
		Workflow and component sharing
		Full/partial automation
	AI Integration and Expansion	AI/ML process mining
		Auto-NLP capabilities
Technical Architecture	Security Management	Confidentiality, integrity, risk assessment
		Application security, accountability
	System Architecture	Local/cloud support
		Virtualization (VMs, containers)
		High availability and disaster recovery
		Network and performance management
		Integration with internal systems
Operation and Management Systems	Automation Process Management	Governance, compliance Operational policies and scheduling
		Error handling, incident response

5 Example Evaluation

We applied the adapted methodology to evaluate several RPA tools within the framework of an evaluation project at our university. All materials generated during the evaluation can be found in [9].

5.1 Initialization

During the Initialization phase, we used the list of RPA tools gathered during the survey and the list of evaluation criteria developed as an outcome of this work (**Update List of Characteristics and Tools**). For reasons of time and scope, 30 tools were selected for evaluation, each with a rating above 4.4 stars in Gartner (**Select Tools to Evaluate**). As the evaluation strategy, it was decided to conduct an exploratory analysis and a theoretical assessment, covering the most critical elements (**Define Evaluation Strategy**). Since the organization is in a very early stage of evaluation, the focus was on quickly eliminating tools that didn't apply to the organizational context and on an initial approach to a couple of them to gain knowledge that could be transferred. For this reason, a practical or quantitative assessment was not performed. The activities considered are those highlighted in Fig. 3.

A set of evaluation criteria was defined as cut-off criteria, which allowed narrowing down the set of tools for more in-depth analysis (**Rank and Select Characteristics**), as shown in Table 3. The requirement column specifies the client's specific requirements. Some additional criteria were considered for reporting, such as the mechanism for defining bots, to provide an initial view of what each tool offers. However, these criteria were not mandatory for selection, as they could be used to refine the evaluation criteria.

5.2 Analysis

The analysis of the 30 RPA tools was conducted based on the defined criteria, gathering information from the providers' official websites, documentation, and videos (**Perform Exploratory Analysis**). Spreadsheets were filled with the information (they can be found in [9]), and as a result, we defined clusters according to the following priority scale:

Priority 0 (6 tools): These are tools that do not apply according to the evaluation interests, which includes tools that: (a) are unavailable, (b) have been discontinued, (c) cannot be used as standalone RPA tools (e.g., RPA is a module within a low-code development platform).

Priority 1 (10 tools): Tools with a low level of interest; they will not be considered for evaluation. These include tools that: (a) are cloud-exclusive (do not allow on-premise installation), (b) are immature (versions less than 2.0), (c) have minimal information to allow a proper evaluation, (d) require a Linux/UNIX environment or other fully proprietary environments (e.g., Oracle), (e) lack regional presence and are not rated by Gartner/Forrester.

riority 2 (9 tools) Tools with a medium level of interest; they could be considered for evaluation, including tools that: (a) are rated by Gartner/Forrester, yet lack sufficient information or regional presence, but are not limited to Microsoft environments or private cloud only, (b) have limited information or meet only some characteristics but have regional presence.

Priority 3 (5 tools): Tools with a high level of interest; they should be considered for evaluation since they meet the most relevant criteria.

Table 3. Considered cut-off criteria for exploratory analysis (results in [9])

Evaluation Items	Criteria	Sub-criteria	Requirement
Capabilities of solution suppliers	Supplier – client technical support system		Regional representation and support
	Available tool documentation		Complete documentation
Technology policy conformity	Hardware/software requirement		Microsoft environment
	System interaction and integration		PDF generation and email sending
Security policy conformity	Consistency with security architecture		LDAP authentication (Active Directory)
Automation process development and convenience	Application functions	Screen scraping	Support for VB 6.0 desktop apps and web apps (Edge/Chrome/Firefox)
Architecture	Local capabilities	Operating system	Windows
		Distributed installation	Local (1st priority)
		Local databases support	Oracle
	Cloud capabilities		On-premise (2nd priority)

As a result of this evaluation, the RPA tools with Priority 3 were: Automation Anywhere, Power Automate, UiPath, Rocketbot, and IBM Robotic Process. To conduct a more detailed evaluation, and given the scope of the work, two of the highest-priority tools were selected: Automation Anywhere and Power Automate. This decision was made because both meet the majority of the client organization's requirements. Although Power Automate is only partially on-premises, the client organization was considering its use, making its inclusion timely.

The evaluation criteria were refined in collaboration with the client, based on the prioritization carried out in the initial stages (**Refine Evaluation Criteria**). Both tools were subsequently theoretically evaluated (**Perform Evaluation**) based on their available official web documentation (further information can be found in [9]). The additional evaluation criteria are shown in Table 4. Since the evaluation was theoretical, the activities **Define Test Cases** and **Specify Case Study** were not performed. Details can be found in [9].

5.3 Documentation

Finally, the evaluation results were documented (**Document conclusions**). All tools that did not apply (Priority 0) were either unavailable or discontinued. Most tools considered of low and medium interest (Priority 1 and 2) were excluded due to the limited availability of information or accessible documentation. In some cases, they also lacked a Microsoft environment or were exclusively private cloud, despite some being rated by Gartner or having regional presence.

Regarding the evaluation of Automation Anywhere and Power Automate, it was observed that both tools satisfactorily meet the majority of the client organization's requirements, as determined through an exploratory analysis.

Table 4. Considered refined criteria for evaluation (excerpt; results in [9])

Evaluation Item	Criteria	Sub-criteria
Economic feasibility	Costs	Licences / Pricing
		RPA tool updates
		Technical support
Vendor capabilities	Free/trial availability	
	Robot management and operability	Robot management functions
		Strategies to scale the number of bots
		Real-time bot monitoring
		Exception management
		Automatic bot updates
	Access management for bot system entry	Protection of comm. between bots
		Self-healing: retry in case of failures
		Self-learning capability
		Scheduling & Load balancing
		Monitoring
Automation development and convenience	API and Other Integration	
	Bot design	
	Application functions	Basic activities (Variables, Write Line...)
		Application Interaction (Click, Type Into, Select Item, Take Screenshot...)
		API and Web Services
AI integration and expansion	AI/ML optimisations, process mining and scalability	
Automation process management	Operational management	Supports versioning
		Analytics & Dashboard

While both Power Automate and Automation Anywhere offer flexible solutions for mixed environments or legacy applications that may require alternative approaches, Power Automate provides more options for direct integrations with the Microsoft ecosystem. For example, regarding the ability of the tool to integrate with existing systems, such as PDF generation and email sending, both tools have similar components for email handling. However, for PDF generation, Power Automate has native PDF connectors and specific connectors, such as Adobe PDF Services. In contrast, Automation Anywhere does not have particular connectors but provides commands and functionalities to interact with third-party applications for PDF manipulation.

Another significant difference lies in representation: both tools have a global presence. In the case of Power Automate, as part of the Microsoft product suite, it has offices in Brazil, ensuring a solid presence. Meanwhile, Automation Anywhere does not have offices in Latin America but relies on its network of local representatives and collaborators to provide support and consultancy.

On the other hand, both solutions offer accessible documentation and free or trial versions to help users familiarize themselves with the platform. They are compatible with Windows and have limited support on Linux. The hardware requirements for Power Automate are slightly lower than those for Automation Anywhere. Regarding software requirements, Power Automate does not require a local database (cloud-based). Overall, the requirements for both tools are similar.

Both can be installed locally; however, in the case of Power Automate, a certain level of connection to Microsoft services is required, although it offers the option to use a secure connection via a Data Gateway. Despite its cloud options, Automation Anywhere requires local devices for bot execution. At the same time, Power Automate can be used fully in the cloud as long as on-premises resources are not needed. Both tools can operate with reduced capabilities without a permanent internet connection, but they require external services or an internal private network for advanced functionalities. In certain cases, it may be necessary to acquire additional licenses to access specific modules or features.

Neither provides a dedicated design tool, nor do they have native self-learning tools; however, both include AI/ML capabilities at an additional cost.

6 Lessons Learned and Roadmap

Regarding the exploratory analysis, the process of evaluating these RPA tools took longer than expected because the providers' websites are often oriented towards product marketing, making it difficult, in some cases, to obtain technical or detailed information. Many providers require direct contact to provide further details. The lack of access to full versions or trial environments limited the scope of practical evaluation; therefore, it is crucial to plan vendor engagement early and use standardized templates and checklists from the outset.

Identifying a minimal subset of cut-off criteria facilitates the primary selection of the candidate tools. Regarding previous experiences in BPM evaluation [4,6], these cut-off criteria are typically associated with aspects of licensing, support, and the existing IT environment, which are the least flexible within the organization. Reusable hierarchical criteria taxonomies and evaluation templates from the project can streamline this phase.

Price and licensing models vary significantly, making direct comparison challenging. Major platforms may meet most criteria, but can be unaffordable for small or medium-sized organizations. Collecting cost and licensing data in comparable formats early and evaluating scenarios that balance functional coverage with return on investment is essential [2]. Public documentation often lacks clarity; documenting assumptions and information gaps explicitly, and adopting confidence scales or value ranges, helps reflect uncertainty in scoring.

Exploratory and theoretical evaluations are necessary, but they are usually insufficient for decision-making. Based on previous experiences, it may be of interest to select a new subset of characteristics of interest and base the process on developing a Minimum Viable Product to verify the tool's suitability.

Several aspects could be considered in a roadmap for further improvements: integrate mechanisms to collect historical usage and performance data, enabling future iterations to adjust criteria and scores based on longitudinal evidence; develop automated test-case templates and dashboards to streamline data collection and result visualization, reducing manual effort; refine quantitative weighting methods (e.g., Analytic Hierarchy Process) for systematic cost – benefit trade-off analysis; and manage uncertainty explicitly (e.g., missing data), defining confidence levels for information and updating scores as new evidence emerges.

7 Conclusions

This paper presents a tailored methodology for evaluating RPA tools, helping organizations select the most suitable solution based on their specific needs. A comprehensive analysis was conducted to identify key vendors and compile a wide range of evaluation criteria, which were then refined into a flexible and adaptable evaluation template. The methodology was enhanced by incorporating insights from existing evaluation approaches.

A BPMS evaluation methodology was successfully adapted for the RPA domain, supporting multiple evaluation strategies, including exploratory, theoretical, and practical analyses, with optional case studies. The methodology was applied to a subset of tools using an exploratory-theoretical strategy, ultimately narrowing the comparison to Automation Anywhere and Power Automate.

Although the study demonstrated the applicability and value of the methodology, several areas for future improvement were identified, including enhancing the handling of uncertainty and incorporating advanced quantitative methods, such as the Analytic Hierarchy Process. Moreover, it could be helpful to validate the scalability and relevance of the evaluation criteria across broader contexts.

Acknowledgements. Partially supported by project "Minería de procesos con automatización robótica e IA generativa para el diseño y sostenibilidad de procesos colaborativos hiperconectados" funded by Comisión Sectorial de Investigación Científica (CSIC), Universidad de la República, Proy I+D 2024, "22520240100504UD", Uruguay.

References

1. Axmann, B., Harmoko, H.: Process and software selection for robotic process automation (RPA). Tehnički glasnik **16**(3), 412–419 (2022). https://doi.org/10.31803/tg-20220417182552
2. Axmann, B., Harmoko, H., Herm, L.V., Janiesch, C.: A framework of cost drivers for robotic process automation projects. In: BPM: Blockchain and Robotic Process Automation Forum, Proceedings, pp. 7–22. LNBIP, Springer, Cham (2021). https://doi.org/10.1007/978-3-030-85867-4_2
3. Basir, K., Khanum, A., Azam, F., Qavi, A.: TAES-COTS: thorough approach for evaluation & selection of COTS products. In: 12th Intelligent Conference on Frontiers of Information Technology, FIT, pp. 91–96. IEEE Comput. Soc. (2014). https://doi.org/10.1109/FIT.2014.26
4. Calegari, D., Delgado, A.: Systematic evaluation of business process management systems. CLEI Electron. J. **21**(2) (2018). https://doi.org/10.19153/cleiej.21.2.7
5. Cernat, M., Staicu, A.N., Stefanescu, A.: Towards automated testing of RPA implementations. In: Proceeding of the 11th ACM SIGSOFT Intelligent Workshop on Automating TEST Case Design, Selection, and Evaluation (2020). https://doi.org/10.1145/3412452.3423573
6. Delgado, A., Calegari, D., Milanese, P., Falcon, R., García, E.: A systematic approach for evaluating BPM systems: case studies on open source and proprietary tools. In: Open Source Systems: Adoption and Impact - 11th IFIP WG 2.13 Intelligent Conference, IFIP Advances in Information and Communication Technology, vol. 451, pp. 81–90. Springer (2015). https://doi.org/10.1007/978-3-319-17837-0_8
7. Eulerich, M., Waddoups, N., Wagener, M., Wood, D.A.: The dark side of robotic process automation (RPA): Understanding risks and challenges with RPA. Account. Horiz. **38**(2), 143–152 (2024). https://doi.org/10.2139/ssrn.4026996
8. Gartner: Gartner magic quadrant for robotic process automation (2024). https://www.gartner.com/en/documents/5656223
9. Gerolami, E., Giaccio, R., Calegari, D.: Systematic evaluation of robotic process automation (RPA) tools (2025). https://github.com/dcalegar/rpaevaluation
10. Jiménez-Ramírez, A.: Humans, processes and robots: a journey to hyperautomation. In: BPM: Blockchain and Robotic Process Automation Forum, Proceedings. LNBIP, vol. 428, pp. 3–6. Springer, Cham (2021). https://doi.org/10.1007/978-3-030-85867-4_1
11. Kim, S.H.: Development of evaluation criteria for robotic process automation (RPA) solution selection. Electronics **12**(4) (2023). https://doi.org/10.3390/electronics12040986
12. Lawlis, P.K., Mark, K.E., Thomas, D.A., Courtheyn, T.: A formal process for evaluating COTS software products. Computer **34**(5), 58–63 (2001). https://doi.org/10.1109/2.920613
13. Morera, D.: COTS evaluation using DESMET methodology & analytic hierarchy process (AHP). In: Product Focused Software Process Improvement, 4th Intelligent Conference, PROFES, Proceedings. LNCS, vol. 2559, pp. 485–493. Springer (2002). https://doi.org/10.1007/3-540-36209-6_40
14. Nabot, A.: Software component selection methods and techniques: a systematic review. Indonesian J. Electr. Eng. Comput. Sci. **33**(3), 1802–1811 (2024). https://doi.org/10.11591/ijeecs.v33.i3.pp1802-1811
15. SEI: T-check: Low-cost approach to technology evaluation. Technical Report 015-001, Software Engineering Institute, Carnegie Mellon University (2010)

16. Taibi, D., Lavazza, L., Morasca, S.: OpenBQR: a framework for the assessment of OSS. In: Feller, J., Fitzgerald, B., Scacchi, W., Sillitti, A. (eds.) OSS 2007. ITIFIP, vol. 234, pp. 173–186. Springer, Boston, MA (2007). https://doi.org/10.1007/978-0-387-72486-7_14
17. Taulli, T.: The robotic process automation handbook: a guide to implementing RPA systems. Springer (2020). https://doi.org/10.1007/978-1-4842-5729-6

From Chaos to Automation: Enabling the Use of Unstructured Data for Robotic Process Automation

Kelly Kurowski(✉), Xixi Lu, and Hajo A. Reijers

Utrecht University, Utrecht, The Netherlands
{k.kurowski,x.lu,h.a.reijers}@uu.nl

Abstract. The growing volume of unstructured data within organizations poses significant challenges for data analysis and process automation. Unstructured data, which lacks a predefined format, encompasses various forms such as emails, reports, and scans. It is estimated to constitute approximately 80% of enterprise data. Despite the valuable insights it can offer, extracting meaningful information from unstructured data is more complex compared to structured data. Robotic Process Automation (RPA) has gained popularity for automating repetitive tasks, improving efficiency, and reducing errors. However, RPA is traditionally reliant on structured data, limiting its application to processes involving unstructured documents. This study addresses this limitation by developing the UNstructured Document REtrieval SyStem (UNDRESS), a system that uses fuzzy regular expressions, techniques for natural language processing, and large language models to enable RPA platforms to effectively retrieve information from unstructured documents. The research involved the design and development of a prototype system, and its subsequent evaluation based on text extraction and information retrieval performance. The results demonstrate the effectiveness of UNDRESS in enhancing RPA capabilities for unstructured data, providing a significant advancement in the field. The findings suggest that this system could facilitate broader RPA adoption across processes traditionally hindered by unstructured data, thereby improving overall business process efficiency.

Keywords: RPA · LLM · Unstructured Data · Information Retrieval · Text Extraction

1 Introduction

Robotic Process Automation (RPA) automates repetitive, rule-based tasks by mimicking user interactions at the user interface (UI) level. This allows organizations to quickly improve efficiency and accuracy without altering underlying systems [6].

However, RPA is most effective when processes involve structured, predictable data [5]. In practice, many business documents—such as invoices—are unstructured or semi-structured (e.g., PDFs), making automated processing

I. van de Weerd et al. (Eds.): BPM 2025 Workshops, LNBIP 569, pp. 155–170, 2026.
https://doi.org/10.1007/978-3-032-13426-4_12

Fig. 1. Business-relevant documents, such as invoices, are often captured in unstructured or semi-structured formats (e.g., PDFs or images). Extracting key information like invoice number, total amount, and other essential data is crucial for completing business processes. This figure illustrates this problem using two examples of invoices from LabSC with the relevant information extracted.

difficult [24]. According to IBM, unstructured data now accounts for approximately 80% of all enterprise data [10]. Figure 1 shows an example where business-related documents, such as invoices, are often captured in unstructured or semi-structured formats (e.g., PDFs). Traditional recommendations to address this challenge emphasize the need for companies to ensure that their documents are well organized, structured, and digitally stored [5,7,22]. However, it can be argued that RPA platforms lack the necessary capabilities to effectively process unstructured documents, which limits their potential applications.

While Large Language Models (LLMs) offer strong capabilities for extracting information from unstructured texts, they are expensive to train, require substantial data, are prone to hallucinations, and pose sustainability concerns [11,23]. Sole reliance on LLMs is therefore not viable for many RPA use cases.

We present UNDRESS (UNstructured Document REtrieval SyStem), a framework composed of interchangeable components designed to enable RPA platforms to extract information from unstructured documents. While the individual techniques employed—fuzzy regular expressions, named entity recognition (NER), and LLMs—are well known, their integration in UNDRESS creates a novel and practical solution. Additionally, users can customize UNDRESS by adding their own components or replacing existing ones (e.g., using a different LLM model). Rather than optimizing individual components, our focus is on the overall performance of a pipeline composed of multiple interacting components. While particularly useful for many RPA use cases, UNDRESS is also applicable to a broader range of document processing and information extraction tasks.

We evaluate UNDRESS using two datasets and conduct interviews with RPA developers to validate its practical relevance. Our contribution is a hybrid, extensible system that enables RPA platforms to handle unstructured data more reliably and efficiently. More broadly, we argue that such a hybrid approach supports the development of more robust and sustainable RPA solutions, offers a promising direction for advancing Information Systems Engineering, and encourages the research community to incorporate simpler, more sustainable techniques when building practical systems.

The remainder of this paper is structured as follows: Sect. 2 presents the related work, providing an overview of existing information extraction techniques and approaches. Section 3 discusses the system design, including all its modules and components. Section 4 covers the evaluation of the developed system. In Sect. 5 we discuss interesting insights. Finally, Sect. 6 summarizes our key findings and makes recommendations for future work.

2 Related Work

RPA. Most existing RPA methods either assume that there are already structured tables available for RPA solutions to use or assume that there are semi-structured data, such as detailed logs regarding users' mouse clicks and keyboard inputs or form level input [8,15]. These methods then rely mostly on *rule-based* approaches to build bots and can not directly use unstructured data as input for building RPA bots.

Other works have been studying information retrieval in combination with RPA. They have applied RPA on datasets from specific domains like healthcare [21], finance [2,13], human resources [20], etc. These works use RPA as a helper tool for retrieving information. For example, they use RPA to monitor the emails and file systems of a particular company, make pre-defined *rules-based* decisions to determine whether the expected information has been found and selected in the extracted text, and download and analyze documents for scanned images. Such solution are data/case specific, as the rules of RPA are hardcoded. Additionally, they do not enhance the RPA technology itself but only use RPA to retrieve information.

Unstructured Data and Information Retrieval. Data within organizations exists in a wide range of digital formats, including CSV files, Excel spreadsheets, PDFs, emails, images, invoices, financial reports, and audio recordings, among others. This data generally falls into three primary categories: structured, semi-structured, and unstructured data [14]. Unstructured data includes items like emails, images, audio recordings, or PDFs that lack a consistent layout or identifiable elements. This type of data does not use key-value pairs, may include handwritten text, follows a free-flowing structure, and lacks uniformity [14].

The data extraction process varies for each category. Although numerous methods are available to extract valuable and useful information from data, no standard approach performs equally well across all scenarios [18].

Information extraction techniques are also highly dependent upon the type of document [26]. For instance, rule-based extraction methods are ineffective for unstructured documents, as the position of the data is neither predictable nor fixed, but they are very useful for structured data extraction tasks.

While AI-based approaches show potential in autonomously extracting valuable information from unstructured documents, they face challenges in handling diverse layouts. We have found that many studies rely solely on Optical Character Recognition (OCR) for text extraction, which is considered a template-based method due to its limitations in handling inconsistent document layouts [4,14]. It is also recommended to use preprocessing techniques before applying OCR to documents, especially when they are blurry and the text is not very readable. Some case studies even created predefined templates to extract information from documents [9,13] which makes the solution highly domain dependent.

To address this issue, there is a recommendation for adopting a template-free, AI-based model. Various document features, such as semantic relationships and positional connections between named entities, can be used to create such a model [4].

3 System Design

The system has two main modules: the *text extraction* and *information retrieval* modules, each with specific components.

The *text extraction* module includes the Preprocessing component, OCR Engine, Spell Checker, and OpenAI component. It takes an unstructured document as input and outputs extracted text for the next module.

The *information retrieval* module contains Fuzzy Regular Expression, Named Entity Recognition, and OpenAI components. It receives the extracted text and a user query to retrieve the requested information.

Figure 2 shows the system architecture. The following sections describe each component in execution order.

Preprocessing. To prepare the document for the OCR engine, we initially resize the file to enhance its resolution. Next, we apply a binary threshold to create a clear black and white image, ensuring optimal contrast. Following this, we employ morphological erosion to fill any gaps between letters, enhancing text continuity. Subsequently, we dilate the letters to prevent any distortion or blurring, thus ensuring legibility. Using cv2, the Python interface for OpenCV (the Open Source Computer Vision Library), we identify contours and create a mask around the text area to isolate it for further processing. Finally, we apply a filter to sharpen the image, enhancing the clarity of the text. With these preprocessing steps complete, the document is now ready to be passed onto the OCR Engine.

OCR Engine. The Tesseract-OCR Engine is utilized for optical character recognition through the pytesseract library, an OCR tool for python. Tesseract boasts an accuracy rate of approximately 94% for identifying numbers and 98% for identifying letters. The supported file extensions by the developed software include .pdf, .jpg, .jpeg, .img, .tif, and .png.

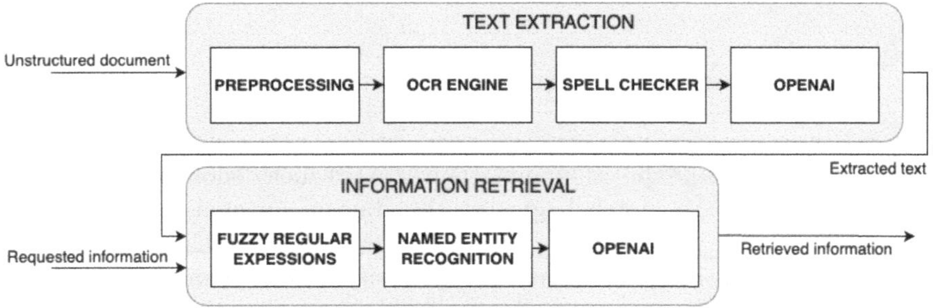

Fig. 2. System Design

The detect function from the Python langdetect library identifies the document's language, either Dutch or English, which helps improve OCR accuracy by specifying the language. This step is also essential for applying the spell checker algorithm to the text.

Spell Checker. We use the Python spell checker library to correct common OCR errors, such as confusing "l" with "i". Words starting with capital letters, often names, are excluded from correction to avoid misprocessing. The spell checker is too simple to handle these cases properly and returns "None", which is undesirable since we want to retain those names.

OpenAI Text Extraction. Finally, we use an OpenAI API Key to correct and format the extracted text. The model used is GPT-3.5-turbo-1106, which is a specific variant of the Generative Pre-trained Transformer (GPT) model developed by OpenAI. The prompt is formulated according to the best practices for prompt engineering with the OpenAI API [16], and is as follows:

```
prompt = f""" Correct spelling mistakes and format the following text below.
Text: "{text}" """
```

Fuzzy Regular Expressions. For information retrieval, we first let the program search for any fuzzy regular expressions (fuzzy RegEx) that match the user input of information to be retrieved. In this component, we focus on "static information", which is the simplest and easiest form of information to retrieve quickly, such as "e-mail address", "phone number" or "website", without the need for any document understanding. We formulated a total of nine expressions. In the code below, an example of a fuzzy RegEx of an e-mail address in Python is given.

```
fuzzy_regexes = {
    "e-mail": r"\b[A-Za-z0-9._%+-]+@[A-Za-z0-9.-]+\.[A-Z|a-z]{2,}\b"
}
```

Breaking down the expression, it starts with \b, which denotes a word boundary, ensuring that the match begins at the start of an email address. Next, [A-Za-z0-9._%+-]+ matches one or more occurrences of alphanumeric characters, dots, underscores, percentage signs, plus signs, or hyphens before the "@" symbol, which is a common pattern in email addresses. After the "@" symbol, [A-Za-z0-9.-]+ matches one or more occurrences of alphanumeric characters, dots, or hyphens, which represent the domain name. ṁatches a literal dot before the top-level domain, which can consist of two or more characters specified by [A-Z|a-z]{2,}. Finally, \b marks the end of the email address, ensuring that it is matched as a whole word.

This regular expression is fuzzy because it matches a wide range of e-mail formats, including those with varying characters and lengths, allowing it to identify addresses even with slight deviations from the standard pattern.

Named Entity Recognition. When a fuzzy RegEx match is not identified, the program proceeds with NER. This component mainly focuses on extracting information such as organizations, companies, persons, cities, places, etc.

We used the "nl_core_news_lg" model from the spaCy library, which boasts the highest named entity precision rate (0.79) among all the Dutch models offered by spaCy. Additionally, we used the "en_core_web_trf" model for English named entities, which also achieves the highest named entity precision rate (0.90) among the English models offered by spaCy.

OpenAI Information Retrieval. When no information is extracted or found by the NER component, we utilize an OpenAI API Key to retrieve the specific information that the user is seeking from the text. We generate the following prompt, adhering to the guidelines provided by OpenAI:

```
prompt = f"""Extract {user_input} from the following text below.
Text: "{text}" {user_input}: """
```

This component is the final part of the Information Retrieval module. By this point, all the information that the user wishes to extract should have been retrieved by the software, if it has not already been obtained by preceding components.

4 Evaluation Experiment

Our evaluation has three main objectives: first, to assess the text extraction module against the ground truth; second, to measure the information retrieval module's effectiveness on various fields (e.g., invoice amount, date) using accuracy, recall, and precision; and third, to explore practical applicability through interviews with five RPA developers. We tested the two modules separately on distinct datasets. Below, we describe the datasets, metrics, and results.

4.1 Datasets

We used two datasets containing unstructured documents for text extraction and information retrieval.

Real Invoices. The first dataset consists of 100 purchase invoices, all with very different layouts, from LabSC, a Dutch company specialized in comprehensive services for laboratory facilities and equipment. LabSC provides on-site inspections of fume hoods, maintenance for lab furniture, and consulting for laboratory setups and air handling systems.

Generated Resumes. The second dataset consists of 400 resumes generated by us using a Python script with the Reportlab and Faker libraries. Faker provides randomized names, addresses, and emails, while labels for these entities vary to reflect unstructured document practices. Document sections and titles are randomized in both position and naming (e.g., a section labeled "Skills" might appear as "Competencies", "Talents", "Skillset", or "Strengths"). Layouts and content vary, with the script choosing from 70 occupations, 50 work experiences, and 30 academic backgrounds to closely mimic unstructured document diversity. The script generates different PDF layouts with adjusted margins, randomly chosen title fonts and sizes, varied heading styles, and decorative horizontal lines for section separation. The script can be found in the `generate_fake_resumes.py` file in the `Data` folder.[1]

4.2 Evaluation Metrics

To evaluate the *text extraction* module for both datasets, we used the Jaccard Similarity Index, a quantitative metric that measures the ratio of common words to total unique words in the extracted set and ground-truth set. The closer the result is to 1, the more similar the two sets are. Each word has an equal weight in this metric, meaning that it does not consider content or semantic relationships. The metric is particularly suited for evaluating whether UNDRESS extracts all the text from the documents. For each document in the dataset, we compute the Jaccard Similarity Index and report the average over all the documents.

To determine the accuracy of the *information retrieval* module, first, we counted the total number of correct outputs—those that matched the ground truth from the document. Then, we computed the accuracy by dividing the

[1] https://github.com/Kelly-Kurowski/UnstructuredDataExtractionTool.

number of correct outputs by the total number of tested documents, which in this case was always 40.

We also report precision and recall for the *information retrieval* module, aiming to assess the system's efficacy in retrieving relevant information. Labels that were correctly retrieved and matched exactly one correct answer were classified as True Positives (TP). If a label is retrieved and returned multiple times, even if the label is included in the ground truth, only one of them was labeled TP, the rest were labeled as False Positives (FP). Additionally, if there was a single incorrect label extracted, it was also labeled as a False Positive (FP). Finally, if no match was found when there should have been information in the document, it was labeled as a False Negative (FN). We calculate Precision $= \frac{TP}{TP+FP}$, and Recall $= \frac{TP}{TP+FN}$.

4.3 Results – Text Extraction

Resumes. Because the resume dataset is artificially generated, it consists of text-based PDFs, allowing for the selection and copying of all text within them. We simply use the extract_text function from the Python pdfminder library to extract the text from each document and use them as our ground truth. Subsequently, we compared the ground truth text with the results obtained from our *text extraction* module using the Jaccard Similarity Index.

We experimented with various prompts in the GPT-3.5 model to determine which one yielded the best results. The first prompt yielded an average Jaccard Similarity Index of 0.90. We observed that 10% of the extracted text from our solution did not align with the original text due to additional symbols accompanying the words. For instance, the Text Extraction module included "satisfaction" in its set, while the PDF extractor included "satisfaction,".

For the second prompt, we removed "and format the following text below" leaving: "Correct spelling mistakes in the following text if there are any." The temperature was set to 0.1 for deterministic responses, favoring conservative corrections. This approach yielded an average Jaccard Similarity Index of 0.92.

For the third prompt, we added a negation, despite following the best OpenAI API prompt practices. The prompt reads: "Correct spelling mistakes in the following text if there are any; do NOT format the text". The third test did not yield a significant improvement, with an average score of 0.91, which was better than the first test but worse than the second.

Table 1 shows the OpenAI prompts with their respective scores. Finally, we used the prompt with the best avarage Jaccard Similarity Index in combination with standard NLP methods by applying tokenization and lemmatization. The resulting average Jaccard Similarity Index was 0.99, achieving a significantly higher score.

Invoices. The invoice dataset contains text in PDFs that is not selectable, preventing it from being copied. Consequently, the Python pdfminer library cannot be used to create the ground-truth sets, as it may not extract all the

Table 1. Results of OpenAI Prompts on Datasets

OpenAI Prompt	Average Jaccard Similarity Index	
	Resumes	Invoices
1) Correct spelling mistakes and format the following text below	0.90	0.69
2) Correct spelling mistakes in the following text if there are any	0.92	0.71
3) Correct spelling mistakes in the following text if there are any, do NOT format the text	0.91	0.71
4) Used Prompt (2) and applied the tokenization and lemmatization rules	0.99	0.81

text. To address this limitation, we utilized Adobe Acrobat Pro to recognize the non-selectable text. We verified manually if the text extracted by Adobe Acrobat Pro did not contain any mistakes.

We found that the extracted text sometimes confused certain letters; for instance, a "c" was mistaken for a "(" symbol. These errors were also corrected manually. We did this manual refinement on 100 documents to create the *ground-truth* texts.

After obtaining the ground-truth texts, we ran the exact same four tests as for the *Resumes* dataset. The prompt "Correct spelling mistakes in the following text if there are any" yielded an average Jaccard Similarity Index of 0.71. We also tested the prompts "Correct spelling mistakes and format the following text below" and "Correct spelling mistakes in the following text if there are any, do NOT format the text", this gave an Index of 0.69 and 0.71 respectively.

In the fourth test, we applied the same rules used for the resume dataset. Combining these rules with the second prompt (which had the highest Jaccard Similarity Index) improved the score to an average of 0.81.

In Table 1, the reader can find a concise overview of the four tests that were run with the specified prompt per dataset, excluding the mitigation of special symbols. Note that employing prompt engineering techniques could have led to even better results, but this was not the main objective of this research.

4.4 Results – Information Retrieval

Resumes. In the resume dataset, we extracted personal information as done in the works of Roopesh et al. [20], Barducci et al. [3], Wosiak [25] and Pudasaini et al. [17], such as the candidate's name, address, e-mail, and phone number. Furthermore, we were interested in identifying the candidate's educational background, (current) job position, known languages, and skills. The retrieval techniques chosen for each field are done in a sequential manner (i.e., first try Fuzzy regex, then NER, then LLM), as discussed in Sect. 3.

Table 2 lists the results for each field. The field "Name" achieved an accuracy score of 83%. The fields "Address", "E-mail", "Phone number" and "Language" each had a perfect score of 100%. Additionally, "Job title" demonstrated strong

Table 2. Accuracy, Precision, and Recall for the resume dataset

Field	Technique	Accuracy	Precision	Recall
Name	NER	0.83	0.83	1.00
Address	Fuzzy regex	1.00	1.00	1.00
E-mail	Fuzzy regex	1.00	1.00	1.00
Phone number	Fuzzy regex	1.00	1.00	1.00
Education	LLM	0.98	0.98	1.00
Hard skills	LLM	0.93	0.93	1.00
Soft skills	LLM	0.88	0.88	1.00
Job title	LLM	0.95	0.95	1.00
Language	NER	1.00	1.00	1.00

Table 3. Accuracy, Precision, and Recall for the invoice dataset

Field	Technique	Accuracy	Precision	Recall
Invoice number	LLM	0.90	0.90	1.00
Invoice date	Fuzzy regex	0.80	1.00	0.77
Total amount	Fuzzy regex	0.65	0.72	0.87
IBAN	Fuzzy regex	0.80	0.87	0.87
Seller	LLM	0.83	0.83	1.00

performance with a 95% accuracy score, and "Education", yielded an impressive 98% score. For skills, we considered "Soft skills" and "Hard skills" in the resume. The corresponding precision and recall for this dataset can be found in Table 2.

Invoices. For the invoice dataset, we took the intersection of the terms evaluated by Keturis et al. [12], Arslan [1], and Rohaime et al. [19], who also used an invoice dataset. This resulted in the terms "Invoice number", "Invoice date", and "Total amount". Additionally, we retrieved the international bank account number ("IBAN"), evaluated by Arslan [1], and the name of the company that sent the invoice ("Seller"), which was evaluated in the work of Kerutis et al. [12].

The extraction accuracy for various fields was measured across 40 documents. The field "Invoice number" achieved a 0.90 accuracy rate, while "Invoice date" was correctly extracted 0.80 of the time. The accuracy for "Total amount" stood at 0.65. The "IBAN" field was accurately identified 0.80 of the time, and the "Seller" field had an extraction accuracy of 0.83. The corresponding precision and recall can be found in Table 3. A comparison of our system components with other works in the context of RPA can be found in Table 5.

LLM Versus Fuzzy Regex and NER. We also compared the performance of LLM to the performance of Fuzzy Regex or NER, since it is possible to use the LLM component for each field. Figures 3 and 4 show the results for the *Resume* and *Invoice*, respectively. For most of the fields (e.g., Name, total amount, IBAN), LLM seems to outperform NER or Fuzzy regex. Interestingly, when the name of the field can be interpreted in different ways, LLM (Chat-GPT3.5) seems to be confused. In our case, when we ask to retrieve "Language", the LLM component retrieves the language of the document, instead of the languages that the candidates speak, achieving a significantly lower accuracy than NER. The user could use a different LLM model to potentially mitigate this specific error. Another observation worthy of mentioning may be that for the invoice date field, the Fuzzy Regex component achieves a higher precision (i.e., 1.00) than the LLM component (i.e., 0.89). It should be noted that the LLM component achieves a better recall (0.94 vs. 0.8).

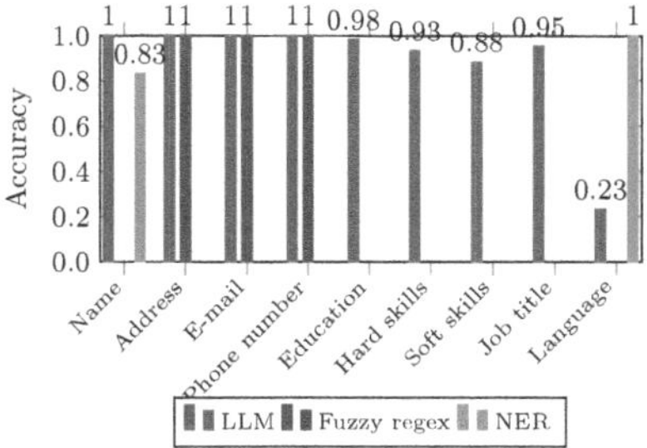

Fig. 3. Accuracy results per extraction method for resume fields

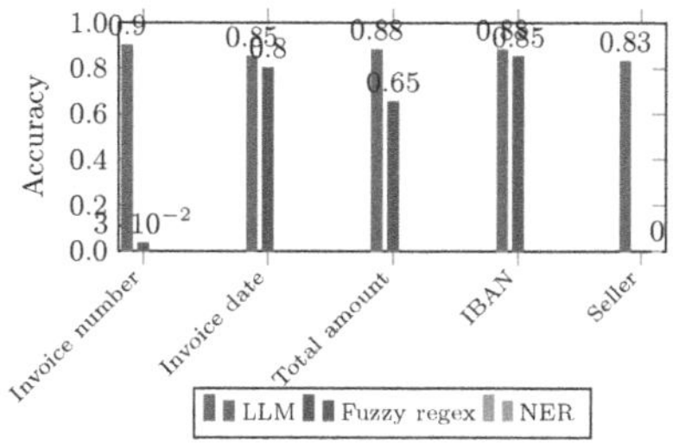

Fig. 4. Accuracy results per extraction method for invoice fields

4.5 Results – Qualitative Evaluation

The primary goal of the qualitative evaluation was to assess the value of UNDRESS for RPA developers in their work activities. To achieve this, we demonstrated the system to five RPA developers: three from a large academic hospital in Utrecht, the Netherlands, and two from an RPA consultancy in Amsterdam, the Netherlands. A concise overview of the developers and their work experience is provided in Table 4.

Table 4. RPA Developers

Developer	Organization	Experience (Years)
Developer 1	UMCU[a], Utrecht, the Netherlands	4
Developer 2	UMCU, Utrecht, the Netherlands	4
Developer 3	UMCU, Utrecht, the Netherlands	1
Developer 4	Tacstone[b], Amsterdam, the Netherlands	5
Developer 5	Tacstone, Amsterdam, the Netherlands	2

[a] *UMCU is a large academic hospital.* [b] *Tacstone is an RPA Consultancy.*

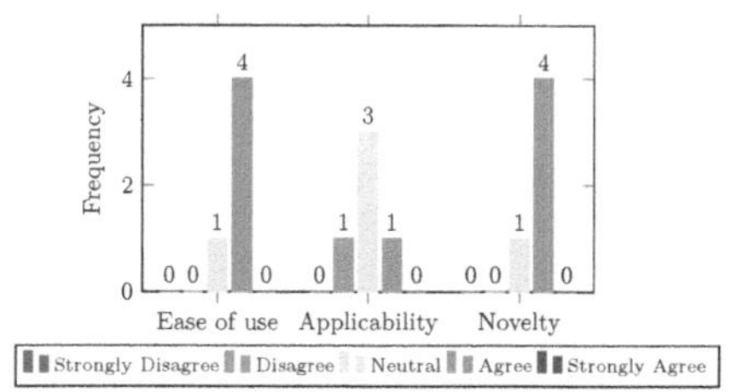

Fig. 5. Survey results for RPA Developers by statement

After the demo session, there was room for questions and an open discussion. Next, each developer was asked to fill in a 5-point rating scale (i.e., strongly disagree, disagree, neutral, agree, strongly agree) on the following statements, which focused on ease of use, applicability, and novelty:

1. The graphical user interface of UNDRESS is intuitive and easy to navigate *(Ease of use)*.
2. UNDRESS could be used to automate many more business processes than are currently possible *(Applicability)*.
3. UNDRESS is a significant addition to the current activities on RPA platforms *(Novelty)*.

Finally, we asked all developers why they provided the answers they did and what they would suggest for further improvement.

Figure 5 illustrates the results of the survey. Four developers found the system easy to navigate, while one developer had a neutral opinion. This developer suggested adding annotations to clarify the system's function and use of multiple arguments in the extraction field. The others mentioned that the errors and gray text in the field boxes are helpful for intuitive use.

Three out of five developers expressed a neutral opinion on the second statement. The developers highlighted the phrase "many more processes" from the statement, noting that several industrial solutions already facilitate information extraction from documents. One developer mentioned Klippa, a company that automates finance and compliance processes, focusing on unstructured documents such as invoices, IDs, and declarations, but not many more types of documents. A general tool for handling diverse unstructured documents across departments is still lacking. Most developers agreed that while information extraction is feasible through various industrial vendors, UNDRESS significantly simplifies the process.

Regarding the third statement, four out of five developers agreed that it is a valuable addition to current RPA platform activities. Two developers praised the sequence in which information is extracted, noting that it progresses from simpler methods (fuzzy regex and NER) to more complex ones (AI). They remarked, "Most solutions focus solely on AI, which can sometimes be unnecessarily complex when a label could be extracted more easily with regex. I find this solution very effective in that regard." One developer mentioned frustration with UiPath's Document Understanding library, noting that the AI sometimes complicates the process and makes it difficult to extract a label, when a simpler regular expression could achieve the exact same result more effectively.

Table 5. Text extraction and information retrieval: comparison of different works

		Text extraction				Information retrieval			
Work	Year	OCR	LLM-Extraction	Preprocessing	Spell Checker	Fuzzy	NER	LLM-Retrieval	Data set
UNDRESS	2024	✓	✓	✓	✓	✓	✓	✓	Invoice, resume
Kerutis et al. [12]	2022	✓	✗	✗	✗	✗	✗	✗	Invoice
Roopesh et al. [20]	2021	✓	✗	✗	✗	✗	✓	✗	Resume
Rohaime et al. [19]	2022	✓	✗	✓	✗	✗	✗	✗	Invoice

5 Discussion

In this section, we discuss the results and describe our insights into the performance of the system and its modules.

Our text extraction module demonstrated competitive performance compared to state-of-the-art solutions. For the resume dataset, it achieved a Jaccard

Similarity Index of 0.99, while for the invoice dataset, the score was 0.81. While Kerutis et al. [12] reported that 83% of invoices were processed correctly, the lack of clarity regarding their metric makes direct comparisons challenging. Our solution did outperform Kerutis et al. [12] on fields such as "Invoice number" (0.90 vs. 0.68) and "Seller field" (0.83 vs. 0.33). Rohaime et al. [19] achieved perfect scores for key invoice fields, but their dataset was more structured than ours.

Specific fields in the invoice dataset presented unique challenges. For instance, while our solution achieved perfect precision (1.00) for the "Invoice date" field, its accuracy (0.80) was lower due to variations in label alignment, such as when labels were top-aligned rather than left-aligned. Similarly, errors in the "IBAN" field (0.80 accuracy) often resulted from character misinterpretations, such as confusing "0" with "O". Additionally, multiple "Total amount" labels in some invoices led to the extraction of redundant values, highlighting a limitation of fuzzy regular expressions. These results demonstrate the *trade-offs in using different techniques* and underscore the need for *field-specific adjustments* to improve accuracy.

The performance difference between resume and invoice datasets likely stems from document characteristics. Resumes have fewer numerical values, making them simpler to extract, while invoices are more complex due to their heavy use of numbers, increasing the chance of extraction errors. Some invoices were scanned, introducing noise and blurriness, while the resume dataset was synthetically generated, ensuring cleaner input. Despite these challenges, the results are fair, as real-world resumes are typically well-readable.

Our approach demonstrates the *versatility* of combining LLM, fuzzy regular expressions, and NER. For instance, Fig. 3 illustrates that fuzzy regular expressions achieve accuracy comparable to LLMs for fields such as "Address", "Email", and "Phone number", while NER even outperforms the LLM in extracting specific fields, like "Language". This highlights that *a solution based solely on LLMs is not necessarily required.*

The use of LLMs and a spell checker algorithm was also a distinctive feature of our approach, enabling us to process datasets in two different languages. In addition, we are the first to use an LLM integrated hybrid approach in RPA context. The proposed system could benefit RPA by processing hundreds of documents automatically. Moreover, the retrieved information could be directly useful for real-life applications, such as automating financial reporting or streamlining HR processes.

However, LLMs introduced unique challenges. For instance, the OpenAI component often formatted text despite explicit prompts to avoid doing so, leading to inconsistencies. Interestingly, even when explicitly instructed not to format the text, there was no significant improvement, *indicating the difficulty of controlling the behavior of LLM.* By mitigating special symbols in the text, we achieved a 0.07 improvement in the Jaccard Similarity Index for the resume dataset and a 0.10 improvement for the invoice dataset. These findings also highlight the importance of *balancing LLM capabilities with simpler, more controllable methods to avoid unnecessary complexity.*

6 Conclusion

We developed and evaluated UNDRESS, a system that enables RPA to work effectively with unstructured documents. The architecture centers on two key components: text extraction and information retrieval. Our primary contribution lies in the novel integration of fuzzy regular expressions, NER, and LLMs. This hybrid approach outperforms methods focused on a single technique, particularly across diverse document types.

Whereas prior work often limits scope to a single domain—such as invoices, where regular expressions may suffice—we show that this does not generalize to other formats like resumes, which require more semantic interpretation, favoring NER. Our results validate the effectiveness of our method on both synthetic resume and invoice datasets, achieving perfect accuracy (1.00) for personal information (e.g., addresses, emails, phone numbers), and high scores for job titles (0.95), education (0.98), invoice numbers (0.90), and sellers (0.83).

Importantly, UNDRESS demonstrates that high accuracy is achievable without full reliance on LLMs, which are expensive to train, data-intensive, and environmentally burdensome. By combining simpler, interpretable methods with optional LLM components in a modular framework, our system offers a customizable, efficient, and sustainable solution for real-world RPA applications. With this work, we aim to demonstrate to the research community that LLMs are not the only viable path to high-performing document automation. Instead, based on the evaluation results, a balanced hybrid strategy can perform just as well.

A qualitative evaluation with RPA developers revealed that the system would significantly help them in their jobs by simplifying the extraction of information from unstructured data. The developers acknowledged that the system effectively simplifies the extraction of information from unstructured data. They appreciated the progression from simpler methods to more complex AI techniques, noting that UNDRESS avoids unnecessary complexity.

For future work, we propose enhancing label-entity alignment through spatial analysis, improving handling of duplicate or ambiguous labels, and refining the system's decision-making about which techniques to apply. The ability to seamlessly switch between methods—based on context or performance—underscores the strength of our hybrid design and opens up promising opportunities for further optimization.

Acknowledgement. We would like to thank Inge van de Weerd for her valuable contribution to the paper.

References

1. Arslan, H.: End to end invoice processing application based on key fields extraction. IEEE Access **10**, 78398–78413 (2022)

2. Baidya, A.: Document analysis and classification: a robotic process automation (RPA) and machine learning approach. In: 2021 4th International Conference on Information and Computer Technologies (ICICT), pp. 33–37 (2021)
3. Barducci, A., Iannaccone, S., La Gatta, V., Moscato, V., Sperlì, G., Zavota, S.: An end-to-end framework for information extraction from Italian resumes. Expert Syst. Appl. **210**, 118487 (2022)
4. Baviskar, D., Ahirrao, S., Potdar, V., Kotecha, K.: Efficient automated processing of the unstructured documents using artificial intelligence: a systematic literature review and future directions. IEEE Access **9**(9402739), 72894–72936 (2021)
5. Costa, D.S., Mamede, H.S., da Silva, M.M.: Robotic Process Automation (RPA) adoption: A systematic literature review. Eng. Manag. Prod. Ser. **14**, 1–12 (2022)
6. Doguc, O.: Robot Process Automation (RPA) and its future. In: Research Anthology on Cross-Disciplinary Designs and Applications of Automation, pp. 35–58. IGI Global (2022)
7. Enríquez, J.G., Jiménez-Ramírez, A., Domínguez-Mayo, F.J., García-García, J.A.: Robotic process automation: a scientific and industrial systematic mapping study. IEEE Access **8**, 39113–39129 (2020)
8. Gao, J., van Zelst, S.J., Lu, X., van der Aalst, W.M.P.: Automated Robotic Process Automation: A Self-Learning Approach. In: Panetto, H., Debruyne, C., Hepp, M., Lewis, D., Ardagna, C.A., Meersman, R. (eds.) OTM 2019. LNCS, vol. 11877, pp. 95–112. Springer, Cham (2019). https://doi.org/10.1007/978-3-030-33246-4_6
9. Gruzauskas, V., Ragavan, D.: Robotic Process Automation for document processing: a case study of a logistics service provider. J. Manag. **36**, 119–126 (2020)
10. IBM: Structured vs. unstructured data. https://www.ibm.com/blog/structured-vs-unstructured-data/ (2021). Accessed 5 Dec 2024
11. Kamath, U., Keenan, K., Somers, G., Sorenson, S.: LLM challenges and solutions. In: Large Language Models: A Deep Dive: Bridging Theory and Practice, pp. 219–274. Springer, Cham (2024). https://doi.org/10.1007/978-3-031-65647-7_6
12. Kerutis, V., Calneryte, D.: Intelligent invoice documents processing employing RPA technologies. In: International Conference on Information and Software Technologies. pp. 235–247. Springer, Cham (2022)
13. Ling, X., Gao, M., Wang, D.: Intelligent document processing based on RPA and machine learning. In: 2020 Chinese Automation Congress (CAC), pp. 1349–1353 (2020)
14. Major, A., Ngalamou, L.: Improving accuracy and efficiency in document handling for business processes. In: Lecture Notes in Networks and Systems, vol. 815 LNNS, pp. 543–562 (2023)
15. Martínez-Rojas, A., Rodríguez-Ruíz, A., Enríquez, J.G., Ramirez, A.J.: What's behind the screen? Unveiling UI hierarchies in process-related UI logs. In: BPM. Lecture Notes in Computer Science, vol. 14940, pp. 256–272. Springer, Cham (2024)
16. OpenAI: Best practices for prompt engineering with the OpenAI API (2024), https://help.openai.com/en/articles/6654000-best-practices-for-prompt-engineering-with-the-openai-api. Accessed 29 Nov 2024
17. Pudasaini, S., Shakya, S., Lamichhane, S., Adhikari, S., Tamang, A., Adhikari, S.: Application of NLP for information extraction from unstructured documents. In: Jeena Jacob, I., Gonzalez-Longatt, F., Kolandapalayam Shanmugam, S., Izonin, I. (eds.) Expert Clouds and Applications. Lecture Notes in Networks and Systems, vol. 209. Springer, Singapore (2022)

18. Pustulka, E., Hanne, T.: Text Mining Innovation for Business. In: Dornberger, R. (ed.) New Trends in Business Information Systems and Technology. SSDC, vol. 294, pp. 49–61. Springer, Cham (2021). https://doi.org/10.1007/978-3-030-48332-6_4
19. Rohaime, N., Abdul Razak, N., Thamrin, N., Shyan, C.: Integrated invoicing solution: A Robotic Process Automation with AI and OCR approach. In: 2022 IEEE 20th Student Conference on Research and Development (SCOReD), pp. 30–33 (2022)
20. Roopesh, N., Babu, C.: Robotic Process Automation for resume processing system. In: 2021 6th International Conference on Recent Trends on Electronics, Information, Communication and Technology (RTEICT). pp. 180–184 (2021)
21. Sreekrishna, M., Jacob, T.: Systematic mapping in improving the extraction of cancer pathology information using RPA orchestration. J. Int. Sci. Technol. **11**(4), 561–561 (2023)
22. Syed, R., et al.: Robotic Process Automation: Contemporary themes and challenges. Comput. Ind. **115**, 103162 (2020)
23. Vartziotis, T., et al.: Learn to code sustainably: an empirical study on LLM-based green code generation. arXiv preprint arXiv:2403.03344 (2024)
24. Wewerka, J., Dax, S., Reichert, M.: A user acceptance model for robotic process automation. In: 2020 IEEE 24th International Enterprise Distributed Object Computing Conference (EDOC), pp. 97–106 (2020)
25. Wosiak, A.: Automated extraction of information from Polish resume documents in the IT recruitment process. Procedia Comput. Sci. **192**, 2432–2439 (2021). Knowledge-Based and Intelligent Information & Engineering Systems: Proceedings of the 25th International Conference KES2021
26. Zaman, G., Mahdin, H., Hussain, K., Rahman, A.: Information extraction from semi and unstructured data sources: a systematic literature review. ICIC Express Lett. **14**(6), 593–603 (2020)

Towards an Actionable Development Method for Robotic Process Automation Using Process Mining

Alexander Skolik(✉)

Paderborn University, Warburgerstr. 100, 33100 Paderborn, Germany
alexander.skolik@uni-paderborn.de

Abstract. Developing Robotic Process Automation bots involves a wide range of skill sets. Besides insights from business process management, software development knowledge like systems interaction and network knowledge is required. For a well functioning process automation these different skill sets must be combined. In a design science research study, concepts from business process management, software development, and best practices are combined to design an actionable development method for RPA. The resulting PM2RPA method structures the development process in four stages: pre-Development, design, development and operations. Within these four stages, 14 activities support product owners, developers, and process experts over the course of the development process. The PM2RPA Method is demonstrated in an environment characterized by frequently changing business processes and heavy resource restrictions due to a lack of skilled workers. The PM2RPA method allows process-driven development while focusing on systems integration and reporting, resulting in a structured and comprehensive method for developing RPA bots. Practitioners can use this method to manage their automation projects. At the same time, researchers benefit from a baseline method aiming to address methodological research challenges and early insights into wider operational strategies for RPA.

Keywords: Process Automation · Robotic Process Automation · Process Mining · Business Process Management

1 Introduction

Robotic Process Automation (RPA) has become a major discipline of BPM within the past decade [25]. Besides knowledge of processes and systems, additional skill sets, like software development and project management, are required to develop and maintain RPA bots [20,32]. Especially with the latest trends aiming to establish operational support by utilizing business processes i.e., combining Process Mining (PM) and RPA, developing new implementation methods becomes more urgent [9,21]. The combination of the two technologies can lie the

I. van de Weerd et al. (Eds.): BPM 2025 Workshops, LNBIP 569, pp. 171–186, 2026.
https://doi.org/10.1007/978-3-032-13426-4_13

groundwork for assessing suitable RPA use cases and sustain the benefits provided by them [11]. Previously, the feasibility of this approach has been tested [11,34], but so far, only objectives for solutions have been verified [9]. Formal methods for the development and operations of RPA bots are currently lacking [32], especially considering the unique skills and tasks a development team must have for a successful RPA project.

This results in the research question: "How must a development method be designed to accommodate the skill and tasks needed for combining process mining and robotic process automation in a successful automation project?".

To answer this research question, a design science research study combining business process management research and best practices from software development is used to create a method called PM2RPA. It is demonstrated as a case study at a regional power grid provider as part of the demonstration phase. The findings from the demonstration are then discussed towards the objectives.

The PM2RPA method contains four phases with 14 activities that are conducted by three groups of stakeholders, leading to a structured, planable, and orchestrated way to implement RPA bots. The method aims to establish a structured approach to find automation worthy processes with process mining, leverages the gained insights to aid the development of the automation and place it in an operational environment. The presented method offers first insights into a formal development method, specifically tailored towards process mining and RPA. Practitioners can use this method to structure their development approach while still adhering to overarching process improvement guidelines like SixSigma.

The remainder of the paper is structured as follows. In the related work, the literature regarding RPA and PM is analyzed, as well as best practices like DevOps and SixSigma. After that, the application of the design science research process is explained and justified. In the results section, objectives for the method are established before the PM2RPA method is explained. After that, the method is demonstrated as an automation project within a regional power grid provider set in Germany. The method is then discussed in regarding the objectives in the discussion section. The outlook section concludes the paper.

2 Related Work

2.1 Process Mining and Automation

Process Automation is an integral part of business process management. RPA allows for a lightweight IT approach towards process automation [12,24]. For example, RPA enables gathering data across different software programs, transforming and transferring them in another system [29]. This means that rather than integrating different IT systems, RPA sits on top of them in a nonintrusive manner [28]. RPA can thus be implemented faster and more cost-effectively within its designed parameters [24,30]. Already existing interfaces are used by RPA within a company's software landscape, most often the graphical user interface [28]. RPA is thus a purely software-based solution that can only process digital in- and outputs [24]. It is also possible that application user interfaces like

REST APIs can connect to different systems [26]. This is especially true in the latest low- and no-code automation solutions [26,29]. Rather than automating end-to-end processes, recommendations indicate that only a few activities should be automated with RPA [37]. An RPA bot then utilizes modules with instructions for automation to act within an application in the information system landscape [13]. RPA works best when a medium amount of cases with just little to medium differences in their process occur [24,34]. This means that most cases have a similar structure, and it is economically viable to cover the differences within an automation [34].

PM can assist in finding and supporting use cases in the development process of RPA and further tracking the bot's performance [11]. PM takes event logs consisting of at least an unique identifier, activity, and time-stamp to understand the as-is execution of a process [15]. However, other attributes can be added to the event log and add more context to an activity [7]. A feasible way to define the life cycle of a PM project is the five stages L* life cycle model [15]. The final stage, called operational support, prescribes that combining process models, event logs, and current data makes it possible to support and intervene in ongoing processes within a company [15]. For an initial implementation of PM the PM^2 method can be used [35]. The method utilizes an initialization phase in which planning and data extraction is done to an iterative process, mine, and analyze data before evaluating it [35]. Their final activity is described as process improvement and support but also requires other competencies than the previous activities [35].

2.2 Software Development Approaches and Best Practices

Due to these changing requirements for RPA projects, related concepts, and best practices can also be considered when developing an actionable method. Agile Methods have already been proven to work with RPA [32], but further focus on software specif skill sets is needed. DevOps is one of the most commonly used software development frameworks [2]. The framework aims to combine development and operation to achieve a broader IT strategy [2]. Between development and operations, three ways can be identified [17]. The first way should enable a fast flow from developers to operations and customers [17]. The second way should enable quick feedback to the developers [17]. A trust culture should be enabled as the third way to support expiration and amplify feedback loops [17]. DevOps is thus suited for highly innovative environments [2]. Within DevOps, the CAMS principle describes that culture, automation, measurement, and sharing aid in the development process [14]. On the business process management side, Six Sigma has earned its place as a framework for process improvement [33]. Within Six Sigma, the DMAIC cycle has become a major problem-solving method for process improvement [5]. As part of the DMAIC cycle, a project is defined, and critical measurements are identified [5]. From this point on root causes are analyzed to improve processes [5]. Controlling is the last activity to sustain the changes made [5]. The DMAIC cycle should be used for empirical problems that are on a larger scale [6]. Creating an RPA bot thus requires different skill sets. From the BPM domain process, reengineering and automation skills are required [35]. From the software development domain, on the one hand, knowledge of system integration and interaction is needed [13,26]. On the other hand, "how to develop" methods like DevOps aid in the development process. Combining these different skill sets together is therefore required to establish a method that enables a structured development approach to RPA and addresses the need for formal methods outlined in ongoing research challenges [32].

3 Research Method

A method is a set of steps to perform a task [18]. Within each step, tasks and results are prepared and subsequently fulfilled [18]. March and Smith (1995) highlight that in system development, a representation of user needs must be turned into system requirements to create system specifications that can be implemented [18]. The goal of a method is to describe proper ways for gathering and analyzing evidence [18]. A proven paradigm to develop methods is design science research.

Figure 1 describes the application of the design science research process based on the design science research method [22]. Since the problem and motivation behind establishing an actionable development method are previously outlined [9,35], an objective-centered entry point is chosen.

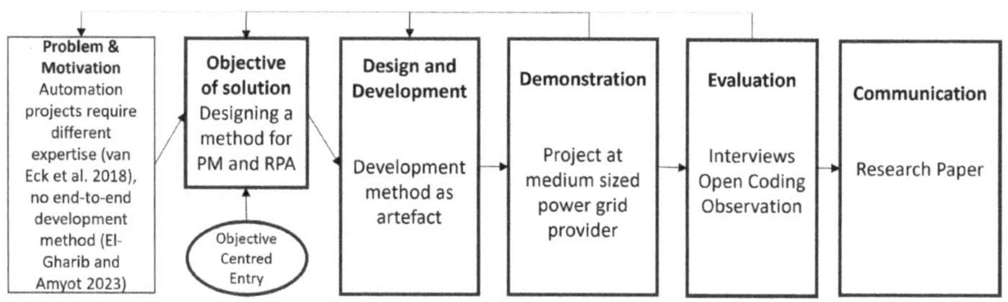

Fig. 1. Application of the Design Science Research Process

Following this entry point, objectives for the solution must be defined. The issues that these objectives must solve include cross-functional expertise in the development process and the need for an end-to-end development method. The objectives stem from related works and were developed with feedback from practitioners. These objectives are then used as an input for the design phase. As a result a method that fulfills these objectives as good as possible is designed. In this case related work and best practices were used to structure the method and derive what must be done in each stage. The method is then demonstrated in a fitting environment, before evaluation takes place. The demonstration was performed at a company that had previously done automation projects based on PM. These projects were structured following agile project management principles but did not follow a specific development method or framework. The project team consisted of two developers and three process experts, alongside a middle manager acting as the product owner. Besides the objectives, the evaluation also included semi-structured interviews from the members of the project team. After the evaluation changes to the objectives and the design can be made. Lastly, the findings are communicated towards researchers and practitioners.

4 Results

4.1 Research Objectives

Following the object-centric DSRM approach, from the extant literature, four objectives can be established that aid in formulating requirements.

Objective one address the lack of formal methods for implementing and adopting RPA especially in combination with PM [32]. Technical considerations specifically for RPA must be included in these methods [32]. Developing an method specific for RPA is thus the objective.

Objective two adds that specific knowledge is needed for process improvement [29,35]. Besides process knowledge, broader IT knowledge like systems integration and network connections are necessary to develop and implement RPA bots [29]. The method must therefore be able to capture and implement the associated knowledge for all development activities.

Objective three highlights the need for support early in development and monitoring once the RPA bot is deployed [9]. Measuring the impact of the interventions by the RPA bot is crucial for the success of automation projects [11]. To overcome this challenge the literature already identified connecting RPA with PM but also highlights that these two technologies were used separated from each other [9,25]. Combining the two technologies for scoping and monitoring tasks is the objective originating from objective three.

Objective four addresses the requirement for a structured development approach. While it is likely that the final artifact deviates from initially planned features and designs, a clear structure of requirements and features should be established [16]. Understanding the process and the underlying information systems should be improved [35] for example by using already developed artifacts like analysis in a PM system [15]. Including test and productive systems in the development is therefore required [17,29]. As an objective a coherent development structure should be part of the method, which allows the users to gradually improve the development of the RPA bots.

4.2 Development

Aligning the outlined theory with recommendations and best practices enables a multi-stage approach that can generally assist in development tasks [16,17,35]. Across the extant literature, four main stages can be identified [16,17,35]. The pre-development stage identifies tasks and systems relevant to automation and is aided by PM results. The design stage aims to structure the development and create a common understanding of what should be developed. The development stage separates the development tasks into test and productive environments. Once this stage concludes, the operations stage implements the developed artifact into the existing systems landscape. Figure 2 highlights the resulting development method PM2RPA.

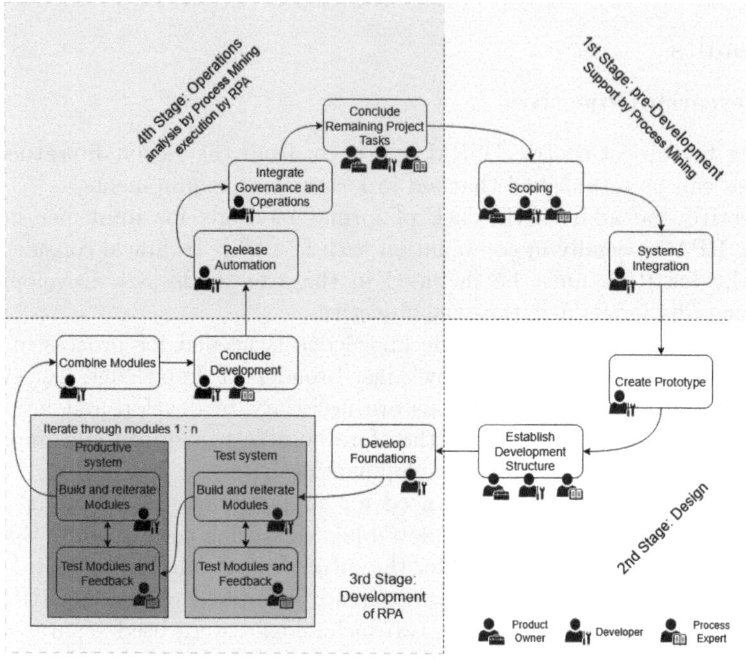

Fig. 2. PM2RPA Development Method

Besides these stages, roles must be established in the development process. The PM^2 method identifies process experts and process analysts as roles [35]. Process experts posses most of the process and domain-specific knowledge [35]. Common software development practices empathize on the different skill sets of developers and distinguish between their expertise [17]. Following agile principles, the developer's role is added to the method. The role also includes tasks similar to process analysts from the PM^2 method [1]. Additionally, it is recommended to have middle and top management support in PM and RPA tasks [27]. Therefore, the role of a product owner is taken from agile principles and should be characterized as someone who can convey the development project to the upper management [1] and prioritize projects.

The first task of the **pre-development stage** is to scope the activities that need to be automated. PM is an ideal technique for this as it gives insights into the as-is process that should be automated [15]. Identified sequences of processes can then be broken down further using, for example, the voice of the customer or requirements analysis to specify the requirements of the project [5,16]. This way, it is possible to gather quantitative data, i.e., key performance indicators (KPI) and monetary values, as well as quantitative insights, recommendations and wishes from the process experts. Similar tasks can be found across other methods and share the goal to identify, quantify, and scope the relevant tasks, data sources, and their nature as well as the involved systems [5,16,17,35]. The latter is especially important as most PM and automation (PM&A) tools at this point receive data as inputs. To allow operational support, the ability to perform actions which provide outputs must be established [15,21]. The scoping activity thus collects information on the process, requirements, and related data sources and systems. It structures them to generate a coherent list of what is needed in the development project as an output. In this activity, all roles take part as operational insights and strategic decisions are required. The insights generated from the scoping activity can then be used to set up and integrate the relevant systems for the automation to function. This can either be additional data from the previously implemented source systems or additional integrations into systems [35]. These implementations can be done directly in the PM&A tool using traditional process automation means [28] or lightweight ones like application programming interfaces (APIs) [26] or low- and no code tools [29]. The insights from the scoping activity are thus used as the inputs to fulfill this activity. As an output direct ways for communication between the PM&A system and the necessary source systems are established. While this is mainly the task of the developer, insights from the process experts on the behavior and rules within the source systems can aid in the integration process. This stage addresses objective three aiming for the utilization of Process and the recommendations of objective two regarding the inclusion multiple skill sets.

After gathering the requirements and setting up the necessary systems, the **design stage** can begin. During this stage the project scope and communication of project members should be cast into a unified development structure and coherent design goal. To do so, a way to make such innovative projects more reachable is the creation of a prototype [27,29]. A simple prototype enables a quick start to the project and highlights the initial value behind it [27]. A proof of concept can thus be delivered as well as a first check on the implemented source systems made [29]. From the initial requirements, more complex tasks can be derived as additional understanding of the interactions within the systems are made [3,27]. Creating such a prototype is up to the developer. As input, the existing requirements and system connections are taken and turned into a presentable prototype that serves as a base for further developments and discussions in later activities. The next activity is establishing a development structure. Structuring how the work is done, reported, and documented is recommended and key in agile project management [1]. One way to structure the work is setting up a design document that aims to gather everything that is learned over the course of the development [38]. The design document should incorporate the project members, a project overview, and the context of the project [38]. Goals and non-goals should be defined and the user impact described [38]. From these goals, milestones and modules can be derived [29,38]. Modules are defined as sequences of activities that should be automated together as they are influenced by each other [29]. The existing and potential solutions can then be defined as user stories and frame the flow of data and communication [38]. The impact of the project as well as the desired testing and validation strategies used later on [38]. The design document enables the incorporation of all relevant information of the design and development process. Therefore, all roles should be present when establishing the design document as it sets the baseline for the development stage. As an input for this activity the knowledge from the previous stages is combined into a single point of truth that incorporates the vision of the project and the structure to fulfill it. This stage highlights the objective one and four, as first and foremost it sets up an RPA specific development project utilizing PM. Furthermore a development structure that enables business process management guided tasks for software development is established.

The **development stage** follows with the activity that aims to establish the basic foundations and enable the development of the modules defined in the previous stage. Additional insights from by PM can aid in selecting and transforming data [35]. As a result, the complexity of the requirements can be reduced as internal and external data can be further identified [35]. Filters and business rules from PM can be transferred to automation and reused to match the identified cases [15]. It is recommended to combine analysis, requirements, and design before beginning with the actual development work [16]. Therefore, the tasks lie solely with the role of the developer. The activity turns the input of a theoretical development structure into a base for all developments that follow in the project. From this point on, development branches into the previously defined modules and iterates through them. Since the modules are independent of each other, work continues on another module once development is stuck on one. To do so each module iterates in the test system between the activities of "building and reiterating" and "testing and providing feedback". The symbiosis of these activities originates from methods native to DevOps like iterative development to include user feedback in the development process [17]. Verifying and validating the data with the original source systems is necessary to establish a functioning artifact [35]. Once a module is fully developed and tested, it can be placed in a live environment where final test and feedback iterations can take place. Especially when it comes to testing the artifact in a productive setting, feedback from end users should be taken seriously, as minor adjustments could maximize the value of the project [37]. After each module has been validated, they can be combined into the final automation, similar to the improvement and providing support activities in the PM^2 method [35]. As part of combining the modules, further tests should be made as well as set-ups for the rollout prepared [17]. Additionally, unfinished documentation should be concluded to provide a complete overview of the project. The roles of the developer and process experts are thus heavily used in these activities as the process expert provides feedback for the developer to act upon. This stage expands on objective one and four. Technical considerations specific for the development of RPA bots are included in this stage. Additionally, an outline of the development on the systems level is provided by highlighting a development pipeline from development to productive systems.

The final stage is the **operations stage** with the first activity to release the automation. This can be done in multiple deployment techniques like environment-based releases that select specific environments or canary environments that utilize user groups [17]. The developer is primarily responsible for this role. However, depending on the usage of scope, other roles and external parties might be involved in the release of the automation. As input, the release-ready automation is operationalized and made available to the users. Following the release, the automation should be incorporated into governance and operations aspects to manage and overview the automation. Additionally it might be useful to include support for change management in this stage. Compliance with the different company guidelines and existing laws should be included [35]. The developer also leads this activity, but depending on the relevancy of the automated activities, it might consist of external parties for compliance reasons. As input, the execution logs and assessments from the automation are taken and incorporated into fitting parts in operations and governance. The proposed method's final activity is to conclude all remaining tasks like documentation, assessments, and company-specific tasks like entries in company databases and documents. Therefore, all roles involved in the project are needed to conclude the development project. This stage goes back to objective two and three. Besides software development knowledge, governance and compliance aspects must be considered widening the required skillsets for a successful RPA development project. Monioring the impact of the intervention on the process is possible due to PM since any changes to the as-is process should be captured by the PM&A tool.

4.3 Demonstration

To demonstrate the PM2RPA method, a regional power grid provider in Germany is chosen. Many of these companies deal with multiple challenges in digitally transforming their processes. Most notably, a lack of skilled employees in the energy industry [4] as well IT-employees [23] clashes with constantly changing requirements from regulators for more sustainable power generation [10,31]. Furthermore, bi-yearly updated market guidelines and new market forms create competitive pressure for the power grid provides [19]. The challenges presented in this specific setting can thus be summarized as a heavily resource-limited environment with changing and evolving processes. The company implemented the PM&A software Celonis including the automation tool Make to optimize business processes. In a previous project, PM was used to analyze the meter-to-cash process, an industry-specific variant of lead-to-cash. The analysis revealed that KPIs regarding meters lacking valid readings significantly prolonged process throughput, disrupted invoicing, and consumed nearly half of an employee's working hours. Given the repetitive nature and medium case frequency of these tasks, they were identified as ideal candidates for automation [34]. Consequently, this project was selected to demonstrate the PM2RPA method. The project team included three process experts, two developers, and one product owner.

The pre-development phase began with an in-depth process analysis using PM. An as-is model was created to define the project frame, following the DMAIC Cycle from Six Sigma. Five areas for the digital transformation of the process were identified: automation for detecting and generating letters, along with reporting and documentation of unsolvable cases, enhanced process monitoring, reducing estimated meter readings and manual tasks, integrating the ERP system, mail system, documentation system, and Microsoft services, and incorporating standardized status texts and alerts. A connection table facilitated setup and integration, confirming ERP connectivity, mail system involvement, and direct letter provisioning. Microsoft services had been integrated in a previous project, and API setup was successfully tested.

The design phase started with developing a minimum viable product in Celonis, including a mock-up for case selection and processing status updates. Initial feedback highlighted the need for automatic status updates based on case events. The design document was then created, outlining the team composition, project context, and current solution. It detailed goals, non-goals, performance indicators, and user stories to guide solution implementation.

The development phase begins with the development of the foundations. In this case, the data had to be prepared. Furthermore, four modules could be derived from the design document that can be developed independently. A classification of meters with multiple estimates must be built. Actions to deal with these cases, like creating letters and alerts, must be developed. An overview for gathering and storing case information and a reporting structure must be established to keep track of the cases implemented. Each module is then developed and tested independently within the development or test system and the production system. In the case of the actions that should be handled with RPA bots, a trigger for each must first be developed. For example, once a meter is classified as multiple times estimated, a letter should automatically be created and sent to the mail services. To do so, the data must be queried from the source system, transformed into the matching format, placed inside the template, and sent to the printing folder for the mail services. Across these iterations, feedback regarding edge cases, usability, and data selection was gathered and implemented. If feedback on one module could not be collected, it was possible to develop another further, thus reducing downtime in the project. The different modules were then combined into the complete artifact and ready for release.

During the operations stage, a canary release strategy was chosen to ensure gradual adoption and minimize risks related to employee interactions. Performance monitoring was integrated using existing tracking modules, enabling long-term impact measurement. The KPIs regarding the workload for tracking the amount meters with multiple estimations dropped from a couple of hours to about 10 min per week. While the impact on the throughput time cannot yet be estimated, it is possible to reliably identify and track the amount of relevant meters fostering a data driven discussion culture. Additionally, governance measures included logging automation activities in the internal control system and risk management processes to ensure stability. The design document, established early on, was finalized as the official project documentation. The method thus enabled a cross-functional team to effectively work together, minimize downtime and lay the foundations for a wider automation strategy which empathizes long lasting process automation.

5 Evaluation and Discussion

The presented method considers multiple skill sets and disciplines. It aligns with the statements regarding the need for separate projects and areas of expertise [35] as well as an overarching deployment of PM and RPA beyond the development of the RPA bot [9]. For example, adding methods from project management is recommended as an area of expertise in BPM [36]. Given the objective centered entry point, these aspects correlate with objective two, which requires the inclusion of specific knowledge. This was also underlined by the developers, empathizing that gathering the right people with the right skills before the project improved the overall working atmosphere.

The categorization into pre-development, design, development, and operation stages suggests a definitive beginning and ending in the project. While this deviates from DevOps, it should be seen as the first stage, where each PM&A project works towards a collection of process optimizations that can be bundled into the operations stage. While these elements point to a DevOps-like software development method, they are closer to the recommendations outlined in the software development life cycle. Establishing a clear development approach thus addresses objective four. Furthermore, it can also be tied into the BPM life cycle [8]. Since the stages are similar to the process discovery, analysis, redesign, and implementation activities in the lifecycle, multiple overarching entry points for the PM2RPA method exist. The method can thus be integrated into a wide range of methods and strategies. Across all strategies, ongoing maintenance of the process optimizations is possible, but ultimately, it must be accommodated on a broader IT and business process management strategy. Additionally, a balance between a feature and value-driven perspective must be found when monitoring the results of an automation environment [11], increasing the importance of an overarching operations stage and strategy PM2RPA is thus a versatile method to aid the development of a wide range of preexisting digitalization and development strategies. Finding a balance between the analysis and automation stage is described by objective three and thus fulfilled by the method. The product owner expands on this topic by explaining how process mining enables a data driven discussion and allows the employees to suggest improvements to the identified issues.

Most of the activities are directly influenced by the previously presented disciplines. By combining the existing theoretical knowledge base with best practices, the PM2RPA method becomes more actionable for practitioners. Since the method was initially designed to work in environments with heavy resource restrictions, i.e., lack of employees, quality as a dimension is neglected. This could be solved by the introduction of quality gates, but could not be demonstrated within the chosen environment, as its introduction would tie more resources to the project. While this might be an issue later on, agile principles advocate for technical excellence throughout the development process [1], rendering the usage of quality gates a useful but ultimately not required addition.

Due to the guided emergence from BPM literature and best practices from software development, the PM2RPA method allows to capture the best of both worlds. It can be used directly after the PM^2 method to translate and expand on the learnings made. Due to the focus on preparing the source systems, skill sets regarding system integration are a cornerstone of the method and extend the required capabilities when transitioning from an process mining to a process automation project. DevOps in its core aims to tie the development and operations side together. Alongside other software development frameworks, these approaches lack the analytical capabilities for BPM projects, specifically required to fulfill BPM specific tasks like the process redesign. SixSigma as a general process improvement framework highlights the need to define the process and highlight root causes before improving on them. The PM2RPA method takes on these insights and gives a clear outline what can be analyzed from process mining and automated with RPA. The PM2RPA method thus brings it unique strengths in a nice fit along side established but more generic methods. In conjunction with the PM^2 method, it solves the skill set issue outlined by van Eck et al. (2015) while BPM specific tasks expand pure software development methods for the usage in RPA. Additionally, PM2RPA fits nicely into existing process improvement paradigms like SixSigma and the BPM life cycle as it can assist one or more of the associated stages there like analysis or improvement and offers support for controlling or monitoring. Furthermore, the specific activities also work well with the framework for implementing RPA as the activities can support the different stages of the framework [12].

The presented method thus adds to the existing knowledge base by providing a suitable method for the development of RPA bots, answering the research challenge, and outlining more methodic approaches towards RPA. It further highlights the need for an overarching orchestration of automation in an operational stage. Additionally, the PM2RPA method can add insights from PM into the development of RPA, thus providing a bridge between PM technologies and RPA. The development method can, therefore, be used when applying frameworks and similar artifacts in this context, i.e., the action-oriented PM framework [21]. Practitioners gain a structured way to develop their RPA bots and create the necessary measures to run and monitor them throughout the operations stage.

6 Outlook

The presented method answers the research question aiming to find which tasks and skills are needed for a successful RPA automation project. To do so the

PM2RPA method consists of 14 activities across four stages, each defining specific tasks and outputs. By leveraging PM insights, the method enables precise scoping and requirement definition for RPA bots. These requirements are visualized in a minimum viable product and structured in a design document, guiding the development process.

During development, a modular approach ensures system integration before the automation is deployed. The operational phase includes governance, performance monitoring, and change management, concluding with comprehensive project documentation. Long-term automation orchestration strategies should follow to ensure sustainability.

A regional energy provider successfully applied the method, demonstrating its effectiveness from process analysis to RPA operationalization. The method's advantages lie in its structured approach, early live integration, and suitability for resource-limited environments, enabling efficient role and task allocation. The company plans to adopt PM2RPA in future automation projects.

However, the method requires validation in environments with stable requirements and fewer resource constraints. While its adaptability is assumed, alternative evaluation criteria, such as quality focus or enhanced process analytics, should be explored. PM maturity is crucial, ensuring that real-time data informs scoping and monitoring activities.

Future research will address these limitations and extend the method to different industries and technologies like agentic automation. Researchers are encouraged to apply PM2RPA in various contexts. Additionally, further investigation into RPA operations is needed, as demographic shifts and labor shortages will drive increased automation. Strengthening the synergy between RPA and PM will be essential for developing frameworks that maximize their combined potential.

Acknowledgments. The author thanks the Enervie Vernetzt GmbH for their assistance and funding.

References

1. Manifesto for agile software development (2020). https://agilemanifesto.org/
2. Alt, R., Auth, G., Kögler, C.: Innovationsorientiertes IT-Management mit DevOps. In: Innovationsorientiertes IT-Management mit DevOps, pp. 21–32. Springer, Wiesbaden (2017). https://doi.org/10.1007/978-3-658-18704-0_3
3. Budde, R., Kautz, K., Kuhlenkamp, K., Züllighoven, H.: What is prototyping? Inf. Technol. & People **6**(2/3), 89–95 (1992). https://doi.org/10.1108/EUM0000000003546
4. Czako, V.: Employment in the energy sector: Status report 2020. JRC science for policy report, Publications Office of the European Union, Luxembourg (2020). https://doi.org/10.2760/95180
5. De Koning, H., De Mast, J.: A rational reconstruction of six-sigma's breakthrough cookbook. Int. J. Qual. & Reliab. Manag. **23**(7), 766–787 (2006)

6. de Mast, J., Lokkerbol, J.: An analysis of the six sigma dmaic method from the perspective of problem solving. Int. J. Prod. Econ. **139**(2), 604–614 (2012). https://doi.org/10.1016/j.ijpe.2012.05.035, compassionate Operations
7. Dumas, M., La Rosa, M., Mendling, J., Reijers, H.A.: Fundamentals of Business Process Management. Springer Berlin Heidelberg, Berlin, Heidelberg (2018). https://doi.org/10.1007/978-3-662-56509-4
8. Dumas, M., La Rosa, M., Mendling, J., Reijers, H.A.: Introduction to Business Process Management. In: Fundamentals of Business Process Management, pp. 1–33. Springer, Heidelberg (2018). https://doi.org/10.1007/978-3-662-56509-4_1
9. El-Gharib, N.M., Amyot, D.: Robotic process automation using process mining – a systematic literature review. Data & Knowl. Eng. **148**, 102229 (2023). https://doi.org/10.1016/j.datak.2023.102229
10. Ethington, J.: The energy industry wants to bounce back — all it needs is workers (2022). https://www.forbes.com/sites/forbesagencycouncil/2022/01/10/the-energy-industry-wants-to-bounce-back--all-it-needs-is-workers/?sh=50dc4855343b
11. Geyer-Klingeberg, J., Nakladal, J., Baldauf, F., Veit, F.: Process mining and robotic process automation: a perfect match. BPM (Dissertation/Demos/Industry) **2196**, 124–131 (2018)
12. Herm, L.V., Janiesch, C., Reijers, H.A., Seubert, F.: From symbolic rpa to intelligent rpa: Challenges for developing and operating intelligent software robots. In: Polyvyanyy, A., Wynn, M.T., Van Looy, A., Reichert, M. (eds.) Business Process Management. BPM 2021, pp. 289–305. Springer, Cham (2021). https://doi.org/10.1007/978-3-030-85469-0_19
13. Hofmann, P., Samp, C., Urbach, N.: Robotic process automation. Electron. Mark. **30**(1), 99–106 (2019). https://doi.org/10.1007/s12525-019-00365-8
14. Humble, J., Molesky, J.: Why enterprises must adopt devops to enable continuous delivery, vol. 24 (2011). https://www.researchgate.net/publication/298620122_Why_enterprises_must_adopt_devops_to_enable_continuous_delivery
15. van der Aalst, W., et al.: Process Mining Manifesto. In: Daniel, F., Barkaoui, K., Dustdar, S. (eds.) BPM 2011. LNBIP, vol. 99, pp. 169–194. Springer, Heidelberg (2012). https://doi.org/10.1007/978-3-642-28108-2_19
16. ISO/IEC JTC 1/SC 7 Software and systems engineering: Systems and software engineering — software life cycle processes (2017–11). https://www.iso.org/standard/63712.html
17. Kim, G., Humble, J., Debois, P., Willis, J., Forsgren, N.: The DevOps Handbook, Second Edition: How to Create World-Class Agility, Reliability, & Security in Technology Organizations. IT Revolution Press, Portland, OR, 2nd ed. edn. (2021). https://permalink.obvsg.at/
18. March, S.T., Smith, G.F.: Design and natural science research on information technology. Decis. Support Syst. **15**(4), 251–266 (1995). https://doi.org/10.1016/0167-9236(94)00041-2
19. Meletiou, A., Cambini, C., Masera, M.: Regulatory and ownership determinants of unbundling regime choice for European electricity transmission utilities. Utilities Policy **50**, 13–25 (2018). https://doi.org/10.1016/j.jup.2018.01.006
20. Noppen, P., Beerepoot, I., van de Weerd, I., Jonker, M., Reijers, H.A.: How to Keep RPA Maintainable? In: Fahland, D., Ghidini, C., Becker, J., Dumas, M. (eds.) BPM 2020. LNCS, vol. 12168, pp. 453–470. Springer, Cham (2020). https://doi.org/10.1007/978-3-030-58666-9_26

21. Park, G., van der Aalst, W.: Action-oriented process mining: bridging the gap between insights and actions. Prog. Artif. Intell. 1–22 (2022). https://doi.org/10.1007/s13748-022-00281-7
22. Peffers, K., Tuunanen, T., Gengler, C.E., Rossi, M., Bragge, J.: The design science research process: a model for producing and presenting information systems research (2006). https://doi.org/10.48550/arXiv.2006.02763
23. Peichl, A., Sauer, S., Wohlrabe, K.: Fachkräftemangel in deutschland und europa: Historie, status quo und was getan werden muss. ifo Schnelldienst **75**(10), 70–75 (2022). https://www.ifo.de/en/publications/2022/article-journal/fachkraeftemangel-deutschland-und-europa-historie-status-quo
24. Penttinen, E., Kasslin, H., Asatiani, A.: How to choose between robotic process automation and back-end system automation? European Conference on Information Systems 2018 (2018). https://publications.aston.ac.uk/id/eprint/33685/
25. Plattfaut, R., Rehse, J.R., Jans, C., Schulte, M., van Wendel de Joode, J.: Robotic process automation – research impulses from the bpm 2023 panel discussion. Process Sci. **1**(1) (2024). https://doi.org/10.1007/s44311-024-00005-1
26. Průcha, P., Skrbek, J.: Api as method for improving robotic process automation. In: Business Process Management: Blockchain, Robotic Process Automation, and Central and Eastern Europe Forum, Lecture Notes in Business Information Processing, vol. 459, pp. 260–273. Springer International Publishing, Cham (2022). https://doi.org/10.1007/978-3-031-16168-1_17
27. Reinkemeyer, L.: How to Get Started. In: Process Mining in Action, pp. 11–14. Springer, Cham (2020). https://doi.org/10.1007/978-3-030-40172-6_2
28. Sibalija, T., Jovanović, S., S Đurić, J.: Robotic Process Automation: Overview and Opportunities (2019)
29. Skolik, A., Löhr, B., zur Heiden, P., Bartelheimer, C.: Nutzung von low- und no-code-anwendungen zur automatisierung von geschäftsprozessen in regulierten energiemärkten. HMD Praxis der Wirtschaftsinformatik **61**(5), 1235–1255 (2024). https://doi.org/10.1365/s40702-024-01101-3
30. Slaby, J.: Robotic automation emerges as a threat to traditional low-cost outsourcing. Hfs Reserach Ltd. (2012). https://www.horsesforsources.com/wp-content/uploads/2016/06/RS-1210_Robotic-automation-emerges-as-a-threat-060516.pdf
31. Smith, O., Cattell, O., Farcot, E., O'Dea, R.D., Hopcraft, K.I.: The effect of renewable energy incorporation on power grid stability and resilience. Sci. Adv. **8**(9) (2022). https://doi.org/10.1126/sciadv.abj6734
32. Syed, R., Suriadi, S., Adams, M., Bandara, W., Leemans, S.J., Ouyang, C., et al.: Robotic process automation: contemporary themes and challenges. Comput. Ind. **115**, 103162 (2020). https://doi.org/10.1016/j.compind.2019.103162
33. Tjahjono, B., et al.: Six sigma: a literature review. Int. J. Lean Six Sigma **1**(3), 216–233 (2010)
34. van der Aalst, W.M.P., Bichler, M., Heinzl, A.: Robotic Process Automation. Bus. & Inf. Syst. Eng. **60**(4), 269–272 (2018). https://doi.org/10.1007/s12599-018-0542-4
35. van Eck, M.L., Lu, X., Leemans, S.J.J., van der Aalst, W.M.P.: PM^2: A Process Mining Project Methodology. In: Zdravkovic, J., Kirikova, M., Johannesson, P. (eds.) CAiSE 2015. LNCS, vol. 9097, pp. 297–313. Springer, Cham (2015). https://doi.org/10.1007/978-3-319-19069-3_19
36. vom Brocke, J., Rosemann, M. (eds.): Handbook on Business Process Management 1. IHIS, Springer, Heidelberg (2015). https://doi.org/10.1007/978-3-642-45100-3

37. Wanner, J., Hofmann, Fischer, M., Imgrund, F., Janiesch, C., Geyer-Klingeberg, J.: Process selection in rpa projects – towards a quantifiable method of decision making. ICIS 2019 Proceedings (2019). https://aisel.aisnet.org/icis2019/business_models/business_models/6
38. Zhang, A.: How to write a good software design doc. freeCodeCamp.org (13072018). https://www.freecodecamp.org/news/how-to-write-a-good-software-design-document-66fcf019569c/

Process Automation and Skills in the Context of Knowledge Work (Short Paper)

Dries Jarijch[1(✉)], Mieke Jans[1,2], and Jan Mendling[3,4,5]

[1] Hasselt University, Hasselt, Belgium
{dries.jarijch,mieke.jans}@uhasselt.be
[2] Maastricht University, Maastricht, The Netherlands
[3] Humboldt-Universität zu Berlin, Berlin, Germany
jan.mendling@hu.berlin.de
[4] Weizenbaum Institute, Berlin, Germany
[5] Vienna University of Economics and Business, Vienna, Austria

Abstract. The rise in digitization has significantly expanded the application of process automation beyond traditional engineering, as there is now a substantial increase in automation tools available for white-collar professionals. In this study, we aim to gain a better understanding of the interaction between process automation and skills in the context of applied knowledge work. Different relevant theoretical models relating to process automation, from the fields of engineering, information systems, and the applied domain of accounting, are examined. Insights from these models are then combined into a single unified model describing process automation. This short paper reports on a pre-study to closely examine in which way elements of automation affect knowledge worker skills. We also highlight two gaps in the literature regarding the context in which optimal automation effects occur and the lack of research regarding reskilling.

Keywords: Process Automation Effects · Unified model · Knowledge worker skills

1 Introduction

The exploration of process automation originated in engineering, an area where it has been thoroughly examined, particularly regarding airplane navigation. The aim of process automation is to relieve humans of complex or repetitive tasks by leveraging machines. This automation is known to offer potential advantages for task performance, including enhanced efficiency and improved decision-making effectiveness [2]. However, in addition to these advantages, there are detrimental effects associated with process automation, including accidents reported in flight and aviation due to skill degradation [3].

I. van de Weerd et al. (Eds.): BPM 2025 Workshops, LNBIP 569, pp. 187–195, 2026.
https://doi.org/10.1007/978-3-032-13426-4_14

With digitization on the rise, process automation is finding growing applicability beyond traditional engineering domains. As technology becomes integral to the fabric of organizations, embedded in ubiquitous information systems, organizations are increasingly leveraging process automation to aid knowledge workers. Consequently, research concerning process automation has extended into the realm of information systems as well as applied areas such as accounting [5,8]. These studies focus on the acceptance of process automation tools and their effects on individuals. However, the influence of process automation on the skills of knowledge workers is not completely understood. Although we recognize potential for harm, the specific circumstances under which certain benefits or adverse effects manifest remain unclear.

This research seeks to gain a deeper understanding of the interaction between process automation and skills within the context of knowledge work. Our approach is divided into two phases. In this first phase we synthesize empirical findings from neighboring research fields concerning process automation. We evaluate diverse theoretical models from engineering, information systems, and the applied field of accounting. By merging insights from these models, we establish a unified model delineating how automation may result in deskilling, upskilling, or reskilling. In a follow-up phase, we will leverage this preliminary study to thoroughly investigate how elements of process automation influence the skills of knowledge workers.

The remainder of the paper is structured as follows. Section 2 first provides background on a real-life case as a specific instance of the research problem. It then outlines the various relevant insights derived from models in the disciplines of engineering, information systems, and accounting—a field typical for professionals with knowledge workers. Section 3 provides an overview of the conceptual integration of these models into a cohesive model, along with the model itself. Section 4 features a discussion of the model and explores potential directions for further research to substantiate the proposed model.

2 Background

In this section, we first introduce a real-world example of an audit company where it has become relevant to examine the effects of process automation on knowledge workers. Second, we elaborate on five different theoretical models regarding process automation from different research fields.

2.1 Real-World Example

We illustrate the research challenge by presenting a real-world example that highlights various elements of process automation pertaining to knowledge workers. This instance is set within the context of financial auditing. Conducting an audit encompasses numerous sub-processes that lend themselves well to automation. Thus, one of the European Audit Authorities, responsible for auditing the structural funds allocated by the European Commission, has initiated a project to automate segments of its audit process. This Audit Authority (AA) is tasked with auditing Management Authorities (MA), which are responsible for the distribution of European funds to appropriate projects. Consequently, there lies an opportunity to enhance the efficiency of both the operation of the different MAs and their respective audits. Undertaken by one of the Big Four audit firms, this project involves activities such as mapping the current processes of both the MAs and their audits, redesigning these processes if it proves beneficial, pinpointing tasks that could potentially be automated, and critically, deciding the extent of automation for these potential tasks.

2.2 Process Automation Models

For the scenario of knowledge work, various theoretical perspectives are relevant, as described by the following theories: the Model of Human Interaction with Automation, the Theory of Effective Use, the Theory of Technostress, the Theory of Technology Dominance, and the Model of Skill Erosion.

To examine process automation, we start in the field of engineering. The model of Human Interaction with Automation, proposed by Parasuraman, et al. (2000), describes 10 different levels of automation [3]. At level 1 of process automation, there is no assistance offered by a computer at all. The level of intervention by the computer increases up to level 10, where there is no longer any human input possible and, additionally, the human is not even being informed. Between these two extremes, different levels of automation are formulated. For example, an audit support system that detects an error in a reimbursement claim and suggests rejecting this claim would qualify as level 4 automation. Aside from the levels of automation, four stages of human information processing are proposed, in each of which automation can occur. The stages are information acquisition, information analysis, decision selection, and action implementation. The theory also proposes that there is an optimal level range of automation for each stage in information processing that leads to the maximal benefit for human and system performance [3]. Within knowledge work, both information analysis and decision selection are the most crucial steps of information processing.

A framework that focuses more on the use of automation tools is the Theory of Effective Use, proposed by Trieu, et al. (2022) [8]. The model originates from the field of information systems, where it examines the drivers for people to use an information system to its fullest potential and use it in the most effective way, and how effective use impacts the efficiency and effectiveness of decision-making. The model breaks down the drivers of reliance –which is seen as a prerequisite for use– into three broad categories: external constraints, learning actions, and effective use factors. The external constraints include aspects of the system being used and the management culture. The learning actions include all actions a user can take to improve the use of a system. This includes learning the system, learning the fidelity of the output, or learning how to leverage the output of the system in their decisions. The effective use factors examine the way a user interacts with a system and how that improves reliance upon it [8].

Another framework from the information systems field, relevant to process automation, is the Theory of Technostress, proposed in Tarafdar et al. (2019) [6] and focused on the reliance on automation technology. According to this theory, one could assess an individual's willingness to use technology based on a user's feelings of stress towards the technology. Stress is categorized in one of two ways. The first is eustress [7]. This happens when a user feels they are challenged and supported by information systems. This provides them with positive outcomes and leads to more reliance. The other type of stress is distress. This occurs when a user feels their work is being threatened by an information system. It makes workers less likely to use an IS to its fullest potential. This will lead to diminished benefits and, as a result, worse outcomes [6].

A process automation framework from an applied business field comes in the form of the Theory of Technology Dominance (TTD), originally proposed in 1998 by Arnold, et al. [1]. It originates from the field of accounting, where knowledge work is a primary characteristic. The theory was then later extended by Sutton, et al. (2022) into TTD2, which is the most extensive model on process automation [5]. It examines three phases of process automation systems. The first phase discusses requirements for relying on process automation, which includes four factors: task expertise, task complexity, familiarity with the automation tool, and cognitive congruence. The second phase describes short-term effects of process automation on decision-making performance and skills of knowledge workers. In the third phase, the long-term effects of process automation are discussed in the form of deskilling [5].

Besides the Theory of Technology Dominance, the Model of Skill Erosion, proposed by Rinta-Kahila, et al. (2023), also examines the potential effects of process automation from a knowledge work perspective [4]. The model first describes what knowledge workers drive to rely on process automation. These include the burdensomeness of tasks, the ability of an automation tool to handle the complexity of burdensome tasks, the reliability of the process automation tool, and the explanation of features of the tool. Second, the model describes how reliance can turn into complacency over time. This is a form of conduct where a user fails to monitor the system to an appropriate degree. Third, if complacency is allowed to persist, the model states this will lead to long-term skill erosion. Finally, the model states that complacency is not the only possible outcome of process automation. If a worker is required to conduct tasks mindfully, complacency can be prevented [4].

In conclusion, there is a diverse spectrum of process automation models presented in literature. Our objective is to conceptually integrate these insights. This enables studying the topic of process automation in the context of knowledge work in a profound manner.

3 Conceptual Integration

To integrate the insights of the different frameworks on process automation, a unified model is constructed (presented in Fig. 1). The model is divided into three separate phases, parallel to the ones proposed in the Theory of Technology Dominance, but they have a clearer indication of when a phase ends and a new phase starts. The first phase is where use of the automation tool is increasing. In the next phase, tool domination increases. Lastly, in the long term, effects on skilling take place. It is important to note that this model is not strictly sequential, but is intended to show how the effects of process automation progress. In the following sections, we discuss the three phases.

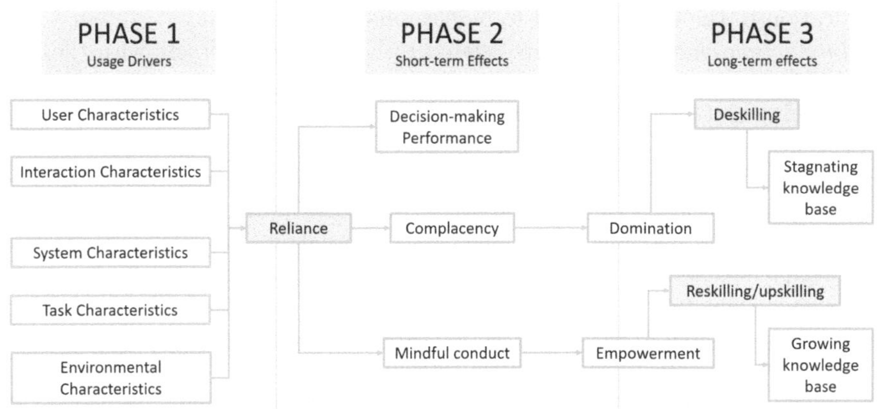

Fig. 1. Unified model for effects of process automation in knowledge work

3.1 Phase 1 - Usage Drivers

The first phase of the model presented in Fig. 1, describes what drives knowledge workers to rely on process automation tools. Throughout the different models, different drivers of reliance are proposed. In general, they can be broadly categorized into five distinct groups: user characteristics, system characteristics, interaction characteristics, task characteristics, and environmental characteristics.

The Theories of Effective Use, Technology Dominance, and Technostress all mention reliance drivers related to *user characteristics*. A user characteristic can be summarized as anything that falls under knowledge, actions, or feelings that a user of the system exhibits. Examples of these types of characteristics include: expertise of users, learning activities performed by users, or technostress experienced by users. Higher expertise in a task that is being automated, decreases the speed at which reliance happens [5]. The same is true for a user that is experiencing techno-distress [6]. A user experiencing techno-eustress, on the other hand, or a user performing learning activities for a system and its output will experience increased reliance [6,8].

Drivers related to *system characteristics* are present in the model of Technology Dominance, Skill Erosion, and Effective Use. They all relate to how a system is designed and what features it has or lacks. The primary examples of these characteristics are system quality, system reliability, system transparency, and collaborative system design. System quality measures a system based on availability, responsiveness, and features [4,8]. System reliability determines how reliably correct the output of the system is [4]. System transparency is a more specific feature that relates to how automation technology communicates its actions [4,5]. A system that is available, responsive, and transparent in its communication to the user will lead to higher reliance from users.

Interaction characteristics are related to how a user interacts with the system. This interaction between user and system can occur in the following ways: physical interaction with the system, familiarity with the system, or cognitive congruence with the system. If the physical interaction between a system and a user is optimal, this means a user is able to access all features they need of the system unimpeded by the systems surface [8]. Familiarity is the degree to which a user is comfortable with a given system based on prior experience and/or training [5]. Cognitive congruence is the degree to which the cognitive process of a system matches with the cognitive process an expert in that task would use. Having optimal physical interaction, higher familiarity, and high cognitive congruence will increase reliance on a system.

Reliance drivers originating from *task characteristics* include all aspects of the task that could lead users to let the system automate it for them. Task complexity and task burdensomeness are the only characteristic discovered, and are presented by the Theory of Technology Dominance and the Model of Skill Erosion. If a task is experienced by users as more complex or burdensome, reliance on a process automation tool is more likely [4,5].

Finally, *environmental characteristics* are currently only presented in the Theory of Effective Use. The environmental characteristic is described as the management culture in an organization. A management culture that promotes, or requires, the use of a process automation tool will lead to increased reliance on said tool [8].

3.2 Phase 2 - Short-Term Effects of Process Automation

The second phase of the model describes effects of process automation that occur in the short-term once knowledge workers are relying on the system. The types of effects that take place in the short-term can be either effects on decision-making or effects on work conduct.

The effect of process automation on decision-making can be in the form of decision-making efficiency or effectiveness. The effect of process automation is almost unanimously positive. The most beneficial impacts are observed if knowledge workers are able to collaborate with the system and substitute their own knowledge when the system falls short [5]. With the assistance of process automation, decisions can be made faster, with less effort, and the resulting outcome of decisions will be more effective [2,8].

Besides decision-making, process automation also has an effect on the conduct of workers. According most theories, process automation encourages complacency in knowledge workers [2,5]. Multiple models report that complacency occurs when automation is highly, but not perfectly, reliable [2,4]. A high level of reliability creates the illusion that there are no negative performance consequences if the system is not monitored. As a result, users will fail to detect errors made by the automation tool [2,4,5].

In contrast, a type of conduct that is only discussed in the Model of Skill Erosion, is mindful conduct [4]. Mindful conduct consists of three behaviors that a knowledge worker must exhibit to avoid complacency: activity awareness, competence maintenance, and output assessment. *Activity awareness* includes both the execution and supervision of task activities. *Competence maintenance* includes the active upholding of domain competences. *Output assessment* involves ensuring that the output of tasks is in compliance with the expected performance [4].

3.3 Phase 3 - Long-Term Effects of Process Automation

As can be seen in phase 3 of the unified model, prolonged use of process automation tools leads to different long-term effects depending on the type of conduct a knowledge worker showed. Different models show that a user being complacent in completing a task, will start experiencing skill degradation. Skill erosion will express itself through the forgetting of previously learned skill and through a failure to adapt to new environmental changes. Process automation may make some skills fully obsolete, in which case skill degradation is not undesirable, but other skills are an essential part of the work.

Besides skill degradation, the Model of Skill Erosion dictates that skill maintenance is another possible long-term effect [4]. Skill maintenance is the result of mindful conduct and includes any positive impact on skills. While not explicitly mentioned in the literature, skill maintenance can be categorized into two types: upskilling and reskilling. The term *upskilling* is used for describing positive effects on skills directly linked to the task being automated. An example of this is when the automation tool functions as an electronic colleague that provides advice and exchanges feedback in order to facilitate final judgments [5]. This type of skill maintenance is most prominently studied in literature. *Reskilling* is used when referring to positive impacts on skills not related to the automated task, but the tasks surrounding it. Minor attention given to reskilling by Parasuraman et al. (2000), Rinta-Kahila et al. (2023), and a study from Vu et al. (2023). The studies report how the automation of a certain task leads to increased performance in unrelated tasks [2,4,9].

Despite the well-known behavior behind skill degradation and skill maintenance, there is currently no research that describes what level of automation encourages which type of conduct. Parasuraman et al. (2000) postulates that for each stage of information processing, there exists an optimal range of process automation that optimizes the benefits for both human skill and decision-making. This currently forms a gap in the literature.

4 Conclusion

Insights on process automation, stemming from different research fields, have been brought together in a unified model on process automation in the context of knowledge work. Namely, our analysis of the different models of process automation from the fields of engineering, information systems, and accounting, revealed a large amount of overlap. This overlap is mainly present in the topics of complacency and skill degradation. However, many drivers of automation reliance are also confirmed across different models.

Our model brings these insights together and allows for a better understanding of the interaction between automation and skills. We also highlight two gaps in the literature regarding the context of when optimal automation effects occur, and the lack of research regarding reskilling. First, from the field of engineering, we know there exists an optimal level of automation to achieve the most benefits while minimizing risks to skills. This optimal level has not been researched in the context of knowledge work. Second, the positive impact automation has on skills not directly related to the automated task, referred to as reskilling, is also not explored in any theory.

This short paper serves as a pre-study to a case study that will be conducted in collaboration with one of the European Audit Authorities. We will examine the effects of process automation within the setting of knowledge work. As has been proposed in this paper, one of the central indicators of expertise in knowledge work is pattern recognition. The envisioned follow-up study will use this insight and focus on the automated process tasks with a high level of pattern recognition.

Acknowledgement. The research of the authors was supported by the Research Foundation - Flanders (FWO) under grant G0AAP24N (ProImpact), by the Einstein Foundation Berlin under grant EPP-2019-524, by the German Federal Ministry of Research, Technology and Space under grant 16DII133, and by Deutsche Forschungsgemeinschaft under grants 496119880 (VisualMine), 531115272 (ProImpact), and SFB 1404/2 (FONDA).

References

1. Arnold, V., Sutton, S.: The theory of technology dominance: Understanding the impact of intelligent decision aids on decision makers' judgments. Adv. Acc. Behav. Res. **1**, 175–194 (1998)
2. Parasuraman, R., Sheridan, T., Wickens, C.: A model for types and levels of human interaction with automation. IEEE Trans. Syst. Man, Cybern. - Part A: Syst. Humans **30**(3), 286–297 (2000). https://doi.org/10.1109/3468.844354, https://ieeexplore.ieee.org/document/844354
3. Parasuraman, R.: Designing automation for human use: empirical studies and quantitative models. Ergonomics (2000). https://doi.org/10.1080/001401300409125, https://www.tandfonline.com/doi/abs/10.1080/001401300409125, publisher: Taylor & Francis

4. Rinta-Kahila, T., Penttinen, E., Salovaara, A., Soliman, W., Ruissalo, J.: The vicious circles of skill erosion: a case study of cognitive automation. J. Assoc. Inf. Syst. **24**(5), 1378–1412 (2023). https://doi.org/10.17705/1jais.00829, https://aisel.aisnet.org/jais/vol24/iss5/2/
5. Sutton, S.G., Arnold, V., Holt, M.: An extension of the theory of technology dominance: capturing the underlying causal complexity (2022). https://doi.org/10.2139/ssrn.4101835, https://papers.ssrn.com/abstract=4101835
6. Tarafdar, M., Cooper, C.L., Stich, J.F.: The technostress trifecta - techno eustress, techno distress and design: Theoretical directions and an agenda for research. Inf. Syst. J. **29**(1), 6–42 (2019). https://doi.org/10.1111/isj.12169, https://onlinelibrary.wiley.com/doi/abs/10.1111/isj.12169
7. Tarafdar, M., Stich, J.F., Maier, C., Laumer, S.: Techno-eustress creators: Conceptualization and empirical validation. Inf. Syst. J. **34**(6), 2097–2131 (2024). https://doi.org/10.1111/isj.12515, https://onlinelibrary.wiley.com/doi/abs/10.1111/isj.12515
8. Trieu, V.H., Burton-Jones, A., Green, P., Cockcroft, S.: Applying and extending the theory of effective use in a business intelligence context. MIS Q. **46**, 645–678 (2022). https://doi.org/10.25300/MISQ/2022/14880
9. Vu, H., Haase, J., Leopold, H., Mendling, J.: Towards a theory on process automation effects. In: Di Francescomarino, C., Burattin, A., Janiesch, C., Sadiq, S. (eds.) Business Process Management Forum. pp. 285–301. Springer, Cham (2023). https://doi.org/10.1007/978-3-031-41623-1_17

9th International Workshop on Business Processes Meet the Internet-of-Things (BP-Meet-IoT 2025)

Incorporating IoT Contexts into Business Processes: A Contextual Classification

Jia Wei[1(✉)], Chun Ouyang[1], and Yannis Bertrand[2]

[1] Queensland University of Technology, Brisbane, Australia
j26.wei@qut.edu.au
[2] Ghent University, Ghent, Belgium

Abstract. Business process management (BPM) is a well-established field dedicated to helping organisations identify, analyse, and improve business processes. The advent of new technologies, such as the Internet of Things (IoT), has resulted in a transformation of traditional BPM, as the IoT can provide valuable contextual information about business processes. So far, most studies have focused on modelling IoT-enhanced processes, with limited attention to converting raw IoT data into meaningful process context data for integration into event logs to support process analysis. This study addresses this gap by proposing a classification for process-relevant IoT contexts developed following a rigorous taxonomy development method. The classification builds on existing context classifications in both the business process and IoT domains, and it is further systematically refined through use cases found in the literature. To evaluate the classification's usefulness, applicability, and robustness, two real-world use cases were analysed, demonstrating the effectiveness of the classification in representing the business process context captured by IoT data. This work has facilitated the integration of IoT into BPM, enabling the analysis of IoT-enhanced processes and advancing data-driven process analytical capabilities, particularly for context-aware process analytics.

Keywords: Business Process · Internet of Things · Context · Classification

1 Introduction

Business Process Management (BPM) is a widely recognised discipline that focuses on the design, analysis, execution, and improvement of business processes [15]. Emerging technologies, such as the Internet of Things (IoT), are transforming traditional BPM with digital innovations and enabling new business models [2]. IoT, defined as a network of interconnected devices with sensors and actuators, facilitates continuous monitoring of physical phenomena [15]. By capturing rich contextual information, IoT data provides real-time insights into physical objects, human resources, and location data involved in process execution [26], supporting more informed analytics and decision-making. For instance,

I. van de Weerd et al. (Eds.): BPM 2025 Workshops, LNBIP 569, pp. 199–216, 2026.
https://doi.org/10.1007/978-3-032-13426-4_15

in a warehouse distribution process, IoT-enabled tracking devices provide real-time visibility into goods movement, improving forecasting and inventory management [38].

However, most existing research focuses on modelling IoT-enhanced processes [6,12,17,38], with limited emphasis on transforming raw IoT data into meaningful process context data for logical integration into event logs. In a manifesto, Janiesch et al. [15] discuss the mutual benefits of IoT and BPM, identifying 16 challenges in bridging the gap between them. Our research aims to address one of these challenges: "*How can IoT data be systematically integrated with business processes?*" To tackle this, we propose a classification for identifying and categorising contextual information captured by IoT data that can be integrated into event logs. We define this type of contextual information as ***process-relevant IoT context***, that is, *information provided by IoT devices during interactions with business processes that may affect process executions.* Specifically, we consider ***interactions between IoT devices and business processes*** as situations in which *IoT devices make observations during process execution, capturing information about business objects, process activities, or the overall process.*

In this study, we adopt a well-established taxonomy development method by Nickerson et al. [23] to construct the process-relevant IoT context classification. The classification includes two interrelated components: the integration of IoT contexts with process contexts, which identifies how IoT devices interact with business processes, and IoT device context, which captures characteristics of IoT devices involved in the process. To validate the classification, we conducted an assessment by systematically examining it through use cases from the literature to ensure it satisfies the ending conditions outlined in the taxonomy development method. For the final evaluation, we applied the classification to two real-world use cases, following the widely recognised evaluation method as surveyed by Kundisch et al. [20]. The evaluation focused on three essential criteria: *usefulness*, assessing the extent to which the classification provides valuable insights for stakeholders [36]; *applicability*, evaluating if the classification is applicable in real-world scenarios [36]; and *robustness*, determining its resilience in handling varying levels of information [35].

Our work contributes to building a conceptual foundation for bridging the gap between low-level IoT data and high-level process execution data. The proposed process-relevant IoT context classification provides guidance on determining which IoT data should be integrated into event logs to produce IoT-enriched event logs, thereby enabling the analysis of IoT-enhanced processes. Instead of incorporating all raw IoT data, the classification ensures that only IoT data capturing contextual information relevant to process executions is included. As a result, the classification supports data-driven process analytics, particularly the context-aware analysis.

The remainder of this paper is structured as follows. Section 2 discusses related work. Section 3 presents the research method used to construct the classification. Section 4 proposes the developed classification, and Sect. 5 focuses on the evaluation of the classification. Finally, Sect. 6 concludes the paper and provides an outlook of future work.

2 Background and Related Work

2.1 Context-Awareness

Context-awareness is crucial in both BPM and IoT. In business processes, context captures environmental changes and attributes affecting process execution [27]. In IoT, context enriches raw data with semantic meaning, enhancing analytical capabilities [34]. A general definition by Abowd et al. [1] describes context as "any information that can be used to characterise the situation of an entity", classifying it into four types: location, identity, time, and activity. As context is conceptualised differently across domains, in the following, we discuss context in BPM and IoT separately.

Context-Awareness for Business Process. There is an increasing amount of literature that discusses the notion of business process context. Van der Aalst and Dustdar [40] propose a classification of contextual factors that are essential for process mining. Rosemann et al. [30] examine different layers of context from the perspective of business operations related to processes. Brunk [8] introduces a taxonomy that discusses dimensions of business process context and characteristics, with a focus on predictive process analysis. Pentland et al. [25] propose a context classification consisting of situational context (essential elements in the process) and sequential context (a relevant sequence of events in the process). Koschmider et al. [19] aim to enhance the quality of event-activity mappings by considering four dimensions of process context: personal and social, task, environmental, and spatial-temporal.

Context-Awareness for IoT. Souabni et al. [34] propose a classification of IoT context into conceptual, operational, and temporal perspectives. From a conceptual perspective, Schilit et al. [31] identify three essential aspects: location-related, resource-related and people-related information. From an operational perspective, Perera et al. [26] distinguish context as either primary (e.g., raw sensor data) or secondary (i.e., information aggregated from the primary context). Henricksen et al. [14] categorise IoT context based on the context's persistence characteristics and data sources, distinguishing between sensed, static, profiled, and derived context. Souabni et al. [34] categorise context distinguishing between past, present, and future. In addition, some studies consider the characteristics of IoT applications. Mirzaie et al. [22] propose four distinct categories of context: inherent, system, organisational, and spatio-temporal. Vodyaho et al. [42] classify context according to the architecture of a mobile computing system, including sensor level, fog level, cloud level and cyber-physical system level.

2.2 IoT and BPM

Most existing works focus on extending business process models with IoT activities and data [10,37]. Schönig et al. [32] propose a method for enriching process models with IoT data, outlining three methods for connecting IoT data and human activities in a business process. Compagnucci et al. [10] present a systematic literature review on modelling notations for IoT-aware business processes. Bertrand et al. [4] define three types of events—IoT events, process events, and context events—and their relationships, aiming to establish a link between IoT and process mining. Vitali and Pernici [41] propose an approach for analysing interconnected business processes in a sensing environment.

Few studies attempt to integrate IoT data into event logs. A relevant work in this regard, Elali et al. [11] present a method to connect sensor data and activity logs by identifying mappings between sensors and activities. In contrast to their work, we propose a classification that enables fine-grained classification of IoT data based on different levels of process context. Mangler et al. [21] introduce an extension of the event log standard format XES named DataStream, aiming to capture relevant IoT data in event logs. Next to this work, Bertrand et al. [5] propose the Native IoT-Centric Event (NICE) log format, a new model for IoT-enhanced event logs. Different from their works, we focus on extracting process-relevant IoT context from raw IoT data. Moreover, in contrast to [21], which is based on the XES schema standard for event logs, our classification can support various event log standards, including, e.g., object-centric event logs.

3 Research Method

We apply the method proposed by Nickerson et al. [23] to develop the process-relevant IoT context classification. This method provides a structured and iterative framework that combines theoretical foundations with empirical insights. While the method is primarily designed for taxonomy development, Nickerson et al. clarify that terms such as taxonomy and classification can be used interchangeably.

The process starts with determining meta-characteristics of the objects of interest, which in this case are process-relevant IoT contexts. Our goal is to establish a classification to identify and categorise process-related contexts that are captured by IoT data for integration into event logs. The meta-characteristics of this classification encompass both the characteristics of process context and IoT context. In the next step, we define ending conditions for terminating the development iterations, which include three objective conditions: 1) "Every dimension is unique and not repeated", 2) "Every characteristic is unique within its dimension", 3) "Each cell (combination of characteristics) is unique and is not repeated", and five subjective conditions (i.e., concise, robust, comprehensive, extensible, and explanatory) outlined in [23].

The method of Nickerson et al. [23] supports two pathways for taxonomy development: "conceptual-to-empirical" and "empirical-to-conceptual". The former is suited for cases with theoretical research but limited empirical data, while the latter is ideal for rich empirical data but limited theoretical foundation. The iterative process continues until all ending conditions are satisfied. Given the limited availability of IoT-enriched event logs but extensive research on IoT and process contexts, we initially adopted the "conceptual-to-empirical" approach.

	Iteration 1	Iteration 2			Iteration 3	Evaluation
Approach	Conceptual-to-empirical	Conceptual-to-empirical			Empirical-to-conceptual	Empirical-to-conceptual
Basis for decision	Existing process context classifications	Inclusion of existing IoT context classifications			Use cases that explore IoT-enhanced business processes	Real-world use cases that apply IoT technologies to business processes
Data source and method	Review and synthesis of existing taxonomies	Review and synthesis of existing taxonomies			A systematic search of existing use cases	Real-world use cases
Deliverables	Process context classification	Refined process context classification	IoT context classification	IoT device context	Assessed process-relevant IoT context classification	Validated process-relevant IoT context classification

Fig. 1. Process-relevant IoT context classification design iterations

Through two iterations, we synthesised insights from the literature on process and IoT context classifications. In the third iteration, we conducted an assessment of the classification derived from the previous two iterations as part of the development phase, carrying out the "empirical-to-conceptual" approach. This involves assessing whether the proposed classification satisfies the predefined ending conditions with use cases from existing literature, a commonly applied method surveyed in [20]. Finally, we performed an evaluation of the assessed classification using real-world use cases. These iterations are further illustrated in Fig. 1, and detailed information about the literature search conducted across the three iterations can be found in the technical report available at https://github.com/JennyJiaW/Process-relevantIoTContextClassification.

1st Iteration. We investigated the process context dimension, starting with the classification by van der Aalst and Dustdar [40]. This paper is widely adopted and provides clear distinctions among levels of contextual information relevant to process analysis, making it a reliable starting point for identifying additional relevant works for our study. It outlines four levels of context factors that may influence the processes: 1) **Instance Context**: details about cases influencing process execution. 2) **Process Context**: attributes associated with the process itself, regardless of any specific cases. 3) **Social Context**: information about people working together within a particular organisation. 4) **External Context**: ecosystem elements outside the organisation's control.

To evaluate and build upon this classification, we conducted a systematic search using backward and forward snowballing [43]. From 102 publications identified in Scopus and Web of Science databases, we observed opportunities to refine the classification to address advancements in IoT integration. Our analysis revealed the following insights:

- **Event Context**: Park et al. [24] propose three context types: *Intrinsic context* (factors inherent to a single event), *Relational context* (factors associated with multiple events) and *External context* (factors that are not directly linked to events but have an influence on their execution). *Intrinsic context* highlights the need for **Event Context**, which isolates event-specific details previously grouped under the broader **Instance Context**.

- **Organisational Context**: Brocke et al. [7] summarise several contextual factors related to organisations, including scope (inter or intra-organisational), size, industry, culture, and resources. Notably, the resource factor is categorised as **Social Context** in [40]. Grisold et al. [13] propose a more refined context framework for organisational contexts, distinguishing between *organisation-external context* (e.g., inter-organisational relationships, policy- and rule-related factors) and *organisation-internal context* (e.g., intra-organisational relationships, structural, and procedural factors). These insights highlight that **Organisational Context** is broader and more inclusive than **Social Context**, as it addresses both intra- and inter-organisational elements, including resource-related considerations that affect processes.
- **IoT Device Context**: IoT advancements enable data collection from sensors/devices relevant to process execution [41]. This necessitates introducing **IoT Device Context**, encompassing IoT-related information such as sensor readings. As a result, this separates IoT-generated data from general external factors previously classified under **External Context**.
- **Process Object Context**: Traditional process analytics often focus on the single-case notion, where a process involves only one object type. Modern applications, however, frequently involve multiple interacting objects, with events tied to these interactions [39]. We replace the **Instance context** with **Process Object context**, better capturing object-level interactions within processes.

By the end of this iteration, we propose the following levels in the process context dimension: **IoT Device Context**, **Event Context**, **Process Object Context**, **Process Context**, and **Organisational Context**.

2nd Iteration. The goal of this iteration is to enrich the classification with the theoretical foundation from the context classification in the IoT domain. We employ the output from the preceding iteration as a foundation and incorporate additional characteristics relating to the IoT setting. Numerous research studies have been conducted to investigate the notion of context-awareness from the IoT perspective [26,29,33]. Thus, in this iteration, we employ the "conceptual-to-empirical" approach again. We selected three recent academic works [28,29,33] that have undertaken systematic literature reviews or surveys on the topic of context-awareness in the IoT domain. These works were chosen for their comprehensive overviews of context-awareness in IoT, providing a solid basis for identifying additional relevant studies. A systematic collection of articles citing the three mentioned papers was conducted using Scopus and Web of Science, resulting in 369 pieces of literature after removing duplicates.

An analysis of these papers reveals that current IoT context classifications are explored from two primary perspectives: conceptual and operational. The conceptual perspective focuses on classifying contextual information based on its semantic meaning and relationships, while the operational perspective addresses how contexts are acquired and processed [9]. The focus in terms of the IoT context dimension is primarily on conceptual classification, as the operational aspects are already covered under the process context dimension (Iteration 1). By reviewing existing IoT context classifications, we identify **Spatial**, **Temporal**, **Human Actor**, and **Environment** information as the most frequently appearing conceptual perspectives. Based on this observation, we propose integrating these categories into the IoT context dimension. In addition, we refine the process context dimension by explicitly including the "activity" performed by IoT devices, a context category frequently mentioned in existing literature. To reflect this refinement, we rename the previously identified **Event Context** into two distinct contexts: **Process Event Context**, which captures context related to process events, and **IoT Event Context**, which captures context observed when IoT devices performing activities.

Several ontologies [3,16,29] have been developed to describe IoT concepts and data structure. Among these, the SOSA ontology [16] introduces a concept of a "feature of interest", representing entities observed by sensors or manipulated by actuators. To incorporate this concept, we introduce the **Physical Object** category in the IoT context dimension to capture information about physical objects monitored by IoT devices. In addition, Bajaj et al. [3] propose five key questions for understanding IoT ontologies: 1) *What* are things involved in the IoT application? 2) *Where* are things located? 3) *When* do the things collect data? 4) *Who* has access to the information in IoT systems? 5) *How* do users or applications interact with things? To address these questions, we introduce characteristics of **IoT device context**. To address the "what" question, we consider the *identifier*, *type* (e.g., actuators, sensors, or tag devices), *name*, *unit*, *state* and *value* of an IoT device. The "when" question relates to the *time* of data collection, while the "where" question concerns the device's *location*. Furthermore, understanding the *interdependencies* among devices and entities is critical for addressing the "how" and "who" questions. Another core concept in the SOSA ontology [16] is the "observable property", which refers to the attribute of an entity monitored by an IoT device. This concept aligns with our process context dimension, which will be explained in Sect. 4.

3rd Iteration. In this iteration, we adopt the "empirical-to-conceptual" approach by assessing the proposed process-relevant IoT context classification with use cases from published research. To ensure comprehensive coverage, we conducted a systematic search following Kitchenham's [18] methodology to collect use cases that explore IoT-aware business processes, resulting in 61 use cases. In assessing the proposed classification, we instantiated it for each use case. Detailed descriptions of the selected use cases and a summary of the instantiations can be found in the previously mentioned technical report.

Overall, the classification effectively categorises existing use cases across different domains, demonstrating its ability to support varying levels of IoT data integration. Our analysis shows that most use cases exhibit contextual information at the **IoT Event**, **Process Event**, and **Organisational** context levels.

In contrast, **Process Context** is less frequently observed, and when present, it primarily captures **environmental**, **temporal**, and **spatial** information. One significant challenge identified during the instantiations was the limited coverage of the **IoT Device Context**. While many use cases specify the types of IoT devices involved (e.g., sensors or actuators), they rarely provide detailed characteristics such as the device's state, time, location, or interdependencies. These characteristics are essential for understanding how IoT devices function and interact within the process. This gap highlights the need for more comprehensive use case documentation to fully represent the role and behavior of IoT devices in IoT-aware business processes.

After this iteration, objective conditions, including "Every dimension is unique and not repeated", "Every characteristic is unique within its dimension", "Each cell (combination of characteristics) is unique" [23] are satisfied, and all five subjective conditions are assessed within the research team.

4 A Classification of Process-Relevant IoT Context

The process-relevant IoT context classification comprises two interdependent components. The first component, illustrated in Fig. 4, comprises two dimensions: the **process context dimension** (see Fig. 2), which represents five levels of process context, and the **IoT context dimension** (see Fig. 3), encompassing categories of IoT context. Each cell at the intersection of these two dimensions (as shown in Fig. 4) specifies the relevant process context and the IoT device responsible for capturing it. The second component, the **IoT device context**, provides detailed specifications for each device. This dual-component structure creates a dynamic interplay: the first part offers a high-level view of how IoT data contribute to different levels of process context, while the second provides granular information about the IoT devices used to capture these contexts. Together, these two components describe twenty-five interactions and nine IoT-specific characteristics, forming an integrated classification for contextualising IoT data in business processes.

4.1 Integrating Process Contexts with IoT Contexts

As illustrated in Fig. 2, the process context dimension is structured into five hierarchical levels. Each level captures a specific aspect of the process that involves or is influenced by IoT devices. Below, we provide examples of each level of process context.

- **IoT Event Context**: The activity "monitor temperature" performed by a temperature sensor, along with the recorded attribute "temperature", are both part of the IoT event context.
- **Process Object Context**: In an Emergency Department (ED) process, objects such as the patient and medication are tracked using unique identifiers (e.g., barcodes). Their attributes, such as the patient's name or the medicine's name, are examples of process object contexts.

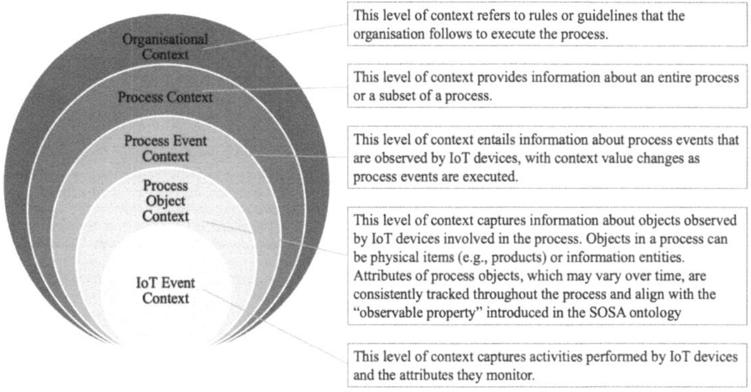

Fig. 2. The five levels of process context and their corresponding definitions

- **Process Event Context**: Events such as "triage in the ED" and "take routine vital signs" involve observable attributes of patients such as heart rate or temperature, collected via devices such as electrocardiograms (ECGs) [44]. Since the values of these attributes change with event execution, they serve as examples of the process event context.
- **Process Context**: In an ED process, the process context could be the hourly arrival rate of the patient, derived from barcode scan records. Such information is valuable for examining the efficiency of the ED process.
- **Organisational Context**: Based on the vital signs checked during triage, a patient may be directed to see a doctor immediately upon arriving at the ED. This reflects predefined rules, informed by IoT data, used to prioritise patients. For example, patients classified as emergencies should not wait more than 10 min to see a doctor[1].

Figure 3 presents the categories in the IoT context dimension. Combined with the process context dimension, this forms the first component of the process-relevant IoT context classification shown in Fig. 4.

4.2 IoT Device Context

This context constitutes the second component of the process-relevant IoT context classification. As illustrated in Fig. 5, it captures the key static characteristics of IoT devices, including identifier, type, name, unit, and location, as well as dynamic characteristics such as state, value, time, and interdependencies. These characteristics describe the devices that were involved in capturing the process-relevant context identified in the first component.

[1] https://www.aihw.gov.au/reports-data/myhospitals/intersection/access/ed.

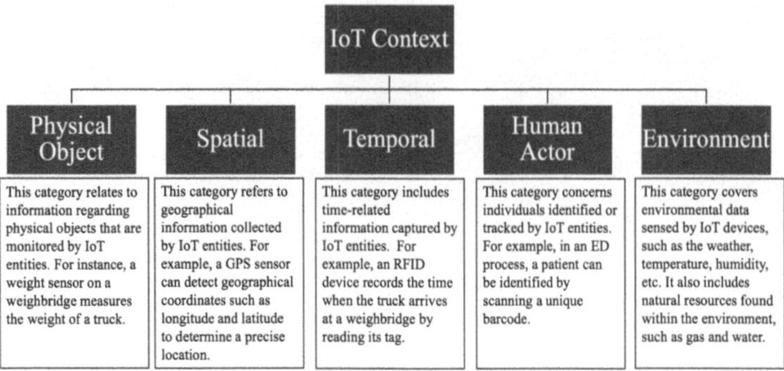

Fig. 3. The five categories of IoT context, along with their definitions and illustrative examples.

	Physical Object	Spatial	Temporal	Human Actor	Environment
Organisational	Org. rules or guidelines related to the attributes of physical objects captured by ***IoT devices*** during process execution	Org. rules or guidelines related to spatial data captured by ***IoT devices*** during process execution	Org. rules or guidelines related to temporal data captured by ***IoT devices*** during process execution	Org. rules or guidelines related to the attributes of human actors captured by ***IoT devices*** involved during process execution	Org. rules or guidelines related to environmental data captured by ***IoT devices*** during process execution
Process	A collection of information about process objects (physical objects) involved in the process provided by ***IoT devices***	Collected spatial information regarding an entire process provided by ***IoT devices***	Collected temporal information regarding an entire process provided by ***IoT devices***	A collection of information about process objects (human actors) involved in the process provided by ***IoT devices***	Collected environment information regarding an entire process provided by ***IoT devices***
Process Event	Information about process objects (physical objects) observed by ***IoT devices*** associated with individual process event	Spatial information observed by ***IoT devices*** associated with individual process event	Temporal information observed by ***IoT devices*** associated with individual process event	Information about process objects (human actors) observed by ***IoT devices*** associated with individual process event	Environment information observed by ***IoT devices*** associated with individual process event
Process Object	Attributes of process objects captured/observed by ***IoT devices*** (when process objects are physical objects)	Spatial information of object captured/observed by ***IoT devices***	Time-related data associated with process objects captured/observed by ***IoT devices***	Attributes of process objects captured/observed by ***IoT devices*** (when process objects are human actors)	Environmental information of process object captured/observed by ***IoT devices***
IoT Event	Activities Performed by ***IoT Devices*** that Capture Information about Physical Objects	Activities Performed by ***IoT Devices*** that Capture Spatial Information	Activities Performed ***by IoT Devices*** that Capture Temporal Information	Activities Performed by ***IoT Devices*** that Capture Information about People	Activities Performed by ***IoT Devices*** that Capture Environmental Information

Fig. 4. The first component of the process-relevant IoT context classification, presenting the definition of each context in relation to process execution and its corresponding IoT category.

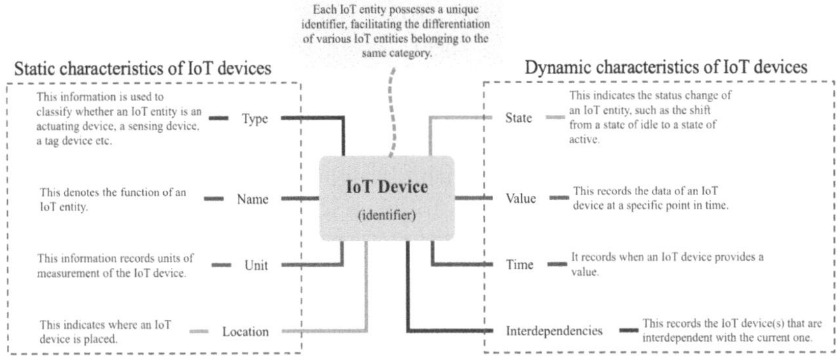

Fig. 5. The second component of the process-relevant IoT context classification, detailing the static and dynamic characteristics of IoT devices involved in the process.

5 Evaluation

During the development phase, the proposed classification was assessed to ensure that it fulfills the subjective and objective ending conditions predefined (in Sect. 3). This section focuses on the evaluation of the finalised classification. Kundisch et al. [20] proposes an extended taxonomy design process that builds upon the approach introduced by Nickerson et al. [23], with an emphasis on taxonomy evaluation. Specifically, Kundisch et al. [20] provide a thorough overview of the existing taxonomy evaluation criteria and methods. For our classification, three essential criteria are considered: 1) applicability [36] indicates whether the proposed classification is "applicable in practice," whereas 2) robustness assesses the classification's ability to handle varying levels of information [35], 3) usefulness relates to the capability of the classification to provide valuable information that is of interest to stakeholders [36]. Among current evaluation approaches, applying classification to represent and/or categorise real-world objects is the most common [23].

To validate the proposed classification, we evaluate its applicability, robustness, and usefulness in two real-world use cases from different domains with varying levels of IoT integration. The instantiations demonstrate the classification's applicability and robustness in capturing diverse levels of context across domains. In addition, its usefulness is highlighted by illustrating how the contextual information provided by the instantiated classification addresses stakeholder questions and delivers actionable insights.

5.1 Cargo Pickup Process

This use case describes the logistics process of cargo pickup at a bulk port in China [45], as illustrated in Fig. 6. The process begins with the customer lodging a pickup plan to schedule trucks for cargo collection. On the scheduled date, each truck arrives, is weighed to record its empty weight, proceeds to the designated silo for loading, and is weighed again to capture its loaded weight. The port issues a weighing ticket and tally sheet before the truck exits. Key business objects involved in this process include cargo, pickup plans, trucks, and silos.

Various IoT devices are integrated into this process and interact with these process objects (Fig. 6). An RFID reader at the entry gate enables automated access control, while a weighbridge with a weight sensor captures truck weights in real time. Historical empty weights stored on RFID tags are read at the weighbridge, allowing alerts to be triggered if the current empty weight significantly deviates from the recorded value. In addition, temperature and humidity sensors in the silos continuously monitor environmental conditions. For example, if the calculated dew point is lower than the grain temperature, pickup is discontinued to protect cargo quality. GPS sensors track truck movements within the port to ensure they remain in authorised areas.

Figure 7 & Fig. 8 illustrate the instantiation of the classification for this use case. To demonstrate the usefulness of this classification, we provide an exemplary scenario of *Weight Anomaly Detection*. Suppose the system flags an abnormal weight for a truck. A logistics expert needs to quickly analyse the cause of this anomaly to ensure compliance and safety. This prompts the question: *What factors could have contributed to this weight anomaly?* By leveraging the context identified in the classification, the following insights about potential root causes of weight anomalies can be derived:

1. The weight anomaly commonly occurs during weighing activities, such as the "weigh the empty truck" or "weigh the loaded truck" events, involving the truck as the physical object. By analysing the **context** of the **physical object** type associated with the **process event**, it becomes evident that the weight sensor detected the anomaly (Fig. 7). Referring to the IoT Device Context (Fig. 8), the weight sensor relies on infrared sensors to ensure proper truck positioning on the weighbridge for accurate measurements. Experts can

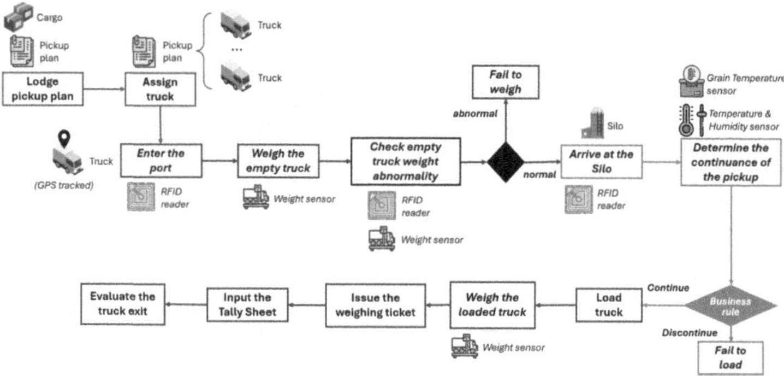

Fig. 6. Control flow of the cargo pickup process, illustrating the interactions between business objects and IoT entities throughout the process execution, adapted from [45].

<table>
<tr><th></th><th colspan="2">Physical object</th><th>Spatial</th><th>Temporal</th><th>Human Actor</th><th colspan="2">Environment</th></tr>
<tr><td>Organisational</td><td colspan="2">Pre-set empty truck weight deviation threshold</td><td>Pre-set route for a truck's pickup operation</td><td>Pre-set duration for a truck's pickup operation</td><td></td><td colspan="2">Pre-set environmental condition rules</td></tr>
<tr><td>Process</td><td colspan="2"></td><td>3
Truck Location Validity
By GPS</td><td></td><td></td><td colspan="2"></td></tr>
<tr><td>Process Event</td><td colspan="2">1
Weigh the empty truck
Weigh the loaded truck
- Truck Weight

By Weight Sensor</td><td></td><td>Enter the port
- Truck inbound time

By RFID Reader

Evaluate the truck exit
- Truck departure time

By RFID Reader</td><td></td><td colspan="2">Determine the continuance of pickup
- Temperature
By Temperature Sensor
- Humidity
By Humidity Sensor
- Grain Temperature
By Grain Temperature Sensor</td></tr>
<tr><td>Process Object</td><td colspan="2">2
A truck:
- Licence plate number

By RFID Reader</td><td>A truck:
- Truck location

By GPS</td><td></td><td>A driver:
- id

By RFID Reader</td><td colspan="2"></td></tr>
<tr><td>IoT Event</td><td>Read tag
- Tag No

By RFID Reader</td><td>Monitor weight
- Weight value

By Weight Sensor</td><td>Track location
- Longitude & latitude

By GPS</td><td>Record timestamp
- Time

By RFID Reader</td><td>Read tag
- Tag No

By RFID Reader</td><td>Monitor temperature
- Temperature

By Temperature Sensor</td><td>Monitor humidity
- Humidity

By Humidity Sensor</td></tr>
</table>

Fig. 7. Instantiation of process-relevant IoT context classification for the cargo pickup process

examine real-time infrared sensor data during the weighing event to assess whether improper truck positioning contributed to the anomaly.

2. The RFID reader captures truck-specific attributes stored on the tag, such as the licence plate. By analysing the **context** of the **physical object** type that represents a **process object** attribute (Fig. 7), experts can assess whether the anomaly is linked to specific truck characteristics, such as a history of structural modifications or tampering, which might have altered its expected weight.
3. GPS sensor continuously tracking the truck's movement within the port. By analysing the **context** of the **spatial** type associated with the truck **process** within the port (Fig. 7), it is possible to determine whether the truck accessed unauthorised areas within the port, potentially to offload illegally added weights or manipulate their weight before arriving at the weighbridge. Experts can detect such deviations by retrieving the value of "truck location validity" and assessing their potential impact on the anomaly.

Name	Identifier	Type	Unit	State	Value	Time	Location	Interdependencies
RFID Reader	rfid#1	device		Idle		t1	Gate #1	
Weight Sensor	WS#1	sensor	Kg	On	2356.0	t2	Weighbridge #1	IR#i
Infrared Sensor	IR#i $(1 \leq i \leq 3)$	sensor		Closed		t2	Weighbridge #1	1
Grain Temperature Sensor	Temp#1	sensor	Celsius	On	5.0	t3	Silo#1	
Temperature Sensor	Temp#1	sensor	Celsius	On	22.0	t1	Yard loc#1	
Humidity Sensor	Humid#1	sensor	Percentage	On	15.0	t1	Yard loc#1	

Fig. 8. Examples of IoT device context for the cargo pickup process

5.2 Chemical Manufacturing Process

This use case presents the production process of a company active in the preparation of chemical products [4]. Their production process can be summarised in four main steps: 1) Preparing raw materials and loading them in the tank; 2) Mixing the raw material in the tank; 3) Circulating the product through filters to remove impurities; and 4) Bottling and packing the finished product.

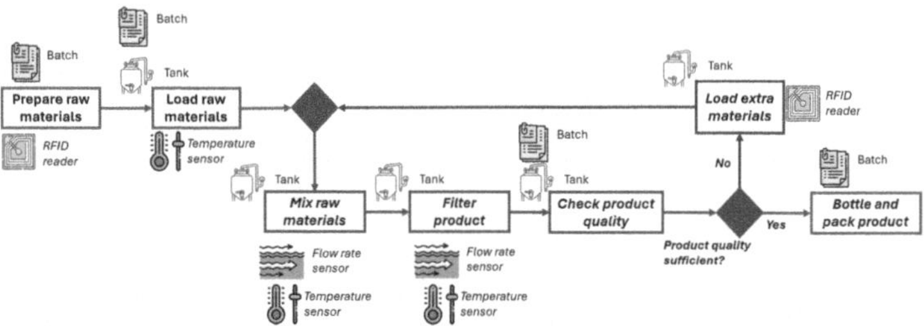

Fig. 9. High-level control flow of the chemical manufacturing process, illustrating the interactions between business objects and IoT entities throughout the process execution.

Sometimes, the quality of the product is not high enough after filtering, i.e., some characteristics of the product do not meet the specifications. In this case, an adjustment is applied by loading additional raw materials into the tank and repeating steps two and three, resulting in the high-level production process depicted in Fig. 9. This seemingly simple process has to be executed with extreme precision and care as the slightest presence of impurities in the finished product greatly diminishes its quality. To demonstrate the usefulness of the classification, one scenario in this use case is *Flow rate monitoring*. In particular, the flow rate of the product through the filters has to remain as stable as possible during the circulation phase, to minimise the risk of impurities being pushed through the filters. To ensure a stable flow rate, strict control limits are defined around a target flow rate value, and operators are constantly monitoring the point value of the flow rate to adjust the flow when necessary. Figure 10 shows an instantiation of the classification and Table 1 depicts the IoT device context for this use case. To prevent such issues from occurring, the following question is raised: *How can the operator evaluate potential causes for changes in flow rate?*

1. The RFID reader fetches relevant details about the raw materials used in the production of a certain batch. By analysing the **context** of the spatial type associated with the raw material **process objects** (e.g., information about the location of raw materials, see Fig. 10), the engineers can make sure that the raw materials used have the required properties and cross-examine data about the supplier to find out possible explanations for the deviations in flow rate.

	Physical object	**Spatial**	**Temporal**	**Identity**	**Environment**
Organisa-tional	Predefined set point for product flow and tolerance intervals (recipe-dependent)		Predefined duration of production (recipe-dependent)		Predefined threshold temperature values
Process				Alarm stops all on-going production *By* **Gyroscope**	Conditions in the clean room Temperature *By* **Temperature sensor**
Process event		Warehouse *By* **RFID reader**	Warehouse - Warehouse start time - Warehouse end time *By* **RFID reader**		
Process object	*A batch* - Flow rate set point - Flow rate tolerance interval *A tank* - Maximum flow rate - Current flow rate *By* **Flow sensor**	*A raw material* *By* **RFID reader** ❶		*An operator* *By* **Gyroscope**	
IoT event	Flow measurement - *Flow value* *By* **Flow sensor** ❷	Displace raw materials *By* **RFID reader**		Phone tilt - Phone orienta-tion measurement *By* **Gyroscope**	Monitor temperature - *Temperature* *By* **Temperature sensor**

Fig. 10. Instantiation of the classification for the chemical manufacturing process.

Table 1. Examples of IoT device context for the chemical manufacturing process

Name	Identifier	Type	Unit	State	Value	Time	Location	Interdependencies
RFID Reader	rfid#1	Device		Idle		t_1	Clean room	
Flow Sensor	FS#1	Sensor	Litres per hour	On	124.3	t_1	Pump#1	
Temperature Sensor	Temp#1	Sensor	Celsius degrees	On	20	t_1	Clean room	
Gyroscope	Gyro#1	Sensor	Degrees per second	On	{2.4, 0.3, 3.1}	t_1	Wearable	

2. The flow rate is measured at various points in the process by flow rate sensors. By analysing the **context** of the **physical object** type associated with the **IoT events**, anomalies can be detected (see Fig. 10). These anomalies can give an indication of the cause of deviations in the flow rate of the product, and flow rate deviations can be solved, e.g., by adjusting the pressure in the tank.

6 Conclusion and Future Research

In this work, we adopt the method introduced by Nickerson et al. [23] to develop the process-relevant IoT context classification. The purpose of our work is to provide guidance for logically integrating low-level IoT data into business processes containing high-level information. The proposed classification consists of two interrelated parts, namely the integration of IoT contexts with process contexts, which classifies IoT-captured context to corresponding process levels, and IoT device context, which specifies the characteristics of IoT devices involved in the process. To evaluate the applicability, robustness, and usefulness of the proposed classification, we applied it to two real-world use cases from different domains with varying levels of IoT integration. Although a key challenge in applying the proposed classification was the limited coverage of the IoT Device

Context in many use cases, the classification overall proved effective in capturing process-relevant IoT contexts across domains. For future work, we focus on how to use this context classification that is to leverage context for process analytics. We plan to extend evaluations through expert feedback and additional real-world cases and promote adoption by researchers and practitioners for further refinement and broader use.

References

1. Abowd, G.D., Dey, A.K., Brown, P.J., Davies, N., Smith, M., Steggles, P.: Towards a better understanding of context and context-awareness. In: HUC, pp. 304–307 (1999)
2. Ahmad, T., Van Looy, A.: Business process management and digital innovations: a systematic literature review. Sustainability **12**(17) (2020)
3. Bajaj, G., Agarwal, R., Singh, P., Georgantas, N., Issarny, V.: 4W1H in IoT semantics. IEEE Access **6**, 65488–65506 (2018)
4. Bertrand, Y., De Weerdt, J., Serral, E.: An expert-validated bridging model for IoT process mining. Bus. Inf. Syst. Eng. 1–20 (2024)
5. Bertrand, Y., Veneruso, S., Leotta, F., Mecella, M., Serral, E.: Nice: the native IoT-centric event log model for process mining. In: ICPM, pp. 32–44. Springer (2023)
6. Bocciarelli, P., D'Ambrogio, A., Panetti, T.: A model based framework for IoT-aware business process management. Future Internet **15**(2), 50 (2023)
7. vom Brocke, J., Zelt, S., Schmiedel, T.: On the role of context in business process management. Int. J. Inf. Manag. **36**(3), 486–495 (2016)
8. Brunk, J.: Structuring business process context information for process monitoring and prediction. In: CBI 2020, pp. 39–48. IEEE (2020)
9. van Bunningen, A.H., Feng, L., Apers, P.M.G.: Context for ubiquitous data management. In: UDM 2005, pp. 17–24. IEEE Computer Society (2005)
10. Compagnucci, I., Corradini, F., Fornari, F., Polini, A., Re, B., Tiezzi, F.: A systematic literature review on IoT-aware business process modeling views, requirements and notations. Softw. Syst. Model. **22**(3), 969–1004 (2023)
11. Elali, R., Kornyshova, E., Deneckère, R., Salinesi, C.: Mining contextual process models using sensors data: a case of daily activities in smart home. In: EMCIS 2022. LNBIP, vol. 464, pp. 409–425. Springer (2022)
12. Gallik, F., Kirikkayis, Y., Reichert, M.: Modeling, executing and monitoring IoT-aware processes with BPM technology. In: ICSS 2022, pp. 96–103 (2022)
13. Grisold, T., van der Aa, H., Franzoi, S., Hartl, S., Mendling, J., vom Brocke, J.: A context framework for sense-making of process mining results. In: ICPM 2024, pp. 57–64. IEEE (2024)
14. Henricksen, K., Indulska, J., Rakotonirainy, A.: Modeling context information in pervasive computing systems. In: Mattern, F., Naghshineh, M. (eds.) Pervasive 2002. LNCS, vol. 2414, pp. 167–180. Springer, Heidelberg (2002). https://doi.org/10.1007/3-540-45866-2_14
15. Janiesch, C., et al.: The internet of things meets business process management: a manifesto. IEEE Syst. Man Cybern. Mag. **6**(4), 34–44 (2020)
16. Janowicz, K., Haller, A., Cox, S.J.D., Phuoc, D.L., Lefrançois, M.: SOSA: a lightweight ontology for sensors, observations, samples, and actuators. J. Web Semant. **56**, 1–10 (2019)

17. Kirikkayis, Y., Gallik, F., Reichert, M.: Modeling, executing and monitoring IoT-driven business rules with BPMN and DMN: current support and challenges. In: EDOC (2022)
18. Kitchenham, B.: Procedures for performing systematic reviews. Keele University, Keele, UK, vol. 33, pp. 1–26 (2004)
19. Koschmider, A., Mannhardt, F., Heuser, T.: On the contextualization of event-activity mappings. In: BPM 2018, vol. 342, pp. 445–457. Springer (2018)
20. Kundisch, D., et al.: An update for taxonomy designers. Bus. Inf. Syst. Eng. **64**, 421–439 (2021)
21. Mangler, J., et al.: Datastream xes extension: embedding IoT sensor data into extensible event stream logs. Future Internet **15**(3) (2023)
22. Mirzaie, M., Behkamal, B., Allahbakhsh, M., Paydar, S., Bertino, E.: State of the art on quality control for data streams: a systematic literature review. Comput. Sci. Rev. (2023)
23. Nickerson, R.C., Varshney, U., Muntermann, J.: A method for taxonomy development and its application in information systems. Eur. J. Inf. Syst. **22**(3), 336–359 (2013)
24. Park, G., Benzin, J., van der Aalst, W.M.P.: Detecting context-aware deviations in process executions. In: BPM 2022 Forum. LNBIP, vol. 458, pp. 190–206. Springer (2022)
25. Pentland, B.T., Recker, J., Wolf, J.R., Wyner, G.M.: Bringing context inside process research with digital trace data. J. Assoc. Inf. Syst. **21**(5), 5 (2020)
26. Perera, C., Zaslavsky, A.B., Christen, P., Georgakopoulos, D.: Context aware computing for the internet of things: a survey. IEEE Commun. Surv. Tutorials **16**(1), 414–454 (2014)
27. Ploesser, K., Peleg, M., Soffer, P., Rosemann, M., Recker, J.: Learning from context to improve business processes. BPTrends **6**(1), 1–7 (2009)
28. Pradeep, P., Krishnamoorthy, S.: The MOM of context-aware systems: a survey. Comput. Commun. **137**, 44–69 (2019)
29. Pradeep, P., Krishnamoorthy, S., Pathinarupothi, R.K., Vasilakos, A.V.: Leveraging context-awareness for internet of things ecosystem: representation, organization, and management of context. Comput. Commun. **177**, 33–50 (2021)
30. Rosemann, M., Recker, J., Flender, C.: Contextualisation of business processes. Int. J. Bus. Process. Integr. Manag. **3**(1), 47–60 (2008)
31. Schilit, B.N., Adams, N., Want, R.: Context-aware computing applications. In: WMCSA, 1994, pp. 85–90. IEEE Computer Society (1994)
32. Schönig, S., Ackermann, L., Jablonski, S., Ermer, A.: IoT meets BPM: a bidirectional communication architecture for IoT-aware process execution. Softw. Syst. Model. (2020)
33. Sezer, O.B., Dogdu, E., Özbayoglu, A.M.: Context-aware computing, learning, and big data in internet of things: a survey. IEEE Internet Things J. **5**(1), 1–27 (2018)
34. Souabni, R., Saâdi, I.B., Ghézala, H.B.: A multidimensional framework to study situation awareness in U-learning systems. Telemat. Inform. **43** (2019)
35. Stoiber, C., Schönig, S.: Improving business processes with the internet of things - a taxonomy of IIoT applications. In: ECIS 2022 (2022)
36. Szopinski, D., Schoormann, T., Kundisch, D.: Criteria as a prelude for guiding taxonomy evaluation. In: HICSS 2020, pp. 1–10. ScholarSpace (2020)
37. Torres, V., Serral, E., Valderas, P., Pelechano, V., Grefen, P.: Modeling of IoT devices in business processes: a systematic mapping study. In: CBI 2020, pp. 221–230. IEEE (2020)

38. Valderas, P., Torres, V., Serral, E.: Modelling and executing IoT-enhanced business processes through BPMN and microservices. J. Syst. Softw. **184**, 111139 (2022)
39. van der Aalst, W.M.P.: Object-centric process mining: unraveling the fabric of real processes. Mathematics **11**(12) (2023)
40. van der Aalst, W.M.P., Dustdar, S.: Process mining put into context. IEEE Internet Comput. **16**(1), 82–86 (2012)
41. Vitali, M., Pernici, B.: Interconnecting processes through IoT in a health-care scenario. In: ISC2 2016, pp. 1–6. IEEE (2016)
42. Vodyaho, A.I., Zhukova, N.A., Abbas, S.A., Kulikov, I.A.: Context aware data collection systems for cyber-physical systems. In: SCM 2021, pp. 183–185 (2021)
43. Webster, J., Watson, R.T.: Analyzing the past to prepare for the future: writing a literature review. MIS Q. **26**(2) (2002)
44. Wei, J., He, Z., Ouyang, C., Moreira, C.: MIMICEL: MIMIC-IV Event Log for Emergency Department (version 2.1.0). PhysioNet (2023)
45. Wei, J., et al.: From conventional to IoT-Enhanced: simulated object-centric event logs for real-life logistics processes (2024)

The PM-EdgeMap: Towards Real-Time Process Mining on the Edge-Cloud Continuum

Hendrik Reiter[1(✉)], Christian Imenkamp[2], Olaf Landsiedel[1], Andrea Maldonado[3], Patrick Rathje[1], and Wilhelm Hasselbring[1]

[1] Kiel University, Christian-Albrechts-Platz 4, 24118 Kiel, Germany
{hendrik.reiter,olaf.landsiedel,patrick.rathje, hasselbring}@email.uni-kiel.de

[2] University of Bayreuth, Bayreuth, Germany
christian.imenkamp@uni-bayreuth.de

[3] School of Engineering and Design, Technical University of Munich, Munich, Germany
andrea.maldonado@tum.de

Abstract. Smart factories are evolving into Cyber-Physical Systems (CPS), demanding increased autonomy. This necessitates real-time decision making, facilitated by insights derived from sensor data. Process mining offers a valuable approach to gain such insights and guide actions. The edge computing paradigm supports this real-time requirement by enabling network communication between sensors and leveraging nearby computing resources. This paper investigates the implications of performing real-time process mining algorithms on the edge. Within this paper, we first propose a formalism to describe relevant datasets and the computing topology. We then evaluate the edge computing approach through a case study involving an edge-based conformance checking algorithm. The results demonstrate the feasibility and benefits of edge-based real-time process mining for enhanced autonomous control in smart factories.

Keywords: Process Mining · Cyber-Physical System · Edge Computing

1 Introduction

The ongoing evolution of industrial automation towards highly autonomous systems within the Industrial Internet of Things (IIoT) represents a significant paradigm shift in manufacturing and operational management [9]. This transformation is largely facilitated by the increasing integration of smart machines and advanced robotics, which, equipped with sophisticated sensing and actuation capabilities, function as core components of Cyber-Physical Systems (CPS) [10]. These systems bridge the physical and digital domains, enabling intricate control

I. van de Weerd et al. (Eds.): BPM 2025 Workshops, LNBIP 569, pp. 217–231, 2026.
https://doi.org/10.1007/978-3-032-13426-4_16

and interaction within complex industrial environments. A fundamental characteristic of these CPS is the pervasive generation of data by numerous sensors. This sensor data exhibits properties aligned with Big Data challenges [24], specifically concerning its volume, velocity, variety, and veracity. For intelligent decision-making and the effective realization of autonomous control, this data requires processing not only in real-time but also with a high degree of accuracy. Traditional, centralized data processing architectures frequently encounter limitations in addressing these demanding requirements, particularly given the scale and rate of data generation.

To address these challenges, the edge computing paradigm has emerged as an architectural solution for contemporary IIoT applications [14] such as real-time machine data analytics, image classification, or real-time anomaly detection [11]. Edge computing [28] involves distributing computational resources closer to the data sources, leveraging a network of heterogeneous, interconnected devices. This distributed architecture offers distinct advantages in fulfilling real-time processing demands by reducing data latency, optimizing network bandwidth utilization by minimizing the transfer of raw data to central repositories, and enhancing data privacy through localized data management. By providing immediate computational capabilities at or near the point of data generation, edge computing [28] aims to support the real-time requirements of autonomous systems. Process mining [1] is a discipline for gaining insights from event data related to operational processes with techniques such as process discovery or conformance checking. Moreover, process mining has expanded to be performed on event streams [12], which processes event data as it is generated, enabling near-real-time analysis.

Considering the intersection between IoT factory automation and Process mining, a notable research gap exists when performing streaming process mining on edge computing topologies. Both disciplines can benefit from a synergistic approach, particularly within the context of IIoT. Conventionally, process mining has been conceptualized primarily as a centralized activity, performing computations on a single, aggregated event log within a central computing instance. In contrast, edge computing operates on distributed and localized data streams, necessitating computations to be performed with only a subset of the complete system data. This architectural divergence between traditional process mining and the distributed characteristics of edge computing presents an unsolved challenge and a significant avenue for research. This paper addresses this research gap by investigating the implications of incorporating edge computing in the context of process mining. We present the Process Mining Edge Map (PM-EdgeMap), a formalization of process mining algorithms and their quality attributes in the realm of edge computing. Thereby, the PM-EdgeMap defines how algorithms interact with edge topologies and their distributed event streams. In summary, the paper contributes the following:

1. The PM-EdgeMap: A formalization of edge computing in the realm of process mining, their quality measures, and distributed event streams in the realm of process mining.

2. A prototype of an edge conformance checking algorithm, designed to demonstrate the suitability of the PM-EdgeMap.

2 Motivation

Consider a modern smart factory producing high-precision automotive components using a network of interconnected robotic workstations. Each workstation is equipped with sensors that continuously log events such as task completions or inter-robot handovers. In such a setting, maintaining tight control over the production process is critical, not only to meet quality standards but also to ensure safety and minimize downtime. A key challenge arises when deviations from the expected process behavior occur, such as unexpected delays, or incorrect task sequences. This is where real-time process mining analysis becomes crucial in tasks such as conformance checking, which detects deviations from the defined production model. Traditional process mining approaches first send the data to a central computing instance. This takes time and requires significant network bandwidth. And in turn, may violate the real-time constraints for safety-critical applications, particularly when video streams or sensor time series have to be transmitted to the central computing instance. However, by deploying these tasks directly on devices close to the machines, i.e., on the edge, these edge devices can detect anomalies immediately and adapt control strategies, without the need to transfer large amounts of raw data to a central server. For example, suppose an edge-based conformance checking algorithm detects that a robotic arm skipped a critical assembly step. In that case, the system can halt the workflow or reroute products before defects propagate downstream. In general, process mining can benefit from edge computing by enabling real-time analysis of several process-related tasks mentioned in the IoT-meets-BPM Manifesto [18], such as online conformance checking, resource utilization optimization, or evaluation of the quality of task execution. Here, real-time analyses provide operational support that allows interactions with the process while it is still running. In this paper, we will argue that process mining can benefit from edge computing by (1) enabling real-time process analysis which supports autonomous control in IIoT systems, (2) utilizing fewer cloud resources which saves computing costs, and (3) more event data can be processed which allows more fine-grained process mining results.

3 Edge Computing

Edge computing [28] represents a distributed computing paradigm that strategically positions computational capabilities closer to the data sources, leveraging a network of heterogeneous, interconnected devices. Thereby it contrasts traditional cloud computing models, in which data is primarily transmitted to and

Table 1. Results from the literature concerning edge computing in the categories main motivations, edge computing topologies, and quality attributes

Objectives [28]	Topologies [4,22]	Quality Attributes [8]
Reduced Latency	Mobile Cloud Comp.	Time Behavior
Low Bandwidth Utilization	Mobile Edge Comp.	Resource Utilization
Privacy & Security	Cloudlet Computing	Load Capacity
Scalability & Reliability		Scalability

processed within central data centers. This section characterizes edge computing by describing its primary motivations, the diverse technical infrastructure it employs, and the critical quality attributes that define its performance and utility.

Edge Computing Objectives. The adoption of edge computing is driven by four key objectives: reduced *network latency*, improved *bandwidth utilization*, enhanced *privacy and security*, and improved *scalability and reliability* [28], as found in literature and summarized in Table 1.

Locating computing resources in closer geographical and network proximity to data generation points reduces *latency* due to the physical distance within the network. This proximity minimizes data transmission delays, leading to lower latency for data processing and subsequent response generation. Edge computing enhances *bandwidth utilization* by reducing the need to transfer all raw data across wide area networks to centralized cloud infrastructures. Techniques such as data filtering, aggregation, and batching can be applied to the edge data before transmitting. For instance, in video surveillance, instead of streaming raw video footage, an edge device can classify objects or detect events locally and transmit only metadata or alerts. By design, edge computing inherently supports improved *data privacy* as processing data closer to its origin means that sensitive or raw information may not need to be transferred beyond the local device or network segment. Furthermore, through local abstraction and aggregation, edge nodes can derive insights or aggregated results, transmitting only this derived, non-sensitive information. This minimizes the exposure of private data to wider networks and central cloud systems, thereby reducing potential attack surfaces and enhancing overall data security. The distributed nature of edge computing contributes to enhanced system *scalability and reliability*: By offloading processing tasks from central cloud servers, edge deployments may handle an increased volume of data, effectively scaling computational capabilities horizontally. Moreover, by performing local processing, edge systems can tolerate temporary network outages or disconnections to the cloud, maintaining operational continuity for critical tasks. This distributed resilience improves the overall reliability of the system, particularly in remote or intermittently connected environments.

Devices at the Edge. Edge computing environments utilize a diverse array of devices, characterized by their heterogeneity in terms of computational capabilities. These devices range from highly resource-constrained entities, such as embedded microcontrollers and single-board computers (e.g., Raspberry Pi), to more powerful local servers or mini-data centers. An edge node typically comprises hardware components for computing (e.g., CPUs, GPUs), storage (e.g., solid-state drives, volatile memory), and network connectivity. Many modern edge devices also incorporate specialized accelerators, such as GPUs for parallel processing or Software-Defined Networking (SDN) components for optimized network routing and management, to enhance their performance for specific tasks. Edge computing is frequently viewed as an extension of cloud computing, forming a layered architecture known as the edge-cloud continuum [4]. This continuum typically comprises distinct layers based on geographical proximity to data sources and computational capabilities: The Edge Layer consists of devices directly at the periphery of the network, such as sensors, mobile devices, switches, and routers. These are the closest to the data generation. The Fog Computing Layer is positioned between the edge and the centralized cloud, involving intermediary nodes like servers or smaller data centers in closer geographical proximity to edge devices than the remote cloud. These nodes offer more substantial computing and storage capabilities than individual edge devices. The Cloud Layer is the uppermost layer. It is characterized by large, centralized data centers with extensive and highly scalable computational resources, with immense processing power. The edge-cloud continuum is not limited to hierarchical algorithms but also peer-to-peer models [20], facilitating direct inter-device communication.

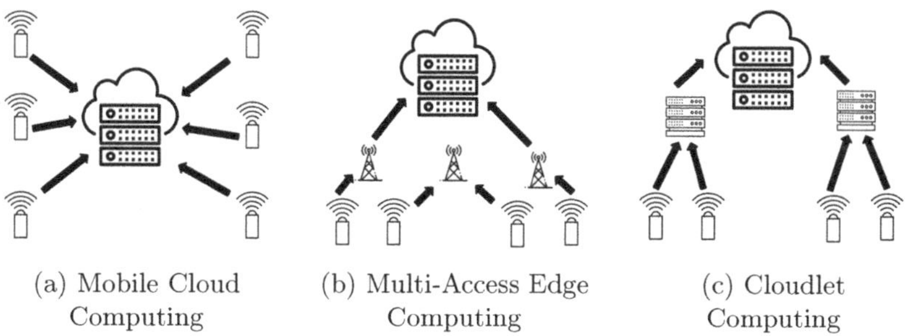

(a) Mobile Cloud Computing (b) Multi-Access Edge Computing (c) Cloudlet Computing

Fig. 1. The three process mining topologies differ in computing and communication allocation, with Distributed PM leveraging data sources' inherent resources.

Within the edge-cloud continuum, various topological instantiations [4,22] exist and each topology comes with specific characteristics: *Mobile Cloud Computing (MCC)* as shown in Fig. 1a refers to mobile devices or sensors offloading computationally intensive operations to remote cloud servers by transmitting relevant data. The cloud acts as an extension for resource-constrained mobile devices. *Multi-Access Edge Computing (MEC, Fig.* 1*b)* primarily concerns mobile devices and sensors connecting to the network via access points (e.g., cellular base stations, Wi-Fi routers) that are equipped with computing, storage, and networking capabilities. MEC servers are deployed at the base station level or aggregation points to provide cloud-like services with low latency. *Cloudlets* (Fig. 1c) are small-scale, decentralized data centers that provide cloud-like computing and storage capabilities at the network edge, often in close physical proximity to mobile users or IoT devices. Cloudlets represent a form of fog computing. This paper's evaluation employs all three topologies in the context of conformance checking.

Quality Attributes at the Edge. Understanding the elementary quality attributes is essential for designing and evaluating edge computing systems. According to a structured mapping study by Ashouri et al. [8], the most prominent quality measures in edge computing are time behavior, functional suitability, resource utilization, and load capacity. While other attributes, such as reliability, security, and maintainability, also play a role, they appear with comparatively lower frequency in the surveyed literature.

Time Behavior encompasses various metrics related to the timeliness of operations, including latency (the delay between an event and a system's response), throughput (the rate at which data is processed or transmitted), and response time (the total time taken for a system to respond to a request). Real-time requirements in many IIoT applications make time behavior a paramount concern. *Functional Suitability* refers to the degree to which a system provides functions that meet stated and implied needs when used under specified conditions. In edge computing, this often relates to the ability of edge devices to perform specific tasks accurately. In the realm of process mining, functional suitability could also refer to the integration of metrics such as fitness and precision [1]. *Resource Utilization* quantifies how efficiently computing, storage, or network components are being used in proportion to their maximal possible load. Efficient resource utilization is crucial for optimizing the cost and performance of edge deployments, especially given the potentially constrained nature of edge devices. *Load Capacity* relates to the maximum workload or data volume a system can handle before its performance degrades unacceptably or fails. For edge systems, understanding load capacity is vital for ensuring that the distributed infrastructure can accommodate peak loads and maintain required service levels.

4 Requirements for an Edge Process Mining Formalization

The characteristics of edge computing environments necessitate a reevaluation of traditional process mining algorithm design principles. Classical process mining tools and methodologies are developed under the assumption of centralized data storage and computation. Deploying process mining algorithms at the edge introduces new design challenges. These implications primarily concern the distributed nature of data and computational resources, the need to incorporate edge computing quality measures, and the influence of varying hardware topologies. This section presents requirements to extend the current process mining formalism to edge computing.

R1) Distributed Nature of Data. Traditionally, process mining algorithms operate on event data aggregated and stored in a central event log. In contrast, the distributed nature of data in edge computing environments implies that event data originates from multiple, geographically dispersed sources. This necessitates a shift towards a new notion of *distributed event logs*, conceptually aligned with principles found in federated process mining [2]. Furthermore, given the real-time requirements, this concept must be extended to *distributed event streams*, where events are processed continuously as they are generated across the network.

R2) Distributed Nature of Algorithms. Classical process mining algorithms typically assume complete and instantaneous access to all relevant event data. However, in an edge computing deployment, an algorithm initially has access only to the data originating from or localized within its own host edge device. To process data from other distributed devices or to gain a global perspective of a process, explicit inter-device communication is required. This means that algorithms must be designed to initiate or respond to network requests for data exchange. This distributed operational model introduces network communication between the edge nodes.

R3) Modelling of a Heterogeneous Compute Topology. Unlike classical process mining, which typically presumes computation on a single machine with uniform access to data, the heterogeneous compute topology of edge environments becomes relevant. The performance of a process mining algorithm is influenced by where it is executed within the edge-cloud continuum, whether on a resource-constrained sensor, an intermediate fog node, or a centralized cloud server. Consequently, a formal notion for describing network requests and the underlying heterogeneous computing topology is essential. Such a formalization would enable systematic analysis and comparison of different deployment strategies and data distribution patterns across the edge-cloud continuum, allowing for optimized allocation of computational tasks.

R4) Integration of Edge Computing Quality Measures. The deployment of process mining algorithms at the edge introduces new requirements concerning their performance and resource consumption. Algorithms must be designed to operate effectively under real-time constraints, ensuring timely insights and actions. Furthermore, they must adhere to the load capacity limitations of the underlying infrastructure. Therefore, the design of edge process mining algorithms must consider and optimize for edge computing quality attributes, such as low latency, efficient resource utilization, and high load capacities and scalability.

5 PM-EdgeMap

This section introduces a set of formal definitions intended to describe process mining algorithms within an edge computing context. The primary focus of this formalism is on modeling and analyzing real-time requirements. While other important concerns, such as data privacy, long-term persistence, or energy efficiency, are acknowledged, they are considered secondary within the scope of this specific formalization. The presented framework specifically models key quality measures, namely processing time, resource utilization, load capacity, and scalability. The overarching design goal is to provide a comprehensive and intuitive means to compare the performance of different process mining topologies and algorithms in distributed edge environments. It is important to state the delimitations of this formalism. It does not aim to provide a fully detailed simulation of the intricate dynamics of an edge environment, which would necessitate the employment of complex modeling techniques such as queuing theory [3], thereby significantly increasing model complexity. Furthermore, this formalism does not explicitly account for overutilization scenarios where existing queues might buffer tasks, but rather focuses on peak load capacities.

Distributed Event Stream. An Event $e = (c, a, t, l)$ is a tuple of case $c \in \mathcal{C}$, activity $a \in \mathcal{A}$, timestamp $t \in \mathcal{T}$ and a location $l \in \mathcal{L}$. Thereby, the location indicates the data source (e.g., a sensor) from which the event originates. Let $\mathcal{E}$ denote the set of all possible events defined as $\mathcal{E} := \mathcal{C} \times \mathcal{A} \times \mathcal{T} \times \mathcal{L}$. The function $\pi_l(e)$ returns the location of the event e. An Event Stream S is a function from the natural numbers to an event $e \in \mathcal{E}$, i.e., $S := \mathbb{N} \rightarrow \mathcal{E}$, with $S(i)$ being the i-th element of the event stream. The event stream S_l located at $l \in \mathcal{L}$ is defined as a subset of the event stream S, where all events are located at l, i.e., $S_l := \{e | i \in \mathbb{N}, e = S(i), \pi_l(e) = l\}$. We refer to the union of all Located Event Streams as a Distributed Data Stream: $S_D := \bigcup_{l \in \mathcal{L}} S_l$. Further, we define the velocity of an event stream as the number of events emitted in a certain period of time Δt as a function $v_{\Delta t} : S \rightarrow \mathbb{N}$.

Computing Topology. We denote N as the set of available computing nodes and HC as the set of hardware components $hc = (node, t_{init}, r_{init}, tp, type)$ as a tuple of the $node \in N$ where the hardware component belongs to, the initial processing delay t_{init}, the initial resource usage r_{init}, and the throughput tp and a type $type \in \{storage, compute, network\}$. To access a property from hc a function with the property name is defined, e.g. to get the throughput the function $tp : HC \rightarrow \mathbb{R}$ exists. An *edge topology* $\mathcal{T} \subseteq \mathcal{P}(HC)$ is subsequently defined as the set of all interconnected edge nodes within the system. A *hardware instruction* $hi \in HI \subseteq HC \times \mathbb{R}$ denotes a tuple of a hardware component and a payload size value. These hardware instructions are used when translating the pseudocode of an algorithm to the set of invoked functions. Therefore, we define an *algorithm execution* $\mathcal{A} : E \rightarrow \mathcal{P}(HI)$ for a single event E as the ordered sequence of all hardware instructions that are made by the algorithm while processing that event. Further, we describe the function $payload : HI \rightarrow \mathbb{R}$ and the function $hw : HI \rightarrow HC$, which return the payload and the hardware component of a hardware instruction.

Quality Measures. Based on the defined formalism, we model the edge quality attributes *processing time*$(t_{process})$, *resource utilization*(r), as well as the load capacity and scalability: For a given event $e \in E$ and an algorithm $\mathcal{A}$, the *processing time* $t_{process}(\mathcal{A}, e)$ is defined as the sum of the initial delays and the processing times for all hardware calls within the execution path. Assuming sequential execution, the processing time is given by:

$$t_{process}(\mathcal{A}, e) = \sum_{step \in (\mathcal{A}(e))} \left(t_{init}(hw(step)) + \frac{payload(step)}{tp(hw(step))} \right)$$

The resource utilization r is determined per hardware component HC over a time unit Δt. For an event stream S with velocity $v(S)$, and considering all hardware calls hi for events E within Δt that utilize hardware components. Hence, the utilization of a hardware component is given by:

$$r(S, \mathcal{A}, hc) = \sum_{i \in \mathbb{N}} \sum_{\substack{step \in \mathcal{A}(S(i)) \\ hw(step)=hc}} \frac{v(S) \cdot (r_{init}(hw(step)) + payload(step))}{tp(hw(step))}$$

The **Load Capacity** of a system is defined via a service level objective (SLO). An exemplary SLO is that the resource utilization should not exceed 100% for any component, or that the response time should stay below 100 milliseconds. The *capacity* is then defined as the maximum event stream velocity v_S without violating that SLO. The *scalability* in this context, describes how the load capacity changes when the resource throughput of individual hardware components $hc \in HC$ is increased [17]. It quantifies the system's ability to improve performance as resources are added or enhanced, indicating how effectively the system can grow to handle higher event stream velocities.

6 Discussion of an Edge Conformance Checking Prototype

To provide a concrete illustration of how process mining can be adapted for edge computing environments, this section outlines a specialized conformance checking algorithm designed to adhere to the requirements for edge process mining algorithms outlined in the preceding discussion. Conformance checking was selected as the focus for this implementation for several key reasons. Firstly, it directly reflects potential real-time requirements, particularly when applied in scenarios such as anomaly detection within a smart factory. In such contexts, deviations from an expected process model (i.e., a drop in conformance below a defined threshold) may necessitate immediate actions, such as halting production, thereby demanding stringent real-time analysis. Secondly, not all process mining tasks inherently require real-time processing; a process analyst might tolerate a certain degree of data outdatedness, for instance, up to one minute, for tasks like periodic performance monitoring. Conformance checking, however, can critically inform immediate operational decisions.

The design of this edge conformance checking algorithm draws inspiration from existing work, specifically from the federated conformance checking algorithms proposed by [25] and the streaming conformance checking approaches

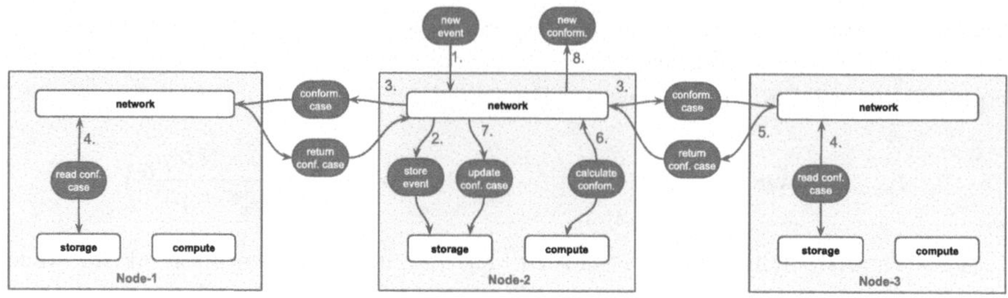

Fig. 2. Sketch of the algorithm execution for checking the conformance for an incoming event. The invoked node sends requests to other participants to check whether they observed events with the same case id and request their conformance.

developed by [13]. The algorithm operates through a two-phase design: a training phase and a conformance phase. The training phase is dedicated to recording and analyzing normal process behavior within the smart factory use case, from which a DFG is constructed. Subsequently, the conformance phase continuously checks the conformance of currently running process instances against the learned model. Figure 2 visualizes the algorithm's conformance checking phase.

During the training phase, a significant departure from traditional approaches is observed. Instead of mining a single, global process model, each instance of the algorithm, typically residing on a specific edge node, learns and maintains its own localized DFG. When a new event is processed at a particular edge node, the algorithm must identify its predecessor within the associated case, which may have been observed on a different node. This necessitates a distributed lookup: a network request is initiated to all available nodes to ascertain whether they have observed an event belonging to the same case. The event with the timestamp closest to, but preceding the currently processed event, is then identified as the predecessor and subsequently integrated into the local DFG. This distributed learning mechanism enables the algorithm to adapt to localized process variations while contributing to a collective understanding of a process's flow.

The Conformance Phase is responsible for continuously tracking and evaluating the conformance for each active process instance. To achieve this, the current conformance state of every case is maintained in memory on the respective edge nodes. When an event represents an "inbound activity" (i.e., its predecessor was observed on a different edge node), a network request is dispatched to the predecessor node. This request queries the current conformance status of the running trace on that remote node, allowing the algorithm to aggregate conformance information across distributed segments of the process instance. This mechanism ensures that even for cases spanning multiple edge devices, a real-time assessment of conformance can be maintained.

The algorithm is implemented in Python together with a simulation of the PM-EdgeMap formalism. Both are publicly available on GitHub[1]. The evaluation has been run on the IoT data set presented in [23]. In this smart factory scenario, the machine type divides the events into a distributed event log, and the Distributed Event Factory disseminates the data stream [27]. We evaluated three different edge topologies: mobile edge computing, mobile cloud computing, and cloudlet. Table 2 holds the setup and the evaluation results.

Table 2. The setup of the edge computing topologies together with the corresponding quality metrics, processing time, and load capacity. The tuple for the hardware components describes the initial latency per request, the initially consumed resources, and the throughput of the component.

	MCC	MEC	Cloudlet
$network_{data}$	$(0.025s, 2, 1000\frac{1}{s})$	$(0.001s, 1, 250\frac{1}{s})$	$(0.025s, 1.5, 500\frac{1}{s})$
$network_{control}$	$(0.005s, 1, 1000\frac{1}{s})$	$(0.025s, 2, 250\frac{1}{s})$	$(0.025s, 1.5, 500\frac{1}{s})$
cpu	$(10^{-5}s, 1, 10^4\frac{1}{s})$	$(10^{-4}s, 1, 10^4\frac{1}{s})$	$(2 \cdot 10^{-5}s, 1, 5 \cdot 10^4\frac{1}{s})$
$storage$	$(10^{-4}s, 1, 10^4\frac{1}{s})$	$(10^{-3}s, 1, 10^3\frac{1}{s})$	$(2 \cdot 10^{-4}s, 1, 5 \cdot 10^3\frac{1}{s})$
$t_{process}$	0.036 s	0.043 s	0.027 s
$capacity$	$83\frac{events}{s}$	$138\frac{events}{s}$	$174\frac{events}{s}$

In the MCC topology, all sensors are connected directly via a central data network. Conversely, in the MEC and Cloudlet topologies, data sources are distributed among four edge nodes, with each node connected to between two and four individual data sources. The specification of the nodes can be retrieved from Table 2. The evaluation yielded distinct performance characteristics across the assessed topologies. Processing time was highest in MEC environments (0.043 s per event), while Cloudlet-based architectures demonstrated the lowest processing times (0.027 s/event). Cloudlet deployments exhibited the highest capacity (174 events/s), whereas MCC showed the lowest(83 events/s). The primary limiting factor for load capacity has been the data network in most scenarios. An exception is MEC, where the control network was the bottleneck. Another insight is that CPU resource consumption was predominantly consumed in the MCC scenario. We attribute this heightened consumption to the increased complexity of conformance checking alignments resulting from a larger data basis. Due to the performant CPUs in the modeled cloud, that fact did not influence the overall performance.

The PM-EdgeMap formalization and its prototype edge conformance checking algorithm are validated through fulfilling four key requirements. This includes the distributed processing of an IIoT datastream across computing locations (R1), the algorithm's efficient operation on data subsets (R2), a comparative analysis of edge computing topologies (R3), and the evaluation of processing time and load capacity as quality measures (R4).

[1] https://github.com/cau-se/PM-EdgeMap/.

7 Future Research Directions and Improvements

Within this formalism's application, several threats to validity are identified, concurrently highlighting avenues for future work. For one, the performance of edge computing quality attributes is highly dependent on the assumed edge computing topology. Currently, processing times are predominantly limited by data network bandwidth, with compute and storage capabilities playing a minor role. This dynamic would fundamentally change with datasets comprising unprocessed, unstructured data, such as video or sensor streams, which are more resource-intensive for storage and demand greater compute for tasks like machine learning inference. Consequently, realistic evaluations necessitate execution on actual edge hardware, but given the limited access to edge testbeds, extending analysis to edge computing simulators [19] without increasing system complexity becomes crucial.

Furthermore, the presented edge conformance checking algorithm serves as a foundational example, illustrating core principles of distributed process mining. Its current simplification lacks advanced capabilities like loop or parallelism detection, vital for modeling complex real-world processes. Future designs must extend this framework to incorporate such functionalities. Additionally, the reliance on artificial data for evaluation limits external validity, emphasizing the need for comprehensive, representative distributed event logs from real IIoT scenarios or the development of an advanced event log generator. This would allow precise control over input parameters, including event velocity and data heterogeneity. Moreover, IIoT process mining often involves unstructured data, where preliminary pre-processing for event and case identification introduces additional computational overhead that must be accurately integrated into performance models. Lastly, rigorous validation ideally requires real hardware testing. Therefore, employing realistic simulation environments that emulate distributed, heterogeneous, and resource-constrained edge deployments is imperative. The integration of data streaming middleware would provide more realistic insights into performance, resource consumption, and scalability under operational IIoT conditions, thereby enhancing the external validity of research findings.

8 Related Work

This paper lays the groundwork for a new research field: process mining within the edge-cloud computing continuum. Because this area is so new, closely related works are rare. However, there is relevant research in distributed process mining, real-time process mining on data streams, and applications of IoT data processing on the edge-cloud-continuum. Distributed process mining can be subdivided into two main types: distribution of data, like in federated process mining [2,26], and distribution algorithms. Federated process mining differs from our approach as it analyzes static event logs without considering real-time needs or the computing infrastructure. When algorithms are distributed, techniques such as MapReduce [15,16] are often used to make calculations faster and more efficient. Unlike our approach, these methods do not work on logically distributed data. Instead, they split data from a single event log for computations. While algorithms like EdgeMiner [5] and CheckMyFlow [6] do operate on distributed data and perform computations in a distributed manner, they focus on creating footprint matrices in a distributed way. Hence, they rather focus on preprocessing than on directly distributing the process mining algorithms. In the area of real-time process mining [12], algorithms such as streaming process mining are used for process discovery and conformance checking. However, unlike our approach, these methods are not applied to distributed data. Other data processing communities, such as machine learning, have already established paradigms for distributing their algorithms across the edge-cloud continuum for IoT data processing [7]. This is exemplified by techniques such as federated learning [21] or TinyML [29]. While Federated Learning enables distributed model training on decentralized datasets while preserving privacy, TinyML focuses on reducing the computational complexity to allow execution on resource-constrained devices. These fields of research may be used as inspiration for further development of process mining algorithms on the edge-cloud continuum.

9 Conclusion

In this paper, we explored the synergistic integration of process mining and edge computing within the context of large-scale IIoT data. We highlighted how edge computing offers significant advantages by enabling low-latency and low-bandwidth data processing, while simultaneously fostering privacy-aware and scalable data handling. Our investigation systematically identified key implications for the design of process mining algorithms when deployed at the edge. These implications encompass the inherently distributed nature of event data and the algorithms themselves, along with the necessity to incorporate the underlying computing topology into the formal framework.

Building upon these insights, we derived a set of critical quality attributes specifically tailored for edge process mining, including processing time, resource utilization, load capacity, and scalability. To demonstrate the feasibility and practical applicability of our proposed formalism, we presented a case study centered on a real-time conformance checking algorithm. This demonstration effectively showcased how variations in the underlying edge-cloud topology, as well as adjustments to algorithmic parameters, directly influence performance within such distributed environments.

Looking ahead, our future work intends to advance the concept of edge process mining further. We plan to develop a more sophisticated edge conformance checking algorithm that explicitly incorporates advanced features such as parallelism and loop detection, crucial for handling the complexities of real-world industrial processes. Furthermore, we aim to enhance the validity and robustness of our design by conducting rigorous benchmarks on actual edge hardware, moving beyond simulated environments. Concurrently, our efforts focus on testing these algorithms with authentic distributed IIoT datasets to ensure their practical efficacy. Ultimately, our overarching goal is to enable the extraction of actionable, real-time process insights from the vast and intricate datasets characteristic of modern IIoT landscapes.

Acknowledgments. This work received funding from the Deutsche Forschungsgemeinschaft (DFG), grant 496119880.

References

1. van der Aalst, W.M.P.: Process Mining: A 360 Degree Overview, pp. 3–34. Springer (2022). https://doi.org/10.1007/978-3-031-08848-3_1
2. van der Aalst, W.M.: Federated process mining: exploiting event data across organizational boundaries. In: 2021 IEEE International Conference on Smart Data Services (SMDS). IEEE (2021). https://doi.org/10.1109/smds53860.2021.00011
3. Adan, I., Resing, J.: Queueing theory. Eindhoven University of Technology, vol. 180 (2002)
4. Al-Dulaimy, A., et al.: The computing continuum: from IoT to the cloud. Internet Things **27**, 101272 (2024). https://doi.org/10.1016/j.iot.2024.101272
5. Andersen, J., Rathje, P., Imenkamp, C., Koschmider, A., Landsiedel, O.: EdgeMiner: Distributed Process Mining at the Data Sources, pp. 705–713. Association for Computing Machinery, New York (2025). https://doi.org/10.1145/3672608.3707873
6. Andersen, J., Rathje, P., Landsiedel, O.: Check My Flow: Distributed Conformance Checking at the Source, pp. 101–112. Springer (2025). https://doi.org/10.1007/978-3-031-78666-2_8
7. Arzovs, A., Judvaitis, J., Nesenbergs, K., Selavo, L.: Distributed learning in the IoT–edge–cloud continuum. Mach. Learn. Knowl. Extr. **6**(1), 283–315 (2024). https://doi.org/10.3390/make6010015
8. Ashouri, M., Davidsson, P., Spalazzese, R.: Quality attributes in edge computing for the internet of things a systematic mapping study. Internet Things **13**, 100346 (2021). https://doi.org/10.1016/j.iot.2020.100346
9. Babayigit, B., Abubaker, M.: Industrial internet of things: a review of improvements over traditional scada systems for industrial automation. IEEE Syst. J. **18**(1), 120–133 (2024). https://doi.org/10.1109/jsyst.2023.3270620
10. Baheti, R., Gill, H.: Cyber-physical systems. Impact Control Technol. **12**(1), 161–166 (2011)
11. Bayar, A., Şener, U., Kayabay, K., Eren, P.E.: Edge Computing Applications in Industrial IoT: A Literature Review, pp. 124–131. Springer (2023). https://doi.org/10.1007/978-3-031-29315-3_11
12. Burattin, A.: Streaming Process Mining, pp. 349–372. Springer (2022). https://doi.org/10.1007/978-3-031-08848-3_11
13. Burattin, A., van Zelst, S.J., Armas-Cervantes, A., van Dongen, B.F., Carmona, J.: Online Conformance Checking Using Behavioural Patterns, pp. 250–267. Springer (2018). https://doi.org/10.1007/978-3-319-98648-7_15
14. Chalapathi, G.S.S., Chamola, V., Vaish, A., Buyya, R.: Industrial Internet of Things (IIoT) Applications of Edge and Fog Computing: A Review and Future Directions, pp. 293–325. Springer (2021). https://doi.org/10.1007/978-3-030-57328-7_12

15. Evermann, J.: Scalable process discovery using map-reduce. IEEE Trans. Serv. Comput. **9**(3), 469–481 (2016). https://doi.org/10.1109/tsc.2014.2367525
16. Evermann, J., Rehse, J.R., Fettke, P.: Process discovery from event stream data in the cloud - a scalable, distributed implementation of the flexible heuristics miner on the amazon kinesis cloud infrastructure. In: 2016 IEEE International Conference on Cloud Computing Technology and Science (CloudCom). IEEE (2016). https://doi.org/10.1109/cloudcom.2016.0111
17. Henning, S., Hasselbring, W.: A configurable method for benchmarking scalability of cloud-native applications. Empir. Softw. Eng. **27**(6) (2022). https://doi.org/10.1007/s10664-022-10162-1
18. Janiesch, C., Koschmider, A., Mecella, M., Weber, B.: The internet of things meets business process management: a manifesto. IEEE Syst. Man Cybern. Mag. **6**(4), 34–44 (2020). https://doi.org/10.1109/msmc.2020.3003135
19. Jha, D.N., et al.: Iotsim-edge: a simulation framework for modeling the behavior of internet of things and edge computing environments. Softw. Pract. Exp. **50**(6), 844–867 (2020). https://doi.org/10.1002/spe.2787
20. Karagiannis, V., Venito, A., Coelho, R., Borkowski, M., Fohler, G.: Edge computing with peer to peer interactions: use cases and impact. In: Proceedings of the Workshop on Fog Computing and the IoT, pp. 46–50. CPS-IoT Week 2019, ACM (2019). https://doi.org/10.1145/3313150.3313226
21. Li, L., Fan, Y., Tse, M., Lin, K.Y.: A review of applications in federated learning. Comput. Ind. Eng. **149**, 106854 (2020). https://doi.org/10.1016/j.cie.2020.106854
22. Mahmud, R., Kotagiri, R., Buyya, R.: Fog Computing: A Taxonomy, Survey and Future Directions, pp. 103–130. Springer, Singapore (2017). https://doi.org/10.1007/978-981-10-5861-5_5
23. Malburg, L., Grüger, J., Bergmann, R.: An IoT-enriched event log for process mining in smart factories (2022). https://doi.org/10.48550/ARXIV.2209.02702
24. Qi, Q., Xu, Z., Rani, P.: Big data analytics challenges to implementing the intelligent industrial internet of things (IIoT) systems in sustainable manufacturing operations. Technol. Forecast. Soc. Change **190**, 122401 (2023). https://doi.org/10.1016/j.techfore.2023.122401
25. Rafiei, M., Pourbafrani, M., van der Aalst, W.M.: Federated conformance checking. Inf. Syst. **131**, 102525 (2025). https://doi.org/10.1016/j.is.2025.102525
26. Rafiei, M., Van Der Aalst, W.M.P.: An abstraction-based approach for privacy-aware federated process mining. IEEE Access **11**, 33697–33714 (2023). https://doi.org/10.1109/access.2023.3263673
27. Reiter, H., Imenkamp, C., Koschmider, A., Hasselbring, W.: Distributed event factory: a tool for generating event streams on distributed data sources. In: ICPM Doctoral Consortium and Demo Track 2024. Workshop Proceedings (2024). https://ceur-ws.org/Vol-3783/paper_323.pdf
28. Satyanarayanan, M.: The emergence of edge computing. Computer **50**(1), 30–39 (2017). https://doi.org/10.1109/mc.2017.9
29. Zaidi, S.A.R., Hayajneh, A.M., Hafeez, M., Ahmed, Q.Z.: Unlocking edge intelligence through tiny machine learning (tinyml). IEEE Access **10**, 100867–100877 (2022). https://doi.org/10.1109/access.2022.3207200

IoT Miner – Intelligent Extraction of Event Logs from Sensor Data for Process Mining

Edyta Brzychczy[1], Urszula Jessen[2,3], Krzysztof Kluza[1(✉)], Sridhar Sriram[2], and Manuel Vargas Nettelnstroth[4]

[1] AGH University of Krakow, Mickiewicza Av. 30, 30-059 Krakow, Poland
{brzych3,kluza}@agh.edu.pl

[2] process.science GmbH & Co. KG, Finkenau 1, 22081 Hamburg, Germany
{uj,sridhar.sriram}@process-science.com

[3] Eindhoven University of Technology, Eindhoven, The Netherlands
u.a.jessen@tue.nl

[4] talpasolutions GmbH, Bismarckstraße 57, 45128 Essen, Germany
manuel@talpa-solutions.com

Abstract. This paper presents *IoT Miner*, a novel framework for automatically creating high-level event logs from raw industrial sensor data to support process mining. In many real-world settings, such as mining or manufacturing, standard event logs are unavailable, and sensor data lacks the structure and semantics needed for analysis. IoT Miner addresses this gap using a four-stage pipeline: data preprocessing, unsupervised clustering, large language model (LLM)-based labeling, and event log construction. A key innovation is the use of LLMs to generate meaningful activity labels from cluster statistics, guided by domain-specific prompts. We evaluate the approach on sensor data from a Load-Haul-Dump (LHD) mining machine and introduce a new metric, Similarity-Weighted Accuracy, to assess labeling quality. Results show that richer prompts lead to more accurate and consistent labels. By combining AI with domain-aware data processing, IoT Miner offers a scalable and interpretable method for generating event logs from IoT data, enabling process mining in settings where traditional logs are missing.

Keywords: Process Mining · Sensor Data · IoT · Event Log Creation · Large Language Models

1 Introduction

Industrial processes generate vast volumes of low-level data as a result of machine operations and monitoring equipment. While these low-level data, such as motor currents, location data, or velocity readings, offer detailed insights into process dynamics, they lack semantic clarity. Sensor data in its raw form is unsuitable for standard process mining (PM) techniques, which require well-defined, high-level event logs to develop process models and provide in-depth process analysis [1,25].

I. van de Weerd et al. (Eds.): BPM 2025 Workshops, LNBIP 569, pp. 232–246, 2026.
https://doi.org/10.1007/978-3-032-13426-4_17

Bridging the semantic gap between raw sensor readings and high-level event labels remains one of the main challenges in the Business Process Management (BPM) domain [11,17]. To bridge this gap, a preprocessing step known as event abstraction is typically applied, which involves mapping fine-grained data into meaningful process activities [14,27].

Event abstraction is a challenging task, often reliant on expert rules (as a supervised task) or data clustering (as an unsupervised task) [8]. Moreover, traditional methods for event abstraction are time-consuming and difficult to scale across different processes, requiring domain knowledge to create rules or label the discovered clusters [4]. This challenge is particularly evident in industrial contexts, where data overload and lack of expert knowledge hinder effective process analysis. Recent case studies show how integrating AI techniques, including LLMs and process mining, can help non-experts interact with complex manufacturing data and obtain rapid insights [12].

To overcome the mentioned disadvantages in event abstraction, we propose an IoT Miner, solution for unsupervised analysis of raw sensor data and event abstraction with the use of LLMs. IoT Miner enables conversion, step by step, of low-level event data into high-level event logs. For this purpose, we use the following analytical pipeline: (1) raw data preprocessing, (2) clustering, (3) labeling, and finally, (4) event logs creation.

In recent years, LLMs have demonstrated high abilities in language processing, pattern recognition, and semantic labeling, also for BPM and PM domains [3,5,10,24]. Their potential to interpret textual and structured input and adapt to new domains suggests a promising direction for the abstraction task [9,18,21]. Our first attempt to use LLM for raw sensor data labeling using automatically generated rules for event abstraction was presented in [7]. However, in this approach, the labels for process activities were a prerequisite for LLM.

Hence, in the next step, in IoT Miner, we designed a pipeline in which the LLM automatically generates meaningful labels for the discovered clusters. Several prompt versions are evaluated, progressively enriched with contextual information to assess how contextual information influences label quality. In evaluation, we use the real-life Load-Haul-Dump (LHD) machine dataset with ground truth data as a benchmark for evaluating the semantic similarity and consistency of the generated labels.

The paper is structured as follows: Sect. 2 presents related work regarding event abstraction of low-level data and LLMs usage. Section 3 describes in detail the IoT Miner solution and its architecture. Section 4 contains evaluation with an experimental setup, results, and discussion. Section 5 concludes the paper and highlights future work.

2 Related Work

The evolution of IoT research has progressed from basic sensing in constrained environments towards intelligent systems capable of real-time analytics. Initial IoT applications, rooted in Wireless Sensor Networks (WSNs), emphasized energy-efficient data aggregation and simple statistical methods [15, 26]. With increased sensor deployments, cloud computing facilitated classical machine learning (ML) and time-series analytics [16,22], and subsequent innovations like real-time stream processing and fog computing addressed latency demands [19]. Recent advances including TinyML, federated learning, and hybrid AI approaches integrate local inference with semantic reasoning, forming a strong foundation for connecting IoT with business process analytics [2,15]. However, a significant gap persists: methods to semantically abstract and align IoT-generated data with high-level business processes remain underdeveloped, limiting operational and organizational actionability.

In process mining, structured event logs typically originate from ERP systems or workflow engines [1], but IoT introduces opportunities to enhance this analysis with detailed sensor observations, bridging physical and digital domains [6]. Despite this potential, IoT data's volume, heterogeneity, and lack of structure complicate integration into traditional process mining methods [6]. To address this, frameworks like the three-phase model of Diba et al. [8] and Bertrand et al.'s conceptual UML-based model have emerged [4]. Recent studies further enhance abstraction and real-time analysis through methods by Koschmider et al. [13], Seiger et al. [20], and others [4,7,23]. Nonetheless, the challenge of creating generalizable, scalable, and semantically enriched event logs from IoT sensor data persists, often limited by reliance on static rules or domain-specific heuristics.

In this work, we introduce a novel approach to bridge the semantic gap between raw IoT outputs and business process constructs, with particular attention to context modeling and event granularity. The following sections detail the foundation, methodological design, and evaluation of our proposed technique.

3 The IoT Miner Approach

To overcome this difficulty, we present a hybrid, modular method for semantic event abstraction that combines large language models (LLMs), unsupervised clustering, and statistical preprocessing. With the help of this technique, noisy IoT signals can be automatically converted into semantically meaningful event logs, which makes it easier to use them directly for process mining and analysis.

3.1 System Pipeline

IoT Miner implements an analytical pipeline transforming raw industrial sensor data into an event log suitable for process mining purposes (Fig. 1). The system connects high-frequency IoT readings with activity-level abstractions required for workflow discovery and analysis.

The pipeline integrates: (1) domain-aware preprocessing and feature engineering, (2) comparative clustering for activity discovery, (3) LLM-powered semantic labeling, and (4) intelligent event log construction with automated case segmentation. Each stage incorporates industrial domain knowledge while maintaining cross-context adaptability.

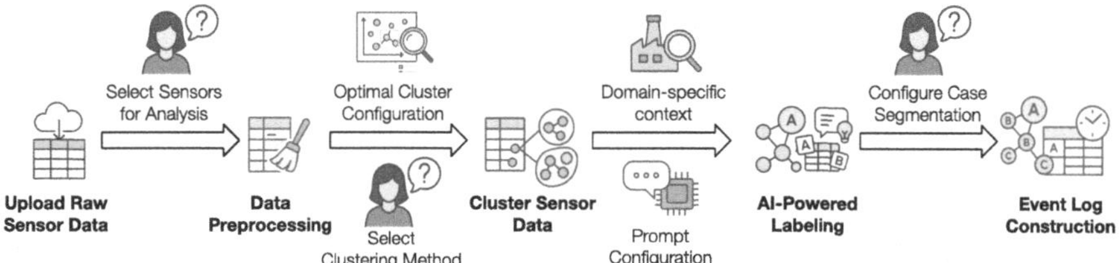

Fig. 1. IoT Miner pipeline

3.2 Data Preprocessing

Industrial sensor data presents various challenges for process mining due to its raw, unstructured nature [4]. IoT Miner implements a comprehensive preprocessing pipeline to transform this data into a format suitable for meaningful pattern extraction and activity identification. Our preprocessing approach addresses three key challenges: (1) heterogeneous data formats and quality issues, (2) high dimensionality with numerous irrelevant signals, and (3) the need to capture temporal patterns that indicate process activities. The preprocessing pipeline consists of several designed stages:

1. Data cleaning and integration—we implement automatic detection of data types, delimiters, and encoding formats to support various input sources (CSV, Excel, JSON). For missing values, context-aware interpolation is applied based on the sensor type and operational characteristics,
2. Temporal feature engineering—we transform the data to better reflect state changes by converting continuous sensor values to binary movement indicators using differential coding, computing first and second-order derivatives to capture rate of change information, and introducing sliding window aggregations to detect sustained patterns versus transient noise,
3. Sensor selection—the system automatically identifies sensor columns by excluding common metadata fields (timestamps, IDs) and applying statistical measures to detect meaningful variation.

Another key step is normalization, which ensures that different signals are on comparable scales–important for effective clustering. IoT Miner supports several normalization methods, including standard scaling (mean-zero, unit variance), min-max normalization, and more robust techniques based on medians and quartiles. These options help adapt the pipeline to various types of sensor data, especially in the presence of noise or outliers.

The preprocessing module is made to be both automated and adaptable. The pipeline can be adjusted by domain experts to fit particular machines, industries, or data properties, but default configurations often function well. Because of its adaptability, IoT Miner can be used in a variety of sensor environments while still staying focused on the requirements of actual industrial processes.

3.3 Clustering and Analysis

After preprocessing, IoT Miner uses unsupervised learning techniques to identify meaningful patterns in the sensor data that correspond to operational activities. The key challenge is determining the appropriate abstraction level–too fine-grained clustering captures noise rather than activities, while too coarse-grained clustering misses important operational distinctions. To address this challenge, we implement a comprehensive comparative clustering approach that automatically evaluates multiple configurations across different algorithms and parameters to identify the optimal clustering strategy for a given dataset. This approach eliminates the need for manual tuning of clustering parameters, which is typically a bottleneck in industrial applications.

The system integrates two well-established clustering algorithms–K-means and DBSCAN–each offering distinct strengths for analyzing industrial sensor data [15]. For each algorithm, IoT Miner explores a wide range of configurations by varying both normalization methods and algorithm-specific parameters such as distance metrics or density thresholds. Each configuration is evaluated using standard internal validation metrics, including the Silhouette Score, Davies-Bouldin Index, and Calinski-Harabasz Index. These measures help identify the most coherent and well-separated cluster structures, laying a strong foundation for the subsequent semantic labeling of operational activities. The system automatically selects the best algorithm for each dataset, as optimal clustering approaches may vary depending on the nature of the industrial process.

Once the optimal clustering configuration is identified, IoT Miner generates detailed statistical profiles for each cluster, capturing the distinctive sensor characteristics that define different operational activities. These profiles provide a comprehensive characterization of each activity, including basic statistics like min, max, mean, median, and standard deviation, quartiles (Q_1, Q_3), helping to distinguish between different operational modes. To visualize high-dimensional cluster structures and validate their separation, we employ dimensionality reduction techniques (like Principal Component Analysis (PCA) and t-Distributed Stochastic Neighbor Embedding (t-SNE)). These visualizations in both 2D and 3D help domain experts interpret the discovered patterns and validate the clustering results (Fig. 2).

Unlike previous approaches that rely on predefined thresholds or fixed parameters, our method dynamically adapts to the statistical characteristics of each specific dataset. This adaptability is crucial for industrial settings where sensor data characteristics can vary significantly between different equipment, processes, and operational conditions.

3.4 AI-Powered Labeling

IoT Miner's key innovation is automated generation of semantically meaningful activity labels, bridging statistical cluster discovery with domain-appropriate terminology and eliminating manual interpretation bottlenecks.

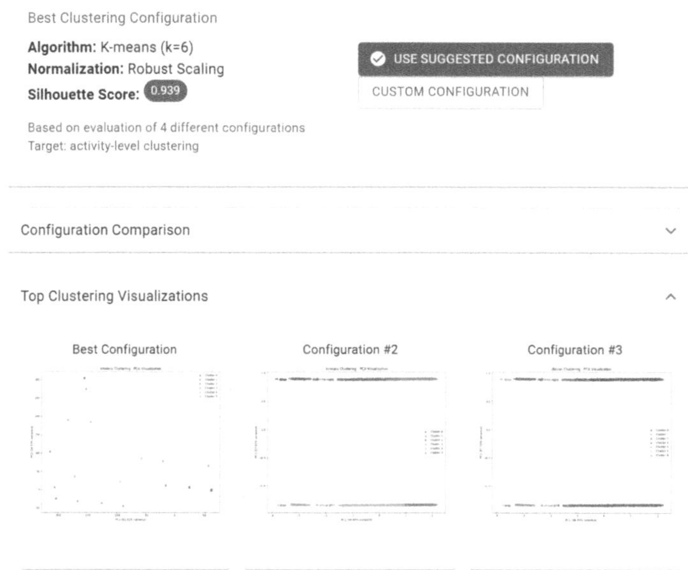

Fig. 2. Clustering results window

Generated statistical profiles of discovered clusters are automatically incorporated into the labeling prompt, which is extended with a user-provided context for the language model (Fig. 3). The labeling window provides the following configuration options:

- Model Selection—choice between different GPT models (GPT-4, GPT-3.5) based on complexity requirements,
- Temperature Setting—controls randomness in generation (0.0–1.0), with lower values producing more deterministic outputs,
- Token Limits—maximum response length configuration (typically 400–800 tokens) ensuring concise but complete labels,
- Prompt Pool—structured template for guiding the model toward appropriate industrial terminology.

The IoT Miner transmits configured prompts through Azure OpenAI API. The API integration handles authentication, request formatting, and response processing while maintaining secure communication channels.

The language model processes combined statistical and contextual information to generate activity labels. This automated labeling pipeline transforms abstract statistical clusters into interpretable activity descriptions, significantly reducing the expertise and time required for cluster interpretation.

3.5 Event Log Construction

The final stage transforms labeled data into event logs through structured case segmentation and temporal sequence construction, enabling standard process

Fig. 3. LLM labeling options window

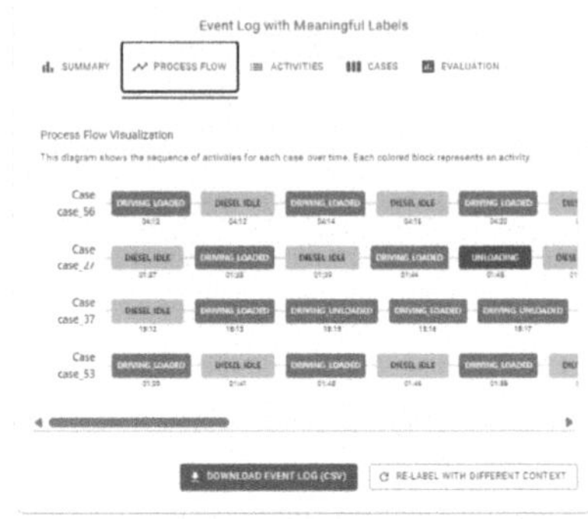

Fig. 4. Event log construction interface showing fragment of created event log

mining tool analysis. This step allows configuring segmentation parameters, including the method of case detection (e.g., based on time gaps, days, or sensor changes), the sensitivity threshold for detecting significant changes, the minimum number of activities per case, and the maximum case duration. Additionally, consecutive identical activities can be optionally merged to reduce noise and improve event granularity.

The IoT Miner monitor key sensors for deviation patterns indicating operational transitions, identifies major activity transitions as natural boundaries, and applies configurable temporal constraints ensuring meaningful operational sequences. This addresses continuous industrial process challenges where traditional case boundaries lack a clear definition. Constructed event logs reveal operational patterns previously invisible in raw sensor data, automatically identifying frequent activity transitions and enabling workflow discovery (Fig. 4). Generated event logs conform to standard XES format requirements (containing case ID, activity and timestamp), enabling direct import into established process mining tools (ProM, Celonis, Disco) [1].

In the case of having the ground truth labels for dataset user can compare generated event logs against operational monitoring records, employing temporal matching and semantic similarity assessment.

4 Evaluation

4.1 Dataset and Machine Description

The dataset utilized in this study was collected from a room and pillar underground oil shale mine. It originates from a Load-Haul-Dump (LHD) machine, specifically the *Scooptram ST1030* manufactured by *Epiroc*. This LHD is designed for heavy-duty load and haul operations and features a nominal payload capacity of 10 tons. It is equipped with a diesel engine and an articulated steering mechanism optimized for confined underground conditions. The Scooptram ST1030 operates alongside various other mining equipment, including drill rigs, roof bolters, and additional LHDs. Within this ecosystem, the LHD performs repeated loading, transporting, and dumping cycles under dynamically changing operational conditions.

The dataset consists of raw signals captured via the machine's Controller Area Network (CAN) bus. The sensor streams offer a detailed view of the LHD's mechanical and operational states. A sample with key recorded engine and transmission parameters is presented in Table 1. These signals, such as engine speed (**ES**), torque (**TQ**), and fuel rate (**FR**), are crucial for assessing the machine's operating conditions and performance patterns during mining operations.

Table 1. Sample data collected from the LHD machine's engine and transmission system. Abbreviations: **ES** Engine Speed (RPM), **OP** Oil Pressure (kPa), **TQ** Torque (%), **FR** Fuel Rate (L/h), **APP** Accelerator Pedal Position (%), **DIT** DPF Intake Temp (°C), **DOT** DPF Outlet Temp (°C), **RS** Regeneration Status, **MP** Manifold Pressure (kPa), **MT** Manifold Temp (°C).

Timestamp	ES	OP	TQ	FR	APP	DIT	DOT	RS	MP	MT	...
241001T06:03:02	712.875	456	35	9.15	0	25.809	5.535	0	10	11	...
241001T06:03:03	725.875	456	36	6.6	0	26.181	5.566	0	10	11	...
...	...	...	...	...	...	...	...	...	...	...	...

These parameters collectively form a multi-dimensional time series that captures the low-level physical behavior of the machine during operation. As is typical for industrial sensor data, these recordings do not contain explicit information about tasks or activities, making them unusable for process mining in their raw form. These signals exhibit, however, characteristic temporal and statistical patterns, which support the segmentation of machine behavior into distinct operational phases such as idling, loading, hauling, and dumping. As such, the dataset provides an effective benchmark for evaluating sensor-based event abstraction techniques under real-world industrial conditions.

4.2 Experimental Setup

To carry out our experiments, we first loaded time-series sensor data collected from an LHD machine. We focused our analysis on five key engine-related signals: accelerator pedal position, engine speed (RPM), engine oil pressure, fuel rate, and engine torque output. Based on these inputs, we applied clustering to discover recurring activity patterns. The optimal number of clusters was determined to be six, using K-means with Robust Scaling as the best-performing configuration (Silhouette Score: 0.939). Next, the clustered data was segmented into activity cases using an automated sensor-based case detection method with the default IoT Miner parameters.

To explore how prompt quality and contextual information affect label generation for clusters, we designed three experimental conditions with increasing levels of instruction and domain-specific guidance.

1. Experiment 1 – Basic Prompt without Task Clarification
   The model received a minimal prompt asking it to assign activity labels based on sensor statistics from clustered time-series data of an LHD machine. No domain-specific context, examples, or constraints were provided (Fig. 3).
2. Experiment 2 – Prompt with Labeling Instructions
   This version extended the basic prompt by including a labeling instruction section that provided relevant activity examples and instructed the model to avoid ambiguous labels (e.g., those containing the word "or").
3. Experiment 3 – Prompt with Context and Operational Guidance
   In addition to the improvements from Experiment 2, this prompt included detailed background information about the LHD machine's operational cycle and interpretive guidelines for reading sensor patterns. It emphasized specific mappings between sensor values and mining-related activities and encouraged unambiguous, domain-appropriate labeling (see Prompt Box 1).

Prompt 1: Prompt for Experiment 3

```
We have time-series sensor data collected from a Load-Haul-Dump
(LHD) machine operating in an underground mining environment.
The machine follows a repetitive operational cycle consisting of
distinct phases: loading blasted rock, hauling it through tunnels,
dumping it, and returning to the loading point. The machine may
also spend time idling or stopped between activities.
This data has been clustered into several distinct groups based on
patterns in the following engine-related sensor values:
- engine 1 accelerator pedal position 1: Degree to which the
operator is pressing the accelerator pedal (0100%)
- engine 1 engine speed: Revolutions per minute (RPM) of the
engine
[here more description of sensor values]
Use mining-related terminology to describe each operational
context
[here more description of mining-related terminology]
Consider the following operational insights when naming the
clusters: Engine speed (RPM) alone does not distinguish phases.
Accelerator pedal position indicates operator intent or system
command. A high value suggests active tramming or bucket work;
low values suggest coast, idle, or no operator input. Fuel rate
and torque increase under higher load demands, such as lifting,
tramming uphill, or carrying heavy material.
[here more operational description of the task]
```

For each experiment, we prompted the GPT-4 model using six different temperature values (ranging from 0.0 to 1.0 in steps of 0.2), generating 10 labeled event logs per temperature to enable consistent comparison.

In our experiments, due semantic variations between the predicted and ground truth activity labels, a direct one-to-one label matching was not feasible.

To address the challenge of non-aligned labels between predicted and reference activity names, we introduce a metric that accounts for their semantic similarity. Instead of relying on exact string matches, this approach assigns partial credit based on how closely the labels relate in meaning. We refer to this metric as Similarity-Weighted Accuracy (SWA), and define it formally as follows:

$$\mathrm{SWA} = \frac{1}{N} \sum_{i=1}^{N} \left(\mathbb{1}_{[s_i \geq T]} \cdot s_i \right),$$

where:

- N is the total number of reference instances,
- $s_i \in [0, 1]$ is the similarity score between the predicted and reference label for instance i,
- $T \in [0, 1]$ is the similarity threshold,
- $\mathbb{1}_{[s_i \geq T]}$ is the indicator function: it equals 1 if $s_i \geq T$, and 0 otherwise.

To measure the similarity score s_i between the predicted and reference labels for each instance, we used Google's `models/embedding-001` text embedding model. This formulation discards similarity scores below the threshold and retains the full value of those above it, allowing partial credit only for sufficiently similar predictions.

Figure 5 presents an example of a similarity-weighted accuracy matrix used to evaluate the alignment between predicted and ground truth labels. Since the predicted labels come from unsupervised clustering, they are not guaranteed to align one-to-one with the actual activity classes–multiple ground truth classes can be grouped into a single cluster, or a single class may be split across several clusters. Additionally, the event distribution in the log is imbalanced, which may also affect the density of values in the matrix. The resulting matrix reflects the product of semantic similarity scores and the corresponding frequencies of label co-occurrence, highlighting meaningful overlaps between predicted and ground truth classes (the color intensity indicates regions of higher weighted agreement).

4.3 Results

To ensure robustness of the evaluation and account for prediction variability, each experimenttemperature configuration was tested in 10 independent runs.

The resulting performance trends are visualized in Fig. 6, which shows the average similarity-weighted accuracy across different temperature levels for each experiment. The shaded areas around the lines represent the standard error of the mean (SE), reflecting how much the average score might vary due to randomness across runs. Narrower bands suggest more consistent and reliable performance under that condition.

To further explore variability and stability, Fig. 7 presents a distribution of the similarity-weighted accuracy across the three separate experiments. Each boxplot shows the accuracy distributions for various temperature settings presenting variability and performance consistency within and between experiments.

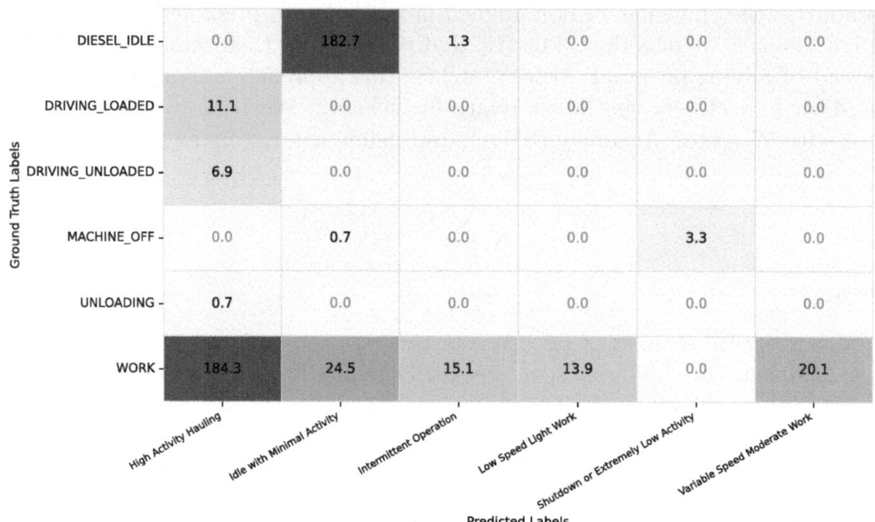

Fig. 5. Similarity-weighted accuracy heatmap showing the correspondence between predicted and ground truth labels.

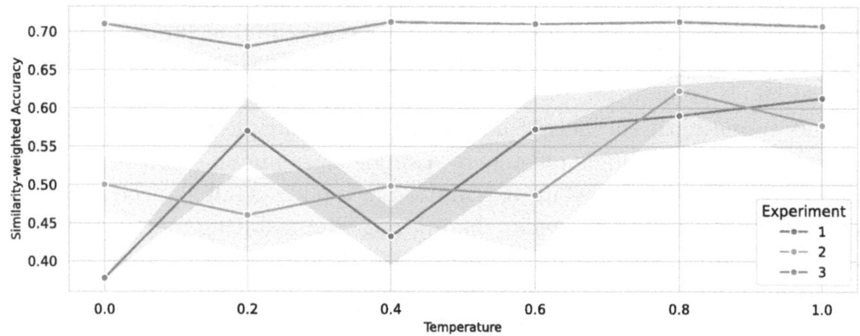

Fig. 6. Average similarity-weighted accuracy by temperature per experiment.

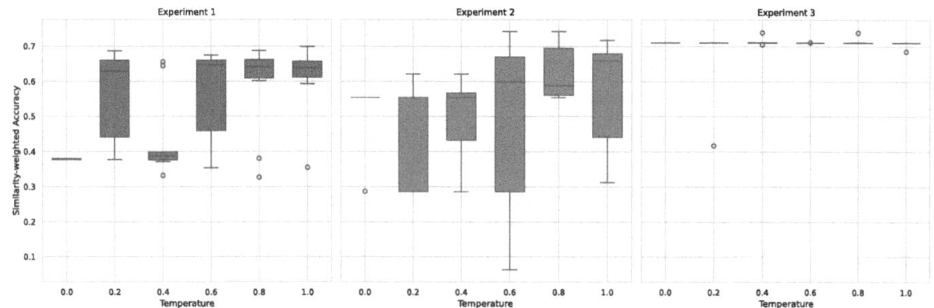

Fig. 7. Distribution of similarity-weighted accuracy for each experiment across different temperature settings.

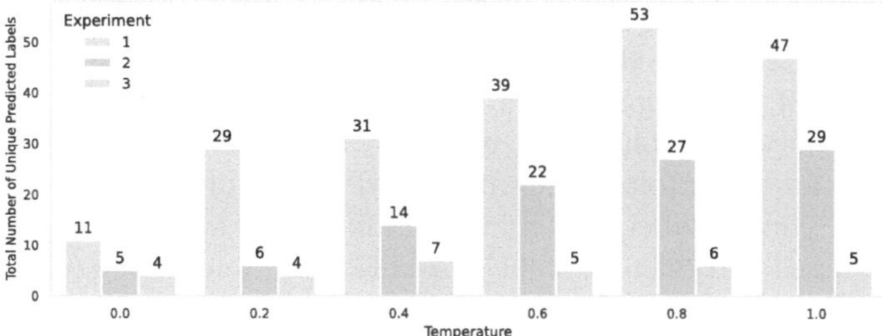

Fig. 8. Total number of unique predicted activity labels in experiments per temp.

Beyond accuracy alone, we also examined the diversity of predicted activity labels across conditions. As shown in Fig. 8, the number of distinct labels (aggregated over 10 runs per temperature) varies notably with both temperature and prompt quality. The results show that the basic prompt (Experiment 1) consistently produces a higher number of unique labels, particularly at higher temperatures, reflecting a more diverse and unconstrained interpretation of cluster semantics. In contrast, Experiment 3, which includes detailed operational context and labeling guidance, tends to result in fewer and more consistent labels–indicating that domain-specific instructions may help the model converge toward a narrower, more uniform naming scheme.

4.4 Discussion and Limitations

Our approach assumes that the input IoT data consists mainly of numerical or boolean time-series data (e.g., RPM, fuel rate, pressure), as commonly found in industrial systems. This makes it well-suited for industrial sensor streams, but less applicable to other data types like images, audio, or complex inputs. This limits the generalizability of the approach to environments where sensor signals show temporal and statistical patterns that can be grouped using clustering.

The approach uses ML methods such as clustering and LLMs, which are generalizable and can be applied to different datasets. However, the formulation of effective prompts remains a critical factor for label quality. In our setup, prompt creation is left to the user, including how to describe the sensors, explain the machine's operation, and guide the label generation process. While our tests show that well-written prompts improve performance, the current version does not provide built-in help for this step.

Our pipeline includes configurable parameters at multiple stages. Although the default settings often produce satisfactory results, selecting appropriate parameters or case segmentation settings may still require expert input and can be challenging for non-expert users without system support. Moreover, our evaluation focused on a single, yet real-world mining use case. This domain offers a rich source of sensor data, it is also highly specific and complex, with limited representation in general LLM training data. As a result, generating accurate and meaningful labels can be more difficult compared to more common and well-documented domains. The broader applicability of the approach in other industrial contexts still needs to be validated.

In the case of evaluation-related limitations, the ground truth labels may include uncertainty or simplification, especially in industrial settings where activity boundaries are fuzzy (often unclear or overlapping). This makes it difficult to assign a single correct label, which in turn affects the accuracy of comparisons between predicted and reference labels. Additionally, our results rely on specific versions of LLMs accessed via external APIs. Any changes to model behavior, availability, or access policies could impact the reproducibility and consistency of the results. Even when provided with clear instructions, LLMs may still generate inconsistent or misleading labels, especially at higher temperature settings or when prompts lack sufficient context. This may raise concerns about the reliability of the output. To address these challenges, more support in writing prompts, testing in other domains, and guiding users are recommended.

5 Conclusion and Future Work

In this paper, we introduced IoT Miner, an unsupervised framework that transforms raw industrial sensor data into high-level event logs suitable for process mining. Our approach combines domain-aware preprocessing, comparative clustering, and semantic labeling powered by LLMs. This enables automatic discovery and interpretation of operational activities from raw sensor streams without requiring expert-defined rules or labeled data.

The experimental evaluation on real-world data from an LHD mining machine demonstrated the effectiveness of IoT Miner. The automatically discovered best clustering configuration produced highly cohesive activity clusters, and LLM labeling showed that more detailed prompts lead to more accurate and consistent labels, highlighting the importance of context when using LLMs in industry.

With flexible configuration options at various stages, IoT Miner adapts to diverse industrial settings–from manufacturing to energy production–without extensive manual setup. Overall, our approach automates transformation of high-frequency industrial sensor data into semantically meaningful process representations, addressing critical gaps in industrial process mining while maintaining domain interpretability and tool compatibility.

In future work, we plan to integrate additional data sources–such as images or operator logs–to improve clustering and labeling accuracy. We also aim to benchmark IoT Miner across a range of industrial datasets to evaluate its generalizability. Furthermore, optimizing the pipeline for real-time and edge use would enable fast, on-site monitoring, while incorporating optional expert feedback could support label verification, combining automation with human insight.

References

1. van der Aalst, W.M.P.: Process Mining: A 360 Degree Overview, pp. 3–34. Springer, Cham (2022). https://doi.org/10.1007/978-3-031-08848-3_1
2. An, T., Zhou, Y., Zou, H., Yang, J.: IoT-LLM: Enhancing Real-World IoT Task Reasoning with Large Language Models. Preprint (2024). https://doi.org/10.48550/arXiv.2410.02429
3. Berti, A., Schuster, D., van der Aalst, W.M.P.: Abstractions, scenarios, and prompt definitions for process mining with LLMs: a case study. In: De Weerdt, J., Pufahl, L. (eds.) Business Process Management Workshops, pp. 427–439. Springer, Cham (2024)
4. Bertrand, Y., De Weerdt, J., Serral, E.: A bridging model for process mining and IoT. In: Munoz-Gama, J., Lu, X. (eds.) Process Mining Workshops, pp. 98–110. Springer, Cham (2022)
5. Brennig, K.: Revealing the unspoken: Using LLMs to mobilize and enrich tacit knowledge in event logs of knowledge-intensive processes. In: AMCIS 2025 Proceedings (2025). https://aisel.aisnet.org/amcis2025/sig_svc/sig_svc/11, paper 11
6. Brzychczy, E., Aleknonytė-Resch, M., Janssen, D., Koschmider, A.: Process mining on sensor data: a review of related works. Knowl. Inf. Syst. 1–34 (2025)
7. Brzychczy, E., Kluza, K., Szała, L.: Enhancement of low-level event abstraction with large language models (LLMs). In: Gdowska, K., Gómez-López, M.T., Rehse, J.R. (eds.) Business Process Management Workshops, pp. 209–220. Springer, Cham (2025)
8. Diba, K., Batoulis, K., Weidlich, M., Weske, M.: Extraction, correlation, and abstraction of event data for process mining. WIREs Data Mining Knowl. Discov. **10**(3) (2020). https://doi.org/10.1002/widm.1346
9. Fani Sani, M., Sroka, M., Burattin, A.: LLMs and process mining: challenges in RPA. In: De Smedt, J., Soffer, P. (eds.) Process Mining Workshops, pp. 379–391. Springer, Cham (2024)
10. Grohs, M., Abb, L., Elsayed, N., Rehse, J.R.: Large language models can accomplish business process management tasks. In: De Weerdt, J., Pufahl, L. (eds.) Business Process Management Workshops, pp. 453–465. Springer, Cham (2024)
11. Janiesch, C., et al.: The internet of things meets business process management: a manifesto. IEEE Syst. Man Cybern. Mag. **6**(4), 34–44 (2020). https://doi.org/10.1109/MSMC.2020.3003135
12. Jessen, U., Schroth, L., Mühllechner, M.: From data to actionable insights: utilizing AI and process mining in manufacturing processes. In: International Conference on Business Process Management, pp. 462–471. Springer (2024)
13. Koschmider, A., Janssen, D., Mannhardt, F.: Framework for process discovery from sensor data. In: 10th International Workshop on Enterprise Modeling and Information Systems Architectures, EMISA 2020, pp. 32–38. CEUR-WS.org (2020)
14. Koschmider, A., Mannhardt, F., Heuser, T.: On the contextualization of event-activity mappings. In: Daniel, F., Sheng, Q.Z., Motahari, H. (eds.) Business Process Management Workshops, pp. 445–457. Springer, Cham (2019)
15. Krishnamurthi, R., Kumar, A., Gopinathan, D., Nayyar, A., Qureshi, B.: An overview of IoT sensor data processing, fusion, and analysis techniques. Sensors **20**(21), 6076 (2020)
16. Mahdavinejad, M.S., Rezvan, M., Barekatain, M., Adibi, P., Barnaghi, P., Sheth, A.P.: Machine learning for internet of things data analysis: a survey. Digit. Commun. Netw. **4**(3), 161–175 (2018)

17. Mangler, J., et al.: From internet of things data to business processes: challenges and a framework (2024)
18. Rebmann, A., Schmidt, F.D., Glavaš, G., van der Aa, H.: On the potential of large language models to solve semantics-aware process mining tasks. Process Sci. **2**(1), 10 (2025). https://doi.org/10.1007/s44311-025-00019-3
19. Sasaki, Y.: A survey on IoT big data analytic systems: current and future. IEEE Internet Things J. **9**(2), 1024–1036 (2021)
20. Seiger, R., Franceschetti, M., Weber, B.: An interactive method for detection of process activity executions from IoT data. Future Internet **15**(2), 77 (2023). https://doi.org/10.3390/fi15020077
21. Shirali, M., Sani, M.F., Ahmadi, Z., Serral, E.: LLM-based event abstraction and integration for IoT-sourced logs. In: Gdowska, K., Gómez-López, M.T., Rehse, J.R. (eds.) Business Process Management Workshops, pp. 138–149. Springer, Cham (2025)
22. Suryavansh, S., Benna, A., Guest, C., Chaterji, S.: A data-driven approach to increasing the lifetime of IoT sensor nodes. Sci. Rep. **11**(1), 22459 (2021)
23. Valderas, P., Torres, V., Serral, E.: Towards an interdisciplinary development of IoT-enhanced business processes. Bus. Inf. Syst. Eng. **65**(1), 25–48 (2023). https://doi.org/10.1007/s12599-022-00770-y
24. Vidgof, M., Bachhofner, S., Mendling, J.: Large language models for business process management: opportunities and challenges. In: Di Francescomarino, C., Burattin, A., Janiesch, C., Sadiq, S. (eds.) Business Process Management Forum, pp. 107–123. Springer, Cham (2023)
25. Weerdt, J.D., Wynn, M.T.: Foundations of Process Event Data. Lecture Notes in Business Information Processing, vol. 448, pp. 193–211. Springer (2022). https://doi.org/10.1007/978-3-031-08848-3_6
26. Yao, Y., Gehrke, J., et al.: Query processing in sensor networks. In: CIDR, pp. 233–244 (2003)
27. van Zelst, S.J., Mannhardt, F., de Leoni, M., Koschmider, A.: Event abstraction in process mining: literature review and taxonomy. Granular Comput. **6**(3), 719–736 (2021). https://doi.org/10.1007/s41066-020-00226-2

5th International Workshop on Change, Drift, and Dynamics of Organizational Processes (ProDy 2025)

A General Framework for Neuro-Symbolic Predictive Process Monitoring

Jamila Oukharijane(✉), Ivan Donadello, and Fabrizio Maria Maggi

Free University of Bozen-Bolzano, Bolzano, Italy
{jamila.oukharijane,ivan.donadello,fabriziomaria.maggi}@unibz.it

Abstract. Concept drift presents major challenges for Predictive Process Monitoring (PPM), as predictive models often struggle to make accurate predictions on traces that differ from the event log they were originally trained on. Nevertheless, some background knowledge can be mined from the drifting traces and be used for improving PPM algorithms. In this paper, we propose a general Neuro-Symbolic framework for multi-attribute suffix prediction that explicitly contextualizes the neural predictions with both declarative and procedural background knowledge. Our framework combines the ability to learn from historical data (the neural component) with the capacity to reason over background knowledge (the symbolic component), aiming to combine the robustness of neural networks with the compliance-checking capabilities of symbolic knowledge. This framework enables more flexible suffix prediction, better suited to the variability of real-world processes, which continuously evolve due to concept drift, and may exhibit new behavioral variants over time. The experimentation on real event logs with a natural concept drift show that incorporating symbolic knowledge, generally improves the performance of suffix prediction.

Keywords: Process Mining · Predictive Process Monitoring · Deep Learning · Symbolic Background Knowledge · Concept Drift

1 Introduction

Predictive Process Monitoring (PPM) leverages historical process execution data to predict how ongoing executions will continue until their completion [5]. One of the main tasks in this domain is suffix prediction (SP), which involves predicting the remaining sequence of events (activities and potentially other attributes attached to them) that will occur in an ongoing process instance.

Recently, there has been significant interest in applying deep learning techniques to multi-attribute SP in PPM [10,12]. These data-driven approaches typically involve a training phase, during which a Neural Network (NN) model learns patterns from historical data, followed by a prediction phase where the trained model is used to make predictions for ongoing cases. While these methods can achieve high accuracy, they face limitations, especially in scenarios where

I. van de Weerd et al. (Eds.): BPM 2025 Workshops, LNBIP 569, pp. 249–261, 2026.
https://doi.org/10.1007/978-3-032-13426-4_18

behavior in the test set is under-represented in the training data, such as when the process undergoes concept drift–that is, changes in process behavior over time. These behavioral changes may not be reflected in the training log but can often be captured through symbolic background knowledge. In many real-world scenarios, additional case-specific background knowledge about the execution context is available and can be used to enhance the predictive power of PPM techniques [6,21]. This background knowledge, often found in guidelines and documents, can help characterize process behavior in exceptional situations and improve predictions under concept drift. For example, in a hospital scenario, new medical guidelines may suddenly necessitate a specific screening prior to surgery, a patient's allergy might preclude the administration of a particular treatment, or an essential hospital worker's unavailability could affect both resource allocation and process control-flow.

This is where Neuro-Symbolic (NeSy) approaches [19] can be particularly beneficial. In NeSy systems, the *neuro* component corresponds to a predictive model (e.g., an NN), while the symbolic component consists of background knowledge ($\mathcal{BK}$), such as constraints or logical rules. NeSy methods can be effective when the behavior seen in the testing set is under-represented in the training set and therefore might not be correctly learned by the predictive model. Such behavior, however, may be accurately captured by the $\mathcal{BK}$. This situation is typical in SP: while a process model captures the expected behavior during process execution, an event log is only a temporal snapshot of such behavior, in which some expected behavior may be absent or represented by only a few traces.

There are only a few contributions on NeSy approaches for SP in the literature. In [6,21], the authors leverage $\mathcal{BK}$ in the form of DECLARE constraints, either during training or as a post-prediction filter. However, these approaches are restricted to a single type of $\mathcal{BK}$ and focus solely on single-attribute (i.e., activity) SP.

In this paper, we address the problem of SP in the presence of concept drift by presenting a general NeSy framework that falls within the Symbolic[Neuro] category according to Kautz's taxonomy [19, Section 2], where an NN model is invoked as a subroutine within a symbolic reasoner component. The key features of our framework are the following:

- It supports both single-attribute (e.g., activity) and multi-attribute (e.g., activity and resource) SP;
- It allows integration of various types of $\mathcal{BK}$, including DECLARE [17], MP-DECLARE (multi-perspective DECLARE) [4], PROBDECLARE (probabilistic DECLARE) [1], procedural models such as Petri nets, and, in principle, even fuzzy background knowledge [7];
- It supports various prefix encoding methods and neural architectures (LSTM (Long Short-Term Memory) [8] and Transformer [22]);
- It enables the contextualization of neural predictions with $\mathcal{BK}$ during the SP process, capturing drifts over time and improving compliance in dynamic environments.

The paper is organized as follows. Section 2 introduces the preliminary concepts that we will use throughout the paper. Section 3 presents the architecture of the proposed framework and details the beam search algorithm used to integrate neural predictions with $\mathcal{BK}$. Section 4 presents the experimental results. Finally, Sect. 5 discusses related works, and Sect. 6 concludes the paper.

2 Background

The starting point of PPM is an event log $\mathcal{L}$, which is defined as a set of traces. A trace is a sequence of events, where each event is represented as a tuple $e = (c, a, t, r)$ with c as the case id, a as the activity name in $\mathcal{A}$, t as the timestamp of the event, and r as the allocated resource in $\mathcal{R}$ for activity a. We denote by $\mathcal{E}$ the universe of possible events and write $e.x$ with $x \in \{c, a, t, r\}$ to refer to elements of an event. A trace is a non-empty sequence of events $\sigma = \langle e_i \rangle_{i=1,\ldots,n}$ such that $\forall i,\ e_i \in \mathcal{E}$; $\forall i, j \in 1, \ldots, n,\ e_i.c = e_j.c$; and $i < j \Rightarrow e_i.t < e_j.t$. The prefix $\sigma_{\leq k}$ of length $k \in [1, n]$ of σ is the sub-trace including the first k events of σ, i.e., $\sigma_{\leq k} = \langle e_i \rangle_{i=1,\ldots,k}$, with $length(\sigma_{\leq k}) = k$. The suffix $\sigma_{>k}$ of σ is the sub-trace obtained by removing the events of $\sigma_{\leq k}$, i.e., $\sigma_{>k} = \langle e_i \rangle_{i=k+1,\ldots,n}$, with $length(\sigma_{>k}) = n - k$. Given an event log $\mathcal{L}$, the prefix log $\mathcal{L}^{<}$ is the event log $\mathcal{L}^{<} = \{\sigma_k : \sigma \in \mathcal{L},\ \text{with } 1 \leq k \leq length(\sigma)\}$ that contains all the prefixes of $\mathcal{L}$.

Definition 1 (Next-Attribute Prediction (NAP) task). *The Next-Attribute Prediction (NAP) task is designed to predict the next attribute x, either activity a or resource r, in a trace. Given a prefix $\sigma_{\leq k} \in \mathcal{L}^{<}$ of a trace $\sigma \in \mathcal{L}$, the next attribute prediction function $\mathcal{F}_{\mathcal{X}_\perp} : \mathcal{L}^{<} \to [0, 1]^{|\mathcal{X}_\perp|}$ returns a probability vector $\pi = \langle p(x_1|\sigma_{\leq k}), \ldots, p(x_{|\mathcal{X}_\perp|}|\sigma_{\leq k}) \rangle$ for all attribute values $x \in \mathcal{X}_\perp$, with $1 \leq i \leq |\mathcal{X}_\perp|$, and $\mathcal{X}$ being a set of activities $\mathcal{A}$ or a set of resources $\mathcal{R}$, where $\mathcal{X}_\perp$ denotes the corresponding set $\mathcal{X}$ augmented with a termination label $\perp$. The NAP task for prefix $\sigma_{\leq k}$ is a function $\mathcal{NAP} : [0, 1]^{|\mathcal{X}_\perp|} \to \mathcal{X}_\perp$ returning the value $\hat{x}_{k+1}$ for the prefix $\sigma_{\leq k}$, where $\hat{x}_{k+1} = \arg\max_{x \in \mathcal{X}_\perp} \mathcal{F}_{\mathcal{X}_\perp}(\sigma_{\leq k})$.*

The NAP task provides the basis for suffix prediction (SP) tasks, such as activity suffix prediction and multi-attribute suffix prediction, which aim to predict the entire suffix of a prefix trace in an ongoing process execution.

Definition 2 (Activity Suffix Prediction task). *Given a prefix $\sigma_{\leq k} \in \mathcal{L}^{<}$ of a trace $\sigma \in \mathcal{L}$ and a NAP task function $\mathcal{NAP} : [0, 1]^{|\mathcal{A}_\perp|} \to \mathcal{A}$, the suffix prediction task is a function $\mathcal{SP} : \mathcal{L}^{<} \to (\mathcal{A}_\perp)^*$ returning a predicted label sequence $\overline{\sigma} = \langle a_1, \ldots, a_k, \hat{a}_{k+1}, \ldots, \hat{a}_n, \perp \rangle$, where each label $\hat{a}_i \in \mathcal{A}$ with $k + 1 \leq i \leq n$ in suffix $\sigma_{>k}$ is obtained by recurrently applying $\mathcal{NAP}$ until the termination label $\perp$ is observed.*

Definition 3 (Multi-Attribute Suffix Prediction task). *Given a prefix $\sigma_{\leq k} \in \mathcal{L}^{<}$ of a trace $\sigma \in \mathcal{L}$ and a NAP task function for activity and resource $\mathcal{NAP} : [0, 1]^{|\mathcal{A}_\perp \times \mathcal{R}_\perp|} \to \mathcal{A} \times \mathcal{R}$, the multi-attribute sequence prediction task is a function $\mathcal{SP} : \mathcal{L}^{<} \to (\mathcal{A}_\perp \times \mathcal{R}_\perp)^*$ returning a predicted multi-attribute sequence*

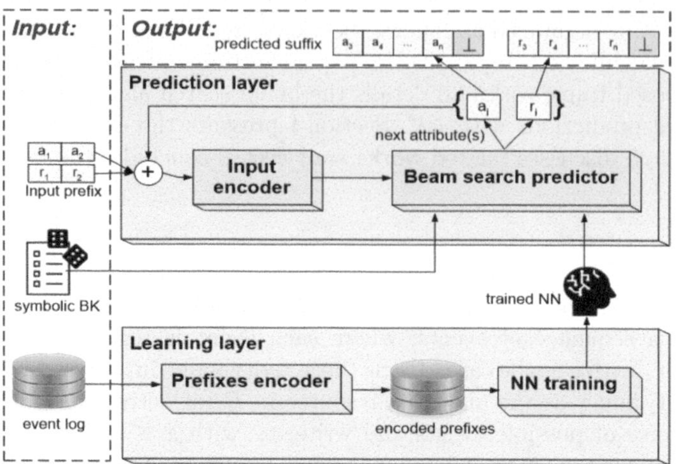

Fig. 1. Conceptual Architecture of our NeSy framework for suffix prediction.

(a.k.a. a suffix), $\overline{\sigma} = \langle (a_1, r_1), \ldots, (a_k, r_k), (\hat{a}_{k+1}, \hat{r}_{k+1}), \ldots, (\hat{a}_n, \hat{r}_n), (\perp, \perp) \rangle$, *where each pair* $(\hat{a}_i, \hat{r}_i)$ *for* $k+1 \leq i \leq n$ *in suffix* $\sigma_{>k}$ *is obtained by recurrently applying the prediction functions for activities and resources until the termination pair* $(\perp, \perp)$ *is observed.*

Definition 3 focuses only on activity and resource attributes but can be easily extended to incorporate other attributes, such as timestamps.

Note that in Definitions 2 and 3, we consider the so-called *autoregressive* approach, which sequentially predicts the next attributes based on the history seen so far. This approach defines $\mathcal{F}_{\mathcal{X}_\perp}$ as a trained NN, where, at each step, it selects the most probable next activity or activity-resource pair, appends it to the prefix, and continues this process until the suffix is fully generated.

3 The Proposed Framework

Figure 1 illustrates the conceptual architecture of our Symbolic[Neuro] framework (hereafter referred to as NeSy), designed for autoregressive SP in dynamic environments affected by concept drift. The framework operates in two stages: the *learning layer*, whose output is a neural network called as a subroutine by the *prediction layer*.

3.1 The Learning Layer

The *learning layer* starts with a *prefix encoder* that encodes traces from the given event log into numeric vectors $\boldsymbol{v} = \langle \boldsymbol{x}_1, \ldots, \boldsymbol{x}_n \rangle$ using one of the following methods: *one-hot*, *index-based*, *shrinked index-based*, or *multi-encoders*. In the one-hot encoding, for each event $e_j = \langle a_j, r_j \rangle$ in trace $\sigma = \langle e_1, \ldots, e_n \rangle$, a binary vector $\boldsymbol{x}_j = [\boldsymbol{x}_{a_j}, \boldsymbol{x}_{r_j}]$ is constructed by concatenating one-hot vectors $\boldsymbol{x}_{a_j}$ and $\boldsymbol{x}_{r_j}$ for activity $a_j \in \mathcal{A}$ and resource $r_j \in \mathcal{R}$, respectively. The encoding vector $\boldsymbol{x}$ for trace σ is a matrix whose rows are the individual $\boldsymbol{x}_j$ vectors. In the index-based encoding, each event e_j is represented as a numeric vector $\boldsymbol{x}_j = [idx_{a_j}, idx_{r_j}]$, where idx_{a_j} and idx_{r_j} are the indices of a_j and r_j in $\mathcal{A}$ and $\mathcal{R}$, respectively. The encoding vector $\boldsymbol{x}$ is the concatenation of the individual $\boldsymbol{x}_j$ vectors. The shrinked index-based encoding assigns a unique integer index to each activityresource pair (a_j, r_j) using a joint index function idx_{AR}, resulting in $x_j = idx_{AR}(a_j, r_j)$. The encoding vector $\boldsymbol{x}$ is the concatenation of the individual x_j values. The multi-encoders create separate embeddings $\mathbf{E}_a$ and $\mathbf{E}_r$ for activities and resources, with modulated representations obtained as $\boldsymbol{x} = \tilde{\mathbf{E}}_a \cdot b_a + \tilde{\mathbf{E}}_r \cdot b_r$, where $\tilde{\mathbf{E}}_a = \mathbf{E}_a \oplus (\mathbf{E}_a \otimes \mathbf{E}_r)$ and $\tilde{\mathbf{E}}_r = \mathbf{E}_r \oplus (\mathbf{E}_r \otimes \mathbf{E}_a)$ are combined embeddings for activities and resources, and b_a and b_r are alignment weights computed via a shared modulator [10,12]. After that, a prefix log is built from the encoded traces, with zero-padding applied to achieve a fixed-size input matrix. These encoded prefixes are used by the *NN training* component to train a neural network to predict the next event (a_i, r_i).

3.2 Prediction Layer

At runtime, the *prediction layer* first encodes a given input test prefix using the same encoding method employed during learning. Then, the *Beam search predictor* (the symbolic component) explores multiple possible suffix continuations from the test prefix using a beam search algorithm, as detailed in Algorithm 1. Note that this component is designed to predict both activity and resource suffixes but can also be used to predict only activity suffixes.

Algorithm 1. Neuro-Symbolic Beam Search for suffix prediction

Require: $\sigma_{\leq k}$, NN, $\mathcal{BK}$, $\mathcal{A}_\bot$, $\mathcal{R}_\bot$, $bSize$, max, w

$h \leftarrow 0$
$branches \leftarrow \{(\sigma_{\leq k}, 1)\}$
while $(h \leq max)$ and $(branches \neq \emptyset)$ **do**
    $branches \leftarrow$ ExpandBranches$(branches, \text{NN}, \mathcal{BK}, \mathcal{A}_\bot, \mathcal{R}_\bot, \mathcal{C}, w)$
    $top\_branches \leftarrow$ TopRank$(branches, bSize)$
    $branches \leftarrow \emptyset$
    $rank \leftarrow 0$
    for all $(\sigma_{\leq k+h}, score_{\sigma_{\leq k+h}}) \in top\_branches$ **do**
        if LastSymbol$(\sigma_{\leq k+h}) \neq \bot$ **then**
            $branches \leftarrow branches \cup \{(\sigma_{\leq k+h}, score_{\sigma_{\leq k+h}})\}$
        else if $rank = 0$ and $\mathcal{C}(\sigma_{\leq k+h}, \mathcal{BK}) = 1$ **then**
            return $(\sigma_{\leq k+h}, score_{\sigma_{\leq k+h}})$
        $rank \leftarrow rank + 1$
    $h \leftarrow h + 1$

The algorithm takes as input a prefix $\sigma_{\leq k}$, the background knowledge $\mathcal{BK}$, a trained neural model NN, the activity and resource alphabets $\mathcal{A}_\bot$ and $\mathcal{R}_\bot$, together with the parameters $bSize$, the maximum number of branches that

Algorithm 2. ExpandBranches

Require: *branches*, NN, $\mathcal{BK}$, $\mathcal{A}_\perp$, $\mathcal{R}_\perp$, $\mathcal{C}$, w
1: $new\_branches \leftarrow \emptyset$
2: **for** $(\sigma_{\leq k+h}, score_{\sigma_{\leq k+h}}) \in branches$ **do**
3: **for all** $a \in \mathcal{A}_\perp$, $r \in \mathcal{R}_\perp$ **do**
4: $\sigma_{\leq k+h+1} \leftarrow \langle \sigma_{\leq k+h}, a, r \rangle$
5: $\text{NN}(\sigma_{\leq k+h+1}) \leftarrow \mathcal{G}(\text{NN}(\sigma_{\leq k+h}, a), \text{NN}(\sigma_{\leq k+h}, r))$
6: $score_{\sigma_{\leq k+h+1}} \leftarrow score_{\sigma_{\leq k+h}} \cdot \text{NN}(\sigma_{\leq k+h+1})^{1-w} \cdot \mathcal{C}(\sigma_{\leq k+h+1}, \mathcal{BK})^{w}$
7: $new\_branches \leftarrow new\_branches \cup \{(\sigma_{\leq k+h+1}, score_{\sigma_{\leq k+h+1}})\}$
8: **return** $new\_branches$

can be explored by the beam search algorithm at the same time, *max*, the maximum number of allowed iterations, and $w \in [0, 1]$ a weight that balances the contextualization giving more weight to the NN or to the $\mathcal{BK}$. The algorithm builds the suffix $\sigma_{\leq k}$ by iteratively appending to the input prefix $\sigma_{\leq k}$ an activity symbol $a \in \mathcal{A}_\perp$ and a resource symbol $r \in \mathcal{R}_\perp$ predicted by the invoked NN and modulated with the $\mathcal{BK}$. This is achieved by iterating over the set *branches* (i.e., the branches of the beam search) of pairs of prefixes and their scores (line 3), which is initialized with $(\sigma_{\leq k}, 1)$ (line 2). New branches are generated by the ExpandBranches procedure (Algorithm 2 called at line 4 of Algorithm 1), which extends each prefix with activity symbols from $\mathcal{A}_\perp$ and resource symbol from $\mathcal{R}_\perp$ (line 3). After h iterations, the prefix $\sigma_{\leq k+h}$ is expanded to $\sigma_{\leq k+h+1}$ and its score is computed based on the score of $\sigma_{\leq k+h}$ as (line 6 of Algorithm 2):

$$score_{\sigma_{\leq k+h+1}} = score_{\sigma_{\leq k+h}} \cdot \mathcal{G}(\text{NN}(\sigma_{\leq k+h+1}))^{1-w} \cdot \mathcal{C}(\sigma_{\leq k+h+1}, \mathcal{BK})^{w} \quad (1)$$

where $\mathcal{G}(\text{NN}(\sigma_{\leq k+h+1}))$ is the aggregated probability of the next attributes, computed using an aggregation function $\mathcal{G}$. This aggregation combines the probabilities of both the activity and the resource, i.e., $p(a \mid \sigma_{\leq k+h})$ and $p(r \mid \sigma_{\leq k+h})$, as predicted by the *trained NN* for a given prefix $\sigma_{\leq k+h}$. In our NeSy framework, $\mathcal{G}$ is implemented as the average of the two probabilities; however, other aggregation strategies are also possible.

The function $\mathcal{C}(\sigma_{\leq k+h+1}, \mathcal{BK})$ is a compliance function that measures how well the extended prefix $\sigma_{\leq k+h+1}$ aligns with $\mathcal{BK}$. It returns a value in $[0, 1]$, which adjusts the NN output by incorporating $\mathcal{BK}$, thereby enabling the beam search to leverage external knowledge. As a result, prefixes that align more closely with this knowledge are favored during the search process. We recall that, in our framework, the compliance function $\mathcal{C}$ supports various compliance checkers, such as the (MP-)Declare conformance checker [4] for (MP) declarative $\mathcal{BK}$, the ProbDeclare checker for probabilistic declarative $\mathcal{BK}$, the conformance checker [2] for procedural $\mathcal{BK}$.

From an implementation point of view, the inner loop of ExpandBranches, explicitly represented at line 3 of Algorithm 2, is realized in the proposed NeSy framework as two separate calls:

- The first call invokes the *trained NN* model as a subroutine, which takes $\sigma_{\leq k+h}$ as input and returns a vector of activity and resource probabilities $\pi = \langle p(a_1|\sigma_{\leq k+h}), \ldots, p(a_i|\sigma_{\leq k+h}), \ldots p(a_{|\mathcal{A}_\perp|}|\sigma_{\leq k+h})\rangle \oplus \langle p(r_1|\sigma_{\leq k+h}), \ldots, p(r_i|\sigma_{\leq k+h}), \ldots p(r_{|\mathcal{R}_\perp|}|\sigma_{\leq k+h})\rangle$ (cf. Definition 1) as predicted by the trained NN.

- The second call executes a *compliance checker* function within the symbolic component, which also takes $\sigma_{\leq k+h}$ as input and returns a vector of compliance values $\varphi = \langle \mathcal{C}(\langle \sigma_{\leq k+h}, a_1, r_1\rangle, \mathcal{BK}), \ldots, \mathcal{C}(\langle \sigma_{\leq k+h}, a_i, r_i\rangle, \mathcal{BK}), \ldots\rangle$, quantifying how well each possible extension aligns with $\mathcal{BK}$.

To avoid underflow problems during the computation of $score_{\sigma_{\leq k+h+1}}$, Eq. 1 is implemented by applying the logarithm to the right-hand side, thus transforming multiplications into summations.

After computing the score of the extended prefix, the beam search algorithm ranks the prefixes according to their scores, and only the top *bSize* prefixes are retained (line 5 of Algorithm 1). This step is necessary to limit the search space. For each of the top-ranked prefixes (line 8), if the last predicted symbol is the termination symbol ($\perp$) and the suffix is compliant, the trace (i.e., the prefix and predicted suffix) and its associated score are returned as the prediction result (line 12). Otherwise, the prefix is added to *branches* (line 10), and the beam search continues until the set of prefixes and scores is empty or the maximum number of iterations *max* is reached (line 3).

4 Experiments

In this section, we evaluate the performance of our NeSy framework for single- and multi-attribute SP under concept drift. To demonstrate its flexibility, the framework has been implemented in *NeSy4PPM*, the first general-purpose Python library for Neuro-Symbolic PPM which is available online via GitHub[1] and PyPI[2]. We conducted experiments using DECLARE and MP-DECLARE as $\mathcal{BK}$. To this end, we first present the datasets and the procedure for extracting $\mathcal{BK}$ representations that capture drifts. This is followed by a description of our empirical evaluation procedure and a discussion of the results.

4.1 Datasets and Background Knowledge

We evaluated the performance of the proposed framework on two benchmark event logs publicly available at the 4TU Research Data repository:[3] Helpdesk and Sepsis. For each log, we sorted the traces chronologically, using the first 80% of the data for training and the remaining 20% for testing. To simulate concept drift, a $\mathcal{BK}$ was derived from under-represented traces in the training set, and the test set was filtered such that all retained traces are compliant with $\mathcal{BK}$.

More specifically, constraints with support lower than 20% in the training set were discovered using the *DeclareMiner*[4] tool. We obtained 5 and 3 DECLARE

[1] https://github.com/JamilaOUKHARIJANE/NeSy4PPM.
[2] https://pypi.org/project/nesy4ppm/0.1/.
[3] https://data.4tu.nl/repository/collection:event_logs_real.
[4] https://rulemining.org.

constraints for Helpdesk and Sepsis, respectively, and 2 MP-DECLARE constraints for both datasets. All the retained traces in the corresponding test sets are therefore compliant with these constraints, thus inducing a drift from the training set to the test set.

The DECLARE-filtered Helpdesk test set contains 320 traces, whereas the corresponding Sepsis test set contains 63 traces. The corresponding MP-DECLARE-filtered test sets contain 820 traces for Helpdesk and 64 for Sepsis. The procedural knowledge (in the form of a Petri net) was extracted from test traces filtered with the DECLARE constraints using the Inductive Miner algorithm [11].

4.2 Experimental Setup

We performed the experiments using our NeSy framework, which we refer to as BS_{BK}. Specifically, we instantiate it with a transformer [22] as the NN, due to its promising results in NAP [3,10]. The employed transformer model consists of a 6-layer encoder with multi-head attention (8 heads, hidden size 64), residual connections, and layer normalization. The encoder output is passed through global max pooling. The transformer has two output layers (for predicting activities and resources), each ending with a softmax activation function and optimized using Adam with a learning rate of 0.001 and early stopping.

For prediction, we run Algorithm 1 with a beam size $bsize = 3$ and perform hyperparameter optimization for the weight w assigned to $\mathcal{BK}$, conducting a grid search in the range $[0, 1]$ with a step size of 0.1. To evaluate the effectiveness of BS_{BK}, we compare it against three alternative methods:

- *SAP*: a Simple Autoregressive sequence Prediction approach introduced in [20] for activity SP, and extended in [10,12] to support multi-attribute SP using transformers.
- *BS*: an ablation version of our NeSy framework in which the compliance checker is removed, leaving only the beam search driven by the Transformer.
- BS_{filter}: the method proposed in [6], which applies $\mathcal{BK}$ to filter non-compliant suffixes only after beam search. We adapt this method to also predict resources and to use MP-DECLARE for compliance checking.

As evaluation metrics, we consider: (i) the **Damerau-Levenshtein Similarity (DLS)** between the predicted suffix $\hat{\sigma}_{>k}$ and the ground truth suffix $\sigma_{>k}$ (averaged over all prefixes); (ii) the **Compliance**, defined as the proportion of predicted traces (i.e., the prefix concatenated with the predicted suffix) that satisfy $\mathcal{BK}$ (i.e., DECLARE or MP-DECLARE constraints); and (iii) the **Fitness**, representing the degree to which the predicted traces align with the procedural Petri net model discovered from the test set.

4.3 Results

We report results for both single-attribute (activity) and multi-attribute (activity and resource) SP under concept drift. For BS_{BK}, we use the value of w that yields the best DLS on the test set. The optimal value of w falls within the range $[0.5, 0.7]$ when the drift occurs infrequently in the training set, and increases to 0.9 when the drift is entirely absent from the training set.

Table 1 presents the average results for DLS, compliance, and fitness for single-attribute SP, comparing the three baselines (SAP, BS, and BS_{filter}) against the proposed NeSy framework (BS_{BK}), using both one-hot and index-based encodings. The results demonstrate that the BS_{BK} method, which combines NN predictions with $\mathcal{BK}$ (either Petri nets or DECLARE), consistently achieves the highest DLS and fitness scores across both logs. Notably, this configuration also maintains high compliance levels, with $\mathcal{BK}$ (DECLARE) achieving the best compliance. Table 2 presents the results for multi-attribute SP, where both activities and their corresponding resources are predicted simultaneously. The table reports the average DLS scores for each attribute and compliance with MP-DECLARE $\mathcal{BK}$ across the SAP, BS, BS_{filter}, and BS_{BK} methods, using all considered encodings. These results demonstrate the effectiveness of integrating symbolic $\mathcal{BK}$ into the beam search algorithm. Notably, BS_{BK} with MP-DECLARE $\mathcal{BK}$ achieves the best performance across all metrics. It yields the highest DLS scores for resource prediction (e.g., 0.672 for Helpdesk and 0.618 for Sepsis with index-based encoding), while also maintaining perfect compliance across both logs.

Table 1. Single-attribute suffix prediction results.

Method	Encoder	Helpdesk			Sepsis		
		DLS	Compliance	Fitness	DLS	Compliance	Fitness
SAP	One-hot [20]	0.767	0.256	0.896	0.136	0.009	0.852
	Index-based	0.769	0.257	0.897	0.151	0.016	0.864
BS	One-hot	0.847	0.496	0.928	0.233	0.009	0.876
	Index-based	0.846	0.492	0.927	0.139	0.019	0.881
BS_{filter}	One-hot [6]	0.847	0.496	0.928	0.233	0.009	0.876
	Index-based	0.847	0.498	0.928	0.139	0.019	0.881
BS_{BK} (Petri nets)	One-hot	**0.992**	**1.0**	**1.0**	0.327	0.03	0.93
	Index-based	**0.992**	**1.0**	**1.0**	0.195	0.09	0.924
BS_{BK} (DECLARE)	One-hot	**0.992**	**1.0**	**1.0**	**0.497**	**1.0**	**1.0**
	Index-based	**0.992**	**1.0**	**1.0**	**0.487**	**1.0**	**0.998**

In contrast, the baseline methods (SAP and BS) struggle with resource prediction, confirming that NN models alone fail to capture drifts in resource allocation. Although BS_{filter} applies MP-DECLARE constraints as a post-prediction filter, its overall performance remains similar to BS in terms of both prediction accuracy and compliance. This limited improvement can be attributed to the restricted beam size: when activity-resource pairs representing drift are rare or unseen during training, the NN model assigns them low probabilities. As a result, these pairs are often excluded from the beam due to the prioritization of higher-probability candidates.

Overall, the results underscore the value of integrating $\mathcal{BK}$ directly into the prediction process rather than using it solely as a post-prediction filter.

Table 2. Multi-attribute suffix prediction results for six configurations.

Method	Encoder	Helpdesk			Sepsis		
		DLS (Acts)	DLS (Res)	Compliance	DLS (Acts)	DLS (Res)	Compliance
SAP	One-hot [10]	0.815	0.169	0.0003	0.308	0.283	0.336
	Index-based [10]	0.812	0.171	0.0003	0.471	0.463	0.635
	Shrinked index-based	0.808	0.162	0.0003	0.194	0.179	0.099
	Multi-encoders [10, 12]	0.805	0.171	0.0003	0.296	0.284	0.016
BS	One-hot	0.818	0.169	0.0003	0.166	0.149	0.04
	Index-based	0.817	0.17	0.0003	0.27	0.25	0.036
	Shrinked index-based	0.812	0.162	0.0003	0.353	0.319	0.397
	Multi-encoders	0.806	0.17	0.0003	0.193	0.176	0.0
BS_{filter}	One-hot	0.813	0.157	0.003	0.166	0.149	0.04
	Index-based	0.814	0.184	0.014	0.275	0.254	0.047
	Shrinked index-based	0.812	0.162	0.0005	0.319	0.326	0.397
	Multi-encoders	0.812	0.181	0.012	0.193	0.176	0.0
BS_{BK} (MP-DECLARE)	One-hot	**0.83**	0.67	**1.0**	0.674	0.6	0.979
	Index-based	0.829	**0.672**	**1.0**	**0.692**	**0.618**	**0.983**
	Shrinked index-based	0.822	0.657	**1.0**	0.68	0.603	0.909
	Multi-encoders	0.826	0.669	**1.0**	0.67	0.6	0.413

5 Related Work

Recent studies have begun addressing the challenge of PPM under concept drift using various strategies. We can classify these contributions based on the adapted PPM phase: either the *learning* phase or the *prediction* phase.

The first group of approaches addresses concept drift by adapting the model training process using *continual* or *incremental* learning. Continual learning techniques aim to integrate new knowledge while preserving historical data during training. In [9], the authors propose a continual learning approach that integrates an adaptive memory mechanism to retain relevant historical knowledge while continuously learning from new process behaviors. The work in [24] introduces a task-free continual learning approach for online next-activity prediction, employing an adaptive memory mechanism and a dynamic loss function to enable the model to adapt to evolving process behaviors. [23] extends this work by using prompts to handle temporal dependencies during continual learning. A key drawback of continual learning approaches is the expensive finetuning process.

In contrast, incremental learning methods update a previously trained model with newly observed data without retraining from scratch. The works in [14, 18] explore several strategies for incrementally updating prediction models to handle previously unseen process behavior. The authors in [16] investigate incremental learning strategies for NN by reusing existing next-activity prediction models and adapting them with newly observed data. Similarly, [15] proposes a strategy to detect concept drift and adapt an NN model to address next-activity prediction in dynamic process data streams, while [13] investigates the next-activity prediction task in the presence of unseen data variability. As shown in [9,18], this first group of approaches is primarily effective for gradual or recurring process drift, which limits their scalability in fast-evolving environments.

To address this limitation, the second group of approaches includes a few contributions that tackle drift by integrating symbolic $\mathcal{BK}$ into the prediction process. These works fall under the umbrella of Symbolic[Neuro] systems, which aim to combine prediction models with symbolic $\mathcal{BK}$ for enhanced SP. One of the earliest works in this group is [6], which applies crisp DECLARE constraints as a post-prediction filter to remove non-compliant suffixes predicted by an LSTM. Our framework belongs to this second category of approaches and is general in the sense that it can handle multi-attribute suffix predictions and use any type of $\mathcal{BK}$ supported by a conformance checker (that needs to be integrated in the prediction layer of the framework).

Other NeSy systems integrate DECLARE knowledge into the loss function of neural systems [21]. These systems cannot naturally deal with concept drift since the $\mathcal{BK}$ needs to be injected at training time. However, it may be possible to finetune such systems using $\mathcal{BK}$ about the concept drift (when available), encoded as a semantic loss, without the need for sample traces and with a lower finetuning time compared to continual training.

6 Conclusion

This paper introduced a NeSy framework for SP in PPM, which leverages symbolic $\mathcal{BK}$ in the form of declarative or procedural process models. Motivated by the limitations of purely data-driven approaches – particularly in scenarios affected by concept drift – our framework integrates $\mathcal{BK}$ during SP to guide the beam search toward more likely and compliant suffixes. This integration supports a broad range of $\mathcal{BK}$ representations, including DECLARE, MP-DECLARE, PROB-DECLARE, and Petri net models, enabling reasoning over both declarative and procedural models in dynamic environments. Experimental results demonstrate that incorporating $\mathcal{BK}$ can significantly improve the accuracy of SP, especially in the presence of substantial changes in the distribution of different trace variants between the training and test sets. As future work, we plan to extend our evaluation to a broader set of real-world event logs and investigate the impact of integrating PROBDECLARE $\mathcal{BK}$ during SP. Additionally, we aim to extend the framework to support the fuzzy LTL_f checker [7], enabling reasoning over fuzzy declarative models to better handle uncertainty in process behavior.

Acknowledgements. This study was partially funded by the European Union - NextGenerationEU, in the framework of the iNEST - Interconnected Nord-Est Innovation Ecosystem (iNEST ECS00000043 CUP I43C22000250006). The views and opinions expressed are solely those of the authors and do not necessarily reflect those of the European Union, nor can the European Union be held responsible for them. The study was also supported by Fondazione Cariverona within the ReSS-Pro project.

References

1. Alman, A., Maggi, F.M., Montali, M., Peñaloza, R.: Probabilistic declarative process mining. Inf. Syst. **109**, 102033 (2022)
2. Berti, A., van der Aalst, W.M.P.: Reviving token-based replay: increasing speed while improving diagnostics. In: ATAED@Petri Nets/ACSD, pp. 87–103 (2019)
3. Bukhsh, Z.A., Saeed, A., Dijkman, R.M.: ProcessTransformer: predictive business process monitoring with transformer network. CoRR abs/2104.00721 (2021)
4. Burattin, A., Maggi, F.M., Sperduti, A.: Conformance checking based on multi-perspective declarative process models. Expert Syst. Appl. **65**, 194–211 (2016)
5. Ceravolo, P., Comuzzi, M., De Weerdt, J., Di Francescomarino, C., Maggi, F.M.: Predictive process monitoring: concepts, challenges, and future research directions. Process Sci. **1**(1), 2 (2024)
6. Di Francescomarino, C., Ghidini, C., Maggi, F.M., Petrucci, G., Yeshchenko, A.: An eye into the future: leveraging a-priori knowledge in predictive business process monitoring. In: Carmona, J., Engels, G., Kumar, A. (eds.) BPM 2017. LNCS, vol. 10445, pp. 252–268. Springer, Cham (2017). https://doi.org/10.1007/978-3-319-65000-5_15
7. Donadello, I., Felli, P., Innes, C., Maggi, F.M., Montali, M.: Conformance checking of fuzzy logs against declarative temporal specifications. In: BPM, vol. 14940, pp. 39–56 (2024)
8. Hochreiter, S., Schmidhuber, J.: Long short-term memory. Neural Comput. **9**(8), 1735–1780 (1997)
9. Iman, A.N., Kamal, I.M., Kim, D., Bae, H.: Continual learning approach with adaptive memory mechanism for predictive process monitoring in dynamic business environments. Available at SSRN 5026481
10. Lazo, G.R., Nanculef, R.: Multi-attribute transformers for sequence prediction in business process management. In: DS, vol. 13601, pp. 184–194 (2022)
11. Leemans, S.J.J.: Robust Process Mining with Guarantees - Process Discovery, Conformance Checking and Enhancement, vol. 440 (2022)
12. Lin, L., Wen, L., Wang, J.: Mm-pred: a deep predictive model for multi-attribute event sequence. In: SDM, pp. 118–126. SIAM (2019)
13. Mangat, A.S., Rinderle-Ma, S.: Next-activity prediction for non-stationary processes with unseen data variability. In: EDOC, pp. 145–161 (2022)
14. Márquez-Chamorro, A.E., Nepomuceno-Chamorro, I.A., Resinas, M., Ruiz-Cortés, A.: Updating prediction models for predictive process monitoring. In: CAiSE, pp. 304–318 (2022)
15. Pasquadibisceglie, V., Appice, A., Castellano, G., Malerba, D.: DARWIN: an online deep learning approach to handle concept drifts in predictive process monitoring. Eng. Appl. Artif. Intell. **123**(Part C), 106461 (2023)
16. Pauwels, S., Calders, T.: Incremental predictive process monitoring: the next activity case. In: Polyvyanyy, A., Wynn, M.T., Van Looy, A., Reichert, M. (eds.) BPM 2021. LNCS, vol. 12875, pp. 123–140. Springer, Cham (2021). https://doi.org/10.1007/978-3-030-85469-0_10

17. Pesic, M., Schonenberg, H., van der Aalst, W.M.P.: DECLARE: full support for loosely-structured processes. In: EDOC, pp. 287–300 (2007)
18. Rizzi, W., Di Francescomarino, C., Ghidini, C., Maggi, F.M.: How do I update my model? On the resilience of predictive process monitoring models to change. Knowl. Inf. Syst. **64**(5), 1385–1416 (2022)
19. Sarker, M.K., Zhou, L., Eberhart, A., Hitzler, P.: Neuro-symbolic artificial intelligence: current trends. AI Commun. **34**(3), 197–209 (2022)
20. Tax, N., Verenich, I., La Rosa, M., Dumas, M.: Predictive business process monitoring with LSTM neural networks. In: Dubois, E., Pohl, K. (eds.) CAiSE 2017. LNCS, vol. 10253, pp. 477–492. Springer, Cham (2017). https://doi.org/10.1007/978-3-319-59536-8_30
21. Umili, E., Licks, G.P., Patrizi, F.: Enhancing deep sequence generation with logical temporal knowledge. In: PMAI@ECAI, vol. 3779, pp. 23–34 (2024)
22. Vaswani, A., et al.: Attention is all you need. In: NIPS, pp. 5998–6008 (2017)
23. Verbeek, T., Hassani, M.: Handling catastrophic forgetting: online continual learning for next activity prediction. In: CoopIS, vol. 15506, pp. 225–242 (2024)
24. Verbeek, T., Yao, R., Hassani, M.: Task-free continual learning with dynamic loss for online next activity prediction. In: ICPM, pp. 693–705 (2024)

Resource-Oriented Workaround Analysis: A Case Study

Wouter van der Waal(✉) and Hajo A. Reijers

Utrecht University, Utrecht, The Netherlands
w.g.vanderwaal@uu.nl, h.a.reijers@uu.nl

Abstract. Workarounds can show how workers solve local issues in designed processes and may therefore be used for general process improvements. Recent advances into workaround mining have shown data-driven approaches can both help discover workarounds and analyze them over long periods. However, earlier studies on workarounds have neglected the resource perspective. In this work, we use information about resource roles to find additional perspectives on workarounds. With a detailed analysis of a single workaround during a case study at an Emergency Room, we find clear differences in how various resource roles adopt it. We interview domain experts to further understand the motivations behind the use of the workaround. Following organizational theory, we find that the hierarchical power of their role is important in how resources approach workarounds, resulting in strongly different adoption speeds. We propose future work to enhance the research technique and suggest directions that may lead to new insights about workarounds.

Keywords: Workarounds · Resources · Healthcare · Business Processs Management · Routine Dynamics

1 Introduction

Workarounds are creative ways to handle unforeseen obstacles during work [2,27]. Although workers typically have good intentions when using workarounds [26], there may be unforeseen negative consequences at a later time [4]. As such, the management of workarounds is important for organizations. In a previous study, we investigated how workarounds change over a period of years [26]. By measuring how often workarounds occurred compared to the normative process, we discovered that workarounds, and the underlying process, could change drastically after organizational and system changes. However, even when there are no discernible changes, workers may increase their use of the workaround, potentially changing an incidental workaround into a common part of the process.

Our previous study also revealed that analyzing only the control-flow of the process was not always sufficient to understand the evolution of a workaround. For example, a workaround where activities were performed after discharge

I. van de Weerd et al. (Eds.): BPM 2025 Workshops, LNBIP 569, pp. 262–273, 2026.
https://doi.org/10.1007/978-3-032-13426-4_19

looked stable, with only a temporary increase in how often it was used after a Hospital Information System (HIS) update. However, when zooming in on the change, we found that initially nurses were involved but especially secretaries applied the workaround after.

In the field of Business Process Management (BPM), workarounds are commonly studied from a data perspective [27,28]. Where BPM is able to use historical data to study long term changes, there is little work studying the effect of resources, even though this perspective is considered important [19]. On the other hand, with their high granularity through detailed interviews and observations, routine dynamics often studies differences between individuals [20,24] but struggles to study long term change. In this work, we aim to bridge the gap and investigate how workarounds change over time, considering resource roles.

In a case study at an Emergency Room (ER) we analyze one workaround in detail. By adding information about resource roles to an existing data analysis technique, we investigate changes in workarounds. Then, we conduct interviews to investigate the motivations and considerations for the workaround. By focusing on the resource perspective of workarounds during this case study, we gain a better understanding of how we can find differences between resource roles and how these influence their way of working. Practically, such differences between these roles can help tailor the management of workarounds better to roles.

In Sect. 2, we start with an overview of the current state of the art for the adoption of workarounds and how information about resource roles is currently used in BPM and routine dynamics. We then explain our technique in Sect. 3 and show the results of our case study in Sect. 4. We discuss our findings and limitations in Sect. 5 before concluding our study in Sect. 6.

2 Related Work

We start this section with an overview of how workarounds get adopted. As we are inspired by both BPM and routine dynamics, we will discuss how resource roles are used in these fields outside of workarounds. We will primarily use BPM terminology in this work. That is, we use *resource* to refer to a human resource or worker. However, to describe their designed job function, we use *role*, largely following one definition according to Organizational Role Theory [6].

2.1 Workarounds

There has been limited research into the adoption of workarounds. In general, workarounds seem to originate as temporary improvisations, adopted by various resources, and, once one has grown enough, it is formally accepted or rejected [2, 23,28]. There are various ideas about how they spread over time. One theory suggests that sharing is initiated by anyone who knows of the workaround [23], while another states that workarounds are shared through teams [2,28]. In both cases, once new people learn about the workaround, they will start using it. However, recent work has shown that sharing may not be the leading cause of the spread of workarounds; instead the use of a workaround may only grow if more workers feel the need to work around obstacles [26].

2.2 The Resource Perspective in BPM

If we take a broader look at the field of BPM, we note multiple calls for resource-oriented research. It is generally accepted that information about resources is relevant for BPM [8]. To further understand process dynamics, their behavior is even considered crucial [14]. Further highlighting both the potential value and the limited research into resource-oriented research, a large Delphi study [18] notes "Analyzing business processes from the resource perspective" as an opportunity rated as extremely relevant by many international experts.

Two sub-fields of BPM take the resource perspective into account by design: Human Resource Mining and Resource Allocation. The former aims to leverage event logs to identify aspects of individual resources to suggest how teams of resources may work together better [18]. One of the more straightforward resource aspects in this field is their role within the organization [9]. Also, in the Resource Allocation field, the formal role is an important consideration [5,22].

While many conformance checking models include control-flow and data perspectives, the resource perspective is often suggested as future work [1,7,12]. When this perspective is used, the role is often only used to approximate permissions [17]. For example, physicians and nurses may record patient tests, while secretaries are generally not allowed to do so. Instead of direct conformance, another angle is to investigate differences between resource roles. One such approach found that different roles can have vastly different ways to execute the same process, based on experience and training differences between them [13].

2.3 The Resource Perspective in Routine Dynamics

Where BPM starts from the managerial side of the process, routine dynamics tends to approach the same topic from individuals. In this way, tensions between individuals are observed to change the underlying process [20,24]. Further information, such as role and power dynamics about individuals in specific contexts can further help with understanding processes [24]. Variances in resource roles often result in differences within the same process. On a process design level, this can be seen as organizations tend to only formally alter processes once resources with high power express that they consider it needs to change [21].

However, even on a lower level these differences are clear. Given the same process, resource aspects such as gender and role strongly affect how and if workers vocalize experienced mistreatment through a designed "remedial voice mechanism" [15]. Besides the higher comfort expressing their frustrations, workers with more power also tend to be more open to altering their process executions creatively without fear of rejection by other, more powerful, colleagues [10]. Similarly, the notion of role-routine ecologies describes that in complex scenarios, similar routines often emerge within resources with the same role [16].

To summarize, we find a broadly supported interest in the resource roles in both fields. Where BPM finds differences between roles, routine dynamics focuses on the similarities within them. In our work we will continue this focus to find how various resource roles behave when performing the same process.

3 Approach

To investigate how different resource roles use workarounds, we adopt a case study approach. Case studies are particularly suitable for how and why questions about complex, real-world phenomena [29]. In our study, we aim to understand both the variation in workaround behavior across roles and the underlying reasons for such differences. This case study consists of two parts: a quantitative analysis of event data and a qualitative analysis of semi-structured interviews with domain experts. Our goal is to identify and understand differences in how resource roles engage with workarounds.

3.1 Context

The case study was conducted at the Emergency Room (ER) of the University Medical Center Utrecht (UMCU). This academic teaching hospital employs 12.000 people and provides care to over 220.000 patients annually. The ER consists of 19 treatment rooms and treats around 18.000 patients per year. The hospital uses HiX[1] as its Hospital Information System (HIS). This study was approved by the Medical Research Ethics Committee (MREC) NedMec (research protocol number 22/1055).

3.2 Data Collection and Preparation

For our data analysis, we use an event log enriched with resource role information. We classify each trace as either workaround or normative, based on prior, expert defined rules [26,27]. To analyze the process, we view the process from three different resource-oriented angles to explore a single workaround.

Process Execution. To determine how to measure the relevant resource for all traces, we find which event would be considered the workaround event. For example, if experts consider a late discharge of a patient a workaround, the discharge is labeled as the workaround event. We then generate an overview of all process executions, including both workarounds and normative traces, by calculating the proportion of traces in which each resource role performs the event. This enables us to find general changes in resource behavior.

Workaround Execution. Next, we create a similar overview for traces marked as workarounds. This, again, allows us to find changes in resource behavior, but from a different perspective: Comparing this with the process execution plot reveals which resource roles approach workarounds differently. The plots also provide a complete overview of the roles relevant to investigate the workaround.

[1] https://www.chipsoft.com/en.

Workaround Ratio. To sharpen our resource perspective, we calculate the ratio of workaround to normative process executions for each resource role. This allows us to determine precise changes in workaround behavior, extending the approach introduced in [26] by explicitly accounting for differences in resource roles.

4 Case Study

4.1 Background

The workaround we investigate in this study concerns the registration of pain scores during visits to the ER. To ensure that treatment is effective, patients should be asked about their pain levels at least twice: once during triage at the start of the process and once again at discharge. This process is embedded in the HIS, which evaluates pain score registration before discharge.

This workaround was discovered in a previous study using the Semi-automated WORkaround Detection (SWORD) framework [27] and later further analyzed [26]. In the present study we build on these findings by conducting a more detailed analysis of how the workaround changes over time, with a focus on the roles of the resources. We specifically selected this workaround because the HIS enforces the use of pain scores, which can only be circumvented manually. In other words, any deviation from the normative process must be a conscious choice, removing any accidental, non-workaround deviations from the data.

As illustrated in Fig. 1, when discharging a patient, a user should drag a patient card from the room they are currently in to the Discharge field ("Ontslagen" in Dutch). This action starts the formal discharge procedure, which includes a check for pain score registration. If fewer than two pain scores have been registered during the ER visit, the system prompts to enter additional pain scores and prevents the actual discharge until this requirement is met. However, users can bypass this control by right-clicking the patient card to access a drop-down menu. From this, they can forcibly move the patient, circumventing any system checks. In doing so, they work around the pain score requirement.

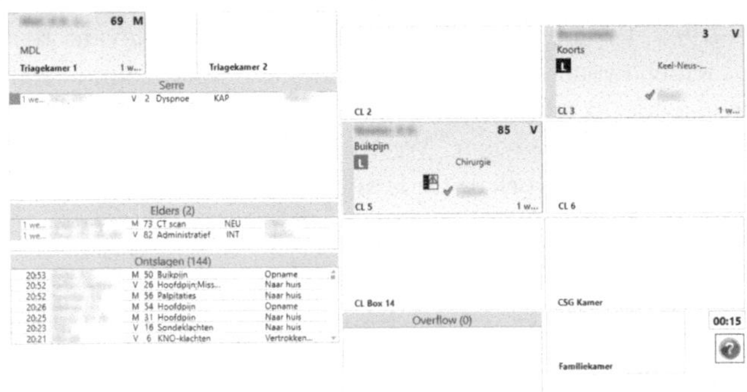

Fig. 1. Screenshot of the process in HiX. The blue cards can be dragged to move patients to various rooms (e.g., "CL 2"), or discharge ("Ontslagen"). (Color figure online)

4.2 Data Extraction

To follow patients, every ER visit is assigned a unique visit ID. We use this as a Case ID in our analysis. For each case, we also extract the pain score registrations and the discharge event. For the discharge event, we record the resource role of the employee that performed the discharge. We classify each trace as a workaround if fewer than two pain scores were registered. Otherwise, traces are labeled as normative.

4.3 Data Results

Process Execution by Resource Role. As shown in Fig. 2, the discharge process is primarily executed by nurses. In 2013, approximately 80% of the patients are discharged by nurses, 15% by secretaries, and 5% by physicians. In July 2014, a sharp increase occurs: the proportion of discharges completed by nurses increases to over 95%. This moment of sudden change coincides with a previously discovered HIS update, which introduced a system constraint: users could only discharge patients if enough pain scores had been registered [26].

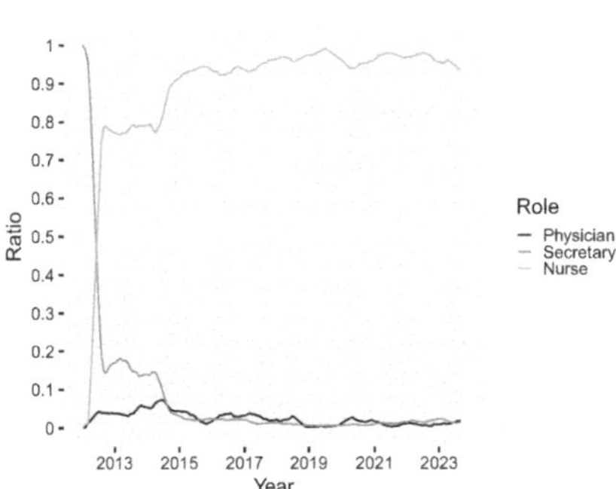

Fig. 2. Process executions per resource role

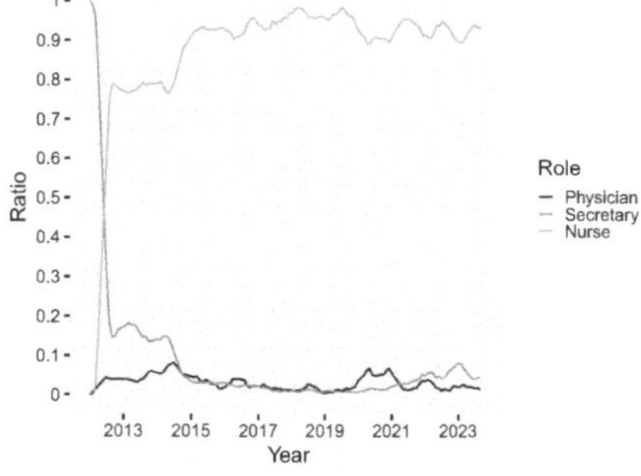

Fig. 3. Workarounds per resource role

Workaround Execution by Resource Role. Figure 3 shows the distribution of resources roles for workaround cases. Before the intervention, the role distribution ratios are similar to the overall process. However, notable differences emerge after the system update in July 2014. Then, nurses still perform most of the discharges, but their share of workarounds is usually lower than their share of the discharges. This difference is especially notable after 2020, where first physicians and later secretaries perform the workaround in more than 6% of the cases, despite neither of them performing more than 3% of the overall cases. This divergence indicates that secretaries and physicians have a higher tendency to use this workaround than nurses after the HIS update.

Workaround Ratio by Resource Role. To gain a deeper understanding of role-specific behavior, we zoom in further on the resources by investigating the ratio of workarounds per role in Fig. 4. Before the intervention, this ratio is close to 100% across all roles, as pain scores were rarely logged prior to being enforced by the system. Directly after the intervention in 2014, the workaround ratio sharply decreases to 15% and gradually lowers further to 10% in 2017 across all roles. We then see strong differences between the roles in how they adopt the workaround:

- Nurses only show gradual adoption of the workaround over five years up to 25%. This averages to 3%pt per year.
- Physicians start using the workaround commonly relatively early in 2018. Then they apply the workaround up to 75% of the time after four years. This averages to 16%pt per year.
- Secretaries do not strongly adopt the workaround until 2020, but they adopt it much faster than physicians and nurses. They ratio grows from 20% to 85% in two years. This averages to 32%pt per year.

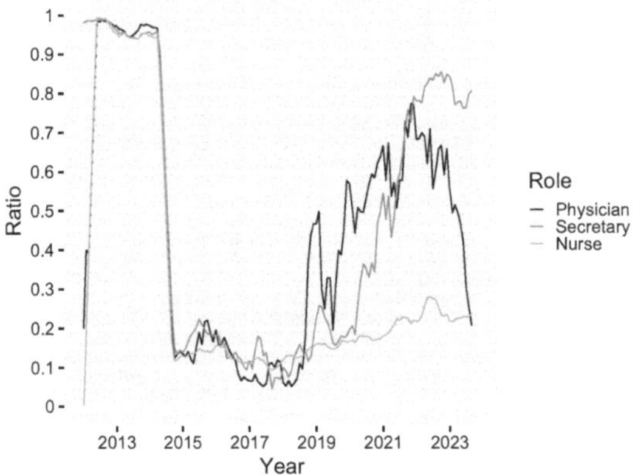

Fig. 4. The ratio of workarounds to normative process executions for each role

Note that the workaround ratios of the physicians and secretaries fluctuate more sharply than those of the nurses. This can be explained as there are months where the former discharge few patients, resulting in ratios that change stronger. Despite this variability, the general changes in workaround ratio are clear.

4.4 Interviews

To understand the motivations behind the workaround behavior observed in the data, we interviewed two domain experts: one ER physician who has worked for 12 years at the UMCU and one nurse who has worked at the ER for 20 years, the latter also serving as the product owner of the HIS for the last six years. Both experts confirmed that they have performed the workaround themselves.

Discharge Responsibilities and Role Dynamics. The interviewees confirmed the general pattern shown in Fig. 2: Nurses are typically responsible for discharging a patient. While both nurses and physicians have permission to perform all tasks related to the discharge, such as registering pain scores with patients. Physicians often perform more specialized care. This makes nurses the more logical choice for these more general tasks that require a good overview of individual patients. As such, if a physician handles the discharge, the case is already exceptional.

While secretaries do not have permission to register measurements such as pain scores, they can discharge patients, typically in edge cases. For example, secretaries may discharge patients who leave the hospital against medical advice or they handle patients who were not properly discharged by anyone else. In this sense, secretaries often function as a "back-stop" and discharge remaining patients to make sure the log of patients at the ER is up to date.

Recognition of Workarounds as Alternative Practices. Both experts clearly distinguish between the normative process, where patients are discharged with pain scores during triage and discharge, and the workaround, where patients are manually discharged with fewer than two pain scores. Besides these options, both experts noted that especially nurses use other strategies to satisfy the HIS requirements. Most notably, they may register placeholder pain scores, such as "n/a" (not available), when the patient is no longer present. While this option is designed for patients who are present but not capable of reporting pain, it is also used as a workaround. Alternatively, the nurse mentioned that some colleagues consistently register two pain scores during triage so they will not run into this issue at all later, already planning ahead and solving the issue beforehand.

Motivations for Using Workarounds. Both interviewees report the same reasons for using any workaround: If the patient has left and it is found that there were not enough pain scores, no normative option (i.e., asking the patient) is available and people need to choose a workaround. This can happen regularly as the discharge procedure may get postponed while patients get sent home during a temporary peak in patients or if there is no computer present at the time.

Physicians often choose the manual discharge workaround as it is quick. The physician noted that they were explicitly instructed not to use this workaround, but they still did so regularly due to time pressure. In contrast, the nurse noted that most nurses are unaware of the manual option and typically resolve missing data through other means. The nurses who are aware of the workaround tend to use it if multiple forms are missing and manual discharge is more efficient than addressing each issue individually. For secretaries, the manual workaround is the only available option when discharging patients with missing pain scores, as they lack the permission to register additional measurements.

Perceived Impact on Patient Care. Neither expert could think of any direct negative impact on the quality of care resulting from this workaround. They are confident in the quality of care as patients are continuously monitored. They may not always log pain scores, but if patients state that their pain is manageable, nurses and physicians understand that no further treatment is necessary. In addition, patients are usually checked at least informally before they go home.

However, the physician did highlight a broader concern: while workarounds at discharge are typically harmless, similar behavior during intake could lead to more serious consequences. For example, skipping questions about antibiotic-resistant bacteria could pose significant risks if done improperly. This contrast underscores that not all workarounds carry the same level of risk, depending on the stage of the process and the nature of the information omitted.

5 Discussion

To interpret our findings, we further discuss our work first from a theoretical angle. After this, we consider the practical contributions and finish this section by discussing the limitations of our study.

Theoretical Contributions. We found differences in workaround adoption among the different resource roles. One explanation could be found in existing theory: Roles with higher power adjust their process with less fear of repercussions than those with low power [11]. As such, secretaries would be hesitant to use the workaround, explaining their late adoption. However, as resources with less power are expected to align their work to those with more power [10], it makes sense that secretaries use the workaround often, as they have no other options to discharge patients without sending work back to nurses or physicians.

The way nurses work strongly follows the temporal coordination theory in complex role-routine ecologies [16]. Following this theory, nurses could either try to follow the normative sequence or optimize timing. However, trying to follow both will lead to local conflicts, such as when a patient could leave without being formally discharged. In such cases, theory suggests that nurses would solve this through role-based prioritizing: They choose based on who benefits [16]. While sequence is important to management, timing is more important for the patient, who would go home earlier, and colleagues, who would have a less crowded ER.

Practical Contributions. Our theoretical findings have direct practical implications related to workaround management. The case study organization was already aware of this workaround, but our data analysis has shown that their attempts to minimize its usage have not worked over time. To manage workarounds more effectively it may be important to keep the resources roles in mind. Although physicians were explicitly told not to use it, they still do so as they feel comfortable deciding for themselves due to their high power. As such, threats of repercussions would have limited effect. Instead, discussing the effects on colleagues and the organization would likely have more effect [21]. Strict instruction could have an effect on low power roles like secretaries, although they would need alternative ways to align their process with their higher power colleagues.

In March 2024, the UMCU had a large HIS update when they moved from a Custom-Built system to the Standard-Content version of the same HIS. This new version standardizes many processes, including the intake and discharge of patients. Various questions, like pain scores, are not enforced anymore. For this workaround, the change is likely positive, given that registering pain scores is unlikely to negatively impact the process. However, during intake, questions about antibiotic-resistant bacteria may now also be skipped without a workaround, which may have potential negative effects. This emphasizes the need for ways to monitor workarounds, as their usage may change unpredictably.

Limitations. The primary limitation of our work is its scope: We only inspected one workaround in a single organization and interviewed two domain experts. Investigating more workarounds and holding more interviews would broaden this study, making more generalizations possible.

In this study, we only used existing visual inspections to find differences in the workaround ratios for the various resource roles. In this case, the differences between roles are large enough to discover these without further statistical proof. However, measures such as cross-correlation [30] or change point detection [3], would provide a more rigorous way to determine such differences.

6 Conclusion

In this resource role-oriented study, we performed a case study at an ER. We looked into the discharge process of patients which should have at least two pain scores. We find that besides the designed differences in how often various roles discharge patients, physicians and secretaries adopt the workaround more quickly than nurses. The findings are in line with IS literature, stating that roles with more hierarchical power tend to alter their personal process quickly without fear of repercussions, while roles with low power may change their process to support those with higher power.

While the resource perspective has already led to novel insights, we can extend this work further in various ways: First, we could discover more about this specific workaround with a further study into the alternative pathways for this process. Batch detection [25] could discover multiple pain scores registered during triage, while rule-based detection [27] could find "not available" pain scores. In addition, a new analysis with more recent data could show new insights into how the process changed, especially given that the system requirements that enforced the number of pain scores is not present anymore.

Second, while we focused on resource roles, similar techniques could be used to find differences between individual resources. This could provide new insights into how workarounds are shared between individuals and when they are used. Combining this with additional resource characteristics, such as quality or experience [31], could help organizations manage workarounds further.

Finally, in this study, we use expert-defined rules to classify traces as workarounds or normative. While this approach manages to identify instances of a specific path, interviews showed that alternative workarounds can be missing. By repeating the cycle of data-analysis and interviews, we could get a more complete view of workaround behavior within a single process.

Acknowledgement. We would like to express our gratitude to B.E.L. Vrijsen MD, PhD and C.M. van Assenbergh for their invaluable insights regarding our findings. Their expertise was instrumental in refining our study and clarifying key interpretations.

This publication is part of the WorkAround Mining (WAM!) project with project number 18490 which is (partly) financed by the Dutch Research Council (NWO).

Disclosure of Interests. The authors have no competing interests to declare that are relevant to the content of this article.

References

1. Alizadeh, M., Lu, X., Fahland, D., Zannone, N., van der Aalst, W.M.P.: Linking data and process perspectives for conformance analysis. Comput. Secur. **73**, 172–193 (2018)
2. Alter, S.: Theory of workarounds. Commun. Assoc. Inf. Syst. **34** (2014)
3. Aminikhanghahi, S., Cook, D.J.: A survey of methods for time series change point detection. Knowl. Inf. Syst. **51**(2), 339–367 (2017)
4. Bartelheimer, C., Löhr, B., Reineke, M., Aßbrock, A., Beverungen, D.: Workarounds as a cause of mismatches in business processes–: insights from a multiple case study. In: Business & Information Systems Engineering (2025)
5. Bellaaj Elloumi, F., Sellami, M., Bhiri, S.: Avoiding resource misallocations in business processes. Concurr. Comput. Pract. Exp. **32**(15) (2018)
6. Biddle, B.J.: Recent developments in role theory. Ann. Rev. Sociol. **12**(1), 67–92 (1986)
7. Borrego, D., Barba, I.: Conformance checking and diagnosis for declarative business process models in data-aware scenarios. Expert Syst. Appl. **41**(11), 5340–5352 (2014)
8. vom Brocke, J., Zelt, S., Schmiedel, T.: On the role of context in business process management. Int. J. Inf. Manag. **36**(3), 486–495 (2016)
9. Cabanillas, C., Ackermann, L., Schönig, S., Sturm, C., Mendling, J.: The RALph miner for automated discovery and verification of resource-aware process models. Softw. Syst. Model. **19**(6), 1415–1441 (2020). https://doi.org/10.1007/s10270-020-00820-7
10. Danner-Schröder, A.: Without actors, there is no action: How interpersonal interactions help to explain routine dynamics. RMS **15**(7), 1913–1936 (2020). https://doi.org/10.1007/s11846-020-00408-x
11. Dionysiou, D.D., Tsoukas, H.: Understanding the (re)creation of routines from within: a symbolic interactionist perspective. Acad. Manag. Rev. **38**(2), 181–205 (2013)
12. Dunzer, S., Stierle, M., Matzner, M., Baier, S.: Conformance checking: a state-of-the-art literature review. In: Proceedings of the 11th International Conference on Subject-Oriented Business Process Management. ACM Press (2019)
13. de la Fuente, R., et al.: Control-flow analysis of procedural skills competencies in medical training through process mining. Postgrad. Med. J. **96**(1135), 250–256 (2019)
14. Grisold, T., van der Aa, H., Franzoi, S., Hartl, S., Mendling, J., vom Brocke, J.: A context framework for sense-making of process mining results. In: International Conference on Process Mining, pp. 57–64 (2024)

15. Harlos, K.: If you build a remedial voice mechanism, will they come? Determinants of voicing interpersonal mistreatment at work. Human Relat. **63**(3), 311–329 (2010)
16. Kremser, W., Blagoev, B.: The dynamics of prioritizing: how actors temporally pattern complex role-routine ecologies. Adm. Sci. Q. **66**(2), 339–379 (2021)
17. Mannhardt, F., de Leoni, M., Reijers, H.A., van der Aalst, W.M.P.: Balanced multi-perspective checking of process conformance. Computing **98**(4), 407–437 (2016)
18. Martin, N., Beerepoot, I.: Unveiling use cases for human resource mining: a framework of past and future research. In: Business & Information Systems Engineering (2024)
19. Martin, N., et al.: Opportunities and challenges for process mining in organizations: results of a Delphi study. Bus. Inf. Syst. Eng. **63**(5), 511–527 (2021). https://doi.org/10.1007/s12599-021-00720-0
20. Nardelli, G.: Innovation dialectics: an extended process perspective on innovation in services. Serv. Ind. J. **37**(1), 31–56 (2017)
21. Nigam, A., Huising, R., Golden, B.: Explaining the selection of routines for change during organizational search. Adm. Sci. Q. **61**(4), 551–583 (2016)
22. Pufahl, L., Stiehle, F., Ihde, S., Weske, M., Weber, I.: Resource allocation in business process executions-a systematic literature study. Inf. Syst. **132**, 102541 (2025)
23. Safadi, H., Faraj, S.: The role of workarounds during an opensource electronic medical record system implementation. In: Thirty First International Conference on Information Systems (2010)
24. Tuominen, T., Edvardsson, B., Reynoso, J.: Institutional change and routine dynamics in service ecosystems. J. Serv. Mark. **34**(4), 575–586 (2020)
25. van der Waal, W., et al.: Putting the SWORD to the test: finding workarounds with process mining. Bus. Inf. Syst. Eng. **67**(2), 171–190 (2024)
26. van der Waal, W., van de Weerd, I., Beerepoot, I., Reijers, H.A.: The emergence and evolution of workarounds: a study of stability and change. In: International Conference on Information Systems (2024)
27. van der Waal, W., van de Weerd, I., Haitjema, S., Kappen, T., Reijers, H.A.: Whetting the SWORD: detecting workarounds by using active learning and logistic regression. In: Hawaiian International Conference on System Sciences, pp. 3687–3696 (2024)
28. Weinzierl, S., Wolf, V., Pauli, T., Beverungen, D., Matzner, M.: Detecting temporal workarounds in business processes – a deep-learning-based method for analysing event log data. J. Bus. Anal. **5**(1), 76–100 (2021)
29. Yin, R.K.: Case Study Research: Design and Methods, 5th edn. SAGE Publications, Thousands Oaks (2013)
30. Yoo, J.C., Han, T.H.: Fast normalized cross-correlation. Circ. Syst. Signal Process. **28**(6), 819–843 (2009)
31. Zhao, W., Liu, H., Dai, W., Ma, J.: An entropy-based clustering ensemble method to support resource allocation in business process management. Knowl. Inf. Syst. **48**(2), 305–330 (2015). https://doi.org/10.1007/s10115-015-0879-7

Linking Actor Behavior to Process Performance over Time

Aurélie Leribaux[1(✉)], Rafael Oyamada[1], Johannes De Smedt[1], Zahra Dasht Bozorgi[2], Artem Polyvyanyy[2], and Jochen De Weerdt[1]

[1] Research Centre for Information Systems Engineering, KU Leuven, Leuven, Belgium
aurelie.leribaux@kuleuven.be

[2] The University of Melbourne, Parkville, VIC 3010, Australia

Abstract. Understanding how actor behavior influences process outcomes is a critical aspect of process mining. Traditional approaches often use aggregate and static process data, overlooking the temporal and causal dynamics that arise from individual actors' behaviors. This limits the ability to accurately capture the complexity of real-world processes, where individual actor behavior and interactions between actors significantly shape performance. In this work, we address this gap by integrating actor behavior analysis with Granger causality to identify correlating links in time series data. We apply this approach to real-world event logs, constructing time series for actor interactions (i.e., continuation, interruption, and handovers) and process outcomes. Using Group Lasso for lag selection, we identify a small but consistently influential set of lags that capture the majority of causal influence, revealing that actors' behaviors have direct and measurable impacts on process performance, particularly in terms of throughput time. These findings demonstrate the potential of actor-centric, time series-based methods for uncovering the temporal dependencies that drive process outcomes, offering a more nuanced understanding of how individual behaviors impact overall process efficiency.

Keywords: Process performance · actor behavior · Granger causality · time series

1 Introduction

Process performance analysis, which focuses on evaluating performance indicators such as waiting times, response times, throughput times (TT), bottlenecks, and case outcomes, is an essential component of process mining [1]. Despite its importance, the role of actor behavior in these analyses remains relatively underexplored [11]. Traditional process mining generally assumes that all events in a process instance follow a single, totally ordered, and causally dependent control flow [16]. Therefore, they often focus on aggregate performance metrics, which collapse diverse forms of actor behavior into a single summary measure. These

I. van de Weerd et al. (Eds.): BPM 2025 Workshops, LNBIP 569, pp. 274–287, 2026.
https://doi.org/10.1007/978-3-032-13426-4_20

metrics typically overlook distinctions between, for example, uninterrupted work by the same actor, work resumed after an interruption, or handovers between different actors. This aggregation approach risks overlooking the significant influence that diverse actor behaviors can have on both performance metrics and overall process outcomes.

Recent work has taken an important step toward bridging this gap by introducing a framework for decomposing process performance based on actor behavior [11]. The approach captures different types of actor interactions, including continuations, interruptions, and handovers, providing valuable insights into how actors influence performance metrics and process outcomes. However, this method primarily focuses on static performance metrics and behavioral patterns, without explicitly modeling the temporal and causal relationships between these behaviors and process outcomes or performance metrics. This limits the ability to identify time-dependent causal effects, a perspective that is valuable for understanding when certain actors' behavior influences process performance (e.g., delays and bottlenecks).

To address this gap, our work extends this actor-centric perspective by incorporating time series analysis. Specifically, we apply Granger causality [7] to time series representing actor behaviors and process outcomes. Unlike aggregation and static case-level approaches, this method captures both the frequency and the timing of interactions, providing a more comprehensive view of the causal mechanisms at play. Our main contributions can be summarized as follows:

- We present a novel framework for the integration of actor behavior classification and Granger causality analysis to uncover temporal dependencies between actor interactions and process performance.
- We validate our framework using real-world data from three diverse event logs (BPIC 2011, BPIC 2017, BPIC 2019), demonstrating its applicability across multiple industries.

The remainder of this paper is structured as follows. Section 2 introduces the necessary terms and methods. Then, Sect. 3 discusses the related work. Section 4 thoroughly describes the methodology, followed by the results in Sect. 5 and a discussion in Sect. 6. Finally, Sect. 7 concludes this paper.

2 Background

In this section, we introduce a definition of event logs and how to decompose actor behavior from them. Subsequently, we describe the construction and properties of time series for behavioral and performance contexts, including the roles of lags and a TT metric.

2.1 Event Logs and Actors

A process-aware information system records execution traces in the form of event logs. An event log E is a set of traces, where each trace captures the sequence of events that occurred during the execution of a single process instance (case). An event is a tuple, denoted as $e_i = (c, a, t, r)$, where c is the identifier of the process case, $a \in \mathcal{A}$ is the label of the executed activity that triggered the event, t is the timestamp at which the event occurred, and $r \in \mathcal{R}$ is the actor (a.k.a., resource) that performed the activity that triggered the event. Thus, a trace $\sigma \in E$ is a sequence of all events $\sigma_c = \langle e_1, e_2, \ldots, e_n \rangle, n \in \mathbb{N}$, with case identifier c ordered by their timestamps.

2.2 Actor Behavior Classification

Unlike traditional approaches in process mining, where traces are regarded as isolated case sequences, our analysis emphasizes actor participation across cases. Each actor induces their own path of events [11,17], enabling the study of the interaction patterns of actors. To analyze the interaction patterns of actors, we introduce a behavioral classification based on actor transitions between consecutive events within the same case. This behavioral classification framework is inspired by the approach described in paper [11], generalized to a diverse set of event log data to systematically analyze actor interactions and resource usage.

Let $\mathcal{E}$ be the collection of all events in event log E. Consider two events $e_i = (c_i, a_i, t_i, r_i)$ and $e_j = (c_j, a_j, t_j, r_j)$ from the same trace (i.e., $c_i = c_j$) in E such that e_i is followed by e_j. We identify four classes of interactions between actors in events e_i and e_j listed below.[1]

- **Continuation (C):** The same actor continues the event sequence without processing any other case in between:

$$f_C(e_i, e_j) \iff (r_i = r_j) \wedge (\nexists e_k \in \mathcal{E} : r_i = r_k,\, t_i < t_k < t_j)\,.$$

- **Interruption (I):** The same actor continues the event sequence, but performs another activity from a different case in between:

$$f_I(e_i, e_j) \iff (r_i = r_j) \wedge (\exists e_k \in \mathcal{E} : r_i = r_k,\, t_i < t_k < t_j,\, c_i \neq c_k)\,.$$

- **Handover Idle (HI):** A different actor continues the event sequence, and that actor was idle during the handover period:

$$f_{HI}(e_i, e_j) \iff (r_i \neq r_j) \wedge (\nexists e_k \in \mathcal{E} : r_j = r_k,\, t_i < t_k < t_j)\,.$$

- **Handover Busy (HB):** A different actor continues the event sequence, and that actor was busy with other cases during the handover period:

$$f_{HB}(e_i, e_j) \iff (r_i \neq r_j) \wedge (\exists e_k \in \mathcal{E} : r_j = r_k,\, t_i < t_k < t_j, c_i \neq c_k)\,.$$

This classification serves as the basis for constructing time series of behavioral indicators of interactions between actors.

[1] By c_k, t_k, and r_k, we refer to the case identifier, the timestamp, and the actor of event e_k, respectively.

2.3 Time Series Construction, Lags, and Throughput Time

Let $T = \{1, \ldots, N\}$ be a set of time points that can be totally ordered. A *time series* $\mathcal{X}$ is a sequence of values listed in time order, denoted by $\mathcal{X} = \{x_t\}_{t \in T}$. For each time series $\mathcal{X} = \{x_t\}_{t \in T}$, we define a corresponding target time series $\mathcal{Y} = \{y_t\}_{t \in T}$, used for the Granger causality analysis.

A *lag* l is the number of time steps before the current one. The lagged value (lag-l value) is the value in the time series l steps before the value in the current step. That is, for a lag $l \geq 1$, the lag-l value of x_t is x_{t-l}. In this paper, we introduce the set of the most influential lags L, $|L| \leq N$. Given a lag l, the series of observed lagged values is defined as $\mathcal{X}' = \{x_{t-l}\}_{t \in (T \setminus \{1, \ldots, l\})}$. To examine how actor behavior evolves over time and how it impacts performance, we convert actor behavior and case outcome metrics into time series.

The main case outcome metric analyzed in this paper is TT. In process mining, TT of a case c is defined as the duration between the timestamp of the first event e_1 and the last event e_n in case c. That is, $TT(c) = t(e_n) - t(e_1)$. In this paper, we restrict our analysis to completed cases only, ensuring that both the first and last event timestamps are available. Ongoing cases, which are still running and have no recorded end event, are excluded to maintain consistency with standard definitions and avoid biases. We first compute $TT(c)$ at the case level. Then, we group the cases by their start date (i.e., the date corresponding to $t(e_1)$) and compute the daily average throughput time for day d as $\mathcal{TT}(d) = \frac{1}{|C_d|} \sum_{c \in C_d} TT(c)$, where C_d is the set of all completed cases that started on day d. Let D denote the set of all days on which at least one completed case started. This results in a daily time series $\{\mathcal{TT}(d)\}_{d \in D}$, where each value reflects the average case duration for that day. Hence, in this paper, one time step corresponds to one calendar day, and a lag $l \in L$ represents looking back l days in time. This approach is straightforwardly extended to other outcome metrics tailored to each event log, which are introduced later in the paper. Together with the behavioral time series (introduced in Sect. 4), the $\mathcal{TT}(d)$ series allows us to test whether past actor behaviors (for example, the number of HB at lag $l = 5$, i.e., five calendar days earlier) Granger-cause variations in TT.

This temporal modeling framework lays the groundwork for our methodology, which involves constructing time series, identifying relevant lags through regularized regression, and applying Granger causality to uncover statistically significant behavioral drivers of process outcomes.

3 Related Work

Granger causality [7] is a foundational method for detecting causal relationships in time series data. It has become a cornerstone of time series analysis, with broad applications in economics, neuroscience, and genomics. In recent years, its adaptability has extended to process mining, particularly due to advances that enable its use in complex data structures such as panel data [12] and spatio-temporal datasets [13].

In process mining, Granger causality has been applied to uncover the causal factors that drive process performance. For instance, Hompes et al. [8] extended the traditional approach to identify cause-effect relationships in business processes, focusing on key performance indicators (KPIs) such as TT and case duration per resource and per activity. While their method effectively captures the process influences, it does not delve into actor-level dynamics, which are essential for understanding how individual behaviors and interactions affect process outcomes.

This limitation has prompted more recent research to shift toward actor-centric analyses. Klijn et al. [11] introduced the concept of actor behavior dimensions, emphasizing the importance of decomposing performance based on the specific actions and interactions of individual process participants. Their framework accounts for various types of interactions, such as handovers, interruptions, and continuations, that influence process efficiency. However, their approach does not explicitly address the temporal causality of these behaviors, an aspect critical to fully understanding process dynamics. Fahland [5] laid the groundwork for this type of analysis by introducing event knowledge graphs, which capture interactions between entities in a process.

Complementing these perspectives, Tour et al. [16] propose an agent-based system mining framework that models organizations as sociotechnical systems, capturing the dynamic interaction between both technical and social (human) components. Their approach relaxes the assumption of a single, fully ordered control flow, thereby enabling the discovery of emergent process behaviors that traditional process mining overlooks. Additionally, Bemthuis et al. [2] introduce an agent-based process mining architecture that integrates process mining techniques with multi-agent systems to capture complex system-wide behaviors. Similarly, the AgentSimulator framework [10] enables the simulation of processes using autonomous and interacting agents, effectively capturing differences in actor behaviors, interaction preferences, and capabilities. Moreover, recent work in resource and collaboration mining emphasizes the importance of analyzing resource interactions and collaboration patterns to understand process performance [3,4,6,9,14]. However, these approaches are often static rather than explicitly modeling temporal dependencies.

Taken together, the literature shows that while Granger causality is a powerful tool for uncovering process-related dependencies, existing approaches often overlook the nuanced, temporal, and actor-specific factors that contribute to process performance. This gap motivates the need for methods that integrate temporal causality with actor behavior analysis, a direction that the proposed methodology explores.

4 Methodology

Starting from preprocessed event data, our methodology comprises three main steps, as illustrated in Fig. 1: (1) construction of time series, (2) preparation of these time series for causal analysis, and (3) Granger causality testing. The following sections provide a detailed description of each step.

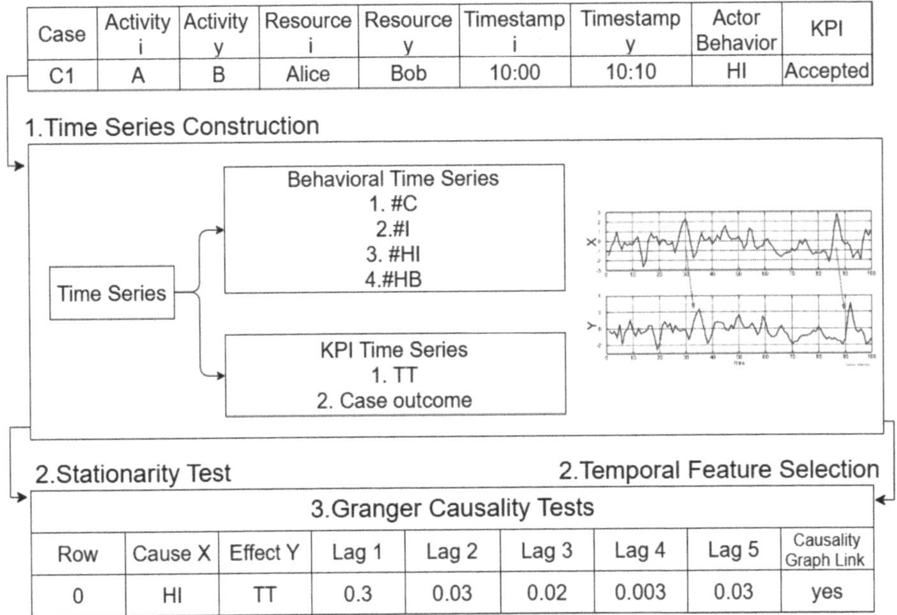

Fig. 1. Schematic visualization of our methodology.

4.1 Step 1: Time Series Construction

The preprocessed event logs are organized into daily time series formats, where each time step corresponds to a calendar day. Events are assigned to time steps based on their recorded timestamp, and each event is treated as an atomic occurrence, meaning that activities are represented as single, instantaneous events. Two categories of time series were constructed from each event log: (1) *Behavioral time series*, which capture the aggregate frequency of each actor behavior type (C, I, HI, and HB) across the entire log as well as per resource and per activity, and (2) *KPI time series*, which capture the average TT of completed cases and the fraction of cases with a predefined event log-specific outcome, both computed by grouping cases based on their start date. This design ensures that all time series share the same daily time steps and are fully aligned for time-dependent analysis and modeling.

As an example, consider the set of actor behaviors HI. Its corresponding time series of daily observed values can be defined as $\mathcal{HI}(d) = \{HI_t\}_{t \in D}$. Such a definition supports a clear temporal understanding of actor behaviors and KPIs, highlighting trends and anomalies across the analyzed processes. The resulting time series were visualized and analyzed using the `DyLoPro` tool [18].

4.2 Step 2: Stationarity Test and Temporal Feature Selection

Before conducting Granger causality analyses, we verified that the time series data satisfied the stationarity assumption [15]. In this context, stationarity implies that the statistical properties of the series, such as mean and variance, remain constant over time. To assess stationarity, we applied the Augmented Dickey-Fuller (ADF) test, which automatically determines the optimal lag length $|L|$ using the Schwarz Information Criterion. For any time series that failed the stationarity test, we employed first-order differencing to achieve stationarity before proceeding with the causality analysis.

Once stationarity was confirmed, the appropriate number of lagged observations was determined prior to the Granger causality test. Selecting too few lags risks omitting relevant causal dependencies, while too many can lead to overfitting and reduced interpretability [15]. To address this, we employed Group Lasso regularization, which treats groups of coefficients collectively rather than individually. This approach hence supports the detection of consistent influences across multiple behavioral variables, allowing lags to be included or excluded as a unit across all variables. As a result, the selected set of lags is $L' \subseteq L$.

4.3 Step 3: Granger Causality Tests

To test whether the behavioral interactions have a causal impact on process performance, we apply Granger causality analysis [7] between the behavioral and KPI time series. A time series $\mathcal{X}$ is said to Granger-cause another series $\mathcal{Y}$ if the past values $\{x_{t-l}\}_{l \in L}$ help to predict $\mathcal{Y}$ better than its past values $\{y_{t-l}\}_{l \in L}$ alone. The test is conducted in three steps:

1. **Baseline prediction (univariate model):** A linear autoregressive model is fitted to $\mathcal{Y}$, using only its own past L values:

$$\mathcal{Y}_t = \sum_{l=1}^{L} \alpha_l y_{t-l} + \epsilon_t \,.$$

2. **Augmented prediction (bivariate model):** A second model that includes both the past values of $\mathcal{Y}$ and $\mathcal{X}$ is constructed:

$$\mathcal{Y}_t = \sum_{l=1}^{L} \alpha_l y_{t-l} + \sum_{l=1}^{L} \beta_l x_{t-l} + \eta_t \,.$$

3. **Statistical comparison:** The prediction errors (ϵ_t and η_t) of the two models are compared using an F-test based on the residual sum of squares (SSR). This test evaluates whether including the lagged values of $\mathcal{X}$ significantly improves the prediction of $\mathcal{Y}$. The F-statistic is computed as:

$$F = \frac{(\text{SSR}_{\text{univariate}} - \text{SSR}_{\text{bivariate}})/L}{\text{SSR}_{\text{bivariate}}/(T - 2L - 1)},$$

where L is the number of lags, and T is the number of observations. A low p-value from the F-test indicates that $\mathcal{X}$ Granger-causes $\mathcal{Y}$.

We perform these tests over the selected lags (Step 2) to determine whether past behavior frequencies Granger-cause changes in performance metrics. For each pair of time series, a relationship is considered significant if the p-value falls below 0.05 at any of the tested lags. A causal graph is then constructed by including only those pairs with at least one significant lag, where a directed edge denotes that $\mathcal{X}$ Granger-causes $\mathcal{Y}$ at one or more lagged observations.

5 Evaluation

We evaluate our approach using three real-life event logs from the Business Process Intelligence Challenge (BPIC) series. These datasets span multiple domains and contain detailed information about both process execution and actor involvement, making them well-suited for analyzing the causal impact of actor behavior on performance outcomes. We implemented the approach in Python, and the code is available on our GitHub repository[2]. The following sections explain the evaluation setup and the results for each dataset.

5.1 Setup

The first dataset, BPIC 2011 (Hospital log)[3], captures patient treatment processes in a Dutch hospital. The second dataset, BPIC 2017[4], documents the handling of loan applications at a Dutch financial institution and serves as a more structured and complete version of the earlier BPIC 2012 dataset. The third dataset, BPIC 2019[5], describes a purchase-to-pay process in a coatings and paint manufacturing company.

For each log, we first identified actor behavior by analyzing every pair of consecutive events within a case. To support outcome-oriented analysis, we then defined KPIs tailored to each dataset. For BPIC 2011, a binary outcome variable was engineered to indicate whether a surgical procedure occurred in a case. This was determined by scanning activity labels for medically relevant Dutch keywords such as `'operatie'`, `'resectie'`, `'excisie'`, and `'extirpaties'`. For BPIC 2017, the process outcome was derived from the final event in each case, which indicates whether a loan application was accepted, rejected, or cancelled, based on event labels prefixed with `'O_'` (e.g., `O_ACCEPTED`). The BPIC 2019 dataset already contains a boolean attribute indicating whether the ordered goods were received, so no additional outcome engineering was necessary.

We constructed two categories of time series (i.e., behavioral and KPI). For all three event logs, we included the frequency of the behaviors and the time series of TT. Additionally, we included the frequency of the behavior types per user and per activity and the fraction of accepted loans (%Acc) in BPIC 2017, the fraction of goods received (%GR) in BPIC 2019, and the fraction of cases

[2] https://github.com/aurelieleribaux-1/ActorBehaviorGranger.

[3] https://doi.org/10.4121/uuid:d9769f3d-0ab0-4fb8-803b-0d1120ffcf54.

[4] https://doi.org/10.4121/uuid:5f3067df-f10b-45da-b98b-86ae4c7a310b.

[5] https://doi.org/10.4121/46a7e15b-10c7-4ab2-988d-ee67d8ea515a.v1.

involving surgical procedures (%OP) in BPIC 2011. To identify the most influential lags L', we tested a broad range of regularization parameters over a maximum lag window of 22 days. Specifically, we varied the group regularization parameter (λ_g), which controls the number of active lag groups, across the set $\lambda_g = \{0.01, 0.1, 0.5, 1, 5, 10\}$. In parallel, the $L1$ regularization parameter (λ_1), which promotes sparsity within those selected groups, was varied over $\lambda_1 = \{0.0, 0.01, 0.1, 0.5, 1\}$. From the resulting models, we selected the five most frequently chosen lags to serve as candidates in the subsequent causality tests.

The following hypotheses guide our evaluation. They test (i) whether past actor behaviors carry predictive information about future performance beyond autocorrelation in the KPI itself, and (ii) whether detected influences are predominantly one-directional rather than merely reflecting mutual co-movement.

1. **Hypothesis 1**: Historical behavioral trends $\mathcal{X}$ at lag $\{x_{t-l}\}_{l \in L'}$ significantly cause changes in process performance outcomes $\mathcal{Y}$ at day t.
2. **Hypothesis 2 (Directionality):** If the lagged values $\{x_{t-l}\}_{l \in L'}$ exhibit significant causal influence on y_t , then the reverse, i.e., lagged $\{y_{t-l}\}_{l \in L'}$ exhibiting significant causal influence on x_t, should not hold. This supports a one-directional effect from behavior to performance.

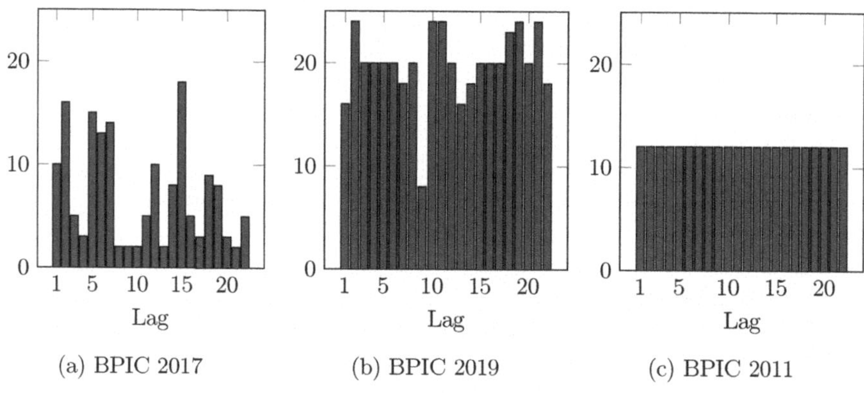

Fig. 2. Lag selection frequency per dataset across all (λ_g, λ_1) combinations.

5.2 Results

In this section, we present the results related to the proposed hypotheses across all datasets. We begin by introducing the lag selection procedure. Figure 2 shows the frequency with which each lag was selected by the Group Lasso method. For the BPIC 2017 and BPIC 2019 datasets, we selected the five most frequently chosen lags: $\{2, 5, 6, 7, 15\}$ for BPIC 2017 and $\{2, 10, 11, 19, 21\}$ for BPIC 2019. For BPIC 2011, where all lags were selected with similar frequency, we used the first five lags: $\{1, 2, 3, 4, 5\}$.

BPIC 2017. The results of the Granger causality analysis are presented in Table 1, revealing noteworthy insights. Consistent with Hypothesis 1, we observe a strong and recurring causal influence of C, HB, and HI on TT. These effects are significant across all lags. Moreover, the influence from I becomes significant for $l = 15$, suggesting a delayed impact on TT. These results support the hypothesis that behavioral trends are associated with subsequent changes in TT. While the influence on %Acc is generally weaker and sporadic, there are still notable findings. In particular, the significant relationship from HB, HI to %Acc at $l = 7$ and $l = 15$ indicates that H may have a delayed influence on loan acceptance.

Figure 4 presents a causality graph of the top 10 most significant influences for BPIC 2017, highlighting how actor behavior affects process outcomes. For instance, User 1's handovers to other resources significantly impact both TT and %Acc. Due to space limitations, similar detailed analyses of the remaining datasets are omitted. The time series in Fig. 3 visually supports the Granger results from the graph and Table 1, with peaks in HI often preceding rises in TT. For example, a HI peak in July 2016 (left) is followed by a TT peak (right), illustrating their lagged relationship.

Hypothesis 2, which posits an asymmetry in causal relationships, was satisfied in 55.55% of the significant cases. This proportion is only slightly above chance, indicating that while some causal links do show directionality, many appear bidirectional or ambiguous. Thus, the support for Hypothesis 2 is limited.

Table 1. BPIC 2017 Granger causality p-values (selected l). Each cell shows $X \rightarrow Y$ with $Y \rightarrow X$ in parentheses only if $X \rightarrow Y$ is significant. Underlined = significant ($p < 0.05$).

l	C → %Acc.	C → TT	HB → %Acc.	HB → TT	HI → %Acc.	HI → TT	I → %Acc.	I → TT
2	0.858	0.001 (0.089)	0.855	0.002 (0.050)	0.619	0.001 (0.061)	0.991	0.180
5	0.799	0.002 (0.009)	0.652	0.004 (0.009)	0.953	0.008 (0.036)	0.998	0.101
6	0.074	0.005 (0.015)	0.076	0.010 (0.613)	0.166	0.022 (0.950)	0.556	0.259
7	0.075	0.006 (0.014)	0.044 (0.004)	0.012 (0.684)	0.210	0.026 (0.973)	0.652	0.153
15	0.254	0.005 (0.003)	0.145	0.007 (0.133)	0.040 (0.050)	0.038 (0.559)	0.299	0.024 (0.027)

BPIC 2019. Granger causality results (Table 2) support Hypothesis 1: HB → TT is significant at lag 21 ($p = 0.039$), suggesting a delayed effect of busy handovers, while HI → TT is significant at lag 2 ($p = 0.031$), indicating a more immediate impact during idle periods. Additionally, I → %OP shows significance at lags 19 ($p = 0.025$) and 21 ($p = 0.002$), suggesting that interruptions may disrupt process accuracy or completion.

With respect to Hypothesis 2, the asymmetric causality condition was satisfied in 50% of the significant cases. This is equivalent to chance, indicating no clear evidence of directionality.

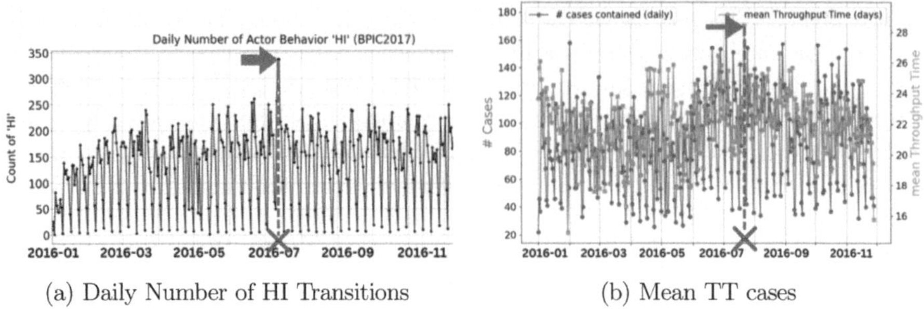

(a) Daily Number of HI Transitions

(b) Mean TT cases

Fig. 3. Comparison of daily actor behavior HI and mean TT for BPIC 2017.

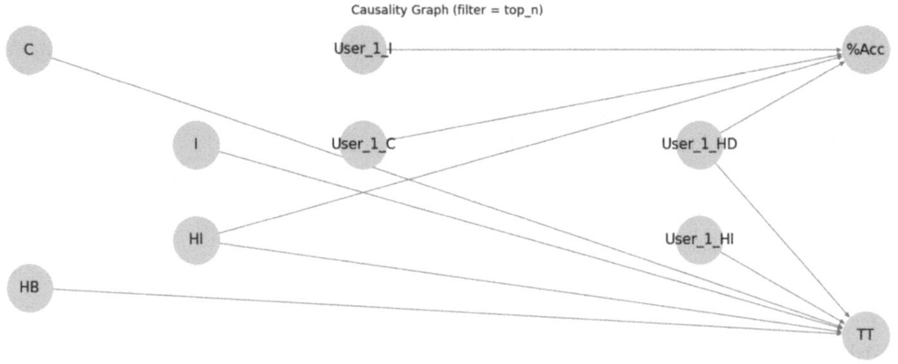

Fig. 4. Causality graph.

BPIC 2011 Hospital Log. For BPIC 2011, detailed Granger causality results are reported in Table 3. Across lags 1 to 5, nearly all behavior-to-performance pathways are statistically significant, providing strong support for Hypothesis 1. In particular, C, I, and both handover types (HI and HB) show consistent and highly significant effects on TT, while several also influence the fraction of operations completed (%OP). These findings indicate that actor dynamics have an immediate and measurable impact on clinical process performance. For instance, frequent task switching or handovers across cases can reduce efficiency, leading to longer case durations and a lower proportion of completed operations.

Regarding Hypothesis 2, the assumption of causal asymmetry is satisfied in 53.33% of the significant cases. This proportion is only slightly above half, suggesting that while some relationships do exhibit directionality, many remain bidirectional or ambiguous. Thus, the evidence for clear asymmetry is again limited.

Table 2. BPIC 2019 Granger causality p-values (selected l). Each cell shows $X \rightarrow Y$ with $Y \rightarrow X$ in parentheses only if $X \rightarrow Y$ is significant. Underlined = significant ($p < 0.05$).

l	C → %GR	C → TT	HB → %GR	HB → TT	HI → %GR	HI → TT	I→ %GR	I → TT
2	0.091	0.063	0.081	0.079	0.170	0.031 (0.520)	0.177	0.368
10	0.167	0.063	0.199	0.318	0.159	0.087	0.626	0.252
11	0.204	0.059	0.194	0.229	0.098	0.080	0.302	0.205
19	0.031 (6e-4)	0.163	0.080	0.083	0.433	0.121	0.025 (0.213)	0.575
21	0.061	0.064	0.021 (3e-7)	0.039 (5e-3)	0.569	0.121	0.002 (0.093)	0.526

Table 3. BPIC 2011 Granger causality p-values (selected l). Each cell shows $X \rightarrow Y$ with $Y \rightarrow X$ in parentheses only if $X \rightarrow Y$ is significant. Underlined = significant ($p < 0.05$).

l	C → %OP	C → TT	HB → %OP.	HB → TT	HI → %OP	HI → TT	I → %OP	I → TT
1	0.465	0.006 (0.901)	0.281	1.7e-5 (0.572)	0.652	0.001 (0.258)	0.783	2e-4 (0.911)
2	0.403	0.0889	0.515	0.001 (0.258)	0.901	0.017 (0.869)	0.275	4e-5 (0.078)
3	0.015 (2e-5)	0.004 (0.360)	1e-3 (0.050)	1e-5 (0.904)	0.076	0.003 (0.670)	1e-6 (0.295)	3.1e-14 (0.002)
4	0.030 (1e-5)	9.3e-5 (0.026)	1.4e-5 (0.009)	1.1e-8 (0.838)	0.042 (1e-4)	5e-5 (0.125)	1e-6 (2.5e-4)	6.4e-13 (0.128)
5	2.4e-4 (1.1e-5)	1e-6 (9e-4)	1.3e-5 (0.014)	3.5e-8 (0.887)	2.8e-4 (1.1e-5)	1.2e-7 (0.002)	2e-6 (0.001)	3.4e-10 (0.002)

6 Discussion

The results presented in Sect. 5 reveal several important insights into the causal influence of different actor behavior dynamics towards process outcomes across different event logs. The most consistent finding is the strong causal influence of handovers, both HB and HI, on TT. This is evident across multiple datasets and lag configurations, intuitively implying that a higher number of handovers increases TT, and vice versa. Moreover, several KPIs' outcomes show promising potential, like in BPIC 2017, where handovers lead to a long-term dependency on %Acc. The one-directionality was satisfied in all datasets. These findings highlight the crucial role of actor behavior in enhancing process efficiency, particularly in complex domains such as healthcare, finance, and procurement. Moreover, the approach scales to large event logs and can be applied in real-world settings using standard event log data, enabling resource-level behavior to inform system-level (e.g., TT) and case-level (e.g., remaining time) predictions.

Despite these promising results, several limitations should be noted. First, we rely on Granger causality, which does not account for latent confounding effects and cannot capture multivariate or non-linear relationships. Additionally, as discussed in Sect. 3, no other time-dependent frameworks focusing specifically on actor behavior exist for direct comparison, limiting our ability to benchmark our framework. Finally, the classification of actor behaviors itself is dependent on the precision of the event log timestamps and task definitions. This can lead to misclassifications if timestamps are coarse, tasks are imprecisely defined, or actors handle multiple tasks simultaneously. The current framework assumes that actors work on only one task at a time and treats tasks spanning multiple cases as separate, potentially overestimating the frequency of busy handovers.

Future work should focus on integrating more flexible, non-linear causal inference methods and extending the framework to handle multi-tasking actors and continuous tasks more effectively.

7 Conclusion

In this paper, we examined how actor behavior influences process performance across loan application (BPIC 2017), purchase-to-pay (BPIC 2019), and hospital processes (BPIC 2011) using Granger causality. Actor behavior is decomposed into continuation, interruption, handover idle, and handover busy. Time series are constructed based on the number of behaviors and KPIs of the process, between which Granger causalities are tested. Collectively, the findings highlight the crucial role of actor behavior in process efficiency. Handovers mainly have distinct, lag-dependent impacts on TT and other process outcomes, reflecting complex interactions between task transfers, actor availability, and coordination. This understanding can improve predictive modeling by anticipating bottlenecks, optimizing resource allocation, and improving overall process performance. Future work could explore how these (handover) behaviors help improve predictive modeling or how they interact with other factors, like case complexity, resource availability, and workload distribution, to further refine process insights.

References

1. van der Aalst, W.M.P.: Process mining: a 360 degree overview. In: Lecture Notes in Business Information Processing, vol. 448, pp. 3–34. Springer, Heidelberg (2022). https://doi.org/10.1007/978-3-031-08848-3_1
2. Bemthuis, R.H., Koot, M., Mes, M.R.K., Bukhsh, F.A., Iacob, M.E., Meratnia, N.: An agent-based process mining architecture for emergent behavior analysis. In: 23rd International Enterprise Distributed Object Computing Workshop, pp. 54–64. IEEE (2019). https://doi.org/10.1109/EDOCW.2019.00022
3. Benzin, J., Rinderle-Ma, S.: Towards standardized modeling of collaboration processes in collaboration process discovery. In: Process Mining Workshops – ICPM 2024. Lecture Notes in Business Information Processing, vol. 533, pp. 171–183. Springer, Heidelberg (2024). https://doi.org/10.1007/978-3-031-82225-4_13
4. Corradini, F., Pettinari, S., Re, B., Rossi, L., Tiezzi, F.: A technique for discovering BPMN collaboration diagrams. Softw. Syst. Model. **23**(6), 1323–1343 (2024). https://doi.org/10.1007/s10270-024-01153-5
5. Fahland, D.: Process mining over multiple behavioral dimensions with event knowledge graphs. In: Lecture Notes in Business Information Processing, vol. 448, pp. 274–319. Springer, Heidelberg (2022). https://doi.org/10.1007/978-3-031-08848-3_9
6. Fan, S., Li, X., Zhao, J.: Collaboration process pattern approach to improving teamwork performance: a data mining-based methodology. INFORMS J. Comput. **29**(3), 438–456 (2017). https://doi.org/10.1287/ijoc.2016.0739

7. Granger, C.: Investigating causal relations by econometric models and cross-spectral methods. Econometrica **37**(3), 424–438 (1969)
8. Hompes, B., Maaradji, A., La Rosa, M., Dumas, M., Buijs, J., Aalst, W.: Discovering causal factors explaining business process performance variation. In: Advanced Information Systems Engineering, pp. 177–192. Springer, Heidelberg (2017). https://doi.org/10.1007/978-3-319-59536-8_12
9. Jooken, L., Depaire, B., Jans, M.: Mining recency–frequency–monetary enriched insights into resources' collaboration behavior from event data. Eng. Appl. Artif. Intell. **126**, 106765 (2023). https://doi.org/10.1016/j.engappai.2023.106765
10. Kirchdorfer, L., Blümel, R., Kampik, T., Van der Aa, H., Stuckenschmidt, H.: AgentSimulator: an agent-based approach for data-driven business process simulation. In: 6th International Conference on Process Mining (ICPM), pp. 97–104. IEEE (2024). https://doi.org/10.1109/icpm63005.2024.10680660
11. Klijn, E.L., Tentina, I., Fahland, D., Mannhardt, F.: Decomposing process performance based on actor behavior. In: 6th International Conference on Process Mining (ICPM), pp. 129–136. IEEE (2024). https://doi.org/10.1109/icpm63005.2024.10680657
12. Lopez, A., Weber, E.: Testing for Granger causality in panel data. Stand Genomic Sci. **18**(4), 804–818 (2018)
13. Pavasant, N., Morita, T., Numao, M., Fukui, K.I.: Granger causality-based cluster sequence mining for spatio-temporal causal relation mining. Int. J. Data Sci. Anal. **17**(3), 275–288 (2023). https://doi.org/10.1007/s41060-023-00411-x
14. Schubert, P., Blatt, J., Just, M., Delfmann, P.: Social process mining: deriving collaborative work processes from the event data of enterprise collaboration systems (2024)
15. Shojaie, A., Fox, E.B.: Granger causality: a review and recent advances. Ann. Rev. Stat. Appl. **9**, 289–319 (2022). https://doi.org/10.1146/annurev-statistics-040120-010930
16. Tour, A., Polyvyanyy, A., Kalenkova, A.: Agent system mining: vision, benefits, and challenges. IEEE Access **9**, 99480–99494 (2021). https://doi.org/10.1109/access.2021.3095464
17. Tour, A., Polyvyanyy, A., Kalenkova, A.A., Senderovich, A.: Agent miner: an algorithm for discovering agent systems from event data. In: Business Process Management - 21st International Conference. Lecture Notes in Computer Science, vol. 14159, pp. 284–302. Springer, Heidelberg (2023). https://doi.org/10.1007/978-3-031-41620-0_17
18. Wuyts, B., Weytjens, H., vanden Broucke, S., Weerdt, J.D.: DyLoPro: profiling the dynamics of event logs. In: Business Process Management – 21st International Conference. Lecture Notes in Computer Science, vol. 14159, pp. 146–162. Springer, Heidelberg (2023). https://doi.org/10.1007/978-3-031-41620-0_9

Understanding the Dynamics of a Process Mining Project Analyzing Log Data of a Process Mining Platform

Alexander Skolik(✉) and Bernd Löhr

Paderborn University, Warburger Straße 100, 33098 Paderborn, Germany
{alexander.skolik,bernd.loehr}@uni-paderborn.de

Abstract. Process mining proved to be valuable for enabling transparency in business processes and to help to manage the everyday process dynamics. But what about the dynamics of a process mining project itself. In this paper, we present insights of a process mining introduction project spanning two years. For that we analyze the logs of the process mining platform supported by interviews of the developers and participants as part of our case study research. Based on this, our findings indicate four actions that impact a successful process mining project and the underlying dynamics. (1) Two development phases in a test and productive environment can lead to data driven process improvements. (2) Maintenance and the associated technical debt can cause process drift. (3) Scope creep of the project is easily identifiable in such logs and hinders the complete process mining initiative and (4) a sufficient user base and constant interaction with allows for bottom up process change. These results provide quantitative insights into the development and adoption cycles of the software and the direct impact on the processes as well as the business process management initiative. From this initial analysis researchers can benefit from first insights into the quantitative side of a process mining project and our categorization of the findings. Practitioners can use the findings as a blueprint or source for improvements to their process mining projects.

Keywords: Process mining · Business Process Management · Process dynamics

1 Introduction

Process mining is one of the most disruptive technologies business process management offers. With comparatively little effort as-is processes can be discovered and compared to their to-be counter parts [27]. Process mining initiatives and projects thus aim to enhance processes and steer their dynamics to improve the business process outcomes [12,24]. Previously such initiatives would only derive their findings from key performance indicators, metrics and qualitative approaches such as interviews [7,23]. However, besides analyzing the dynamics of processes, process mining projects exhibit dynamics of their own.

I. van de Weerd et al. (Eds.): BPM 2025 Workshops, LNBIP 569, pp. 288–299, 2026.
https://doi.org/10.1007/978-3-032-13426-4_21

Quantitative data like development logs from the process mining system itself on the progression and inner workings of a process mining project has to the best of our knowledge not been analyzed yet. Such data combined with qualitative insights can help to create a more objective view on the behavior of such process mining projects. Due to these missing insights, the outcomes of a process mining project can be observed and qualitative success factors can be established, but quantitative measures to underline these findings are hard to come by. Therefore we aim to answer the research question "What quantitative insights can be gathered from the inner workings of a process mining project?".

To answer this research question, we analyze a case study that includes the system log data from a process mining project. The case study takes place at a medium sized power grid provider in Germany. Together with the process experts the researchers were able to extract a system log from the process mining platform. The system log was processed to highlight when new artifacts were developed, updated or maintained and the users added to the system or changes to their permissions made. From these logs we identify that (1) a development- and productive system split can lead to more data driven process improvements. (2) The amount of maintenance tasks can be underestimated and build up over time as technical debt. (3) Feature requests must be carefully managed as scope creep can quickly build up and hinder the project process. (4) A sufficient user base must be present with each development until a saturation within the department kicks in, otherwise the developments will not be used. The existing literature thus gains initial insights into the quantitative workings of a process mining project alongside factors that can be crucial for the success, failure and adoption of a process mining project. Additionally, practitioners receive early warning signs for these factors, which help to steer the projects away from failures.

The remainder of this paper is structured as follows. Section two highlights the related work including an introduction to process mining and previously identified success factors. Section three highlights our research method and introduces our case study. Section four then describes our results by describing the case and the analysis of the data in conjunction with the presented interviews. Followed by this is section five with a formalization and discussion of our findings and section six with a conclusion, the limitations and an outlook on our future work.

2 Dynamics in Business Process Management and Process Mining

Modern organizations must be agile to keep pace with technological innovations and digital transformation. As digital technologies permeate business operations, information systems have become deeply intertwined with business processes, making it possible to trace, analyze, and even forecast how these processes evolve over time [14,24,25]. The study of such process dynamics builds on routine dynamics theory [13], using both routines and business processes as frameworks to understand how work unfolds across actors in organizational settings [9,34].

Although BPM remains a valuable tool for controlling and improving processes [9,21], earlier assumptions of stability and linear improvement are challenged by today's dynamic, rapidly changing conditions [26,29,33]. BPM scholars face the challenge of addressing this growing complexity and reconciling the need for reliable operations with the imperative to innovate and adapt, which is true for the daily operation as well as conducting projects [4,14].

Technologies such as AI, Robotic Process Automation (RPA), and especially process mining, offer new capabilities to analyze and respond to process dynamics with greater detail and flexibility [1,16,32]. Consequently, BPM research is increasingly focused on understanding how processes develop in real-time and how organizations can evolve their capabilities and frameworks to manage high-speed, high-complexity operations [4,18]. Process mining enables the reconstruction of real-world processes through event logs and facilitates automated modeling (process discovery), conformance checking, and enhancement of existing process models [1]. Advanced process mining techniques now support comparison, prediction, and prescription of process behaviors [2], offering organizations the ability to adapt and respond to change proactively. These insights also extend to organizational routines, as digital trace data reveals shifts and interactions over time [13,25,34], helping organizations detect "critical events" that signify change dynamics [13].

Self-learning approaches in process mining now outperform traditional methods in handling dynamic contexts and concept drift [15,30]. However, these digital insights need to be complemented with contextual data to fully understand and explain change [13]. Routine dynamics research can help interpret unexpected outcomes from mining applications [12].

From a management standpoint, successful adoption of process mining hinges on understanding benefits versus implementation costs, data privacy concerns, governance structures, and leadership support [12]. Core success factors include sound project management, quality data, skilled process miners, and structured approaches [20]. These have been expanded to include change management, tool capabilities, and adequate training [19]. Additional refinements have identified stakeholder involvement, information availability, and technical expertise as vital elements [19]. Cross-departmental collaboration between IT, BPM, and business units is often necessary, and over time, a dedicated process mining function can enhance institutional capabilities and resource concentration [28]. Process mining also requires organizations to consider implications across technical, organizational, and even ecosystem levels [6], with special attention to non-technical and cultural challenges [22].

This increased process transparency is both chance and challenge. To help with this, bottom-up and top-down management approaches can successfully improve process awareness, which in turn support process participants to properly consider end-to-end processes while acting and reacting to daily challenges [11]. Despite substantial research and available frameworks, many organizations still face difficulties in achieving a mature process mining practice and fully realizing its potential value [6,10,22]. However, recent studies collected information on actions to successfully conduct process mining projects [5]. Three pillars have been identified, which are relevant to achieving business value [3]. This includes the adoption of features that enable continuous monitoring, data-driven, and proactive decision making, while fostering process awareness and involving stakeholders through change management and training. Further, real-time connectivity and transparency allow for faster process improvement compared to classical methods, but achieving full value requires trust in the technology and contextual business knowledge [3].

3 Research Method

Case study research provides a valuable methodology for examining one or multiple real-life instances in depth [31]. By observing case studies, researchers can collect data rooted in real-world settings, enabling them to explore the underlying dynamics of a phenomenon with accuracy and contextual relevance [17]. The primary aim of this approach is to foster a comprehensive understanding of the specific context under investigation and to identify its significant characteristics [8]. To achieve this, an appropriate case is selected and analyzed with regard to the defined unit of analysis [31]. A combination of data sources–such as interviews and performance indicators–is typically employed to examine and interpret the findings [35].

A regional German power grip provider provided systems logs from their process mining platform. These system logs include all developments and changes made to the software. As a focal company the metering department previously got first insights into process mining and aims to leverage the associated capabilities to improve their processes. Following this assessment an process improvement project within the industry specific lead-to-cash process was identified and deemed as great candidate for process improvements. The provided system log originates from this project and shows the first process mining project within the department. Using such a system log has the advantage that everything is recorded and the data can not be changed afterwards. Additionally, information regarding usage and behavior can be captured long after the project is done. Whereas interviews usually take place shortly after the release of an artifact, the logs record further usage of the artifact and any associated changes. Nevertheless, interviews with the product owner, one process expert and one developer were conducted to gain qualitative insights and expand on the findings.

The provided system log file was structured as a comma separated value file with additional JSON code as one of the values. After processing the file in a suitable data frame 204,815 events were identified in the file. From this file the data regarding the M2C-project was filtered by selecting all appropriate users that were at some point involved in the project. After the data clean up, a total of 23,317 events from a time frame of the beginning of 2022 until the end in 2023 were identified across of 44 different artifacts and 30 event types. The different event types were categorized into “Studio Developments”, “Studio Updates” and “Studio Maintenance” as well as “User Info”. With the “studio” being the development environment of the process mining platform, development tasks were classified as all events in which a new asset was created or duplicated since such duplications were done in preparation to switch from an development to a productive environment. "Studio Updates" are characterized as a new feature or updated version of the developments made available to test or productive users. "Studio Maintenance" refers to all events in which an asset was deleted or moved. "User Info" is defined as all events in which a user was registered to the system or an update to the permissions was given.

The data matches the information gained through the insights from the project. The validity can thus be confirmed externally and internally. External validation can be reached by comparing time slots with frequent events e.g.: around the Christmas holidays the number of events drops to almost zero. Internal validity expands on this topic since a development pause takes place in December. Furthermore, events like summer vacation in September impact the number of events. Additionally, a two steps development approach with prototyping and relying in user feedback as its main development pattern is used. The data especially in the first and second development phase shows this behavior, as the user and development events go well together.

4 Results

4.1 Case Study Description

The highlighted case study takes place at a regional power grid provider in Germany from the beginning of 2022 to the end of 2023. Following a few minor process mining pilot projects, the meter reading department hired two process mining experts in March of 2023. Due to ongoing regulatory changes from the legislators, the business processes must be flexible and able to adhere to these changes on quick notice. To do so, the meter-to-cash (M2C) process, a energy industry specific lead-to-cash process, was scoped as the main process for improvement. Besides the process mining experts, two domain experts and the department leader joined the project to coordinate the initiative. The project members are characterized as the stakeholders of the initiative. From this system log, data was shared with the researchers, including a total of 204,815 logged events. Additionally, at the end of the projects interviews were conducted to gather qualitative insights from the process mining project.

4.2 Case Analysis

Figure 1 now shows the cumulative amount of events from 2022 and 2023 as a general overview on the project. Besides the mentioned event types, the rough outline of the project is marked. The overarching center of excellence conducted some preparations and developed a few prototypes before the newly hired process experts took over in March of 2022.

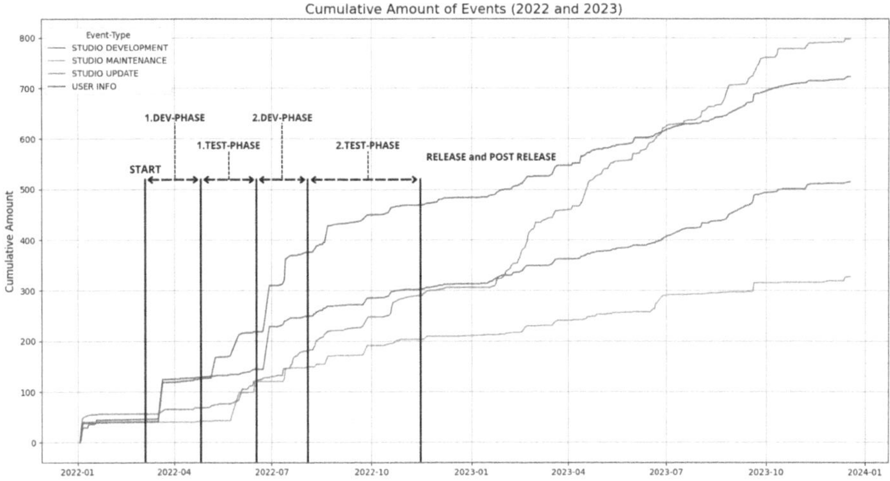

Fig. 1. Cumulative Events from 2022 to 2023

After scoping and set-up tasks the 1st development phase begun, indicated by the influx in development events, additionally a first set of users was introduced to the platform. The first test phase matches with additional users and permissions assigned to the test users. Additionally, the increase in maintenance tasks towards the second development phase indicates the transition towards the productive system. The second development phase then again has seen an influx in users and developments, together with an almost linear development of updates into the second test phase. Once most of the relevant users are on the process mining platform the user info events mostly stagnate after the artifact is released. From these insights two findings can be generated. On one hand, splitting the development in two phases as part of the development and productive environment is usually accompanied with an influx in users and user permissions. This split allows for a greater focus on intermediate results and allows "a step by step approach to the project" as highlighted by the process expert. The chosen approach was perceived as an advantage. On the other hand, however, a major point to look out for is the introduction of scope or feature creep after the project. The process expert highlighted that "add something nice to have on top" and "lead to positives for the whole department" as the product owner expands on. From the graph, however, it can be seen that in the beginning of 2023 users and developments just slightly increase but studio updates greatly expand. Such a form of scope creep consumes development time and "small improvements made it difficult to focus on the development of other projects" according to one developer. Such behavior can be a threat to the process mining initiative, since more and more small feature requests take away from larger more value adding projects.

As a deep dive into each specific month Fig. 2 shows the different event types. The development phases stay the same when compared to Fig. 1. Two additional findings can be derived from this overview. Firstly, the amount of maintenance tasks increases over time, especially frequently in the post release phase of the project. The developer highlighted that the amount of maintenance tasks, even for a smaller team and development project was underestimated. Due to the need for quick wins towards the employees and a prototyping like development approach, quick fixes for issues and short term solutions were preferred. This so called technical debt can build up over time and hinder further developments. Thus, in the later stages the development team opted to gather all maintenance tasks and periodically work on them rather than in addition to their daily doings. As the developer highlights such an approach offers a more planable maintenance of the developments but the initial problem of technical debt must be considered carefully. Secondly, from the graph it can be seen that the user and development events especially in the beginning of the project go well together. Due to the prototyping development pattern user feedback greatly supports the development. A sufficient user base for each phase is thus necessary to generate this feedback, therefore reaching a sufficient user base for each stage is crucial for the project. New users were brought into the system during the development phase who could test the developments during the testing phase. Since with the productive system a wider user base was required the highest peaks are recorded in this time. Together with Fig. 1 it can also be seen that at some point a saturation is reached and rather than bringing new user into the system additional permissions are granted to the users. The product owner highlighted the benefits of taking new users in at crucial points as this way the employees do not feel left out of the development.

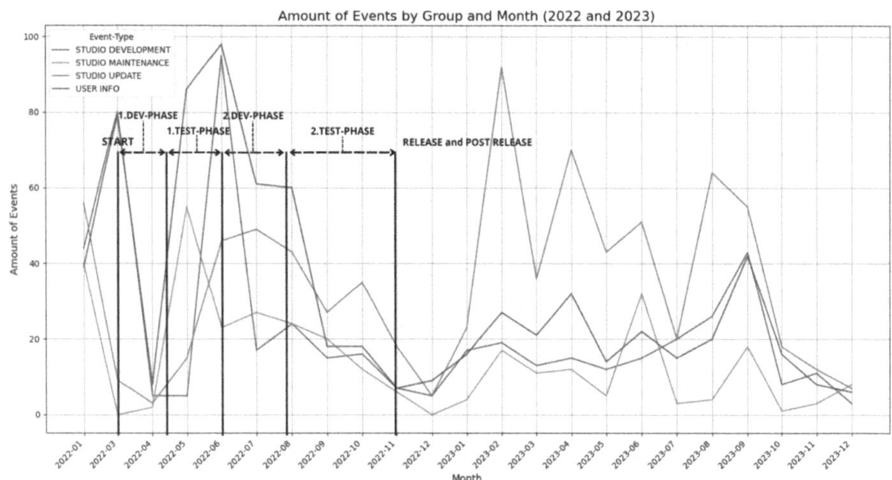

Fig. 2. Number of Events by Type and Month

5 Formalization and Discussion

Table 1 now categorizes these findings with a description and an indicator of their origin. The two development phases were perceived as an advantage and highlight that within a short amount of time a wide range of developments for such a project can be conducted. Such a development approach has in its test stage little impact on the focal process. The main impact and change arrives with the push to the productive system. From this point on the dynamics of the process shift towards more data driven discussions, since key performance indicators and automation rates become believable metrics for discussions, as the product owner and developer agree upon.

Table 1. Formalization of Findings

Finding/ Phenomenon	Description	Origin	Effect on Process Dynamics
Two Development Phases	A development and productive system development approach allows to develop intermediate solutions	Development peaks and increased user base	Rapid process advancements through intermediate solutions
Technical Debt	Maintenance of a process mining project slowly becomes more important, happens frequently	Recurring peaks in maintenance	Process Drift - focus shifts from development to maintenance
Scope and Feature Creep	An over proportional influx in feature updates points to scope and feature creep and takes development time away from main projects	Feature updates take over all development tasks	Diminishing returns for the process, yet rising development efforts
Sufficient User Base	Establish a proper user base for each phase	Peaks in user info according to phases	Successful implementation into the process

Technical debt in its early form is underestimated. The graphs and interviews highlight that a lack of maintenance for the development builds up over time. Managing and mitigating such circumstances should be planned beforehand, otherwise underestimating maintenance tasks can become a threat to the whole process mining initiative in the long run. Especially since other projects and data pipelines can be obstructed by this technical debt. Depending on the way technical debt is dealt with, the focus process can greatly suffer. In the worst case the developer points out that the focus process drifts back into previous patterns since the newly developed solutions are not reliable enough to convince the employees to use them.

Another example for an early threat in a process mining project is the topic of scope or feature creep. Once the intended development cycle concludes it is easy to fall into a "one-more-thing" trap that extends the project beyond the originally intended scope. Rather than working on other areas of the process and establishing more valuable projects, smaller but more complicated tasks take development time away and lead to highly task or user specific solutions. Such a threat can spiral out of control and lead to unsatisfactory results for most of the involved parties, as highlighted by the product owner. Thus, scope and feature creep can evolve into substantial road blocks as rather the more and more incremental improvements add little value to the process improvement project.

The stakeholder involvement, and in this case a sufficient user base is a necessity for the each phase to function [19]. Selecting the appropriate measures to set the user base up, depends on the development method and should be thought about in earlier project stages. For a prototyping development approach an influx in users is beneficial for gathering feedback and setting up the test stages. However, with regards to the change management [19], a careful balance between enabling new users and taking their requests must be found otherwise scope creep can occur. A gradual increase in features and use cases has been a successful strategy [5]. If this balance is found the users are one of the most valuable sources to drive process change. As the process expert explained "once we understood what was possible with the software, we could always find additional ways to improve our work". A well adopted user base thus directly enables bottom up process change.

These early findings show that besides the pure analysis and improvement of a process mining or BPM project in general, aspects different than outcome based metrics can be found. Throughout such a project the dynamics between development, process analysis and improvement are much more delicate to balance as otherwise projects and wider initiatives could work well on the outside but posses higher issues on the inside. Such projects might highlight the benefits of their approaches, but quantitative insights into topics like scope creep, technical debt and platform adoption can paint a different picture. In the highlighted case study, employees and key performance indicators praised the development approach and qualitative aspects of the project. Only the logs as quantitative measures are able to reveal the dynamics of the project and give hints what to look out for.

6 Conclusion and Outlook

The presented case study utilizes system logs of a process mining platform to identify quantitative insights and the impact on process dynamics by a process improvement project. Together with additional insights from interviews four initial findings can be derived. (1) Two main development phases foster a secure development environment offering users and developers alike to test different features and skills. This finding has to potentials to change the dynamics of a focal process once any improvements reach the productive system. (2) However, such process improvements can be short lived, if the occurring technical debt is not dealt with. Ever increasing maintenance tasks can signal the users that the new solution is not sufficient, leading to a drift to the old process. (3) Scope and feature creep can happen without the project members noticing. Such behavior can become a roadblock in the process improvement project as rather then working on larger issues, smaller but more time consuming improvements are made. (4) While such behavior should not be encouraged, it shows that a sufficient user base is able to provide bottom up process innovation once the process mining platform and its possibilities are understood.

While this study shows an early insight into the inner workings of a process mining project it does come with some limitations. Since it is a single case study, only one project within the company has been observed, the generalization of the findings thus is limited. Other companies might take different approaches and thus face different challenges. Additionally, in this study only the development side has been analyzed, adding the impacts of the developments on the process would yield an additional point of view.

Therefore to overcome these issues we aim to investigate two research objectives. On the one hand, while this paper focuses on one project, we received additional system logs spanning almost the entire duration of the process mining platform. Thus, is it is possible to look at different projects, analyze their impact on the processes and give an overview on the long term value of a process mining initiative. On the other hand, the findings indicate threats to a successful process mining project and the data to establish early warning signs. Identifying a class of such threats including early ways to mitigate them describes our second research objective.

Acknowledgments. First, the Authors want to thank the Enervie Vernetzt GmbH for their assistance and funding. Second, as part of the Change.WorkAROUND project (promotional sign 02J21C166), this research was funded by the German Federal Ministry of Education and Research.

References

1. van der Aalst, W.M.P.: Process Mining - Data Science in Action. Springer, Heidelberg (2016). https://doi.org/10.1007/978-3-662-49851-4
2. van der Aalst, W.M.P.: Process mining: a 360 degree overview. In: van der Aalst, W.M.P., Carmona, J. (eds.) Process Mining Handbook, vol. 448, pp. 3–34. Springer, Cham (2022). https://doi.org/10.1007/978-3-031-08848-3_1
3. Badakhshan, P., Wurm, B., Grisold, T., Geyer-Klingeberg, J., Mendling, J., Vom Brocke, J.: Creating business value with process mining. J. Strateg. Inf. Syst. **31**(4), 101745 (2022)
4. Beverungen, D., et al.: Seven paradoxes of business process management in a hyper-connected world. Bus. Inf. Syst. Eng. **63**(2), 145–156 (2021). https://doi.org/10.1007/s12599-020-00646-z
5. Brock, J., Brennig, K., Löhr, B., Bartelheimer, C., von Enzberg, S., Dumitrescu, R.: Improving process mining maturity-from intentions to actions. Bus. Inf. Syst. Eng. **66**(5), 585–605 (2024)
6. vom Brocke, J., Jans, M., Mendling, J., Reijers, H.A.: A five-level framework for research on process mining. Bus. Inf. Syst. Eng. **63**(5), 483–490 (2021). https://doi.org/10.1007/s12599-021-00718-8
7. Brockhoff, T., et al.: Process Mining in Textile Production: Insights from Penn Textile Solutions, pp. 87–103. Springer, Heidelberg (2025).https://doi.org/10.1007/978-3-031-80793-0_7
8. Cousin, G.: Case study research. J. Geogr. High. Educ. **29**(3), 421–427 (2005). https://doi.org/10.1080/03098260500290967
9. Dumas, M., La Rosa, M., Mendling, J., Reijers, H.A.: Fundamentals of Business Process Management. Springer, Heidelberg (2018). https://doi.org/10.1007/978-3-662-56509-4

10. Dunzer, S., Zilker, S., Marx, E., Grundler, V., Matzner, M.: The status quo of process mining in the industrial sector. In: Ahlemann, F., Schütte, R., Stieglitz, S. (eds.) WI 2021. LNISO, vol. 48, pp. 629–644. Springer, Cham (2021). https://doi.org/10.1007/978-3-030-86800-0_43
11. Eggers, J., Hein, A., Böhm, M., Krcmar, H.: No longer out of sight, no longer out of mind? How organizations engage with process mining-induced transparency to achieve increased process awareness. Bus. Inf. Syst. Eng. **63**(5), 491–510 (2021). https://doi.org/10.1007/s12599-021-00715-x
12. Grisold, T., Mendling, J., Otto, M., vom Brocke, J.: Adoption, use and management of process mining in practice. Bus. Process Manag. J. **27**(2), 369–387 (2021). https://doi.org/10.1108/BPMJ-03-2020-0112
13. Grisold, T., Wurm, B., Mendling, J., vom Brocke, J.: Using process mining to support theorizing about change in organizations. In: Bui, T. (ed.) Proceedings of the 53rd Hawaii International Conference on System Sciences. Proceedings of the Annual Hawaii International Conference on System Sciences, Hawaii International Conference on System Sciences (2020). https://doi.org/10.24251/HICSS.2020.675
14. Grisold, T., Wurm, B., vom Brocke, J., Kremser, W., Mendling, J., Recker, J.: Managing process dynamics in a digital world: integrating business process management and routine dynamics in is curricula. Commun. Assoc. Inf. Syst. **51**, 637–656 (2022). https://doi.org/10.17705/1CAIS.05127
15. Heinrich, K., Zschech, P., Janiesch, C., Bonin, M.: Process data properties matter: introducing gated convolutional neural networks (GCNN) and key-value-predict attention networks (kvp) for next event prediction with deep learning. Decis. Support Syst. **143**, 113494 (2021). https://doi.org/10.1016/j.dss.2021.113494
16. Janiesch, C., Zschech, P., Heinrich, K.: Machine learning and deep learning. Electron. Mark. **31**(3), 685–695 (2021). https://doi.org/10.1007/s12525-021-00475-2
17. Kaplan, B., Maxwell, J.A.: Qualitative Research Methods for Evaluating Computer Information Systems, pp. 30–55. Springer, Heidelberg (2005). https://doi.org/10.1007/0-387-30329-4_2
18. Kerpedzhiev, G.D., König, U.M., Röglinger, M., Rosemann, M.: An exploration into future business process management capabilities in view of digitalization. Bus. Inf. Syst. Eng. **63**(2), 83–96 (2021). https://doi.org/10.1007/s12599-020-00637-0
19. Mamudu, A., Bandara, W., Wynn, M.T., Leemans, S.J.J.: A process mining success factors model. In: Di Ciccio, C., Dijkman, R., del Río Ortega, A., Rinderle-Ma, S. (eds.) Business Process Management, vol. 13420, pp. 143–160. Springer, Cham (2022). https://doi.org/10.1007/978-3-031-16103-2_12
20. Mans, R., Reijers, H., Berends, H., Bandara, W., Rogier, P.: Business process mining success. In: ECIS 2013 Completed Research. No. 89 (2013)
21. Maris, A., Ongena, G., Ravesteijn, P.: Business process management maturity and process performance - a longitudinal study. In: Di Francescomarino, C., Burattin, A., Janiesch, C., Sadiq, S. (eds.) Business Process Management Forum, pp. 355–371. Springer, Cham (2023). https://doi.org/10.1007/978-3-031-41623-1_21
22. Martin, N., et al.: Opportunities and challenges for process mining in organizations: results of a Delphi study. Bus. Inf. Syst. Eng. **63**(5), 511–527 (2021). https://doi.org/10.1007/s12599-021-00720-0
23. Nguyen, G.T.: Siemens: Driving Global Change with the Digital Fit Rate in Order2Cash, pp. 49–57. Springer, Heidelberg (2020). https://doi.org/10.1007/978-3-030-40172-6_9
24. Pentland, B.T., Liu, P., Kremser, W., Haerem, T.: The dynamics of drift in digitized processes. MIS Q. **44**(1), 19–47 (2020). https://doi.org/10.25300/MISQ/2020/14458

25. Pentland, B.T., Vaast, E., Wolf, J.R.: Theorizing process dynamics with directed graphs: a diachronic analysis of digital trace data. MIS Q. (2021). https://doi.org/10.25300/MISQ/2021/15360
26. Recker, J., Rosemann, M., Indulska, M., Green, P.: Business process modeling- a comparative analysis. J. Assoc. Inf. Syst. **10**(04), 333–363 (2009). https://doi.org/10.17705/1jais.00193
27. Reinkemeyer, L.: Process Mining in a Nutshell, pp. 3–10. Springer, Heidelberg (2020). https://doi.org/10.1007/978-3-030-40172-6_1
28. Reinkemeyer, L., Grindemann, P., Egli, V., Röglinger, M., Marcus, L., Fabri, L.: Accelerating Business Transformation with a Process Mining Center of Excellence (CoE) (2022). https://www.celonis.com/report/fraunhofer-study/
29. Rosemann, M., Recker, J., Flender, C.: Contextualisation of business processes. Int. J. Bus. Process Integrat. Manag. **3**(1), 47 (2008). https://doi.org/10.1504/IJBPIM.2008.019347
30. Sato, D.M.V., De Freitas, S.C., Barddal, J.P., Scalabrin, E.E.: A survey on concept drift in process mining. ACM Comput. Surv. **54**(9) (2021). https://doi.org/10.1145/3472752
31. Schoch, K.: Case study research. In: Burkholder, G.J., Cox, K.A., Crawford, L.M., Hitchcock, J.H. (eds.) Research Design and Methods, pp. 245–258. Sage, Thousand Oaks (2020)
32. Syed, R., Suriadi, S., Adams, M., Bandara, W., Leemans, S.J., Ouyang, C., ter Hofstede, A.H., van de Weerd, I., Wynn, M.T., Reijers, H.A.: Robotic process automation: contemporary themes and challenges. Comput. Ind. **115**, 103162 (2020)
33. vom Brocke, J., Schmiedel, T., Recker, J., Trkman, P., Mertens, W., Viaene, S.: Ten principles of good business process management. Bus. Process. Manag. J. **20**(4), 530–548 (2014). https://doi.org/10.1108/BPMJ-06-2013-0074
34. Wurm, B., Grisold, T., Mendling, J., vom Brocke, J.: Business process management and routine dynamics, pp. 513–524. Cambridge University Press, Cambridge (2021). https://doi.org/10.1017/9781108993340.042
35. Yin, R.K.: Case Study Research and Applications: Design and methods, 6th edn. SAGE Publications Inc., Thousand Oaks (2018)

1st International Workshop on Distributed Ledger Technologies in Business Process Management (DLT4BPM 2025)

Beyond the Hype: Blockchain Meets BPM - Challenges on the Plains

Julius Köpke(✉)

Department of Informatics Systems, University of Klagenfurt, Klagenfurt, Austria
julius.koepke@aau.at
https://www.aau.at/isys/ics

Abstract. With the emergence of early blockchain platforms, such as Bitcoin and Ethereum, blockchain technology has attracted significant attention from the industry, media, and researchers. Early narratives anticipated a profound disruption of existing business models, predicting that distributed ledgers would render trusted intermediaries obsolete. Yet more than a decade later, intermediaries, such as online marketplaces and hotel-booking platforms, remain resilient, often stronger than before.

The keynote begins by addressing early misconceptions about the technology, discusses technical challenges, reflects on selected research works at the intersection of BPM and blockchain, and outlines potential directions for future research on blockchain technology from a Business Process Management perspective.

Keywords: Blockchain · BPM · Smart Contract · Distributed Ledger

1 Introduction

A blockchain is a fully replicated, distributed, append-only database that stores state-changing transactions in data blocks. Each block contains a cryptographic hash of the previous block, resulting in a chain-like structure. Distribution and replication require the use of consensus protocols to agree on the state of the ledger. The combination of specific consensus protocols and the chain structure makes blockchains practically tamper-resistant.

Public blockchains such as Bitcoin [22] or Ethereum [2] support digital currencies as well as custom transactions (typically referred to as Smart Contracts). Smart Contracts are deployed and then executed exactly as specified. Once deployed, Smart Contracts are immutable.

It soon became apparent that this architecture has the potential to disrupt established business models: Actors could secure their collaboration using Smart Contracts. They could then trust in the correct execution of the contract, regardless of whether they trust their partners or not. Any deviation from the agreed behavior is rendered impossible. Consequently, any business model fundamentally acting as a trusted intermediary - such as online marketplaces, hotel-booking platforms, notaries, or banks - was considered at risk, or at least

I. van de Weerd et al. (Eds.): BPM 2025 Workshops, LNBIP 569, pp. 303–310, 2026.
https://doi.org/10.1007/978-3-032-13426-4_22

expected to undergo significant change. Today, we can make the test of time: We can see that such a large-scale disruption has not occurred. However, which properties of blockchains were misunderstood? From a business perspective, acting as a trusted third party is indeed a key function of an online marketplace. However, other functions, such as marketing and logistics, also play a major role. But more importantly, also from the technical perspective, there are fundamental challenges that hinder practical applications beyond blockchain-native use cases such as cryptocurrencies. This keynote will shed light on fundamental problems, discuss existing works addressing the problems, and present future directions for research on the intersection of BPM and blockchain.

2 Challenges

Early assumptions about blockchain technology had a certain simplicity and appeal. However, a closer look soon revealed that widespread adoption would require addressing several substantial challenges. In this talk, we focus on three of them: The Oracle Problem, privacy, and flexibility.

2.1 Oracle Problem

A Smart Contract is essentially a blueprint for custom transactions on the blockchain. At runtime, a transaction is issued by an external account identified by a private key and may include input parameters. The blockchain system then processes the transaction, which can involve reading from and writing to permanently stored on-chain data. The underlying code must always be deterministic; otherwise, the blockchain nodes would be unable to agree on the outcome of the transaction.

This technical requirement, however, limits the usefulness of Smart Contracts in untrusted environments. Data is either provided by an external account or is already stored on the blockchain. In other words, any entity supplying data from the outside effectively acts as a trusted third party. Consequently, such values should only be trusted if there are valid reasons to do so. Entities that provide off-chain data to the blockchain are referred to as oracles [3,21].

A common approach to mitigating this issue is not to rely on a single entity for off-chain data but instead to require a consortium of off-chain entities to reach an agreement before adding the data to the blockchain. This concept is known as a distributed oracle [6]. Nevertheless, it still shifts the trust provided by the blockchain network to a comparatively small set of entities taking part in the oracle.

This limitation implies that the promise of "trust in trustless environments" applies primarily to fully on-chain applications, such as cryptocurrencies, unless the correctness of off-chain data can be verified by the blockchain network. Depending on the type of data provided by the oracle, advanced cryptographic methods can be employed to ensure correctness. These include trusted computing platforms and zero-knowledge proofs [7,23,26], which enable the blockchain system to verify the validity of the provided input.

2.2 Privacy

Following blockchain principles, any transaction, its input and output, as well as any value that has ever been part of the blockchain state, is permanently stored and remains accessible to all members of the blockchain. In the case of public blockchains, all such values are publicly accessible indefinitely. This severely limits the suitability of blockchains for applications with privacy requirements (e.g., under the GDPR).

A potential way to address this issue is the use of encryption for on-chain data. However, encryption introduces significant challenges: it effectively turns on-chain data into off-chain data. If only off-chain entities can decrypt the encrypted on-chain data, the blockchain itself cannot process it; conversely, if the blockchain network can decrypt the data, it becomes public.

Off-chain data is again subject to the oracle problem. Nevertheless, approaches that combine storing only a cryptographic digest on-chain with the use of zero-knowledge proofs [7,23,26] can help mitigate these challenges by enabling verification without revealing the underlying sensitive data.

2.3 Flexibility

A primary motivation for securing business processes with blockchains is the guarantee that their prescribed behavior is enforced by the blockchain system. While this property is crucial in zero-trust environments, it conflicts with the need for flexibility.

The real world is constantly evolving. To mention just a few examples: business partners may go out of business; technical failures, including the loss of cryptographic keys, may occur; off-chain objects (physical or digital) may change unpredictably; or new regulations may be introduced. Any of these factors can render the originally prescribed behavior impossible.

Because the behavior is strictly enforced by the blockchain system, it may happen that a process is initiated, potentially involving escrows, but a required releasing action can no longer be performed. This can lead to permanently blocked processes and, in some cases, to irretrievably "burned" cryptocurrency assets.

For real-world applications, it is therefore typically not feasible to ignore the need for flexibility. At the same time, flexibility poses a significant challenge in zero-trust environments: if participants can collectively agree to arbitrary changes, the enforcement guarantees of the blockchain system can be undermined. Consequently, it is essential to strike an appropriate balance between flexibility and enforcement.

3 Opportunities

Based on these challenges, we can conclude that supporting trust in trustless environments is not an out-of-the-box feature of blockchains for most applications. Instead, sophisticated solutions are required to balance partially conflicting requirements.

In light of these issues, several promising paths emerge for exploring the intersection of BPM and blockchain technology.

Path 1: Focus on domains where the identified problems are minimal or do not exist at all. This includes fully on-chain applications such as cryptocurrencies, fintech solutions, and gambling platforms. For example, process mining has already been successfully applied to analyze the behavior of blockchain-based applications [8].

Path 2: Shift from purely no-trust settings to low-trust or partial-trust scenarios. This approach also implies moving away from the extremes of placing everything on-chain or off-chain, toward carefully designed hybrid systems that determine which components should reside on-chain and which should remain off-chain. These systems must strike a balance between privacy, enforcement, and flexibility, tailored to the specific application requirements. This highlights opportunities for conceptual modeling and MDE-based approaches.

Path 3: Attack the fundamental problems.

3.1 From No-trust to Low-trust

We will now focus on Path 2. This path has already been addressed by the BPM community over the previous years. It explores, on the one hand, how to cope with the discussed technical limitations in blockchain-based Business Processes. On the other hand, it examines how BPM can benefit from blockchain technology even in fields that are not characterized by a fundamental lack of trust. Notably, blockchain systems provide a very welcome property for the implementation of cross-organizational processes: They are physically fully distributed but still provide a logically central state. The lack of a global state is a major problem in choreographies - especially concerning data [11].

We will now discuss selected existing works on this path, focusing on the author's previous works.

Privacy. We have discussed conflicts between privacy and enforceability for blockchain-based processes in [10]. The approach identified the problem, defined degrees of privacy in terms of privity spheres, and proposed the combination of encryption or off-chain storage and distributed oracles. A key problem is the dynamic phenomena of a process: When storing some data value during a process execution, it may not be known which other participants should subsequently have access to the value. The implementation of the various degrees of privacy identified in [10] using Hyperledger Fabric's channels was discussed in [9]. Other approaches supporting fine-grained data confidentiality using encryption were presented in works such as [19] and [15].

Modeling of Hybrid On-and Off-Chain Processes. While early approaches for the execution of Business Processes on blockchain, such as [18,27], followed an all-or-nothing approach, it is obvious that for real-world applications in low-trust environments, hybrid approaches are required, where some parts of the process are executed on-chain others are executed off-chain.

We have proposed the modeling method SecBPMN2BC for such processes in [12,20]. The starting point of the approach is to model processes, including security- and blockchain-specific requirements [10], using an extension of BPMN.

A tool is used to detect conflicting requirements and then to assign which portions of the process should be executed on or off-chain. Finally, the corresponding on-chain and off-chain implementations of the processes are created or generated [14].

One way to address enforcement requirements for decisions over off-chain data is the use of distributed oracles. This implies the need to balance privacy and enforceability. Our approach in [16] allows us to measure the privacy impacts of specific sets of oracle members with the goal of minimizing these impacts.

Flexibility: The work in [17] proposes an approach for controlled flexibility of blockchain-based business processes. It includes the ability to dynamically change actors, to replace activities or sub-processes, or to change the control-flow of the process at specific decision points. Participants can agree upfront by defining policies for changes. The actual instantiation of a change at runtime is agreed upon using voting. The approach in [4] provides additional degrees of flexibility for blockchain-based choreographies. Participants can, at runtime, agree on changing the rules of the choreography. Accordingly, [17] emphasizes more on trust, while [4] offers higher degrees of flexibility. However, the guarantee that a process can only deviate in a prescribed manner does not hold.

Recently, we have published the approach [13]. It provides a solution for exceptions arising from the fact that blockchain-based processes can provide only partial enforcement. On the one hand, the blockchain-based process has certain assumptions on the states of objects (physical or data); on the other hand, the blockchain cannot enforce the prescribed state. It is therefore likely that the real-world state deviates from the one assumed by the blockchain, leading to exceptions. The approach addresses the problem by accompanying classical imperative on-chain processes with declarative object life-cycles representing contractual state changes of objects. This way, repair plans can be generated to recover from object state exceptions. Since participants agree beforehand on the allowed state changes in a declarative form, the approach allows for balancing enforcement and flexibility.

4 Conclusion and Future Directions

For a widespread application of blockchain technology in cross-organizational business processes, a number of problems, including the oracle problem, privacy, flexibility, and scalability, have to be solved. While existing research works have typically addressed these concerns only partially or in isolation, actual applications have to deal with combinations of these problems. This adds an additional layer of complexity and demands integrated modeling approaches. These approaches likely have to go beyond classical process models. E.g., goals of a collaboration may have an influence on permissible changes in a process. This strives for approaches integrating Enterprise Modeling [5] and Process Modeling for blockchain applications. When staying on the process level, methods integrating imperative and declarative modeling paradigms [1] as well as object-centric or artifact-centric process models [25] can be valuable for addressing the required levels of flexibility.

In addition, the application of zero-knowledge proofs [7,23,26] for the requirement-driven design of hybrid on-chain and off-chain processes needs further investigation and integration.

One substantial problem is the added levels of complexity for designing such applications. A promising approach in this direction is the combination of generative AI and classical model checking as realized for conversational process modeling in [24]. Such approaches have the potential to reduce the burden of modeling complex applications for users.

References

1. Alman, A., Maggi, F.M., Rinderle-Ma, S., Rivkin, A., Winter, K.: Towards a multi-model paradigm for business process management. In: Advanced Information Systems Engineering, pp. 178–194. Springer, Cham (2024). https://doi.org/10.1007/978-3-031-61057-8_11
2. Buterin, V.: Ethereum: A next-generation smart contract and decentralized application platform (2014). https://ethereum.org/en/whitepaper/. Accessed 28 Oct 2021
3. Caldarelli, G.: Understanding the blockchain oracle problem: a call for action. Information **11**(11), 509 (2020)
4. Corradini, F., Marcelletti, A., Morichetta, A., Polini, A., Re, B., Tiezzi, F.: A flexible approach to multi-party business process execution on blockchain. Future Gener. Comput. Syst. **147**, 219–234 (2023). https://doi.org/10.1016/J.FUTURE.2023.05.006
5. Curty, S., Fill, H.: A domain-specific e^3value extension for analyzing blockchain-based value networks. In: The Practice of Enterprise Modeling - 16th IFIP Working Conference, PoEM 2023, Vienna, Austria, 28 November–1 December 2023, Proceedings. Lecture Notes in Business Information Processing, vol. 497, pp. 74–90. Springer, Heidelberg (2023). https://doi.org/10.1007/978-3-031-48583-1_5
6. Ezzat, S.K., Saleh, Y.N.M., Abdel-Hamid, A.A.: Blockchain oracles: state-of-the-art and research directions. IEEE Access **10**, 67551–67572 (2022). https://doi.org/10.1109/ACCESS.2022.3184726
7. Henry, T., Tucci Piergiovanni, S.: Secure proof verification blockchain patterns. In: Business Process Management: Blockchain, Robotic Process Automation, Central and Eastern European, Educators and Industry Forum - BPM 2024 Blockchain, RPA, CEE, Educators and Industry Forum, Krakow, Poland, 1–6 September 2024, Proceedings. Lecture Notes in Business Information Processing, vol. 527, pp. 71–88. Springer, Heidelberg (2024). https://doi.org/10.1007/978-3-031-70445-1_5

8. Hobeck, R., Berti, A., Weber, I., van der Aalst, W.M.P.: Object-centric process mining for blockchain applications extracting and representing ethereum execution data in OCEL 2.0. Enterp. Model. Inf. Syst. Archit. Int. J. Concept. Model. **20** (2025). https://doi.org/10.18417/EMISA.20.2
9. Köpke, J., Brdanin, A.: On storing data objects of business processes on blockchain channels. In: Proceedings of the PoEM 2022 Workshops and Models at Work co-located with Practice of Enterprise Modelling 2022, London, United Kingdom, 23–25 November 2022. CEUR Workshop Proceedings, vol. 3298. CEUR-WS.org (2022)
10. Köpke, J., Franceschetti, M., Eder, J.: Balancing privity and enforceability of bpm-based smart contracts on blockchains. In: Di Ciccio, C., Gabryelczyk, R., García-Bañuelos, L., Hernaus, T., Hull, R., Indihar Štemberger, M., Kő, A., Staples, M. (eds.) BPM 2019. LNBIP, vol. 361, pp. 87–102. Springer, Cham (2019). https://doi.org/10.1007/978-3-030-30429-4_7
11. Köpke, J., Franceschetti, M., Eder, J.: Optimizing data-flow implementations for inter-organizational processes. Distrib. Parallel Databases **37**(4), 651–695 (2019). https://doi.org/10.1007/S10619-018-7251-3
12. Köpke, J., Meroni, G., Salnitri, M.: Designing secure business processes for blockchains with secbpmn2bc. Future Gener. Comput. Syst. **141**, 382–398 (2023). https://doi.org/10.1016/J.FUTURE.2022.11.013
13. Köpke, J., Meroni, G., Salnitri, M.: Towards automated handling of object state exceptions in smart contracts. In: Business Process Management: Responsible BPM Forum. Process Technology Forum, Educators Forum, pp. 168–183. Springer, Cham (2026). https://doi.org/10.1007/978-3-032-02936-2_13
14. Köpke, J., Trattnig, S.: Transformation rules for the decentralization of a blockchain-extended global process model. CoRR arxiv:2312.07388 (2023). https://doi.org/10.48550/ARXIV.2312.07388
15. Kryston, M., et al.: MARTSIA: a tool for confidential data exchange via public blockchain. In: Intelligent Information Systems - CAiSE 2025 Forum and Doctoral Consortium, Vienna, Austria, 16–20 June 2025, Proceedings. Lecture Notes in Business Information Processing, vol. 557, pp. 173–180. Springer, Heidelberg (2025). https://doi.org/10.1007/978-3-031-94590-8_21
16. Köpke, J., Nečemer, M.: Measuring the Effects of Confidants on Privacy in Smart Contracts, pp. 84–99 (2022). https://doi.org/10.1007/978-3-031-16168-1_6
17. López-Pintado, O., Dumas, M., García-Bañuelos, L., Weber, I.: Controlled flexibility in blockchain-based collaborative business processes. Inf. Syst. **104**, 101622 (2022). https://doi.org/10.1016/J.IS.2020.101622
18. López-Pintado, O., García-Bañuelos, L., Dumas, M., Weber, I., Ponomarev, A.: Caterpillar: a business process execution engine on the ethereum blockchain. Softw. Pract. Exp. **49**(7), 1162–1193 (2019). https://doi.org/10.1002/SPE.2702
19. Marangone, E., Spina, M., Ciccio, C.D., Weber, I.: CAKE: sharing slices of confidential data on blockchain. In: Intelligent Information Systems - CAiSE Forum 2024, Limassol, Cyprus, 3–7 June 2024, Proceedings. Lecture Notes in Business Information Processing, vol. 520, pp. 138–147. Springer, Heidelberg (2024).https://doi.org/10.1007/978-3-031-61000-4_16
20. Meroni, G., Dalskov, A.P.K., Norta, A.: Secbpmn2bc online editor: a web-based tool for designing secure business processes on blockchains. In: Intelligent Information Systems - CAiSE 2025 Forum and Doctoral Consortium, Vienna, Austria, 16–20 June 2025, Proceedings. Lecture Notes in Business Information Processing, vol. 557, pp. 197–204. Springer, Heidelberg (2025). https://doi.org/10.1007/978-3-031-94590-8_24

21. Mühlberger, R., et al.: Foundational oracle patterns: connecting blockchain to the off-chain world. In: Asatiani, A., et al. (eds.) BPM 2020. LNBIP, vol. 393, pp. 35–51. Springer, Cham (2020). https://doi.org/10.1007/978-3-030-58779-6_3
22. Nakamoto, S.: Bitcoin: a peer-to-peer electronic cash system (2009). http://www.bitcoin.org/bitcoin.pdf
23. Petto, O., Preindl, T., Kjäer, M.: Interpreted and confidential execution of process choreographies on a blockchain. In: Di Ciccio, C., et al. (eds.) Business Process Management: Blockchain, Robotic Process Automation, Central and Eastern European, Educators and Industry Forum, pp. 40–54. Springer, Cham (2024). https://doi.org/10.1007/978-3-031-70445-1_3
24. Safan, A., Köpke, J.: Bpmn-chatbot++: Llm-based modeling of collaboration diagrams with data. In: BPM 2025 Best Dissertation Award, Doctoral Consortium, and Demonstration & Resources Forum (2025)
25. de Sousa, V.A., Burnay, C., Snoeck, M.: Artifact-centric modeling and implementation of blockchain-enabled business processes. Bus. Inf. Syst. Eng. (2024). https://doi.org/10.1007/s12599-024-00885-4
26. Sun, X., Yu, F.R., Zhang, P., Sun, Z., Xie, W., Peng, X.: A survey on zero-knowledge proof in blockchain. IEEE Netw. **35**(4), 198–205 (2021). https://doi.org/10.1109/MNET.011.2000473
27. Tran, A.B., Lu, Q., Weber, I.: Lorikeet: a model-driven engineering tool for blockchain-based business process execution and asset management. In: Proceedings of the Dissertation Award, Demonstration, and Industrial Track at BPM 2018 co-located with 16th International Conference on Business Process Management (BPM 2018), Sydney, Australia, 9–14 September 2018. CEUR Workshop Proceedings, vol. 2196, pp. 56–60. CEUR-WS.org (2018). https://ceur-ws.org/Vol-2196/BPM_2018_paper_12.pdf

Gas Management Patterns in Blockchain-Enabled Process Execution

Hassan Atwi[(✉)] and Cesare Pautasso

Software Institute, Università della Svizzera italiana, Lugano, Switzerland
Hassan.Atwi@usi.ch, c.pautasso@ieee.org

Abstract. In this paper, we present a methodology for modeling efficient gas management in blockchain-enabled collaborative business processes. We introduce four patterns designed to optimize and manage gas fees throughout business process execution. These patterns are formally represented using BPMN to provide a clear visual framework for integration into business workflows. Furthermore, we translate these patterns into Solidity smart contracts and evaluate their performance within a real-world business scenario. Our approach aims to enhance the efficiency and cost-effectiveness of blockchain-based process execution.

Keywords: Blockchain · Gas · Solidity · Collaborative Processes · BPMN

1 Introduction

Blockchain technology [11] has gained attention across many use cases due to key characteristics such as transparency, immutability, and tamper-resistance. One area where blockchain has shown strong potential is Business Process Management [1] (BPM). Smart contracts [2] allow collaborative business processes to be encoded as deployable programs that enforce process logic directly on the blockchain. This enables transparent and immutable execution of collaborative processes, helping ensure trust and compliance among all participants.

As a result, blockchain-based workflow engines [6,9] compile business processes into smart contracts to execute them on-chain. A key concern in writing smart contracts is their execution cost. Unlike traditional workflow engines that run on local infrastructure, blockchain-based execution requires the payment of gas fees, which are determined by code complexity. This makes process execution potentially expensive [12]. Therefore, making gas usage visible at the process modeling level can help reduce business operation costs for blockchain execution.

In this paper, we propose four design patterns aimed at managing and optimizing gas consumption in blockchain-based processes: event logging, guard checking, partial recovery, and gas sponsorship. These patterns (Fig. 1) are intended for both business practitioners and blockchain developers designing processes for on-chain execution. They are BPMN specific patterns and can be applied across various business scenarios in process modeling.

I. van de Weerd et al. (Eds.): BPM 2025 Workshops, LNBIP 569, pp. 311–326, 2026.
https://doi.org/10.1007/978-3-032-13426-4_23

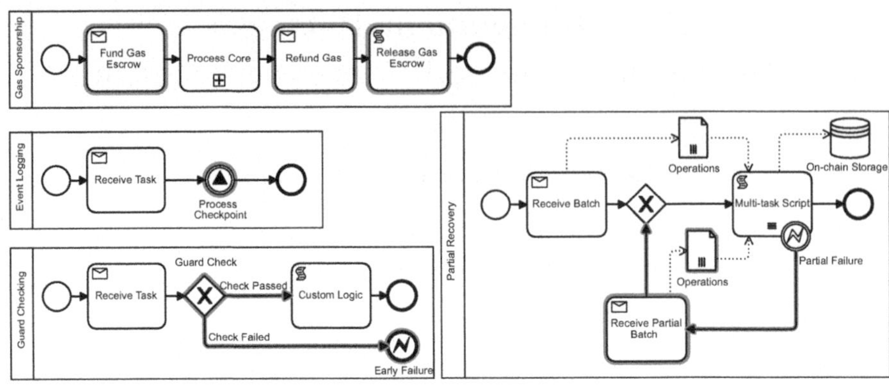

Fig. 1. Gas management design patterns modeled in BPMN (highlighted in blue). (Color figure online)

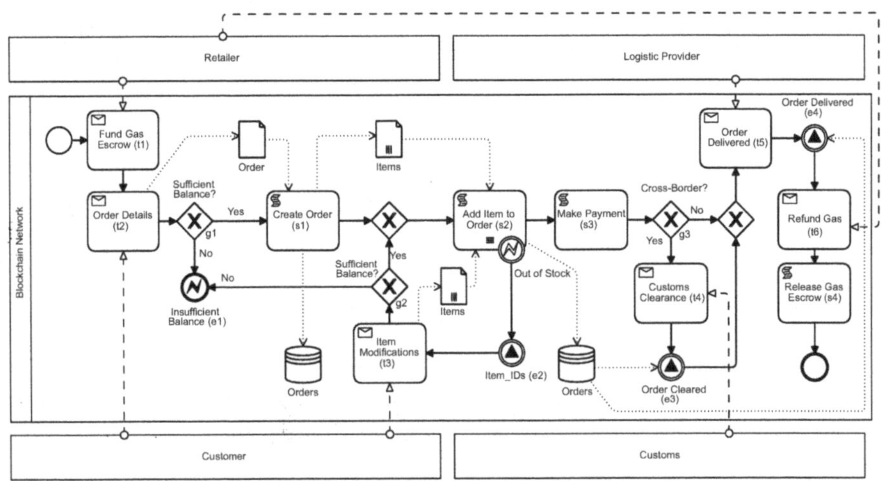

Fig. 2. BPMN diagram representing a supply chain collaborative process in which the four gas management patterns have been introduced.

To demonstrate these patterns, we apply them to a collaborative process scenario involving four participants (Fig. 2): Retailer, Logistics Provider, Customer, and Customs. These participants interact through a blockchain network that provides a shared view of the core supply chain process. In the scenario, the Customer places an order with multiple items. The order is validated based on stock availability and the Customer's balance. If the order is approved and it involves a cross-border transaction, Customs issues a clearance on-chain. The Logistics Provider then logs the delivery on the blockchain.

The process is compiled into a Solidity smart contract and deploy on a local Ethereum network. We execute 500 traces of the process to evaluate the impact of each design pattern on both deployment and execution gas costs. Our results show which pattern combinations improve gas efficiency, while others may introduce additional costs.

The paper is organized as follows: In Sect. 2, we formalize the semantics of a blockchain-enabled collaborative process using BPMN so that its gas consumption can be estimated. In Sect. 3, we introduce the design patterns illustrating their application within the use case scenario. Section 4 presents an experimental evaluation of their benefits in terms of gas usage during deployment and execution. In Sect. 5, we discuss the results before concluding the paper in Sect. 6.

2 Background and Motivation

2.1 Blockchain-Enabled Business Process

To explain process execution costs, we introduce a set of assumptions on how various blockchain-related aspects are mapped to BPMN elements. In particular, we designate one pool to represent the on-chain logic. All other pools represent off-chain business processes, locally executed by each participant. Formally, the blockchain pool B is defined as:

$$B = (T, G, E, P, F, \iota)$$

where:

- T is the set of tasks, with $T_R \subseteq T$ as Receive Message Tasks (from off-chain participants), and $T_S \subseteq T$ as Script Tasks (deterministic on-chain logic),
- G, E: sets of gateways and events, respectively, where $E_R \subseteq E$ is the set of error events
- P: set of participants
- $F \subseteq (T \cup G \cup E) \times (T \cup G \cup E)$: control-flow edges (sequence flows),
- $\iota : T_R \rightarrow P$: maps each receive task to its initiating participant,

A blockchain transaction begins with a receive task and terminates at either another receive task or an end event (end event may be an error event). Formally, it is defined as a tuple:

$$\tau = (t_{\text{start}}, \sigma, \pi, \sigma', n_{\text{end}})$$

where:

- $t_{\text{start}} \in T_R$ is the initiating receive task,
- $n_{\text{end}} \in T_R \cup E_R$ is the terminating node, either a receive task T_R (success) or an error event E_R (failure),
- $\pi = \langle n_1, \ldots, n_k \rangle \in (T \cup G \cup E)^*$ is a valid transaction control-flow path such that:

$$(t_{\text{start}}, n_1),\ (n_1, n_2),\ \ldots,\ (n_{k-1}, n_k),\ (n_k, n_{\text{end}}) \in F$$

- $\sigma, \sigma' \in \Sigma$ are the initial and resulting blockchain states,

- Executing π transitions the state from σ to σ', denoted $(\sigma, \pi, \sigma') \in \theta$, where $\theta \subseteq \Sigma \times (T \cup G \cup E)^* \times \Sigma$ is the state transition relation,
- If $n_{\text{end}} \in E_R$, the transaction is reverted: the blockchain state remains unchanged ($\sigma' = \sigma$), and the control flow is rolled back to the initiating receive task t_{start}.

2.2 Gas Cost in Transaction Execution

In blockchain networks, the execution of logic comes with a cost because of the distributed nature of the network. For instance, in Ethereum blockchain networks, to prevent abuse through computationally intensive or potentially unbounded code execution, a fee called gas [16] is applied to all operations performed on-chain. Each transaction is assigned a gas limit and a gas price. The total fee is determined by multiplying the gas consumed during execution by the specified gas price. This fee is paid in ETH and deducted from the transaction sender's balance. If the transaction exceeds the specified gas limit, it is reverted, but the gas consumed up to the point of failure is still paid.

To map gas fees to business processes, we relate them to the BPMN elements executed during a blockchain transaction. Since each element corresponds to an on-chain operation, the total gas cost can be represented as the sum of the individual costs of these operations. Formally, the gas fee can be expressed as:

$$G_{\text{tx}}(\pi) = \sum_{i=1}^{|\pi|-1} G(n_i)$$

where $\pi = \langle t_{start}, \ldots, n_i, \ldots, n_{end} \rangle$ is a valid transaction execution control-flow path. $G(n_i)$ denotes the gas cost of executing each BPMN element n_i along the path. The total gas cost $G_{\text{tx}}(\pi)$ excludes the terminating node n_{end} and represents the sum of gas consumed by all preceding elements in the transaction. This total is paid by the sender of the transaction upon execution of the control flow path triggered by its receipt on the blockchain.

2.3 Related Work and Research Gap

In [10], the BPMN and CMMN notations are used to represent patterns covering blockchain concepts such as oracles, tokenization, and on-chain encryption. The study does not include any gas cost evaluation for the patterns. The pattern collections presented in [17,18] provide a systematic overview of design patterns for blockchain-based applications and serve as a foundation for integrating blockchain components into broader software architectures. In [7], a specific category of blockchain patterns is introduced, focusing on payment mechanisms and transfer of funds between participants. While the primary objective of the study is to explore payment patterns rather than transaction costs, it notes the high deployment cost of the patterns. The study does not use business process modeling to represent the patterns. [14] is a collection of Solidity design patterns and best practices derived from real-world decentralized applications. In our work, we adopt the Guard Check pattern from that collection and represent it using BPMN.

To optimize the cost of executing business processes on blockchain, the authors of [3] transform existing BPMN models into Petri nets and apply optimization rules to enhance execution efficiency on the blockchain. The results are empirically compared to a baseline by replaying execution logs and measuring gas consumption. This work concentrates on low-level transformations of business processes, rather than addressing application and domain specific concerns at the business level. In [8], the authors explore a range of low-level optimization strategies for Ethereum smart contracts. They evaluate strategies for analyzing and minimizing gas consumption during both the contract generation and deployment phases. However, this work remains focused on the technical level and does not address higher-level business concepts as we do in this paper.

3 Gas Management Design Patterns

3.1 Partial Recovery

Context: In many blockchain applications, a participant may need to perform multiple operations that are submitted together in a single transaction, commonly referred to as batching. In BPMN, this concept is often represented using a multi-instance parallel task, where the same task is executed concurrently for multiple items or data elements.

Problem: While batching reduces the overhead of submitting multiple separate transactions, it also introduces dependencies between the batched operations which are executed atomically. If one operation within the batch fails, the entire transaction is reverted due to the atomic (all-or-nothing) nature of transactions. This forces the user to resubmit the whole transaction after resolving the issue, resulting in additional costs. How to avoid the participant having to resubmit the entire batch to reprocess their operations, leading to increased gas fees?

Solution: Operations within a batch transaction are separated and executed individually rather than atomically as a batch. Successful operations are persisted on-chain, while failed ones are flagged and skipped. A dedicated event is emitted containing references to the failed operations. Participants can then resubmit only the failed operations, i.e., performing a partial recovery of the batch, with corrected parameters, avoiding the need to resend the entire batch.

Use Case: In the use-case scenario (Fig. 2), the partial recovery pattern is applied during the process of adding items to a customer order, where multiple items are processed in a single batch. Assuming the customer has sufficient balance to place the order, the transaction τ_{order} may result in one of two execution paths depending on the availability of the requested items:

$$\pi_1 = \langle t_2, g_1, s_1, \{s_2^{(1)}, \ldots, s_2^{(N)}\}, s_3, g_3, n_f \rangle \quad \text{where } n_f \in \{t_4, t_5\},$$
$$\pi_2 = \langle t_2, g_1, s_1, \{s_2^{(1)}, \ldots, s_2^{(N)}\}, e_2, t_3 \rangle$$

Here, $\{s_2^{(1)}, s_2^{(2)}, \ldots, s_2^{(N)}\}$ represents the repeated execution of task s_2 for each item in the original order. N denotes the total number of items in the customer's order. Task s_2 is treated as a multi-instance parallel task, corresponding to the addition of each item individually.

Path π_1 is followed when all requested items are in stock and the transaction is completed successfully. Alternatively, path π_2 is taken when some or all items are out of stock. In this case, the transaction emits event e_2, which carries references to the failed items. When the initial order contains out-of-stock items, the customer submits a follow-up transaction $\tau_{\text{order}'}$ to modify the order with the remaining items. This transaction may follow one of two paths:

$$\pi_3 = \langle t_3, g_2, \{s_2^{(1)}, \ldots, s_2^{(M)}\}, s_3, g_3, n_f \rangle \quad \text{where } n_f \in \{t_4, t_5\},$$
$$\pi_4 = \langle t_3, g_2, \{s_2^{(1)}, \ldots, s_2^{(M)}\}, e_2, t_3 \rangle$$

In these paths, $M \leq N$ refers to the number of items that are still pending and need to be added in the follow-up transaction(s). Each instance $s_2^{(i)}$ corresponds to the processing of a single item, whether it succeeds or fails.

The gas consumed by the customer can be calculated as follows: if all items are available in the initial transaction, the total gas usage is $G_{\text{customer}} = G_{\text{tx}}(\pi_1)$. If at least one item is unavailable, the total gas becomes:

$$G_{\text{customer}} = G_{\text{tx}}(\pi_2) + (\delta - 1) \cdot G_{\text{tx}}(\pi_4) + G_{\text{tx}}(\pi_3)$$

where δ represents the number of attempts required to complete the order.

Application: The partial recovery pattern can be implemented using the multicall [4] approach in blockchain systems. In a multicall, multiple user operations are bundled and executed within a single transaction to reduce overall execution fees. The partial recovery pattern complements this mechanism by allowing individual operations within the bundle to fail without reverting the entire transaction. This ensures that successful operations are preserved while isolating and handling failures independently, thereby saving additional cost, as there is no need to resubmit the entire set of operations in case of partial failure.

3.2 Gas Sponsorship

Context: In blockchain-enabled collaborative processes, multiple participants interact through the blockchain to achieve a shared business objective. Since executing tasks on-chain requires initiating blockchain transactions, participants are responsible for covering the gas fees. These fees can be substantial, especially in high-frequency scenarios.

Problem: Blockchain technology offers many advantages for business processes, such as traceability, decentralization, and immutability. However, these benefits come at the cost of transaction fees. Transaction costs can deter participants from engaging in blockchain-enabled processes, especially in environments where costs are prohibitive and unstable. This challenge may outweigh the advantages of blockchain-enabled processes, leading businesses to revert to centralized systems. How to avoid participants paying transaction fees as they interact with a process?

Solution: To address the drawback of transaction costs in blockchain-based business processes, participants in the collaboration agree to designate one or more gas sponsors responsible for covering the transaction fees of other participants. The agreed-upon process begins with an activity in which the sponsors allocate funds within the smart contract, effectively acting as an escrow. Once the escrow is funded, the process execution continues. At the end of the process, the gas consumption of each participant is measured, and the escrow is released proportionally based on each participant's actual usage. With the help of the business process model, the sponsorship can be made selective based on two factors derived from the process itself. The first is *resource-selective*, identifying the eligible participants who may be refunded. The second is *path-selective*, referring to the specific control-flow path that a transaction has followed (π). Certain paths can be excluded or included in the refunding logic. Both factors can also be combined to enable a process-aware gas sponsorship strategy.

Use Case: In our use-case scenario Fig. 2, the participants agreed to adopt the gas sponsorship pattern within the process. The *retailer* was selected as the sponsor responsible for funding the escrow. Additionally, the participants agreed to apply both resource-selective and path-selective strategies. In the resource-selective strategy, only a defined set of participants are eligible for a refund, specifically: $\{customer, logistics\_provider\}$. In the path-selective strategy, the following control-flow paths are excluded from the refunding logic:

$$\begin{aligned}
\pi_1 &= \langle t_2, g_1, s_1, \{s_2^{(1)}, \ldots, s_2^{(M)}\}, e_2, t_3, g_2, e_1 \rangle, \\
\pi_2 &= \langle t_2, g_1, e_1 \rangle, \\
\pi_3 &= \langle t_4, e_3, t_5 \rangle
\end{aligned}$$

Paths π_1 and π_2 are excluded because they correspond to aborted transactions that revert due to insufficient customer balance. In these cases, the retailer explicitly agreed not to sponsor failed transactions. Path π_3 is excluded as it is initiated by the *customs* participant, who is not eligible for a refund under the agreed resource-selective policy. Therefore, the total gas sponsored by the retailer is the sum of the gas fees for all valid transaction paths, excluding the three excluded ones. Let Π be the set of all valid execution paths in the process, and let $\{\pi_1, \pi_2, \pi_3\} \subset \Pi$ be the set of paths excluded from refunding. The total gas cost G_{retailer} sponsored by the retailer is computed as:

$$G_{\text{retailer}} = \sum_{\pi \in \Pi \setminus \{\pi_1, \pi_2, \pi_3\}} G_{\text{tx}}(\pi)$$

Applications: The gas sponsorship pattern has gained attention in recent research aimed at abstracting users from the complexity and cost of interacting with blockchain systems, particularly in the context of Account Abstraction (AA) [15]. AA introduces a flexible transaction model that enables more user-friendly blockchain interactions. One key component of this model is the Paymaster, a smart contract responsible for sponsoring gas fees on behalf of users. This allows users to interact with decentralized applications (dApps) without needing to hold or manage native tokens for gas, thereby improving accessibility.

3.3 Guard Checking

Context: In blockchain-enabled business processes, task execution consumes gas, regardless of its success. Even when a transaction fails and is reverted, the participant still pays for the operations executed up to the failure point. Early input validation is essential to avoid incurring unnecessary gas costs during task execution.

Problem: A blockchain transaction is executed atomically, and while a failed transaction reverts all state changes, participants still incur the gas costs for the execution up to the point of failure. This is both counterproductive and costly for participants. When critical validations, e.g., balance checks, access permissions, are deferred to later stages of the process, earlier tasks may have already performed multiple expensive, state-changing operations. Even though the transaction is eventually reverted, the participant still incurs gas costs for computation and memory usage up to the point of failure. How to reduce the cost of failed transactions?

Solution: To avoid late failure in a blockchain process, early validation of critical conditions is applied in a process control-flow to ensure that faulty transactions are halted as early as possible, before any expensive state-changing logic is triggered. This pattern make use of decision gateways at the beginning of the execution path to validate preconditions. If the guard fails, the process reverts immediately with minimal gas consumption.

Use Case: In the process shown in Fig. 2, the transaction for placing an order follows the path:

$$\pi = \langle t_2, g_1, s_1, \{s_2^{(1)}, \ldots, s_2^{(N)}\}, s_3, g_3, n_f \rangle \quad \text{where } n_f \in \{t_4, t_5\}$$

Let $\tau = (t_2, s, \pi, s', n_f)$ denote the transaction. If the customer's balance is insufficient, the control flow is redirected to a terminating event via the gateway

g_1. However, if the balance check is deferred until s_3, the transaction proceeds through s_1 and s_2 before failing. These tasks incur significant gas costs due to their storage-intensive operations, i.e., order creation and item insertion, making early validation crucial for cost efficiency.

- Without early guard: If balance validation is deferred until s_3, the gas cost upon failure becomes:

$$G_{\text{fail-late}} = G(t_2) + G(s_1) + \sum_{i=1}^{N} G(s_2^{(i)}) + G(s_3)$$

- With early guard: Placing the check at g_1 ensures early termination if the balance is insufficient:

$$G_{\text{fail-early}} = G(t_2) + G(g_1)$$

The gas savings in case of failure are:

$$\Delta G = G_{\text{fail-late}} - G_{\text{fail-early}} = G(s_1) + \sum_{i=1}^{N} G(s_2^{(i)}) + G(s_3) - G(g_1)$$

This shows how guard checking reduces costs for failing transactions.

Applications: The guard checking pattern is widely adopted in many decentralized application (dApp) smart contract codebases. It typically appears at the beginning of function calls to enforce preconditions. Solidity offers a dedicated "`require()`" statement. In Uniswap [5] early checks are used to validate input conditions, e.g., ensuring sufficient output amounts or valid recipient addresses, before proceeding with more costly operations.

3.4 Event Logging

Context: Blockchain storage writes incur high gas costs, while event logging is cheaper but still suited to track the achievement of key process milestones.

Problem: Participants need visibility into the state of a blockchain-enabled process for monitoring, auditing, or coordination purposes. However, frequently persisting state information on-chain through storage operations is costly in blockchain environments, leading to increased gas consumption. How to reduce the cost for on-chain logging of the process instance state?

Solution: To reduce the cost associated with frequent state modifications in blockchain-enabled processes, we use blockchain events, which are modeled as signal events in BPMN. These events are emitted at specific checkpoints within the process and serve as lightweight markers that communicate progress without altering the contract's state. This approach offers a gas-efficient alternative for broadcasting and auditing the status of a business process on-chain.

Use Case: In our use-case scenario (Fig. 2), the transactions $\tau_{\text{customs\_clearance}}$ and $\tau_{\text{order\_delivered}}$, corresponding to the execution paths $\pi_1 = \langle t_4, e_3, t_5 \rangle$ and $\pi_2 = \langle t_5, e_4, t_6 \rangle$ respectively, demonstrate the application of gas-efficient checkpoint logging. Upon successful customs clearance or order delivery, a signal event is emitted to indicate the occurrence of a checkpoint within the process.

Since this status information, i.e., the order has been cleared or delivered, is not consumed by any on-chain logic or referenced by other smart contracts, persisting it via storage updates (e.g., `order.cleared = true`) incurs unnecessary gas costs. Instead, emitting a signal event offers a lightweight and cost-effective alternative for communicating progress to off-chain participants. Persisting such data on-chain when it serves no purpose in subsequent smart contract logic represents an anti-pattern. Gas-efficient checkpoint logging avoids redundant state changes while still sustaining transparency and traceability of process execution for external observers through the event log.

Applications: Event logging is a widely adopted pattern in decentralized applications (dApps) to minimize state-changing operations and reduce gas costs. Instead of persisting non-critical state updates on-chain, many dApps emit events to signal significant process milestones. A practical example is The Graph [13], a protocol that leverages blockchain-emitted events to index and query contract data efficiently. This approach enables transparency and auditability without incurring the high gas costs associated with on-chain storage operations.

4 Experimental Evaluation

We used the running example to quantitatively evaluate the patterns in terms of gas usage during both deployment and execution. To enable this evaluation, the collaborative process was compiled into a smart contract based on the state machine pattern [14]. The process state is represented by a token that marks the currently active task. The smart contract maintains a mapping from tasks to their corresponding state, i.e., process token. When a task becomes enabled, a token is placed on it. Upon the execution of that task, the token moves to the subsequent task according to the process flow. Public functions represent user-invoked tasks, while internal functions capture the behavior of script tasks, gateways, and events, i.e., callable only from within the contract itself.

During the evaluation, we distinguish between the base contract and the full contract. The base contract implements only the core process logic, i.e., the state machine, without incorporating any of the patterns. For instance, in the absence of the event logging pattern, the base contract persists order status using on-chain storage instead of emitting events. Guard checking is also omitted: control-flow elements such as gateways g_1 and g_2 are not present in the base model. Partial recovery is likewise not supported in the base contract. As a result, when some items are unavailable, the customer must resubmit a transaction with the entire item list. This leads to the execution path such as $\pi_{\text{full}} = \langle t_2, s_1, s_2, e_2 \rangle$,

Table 1. Breakdown of full contract deployment cost.

Component	Deployment Cost (gas)	Deployment Cost Share (%)
Base Contract	2,692,867	62.46%
Patterns		
Event Logging	29,182	0.68%
Guard Checking	176,309	4.09%
Partial Recovery	282,067	6.54%
Gas Sponsorship	1,130,273	26.22%
Full Contract	4,310,698	100%

with $e_2 \in E_R$ being an error end event instead of a signal event. Lastly, the gas sponsorship pattern is not implemented in the base contract. Tasks responsible for funding and refunding participants, e.g., t_1 and t_6, are omitted. In contrast, the full contract includes all four patterns as specified in the process model.

4.1 Deployment Cost

The patterns discussed are designed to manage gas usage in a blockchain-enabled business process. In addition to their execution cost, the deployment cost is equally important. It is essential to evaluate the deployment cost to determine whether implementing these patterns is affordable, particularly in relation to their execution cost and overall profitability. We isolate the pattern from the base contract to inspect the deployment cost of each pattern. We then deploy the base contract along with the individual pattern and compare its deployment cost to that of the base contract. Understanding how much additional gas each pattern requires during deployment, relative to the base contract, is essential for evaluating the trade-offs involved. Table 1 presents the deployment costs for each pattern. The most expensive pattern to implement is the gas sponsorship pattern, with a deployment cost of 1,130,273 gas (26.22%), which incurs higher costs due to the continuous tracking of gas consumption in real-time across the contract's functions and the storage of gas usage by participants. The least expensive pattern to implement is event logging, with a deployment cost of 29,182 gas (0.68%), which is attributed to its simple implementation that involves emitting a native Solidity event when triggered within the control flow. In total, the patterns represent 35.53% of the deployment cost of the base contract, which has a deployment cost of 2,692,867 gas (62.46%).

4.2 Execution Cost

To assess the execution cost of the patterns, we need to run the collaborative process by interacting with the deployed smart contracts. This interaction is simulated through a generated event log, consisting of 500 traces, where each trace represents an execution instance of the process. Each trace includes input

Table 2. Transaction count, average cost, total gas used, and relative difference with respect to the Base Contract.

Component	Transactions		Total Gas Used	Relative Difference (%)
	Count	Avg. Cost (gas)		
Base Contract	3,475	272,667.57	947,519,800	–
Patterns				
Event Logging	3,475	256,525.79	891,427,135	-5.91%
Guard Check	3,475	268,767.43	933,966,831	-1.43%
Partial Recovery	4,594	103,902.50	477,328,105	-49.64%
Gas Sponsorhip	4,318	248,719.16	1,073,969,351	+13.36%
Full Contract	4,318	130,314.79	562,699,263	-40.64%

parameters required to execute the process, such as the retailer's stock levels and item prices, the initial gas amount funded by the retailer, and the customer's Ether balance, which determines whether the purchase can be completed. The number of attempts (δ) made by the customer to successfully fulfill the order is generated as part of each trace, along with whether the order is domestic or cross-border. These parameters are randomly assigned across the traces to simulate different execution scenarios. The same event log is used to simulate each process trace on both the full and base contracts, with the execution path determined by the corresponding input parameters.

To analyze the gas cost impact of each pattern, we deploy contract variants that combine the base process with a single pattern. This setup enables us to isolate the cost contribution of each pattern and understand how it affects execution independently. By comparing these variants with the base contract, we observe the relative increase or decrease in total gas usage. In Table 2, the partial recovery pattern results in the highest gas reduction of 49.64% compared to the base contract, despite introducing the largest number of transactions. Conversely, the Refund Gas pattern results in a 13.36% increase in total gas usage. This is expected, as the pattern's goal is not cost optimization but refund management. It also introduces more transactions than the base contract, due to additional operations for funding and refunding participants. When all patterns are integrated in the full contract, we observe a 40.64% reduction in total gas consumption compared to the base contract, despite an increased number of transactions. This indicates that the combined use of patterns contributes to overall cost efficiency in the process execution.

Looking at the impact of the patterns from a task execution perspective (Fig. 3), we can observe how each pattern affects different parts of the process in terms of gas usage. For instance, in the Order Details task, the gas consumption in the full contract is approximately 66% lower than that of the base contract. This reduction results from the combined effect of the partial recovery and Guard Check patterns integrated within the task's logic. It is also worth noting the gas

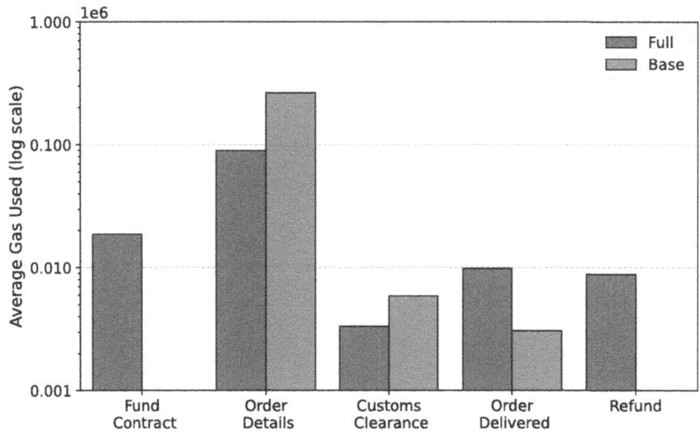

Fig. 3. Comparison of average gas usage by task in full vs base contract.

usage in the Customs Clearance and Order Delivered tasks. Although both tasks incorporate the event logging pattern in the full contract, Order Delivered still consumes more gas than Customs Clearance. This discrepancy is due to the additional logic introduced by the gas sponsorship pattern in Order Delivered, i.e., tracking and storing gas usage on-chain. This observation highlights that certain pattern combinations may not be cost-effective. In this case, the gas sponsorship pattern introduces overhead that offsets the efficiency gains of event logging, nullifying its intended benefit.

Figure 4 illustrates gas usage trends in relation to the number of customer attempts. In the base contract, gas usage increases sharply as the number of attempts grows $(G_{\text{tx}}(\pi_{\text{full}}) \cdot (\delta))$ (Fig. 4a). This behavior is due to the lack of partial recovery pattern. Each failed attempt requires resubmitting the entire order, resulting in redundant execution and higher costs. In contrast, the full contract shows a decreasing trend in gas usage across attempts. Thanks to partial recovery pattern, once certain items are successfully added, they are excluded from future attempts. Thus, only the failed items are retried ($M \leq N$), leading to reduced computational effort and lower cumulative gas costs. Similarly, as the number of items in an order increases (Fig. 4b), the base contract shows a steep rise in gas consumption. Since the full batch is reprocessed with every failure, the cost of each additional item compounds. The full contract maintains a relatively stable profile, as it isolates and reattempts only the necessary operations.

To demonstrate the utility of the gas sponsorship pattern, Table 3 presents the distribution of funds among participants. In this setup, the retailer acts as the sole sponsor, covering the gas costs of the entire process. Due to the adoption of a resource-selective refunding strategy, Customs is excluded from gas reimbursement and therefore receives no refund. Other participants, i.e., the Customer and Logistics, receive only partial refunds. This shortfall arises from certain gas-consuming operations that are not encompassed within the defined sponsorship boundaries, i.e., path-selective. Notably, Logistics consistently exhibits the low-

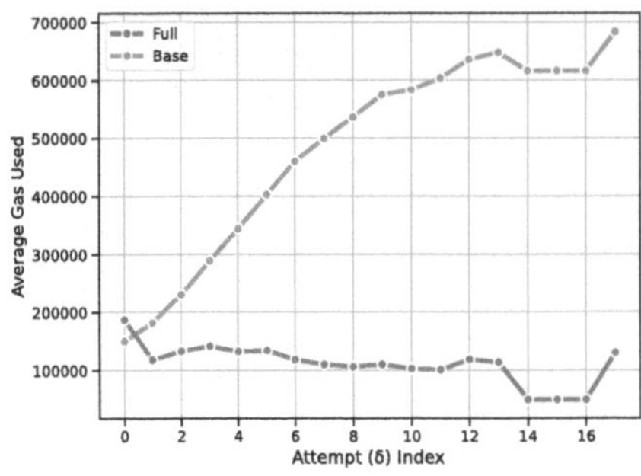

(a) Average gas usage by attempts.

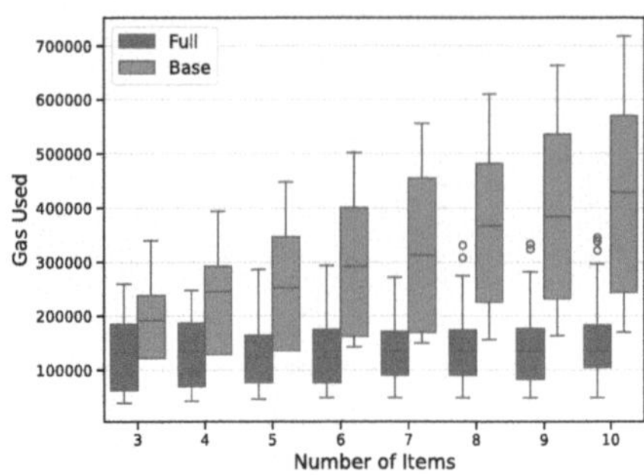

(b) Gas usage by number of items.

Fig. 4. Gas usage scaling across attempts (δ) and item counts.

Table 3. Distribution of funds among participants with their respective gas usage.

Participant	Funded (ETH)	Gas Used (ETH)	Refund (ETH)	Refund (%)
Retailer	295	0.11406309	294.72367810	99.91%
Customer	0	0.34435188	0.25267738	73.36%
Logistics	0	0.03658384	0.02364452	64.63%
Customs	0	0.01223939	0	0.00%

est refund rate. As discussed in Fig. 3, this is attributed to the fact that the gas cost of the logistics task itself is lower than the overhead required to track and process gas usage on-chain, resulting in a refund gap for the participant.

5 Discussion

As observed in the evaluation, adding patterns to the base contract nearly doubles the deployment cost. This increase is expected due to the additional logic introduced by the patterns. However, this higher deployment cost represents an investment that will return significant gas savings during execution.

In some cases, combining patterns leads to a reduction in both execution costs and the number of transactions. Certain patterns may appear costly when applied in isolation, but become more efficient in a combined contract. This is due to the way patterns interact and complement each other, often reducing redundant operations. For example, the Partial Recovery pattern recorded fewer transactions in the full contract compared to its isolated implementation. This is largely due to the presence of a Guard Check, which filters out invalid transactions, e.g., due to low balance, early in the process. Another observation involves the gas sponsorship pattern, which shows significantly higher execution costs when applied alone (almost double) compared to when it is used in combination with other patterns. This is because it misses out on the optimizations introduced by the other patterns.

Just as some patterns work well together, others may have a negative impact when combined. For instance, gas sponsorship can increase the cost of otherwise lightweight patterns such as Event Logging. This overhead stems from the additional write operations needed to track gas usage. One way to address this is to introduce a fixed gas refund for such lightweight tasks when user refunds are necessary, thus avoiding excessive overhead for simple operations.

The presented patterns can act as a guide for process designers aiming to implement blockchain-based workflows while managing gas costs. By applying these patterns, designers can reduce gas usage and make blockchain adoption more attractive to participants who are concerned about transaction fees. Although the patterns are demonstrated within our own smart contract implementation, they should also be tested with other blockchain-enabled workflow engines to assess their general applicability and performance across different environments.

6 Conclusion

In this paper, we presented four BPMN-based gas management patterns for blockchain-enabled processes. These patterns were demonstrated through a use case scenario and evaluated under different settings to assess their effectiveness in reducing gas consumption. The results showed that, while the patterns introduce an increase in deployment cost, they offer significant gas savings during execution. These patterns are BPMN specific and can be applied across various business scenarios involving blockchain-based processes. They may serve as practical guidelines for designing gas-aware and efficient blockchain workflows.

Acknowledgement. This work is supported by the Swiss National Science Foundation (SNSF) funded project "Flexible Choreographies in Multi-chain Environments" (196958).

References

1. Belchior, R., Guerreiro, S., Vasconcelos, A., Correia, M.: A survey on business process view integration: past, present and future applications to blockchain. Bus. Process. Manag. J. **28**(3), 713–739 (2022)
2. Buterin, V., et al.: A next-generation smart contract and decentralized application platform. White Paper **3**(37), 2–1 (2014)
3. García-Bañuelos, L., Ponomarev, A., Dumas, M., Weber, I.: Optimized execution of business processes on blockchain. In: Carmona, J., Engels, G., Kumar, A. (eds.) BPM 2017. LNCS, vol. 10445, pp. 130–146. Springer, Cham (2017). https://doi.org/10.1007/978-3-319-65000-5_8
4. Hughes, W., Russo, A., Schneider, G.: Multicall: a transaction-batching interpreter for ethereum. In: Proceedings of 3rd ACM International Symposium on Blockchain and Secure Critical Infrastructure, pp. 25–35 (2021)
5. Lo, Y.C., Medda, F.: Uniswap and the emergence of the decentralized exchange. J. Finan. Mark. Infrastruct. **10**(2), 1–25 (2021)

6. López-Pintado, O., García-Bañuelos, L., Dumas, M., Weber, I., Ponomarev, A.: Caterpillar: a business process execution engine on the ethereum blockchain. Softw. Pract. Exp. **49**(7), 1162–1193 (2019)
7. Lu, Q., Xu, X., Bandara, H.D., Chen, S., Zhu, L.: Patterns for blockchain-based payment applications. In: Proceedings of 26th European Conference on Pattern Languages of Programs, pp. 1–17 (2021)
8. Mandarino, V., Pappalardo, G., Tramontana, E.: Some blockchain design patterns for overcoming immutability, chain-boundedness, and gas fees. In: 2022 3rd Asia Conference on Computers and Communications (ACCC), pp. 65–71. IEEE (2022)
9. Mendling, J., et al.: Blockchains for business process management-challenges and opportunities. ACM Trans. Manag. Inf. Syst. (TMIS) **9**(1), 1–16 (2018)
10. Milani, F., Garcia-Banuelos, L., Filipova, S., Markovska, M.: Modelling blockchain-based business processes: a comparative analysis of BPMN vs CMMN. Bus. Process. Manag. J. **27**(2), 638–657 (2021)
11. Nakamoto, S.: Bitcoin: a peer-to-peer electronic cash system (2008)
12. Porkodi, S., Kesavaraja, D.: Escalating gas cost optimization in smart contract. Wirel. Pers. Commun. **136**(1), 35–59 (2024)
13. Tal, Y., Ramirez, B., Pohlmann, J.: The graph: a decentralized query protocol for blockchains (2018). https://raw.githubusercontent.com/graphprotocol/research/master/papers/whitepaper/the-graph-whitepaper.pdf
14. Volland, F.: Solidity design patterns. https://fravoll.github.io/solidity-patterns/. Accessed 21 May 2025
15. Wang, Q., Chen, S.: Account abstraction, analysed. In: 2023 IEEE International Conference on Blockchain (Blockchain), pp. 323–331. IEEE (2023)
16. Wood, G., et al.: Ethereum: a secure decentralised generalised transaction ledger. Ethereum Proj. Yellow Paper **151**(2014), 1–32 (2014)
17. Xu, X., Pautasso, C., Lo, S.K., Zhu, L., Lu, Q., Weber, I.: An extended pattern collection for blockchain-based applications. In: Transactions on Pattern Languages of Programming V, pp. 67–117. Springer, Heidelberg (2025). https://doi.org/10.1007/978-3-662-70810-1_2
18. Xu, X., Pautasso, C., Zhu, L., Lu, Q., Weber, I.: A pattern collection for blockchain-based applications. In: Proceedings of 23rd European Conference on Pattern Languages of Programs, pp. 1–20 (2018)

On LLM–Assisted Generation of Smart Contracts from Business Processes

Fabian Stiehle[1(✉)], Hans Weytjens[1], and Ingo Weber[1,2]

[1] School of CIT, Technical University of Munich, Munich, Germany
{fabian.stiehle,hans.weytjens,ingo.weber}@tum.de
[2] Fraunhofer Gesellschaft, Munich, Germany

Abstract. Large language models (LLMs) have changed the reality of how software is produced. Within the wider software engineering community, among many other purposes, they are explored for code generation use cases from different types of input. In this work, we present an exploratory study to investigate the use of LLMs for generating smart contract code from business process descriptions, an idea that has emerged in recent literature to overcome the limitations of traditional rule-based code generation approaches. However, current LLM-based work evaluates generated code on small samples, relying on manual inspection, or testing whether code compiles but ignoring correct execution. With this work, we introduce an automated evaluation framework and provide empirical data from larger data sets of process models. We test LLMs of different types and sizes in their capabilities of achieving important properties of process execution, including enforcing process flow, resource allocation, and data-based conditions. Our results show that LLM performance falls short of the perfect reliability required for smart contract development. We suggest future work to explore responsible LLM integrations in existing tools for code generation to ensure more reliable output. Our benchmarking framework can serve as a foundation for developing and evaluating such integrations.

Keywords: Blockchain · Process Execution · Process Enactment · Workflow · Large language models · Generative AI

1 Introduction

In many fields, LLMs are envisioned to assist in a wide variety of tasks, where so far the training of general machine learning models has been challenging due to the scarcity of specialized data and the large computational effort required (c.f., [4,8,42]).

In the wider field of software engineering, LLMs are anticipated to support all phases of the software engineering process [4]. For code generation, LLMs have arguably made the biggest practical impact so far, testified by the integration of commercial tools like *Github's Copilot*—which builds on seminal research on

I. van de Weerd et al. (Eds.): BPM 2025 Workshops, LNBIP 569, pp. 327–342, 2026.
https://doi.org/10.1007/978-3-032-13426-4_24

LLMs trained on code [11]—into popular development environments like *Visual Studio Code*.

Similarly, within the field of business process management (BPM), Vidgof et al. [42] call to evaluate the combination of LLMs with existing BPM technologies. First results evaluating LLMs on BPM tasks show the large promise, since they perform comparable to or better than existing BPM tools [17].

Blockchain-based business process execution relies on a model-driven paradigm, where process descriptions are transformed into executable artefacts based on rule-based transformation tools [39]. These tools, however, exhibit various limitations such as in their flexibility, e.g., in terms of supported process modelling constructs, their supported output targets, or their support of blockchain-specific features. Considering the wider field of model-driven engineering, LLMs are similarly prospected to have the potential to drive automation [8]. This hope can draw on seminal results from the related field of code-to-code translation (transpilers), where LLM-based approaches were found to outperform traditional rule-based approaches [34,35].

While many positive visions exist, and early results on leveraging LLMs to assist in code generation are impressive [7], significant challenges remain—extending even beyond the well-known hallucination issue (or more precisely: confabulation [36]). For instance, GitHub Copilot can introduce numerous security vulnerabilities into generated code [32]. LLM outputs are inherently non-deterministic [30], making them unreliable for consistent behaviour. Meanwhile, Huang et al. [20] show that generated code may reproduce ethically concerning biases, such as gender-related ones.

Furthermore, proprietary models raise concerns about confidentiality, privacy, and autonomy (c.f. [4,18]). These AI models are often deployed on large, centralised platforms provided by hyperscalers like *AWS*, *Azure*, or *GCP*. Open-source models running on these platforms face the same security concerns. Relying on central deployments may not be a good fit for blockchain-based processes, where decentralisation is a goal [38].

Thus, it is paramount to systematically evaluate LLMs' usefulness and fit of properties for a given task and weigh benefits and drawbacks. Research is called to identify the scenarios where LLMs add true value (c.f. [4,42]). However, evaluation poses a significant challenge, as it often requires manual human investigation and large volumes of labelled or parallel data [9].

Research on using LLMs for smart contract generation is in its infancy. Existing work aims, among other things, to reduce the required specialised programming skills for contract development. However, most of this work focuses on reporting the syntactical correctness of generated code (compilability), not its functional correctness [1,25,28]. In other cases, correctness is assessed through manual inspection of small samples [10,15]. In the case of blockchain-based process execution, early work explores the promise of deriving code from process descriptions, but draws conclusions from a singular case study [15]. Current research furthermore does not make data or code openly accessible.

In this work, we present an exploratory study investigating the use of LLMs to generate smart contract code from business process descriptions. We think it paramount to ground such research in open empirical evidence from larger datasets. Beyond standards of open science, the availability of open repeatable benchmarks and data is especially important in the present case, as LLMs capabilities develop in a fast pace and their output is unpredictable. With this work, we introduce an automated evaluation framework for generating smart contract code from process models. We provide empirical data from larger data sets of process models (165 models filtered and sampled from the collection of SAP-SAM [37] models). We test seven LLMs of different types and sizes in their capabilities of achieving central properties of blockchain-based process enactment (c.f. [39]): enforcing process flow, case data-based conditions, resource allocation, and efficiency.

In general, our results indicate good performance of some models, with those achieving F1 scores of 0.8 or more. Due to the stochastic nature of LLMs, output remains imperfect and unreliable. While such performance may be acceptable in other contexts, blockchain is an unforgiving environment—on public blockchains developers should assume that any weakness will be exploited. As such, we believe this is a fundamental issue of the chosen approach to have LLMs generate smart contract code, which cannot be overcome by LLMs based on the current architectures. We discuss this point further in the paper, including an outlook on roles LLMs could fulfil productively in the generation of smart contracts from process models.

The remainder of the paper is structured as follows. A background on LLMs and relevant terminology is provided in the next section; note that we assume familiarity with blockchain and process enactment on it. Subsequently related work is discussed in Sect. 3, before we present the benchmarking framework in Sect. 4. Based on it, we conduct experiments that we report on in Sect. 5 and discuss in Sect. 6, before Sect. 7 concludes.

2 Background

In this section, we give relevant background on the AI models, their attributes, and related concepts which we use in the body of the paper. Large Language Models (LLMs) are transformer-based neural network systems [41]. LLMs are a specific class of Foundation Models, a class of machine learning models trained on extensive data sets, not for one specific purpose but as a basis for many possible applications [3]. In the case of LLMs, training ingests very large textual corpora, comprising not only natural language, but also programming code (such as Solidity for blockchain smart contracts), and formal representations (such as BPMN for modeling business processes). Due to their generality and the training input, LLMs can perform complex tasks beyond language understanding and generation, including analyzing and creating business process models [19] and smart contracts [12]. Many of the latest LLMs support other modalities (such as images, video, or audio), hence they are sometimes referred to as large multimodal models (LMMs). However, for this paper, the distinction between LLMs and LMMs is of no importance, and hence for the sake of clear communication, we follow the current common practice and refer to them as LLMs.

In many usage scenarios, LLMs deliver high performance out of the box, eliminating the need for fine-tuning or training from scratch with large supervised datasets or significant compute resources. In *zero-shot prompting*, models complete tasks based solely on instructions without prior examples, whereas *few-shot prompting* involves providing a handful of illustrative examples directly within the input [14].

Tokens are the units of input and output for LLMs. Tokens can be whole words, subwords (parts of words), individual characters, punctuation, or special characters [2]. The total number of tokens—both in the input query and the generated output—directly influences the computational load of running these models. Models that perform complex *reasoning* (so called reasoning models) typically generate a plan to answer a query, execute the steps in the plan, and possibly check their work; hence they require many more tokens than regular LLMs. Increasing the model size—measured by the number of parameters, the numeric values representing the strength of connections between "neurons"—generally improves performance but also raises computational demands, leading to greater energy consumption [29]. Balancing model size, token usage, and capability is therefore essential for developing efficient and sustainable LLM-based applications.

LLMs are available in both proprietary and open-source forms [43]. Proprietary models, such as *OpenAI's GPT* and *Anthropic's Claude* model families, are typically accessed via APIs hosted by third parties. In comparison to open-source models, they often deliver superior performance but introduce risks such as data exposure, dependency on external providers, and limited transparency. In contrast, open-source models enable self-hosting and on-premise deployment—an attractive option in blockchain contexts where data sovereignty, trust minimization, and operational independence are essential.

Temperature is a setting for LLMs that controls the randomness of generated text; lower temperatures make outputs more predictable and focused (by selecting the most probable tokens), while higher temperatures encourage more creative and varied responses (by selecting less probable tokens).

3 Related Work

Within the field of BPM, Vidgof et al. [42] outline the opportunities and challenges of integrating LLM-based tools within the BPM lifecycle. Recent work explores an increasingly wide array of BPM applications (see e.g., Pfeiffer et al. [33], which explore four real-world use cases that demonstrate the use of LLMs across modelling, prediction and automation). Within predictive process monitoring, LLMs are explored for their capability to predict future states of processes (e.g., Pasquadibisceglie et al. [31]). In prescriptive process monitoring, LLMs are explored to enhance recommendations with LLM-generated explanations [23].

Orthogonal to our work is the question whether LLMs can assist in deriving accurate models from natural language process descriptions (e.g., Hörner et al. [19]); for an overview see Klievtsova et al. [22]. Closer to our work, Monti et al. [26] propose an LLM-driven pipeline to extract executable scripts (for deployment in a process execution engine) from natural language process descriptions. For the evaluation of their code generation, they use 10 cases and compare the LLM output to a manually implemented script. Additionally, they conducted a human evaluation, assessing the quality of the produced code. A similar study to ours was conducted by Berti et al. [5], which presents a benchmark on the performance of LLMs for different Process Mining tasks, the open-ended nature of these tasks requires a *LLM judge* evaluation approach, where LLMs assess the output of other LLMs.

Research on LLM-assisted smart contract generation is in its infancy. Existing results are limited to reporting the syntactical correctness of generated code (compilability) and the automated detection of known vulnerabilities using existing tools [1,25,28]. A relevant result to our investigation is provided by Luo et al. [25]; their result suggests that augmenting the generation process by a formalised model improves results. Some works go beyond syntactical correctness by manual inspection of code [10,15]. However, this is limited to a few simplistic cases, as it is highly labour intensive. Karanjai et al. [21] extract solidity functions from GitHub repositories and use extracted code comments as prompts; to test the LLM output, they rely on corresponding unit tests present in the mined repository.

None of the aforementioned studies on smart contract generation make their data or evaluation frameworks available.

Our work lies at the intersection of previously outlined fields. To the best of our knowledge, the only directly related work is the recent case study of Gao et al. [15]. They present an approach, based on few-shot prompting, capable of generating a smart contract from a Business Process Modeling Language (BPML) specification (a superset of BPEL), derived from a collaboration diagram. However, their evaluation is limited to one process, which includes start, end, and message events, tasks, and two XOR splits. They do not make their code or data available.

To the best of our knowledge, we are the first to present an open source benchmarking framework to automate the assessment of code generation from process models. We provide an instantiation of it based on the large SAP-SAM data set [37], one-shot and two-shot prompts, and a Ethereum virtual machine (EVM) environment. Using it, we evaluate different proprietary and open source LLMs on 165 cases each. All our data is available and our tests can be repeated (see Footnote 1).

4 Benchmarking Framework

To assess the capabilities of LLMs for smart contract generation, we designed a configurable benchmarking framework and make it openly available along with

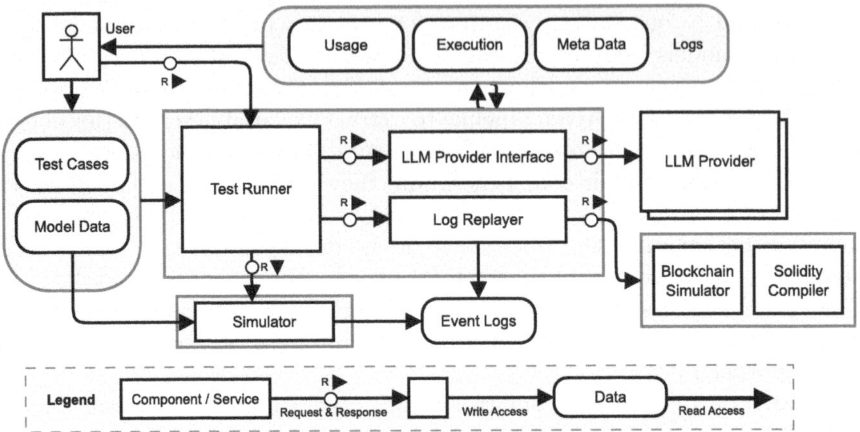

Fig. 1. Main components, services and data of the benchmarking framework architecture as FMC block diagram.

all relevant input and output data.[1] An open framework facilitates repeatability and can be used to judge the capabilities of future model evolutions. We envision our framework to also serve as a foundation for evaluation in future related research (as outlined in Sect. 6). In contrast to previous work, we want to facilitate automated evaluation from large data sets with optimal coverage. An established method to benchmark the correctness of a blockchain-based business process is to replay all possible conforming traces[2] (which the smart contract has to accept) and replay a set of non-conforming traces (which the smart contract has to reject) [39]. Our approach makes use of this method. From a given process model, it generates conforming traces (not always exhaustively, but up to a configurable threshold, as parallelism and loops can result in an intractable search space) and non-conforming traces. All traces are then replayed against the generated smart contracts.

4.1 Architecture Overview

Figure 1 depicts an overview of our architecture. As input, different test cases can be configured. Mainly, a test case is a tuple of: (i) the LLM to benchmark, (ii) the prompt to use, (iii) the process model data set to use.

Interaction with the framework is achieved through a *test runner*. Based on user interaction, the runner coordinates the benchmark execution with the

[1] https://github.com/fstiehle/bpmn-sol-llm-benchmark. An archived version is available at: https://doi.org/10.5281/zenodo.16616694.

[2] For the remainder of the paper, we use common terminology. We loosely denote an event log as a set of events, where each event is associated with a case identifier that groups it into a case. A trace is the ordered sequence of events (activities) that occurred for a specific case. Each event represents a task (activity) in the model. A trace can be said to be in conformance with a process model if it represents a valid execution path through that model.

other internal and external components. From the model data (process models), a *simulator* component generates conforming and non-conforming traces. This simulator component is external to the framework, so it can be swapped based on different model data inputs. The simulator is responsible for generating conforming and non-conforming event logs from the input process models. To generate a non-conforming trace, a conforming trace is randomly chosen and manipulated. The simulator also generates an encoding that maps the events and participants to how they should be represented in the smart contract (`taskIDs` and `participantIDs`, the latter associated with a blockchain address).

This encoding is embedded into the prompt, along with the model data, by the *LLM provider interface*, which calls the external LLM provider as configured in the test cases. The received output is stored in a usage log. For any interaction with an LLM provider, the usage log stores (among other things): a timestamp, the configured test case, the full input and the full output. This allows to reconstruct and rerun a benchmark at a later time. The usage log also records usage statistics (tokens used, price, etc.) as reported by the provider.

From the usage log output, the *log replayer* extracts the smart contract code, compiles and deploys it to an external blockchain environment, and uses the encodings and event logs to perform a benchmark on the deployed contract. The replayer stores the results in execution logs. The framework also extracts metadata on the used process model (e.g., modelling constructs per model, etc.) to aid in the evaluation of the benchmark.

4.2 Instantiation

In the current instantiation of our framework, we support BPMN 2.0 Choreographies. This is a purely practical implementation choice, given that there is no consensus on the best fitting modelling paradigm for blockchain-based execution (c.f. [39]) and given our familiarity with a suitable tool. We instantiate our framework for an Ethereum virtual machine (EVM) blockchain environment, the most widely employed environment [39]. We discuss key design decisions in the instantiation of our architecture.

Simulator. We extend the open source tool *Chorpiler*, first introduced in [40] with simulation capabilities. Chorpiler transforms BPMN Choreographies to smart contracts, generates non-conforming traces from conforming traces, and also generates machine-readable encodings on how to interact with a contract. Chorpiler parses a given Choreography into an interaction net, a special type of labelled Petri net (see [13]), suitable to represent choreographies. We make use of this intermediate presentation to generate conforming traces. Here, we adopt the implementation of *pm4py* [6], a popular Python library for process mining, which includes a *playout* functionality to generate event log traces from Petri nets. The implementation tries to discover new conforming traces with each pass until a threshold of passes is reached.

As we also want to benchmark data-based exclusive gateways (XOR), we had to extend the playout functionality to generate appropriate data manipulation events. To do so, for each outgoing flow (other than the default flow), we generate a boolean decision. During trace generation, once our algorithm encounters a decision transition, it inserts a corresponding data event in the trace.[3]

Test Runner, Replayer and LLM Provider. To provide the replayer with a blockchain environment, we use *hardhat*, a popular Ethereum development framework that allows testing, deployment, and debugging of smart contracts in a locally simulated EVM environment.[4] As LLM provider, we use *OpenRouter*, a platform that provides a unified API across multiple language model providers. This simplifies our integration and gives access to a broad range of state-of-the-art models.[5] We use a *Node.js* environment; the test runner is implemented using *Mocha*, a JavaScript test framework.[6]

5 Experiment

We use the instantiation of our framework to conduct a large scale benchmarking experiment. Our process model data is based on the *SAP Signavio Academic Models Dataset* (SAP-SAM), which was initially introduced in [37]. The dataset contains different model types created through the *Academic Initiative* platform from 2011 to 2021.[7] Thus, the dataset primarily contains process models created by students, researchers, and teaching staff. Still, for BPMN specifically, the dataset's properties (distribution of modelling constructs) are in line with previous research assessing the usage of modelling constructs from diverse sources [27]. The collection includes 4,096 BPMN 2.0 choreography models, to our knowledge, the largest collection of choreography models accessible for research purposes.

5.1 Pre-processing

The SAP-SAM dataset contains many non-standard compliant choreography models. For our purposes, we can relax requirements of ownership and observability present in the standard, as the smart contract provides global ownership and observability (c.f. [24]).[8] Furthermore, the models lack execution-relevant information for exclusive gateways (conditions or labels from which conditions could

[3] Chorpiler implements transactional logic as in [24]; the smart contract makes as much progress as possible after a task is executed; i.e., data-based decisions are made autonomously once the gateway is enabled, and the required data must be already set by then. Thus, data events are inserted preceding any event that leads to a given gateway.

[4] https://hardhat.org, accessed 2025-06-12.

[5] https://openrouter.ai, accessed 2025-06-12.

[6] https://www.npmjs.com, https://mochajs.org, both accessed 2025-06-12.

[7] https://academic.signavio.com, accessed 2025-06-12.

[8] During our initial exploration of the dataset we encountered this issue in many models. The problem is exacerbated by the fact that many participants share the same name in the task bands, but are assigned different participant IDs. We hypothesise that this occurred when a participant's name was entered manually rather than selected from a list of existing ones in the visual editor.

Table 1. Models selected for our experiments, conducted June 11–13, 2025, using the then-current models available through OpenRouter. *Size* refers to the number of parameters in billions (B), where available.

	Provider	Model	Size (B)
Open Source	DeepSeek	DeepSeek-V3 0324	671
	Meta	Llama-3.1-405b-instruct	405
		Llama-3.3-70b-instruct	70
	Alibaba	Qwen3-235b-a22b	235
Proprietary	OpenAI	GPT-4.1	n/a
	Anthropic	Claude Sonnet 4	n/a
	X AI	Grok 3	n/a

be inferred, and default flow markings). Thus, we pre-processed each model. When no default flow was marked, we set the first outgoing flow to the default flow. Then, for all other outgoing flows, we inserted a boolean condition. Furthermore, we removed any Signavio extension elements. To reduce the size of LLM input, we also removed the BPMN 2.0 Diagram Interchange, as it only contains additional information required to visualise the model. Finally, we merged all start and end events, so each model contains only one, to adhere to the implementation limitation of Chorpiler.

From these pre-processed models, we use Chorpiler to assess the syntactic soundness of each model. Simply put, if Chorpiler is able to generate a contract from the model, we consider it for our benchmark. Chorpiler supports all basic elements of BPMN Choreographies[9]. Choreography tasks, start and end event, exclusive, event, and parallel gateways, sub choreographies, and loops in the model. It also ignores issues regarding ownership and observability.

After the filtering steps, 1,427 choreography models remain. We use a sample of 165 models for our benchmark runs. In our sample, on average, each process contains 13 participants (see footnote 8), six tasks, one diverging exclusive gateway, 0.1 diverging event-based gateways, and 0.2 diverging parallel gateways, among others. The largest model in the dataset contains 24 tasks and ten gateways, respectively.

5.2 Benchmark

Prompt. For our benchmark, we developed multiple prompts. To reduce the likelihood of our results being tainted by a poorly performing prompt, we tested, compared, and refined multiple versions in pre-runs, which we conducted with

[9] We use the latest alpha version (https://github.com/fstiehle/chorpiler/tree/release/v2, accessed 2025-06-12).

sets of five to twenty process models. This allowed us to iteratively refine our prompts and test our framework. For any pre-run, in addition to the automated tests, we manually investigated the generated output. This led to many refinements. In summary, our prompts moved from loosely defined (zero-shot) instructions, to (better performing) more specific instructions on how the process model should be interpreted and the contract generated. Through our initial tests, we arrived at a one-shot prompt. Specifically, in our prompt we ask for a Solidity implementation for the given process model, enforcing: (i) the control flow, i.e., the order of tasks, (ii) that only the respective initiator can execute a task, and (iii) the autonomous enforcement of gateways, and the evaluation of data-based decisions.[10] To gauge the effect of prompt-based training, we test a one-shot and a two-shot variant.

Setup. We select a range of top proprietary LLMs[11] as benchmarks and compare them to a host of open source models to evaluate to what extent hosting open source models signifies sacrificing performance for autonomy. Table 1 provides an overview of our benchmarked models. Figure 2 gives an overview of our benchmarking experiment run. For our LLM selection (c.f. Table 1), we benchmark a one-shot and two-shot variant of our prompt with temperature set to 0,[12] on a sample of 165 process models from our pre-processed files. For the generation of conforming process traces, we set a threshold of 2,500 traces per process. We generated and replayed 50 non-conforming traces per process.[13]

We ran our experiment from June 11 to June 13, 2025. For some requests, we had to perform repeated tries, as the provider connection sometimes timed out. We also encountered a period in which OpenRouter experienced an outage. Our framework is set up to retry failed requests on additional runs.

[10] Our prompt also specifies that the state of the contract should be encoded using a bitmasking technique, as it is the most efficient encoding for a token-based execution (c.f. [16]). This variant did, on average, not perform worse than a prompt asking for a more naïve implementation during our pre-runs.

[11] Our initial run also included *Google's Gemini*. However, we were not able to deactivate the output of its reasoning process, which prevented us from reliably parsing a contract from the output automatically.

[12] Leading to quasi-deterministic (c.f. [30]) inference results. Tie breaking between tokens of equal probabilities, floating point variability, etc. may still cause stochasticity.

[13] For process models with loops, the threshold is a necessary upper bound. Our non-conforming trace generation algorithm currently depends on a ground truth to assess whether a manipulated trace is not conforming on accident. For models, where the number of conforming traces exceeds our search threshold, non-conforming traces that are actually conforming can be generated. These must be manually removed.

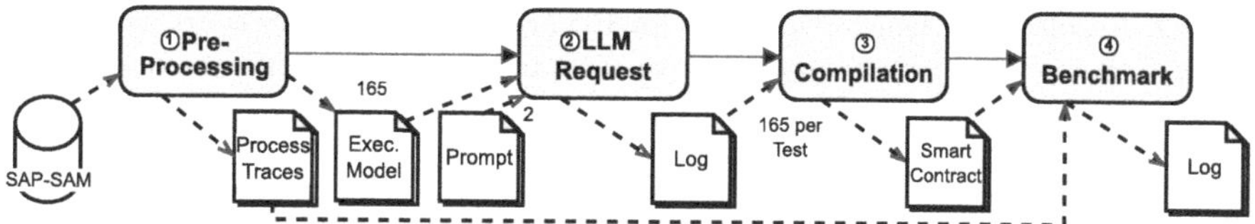

Fig. 2. Process of our benchmark experiment: We pre-process the raw model data from the SAP-SAM dataset to receive executable process models and corresponding traces. We use 165 models and perform requests for one and two-shot prompts, a pair for each LLM. From this, logs are generated including the received output. All output is compiled and deployed and benchmarked against the process traces. The benchmark result is logged.

5.3 Results

To assess the quality of the produced output we compare usage, in terms of cost and tokens used, as charged by OpenRouter.[14] To assess the efficiency of the generated output, we also record gas usage. For a given process model and its generated implementation, we classify the outcome of a trace replay accordingly.

- *True Positive*: Each event in a conforming trace was accepted (led to a state change in the contract), and the whole trace led to the end event.
- *False Positive*: A non-conforming trace was accepted as per above.
- *True Negative*: Any event in the non-conforming trace was rejected, or the trace did not lead to the end event.
- *False Negative*: A conforming trace was rejected as per above.

Using this classification framework, we calculate precision and recall per process case, using standard formulations, and the F1 score (the harmonic mean of precision and recall), common metrics to assess LLM output (see e.g., [9]). In our case, F1 is a suitable choice over metrics like accuracy, since the number of traces is unbalanced.

To assess the overall performance of each model, we calculate the macro F1 (the average of all F1 across all cases). Our results are shown in Table 2. The most obvious aspect is that Grok and Claude achieved F1 scores of 0.8 or more in all variants. Most of the generated code compiled. The cost for translating a process model was on the orders of 0.1 cents to a few cents. Interestingly, the two-shot prompt did not consistently yield better results. As a side effect of the experiment, we observed that the framework performed well in running the benchmark across the diverse set of process and AI models.

---

[14] OpenRouter operates on a 'credits' system; credits are purchased upfront, which are then deducted per model request, according to the underlying provider's token-based rate. OpenRouter charges a fee ($\approx 5\% + \$0.35$) when loading credits., which we did not include in our calculations (https://openrouter.ai/docs/faq, accessed 2025-06-13).

Table 2. Result of our benchmark run with 165 process models. We report the average cost in US$ (as reported by OpenRouter), and tokens used per process model. The overall correctness is reported via the F1 macro. Compilability (Comp.) reports on the percentage of syntactically correct generated contracts.

Shot	Model	(Avg./Process)		Correctness	
		Cost($)	Tokens	F1 Mac.	Comp.(%)
One	grok-3-beta	0.044	10.134	0.918	100.0
	claude-sonnet-4	0.046	11.442	0.862	100.0
	gpt-4.1	0.028	10.326	0.797	99.4
	qwen3-235b-a22b	0.009	18.444	0.648	97.0
	deepseek-chat-v3-0324	0.005	10.483	0.580	99.4
	llama-3.1-405b-instruct	0.010	10.259	0.475	99.4
	llama-3.3-70b-instruct	0.001	10.249	0.399	90.4
Two	grok-3-beta	0.056	14.964	0.861	100.0
	claude-sonnet-4	0.064	17.218	0.853	100.0
	gpt-4.1	0.038	15.410	0.696	100.0
	deepseek-chat-v3-0324	0.007	15.680	0.669	97.6
	qwen3-235b-a22b	0.009	24.415	0.581	93.4
	llama-3.1-405b-instruct	0.016	15.473	0.431	98.8
	llama-3.3-70b-instruct	0.002	15.252	0.370	97.0

6 Discussion, Limitations and Future Work

Our results show that current LLMs can transform executable choreography models into syntactically and functionally correct smart contracts most of the time—even when benchmarked against a realistic and diverse dataset. While the results in terms of F1 score shows promise, it can only serve as a point of departure for future work exploring meaningful integrations within a smart contract generation workflow. As mentioned earlier, blockchain is an unforgiving environment, and smart contract vulnerabilities may become very costly. Indeed, the goal of business process execution via smart contracts is to provide a trusted and secure decentralised platform. These requirements would be undermined by a reckless integration of LLM capabilities.

F1 scores that do not reliably achieve 100% would not be suitable for this context. Say, the approaches would be improved to achieving an average F1 score of 98%; while this would be impressive in many domains, it falls short of the perfect reliability required for blockchain-based smart contracts. Given the financial risks and immutable nature of blockchain transactions, even such a 2% error rate could lead to significant vulnerabilities or losses, making such performance inadequate for real-world deployment. We do not see a way in which this fundamental issue could be resolved with current LLM architectures.

However, we see ways to advance the current direction beyond using output as-is. Future work should explore integrating LLM capabilities into existing smart contract generation tools. For smart contract development, which demands high security, LLM integration must rely on extensive evaluation and robust verification of generated outcomes. This could involve using LLMs to propose code snippets or modifications, which are then rigorously checked against formal specifications (as we demonstrated with our framework) or verified using automated theorem provers, before being considered. LLMs should also generate test cases or identify potential vulnerabilities themselves, identifying common or context-depending issues in smart contracts, augmenting existing verification processes.

Furthermore, LLMs could be used to extend the functionality of existing code generation tools (generating new rules) by: (i) generating more flexible templates based on specific process models, (ii) generating code snippets for edge cases not covered by standard templates, (iii) suggesting optimisations for rules and generated code, and (iv) assisting in translating between different smart contract languages or blockchain platforms. Any such use would still have to be vetted in a suitable form, but has the advantage that rule improvements and extensions are not subject to non-determinism after being included in the code generation tools. This approach combines the reliability and domain-specific knowledge of traditional code generation tools with the flexibility and natural language understanding of LLMs, and hence addresses the limitations mentioned in the introduction.

Our benchmarking framework can serve as a foundation for evaluating these future directions, helping to assess the quality of LLM-generated code, the effectiveness of verification methods, and benchmarking extended code generation tools. Towards this, the capabilities of the benchmarking tool itself must be extended to, e.g., consider other factors such as efficiency of generated code, potential biases present in the LLM, or sustainability factors (c.f. [18]).

Finally, some limitations apply to our performed benchmark. We experimented with different prompts, but cannot guarantee that the selected query was optimal; furthermore, we used the same prompt across all LLMs, which may be suboptimal. Although we included a diverse set of LLMs, our findings should not be assumed to generalise to all current or future LLMs.

7 Conclusions

In this work, we presented an exploratory study investigating the use of LLMs for generating smart contract code from business process descriptions. We introduced an automated evaluation framework and provided empirical data from a large dataset of 165 process models. Our results show that while current LLMs can transform executable choreography models into syntactically and functionally correct smart contracts most of the time, achieving F1 scores of 0.8 or more for top-performing models, this performance falls short of the perfect reliability required for smart contracts. Given the financial risks and immutable nature of blockchain transactions, even small error rates could lead to significant vulnerabilities or losses. We argue that this fundamental issue cannot be resolved with current LLM architectures. Instead, we propose future work to explore responsible LLM integrations in existing tools for code generation, focusing on using LLMs for verification and enhancing current code generation tools rather than replacing them entirely. Our benchmarking framework can serve as a foundation for developing and evaluating such integrations.

Acknowledgments. Generative AI was used to assist in the editing of the manuscript and the implementation of the artifact. Generated output was never taken "as-is", it was reviewed and verified by the authors.

References

1. Alam, M.T., Goswami, S., Singh, K., Halder, R., Maiti, A., Banerjee, S.: Solgen: secure smart contract code generation using large language models via masked prompting. In: Proceedings of the 18th Innovations in Software Engineering Conference, pp. 1–11 (2025)
2. Ali, M., Fromm, M., Thellmann, K., et al.: Tokenizer choice for LLM training: negligible or crucial? In: Findings of the Association for Computational Linguistics: NAACL 2024, pp. 3907–3924 (2024)
3. Bass, L., Lu, Q., Weber, I., Zhu, L.: Engineering AI Systems: Architecture and DevOps Essentials. Addison-Wesley Professional (2025)
4. Belzner, L., Gabor, T., Wirsing, M.: Large language model assisted software engineering: prospects, challenges, and a case study. In: International Conference on Bridging the Gap between AI and Reality, pp. 355–374. Springer (2023)
5. Berti, A., Kourani, H., van der Aalst, W.M.: PM-LLM-benchmark: evaluating large language models on process mining tasks. In: International Conference on Process Mining, pp. 610–623. Springer (2024)
6. Berti, A., van Zelst, S., Schuster, D.: PM4Py: a process mining library for python. Softw. Impacts **17**, 100556 (2023)
7. Brynjolfsson, E., Li, D., Raymond, L.R.: The productivity effects of generative AI: Evidence from a field experiment with GitHub Copilot (2023). https://mit-genai.pubpub.org/pub/v5iixksv/release/2. Accessed 07 June 2025
8. Burgueño, L., Di Ruscio, D., Sahraoui, H., Wimmer, M.: Automation in model-driven engineering: a look back, and ahead. ACM Trans. Softw. Eng. Methodol. (2025)
9. Chang, Y., et al.: A survey on evaluation of large language models. ACM Trans. Intell. Syst. Technol. **15**(3), 1–45 (2024)
10. Chatterjee, S., Ramamurthy, B.: Efficacy of various large language models in generating smart contracts. In: Future of Information and Communication Conference, pp. 482–500. Springer (2025)
11. Chen, M., et al.: Evaluating large language models trained on code. arXiv preprint arXiv:2107.03374 (2021)
12. De Vito, G., D'Amici, D., Izzo, F., Ferrucci, F., Di Nucci, D.: LLM-based generation of solidity smart contracts from system requirements in natural language: The AstraKode case. In: International Conference on Software Analysis, Evolution and Reengineering (SANER), pp. 170–180. IEEE (2025)
13. Decker, G., Weske, M.: Local enforceability in interaction petri nets. In: Alonso, G., Dadam, P., Rosemann, M. (eds.) BPM 2007. LNCS, vol. 4714, pp. 305–319. Springer, Heidelberg (2007). https://doi.org/10.1007/978-3-540-75183-0_22

14. Dong, Q., et al.: A survey on in-context learning (2024). https://arxiv.org/abs/2301.00234
15. Gao, S., Liu, W., Zhu, J., Dong, X., Dong, J.: BPMN-LLM: transforming BPMN models into smart contracts using large language models. IEEE Softw. (2025)
16. García-Bañuelos, L., Ponomarev, A., Dumas, M., Weber, I.: Optimized execution of business processes on blockchain. In: Carmona, J., Engels, G., Kumar, A. (eds.) BPM 2017. LNCS, vol. 10445, pp. 130–146. Springer, Cham (2017). https://doi.org/10.1007/978-3-319-65000-5_8
17. Grohs, M., Abb, L., Elsayed, N., Rehse, J.R.: Large language models can accomplish business process management tasks. In: International Conference on Business Process Management, pp. 453–465. Springer (2023)
18. Haase, J., Klessascheck, F., Mendling, J., Pokutta, S.: Sustainability via LLM right-sizing. arXiv preprint arXiv:2504.13217 (2025)
19. Hörner, L.F.: Towards an LLM-based conversational framework for business process modeling: research approach and preliminary results. In: International Conference on Advanced Information Systems Engineering, pp. 286–293. Springer (2025)
20. Huang, D., Zhang, J.M., Bu, Q., Xie, X., Chen, J., Cui, H.: Bias testing and mitigation in LLM-based code generation. ACM Trans. Softw. Eng. Methodol. (2024)
21. Karanjai, R., Li, E., Xu, L., Shi, W.: Who is smarter? an empirical study of ai-based smart contract creation. In: 2023 5th Conference on Blockchain Research & Applications for Innovative Networks and Services (BRAINS), pp. 1–8. IEEE (2023)
22. Klievtsova, N., Benzin, J.V., Kampik, T., Mangler, J., Rinderle-Ma, S.: Conversational process modelling: state of the art, applications, and implications in practice. In: International Conference on Business Process Management, pp. 319–336. Springer (2023)
23. Kubrak, K., Botchorishvili, L., Milani, F., Nolte, A., Dumas, M.: Explanatory capabilities of large language models in prescriptive process monitoring. In: Business Process Management, pp. 403–420. Springer, Cham (2024)
24. Ladleif, J., Weske, M., Weber, I.: Modeling and enforcing blockchain-based choreographies. In: BPM, vol. 11675, pp. 69–85 (2019)
25. Luo, H., et al.: Guiding LLM-based smart contract generation with finite state machine. arXiv preprint arXiv:2505.08542 (2025)
26. Monti, F., Leotta, F., Mangler, J., Mecella, M., Rinderle-Ma, S.: Nl2processops: towards LLM-guided code generation for process execution. In: BPM, pp. 127–143 (2024)
27. Muehlen, M.z., Recker, J.: How Much Language Is Enough? Theoretical and Practical Use of the Business Process Modeling Notation, pp. 429–443. Springer (2013)
28. Napoli, E.A., Barbàra, F., Gatteschi, V., Schifanella, C.: Leveraging large language models for automatic smart contract generation. In: Computers, Software, and Applications Conference (COMPSAC), pp. 701–710. IEEE (2024)
29. O'Donnell, J., Crownhart, C.: We did the math on AI's energy footprint. here's the story you haven't heard. MIT Technol. Rev. (2025)
30. Ouyang, S., Zhang, J.M., Harman, M., Wang, M.: An empirical study of the non-determinism of chatgpt in code generation. ACM Trans. Softw. Eng. Methodol. **34**(2), 1–28 (2025)
31. Pasquadibisceglie, V., Appice, A., Malerba, D.: LUPIN: a LLM approach for activity suffix prediction in business process event logs. In: ICPM, pp. 1–8 (2024)

32. Pearce, H., Ahmad, B., Tan, B., Dolan-Gavitt, B., Karri, R.: Asleep at the keyboard? Assessing the security of GitHub Copilot's code contributions. Commun. ACM **68**(2), 96–105 (2025)
33. Pfeiffer, P., Rombach, A., Majlatow, M., Mehdiyev, N.: From theory to practice: real-world use cases on trustworthy LLM-driven process modeling, prediction and automation (2025). https://arxiv.org/abs/2506.03801
34. Roziere, B., Lachaux, M.A., Chanussot, L., Lample, G.: Unsupervised translation of programming languages. Adv. Neural. Inf. Process. Syst. **33**, 20601–20611 (2020)
35. Roziere, B., Zhang, J.M., Charton, F., Harman, M., Synnaeve, G., Lample, G.: Leveraging automated unit tests for unsupervised code translation. arXiv preprint arXiv:2110.06773 (2021)
36. Smith, A.L., Greaves, F., Panch, T.: Hallucination or confabulation? Neuroanatomy as metaphor in large language models. PLOS Digit. Health **2**(11), 1–3 (2023)
37. Sola, D., Warmuth, C., Schäfer, B., Badakhshan, P., Rehse, J., Kampik, T.: SAP Signavio academic models: a large process model dataset. In: Process Mining Workshops at ICPM 2022. LNBIP, vol. 468, pp. 453–465. Springer, Cham (2022)
38. Stiehle, F., Klessascheck, F., Kjäer, M., Weber, I.: Business in the age of platform economics: managing decentralised business processes beyond blockchain. In: Innov8BPM'24: International Workshop on Managing Process Innovation and Value Creation in the Era of Digital Transformation at BPM'24 (2024)
39. Stiehle, F., Weber, I.: Blockchain for business process enactment: a taxonomy and systematic literature review. In: BPM: Forum. LNBIP, vol. 459, pp. 5–20 (2022)
40. Stiehle, F., Weber, I.: Process channels: A new layer for process enactment based on blockchain state channels. In: BPM, pp. 198–215. Springer (2023)
41. Vaswani, A., Shazeer, N., Parmar, N., et al.: Attention is all you need. In: Advances in Neural Information Processing Systems, vol. 30 (2017)
42. Vidgof, M., Bachhofner, S., Mendling, J.: Large language models for business process management: opportunities and challenges. In: International Conference on Business Process Management, pp. 107–123. Springer (2023)
43. Wong, E.: Comparative analysis of open source and proprietary large language models: Performance and accessibility. Adv. Comput. Sci. **7**(1), 1–7 (2024)

2nd International Workshop on Managing Process Innovation in the Era of Digital Transformation (Innov8BPM 2025)

Modeling Business Processes: From a BPMN Structured Process Flow to a Declarative Rule-Based ACM Method

Ricardo M. F. Fernandes[1(✉)], Antonio M. Gutiérrez Fernández[2], Marek Szelągowski[3], and Christoph Ruhsam[1]

[1] Applied Applications Research Group, Papyrus Academy Department, ISIS Papyrus Europe AG, Brunn Am Gebirge, Austria
{ricardo.fernandes,christoph.ruhsam}@isis-papyrus.com

[2] Lenguajes y Sistemas Informáticos, Universidad de Sevilla, Seville, Spain
amgutierrez@us.es

[3] Systems Research Institute, Polish Academy of Sciences, Warsaw, Poland
marek.szelagowski@dbpm.pl

Abstract. In the current era of digital transformation, traditional business process management (BPM) often lack the flexibility required to manage dynamic and knowledge-intensive business processes. The purpose of this article is to present the possibilities of overcoming the limitations of traditional business process modeling focused on designing and representing the exact process flow by comparing two approaches: the widely adopted Business Process Modeling and Notation (BPMN) and the declarative, rule-based Adaptive Case Management (ACM) approach. Using a Repair Service Management (RSM) case study, we systematically analyze the strengths and limitations of both approaches regarding expressiveness, adaptability, and change management efficiency. While modeling using ad hoc subprocesses in BPMN offers some flexibility in modeling the flow of a business process, the declarative rule-based method empowers business experts to design and maintain business applications with a focus on the purpose and outcome of the business process rather than on designing its exact flow which is important to handle unforeseen situations. Building on these insights, we offer initial advice to help practitioners and researchers decide when to consider each modeling approach in dynamic business environments, contributing to the ongoing development of BPM methodologies that are essential for the digital transformation of companies.

Keywords: Adaptive Case Management · Dynamic Business Process Management · Business rules · Business Ontology · Business architecture · Value streams · Digital transformation

1 Introduction and Related Work

Business process management (BPM) is a well-established methodology for managing the lifecycle of activities in organizations [1]. Scientific Management is considered the precursor of BPM, focused on structured and repetitive mass production processes.

I. van de Weerd et al. (Eds.): BPM 2025 Workshops, LNBIP 569, pp. 345–359, 2026.
https://doi.org/10.1007/978-3-032-13426-4_25

Since then, BPM has covered all business processes of organizations, regardless of their nature or place in the value chain [2]. With the growing demand for product and service customization in the digital era, organizations increasingly require dynamic, knowledge-driven process management rather than rigid workflows [3–5]. Therefore, in the modern economy, where knowledge is the most competitive asset, restricting knowledge workers (employees who produce value due to their expertise) to operate strictly in accordance with pre-defined standard process flow models results in a *de facto* loss of the use of a significant part of the organization's intellectual capital [6].

Well-established approaches such as Adaptive Case Management (ACM) [7] or Dynamic BPM [2], overcome such limitations by considering the business goals to drive the unpredictable process and create actions at runtime constrained by rules, rather than following an exact flow of predefined actions. To implement the ACM paradigm, various modeling variants have emerged. The Case Management Model and Notation (CMMN), standardized by the Object Management Group (OMG), is the most widely recognized notation for explicitly modeling cases. CMMN allows for the definition of tasks, milestones, and events within a case, enabling flexible execution paths based on real-time context and decisions [8]. Additionally, declarative approaches such as Dynamic Condition Response (DCR) graphs prioritize defining constraints and business rules to govern activity execution, offering a robust framework for managing process variability without enforcing a strict sequential order [9]. Complementing these approaches, Gutiérrez et al. [10] proposed a method that integrates business architecture principles with domain-specific ontology for ACM modeling. This approach leverages the structured ontology to capture the complete value stream, including its goals, actions, and business rules, using a formalized natural business language. This direct business-level definition allows for the instant enactment of the business information model, enabling agile adaptation and ensuring case compliance by guiding knowledge workers with transparently formulated rules.

Previous research [11–13] has examined structured and unstructured processes separately, but comparative studies evaluating BPMN and declarative models in real-world implementation contexts remain limited. Zensen et al. conducted a practical case study comparing BPMN's flexible ad hoc subprocesses with CMMN, demonstrating that CMMN offers a more native and clearer approach for highly flexible processes, albeit with increased modeling complexity [14]. However, their findings are confined to a single case. While their study focused on CMMN, the present study broadens the investigation by exploring a declarative rule-based ACM approach to address this gap, guided by the following research question:

What are the advantages and disadvantages of using a BPMN modeling method versus a declarative rule-based modeling method with ACM?

To answer this question, we model a Repair Service Management (RSM) case study using:

- Business Process Modeling Notation version 2 (BPMN), which enforces a structured process flow [15].
- A declarative, rule-based ACM approach, which avoids predefined sequence of actions, leveraging values streams (from business architecture) and business ontology to model the business data objects [10].

Our comparative analysis examines the impact of each approach on workload, flexibility, and user experience, providing practical insights for BPM practitioners and researchers. This work evaluates how each method addresses the limitations of traditional BPM, particularly rigidity and adherence to predefined workflows, making it a valuable case study [16, 17]. This comparative analysis helps in understanding which method is better suited for certain types of processing and organizational contexts. As noted earlier, due to the importance of processes requiring dynamic management, developing a methodology for their effective modeling is of paramount importance [18]. We discuss the advantages and weaknesses of the two methods from modeling to execution.

The remainder of the article outlines the research methodology, describes and contrasts the two modeling methods, details a Repair Service Management use case and its implementation in both methods, followed by the discussion and conclusion.

2 Research Methodology

This article uses an illustrative case study methodology [17] to present the modeling method and then to comparatively evaluate two different business process modeling approaches: structured process modeling using BPMN and declarative rule-based modeling using ACM. The case study method provides the reader with descriptive details that are important to support the research process and understand the results [19]. It should be emphasized that such publications are surprisingly rare, considering the importance of unstructured processes in the modern economy [5, 20].

To evaluate and compare business process design and execution methodologies, we adopted five key dimensions, each grounded in well-established frameworks from the BPM literature:

Modeling Complexity. The effort required to define the process using each method [21].
Execution Flexibility. The ability to adapt to unforeseen circumstances and process variations [22].
IT Dependency. The level of technical expertise needed to implement the model [23, 24].
Knowledge Worker Autonomy. The degree of control that end users have on process execution [7].
Efficiency in Change Management. How easily processes can be adapted over time [23].

The selection of these five dimensions is motivated by their relevance to the core challenges and distinctions between highly structured (like BPMN) and flexible, adaptive (like declarative ACM) process management approaches, especially within dynamic real-world operational contexts.

The case study is based on Repair Service Management (RSM), a process within the Facility Management industry. The following steps are conducted (i) Modeling Phase – The RSM process was modeled in both BPMN and ACM, following best practices for each methodology. (ii) Implementation & Execution – Each model was simulated in an appropriate system to understand practical implications, (iii) Evaluation & Analysis – The models were compared using the evaluation criteria listed above. The authors of this paper are involved in the case study modeling in dual roles: as researchers, bringing expertise in modeling techniques from both approaches, and as practitioners, providing insights into real-world practices to ensure the model's relevance.

Findings from the case study will be presented in the discussion section, where the strengths and weaknesses of each approach are analyzed in relation to the evaluation criteria. Each criterion will be analyzed through qualitative assessment and empirical insights from the case study implementation. Consistent with the nature of qualitative case studies, this analysis is largely interpretive, reflecting the accumulated perspectives and insights of the experts involved in and observing the process over time, among whom the authors served in both research and practical roles.

The illustrative case study method enables an objective comparison of the usability of both approaches. The detailed conclusions from this comparison can guide researchers and practitioners in identifying, improving, communicating, and implementing business processes that require dynamic management.

3 Modeling Methods

We consider two distinct approaches to model business processes. On one side, formal workflow notations like Business Process Model and Notation (BPMN) [1] provide a structured language for modeling complex workflows. BPMN's standardized graphical representation ensures a shared understanding among stakeholders, improving process transparency and consistency. Its machine-readable format enables automation, reducing manual effort, minimizing errors, and optimizing efficiency by streamlining repetitive tasks. On the other side, Adaptive Case Management (ACM) models processes as a set of goals and rules that guide execution while ensuring compliance with business regulations [25]. ACM systems can integrate AI to learn from user actions and suggest the best next steps to achieve case goals in an optimal way [26].

Both approaches support business application development, designed by analysts and executed by knowledge workers. A typical business application consists of key components—data models, participants, actions, among others. In BPMN, these applications are process models, whereas in the discussed ACM methodology, they are value stream definitions.

3.1 Structured Modeling with BPMN

For structured modeling, we consider BPMN 2.0, a well-known BPM modeling, which is well-suited for structured, predictable processes. This method defines strict task flows within process models, where different parties interact through message flows across distinct pools, with their roles represented as swimlanes within those pools. Processes rely on data objects that serve as inputs or outputs for tasks. Process execution adapts dynamically via conditional expressions (e.g., decision-making, scheduled tasks) visualized in a diagram as decision gates. Tasks or process fragments with an unpredictable course are modeled in BPMN using ad hoc subprocesses, which make it possible to determine, in the modeling phase, a list of tasks from which the process executor will be able to select, at his own discretion, the tasks for subsequent execution, as well as the conditions for completing the ad hoc subprocess. During the application design, experts define process models, and specify relevant data objects (artifacts). Additionally, data modeling involves platform-specific database definitions, requiring advanced IT knowledge during the design. Ultimately, the business application is only partially modeled in BPMN style [1, 6]. Complex decision making is commonly defined out of the scope of BPMN and requires integration with Decision Model systems.

3.2 Declarative Modeling with ACM

ACM modeling is a declarative approach where business processes have no predefined flows [10, 27]. Instead of following a rigid workflow, knowledge workers have full flexibility to decide the next action based on the current situation. Compliance is enforced through business rules, preventing actions that violate regulations or policies. To support decision-making, machine learning algorithms analyze past case executions and suggest the best next action to achieve the case goal, ensuring value delivery to stakeholders [26].

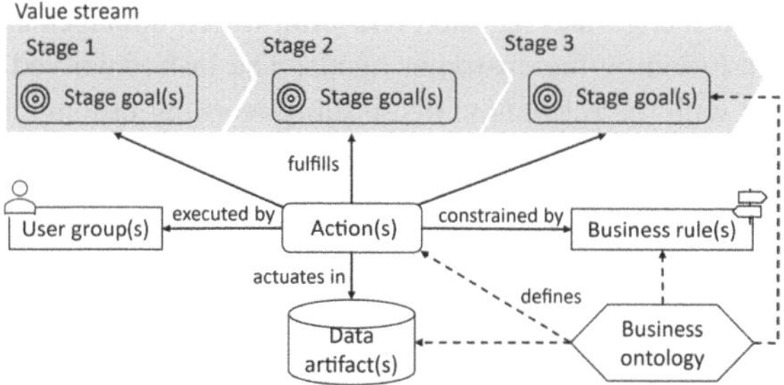

Fig. 1. Main elements of the declarative rule-based ACM modeling.

Figure 1 illustrates the ACM modeling components during the design phase. Business applications are structured as value streams, supported by a business ontology that defines domain-specific concepts and relationships. Although the value stream imposes a certain flow, the presented ACM method allows any arbitrary stage goal to be completed even if previous stages are not closed. Actions and rules are expressed using business terminology, ensuring clarity, as both use elements defined in the business ontology. The business rules within the ACM approach have different levels of enforcement, ranging from mandatory to advisory. This flexibility enables knowledge workers to override rules when necessary to ensure optimal case outcomes. Unlike traditional step-by-step process flow design, business experts using this approach focus on identifying and defining rules that guide actions toward achieving goals. As Ross [28] suggests, these rules are written in natural language using business vocabulary (from the business ontology) to ensure clarity for users. Thus, this declarative ACM approach combines a grammar with concepts and relations defined in the business ontology to create structured natural language rules that are human- and machine-readable [10]. All elements in the system – value streams, goals, actions and rules – are defined and implemented using an ontology. The ontology-driven approach simplifies modeling by standardizing elements and reducing redundancy. Supporting tools ensure consistency and automatic instantiation of concepts, facilitating updates without requiring IT intervention.

4 Business Use Case "Repair Service Management"

Repair Service Management (RSM) from the Facility Management industry was chosen as the case study due to its well-defined yet flexible nature, involving multiple interacting actors such as customers, service agents, technicians, and inventory managers. It follows a structured flow of tasks, events, and decision points but can also be modeled using a declarative approach, where execution is guided by constraints rather than a strict sequence (e.g., repair approval must precede invoicing, but other tasks can occur flexibly). RSM includes conditional flows (e.g., repair approved vs. rejected, spare parts available vs. ordering required) and maintenance services [29] which are a common field for process automation, leveraging BPMS, workflow engines, and declarative modeling techniques.

An RSM company specializes in repair and maintenance services for buildings, including electrical work, gardening, etc. The front office manages customer requests and schedules work based on the customer needs. The tasks involved in RSM include assigning personnel with the relevant skills, issuing working orders and ensuring work is performed according to the customer's requirements. Material orders may need to be approved before work starts, but in some cases, they can be handled in parallel. Role management is an important aspect because supervisors must approve work requests before they are executed.

With its comprehensive approach to repair and maintenance services, the RSM use case serves as a valuable model that can be easily transferred to other business areas. The following subsections present the design of a business application to implement RSM using (i) a structured process modeling method with BPMN 2.0 and (ii) declarative rule-based modeling with ACM.

4.1 BPMN Modeling

For the Repair Service Management (RSM) use case, BPMN provides a standardized framework for designing the underlying business application. It allows us to visualize, define, and communicate the operational flows.

4.1.1 Business Process Model

Defining business process models is the first step in developing a business application with BPMN. We explicitly modeled the process flow, ensuring clear task sequences, predefined subprocesses, and decision gateways for process execution.

Figure 2 depicts a business process model for the RSM service. The process is initiated by a message start event, where the customer submits a request with details of their repair requirements. Within the RSM back-office pool, the clerk begins by performing the *Check Customer Request* task, evaluating the submitted details. The clerk team then assesses these requirements to assemble a team with the skills best suited to the needs. Based on the team composition and requirements, the clerk team prepares a Working Order (WO), which requires verification and approval by the RSM service supervisor. Each activity may involve subprocesses and interactions with customer processes, which are omitted here for brevity. The process concludes with the *Format Customer Letter* task, followed by a message event to notify the customer.

The WO may also specify required materials for the repair (an ad hoc subprocess). Once approved, the clerk team schedules the team members according to the plan in the WO and, if necessary, reserves the required materials. When both the team and materials are prepared, the WO can be submitted to the customer. Because material orders are optional and lack predefined details, they are modeled as an ad hoc subprocess with 2 tasks (*Order Material* and *Order Equipment*). In our model, materials are ordered before the WO is approved. This decision assumes that there is a low risk of work order rejection and that materials are commonly required, with the risk of unnecessary purchases. Alternative workflows, such as ordering materials *after* WO approval, could avoid unnecessary costs but introduce delays if approval takes time. Other workflows could also include preemptive booking personnel before WO approval. Both examples would require maintaining multiple models and updating existing ones, which carries the risk of inconsistency in ongoing case executions, increasing modeling complexity.

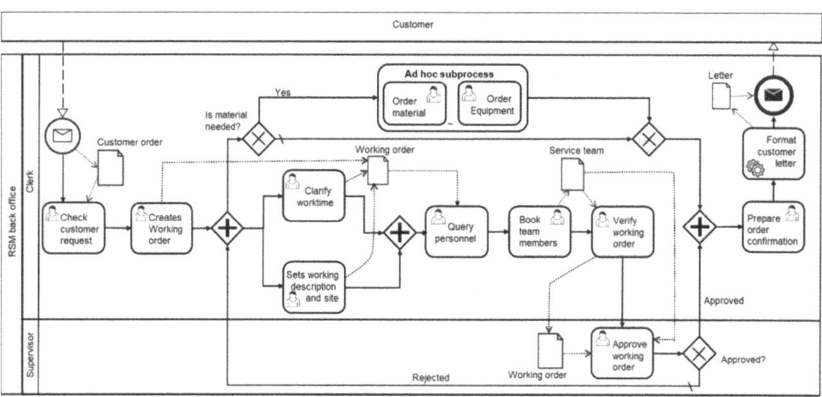

Fig. 2. BPMN for Repair Service Management.

This process highlights the trade-offs between flexibility and complexity. A model designed for maximum flexibility would require numerous subprocess variations, making it complex and error-prone, whereas a simpler model would enforce a rigid execution, reducing adaptability [18].

4.1.2 Defining Participants (Roles)

The RSM application comprises two user groups, namely the *clerk group*, responsible for the customer-facing activities, and the *supervisor group*, responsible for approving certain activities. In the BPMN those are represented as swimlanes. While knowledge worker autonomy is moderate, as workers have some decision-making, their actions remain constrained by the process model. Supervisors provide oversight, particularly for WO approvals, ensuring that process execution maintains control over decisions.

4.1.3 Defining Data Content (Artifacts)

The business application must read, create, or update data objects that reflect its execution state. Thus, the business administrator must determine during the design phase which data objects are relevant to store the case data. In RSM we identify four data objects: (i) **Customer order** (customer name, address, request description, etc.), (ii) **Working order** (working order data, namely the working site, description, etc.), (iii) **Service team** (assigned service team), and (iv) **Service confirmation letter** (file generated by the system and sent to the customer).

4.1.4 Modeling Evaluation

Modeling complexity: Moderate to high, due to the balance between flexibility, process variations, and IT dependencies. Managing multiple models for alternative workflows increases complexity and maintenance efforts with the risk of inconsistencies.
Execution flexibility: Low to moderate. Very dependent on model design. A highly flexible model introduces complexity and error-prone execution, while a simpler model enforces rigidity.
IT dependency: Moderate to high. While BPMS primarily focuses on process modeling, the resulting artifacts must be structured and stored in a database, which requires database development skills, among others.
Knowledge worker autonomy: Moderate. Workers (clerks and supervisors) can make decisions within their roles but remain bound to predefined workflows.
Efficiency in change management: Low to moderate. Increasing model flexibility inherently adds complexity. As a result, adjusting workflows—such as deciding when to order materials or schedule personnel—requires either maintaining multiple models or frequently updating existing ones. This raises the risk of inconsistencies, which can only be

4.2 ACM Modeling

Building on traditional ACM, we model RSM using an enhanced approach that explicitly incorporates elements of business architecture (such as value streams), as described by Gutierrez et al.[27]. This enhancement allows us to structure a given business case into a value stream, where each stage has defined specific goals. Actions to reach the goals can be further constrained by business rules – ensuring a flexible, yet business-compliant workflow.

4.2.1 Value Stream Definition

The *Repair service request* value stream (Fig. 3) delivers the previously explained repair service to customers, structured into three stages: *Requirements defined*, *Service team determined* and *Working order submitted*. Unlike BPMN modeling, execution is not predefined; instead, knowledge workers determine the best sequence of actions within constraints, providing flexibility. Moreover, if business rules allow it, the value stream does not need to be executed sequentially.

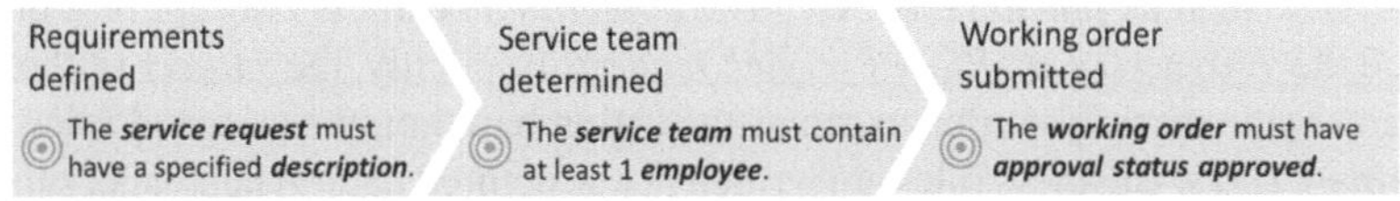

Fig. 3. Repair service request value stream, stages and examples of stage goals.

4.2.2 Business Ontology Definition

The underlying ontology defines key business concepts, properties and their relationships. Figure 4 depicts an extract of the RSM ontology, including (i) concepts (e.g., service request, customer, employee) and (ii) properties of a concept connected with dashed arrows (e.g., *Name* of *customer*). Full arrows denote a relation between two concepts (e.g., *customer places service request*).

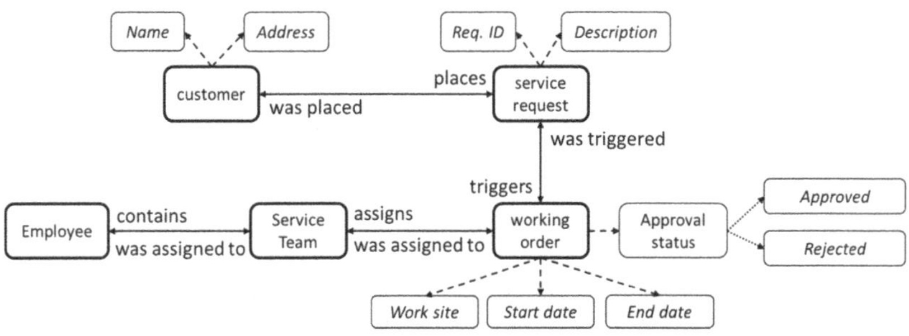

Fig. 4. Extract of the business ontology used in the ACM modeling.

The ontology itself can be shared across an entire business domain (e.g., maintenance services), ensuring consistency and interoperability, while individual applications can be customized for specific use cases (e.g., repair maintenance services) or customers to meet operational needs.

4.2.3 Goals, Actions and Business Rules

The declarative nature of the modeling encompasses defining goals for each stage, actions to achieve these goals, and establishing business rules to govern the execution of the value stream. These elements, including goals, actions, and rules, are derived from the business vocabulary entered in the business ontology.

Goals. Figure 3 also shows some of the goals defined for the stages of the *Repair service request* value stream. The business ontology concepts of *service request*, *service team* and *working order*, with their properties, are used to define the goals. Moreover, on the stage *Service team determined*, the relation *Service team contains Employee*, which is used to define a goal that at least one employee must be part of the service team.

Actions. The accomplishment of goals is done through the execution of actions, which are linked to an ontology business concept with an expression *verb* + *object*. The *verb* can include generic CRUD operations (*create*, *read*, *update*, *delete*) or domain-specific verbs such as *place*, *verify*, etc. The *object* is a business concept or a property on which the verb acts, e.g., *Places service request*. Implicitly, the *subject* of the action expression is the participant that executes the action based on the assigned roles.

Business rules. Business rules are written in a structured natural language, supported by a grammar, that assists business experts in defining rules on actions. Rules combine elements from the business ontology (previously defined by the users) with grammar elements, such as *must*, *have*, etc., to create a structured natural language expression that is simultaneously readable by business users and unequivocally interpreted by the system. These rules are enforced when users attempt to start any actions (entry level) or when finalizing them (completion level). There are different enforcement levels, from mandatory rules to simple guidelines. For example, similarly to the discussion on BPMN modeling, if preparing the order confirmation requires that the equipment is ordered first, we could define a rule such as:

"To prepare order confirmation, the working order must have a specified material."

To modify this requirement, we would simply need to rewrite the business rule. Similarly, if a new regulation mandates that every working order must include a customer's phone number for contact purposes, this would require adding a new mandatory *Phone Number* property to the ***Customer*** concept and updating the business rules to ensure that all new service requests include a phone number before submission.

The execution of actions can be restricted to different roles (e.g., *clerk* and *supervisor*), but we do not detail these constraints here for simplicity.

4.2.4 Modeling Evaluation

Modeling complexity: Moderate to high, but it differs from traditional BPMN-based process models. Instead of relying on an explicit process flow, this approach dynamically manages business rules, constraints, and dependencies.
Execution flexibility: High, enabling multiple valid paths to achieve goals but requiring careful rule management to avoid inconsistencies. AI agents, that learn from users in real time, and support knowledge workers to decide the next action.
IT dependency: Low. Defining the ontology (information model) and the business rules in natural language reduces dramatically the IT dependency. IT has to configure interfaces for data services with core business systems during the initial setup.
Knowledge worker autonomy: High, allowing flexible decision-making within defined constraints.
Efficiency in change management: Moderate to high. Rules simplify updates, but complex interdependencies require careful governance.

5 Discussion

The RSM was implemented using both *BPMN* and *ACM-based modeling*, focusing on five key metrics: Modeling Complexity, Execution Flexibility, IT Dependency, Knowledge Worker Autonomy and Efficiency in Change Management. In this section, we will evaluate both approaches and provide a comparative analysis, summarized in Table 1 below.

Modeling Complexity. Both approaches share moderate to high complexity. The *ACM modeling* introduces complexity in managing rules, but offers greater flexibility in process execution and change dependencies with natural language.

Execution Flexibility. While both approaches support flexibility, *ACM modeling* provides a more inherent and consistent flexibility due to its dynamic rule-based model. *BPMN modeling*, in contrast, requires careful modeling to achieve similar flexibility, but at the cost of introducing many variants and potential errors and inconsistencies.

IT Dependency. *BPMN modeling* relies heavily on BPMS and requires database skills, making it more IT-dependent, while ontology and rule-based modeling offers greater flexibility in IT involvement. Although *ACM modeling* still requires a robust IT infrastructure for rule management, it is less reliant on rigid IT systems compared to BPMN modeling.

Knowledge Worker Autonomy. *ACM modeling* stands out in terms of worker autonomy. It enables a higher degree of decision-making power, allowing workers to navigate the process more independently. However, this autonomy may also lead to a loss of perspective or alignment with the overall goal if not carefully managed. In such cases, AI could be leveraged to provide real-time guidance and support. *BPMN modeling*, on the other hand, limits worker autonomy due to its rigid process structure, requiring workers to follow the predefined workflow with less freedom for process adaptation.

Efficiency in Change Management: In *BPMN modeling*, efficiency is constrained by the need to preserve structural integrity, requiring a balance between control and adaptability. In contrast, *ACM modeling* offers greater efficiency for frequent or small-scale changes due to its declarative nature. However, governance mechanisms must be robust to handle complexity and ensure consistency.

Table 1. Comparison summary.

Metric	BPMN modeling	ACM modeling
Modeling complexity	Moderate to high; rigid process flow	Moderate to high; dynamic rule management
Execution flexibility	Low to moderate; dependent on model design; risk of errors	High; multiple valid paths, requires careful rule management
IT dependency	Moderate to high; requires database modeling for artifacts	Low; natural language rule definition based on ontology modeling

(continued)

Table 1. (*continued*)

Metric	BPMN modeling	ACM modeling
Knowledge worker autonomy	Moderate; tied to workflow, supervised	High; empowered to make decisions within constraints
Efficiency in change management	Low to moderate; process change requires updating flows and dependencies	Moderate to high; rule updates can be more agile, but complexity must be managed carefully

Key Insights:

- **Rigid vs flexible structure:** ACM rule-based modeling consistently offers more execution flexibility and worker autonomy compared to structured process modeling (BPMN). However, this flexibility comes with the challenge of managing business rules and avoiding inconsistencies.
- **IT dependency:** while both approaches require IT support, modeling in BPMN is more IT-dependent due to the BPMS and database design. In contrast, ACM rule-based modeling relies on business domain specific ontologies, requiring IT only for initial data interface definitions.
- **Worker autonomy:** ACM rule-based modeling clearly excels in terms of knowledge worker autonomy. It offers a system that empowers workers to make decisions based on their expertise and understanding of the business rules. Conversely, structured process modeling (BPMN) retains more control over the workflow, thereby limiting worker autonomy.

6 Conclusions

This work explores two distinct modeling methods: a structured process approach with BPMN and a declarative rule-based method with ACM. They differ in their underlying structure and execution flexibility. The BPMN modeling offers some flexibility during execution, allowing knowledge workers to incorporate optional tasks. This method is well-suited for organizations with predictable processes that have some dynamic elements.

In contrast, the ACM modeling method introduces a new paradigm for highly flexible workflows. This approach utilizes a value stream with stage goals and business rules to guide execution. ACM excels in highly dynamic business environments where real-time execution changes frequently and business application rules require frequent updates. In combination with an AI agent, flexibility can be leveraged by best next action suggestions to knowledge workers during run time execution.

The Repair Service Management case study illustrates these benefits in practice, offering concrete insights into how organizations can navigate ongoing change with greater agility and reduced dependency on rigid process structures. The choice between these two methods depends on the nature of the process and the specific needs of the organization. While BPMN modeling is ideal for organizations with processes entirely predictable or predictable with ad hoc exceptions, ACM modeling offers greater flexibility in organizations with highly dynamic workflows by enabling purpose-driven process execution.

Looking ahead, implementing ACM may require additional training for experts due to the business ontology component. Thus, future work could explore integrating Large Language Models (LLMs) to assist with process modeling. Additionally, expanding this research to include typical use cases across different industries and utilizing the Business Process Nature Assessment Framework (BPNAF) [30] could provide valuable insights for selecting the optimal modeling methods for specific organizations.

Acknowledgements. This work was partially supported by FEDER/Ministry of Science, Innovation and Universities/Junta de Andalucía/State Research Agency/CDTI with the following grants: *Data-pl* (PID2022-138486OB-I00), *SENSOLIVE* (PLSQ_00162, *TASOVA PLUS* research network (RED2022–134337-T) and AquaIA (GOPG-SE-23–0011).

References

1. Dumas, M., La Rosa, M., Mendling, J., Reijers, H.A.: Fundamentals of Business Process Management. Springer-Verlag, Heidelberg (2018)
2. Szelągowski, M.: Dynamic Business Process Management in the Knowledge Economy: Creating Value from Intellectual Capital. Springer (2019)https://doi.org/10.1007/978-3-030-17141-4
3. Szelągowski, M., Lupeikiene, A., Berniak-Woźny, J.: Drivers and evolution paths of BPMS: state-of-the-art and future research directions. Informatica. **33**, 399–420 (2022). https://doi.org/10.15388/22-INFOR487
4. Baiyere, A., Salmela, H., Tapanainen, T.: Digital transformation and the new logics of business process management. Eur. J. Inf. Syst. **29**, 238–259 (2020). https://doi.org/10.1080/0960085X.2020.1718007
5. Szelągowski, M., et al.: Adapting to the dynamic nature of business processes in the digital age. In: Di Ciccio, C., et al. (ed.) Business Process Management: Blockchain, Robotic Process Automation, Central and Eastern European, Educators and Industry Forum, pp. 220–234. Springer, Cham (2024). https://doi.org/10.1007/978-3-031-70445-1_14
6. Grisold, T., vom Brocke, J., Gross, S., Mendling, J., Röglinger, M., Stelzl, K.: Digital innovation and business process management: opportunities and challenges as perceived by practitioners. Commun. Assoc. Inf. Syst. **49**, 27 (2021). https://doi.org/10.17705/1CAIS.04927
7. Swenson, K.D., Palmer, N.: Mastering the Unpredictable: How Adaptive Case Management Will Revolutionize The way that Knowledge Workers Get Things Done. Meghan-Kiffer Press, Tampa (2010)
8. Kurz, M., Schmidt, W., Fleischmann, A., Lederer, M.: Leveraging CMMN for ACM: examining the applicability of a new OMG standard for adaptive case management. In: Proceedings of the 7th International Conference on Subject-Oriented Business Process Management. pp. 1–9. ACM, New York (2015). https://doi.org/10.1145/2723839.2723843
9. Hildebrandt, T.T., et al.: EcoKnow: engineering effective, co-created and compliant adaptive case management systems for knowledge workers. In: Proceedings of the International Conference on Software and System Processes, pp. 155–164. ACM, New York (2020). https://doi.org/10.1145/3379177.3388908

10. Gutiérrez Fernández, A.M., et al.: Applying business architecture principles with domain-specific ontology for ACM modelling: a building construction project example. In: Di Francescomarino, C., Dijkman, R., Zdun.U. (eds.) Business Process Management Workshops, pp. 388–399. Springer, Cham (2019). https://doi.org/10.1007/978-3-030-37453-2_32
11. Neubauer, T.: An empirical study about the status of business process management. Bus. Process. Manag. J. **15**, 166–183 (2009). https://doi.org/10.1108/14637150910949434
12. Alotaibi, Y., Liu, F.: Survey of business process management: challenges and solutions. Enterp Inf Syst. **11**, 1119–1153 (2017). https://doi.org/10.1080/17517575.2016.1161238
13. Diamantini, C., Genga, L., Potena, D.: Behavioral process mining for unstructured processes. J. Intell. Inf. Syst. **47**, 5–32 (2016). https://doi.org/10.1007/s10844-016-0394-7
14. Zensen, A., Kuster, J.: A comparison of flexible BPMN and CMMN in practice: a case study on component release processes. In: Proceedings - 2018 IEEE 22nd International Enterprise Distributed Object Computing Conference, EDOC 2018, pp. 105–114. Institute of Electrical and Electronics Engineers Inc. (2018). https://doi.org/10.1109/EDOC.2018.00023
15. OMG: Business Process Model and Notation (BPMN) Version 2.0.2
16. Mertens, D.M.: Research and Evaluation in Education and Psychology: Integrating Diversity with Quantitative, Qualitative, and mixed Methods, 6th edn. SAGE Publications, Thousand Oaks (2024)
17. Yin, R.K.: Case study Research: Design and Methods, 4th edn. SAGE Publications, Thousand Oaks (2009)
18. Antunes, P., Tate, M.: Business process conceptualizations and the flexibility-support tradeoff. Bus. Process. Manag. J. **28**, 856–875 (2022). https://doi.org/10.1108/BPMJ-10-2021-0677
19. Hayes, R., Kyer, B., Weber, E.: The case study cookbook, https://digital.wpi.edu/downloads/3484zh540. Accessed 03 May 2025
20. Olding, E., Rozwell, C.: Expand Your BPM Horizons by Exploring Unstructured Processes. Gartner Technical Report G00172387 (2009)
21. Mendling, J.: Metrics for Process Models. Springer, Heidelberg (2008). https://doi.org/10.1007/978-3-540-89224-3
22. Reichert, M., Weber, B.: Enabling Flexibility in Process-Aware Information Systems. Springer, Heidelberg (2012). https://doi.org/10.1007/978-3-642-30409-5
23. vom Brocke, J., Rosemann, M.: Handbook on Business Process Management 1. Springer, Heidelberg (2015). https://doi.org/10.1007/978-3-642-45100-3
24. Ribeiro, V., Barata, J., da Cunha, P.R.: Modeling inter-organizational business process governance in the age of collaborative networks. Electron. Mark. **34**, 51 (2024). https://doi.org/10.1007/s12525-024-00730-2
25. Kim, T.T.T., Weiss, E., Ruhsam, C., Czepa, C., Tran, H., Zdun, U.: Enabling flexibility of business processes using compliance rules: the case of mobiliar. In: vom Brocke, J., Mendling, J. (eds.) Business Process Management Cases. MP, pp. 91–109. Springer, Cham (2018). https://doi.org/10.1007/978-3-319-58307-5_6
26. Kim, T.T.T., Ruhsam, C., Pucher, M.J., Kobler, M., Mendling, J.: Towards a pattern recognition approach for transferring knowledge in ACM. In: 2014 IEEE 18th International Enterprise Distributed Object Computing Conference Workshops and Demonstrations, pp. 134–138 (2014). https://doi.org/10.1109/EDOCW.2014.28
27. Gutiérrez Fernández, A.M., et al.: Applying adaptive case management to enable energy efficiency performance tracking in building construction projects. In: 17th International Conference of Business Process Management (2019). https://doi.org/10.1007/978-3-030-37453-2_32
28. Ross, R.: Business Rule Concepts: Getting to the Point of Knowledge.4th ed. Business Rule Solutions, LLC, (2013)
29. van der Aalst, W.: Process Mining. Springer, Heidelberg (2016). https://doi.org/10.1007/978-3-662-49851-4

30. Szelągowski, M.: Practical assessment of the nature of business processes. Inf. Syst e-Bus. Manage **19**, 541–566 (2021). https://doi.org/10.1007/s10257-021-00501-y

The Increasing Importance of Knowledge with the Growth of BPM Maturity

Marek Szelągowski[1], Piotr Sliż[2], Marzena Grzesiak[3(✉)], Marek Moszyński[4], Karol Flisikowski[3], and Piotr Senkus[5]

[1] Systems Research Institute of the Polish Academy of Sciences, Warsaw, Poland
[2] Faculty of Management, University of Gdańsk, Sopot, Poland
[3] Faculty of Management and Economics, Gdańsk University of Technology, Gdansk, Poland
marzena.grzesiak@pg.edu.pl
[4] Faculty of Electronics, Telecommunications and Informatics, Gdańsk University of Technology, Gdansk, Poland
[5] Management Institute, Calisia University, Calisia, Poland

Abstract. The main aim of this paper is to analyse in a surveyed group of organisations the correlation between the level of BPM Maturity and the criteria characterising the nature of business processes. In the context of the transformation of organisations in the Industry 4.0/5.0 era, the key role of knowledge-intensive business processes is highlighted as an element supporting the innovation and adaptability of modern organisations. An empirical study was conducted in 33 organisations using two proprietary tools: the Business Process Nature Assessment Framework (BPNAF) and the BPM Maturity Assessment (BPM MA). The results indicate a lack of correlation between BPM Maturity and business process Unpredictability and Knowledge-intensity. At the same time, they indicate a positive correlation between BPM Maturity and the use of knowledge in increasing the efficiency and adaptability of semi-structured and unstructured business processes. This supports the call for integrating BPM and Knowledge Management (KM). The proposed integration promotes a better fit between BPM strategies and the realities of hyper-automation and digital duality. The article contributes to both the development of BPM theory and the practice of implementing process management and knowledge management in organisations with diverse business profiles.

Keywords: BPM · Knowledge Management · BPNAF · BPM Maturity · BPM MA

1 Introduction

Business Process Management (BPM) is currently undergoing an evolution in response to the dynamically changing conditions in which organisations operate in the digital economy era. This transformation is driven by the progressive development of information-communication technologies (ICT), as well as by the operationalisation of technologies characteristic not only of the Industry 4.0 concept, but increasingly also of Industry 5.0

I. van de Weerd et al. (Eds.): BPM 2025 Workshops, LNBIP 569, pp. 360–373, 2026.
https://doi.org/10.1007/978-3-032-13426-4_26

[22]. This results in a discussion about the need to reconfigure existing BPM assumptions, especially in terms of knowledge management and the organisation's ability to adapt processes dynamically. This does not imply a departure from the foundations of BPM, such as customer orientation, the pursuit of efficiency, or continuous improvement, but points to the need to adapt processes and the approach to managing them to the realities of an environment of hyper-automation, interoperability, and instantaneous information processing. According to the results of a study [23], knowledge-intensive business processes (kiBPs) play a key role in the functioning of organisations in an Industry 4.0/5.0 environment. However, they require a dynamic management approach that enables the rapid adaptation of processes to the changing technological and organisational context. The knowledge context appears to be a critical factor not only from the point of view of adapting processes to technological challenges, but also as an impetus for further BPM evolution, including towards an ambidextrous BPM approach. In this view, especially in the exploratory layer, the knowledge component is an immanent feature of the so-called explorative processes that support the innovation and adaptability of the organisation.

It is worth emphasising at this point that, despite the growing importance of kiBPs [23], there is a perceived scarcity of empirical research identifying the association between the share of kiBPs and the level of BPM Maturity. Focusing solely on technology (technology maturity) – even in the area of core processes – may be insufficient if it is not accompanied by a comprehensive implementation of BPM assumptions comprising six basic elements: strategic alignment, governance methods, IT, people, culture, and methods [15, 17]. In this context, identifying and raising the level of BPM Maturity is extremely important.

The research background outlined leads to the formulation of the main research problem: Does a higher level of BPM Maturity enhance the organisation's ability to identify knowledge-intensive and unpredictable business processes?

The main aim of this paper is to analyse changes in the assessment of knowledge-intensity in selected groups of business processes depending on the level of BPM Maturity in the studied group of organisations. The theoretical basis for the adopted research concept is the assumption that increasing process maturity promotes greater awareness of the role of knowledge in processes and more effective management of knowledge-based processes. Confirmation of this thesis could provide a rationale for updating and extending the Six Core Elements of the BPM concept with a component responsible for Knowledge Management – along the lines proposed by Szelągowski and Berniak-Woźny [21]. Such integration could contribute to the development of an integrated BPM framework, considering both efficiency and exploration requirements, which are necessary in the era of digital duality (ambidexterity).

2 Association Between BPM Nature and BPM Maturity

BPM Maturity is widely acknowledged as a critical indicator of organisational capability to manage and improve business process management [19]. Higher levels of BPM Maturity are associated with enhanced flexibility, innovation, and overall organisational performance [6, 7, 15, 19, 25, 26]. Despite the development of over 150 maturity models

[27], their practical applicability remains limited due to inconsistent design principles and a lack of benchmarking potential [16]. The existing models often fail to account for dynamic, unstructured, and knowledge-intensive processes that dominate modern organisational landscapes. Many models are descriptive, often created without empirical validation or sufficient methodological transparency. This results in a research-practice gap, where managers struggle to derive actionable insights from BPM Maturity assessments [19]. To bridge this gap, future BPM Maturity Models (BPM MM) should support iterative assessment cycles and align with BPM implementation lifecycles [10, 12]. They must also incorporate sustainability and resource optimisation elements, especially in the context of Industry 5.0 demands [5]. The integration of artificial intelligence (AI) in tailoring development paths based on maturity levels is one promising direction [13]. Ultimately, BPM Maturity should evolve from a theoretical construct into a practical management tool fostering continuous organisational development [14, 18].

2.1 Characteristics of Business Process Management Maturity Assessment Model

The BPM Maturity Assessment (BPM MA) model proposed by Szelągowski and Sliż [24] constitutes an implementation-oriented framework for evaluating BPM Maturity within organisations. The BPM MA model builds upon the five-level CMMI structure but goes beyond traditional descriptive maturity models by incorporating prescriptive recommendations tailored to each of the 5 maturity levels and the organisational context. It integrates four core assessment dimensions – organisation, people and culture, methods and IT, and knowledge management – thereby ensuring a holistic evaluation aligned with both strategic and operational realities in Industry 4.0/5.0. A main feature of the BPM MA model is its tight integration with BPM implementation methodologies, allowing the assessment to serve not only as a diagnostic tool but also as a strategic roadmap for increasing BPM capabilities. The model adapts to the requirements of Industry 4.0 and 5.0, including automation, artificial intelligence, and sustainability, and explicitly supports dynamic and knowledge-intensive business processes often neglected by existing models. It employs both mandatory and optional criteria, supplemented with over 180 practical recommendations that are adjustable, scalable, and actionable. By enabling repeatable, context-sensitive assessments and guiding organisations along multi-variant developmental paths, BPM MA addresses critical gaps in existing models and aligns process maturity with real-world managerial decision-making and continuous improvement [24].

2.2 Characteristics of Business Process Nature Assessment Framework

The concept of "nature of a thing/phenomenon" is commonly understood as "The basic or inherent features, character, or qualities of something" [14]. The term "nature of business processes" refers to unchanging characteristics, inherent to a given business process, i.e., those that must be considered in absolutely every instance of that process, regardless of the number of variants or the context of occurrence. Not all dimensions of business processes are inherent characteristics [30]. Most of them depend on the context of implementation and execution of the business process [29, 30]. Characteristics that are not determined by the context of process execution, and whose change requires a change in the business model, or the foundations of the organisation's strategy include [21]:

- unpredictability - associated with factors such as repetitiveness, variability or uncertainty,
- knowledge intensity - associated with factors such as creativity or innovation.

BPM implementation requires the selection of methodology and IT tools that are harmonized with the nature of business processes. To operationalise the potential of this harmonisation, a Business Process Nature Assessment (BPNA) application was designed and developed based on the Business Process Nature Assessment Framework [2, 20]. The application assesses the nature of business processes, taking as the main evaluation criteria their unpredictability and the intensity of knowledge use necessary to achieve the objective of the processes [8]. This tool is dedicated to both experts and non-experts in business process management. The application is currently running on the servers of the Gdansk University of Technology dedicated to cooperation with the environment.

The presentation of the results of the study makes it possible to objectively recommend the choice of implementation methodology and IT tools supporting BPM, or human resources management strategy in accordance with the actual nature of business processes in each organisation.

For the purposes of operating the application, two roles have been distinguished:

- Investigator – manages the Investigation Start and Investigations In Progress sections, located on the start page of the application.
- Evaluator – completes the evaluation questionnaire generated by the Investigator, proposes recommendations, generates a report and closes the questionnaire.

In an organisation carrying out an assessment of the nature of business processes, it is possible for these roles to intermingle, i.e. the investigator can also be an assessor or one of the assessors.

Other roles in the application, not directly involved in the research process, are:

- Administrator – responsible for maintaining the application in the cloud and its security, updating the version of the application, instructions and examples in all language versions, having access to the file system representing the questionnaire database, making a security copy, and
- Analyst – having access – in read mode – to all questionnaires and evaluator-generated reports, with the ability to select questionnaires based on criteria such as company ID, evaluator ID, industry, company size, and the authority to export data to open CSV or xml spreadsheet formats for further analysis.

The application includes:

1. User manual,
2. Examples of surveys, some to be completed by the user,
3. A questionnaire generator for starting a survey,
4. A module for managing existing surveys, including comparing survey results and creating final reports.

Metrics identifying the organisation are required to start the survey. The list of industries in BPNAF version 1.76 is based on a list in line with the classification recommended by the American Quality and Productivity Center [1].

An important, and from a practical point of view, the most important, element of the survey is the completion by the Evaluator(s) of recommendations for the implementation or management of business processes. Recommendations can be introduced separately at two levels of detail – general for BPM in the organisation and independently for individual business processes. In both scopes, recommendations may relate to elements of human resource management, use of IT systems and knowledge management.

The survey process begins with the appointment of an Investigator, followed by assessment teams and those responsible for inputting their agreed assessments and recommendations into the application (role: Assessors). Each team then makes assessments of the nature of the business processes and prepares proposed recommendations. This data is entered into the application by the person in the role of Evaluator. In the final step of the study, the Investigator, as part of the sessions in which the evaluation teams participate, reconciles the evaluation results. Ultimately, a single questionnaire should be prepared for the organisation containing the agreed assessments and the recommendations to be implemented.

In the remainder of this article, research carried out using the BPNAF v. 1.76 application is used.

3 Study Design

3.1 Research Data

The research presented in this article was carried out as part of their own projects by researchers from three academic centres in Poland. Two parallel studies were carried out as part of the project. The first concerned the nature of business processes and was conducted using the BPNA tool [8, 20]. While the second study was oriented towards assessing the level of BPM Maturity, Project Management Maturity (PM Maturity) and Readiness for Green BPM. The BPM MA method was used to assess BPM Maturity [24].

3.2 Research Process

The BPM MA study was conducted in Q1 2025, while the BPNA was conducted in Q1 and early Q2 2025. The empirical study was preceded by a literature review and based on the identification of the current state of knowledge, the research problem and objectives were outlined. Following the BPNA and BPM MA studies, the results obtained were integrated and qualitatively assessed and then analysed using statistical methods. It should be emphasised that both studies were conducted almost in parallel, which means that respondents completed separate questionnaires, and the results obtained from BPM MA and BPNA were merged based on a unique respondent ID.

3.3 Research Sample

The study was carried out using a survey-based opinion poll, with a non-random sample of respondents. Selection by convenience was used. The 2025 survey was conducted in parallel with a sample of MBA participants.

The research process consisted of two separate surveys of the organisation's business processes, carried out in close succession. In the first study, a process map had to be prepared and, with BPNAF, the nature of the business processes had to be assessed using a dedicated BPNA application. In the second study, BPM Maturity had to be assessed using the BPM MA approach. After a qualitative analysis of the collected empirical material, 33 organisations were qualified for the study. The structure of the surveyed entities in terms of the size of the organisation, assessed on the basis of the declared number of employees, was as follows: large organisations (23), medium organisations (7), small organisations 2 and microorganisations (1). Organisations were also divided by the number of years of operation in the market: up to 5 years (1), 11 to 20 years (6), 6 to 10 years (1), and more than 20 years (25). The distribution of answers to the question on the dominant business profile was as follows: trade (3), manufacturing (13), and services (17). The vast majority of respondents in the survey were directors (14) and managers (11). The remaining group consisted of team leaders (5), specialists/experts (2), and a member of the organisation's board of directors (1).

The following results were obtained in the context of BMP Maturity level, out of 33 units: level 1 (11), level 2 (3), level 3 (12), level 4 (3), and level 5 (4). This means that the survey yielded a diverse group of organisations in terms of BPM Maturity.

4 Results

The aim of the conducted research process was to examine the correlation between two constructs: "business process" and "BPM Maturity," characterised by three variables:

a) BPM Maturity level – the assessment of BPM Maturity expressed numerically from *1* to *5* according to the BPM MA method (*1* – the lowest level, *5* – the highest level) [24].
b) Unpredictability level – the level of unpredictability of the analysed group of processes, expressed in the study on a numerical scale from *1* – structured, fully predictable processes; *2* – structured with ad hoc exceptions; *3* – unstructured with pre-defined fragments; *4* – unstructured, unpredictable processes [23].
c) Knowledge-intensity (ki) – the intensity of knowledge required to carry out the business process [2].

The collected data allowed for the assessment of two correlations:

1. Association between the BPM Maturity level and Unpredictability level.

Both the analysis of arithmetic means and medians, as well as statistical tests (including variance analysis and correlation tests), did not confirm the existence of strong or systematic relationships between these two variables.

2. Association between BPM Maturity level and Knowledge-intensity

To examine whether the level of BPM Maturity has a statistically significant effect on the level of intensity of knowledge use necessary to implement business processes, a one-way Analysis of Variance (ANOVA) was conducted. This method was chosen due to its suitability for comparing the means of a continuous dependent variable (Knowledge-intensity) across multiple independent categorical groups (BPM Maturity levels, ranging from *1* to *5*). The analysis returned a non-significant result ($F = 0.63$, $p = 0.66$), indicating that there are no statistically significant differences in the average Knowledge-intensity among the different levels of BPM Maturity. This outcome suggests that the degree of BPM Maturity within an organisation does not have a measurable or consistent effect on how knowledge-intensive its processes are. In other words, processes conducted in organisations with high BPM Maturity are not necessarily more (or less) knowledge-intensive than those in organisations with lower maturity levels. The lack of a significant relationship may imply that Knowledge-intensity is determined more by the intrinsic characteristics of specific business processes (e.g., domain complexity, regulatory requirements, or industry type) rather than by the overall maturity of BPM practices. Alternatively, it is possible that the maturity of BPM practices impacts other dimensions of process performance or structure, but not the knowledge demands associated with execution. These findings contribute to the ongoing discussion on the implications of BPM Maturity, suggesting that improvements in maturity may not automatically lead to changes in the cognitive or informational demands placed on process participants. This outcome suggests that BPM Maturity does not have a measurable or consistent effect on how knowledge-intensive organisational processes are. Rather, knowledge intensity may be shaped more by intrinsic process characteristics or industry context than by process maturity itself.

Finally, in the last stage of the analysis, to deepen the understanding of the relationships under investigation, a multi-factorial ANOVA with interaction effects was conducted. This model incorporated several explanatory variables simultaneously: the average level of Knowledge-intensity (ki), the BPM Maturity Level, the number of processes analysed within each case, and a categorical measure of company size. This statistical approach allowed for the examination not only of the main effects of individual variables – Knowledge-intensity (ki value AVE), BPM Maturity Level, Number of Processes, and Company Size – but also of the interaction effect between Knowledge-intensity and BPM Maturity Level.

The inclusion of the interaction term (ki value AVE * BPM M Level) enabled the identification of whether the effect of Knowledge-intensity on the level of process unpredictability varies depending on the degree of BPM Maturity. The analysis revealed that this interaction was statistically significant, indicating that the relationship between Knowledge-intensity and process unpredictability is not uniform across different BPM Maturity levels.

This finding suggests that the impact of Knowledge-intensity on how structured or unstructured a process is may be contingent upon the organisation's BPM Maturity. In more mature BPM environments, knowledge-intensive processes may be managed differently – potentially with greater structure or predictability – than in less mature contexts. This insight highlights the importance of considering contextual organisational factors, such as BPM Maturity, when analysing how knowledge demands influence process characteristics.

Table 1. The results of the Multi-Factor ANOVA

Source of variability	df	SS	MS	F	p-value
ki value	1	0.0023	0.0023	0.028	0.86810
BPM Maturity Level	1	0.0357	0.0357	0.442	0.51241
Number of processes	1	0.1971	0.1971	2.441	0.13080
Company size	1	0.9876	0.9876	12.228	0.00178**
ki value*BPM Maturity Level	1	0.7048	0.7048	8.727	0.00674**
Residuals	25	2.0191	0.0808		

Presented in Table 1 the results of the multifactorial ANOVA indicate that, when considered independently, the variables Knowledge-intensity ($F(1,25) = 0.028$, $p = 0.86810$), BPM Maturity Level ($F(1,25) = 0.442$, $p = 0.51241$), and Number of Processes ($F(1,25) = 2.441$, $p = 0.13080$) do not exhibit statistically significant effects on the dependent variable, Unpredictability Level. The corresponding p-values exceed the conventional $\alpha = 0.05$ threshold, suggesting a lack of sufficient evidence to reject the null hypothesis of equal means across the respective groups.

In contrast, the variable Company Size yields a highly significant effect ($F(1,25) = 12.228$, $p = 0.00178$), indicating that organisational size contributes meaningfully to the variance in Unpredictability Level. This suggests that company size is a critical determinant in explaining differences in process unpredictability, potentially due to structural or operational factors associated with scale.

Moreover, the interaction effect between Knowledge-intensity and BPM Maturity Level is also statistically significant ($F(1,25) = 8.727$, $p = 0.00674$), providing strong evidence of a moderation effect. This result implies that the effect of Knowledge-intensity on Unpredictability Level is not uniform across levels of BPM Maturity. Rather, the influence of knowledge demands on process unpredictability is conditional upon the degree of BPM Maturity, with interaction-driven variation accounting for a significant proportion of the explained variance.

The significance of this interaction term underscores the need to model non-additive effects when analysing organisational process behaviour. Ignoring such interactions would obscure meaningful relationships, as neither Knowledge-intensity nor BPM Maturity Level individually demonstrated a significant main effect. The findings support the hypothesis that BPM Maturity alters the functional relationship between Knowledge-intensity and process unpredictability, potentially through mechanisms such as improved process governance, documentation, or automation capabilities in more mature organisations.

The residual variance (MS = 0.0808) suggests a moderate level of unexplained variability, which could be attributed to factors not included in the current model. Nevertheless, the significant interaction and the effect of company size provide important explanatory power for understanding process unpredictability in organisational contexts.

In summary, while the variables Knowledge-intensity, BPM Maturity Level, and Number of Processes do not exhibit statistically significant individual effects on the Unpredictability Level, the analysis identifies two factors that do contribute meaningfully to the explained variance:

- First, the variable Company Size demonstrates a strong and statistically significant main effect ($F = 12.228$, $p = 0.00178$), indicating that organisational scale has a substantial impact on the predictability of business processes.
- Second, the interaction between Knowledge-intensity and BPM Maturity Level is also statistically significant ($F = 8.727$, $p = 0.00674$), revealing that the effect of knowledge demands on process unpredictability is moderated by the maturity of BPM practices.

Thus, although Knowledge-intensity and BPM Maturity Level alone are not significant predictors, Company Size emerges as a key determinant of process unpredictability, and their combined interaction exerts a significant and non-negligible influence on the same outcome. These findings highlight the importance of modelling interaction effects and organisational context when analysing complex process characteristics.

5 Discussion

The BPM Maturity level does not exhibit a general correlation in the studied group of organisations with either the Unpredictability level or Knowledge-intensity. This confirms that the nature of business processes carried out by an organisation does not depend on BPM Maturity, and consequently, it is not influenced by factors that significantly affect maturity, such as the implementation of corporate governance, the use of ICT, knowledge management practices, and so forth.

The in-depth analysis conducted showed that the impact of Knowledge-intensity on process unpredictability may vary depending on the level of BPM Maturity. The primary differentiating factor is the size of the organisation. This may be because larger organisations have better control systems or more complex business processes due to longer and more intricate value chains or logistics chains, which affect their unpredictability.

An ANOVA approach was used to determine the direction of this relationship. The model explains 39% of the variance in the Unpredictability level. Individually, Knowledge-intensity and BPM Maturity level have a positive effect on unpredictability. However, the interaction between Knowledge-intensity and BPM Maturity level is negative and statistically significant, indicating that the effect of one variable decreases at higher levels of the other.

In larger organisations, the level of unpredictability is lower. This may result from more detailed analyses of business processes, where, to enable automation, such as robotic process automation (RPA), tasks requiring the consideration of unpredictability are isolated and possibly consolidated within selected business processes.

The decision tree model (Fig. 1) was constructed to identify the most significant predictors of the "Unpredictability level AVE" variable in a nonparametric manner, utilising both numerical and label-encoded categorical features from the dataset. This approach enhances the interpretability of the predictive modelling process and can inform subsequent research or practical interventions aimed at managing unpredictability within the system under investigation. The decision tree is a widely used supervised machine learning technique applicable to both classification and regression problems. This non-parametric method recursively partitions the dataset into subsets by selecting features and corresponding threshold values that maximise the homogeneity of the target variable within each subgroup [4]. The resulting model is a tree-like structure, where internal nodes represent decision rules based on input variables, branches correspond to the outcomes of these rules, and leaf nodes provide the final predictions. For regression tasks, such as in the present study, the decision tree algorithm selects splits that minimise the variance of the target variable within each node, thereby improving predictive accuracy [9]. One of the main advantages of decision trees is their interpretability; the model transparently reveals which variables are most influential and how they interact to affect the outcome.

All categorical variables were transformed into numeric representations using label encoding, ensuring that the model could leverage the full spectrum of available information. The resulting tree structure provides a hierarchical visualisation of how different variables contribute to the prediction of unpredictability. The root node of the tree represents the feature with the highest explanatory power, indicating that this variable accounts for the largest reduction in variance of the target variable. Subsequent branches illustrate further splits based on additional features, each contributing incrementally to the model's predictive accuracy. The leaves of the tree correspond to the predicted average values of "Unpredictability level AVE" for observations that satisfy the conditions along the path from the root.

Analysis of the tree reveals which features are most influential in determining unpredictability. Variables that appear near the top of the tree are interpreted as having the strongest association with the target variable. The structure of the tree also highlights potential interactions between predictors, as certain combinations of feature values lead to distinct outcomes in unpredictability levels. It is important to note that the use of label encoding for categorical variables introduces an artificial ordinal relationship among categories, which may not always reflect the true nature of the data. Nevertheless, the decision tree provides valuable insights into the relative importance of both numerical and categorical predictors and offers an interpretable framework for understanding the factors driving unpredictability in the studied context..

In summary, the "Company size code" is the most influential predictor of unpredictability. For smaller companies ("Company size code" $\leq$ 1.5), "ki value AVE" and "Number of processes" further differentiate the unpredictability level. For larger companies ("Company size code" > 1.5), "Age of the organisation" is the key factor. The lowest unpredictability is observed for small companies with low "ki value AVE." The highest unpredictability is observed for large, young organisations. This tree provides a clear, interpretable structure showing how company size, knowledge intensity, number of processes, and organisational age interact to determine unpredictability.

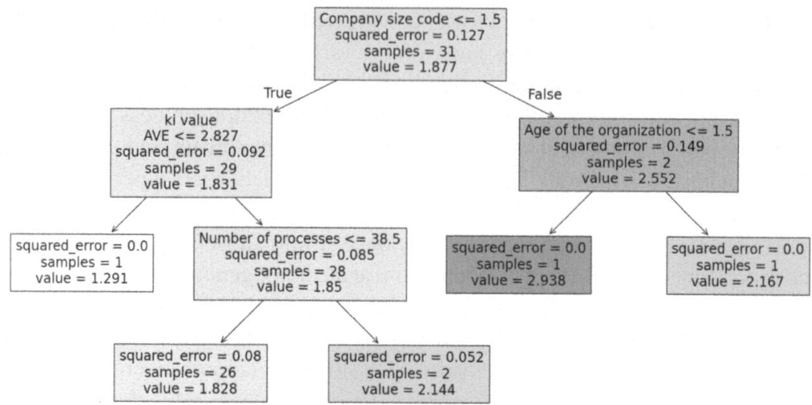

Fig. 1. Decision tree for the median of unpredictability level.

The decision tree version presented in Fig. 1. Was selected as optimal according to the 1-SE rule (which aims to minimise overfitting), as it corresponds to the lowest error. Adding further splits beyond this optimal tree structure increases the error.

6 Conclusion

The study showed that in the surveyed group of organisations, the BPM Maturity level does not correlate with the Unpredictability level and Knowledge-intensity scores. This means that the intuitive expectation that more mature organisations (i.e. with a higher BPM Maturity level) will have lower business process unpredictability due to, among other things, better identified, designed, implemented, and monitored business processes is not true. Similarly, the intuitive expectation that more mature organisations will be characterised by higher knowledge-intensity of the business processes implemented is not true. The absence of these correlations shows that the mere level of an organisation's BPM Maturity does not necessarily translate directly into a reduction in unpredictability or the dependence of the achievement of business process goals on the use of knowledge. This confirms that the nature of business processes, characterised by both unpredictability and knowledge-intensity, results from other factors, e.g. industry characteristics, process complexity, variability of the market environment, or degree of innovation.

At the same time, the results indicate that a change in BPM Maturity affects the functional relationship between Knowledge-intensity and Unpredictability of business processes. This implies, in more mature organisations, a better use of knowledge to manage and continuously improve the efficiency of semi-structured and unstructured processes, due to better management, faster knowledge exchange, and better adaptation of the hyper-automation technologies used to the nature of the processes performed.

This paper contributes to BPM research by demonstrating that BPM Maturity does not directly correlate with knowledge intensity or unpredictability of processes, but this finding highlights the complexity of business process dynamics.

6.1 Theoretical Implications

The theoretical implication of the lack of correlation between BPM Maturity and Unpredictability level and Knowledge-intensity is to demonstrate the independence of the nature of an organisation's business processes from the maturity of the realising organisation. Consequently, this lack of correlation reveals important limitations of approaches based solely on current BPM MM, pointing to the need for a more integrated approach in managing uncertainty and variability and knowledge in business processes. This indicates the need, from a practical point of view, to include in BPM MM and BPM Maturity assessment methods both criteria and, above all, recommendations relating to the relevance to the organisation of knowledge management. This is particularly relevant in the era of hyper-automation technologies in Industry 4.0, enabling real-time knowledge management.

6.2 Managerial Implications

From the perspective of management practice, the outcome of the study provides an important warning for organisations that are investing in the development of BPM Maturity with the hope of greater predictability of business processes. The implementation of BPM tools and structures alone does not guarantee a reduction in operational risks associated with unpredictability. It is necessary to assess the nature of business processes in terms of precise unpredictability or knowledge-intensity, in order to select management methods and tools according to the actual nature of the processes. At the same time, the correlation between Knowledge-intensity and Unpredictability of business processes, together with the rise of BPM Maturity, points to Knowledge Management as an important factor for increasing the efficiency and openness to breakthrough innovations of semi-structured and unstructured business processes. In the Industry 4.0/5.0 era, organisations need to ensure that the right infrastructure is in place to enable the capture and collection (e.g. IoT sensors and ERP or CRM systems) and evaluation and use of knowledge (e.g. information repositories or KM Systems). Raising BPM Maturity in line with the current BPM MM does not automatically ensure a high level of governance in this area.

6.3 Limitations and Future Research

The main limitation of the research presented in this paper concerns the relatively small number of organizations included in the analysis, as well as the non-random nature of the sample selection, which was based on a convenience sampling technique. As a result, the findings apply solely to the subset of organizations that participated in both the BPNAF and BPM MA assessments. Nevertheless, the results provide a strong rationale for further extending this research, both by increasing the sample size and by focusing more specifically on organizations operating within a single business profile. This would allow for more precise conclusions, which should ideally be complemented by qualitative research to deepen the interpretation. The authors also intend to expand the study by introducing an additional component -Project Maturity Assessment-based on the same methodology as BPM Maturity Assessment, in order to explore the relationships within the triad of BPM MA, PM MA, and Business Process Nature Assessment.

Future research should extend this analysis by combining BPM MA and BPNAF within mixed-method designs, involving larger and more diverse samples of respondents across hierarchical levels and functional areas, in order to capture the multifaceted nature of process knowledge-intensity and unpredictability within organisations.

References

1. APQC's Resource Library. https://www.apqc.org/resource-library. Accessed 20 Feb 2024
2. Berniak-Woźny, J., Szelągowski, M.: Towards the assessment of business process knowledge intensity – a systematic literature review. Bus. Process. Manag. J. **28**(1), 40–61 (2022). https://doi.org/10.1108/BPMJ-01-2021-0012
3. Berniak-Woźny, J., Szelągowski, M.: Business processes nature assessment matrix - a novel approach to the assessment of business process dynamism and knowledge intensity. Aslib J. Inf. Manag. **74**(2), 244–264 (2022). https://doi.org/10.1108/AJIM-04-2021-0110
4. Breiman, L., Friedman, J.H., Olshen, R.A., Stone, C.J.: Classification and Regression Trees. Wadsworth, Belmont, CA (1984). https://doi.org/10.1201/9781315139470
5. Breque, M., De Nul, L., Petridis, A.: Industry 5.0. Towards a sustainable, human-centric and resilient European industry. Eur. Comm. (2021). https://doi.org/10.2777/308407
6. Dijkman, R., Lammers, S.V., de Jong, A.: Properties that influence business process management maturity and its effect on organizational performance. Inf. Syst. Front. **18**, 717–734 (2016). https://doi.org/10.1007/s10796-015-9554-5
7. Froger, M., Benaben, F., Truptil, S., Boissel-Dallier, N.: A non-linear business process management maturity framework to apprehend future challenges. Int. J. Inf. Manage. **49**, 290–300 (2019). https://doi.org/10.1016/j.ijinfomgt.2019.05.013
8. Grzesiak, M., Szelągowski, M., Berniak, J., Moszyński, M.: Enhancing business process management through nature assessment: development and deployment of the business process nature assessment tool. In: Di Ciccio, C., et al. Business Process Management: Blockchain, Robotic Process Automation, Central and Eastern European, Educators and Industry Forum. BPM 2024. Lecture Notes in Business Information Processing, vol. 527, pp. 235–249. Springer, Cham (2024). https://doi.org/10.1007/978-3-031-70445-1_15
9. Hastie, T., Tibshirani, R., Friedman, J.: The Elements of Statistical Learning: Data Mining, Inference, and Prediction (2nd ed.). Springer, New York (2009). https://doi.org/10.1007/978-0-387-84858-7
10. Jochem, R., Geers, D., Heinze, P.: Maturity measurement of knowledge-intensive business processes. TQM J. **23**(4), 377–387 (2011). https://doi.org/10.1108/17542731111139464
11. Kerpedzhiev, G., Lehnert, M., Röglinger, M.: The future of business process management in the future of work. AIS eLibrary Research Papers, p. 81 (2016), http://aisel.aisnet.org/ecis2016_rp/81
12. Krivograd, N., Fettke, P., Loos, P.: Development of an intelligent maturity model-tool for business process management. In: 2014 47th Hawaii International Conference on System Sciences, IEEE, pp. 3878–3887 (2014). https://doi.org/10.1109/HICSS.2014.481
13. Maddikunta, P.K., et al.: Industry 5.0: a survey on enabling technologies and potential applications. J. Ind. Inf. Integr. **26**, 100257 (2022). https://doi.org/10.1016/j.jii.2021.100257
14. Oxford Dictionary (n.d.). Nature. https://www.lexico.com/definition/nature.Accessed 18 Sept 2020
15. Paulk, M., Curtis, B., Chrissis, M., Weber, C.: Capability maturity model, version 1.1. IEEE Softw. **10**(4), 18–27 (1993). https://doi.org/10.1109/52.219617

16. Pinto, J., dos Santos, V.: Assessing the relationship between BPM maturity and the success of organisations. In: Silhavy, R., (ed.), Applied Informatics and Cybernetics in Intelligent Systems. Proceedings of the 9th Computer Science On-line Conference 2020, vol. 3, pp. 108–126. Springer, Cham (2020). https://doi.org/10.1007/978-3-030-51974-2_10
17. Pöppelbuß, J., Röglinger, M.: What makes a useful maturity model? A framework of general design principles for maturity models and its demonstration in business process management. In: Tuunainen, V.K., Rossi, M., Nandhakumar, J., (eds.), Proceedings of the 19th European Conference on Information Systems (ECIS 2011). Association for Information Systems (AIS) (2011)
18. Rosemann, M., vom Brocke, J.: The six core elements of business process management. In: vom Brocke, J., Rosemann, M., (eds), Handbook on Business Process Management 1, International Handbooks on Information Systems, 2nd Edn., pp. 105–122. Springer, Berlin (2015). https://doi.org/10.1007/978-3-642-45100-3_5
19. Sliż, P.: Organizacja procesowo-projektowa. Istota, modelowanie, pomiar dojrzałości. Difin (2021)
20. Sliż, P., Szelągowski, M.: Kierunki badań nad oceną dojrzałości zarządzania procesami biznesowymi w Przemyśle 4.0/5.0. E-mentor, **5**(102), 5–14 (2023). https://doi.org/10.15219/em102.1633
21. Szelągowski, M.: Practical assessment of the nature of business processes. Inf. Syst e-Bus. Manage **19**(2), 541–566 (2021). https://doi.org/10.1007/s10257-021-00501-y
22. Szelągowski, M., Berniak-Woźny, J.: BPM challenges, limitations and future development directions – a systematic literature review. Bus. Process. Manag. J. **30**(2), 505–557 (2024). https://doi.org/10.1108/BPMJ-06-2023-0419
23. Szelągowski, M., Berniak-Woźny, J., Lupeikiene, A.: The future development of ERP: towards process ERP systems? In Marrella, A., et al. (eds.) Business Process Management: Blockchain, Robotic Process Automation, and Central and Eastern Europe Forum. BPM 2022. Lecture Notes in Business Information Processing, vol. 459, pp. 326–341. Springer, Cham (2022). https://doi.org/10.1007/978-3-031-16168-1_21
24. Szelągowski, M., et al.: Exploring the diversity of business process nature in organizations Industry 4.0/ 5.0. Future Bus. J. **10**, 118 (2024). https://doi.org/10.1186/s43093-024-00395-5
25. Szelągowski, M., Sliż, P.: Toward BPM maturity assessment integrated with BPM implementation and use. Bus. Process Manage. J. **31**(6), 2285–2338 (2025). https://doi.org/10.1108/BPMJ-04-2024-0249
26. Tarhan, A., Turetken, O., Reijers, H.A.: Business process maturity models: a systematic literature review. Inf. Softw. Technol. **75**, 122–134 (2016). https://doi.org/10.1016/j.infsof.2016.01.010
27. Van Looy, A., De Backer, M., Poels, G.: Which maturity is being measured? A classification of business process maturity models. In: van Dongen, B.F., Reijers, H.A., (eds.), 5th SIKS/BENAIS Conference on Enterprise Information Systems (EIS 2010), pp. 7–16 (2010). https://www.win.tue.nl/eis2010/eis2010_proceedings.pdfngs.pdf (tue.nl)
28. Van Looy, A., Poels, G., Snoeck, M.: Evaluating business process maturity models. J. Assoc. Inf. Syst. **18**(6), 461–486 (2017). https://doi.org/10.17705/1jais.00460
29. vom Brocke, J., Mendling, J.: Frameworks for business process management: a taxonomy for business process management cases. In vom Brocke, J., Mendling, J., (eds.), Business Process Management Cases, Management for Professionals (2018). https://doi.org/10.1007/978-3-319-58307-5_1
30. vom Brocke, J., Baier, M., Schmiedel, T., Stelzl, K., Röglinger, M., Wehking, C.: Context-aware business process management. Bus. Inf. Syst. Eng. **63**, 533–550 (2021). https://doi.org/10.1007/s12599-021-00685-0

Connecting the Digital Dots - Can Customer Journeys Be Analyzed Purely from Event Logs?

Kristoffer Alves Brekke[1], Ragnhild Halvorsrud[2(✉)], Felix Mannhardt[3], Lasse Brurok[4], and Otas Meironas[2]

[1] University of Oslo, Oslo, Norway
[2] SINTEF Digital, Oslo, Norway
ragnhild.halvorsrud@sintef.no
[3] Eindhoven University of Technology, Eindhoven, The Netherlands
[4] Bookis AS, Oslo, Norway

Abstract. Customer journeys increasingly unfold through digital channels. This offers new opportunities for service providers to extract insights from customers' digital traces. However, as customers move across organizational boundaries and modes of interaction, it is difficult to capture the complete end-to-end journey with process mining or similar methods. This experience report investigates how accurately service providers can reconstruct actual customer journeys using only internal system data. We apply a dual-perspective approach that combines an empirical investigation involving customers with a reconstruction of the same journeys based on digital traces from internal service systems. Our findings highlighted key challenges in reconstructing customer journeys. While planned or expected touchpoints were well covered (89% in our case), ad-hoc or deviating touchpoints proved more challenging to capture (33%). Crucially, quality issues tended to arise not within an organization, but in the transitions between them—precisely where visibility is most needed. Effective reconstruction of customer journeys requires a systematic approach to bridge silos and enable a unified view, especially when service delivery is partly outsourced.

Keywords: Customer Journey · Process Mining · Empirical Study · Coverage

1 Introduction

The recent wave of digital transformation has led to customers leaving behind more digital traces than ever before in the information systems of service providers. Every digital interaction generates system-level data, creating new possibilities for analyzing service use and user behavior. Service ecosystems typically involve a main provider and multiple supply-chain partners, each operating their own IT infrastructure. Together, these actors form a Service Delivery

I. van de Weerd et al. (Eds.): BPM 2025 Workshops, LNBIP 569, pp. 374–386, 2026.
https://doi.org/10.1007/978-3-032-13426-4_27

Network (SDN) [11]. This fragmentation of the service system complicates coordination and may result in poor customer experience. Although SDNs, in principle, may leverage digital traces to improve cross-organizational insight, doing so requires substantial coordination and resources. As a result, few attempts are made to track user experiences over time. This lack of holistic, time-aware analysis creates a digital blind spot in understanding how services are encountered by end users. The concept of *customer journeys* is central to this effort, offering an outside-in view of service delivery from the end user's perspective [16]. A customer journey consists of a series of touchpoints—moments when users interact with the SDN, either digitally or physically. While many of these touchpoints leave digital traces, others do not: they may be unlogged, occur offline, or involve actors outside the formal SDN. As a result, significant parts of the journey may remain invisible to the service provider.

In this study, we investigate to what extent service providers can reconstruct actual end-to-end customer journeys based solely on internal system data. We combine two complementary perspectives: an empirical investigation involving real customers, and a retrospective reconstruction of the same journeys based on the digital footprints they leave within the SDN. This dual-perspective design allows us to evaluate how accurately the reconstructed journeys reflect the actual sequence of events experienced by customers. It also provides a basis for identifying potential gaps, overlaps, and blind spots, and contributes to advancing the knowledge needed to automate the discovery and analysis of real-world customer journeys based solely on system-level data. In summary, this paper makes two contributions. First, using a *case study of an online bookstore*, it examines how organizations can structure their systems to enable automated reconstruction of customer journeys from backend data. Second, it presents *empirical findings* on the extent to which such journeys can be extracted from real-world system logs.

2 Background

Customer journey methodology offers a range of approaches to investigate end users' encounters with service offerings. Despite the growth of the field, it remains fragmented and lacks standardized methods and established standards [6,7,16]. Nevertheless, a central feature is the visual representation of journeys as customer journey *maps*—mostly portraying customer touchpoints chronologically along a time axis. The second dimension varies widely and may include elements such as emotions, communication channels, or user strategies. A particular language that emerged is the Customer Journey Modeling Language (CJML), which we adopt in this paper for the empirical investigation. CJML is a domain-specific modeling language developed to represent service processes from the perspective of the end-user[1]. Customer Journey Analysis (CJA) employs CJML as its modeling language to empirically investigate individual service experiences over time and across multiple channels [7]. The process begins with an analysis of the SDN to establish the planned journey(s), typically through methods such as

[1] https://www.cjml.no/.

process mapping, mystery shopping, and service walk-throughs. Customers are then recruited early in their journeys and participate in an initial interview to capture motivations and expectations. They are instructed to keep a *structured diary*, documenting all encounters with the service system. Once the journey is completed, a *follow-up interview* is conducted to review the diary entries and reflect on the actual experience. Touchpoints are chronologically ordered and annotated with relevant attributes, such as instrumental properties and customer feedback. Deviations from the planned journey are categorized as ad hoc touchpoints (unexpected additions), irregularities in sequence or timing, failing touchpoints (unwanted outcomes), and missing touchpoints.

In contrast to CJA, process mining reverse engineers the as-is process behavior from events sourced from information systems [1]. Initially, it was targeted to business processes of an organization, but process mining has seen widespread adoption among many domains including the analysis of customer journeys [2,8,9,12,13]. Journeys have been analyzed, e.g., through web log analysis [12] and also information such as customer emotions or their characteristics have been subject to analysis with process mining methods [3,4]. Zilker et al. [17] noted that customer-centered analysis is still challenging in the case of end-to-end journeys spanning several systems and when including user experience. Case studies on customer journey analysis have been previously published [8,9]. In fact, our previous work [9], reported on an analysis of event data from the same case provider; however, the empirical evaluation involving the actual customers, as done in this paper, is lacking.

There is also empirical work in the field of process mining that investigates the organizational use of process mining [10,14]. Major research directions are the impact of process mining and its use by analysts [10]. Many case studies, also in the domain of customer service, have been reported [5]. Our case study focuses on the data collection phase, which was reported to have a low level of thoroughness in related works [5]. Through the dual-perspective design, we aim to shed light on data accessibility in the customer journey domain. Data availability has previously been identified as a challenge [18]. However, we are not aware of existing work that investigates this in the domain of customer journeys in a real case and combines process mining and CJA methodology.

3 Case

Bookis[2] is a Norwegian consumer-to-consumer (C2C) marketplace for buying and selling used books via web and mobile platforms. The service integrates payments and logistics, aiming to make literature more accessible while promoting reuse. Given its platform model, Bookis has a strong focus on customer experience and is actively working to improve visibility across partner systems. This study was conducted as part of the Smart Journey Mining research project,

[2] https://bookis.com/.

in which Bookis participated as an industry partner. As part of the collaboration, Bookis provided customer journey data and supported the mapping of planned touchpoints. Further details about the platform's business model and functionality are available in previous work [9].

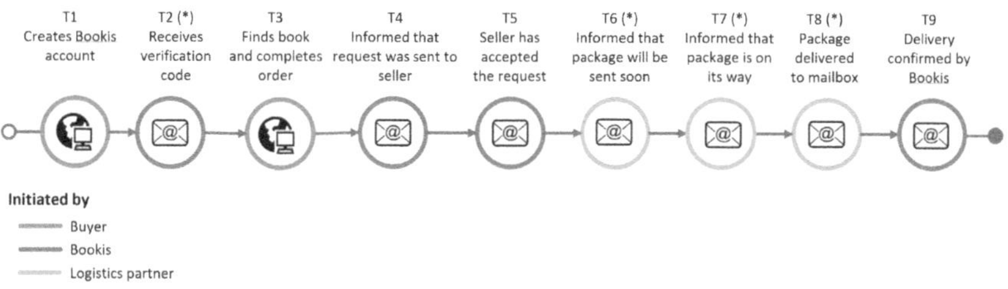

Fig. 1. Planned customer journey for a buyer. Touchpoints are color-coded according to the actor initiating the communication. An asterisk indicates touchpoints where variations occur.

This paper focuses on the buyer's customer journey, that is, the journey of a customer purchasing a book on the Bookis platform. Figure 1 illustrates the planned journey, i.e., the expected sequence of touchpoints, beginning with T1, where the buyer creates an account on the Bookis website. At touchpoint T2, the buyer receives an email containing a verification code to complete the account creation process. Once the account has been created, the buyer can proceed to order a book. At T3, the buyer locates the book, selects the desired version and seller, and completes the payment. The next touchpoint, T4, is an email from Bookis to the buyer confirming that the request to purchase the book has been sent to the seller. T5 is another email from Bookis informing the buyer that the seller has accepted the request. This email also includes information about when the package will be shipped, an option to track the package, and an option to chat with the seller. At touchpoint T6, the logistics partner sends an email to the buyer notifying them that a package will be sent soon. T7 is a subsequent email from the logistics partner indicating that the package is on its way. T8 is an email from the logistics partner confirming that the package has been delivered to the mailbox. Finally, T9 is an email from Bookis confirming delivery.

As indicated in Fig. 1, touchpoints T2 and T6–T8 represent points of variation in the planned journey. T2 will only occur for customers who wish to create an account using their email address; for those who log in with Google, it does not occur. Touchpoints T6-T8 vary in how the logistics partner communicates with the buyer about the package. In some cases, the partner may use one or more channels, such as email, push notifications via the logistics app, or SMS. Regardless of the channels used, the information conveyed and the sequence of T6–T8 remain consistent. Due to these variations, the planned customer journey will contain a different number of touchpoints for different buyers.

4 Method

This study investigates the reconstruction of actual customer journeys based solely on internal data from a SDN. To this end, we adopted a multi-method approach supporting a *dual-perspective* investigation. First, we applied the CJA method [7] to gather detailed, empirical accounts of real customer journeys. This *outside-in perspective* served as the ground truth for the customer journeys. In parallel, we collected all available digital traces related to the same customers from the back-end systems of the SDN. This enabled an independent *inside-out reconstruction* of the journeys, based exclusively on logs, events, and interactions recorded across the infrastructure of the SDN. Ethical approval was granted by SIKT - Norwegian Agency for Shared Services in Education and Research (reference No. 794702).

Empirical Investigation with Customer Journey Analysis. We applied CJA as described in Sect. 2 to the buying journey of Bookis, with us acting as the seller of the books to create a controlled environment. We employed a convenience sampling strategy, recruiting students both for practical reasons and because they represent a key target group for Bookis. Recruitment and data collection took place from December 2024 to March 2025. Participants were recruited via posters on the University of Oslo campus. Written informed consent was obtained from all participants prior to data collection. To be eligible for inclusion, participants had to be currently enrolled students at the University of Oslo, have experience with digital services and online shopping, and not have an existing user profile on Bookis. no, allowing account creation to be included as part of the journey.

A total of 39 individuals signed up during the recruitment period. Of these, one person declined participation due to the study's scope, and twelve were unresponsive to e-mails regarding consent and scheduling. From the initial 39 responses, 21 participants were selected to take part in the study with 20 of them successfully completing. Participants were between 22 and 31 years old (M = 25.0, SD = 2.7). The gender distribution was slightly skewed, with 11 men and 9 women. The participants' fields of study ranged from humanities and social sciences to health sciences and technical disciplines. Most of them were in their fourth or fifth year of study.

Data-Based Reconstruction with Process Mining. The reconstruction process started with understanding Bookis' objectives, the information they were logging and how these data sources could be accessed. Next, Bookis provided example data and demonstrated the structure of their dataset. After several iterations, we identified the essential data that needed to be logged and suggested modifications to achieve this. Once the changes were implemented, we began our study asking the participants to buy used books from us. After the study, Bookis provided the participants' journey logs and obtained shipment logs from the logistics partner for parcel tracking.

Bookis provided data in two distinct files: the shipment logs in JSON format and their own logs in CSV format. To ensure privacy, Bookis removed information such as geolocation, IP addresses, and e-mail addresses. The data was then cleaned to remove irrelevant data and records outside of the observation period. This resulted in the final data structure: userID (assigned participant ID), event (touchpoint), subject/description (touchpoint description), channel, sender, timestamp, and URL. To properly link the shipment data, we extracted the attributes event, description, sender, and timestamp from the transportation events associated with the parcel. Once both data structures were aligned, differences in timestamp formats remained across the datasets. These were standardized using Power Query to ensure consistency. Finally, events were renamed for consistency with the main event log yielding a unified dataset ready for analysis.

To analyze the data, we used the process mapping functionality of the academic version of Apromore[3]. Apromore takes the event log and provides a visual process map indicating the flow of the events. These maps allowed us to visualize the SDN. Furthermore, with the participants' diaries, we were able to compare participant-reported events and system logs.

5 Results

The reconstructed customer journeys revealed a mix of planned and ad-hoc interactions across varying durations and levels of complexity. Participants encountered an average of 9.9 planned touchpoints and 2.7 ad-hoc touchpoints. In total, the number of touchpoints per journey ranged from 9 to 28. The journey spanned an average of 7.8 days per participant, with individual durations ranging from 4 to 22 days. Table 1 provides the detailed breakdown per participant, including the number of planned and ad-hoc touchpoints, total number of touchpoints, and the duration of the journey.

The combination of diary data and follow-up interviews provided detailed accounts of participants' actual journeys and corresponding experiences. Although this paper focuses on the objective touchpoint data rather than the participants' subjective experiences, the rich qualitative input revealed several variations from the planned journey described in Sect. 3. Participants also reported several ad-hoc touchpoints that were not captured in the event logs. Most of the issues reported by the participants were related to T3 (find book and complete order), with one user reporting that the site crashed when trying to complete an order. In addition, touchpoints involving communication with the seller and customer service, as well as package tracking, were frequently mentioned but not consistently captured by the event logs.

The event log consisted of 886 events captured over a three-month period, distributed across 20 distinct cases (each corresponding to a study participant). Each case followed a unique sequence of events, resulting in 20 trace variants. This is likely due to differences in user navigation and variations related to

[3] https://apromore.com/academic-alliance.

Table 1. Overview of planned, ad-hoc, and total touchpoints per participant, and journey duration (days).

Participant	Planned	Ad-hoc	Total	Duration
ID1	8	4	12	7
ID2	11	0	11	6
ID3	10	1	11	5
ID4	10	0	10	5
ID5	11	0	11	11
ID6	11	2	13	4
ID7	9	7	16	5
ID8	10	2	12	6
ID9	9	0	9	9
ID10	11	17	28	22
ID11	10	2	12	7
ID12	11	3	14	7
ID13	10	2	12	7
ID14	10	1	11	9
ID15	8	2	10	6
ID16	10	5	15	6
ID17	9	1	10	11
ID18	9	1	10	6
ID19	10	3	13	6
ID20	10	1	11	10
Sum	197	54	251	
Average	9.9	2.7	12.6	7.8

touchpoints T5-T8. In all cases, a total of 47 unique event types were recorded. Overall, user navigation accounted for 44%, internal logs for 35% and communication with the customer for 21% of the events. The average case duration was 9.5 days, ranging from 4 to 29 days. A substantial portion of the events were related to touchpoints T1 and T3. Customer communication represented the smallest share of recorded events; however, this category also demonstrated weaknesses in the logging process, particularly when customer interactions occurred outside of the planned journey.

Figure 2 shows the overall process map generated from the event log. Because of its size and complexity, we highlight two zoomed-in segments in Fig. 2b and Fig. 2c. Figure 2b shows Bookis' internal system logs related to order completion, along with a customer notification event. These events correspond to touchpoints T3 and T4 in the planned journey. The first event in this segment also reveals an application error captured by Bookis. Figure 2c depicts events from the logistics partner, corresponding to touchpoint T6 and the progression toward touchpoint

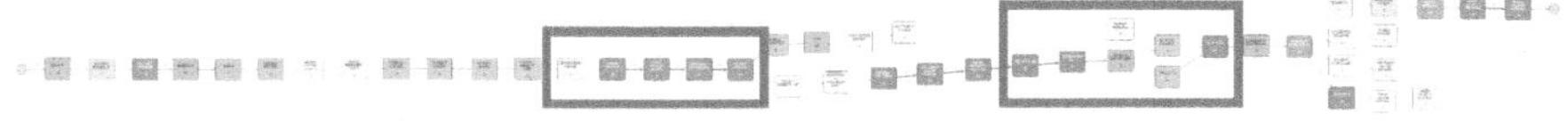

(a) Full process map obtained with Apromore

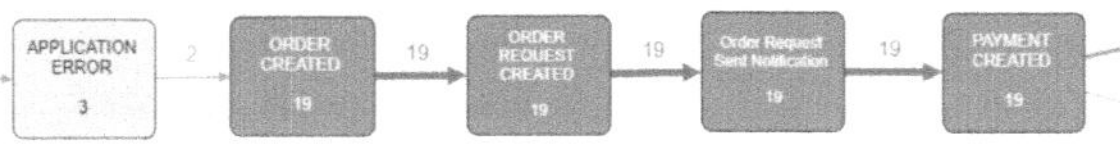

(b) Zoomed-in segment on the left side.

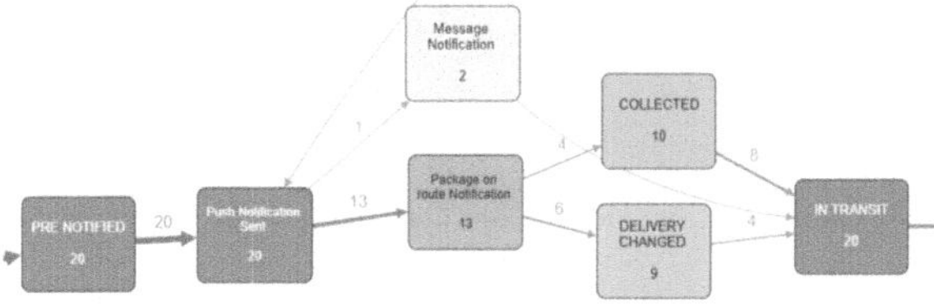

(c) Zoomed-in segment on the right side.

Fig. 2. Composite figure showing the full process map (a) and two zoomed-in segments (b) and (c), corresponding to the areas marked.

T7. The sequence begins with an internal event from the logistics partner, followed by two customer notifications, and continues with events that document the advancement of the delivery process.

Turning from the sequence of events to their classification, Table 2 presents different categories of event types in the event log along with illustrative examples. From 47 unique events, user navigation (C1) amounts to 15 distinct event types. These events are primarily associated with touchpoint T3 and provide insights into how the buyer navigates the platform to achieve their goal. The next category (C2), comprises Bookis' internal logs, which include twelve different event types. Although these events are not directly related to customer interactions, they are crucial for managing internal processes and coordination with logistic partners. In category C3 there are events related to Bookis' communication with the customer, which are very relevant for analyzing the customer journey. These represent interactions in which information is communicated to the customer via email related to touchpoints T2, T4, T5, and T9 from the planned journey and encompass four distinct event types. The internal events from the logistics partner log (C4) capture nine event types related to the delivery handling process. These events range from the receipt of the package from the seller to its final delivery. They primarily serve internal tracking and operational control purposes within the logistics provider. Finally, C5 focuses on customer-facing notifications throughout the delivery process. There are seven

Table 2. Number of event types of different categories present in the event log.

Category	Example Events	#Types
User Navigation Events (C1)	- Search started - Product clicked - Product added to cart	15
Bookis Internal System Logs (C2)	- Payment captured - Order request accepted - Order submitted	12
Bookis Customer Notification (C3)	- Delivery registered notification - Order request approved notification	4
Logistics Partner Internal Logs (C4)	- Collected - Deviation - In transit - Ready for pickup	9
Logistics Partner Customer Notification (C5)	- Package on route notification - Delivery notification	7

event types on activities that ensure that customers receive timely and relevant information about their deliveries.

Comparing the recordings and the empirical study, Table 3 shows the extent to which the planned and ad hoc touchpoints documented by participants in their diaries were also captured in the event data. In total, 197 planned and 54 ad-hoc touchpoints were documented. The number of planned touchpoints ranged from 8 to 11 with an average of 9.9 across participants. Each participant encountered all planned touchpoints and no participant reported fewer touchpoints than those in the planned journey. The coverage of planned touchpoints in the event logs was high on average (89%). This number could have been closer to full coverage if not for challenges in consistently logging touchpoint T1 and the absence of touchpoint T2 from the logging. In contrast, greater variation was observed in the ad-hoc touchpoints, which ranged from 0 to 17 touchpoints with an average of 2,7 across participants. The average coverage for ad-hoc touchpoints was substantially lower (33%). For participants who reported ad-hoc touchpoints, the event logs frequently failed to capture these interactions. The ad-hoc touchpoints not captured in the event logs primarily involved communications with customer service and the seller as well as issues related to tracking. For example, Participant 1 contacted customer service to address issues during the order process, while Participant 10 engaged in repeated communication with the seller through Bookis' chat service to resolve a refund request. Several buyers reported difficulties tracking their packages through the Bookis website.

In conclusion, the company's event log data did not fully capture the breadth of user interactions specifically when it comes to ad hoc interactions.

Table 3. Coverage (%) showing the fraction of planned and ad-hoc touchpoints captured in the event log.

Participant	Count		Coverage (%)	
	Planned	Ad-hoc	Planned	Ad-hoc
ID1	8	4	87	50
ID2	11	0	81	-
ID3	10	1	90	0
ID4	10	0	90	-
ID5	11	0	90	-
ID6	11	2	90	100
ID7	9	7	89	28
ID8	10	2	90	50
ID9	9	0	89	-
ID10	11	17	91	18
ID11	10	2	90	0
ID12	11	3	91	33
ID13	10	2	100	50
ID14	10	1	90	100
ID15	8	2	87	50
ID16	10	5	90	20
ID17	9	1	78	0
ID18	9	1	89	0
ID19	10	3	90	33
ID20	10	1	90	0
Average	9.9	2.7	89	33

6 Discussion

Previous research has shown that service providers often have only partial insight into the customer journeys they are responsible for—sometimes lacking awareness of the sequence of touchpoints or even of their existence [7]. In this case, the main service provider had good control over the planned journey, but we identified variations in touchpoints managed by the logistics partner. These variations were revealed both through the mystery shopping assessment and the empirical study. For instance, the dispatch of notifications depended on whether the customer had installed the logistics partner's mobile app—an external detail that is difficult for the main provider to anticipate or control.

In the case of Bookis and many other new businesses that utilize a C2C-model, ensuring a positive user experience for both sides of the platform is essential. This focus on user experience is crucial for attracting and retaining users, particularly due to the network effects at play. Network effects refer to the phenomenon in which each new user added to the platform increases its value for all existing users [15]. For Bookis, the more users they can attract and retain, the easier it becomes for users to buy and sell books. For Bookis, this gap has direct implications. Our analysis shows that while digital traces of planned touchpoints are largely captured (coverage 89%), deviations remain significantly under-logged (coverage 33%). Insights from the study are already informing improvements in system design and partner coordination, which will better support both buyer and seller experiences on the platform.

To improve coverage, Bookis will (1) implement structured logging for customer service interactions (chat and email), (2) negotiate standardized event formats with logistics partners to ensure visibility into key delivery steps and failures. Already Bookis have (3) implemented customer feedback loops (in-app prompts post-delivery) to validate and enrich journey data. Failures in visibility, especially in transitions between platform and logistics partners, can impact user satisfaction, support load, and ultimately user retention on the platform. From a *managerial perspective*, two main insights emerge: **(1)** Journey continuity depends on partner integration: Capturing full customer journeys requires structured data-sharing and aligned logging standards across the SDN. **(2)** Ad-hoc events need more attention: Internal logging systems must evolve to include non-linear, customer-initiated actions such as support chat and reordering attempts, critical for understanding user frustration. Finally, as an orthogonal but very important concern, responsible data use is key: As journey mining capabilities scale, transparency and alignment with GDPR principles, e.g., through privacy-preserving process mining techniques, are essential for maintaining user trust and ensuring ethical data practices.

Limitations. This study has several limitations. It focuses on a specific C2C marketplace which may differ from other, similar platforms. The buying journey examined is simplified, excluding scenarios such as purchasing multiple books or buying from different sellers. To reduce uncertainty, we deliberately controlled the seller's role and avoided complications such as unaccepted orders or failed deliveries. This enabled comparison against a common, planned journey with minimal variation but reduces the generalizability of the findings. Furthermore, there are multiple ways to delineate steps in a customer journey. For example touchpoint T3 "Finds book and completes order" could reasonably be decomposed in several sub-activities. This simplification is an inherent challenge in modeling and we acknowledge that it can influence the reported coverage. Finally, the data were gathered from a convenience sample of 20 students without existing Bookis accounts. This recruitment strategy further narrows the applicability of our findings to broader user groups or other platforms.

7 Conclusion

This experience report contributes a dual perspective case study on a customer journey in a C2C marketplace for buying and selling used books. Our findings indicate that organizing customer data in terms of individual journeys—by leveraging their continuous digital footprint—can offer service providers valuable insights into customer behavior and reveal opportunities for service improvement. The dual perspective showed to be important in revealing that many ad-hoc interactions are not captured and, consequently, several interesting deviations would not have been possible to analyze with process mining methods alone.

In future work, our aim is to further refine and generalize the applied dual-perspective method beyond this single case study and provide recommendations for a successful integration of both perspectives. Another promising direction for future work lies in investigating whether customer experience itself, and not just a proxy for it in terms of deviating touchpoints, can be inferred from these digital traces. This would open the door to more personalized and responsive service innovation based on process mining methods.

Acknowledgments. We thank Bookis for the fruitful collaboration and in particular Arne-Morten Willumsen for the data extraction. This work is part of the Smart Journey Mining project, funded by the Research Council of Norway (grant no. 312198).

References

1. Aalst, W.V.d.: Process Mining: Data Science in Action. Springer, Cham (2019)
2. Bernard, G., Andritsos, P.: Discovering customer journeys from evidence: a genetic approach inspired by process mining. In: CAiSE Forum. LNBIP, vol. 350, pp. 36–47. Springer, Cham (2019)
3. Bernard, G.: Process-Mining-based Customer Journey Analytics. Ph.D. thesis, University of Lausanne (2020)
4. Bernard, G., Andritsos, P.: Cjm-ex: goal-oriented exploration of customer journey maps using event logs and data analytics. In: BPM (Demos). CEUR Workshop Proceedings, vol. 1920. CEUR-WS.org (2017)
5. Emamjome, F., Andrews, R., ter Hofstede, A.H.M.: A case study lens on process mining in practice. In: OTM Conferences. LNCS, vol. 11877, pp. 127–145. Springer, Cham (2019)
6. Følstad, A., Kvale, K.: Customer journeys: a systematic literature review. J. Serv. Theor. Pract. **28**(2), 196–227 (2018)
7. Halvorsrud, R., Kvale, K., Følstad, A.: Improving service quality through customer journey analysis. J. Serv. Theor. Pract. **26**(6), 840–867 (2016)
8. Hansson, M., Angel, K., Mannhardt, F., Kvale, K.: How can a service provider utilize process mining on customer journeys to gain actionable insights for service delivery improvements? In: BPM Industry Forum. CEUR Workshop Proceedings, vol. 3112, pp. 15–26. CEUR-WS.org (2021)
9. Mannhardt, F., Halvorsrud, R., Meironas, O., Brurok, L.: The quest for the comprehensive customer journey - A case study from a C2C marketplace. In: BPM (Blockchain and RPA Forum). LNBIP, vol. 527, pp. 451–461. Springer, Cham (2024)
10. Mendling, J., Jans, M., Sahling, K.: Structuring empirical research on process mining at the individual level using the theory of effective use. In: ICPM Workshops. LNBIP, vol. 533, pp. 520–532. Springer, Cham (2024)

11. Tax, S.S., McCutcheon, D., Wilkinson, I.F.: The service delivery network (SDN): a customer-centric perspective of the customer journey. J. Serv. Res. **16**(4), 454–470 (2013)
12. Terragni, A., Hassani, M.: Analyzing customer journey with process mining: From discovery to recommendations. In: FiCloud, pp. 224–229. IEEE (2018)
13. Terragni, A., Hassani, M.: Optimizing customer journey using process mining and sequence-aware recommendation. In: SAC, pp. 57–65. ACM (2019)
14. Thiede, M., Fuerstenau, D., Barquet, A.P.B.: How is process mining technology used by organizations? A systematic literature review of empirical studies. Bus. Process. Manag. J. **24**(4), 900–922 (2018)
15. Tiwana, A.: Platform Ecosystems: Aligning Architecture, Governance, and Strategy. Morgan Kaufmann Publishers Inc., San Francisco (2013)
16. Tueanrat, Y., Papagiannidis, S., Alamanos, E.: Going on a journey: a review of the customer journey literature. J. Bus. Res. **125**, 336–353 (2021)
17. Zilker, S., Marx, E., Stierle, M., Matzner, M.: Process mining for advanced service analytics - from process efficiency to customer encounter and experience. In: HICSS, pp. 1–10. ScholarSpace (2022)
18. Zimmermann, L., Zerbato, F., Weber, B.: What makes life for process mining analysts difficult? A reflection of challenges. Softw. Syst. Model. **23**(6), 1345–1373 (2024)

Factors and Impacts of Gender Imbalance in Digital Transformation Projects: A Systematic Literature Review

Muhammad Febrilian Dwi Syahputra[1,2], Rinda Faiz Shabira[1], and E. R. Mahendrawathi[1(✉)]

[1] Institut Teknologi Sepuluh Nopember, Surabaya, Indonesia
{7026241005,6026241022}@student.its.ac.id, mahendra_w@is.its.ac.id

[2] Universitas Negeri Surabaya, Surabaya, Indonesia

Abstract. Inclusivity is a key principle in Sustainable Development Goals (SDGs), especially in accelerating Digital Transformation (DT). Gender imbalance remains both understudied, particularly within the design and execution of digital projects. This study presents a Systematic Literature Review (SLR) that examines how gender imbalance factors emerges in DT projects, and how such imbalances impacts on project innovation. Based on 31 peer-reviewed studies, the review identifies three key thematic dimensions: (1) structural and institutionalized biases in digital work culture, (2) fragile support ecosystems for women in DT projects, and (3) inclusive innovation as a sustainability enabler. These themes are synthesized through the Gioia methodology and integrated into four analytical layers: women's career decisions, organizational dynamics, DT project ecosystems, and institutional policy. The layered structure illustrates how barriers to inclusion are distributed vertically from individual level constraints to systemic policy gaps, reinforcing exclusion across the digital value chain. Findings reveal that gender equality is not only a matter of social justice but also a driver of innovation quality, team adaptability, and long term digital sustainability. This study contributes a novel perspective by positioning gender balance as a foundational design principle in digital transformation. In doing so, it offers actionable insights for researchers, practitioners, and policymakers to build more inclusive and resilient digital futures.

Keywords: Gender Imbalance · Digital Transformation · Systematic Literature Review

1 Introduction

Gender imbalance continues to be a significant issue, especially in the technology sector, where its effects are magnified due to the growing importance of the interaction between Information Technology (IT) and Digital Transformation (DT) across various industries [1]. This disparity is particularly alarming, considering the essential role of IT in fostering

I. van de Weerd et al. (Eds.): BPM 2025 Workshops, LNBIP 569, pp. 387–401, 2026.
https://doi.org/10.1007/978-3-032-13426-4_28

corporate innovation and digital competitiveness [2]. Gender imbalance often stems from non inclusive processes that systematically limit equal participation and representation across genders [3]. Organizations with gender imbalanced teams may experience less innovation, restricted user understanding, and a weakened capacity to develop inclusive solutions [4]. As business process transformation transitions from conventional models to digital first methodologies, the success of these initiatives increasingly relies on the diversity and inclusivity of the participating teams [5]. Diverse teams provide broader perspectives and more thorough solutions, rendering gender balance an issue of equity and a strategic asset in attaining effective and lasting DT [1].

Implementing DT initiatives reveals significant challenges exacerbated by existing gender imbalances within organizational structures [2]. For instance, men often benefit from their past performance and reputation in project funding processes, receiving prioritization for new project approvals, whereas women do not enjoy the same advantage [6]. Additionally, women frequently report having significantly less support and authority to make key decisions, lower satisfaction with compensation, and feeling undervalued within their teams [7]. While men tend to cite technical or project-related obstacles as their main challenges, women more often highlight issues rooted in team dynamics and gender biases [7]. This is intensified by the underrepresentation of women in technical roles and digital leadership positions and the scarcity of mentors, professional networks, and female role models, which are factors that continue to widen the gender gap in digital innovation environments [8].

Numerous studies have emphasized the critical role of project team formation in determining learning outcomes and the overall success of DT initiatives [9]. Teams with gender diversity have consistently been found to be more innovative, collaborative, and capable of balanced decision making [10]. In agile education contexts, for example, team composition directly influences engagement and learning quality [11]. However, women scientists and professionals remain less visible in funded projects, suggesting that forming teams is often not inclusive [12]. This exclusion limits women's participation and diminishes the potential for innovative outcomes, as inclusivity is a fundamental element of sustainable and impactful innovation.

Research also highlights the importance of designing teams with a deliberate mix of gender and skills to create a well-rounded, effective unit. Strategies for forming such teams can involve either self-selection or instructor facilitation [10]. Instructor-formed teams, in particular, are shown to encourage diversity that may not naturally emerge in student or employee led settings [11]. Moreover, differences in focus between genders, where women often emphasize design and process, and men focus on technical architectures and algorithms, illustrate how gender diversity can enrich project perspectives [11]. Nonetheless, managing team composition and group dynamics remains a persistent challenge, especially when aiming for equity and inclusivity [10]. Beyond improving outcomes, diverse teams foster healthy intergroup competition and more resilient collaborative environments [10].

Although many studies have investigated the issue of gender and DT, they do not explicitly address the natural differences in how men and women work, nor consider how the absence of gender balance in project teams can introduce subtle biases into outcomes [13]. Persistent stereotypes, such as the belief that men are inherently more tech oriented than women, continue to influence women's opportunities, representation, and potential contributions to DT projects [14]. Most existing research focuses on identifying barriers and success factors in executing DT projects without examining the gender composition of teams and its impact on project. While various initiatives have been implemented to improve women's participation in the digital sector, there is still a need for targeted strategies that enhance their roles and visibility in DT efforts. To comprehensively understand the current state of knowledge and identify recurring patterns, influencing factors, and existing gaps, this study uses a Systematic Literature Review (SLR), which offers a structured and rigorous method to synthesize existing research and provide evidence based insights.

This paper is organized as follows. Section 1 introduces the research background and the importance of addressing gender imbalance in DT projects. Section 2 describes the research questions, research methodology, including the SLR search protocol and procedure, also coding approach. Section 3 presents the findings and discussion, structured into three main thematic dimensions. Section 4 outlines the theoretical contributions, practical implications, and future research directions. Finally, Sect. 5 concludes the paper with a summary of insights and reflections.

2 Methodology

In recent years, there has been a growing interest in studying gender imbalance within digital transformation initiatives. Although numerous studies have investigated the impact of gender imbalance in DT project, including the underrepresentation of women in technical positions, disparities in project leadership roles, and gender inequality in the technology sector, few have systematically examined this relationship. Then, we aim to explore how gender imbalance occurs in DT projects by investigating the following research questions:

RQ1: What are the key factors contributing to gender imbalance in digital transformation projects?

RQ2: How does gender balance or imbalance impact the sustainability of digital transformation projects?

The SLR was conducted in accordance with the established guidelines proposed by [15], which guaranteed a rigorous and transparent approach to the selection, evaluation, and synthesis of literature. Emerald, Springer, Taylor & Francis, Wiley Online Library, and Sage comprise the five primary academic databases utilized in this review. The SLR structured process is thoroughly described in the supplementary material (Appendix A), which offers complete transparency regarding the search strategy, inclusion and exclusion criteria, and coding process. Table 1 shows the protocol used in the search process and the results obtained for each database.

During the preliminary search, keywords such as "gender imbalance", "information technology", project and digitalization yielded limited relevant studies. Then we changed the search strategy by using the keywords "gender imbalance", "digital transformation", and projects to get more literature. We also applied a snowball sampling to identify additional relevant literature by tracking references and citations from the initially selected articles. After implementing the strategy, we got the ideal number of articles.

Table 1. SLR Search Protocol

Database	Search String Protocol	Total Articles
Emerald	"gender imbalance" AND ("digital transformation ") AND (project)	22
Springer	"gender imbalance" AND "digital transformation" AND project	22
Taylor & Francis	[All: "gender imbalance"] AND [All: " digital transformation "] AND [All: project]	11
Wiley	""gender imbalance"" anywhere and "" digital transformation "" anywhere and "project" anywhere	11
Sage	"gender imbalance" AND "digital transformation" AND project	13
Snowball Sampling	We search for random samples that are relevant to the research question	3
Total		79

Figure 1 presents the PRISMA (Preferred Reporting Items for Systematic Reviews and Meta Analyses) flow diagram illustrating the process of identifying, screening, and selecting studies for inclusion in this SLR [16]. The diagram is divided into two primary identification methods: database searching and other methods, specifically citation searching (snowballing). From database searching, a total of 79 article were identified. After applying the inclusion criteria specifically focusing on publication years (2015–2025), journal articles selection only, and keywords correspond with combination criteria (title, abstract, and contributor), 22 journal article were excluded, leaving 57 journal article for further assessment. No duplicates or irrelevant journal article were identified.

All 57 remaining articles were eliminated by subject area (e.g. including computer science and management journal, excluding medical and physics journal), leading to the exclusion of 37 articles because the articles only addressed some aspects of the topic and did not include a direct link between gender imbalance and digital transformation projects. Some focus only on gender issues in education or science in general without linking the context to digital projects or innovation. Other articles discussed digital transformation from a technical or managerial perspective, but did not address issues of gender representation, equality or women's participation. In addition, some articles partially used relevant keywords, but upon further analysis through the abstract and content, did not directly contribute to the proposed research questions.

Finally, 18 additional journal article were identified through citation searching. After initial screening, 7 of these were excluded for similar reasons (not relevant to the research questions), and 11 were retained and included in the final review as part of the snowballing strategy. In total, 31 studies were included in the final synthesis: 20 from database searches and 11 from snowballing, reinforcing the necessity of using multiple identification strategies to capture comprehensive insights on the research topic of gender imbalance in digital transformation projects.

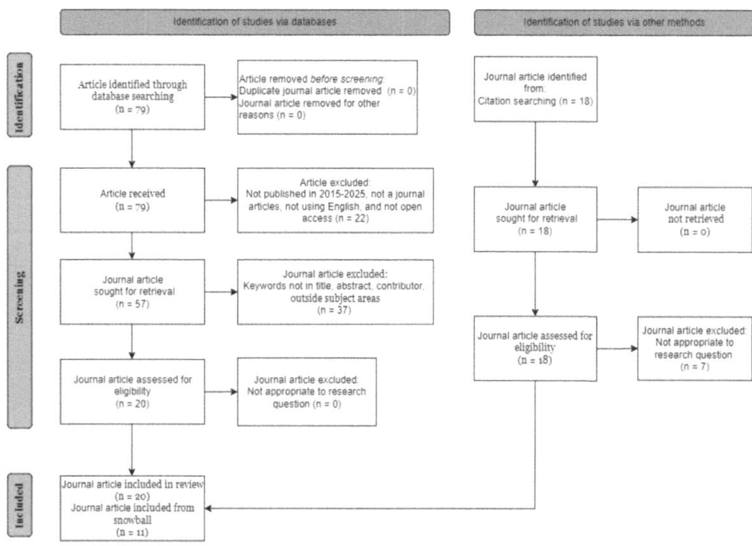

Fig. 1. Article Selection Using Prisma Method

To systematically structure and synthesize the findings, this study employed the Gioia methodology as a qualitative coding framework [48]. The process begins with extracting exemplary verbatim, which are direct quotations from the reviewed literature that reflect key concepts or observations. These verbatim then abstracted into first order thematic codes that remain close to the original language used in the sources.

Subsequently, second order themes are developed through interpretive analysis by grouping related first order codes into broader, conceptual categories. Finally, these second order themes are synthesized into higher level aggregate dimensions that capture the overarching patterns emerging from the data. This approach enables a clear and traceable link between empirical evidence and conceptual insight, supporting the development of a robust and theory informed model. An example of the coding process is provided to illustrate how the themes were constructed, as shown in Table 2. The complete coding scheme can be seen in the appendix B.

Table 2. Gioia Methodology Coding Process Example

Exemplary Verbatim	1st-orders Thematic Analysis	2nd-order Thematic Analysis	Aggregate Dimension	Source

(*continued*)

Table 2. (*continued*)

Exemplary Verbatim	1st-orders Thematic Analysis	2nd-order Thematic Analysis	Aggregate Dimension	Source
Balancing the gender ratio would also make BPM teams more diverse, which, on the one hand, would lead to "superior productivity and financial performance compared with homogeneous teams"	Balancing gender ratio can increase productivity and team efficiency	Collaboration and Communication Dynamics	Inclusive Innovation as a Sustainability Enabler	28

3 Findings and Discussion

In visualizing the findings, this study adapts the conceptual approach of the UNDP policy brief [47], which emphasizes the importance of inclusivity in digital transformation architecture. This approach allows the development of a conceptual model that explains the relationship between gender inequality and the sustainability of DT projects in modern organizations and institutions.

3.1 SLR Findings and Conceptualization

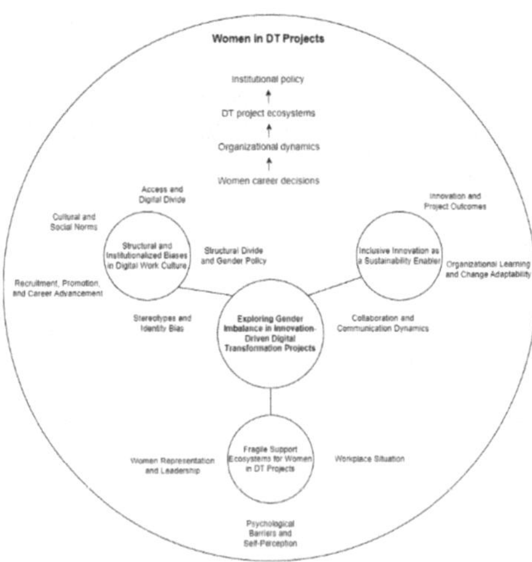

Fig. 2. Conceptualization of Gender Imbalance in DT Projects

As shown in Fig. 2, the conceptualization was developed to illustrate how gender imbalance in innovation based DT projects is not the result of a single cause, but rather a series of interrelated and systemic factors. Figure 2 was developed to represent the integrated findings of this study and was inspired by the layered framework in the UNDP Policy Brief. This figure visualizes gender imbalance DT projects as a multidimensional issue situated within interconnected systemic layers. These thematic clusters are embedded within four concentric layers, women career decisions, organizational dynamics, DT project ecosystems, and institutional policy, which represent a vertical hierarchy from operational to strategic influence. The placement of these layers reflects how individual level experiences are shaped by, and in turn shape, broader structural and policy level conditions.

The model consists of three main thematic dimensions developed through the Gioia methodology. **Structural and institutionalized biases in digital work culture** and **fragile support ecosystems for women in DT projects** primarily **answer RQ1**, which investigates the key factors contributing to gender imbalance in digital transformation projects. Meanwhile, the third theme, **inclusive innovation as a sustainability enabler**, **addresses RQ2** by illustrating how gender balance or its absence impacts the sustainability and long term success of digital transformation initiatives.

The first theme, **structural and institutionalized biases in digital work culture**, refers to the entrenched cultural, organizational, and systemic factors that limit women's full participation in digital environments. These biases are not isolated or overt, but rather embedded in everyday norms, expectations, and practices that shape who gets access, recognition, and authority in digital innovation spaces. **Fragile support ecosystems for women in DT projects**, captures the lack of enabling conditions that allow women to thrive. Even when women enter the digital workforce, they often find themselves without sufficient mentorship, representation, or psychological safety. This absence of structural support and affirmation leads to under recognition, limited influence, and higher exit rates from digital careers. The last, **inclusive innovation as a sustainability enabler**, highlights that achieving gender balance is not only a matter of fairness, but also a catalyst for better innovation and long term project success. When teams are diverse and inclusive, they generate richer ideas, solve problems more holistically, and adapt more effectively to change. Thus, gender inclusivity strengthens not just social equity but also the sustainability of digital transformation efforts.

The three overarching themes are shaped by multiple, interrelated layers of influence that operate across individual to systemic levels. RQ1 is primarily addressed in the lower two layers, women career decisions and organizational dynamics, where many structural and support related issues occur. Then, RQ2 visible in the upper layers, particularly in DT project ecosystems and institutional policy, where decisions about innovation, governance, and long term project success are made. At the foundational layer lies **women's career decisions**, shaped by early experiences, self-perception, and perceived opportunity structures. These individual choices are deeply affected by the second layer, **organizational dynamics**, including team culture, leadership practices, and workplace inclusivity. Moving further up, the third layer is the **DT project ecosystem**, where norms around collaboration, innovation, and agility can either reinforce or challenge gendered structures.

3.2 Structural and Institutionalized Biases in Digital Work Culture

Gender imbalance in digital transformation (DT) projects is deeply rooted in struc-tural and cultural systems that shape women's opportunities and constraints across various contexts. Cultural norms often place dual expectations on women to partici-pate economically while managing domestic responsibilities creating persistent ten-sion in their career trajectories [25, 41]. These pressures begin early; gendered toys and expectations influence future behavior and skill development [38], while social norms in rural communities can restrict women's access to even basic technologies [34]. Work environments tend to reflect these dynamics. Competitive digital cultures, such as those encouraged by gamified systems like Stack Overflow, often favor male participation and discourage collaboration [42]. Rigid work structures, lack of men-torship, and informal male dominated networks further hinder women's retention and advancement [45].

Stereotypes continue to frame technical roles as masculine, while undervaluing attributes traditionally associated with women, such as communication and creativity [28]. These biases affect not only career aspirations but also external perceptions, investors may view women as less competent in management and finance [22]. In patriarchal societies, limited access to education and ICT training exacerbates these challenges [31], while misconceptions that computing lacks social relevance deter many girls from engaging in digital careers [17, 41]. Access related disparities form another layer of exclusion. Women are less represented in digital specialist roles and are widely perceived to have lower technical skills [17]. They also face barriers in owning devices and affording connectivity, especially in low income settings [32, 34]. This limits their ability to use technology productively or securely, as awareness of digital privacy remains significantly lower among women [36].

Institutionally, women continue to be underrepresented in leadership and technical roles [33]. Workplace engagement strategies often neglect gendered needs, making it harder for women to thrive [23]. Many interventions treat women as a single demographic, ignoring differences across age, location, and economic status [1, 31]. In public digital services, the lack of gender sensitive design further marginalizes under-served women [37]. Biases also pervade recruitment and promotion processes. Discriminatory screening, especially through social media can disadvantage women unconsciously [21]. The glass ceiling remains intact, limiting their career progression [28]. Often, advancement only occurs due to external advocacy, not structural inclusion [43]. For others, the absence of visible pathways means leadership is never considered a viable option [43].

These findings underscore how organizational culture and institutional structures in digital transformation projects reproduce gendered barriers at multiple levels, from hiring practices and team dynamics to leadership pathways. The persistence of these biases signals a deeper misalignment between current digital work environments and the principles of equity and inclusivity [49]. Addressing these challenges requires more than policy change, it demands a cultural shift that integrates gender sensitive values into the core of organizational routines and decision making [49].

3.3 Fragile Support Ecosystems for Women in DT Projects

The underrepresentation of women in DT projects is closely tied to the fragility of support ecosystems within which they operate. A key limitation lies in the absence of women in visible leadership and strategic roles, which leads many young women to feel disconnected from the field of technology [19]. Women in leadership often face higher scrutiny and shifting performance standards, leading them to work harder for equal recognition compared to their male counterparts [20]. In entrepreneurship, they often experience role conflict, as they are disproportionately burdened with multitasking demands in an already gendered professional landscape [26]. Gender diversity is often not viewed as a strategic priority [24], resulting in limited exposure to female leaders and diminished access to their strategic insights [27]. This lack of visibility is reinforced by the enduring perception that technical roles are inherently masculine, which discourages women's participation in skill based domains [30].

These structural limitations mirror broader patterns of political exclusion, such as the lack of female political leaders in countries like Mongolia, highlighting systemic barriers to female empowerment at the institutional level [36]. In the entrepreneurial space, women remain underrepresented and under acknowledged; most high profile success stories emerge from male dominated cultures, particularly in startup ecosystems labeled as "tech bros" [38]. In legacy male led industries, women's contributions remain undervalued due to the absence of professional lineages or established role models [19], which makes their work less recognized despite its critical nature [43]. Even when they reach executive positions, women are often discouraged from taking on risk heavy decisions, reinforcing narrow assumptions about gendered leadership behavior [44].

Beyond structural issues, psychological barriers and self perception significantly affect women's participation. Impostor syndrome is disproportionately reported among women in science and tech fields, particularly in environments that reinforce stereotypes about their limited competence [17]. Confidence gaps and pessimism around adopting high-tech products also affect engagement, often linked to height-ened risk aversion [34]. These feelings are compounded by higher levels of tech-nostress and technophobia, which reflect anxiety and strain in adapting to digital environments [32].

Another constraint is the limited network awareness reported among women in academia and professional settings, which curtails access to informal mentoring and collaborative spaces [29]. Additionally, women often face a paradox: if they emulate male behavior to succeed in male dominated roles, they risk being perceived as un-likeable or nonconforming [39]. Among younger women, perceptions that tech ca-reers hinder social life contribute to disengagement from early digital education [41]. This is further reinforced by organizational norms and exclusion perceptions of IT as a male-dominated field, which contribute to underrepresentation of women in technical roles [40], then also reinforced by structural biases that position them as more suited for communication or coordination tasks [45]. These patterns reflect broader issues of digital confidence. Despite interest in IT, many women lack pro-gramming skills and practical experience, often due to gaps in early exposure or sys-temic exclusion from technical tracks [41]. Survey data also reveals that women report significantly lower confidence in operating digital systems compared to men [32].

These insights reveal that the barriers faced by women in DT projects extend beyond formal structures into the less visible, yet equally critical, domains of culture, self perception, and informal support. The absence of role models and networks, the psychological toll of underrepresentation, and limited access to strategic mentorship all point to the urgency of cultivating inclusive support ecosystems. Fostering such environments requires organizations to move beyond compliance and embed equity within their talent development strategies, from early exposure and digital literacy to leadership pathways. It also demands a reconfiguration of organizational culture that validates diverse leadership styles and dismantles the implicit norms that disadvantage women. Through proactive change management, institutions can create psychologically safe spaces that not only retain women but empower them to lead, innovate, and thrive in digital transformation contexts.

3.4 Inclusive Innovation as a Sustainability Enabler

Inclusive innovation plays a vital role in enabling sustainability within DT projects, particularly by fostering diversity, collaboration, and creativity. A balanced gender composition in project teams not only increases productivity and efficiency, but also promotes inclusive decision making and better innovation outcomes. Gender-balanced teams outperform homogeneous ones in productivity, innovation, and financial performance [28]. Women contribute cooperative behavior, supportive communication, and knowledge sharing traits that enhance team dynamics in BPM and digital contexts [42, 45]. The COVID-19 pandemic accelerated the use of digital collaboration tools, allowing more inclusive and sustainable teamwork, especially among women academics and leaders [29]. These platforms help reshape power dynamics and foster equitable collaboration models. However, digital gender gaps still persist, limiting women's participation and hindering inclusive public services [36]. Despite structural challenges, women play strategic roles balancing emotional labor and task focus to maintain team harmony under pressure [39]. They show resilience and adaptability by navigating workplace bias, often finding creative workarounds to ensure team success, even in male dominated environments [43].

Gender diversity fuels innovation by introducing varied perspectives [17] and broader problem solving approaches [28, 42]. A lack of diversity leads to homogeneity and weak innovation outcomes [40, 46]. Including women in tech development improves artefact usability and societal relevance, especially since women are major technology users but underrepresented as creators [1, 42]. Firms with balanced leadership demonstrate stronger innovation outcomes [38], and women often contribute insights overlooked in male led settings [43]. The assumption about women are not always risk-averse show that diverse teams can lead IT projects [44]. Women also display high commitment and flexibility, often adopting multiple roles, task driven and nurturing to meet tight deadlines while sustaining team morale [39]. Investing in women's digital skills not only enhances development quality but also promotes sustainable innovation [31].

Gender balance in digital skills training fosters psychological empowerment enhancing competence, autonomy, and purpose, especially in virtual settings [35]. Empowered women are more engaged in organizational innovation and change efforts. On the other hand, gender imbalance creates discomfort and reduces participation, particularly for women isolated in technical teams [25]. Perceived gender equity boosts well-being for all, but especially for women [23]. Excluding women from leadership also wastes global talent and impairs organizational effectiveness [44]. In digital governance, lack of gender diversity weakens project sustainability by narrowing the range of perspectives in system design [37]. Broader exclusion from IT fields carries long term social, economic, and scientific costs [41].

When women are integrated meaningfully into project teams, organizations benefit from more holistic decision making, stronger resilience, and wider reaching innovations. To harness this potential, organizations must embed inclusive practices within change management strategies, ensuring that digital transitions are not only technologically sound but socially responsive. Organizational culture must be reframed to recognize diverse contributions as core to innovation, shifting away from masculine coded norms toward collaborative and adaptive models. Inclusive innovation thus emerges as a critical pathway for both digital and organizational sustainability.

3.5 Women in Digital Transformation Project Layers

Understanding women's roles and experiences in DT projects requires a multi-layered perspective that reflects both vertical progression and contextual interaction across organizational and institutional domains. We conceptualize four interrelated layers: **women's career decision making, organizational dynamics, DT project ecosystems**, and **institutional policy**. These layers represent a vertical continuum from operational and individual level experiences at the base to macro level strategic frameworks at the top.

Fig. 3. Women in DT Project Layers

As shown in Fig. 3, at the foundational level, women's career decisions are shaped by internal motivations, social expectations, and perceived opportunities or constraints in digital fields. These decisions are often influenced by prior exposure to digital skills training, individual psychological empowerment, and support structures within educational or early professional contexts [35]. Gender imbalance at this level may deter women from entering or remaining in DT related careers, creating a pipeline problem that restricts diversity in upper layers [25, 41].

The third layer, DT project ecosystems, refers to the collaborative networks, technology development practices, and agile team configurations that define how digital transformation unfolds. At this level, women's participation ensures that diverse user perspectives are embedded into the development of IT artefacts, improving inclusivity, functionality, and social impact [1, 42]. A lack of gender diversity here risks perpetuating homogeneous thinking and suboptimal design outcomes [40, 46]. Moreover, diverse ecosystems are not only ethically desirable but strategically advantageous [28], as they fuel innovation and enhance project sustainability [31, 38].

At the strategic apex lies institutional policy, which frames the broader regulatory, economic, and educational contexts in which digital transformation projects operate.

Policies that promote gender equity in leadership, digital literacy, and workforce development play a decisive role in shaping the conditions for inclusion. Exclusionary institutional cultures or insufficient policy mandates can hinder long term innovation and lead to negative economic and scientific consequences [41, 44]. Conversely, policies that support gender balanced leadership and equitable training programs can amplify women's agency and sustain their roles across DT project layers [35, 37].

For instance, the career decisions women make are directly affected by how inclusive communication and collaboration practices are at the organizational level. Similarly, innovation outcomes are shaped by both the presence of diverse contributors within project ecosystems and the enabling role of institutional support. Finally, the adaptability of organizations in learning from diverse talent and in institutionalizing that learning is contingent on strategic alignment across all layers. Each layer represents a critical point of intervention. While bottom up initiatives (such as digital upskilling) empower women at the operational level, top down mechanisms (like institutional policies) are needed to dismantle systemic barriers.

4 Future Research Directions

The strong concentration of findings related to structural and institutionalized biases (RQ1) signals the need for more empirical studies to validate and contextualize these issues within real world DT initiatives. Future research could conduct in depth case studies, longitudinal tracking of women's career trajectories, or ethnographic observations of gender dynamics in technology teams to enrich the current understanding grounded in conceptual synthesis. Second, there is a significant opportunity to expand inquiry into the sustainability value of inclusive innovation (RQ2). While this study identifies that gender balanced teams improve innovation and long-term project outcomes, empirical evidence remains sparse. Future studies should examine how diverse teams influence decision making, resilience, and system design in various digital contexts, especially in low and middle income countries where structural challenges are compounded by economic constraints.

From a theoretical view, several gaps remain. Some of the literature refers to Ahuja's gendered theory of IT career stages [1, 50], critical mass theory [20], and social role theory [23]. Ahuja's gendered theory of IT career stages could offer a powerful lens to analyze how gendered barriers across career phases affect women's participation and progression in DT projects. Similarly, the Individual Differences Theory of Gender and IT remains underutilized in explaining how gendered cognitive, affective, and behavioral traits influence women's engagement with digital tools, their motivation in pursuing technology related careers, and their autonomy in digital decision making processes [1].

5 Conclusion

This study conducted an SLR to explore the contributing factors and impacts of gender imbalance in DT projects. Based on a comprehensive analysis of 31 studies, the findings demonstrate that gender imbalance in DT is not the result of isolated incidents but rather a consequence of intersecting structural, cultural, and psychological barriers operating across multiple levels, from individual career decisions to institutional policies. Three aggregate dimensions were identified: structural and institutionalized biases in digital work culture, fragile support ecosystems for women in DT projects, and inclusive innovation as a sustainability enabler. These themes reveal how deeply embedded cultural norms, gendered stereotypes, unequal access to digital resources, and exclusionary organizational practices continue to marginalize women. Moreover, psychological barriers and unsupportive environments further restrict women's participation and advancement in digital innovation processes.

This study uncovers how the sustainability of digital transformation projects is intrinsically linked to structural inclusivity, support ecosystems for underrepresented talent, and the strategic integration of gender balanced teams as innovation drivers. The research highlights new pathways where gender equity is not only a social goal but a critical design principle for digital sustainability. To further conceptualize these findings, a layered model was developed, encompassing four vertical levels: women's career decisions, organizational dynamics, DT project ecosystems, and institutional policy. This model illustrates how barriers to inclusion operate hierarchically, from operational to strategic levels, and how each layer must be addressed in an integrated manner to enable systemic change.

Appendix: Supplementary Material

Supplementary material for this article is available online at s.id/Innov8BPMSup-plementaryMaterial.

References

1. Gorbacheva, E., Beekhuyzen, J., vom Brocke, J., Becker, J.: Directions for research on gender imbalance in the IT profession. Eur. J. Inf. Syst. **28**, 43–67 (2019)
2. Belas, J., Kliestik, T., Dvorsky, J., Streimikiene, D. Exploring gender-based disparities in the digital transformation and sustainable development of SMEs in V4 countries. J. Innov. Knowl. **10** (2025)
3. Kalkanci, B., Rahmani, M., Toktay, L.B. The role of inclusive innovation in promoting social sustainability. SSRN Electron. J. (2018)
4. Peng, Y., et al.: Impact of digitalization on process optimization and decision-making towards sustainability: the moderating role of environmental regulation. Sustainability **15**, 15156 (2023)
5. Dobrovic, Z.: The Role of Business Processes in Digital Transformation of the Organization. (Croatian Society for Information, Communication and Electronic Technology – MIPRO) (2021)
6. Liao, C.H., Lian, J.W.: Gender inequality in applying research project and funding. J. Inf. Sci. **50**, 546–554 (2024)
7. Guzmán, E., Fischer, R.A.L., Kok, J.: Mind the gap: gender, micro-inequities and barriers in software development. Empir. Softw. Eng. **29** (2024)
8. Alam, K., Ali, M.A., Erdiaw-Kwasie, M.O., Murray, P.A., Wiesner, R.: Digital transformation among SMEs: does gender matter? Sustainability (Switzerland) **14** (2022)
9. Løvold, H.H., Lindsjørn, Y., Stray, V.: Forming and assessing student teams in software engineering courses. In: LNBIP, vol. 396, pp. 298–306. Springer, Cham (2020)

10. Yalina, N., Graham, G., Ghobadi, S.: Barriers, Challenges, and Benefits: Gender Diversity in Technology-Based New Venture Team Innovation (2024)
11. Sæter, G.E., Lund, C.K. Stray, V.: Agile software engineering capstone courses: exploring the impact of gender. In: LNBIP, vol. 524, pp. 150–158. Springer, Cham (2025)
12. Wu, C., Yan, E., Zhu, Y., Li, K.: Gender imbalance in the productivity of funded projects: a study of the outputs of national institutes of health R01 grants. J. Assoc. Inf. Sci. Technol. **72**, 1386–1399 (2021)
13. Mennega, N., de Villiers, C.: A quarter century of gender and information systems research: the role of theory in investigating the gender imbalance. Gend. Technol. Dev. **25**, 112–130 (2021)
14. He, J., Freeman, L.A.: Are Men More Technology-Oriented Than Women? The Role of Gender on the Development of General Computer Self-Efficacy of College Students. (2010)
15. Kitchenham, B., et al.: Systematic literature reviews in software engineering - a systematic literature review. Inf. Softw. Technol. **51**, 7–15 (2009)
16. Page, M.J., et al.: The PRISMA 2020 statement: an updated guideline for reporting systematic reviews. Int. J. Surg. **88** (2021)
17. Akhmadi, S., Tsakalerou, M.: Exploring gender imbalances in innovation and entrepreneurship: evidence from a global south country. Int. J. Gend. Entrep. **15**, 275–292 (2023)
18. Madichie, N.O., Bolat, E., Taura, N.: Digital transformation in West Africa: a two country, two-sector analysis. J. Enterprising Commun. **15**, 246–257 (2021)
19. Vainionpää, F., Kinnula, M., Iivari, N., Molin-Juustila, T.: Girls in IT: intentionally self-excluded or products of high school as a site of exclusion? Internet Res. **31**, 846–870 (2020)
20. Zajiji, Z., Wilson-Prangley, A., Ndletyana, D.: Board level (in)visibility and critical mass in South African companies. Gend. Manag. **36**, 149–168 (2021)
21. AbdulKareem, A.K., et al.: Investigating ICT adoption and public value of e-recruitment in the public sector: the role of social media use. Int. J. Public Sect. Manag. **37**, 284–304 (2024)
22. Nigam, N., Shatila, K.: Entrepreneurial intention among women entrepreneurs and the mediating effect of dynamic capabilities: empirical evidence from Lebanon. Int. J. Entrepreneurial Behav. Res. **30**, 916–937 (2024)
23. Bhargava, S., Sharma, R., Kulshreshtha, M.: Promoting subjective well-being of IT professionals through gratitude practice: a moderated mediation analysis of gender and employee engagement. Manag. Res. Rev. **47**, 559–580 (2024)
24. Martzoukou, K., Luders, E.S., Work, F., Kostagiolas, P.A., Johnson, N.: Digital divides in nursing students: an exploration of the relationship between self-perceived digital competencies and digital barriers. J. Documentation **81**(2), 330–350 (2025). https://doi.org/10.1108/JD-09-2024-0209
25. Sońta, M.: "Stop talking about gender:" toward positive diversity and inclusion experience of female IT professionals in Poland. Equality, Divers. Incl. **42**, 1021–1037 (2023)
26. Shukla, A., Kushwah, P., Jain, E., Sharma, S.K.: Role of ICT in emancipation of digital entrepreneurship among new generation women. J. Enterprising Commun. **15**, 137–154 (2021)
27. Stefanelli, V., Manta, F., D'Amato, A.: Female CEO and FinTech performance: are senior directors more inclusive? Corp. Gov. (Bingley) **24**, 327–345 (2024)
28. Gorbacheva, E., Stein, A., Schmiedel, T., Müller, O.: The role of gender in business process management competence supply. Bus. Inf. Syst. Eng. **58**, 213–231 (2016)
29. Brown, C., et al.: Academic women co-designing education futures in a postdigital world. Postdigit. Sci. Educ. **6**, 300–320 (2024)
30. Yusif, S., Abunyewah, M., Erdiaw-Kwasie, M.O.: Challenges faced by minority technology entrepreneurs women IT entrepreneurs in South Africa post-apartheid era. J. Int. Entrepreneurship (2024)

31. Mukherjee, T., Ilavarasan, P.V., Kar, A.K.: Empowering through digital skills training: an empirical study of poor unemployed working-age women in India. Inf. Technol. Dev. **30**, 562–583 (2024)
32. Gupta, M., Kiran, R.: Reflection of Gender Digital Divide on Digital Financial Inclusion in Context of Indian Bankers: An Empirical Analysis. Sage Open **14** (2024)
33. Kerrigan, P., Liddy, S., O'Brien, A.: Tools and measures for diversity and inclusion in media industries: International best practice and informing policy change in the Irish film and television sector. Eur. J. Commun. **38**, 217–236 (2023)
34. Mapiye, O., Makombe, G., Molotsi, A., Dzama, K., Mapiye, C.: Information and communication technologies (ICTs): the potential for enhancing the dissemination of agricultural information and services to smallholder farmers in sub-Saharan Africa. Inf. Dev. **39**, 638–658 (2023)
35. Deja, M., Bobkowski, P., Huvila, I., Mierzecka, A.: Empowering through digital skills: a case of alumni in the business services sector. J. Assoc. Inf. Sci. Technol. (2024)
36. Buyannemekh, B., Chen, T.: Digital governance in Mongolia and Taiwan: a gender perspective. Inf. Polity **26**, 193–210 (2021)
37. Senshaw, D., Twinomurinzi, H.: How women circumvent systemic constraints: patriarchy's extension to the adoption of digital government innovations. Inf. Polity 1–19 (2024)
38. Kovaleva, Y., Hyrynsalmi, S., Saltan, A., Happonen, A., Kasurinen, J.: Becoming an entrepreneur: a study of factors with women from the tech sector. Inf. Softw. Technol. **155** (2023)
39. Wijayawardena, K., Wijewardena, N., Samaratunge, R.: Compromising gender identities: stay strategies of women in gender-atypical information technology firms in Sri Lanka. Inf. Technol. People **30**, 246–264 (2017)
40. Sperber, S., Linder, C.: Gender bias in IT entrepreneurship: the self-referential role of male overrepresentation in digital businesses. Eur. J. Inf. Syst. **32**, 902–919 (2023)
41. Hur, J.W., Andrzejewski, C.E., Marghitu, D.: Girls and computer science: experiences, perceptions, and career aspirations. Comput. Sci. Educ. **27**, 100–120 (2017)
42. Zolduoarrati, E., Licorish, S.A.: On the value of encouraging gender tolerance and inclusiveness in software engineering communities. Inf. Softw. Technol. **139** (2021)
43. Vincent, J.: "She does a good job for a woman"–the challenges for women enablers in the era of internet histories. Internet Histories (2024)
44. Mukarram, S.S., Ajmal, T., Saeed, A.: Women directors' propensity towards risk in technology firms. Corp. Gov. (Bingley) **18**, 353–367 (2018)
45. Tretiakov, A., Jurado, T., Bensemann, J.: Women in IT: a work ecosystem perspective. J. Comput. Inf. Syst. (2024)
46. Young, E., Wajcman, J., Sprejer, L.: Mind the gender gap: Inequalities in the emergent professions of artificial intelligence (AI) and data science. New Technol. Work Employ. **38**, 391–414 (2023)
47. Lister, S., et al.: Inclusive by Design: Accelerating Digital Transformation for the Global Goals (2022)
48. Magnani, G., Gioia, D., University of Pavia., Penn State University.: Using the Gioia methodology in international business and entrepreneurship research. Int. Bus. Rev. **32**, 102097 (2023)
49. Widiati, R., Costantini, A., Soetjipto, B.W., Siscawati, M.: Fostering digital innovation among female managers: the interplay of psychological capital, gender equality policies, and leader-member exchange. Gender Manage. Int. J. (2025)
50. Armstrong, D.J., Riemenschneider, C.K., Giddens, L.G.: The advancement and persistence of women in the information technology profession: an extension of Ahuja's gendered theory of IT career stages. Inf. Syst. J. **28**, 1082–1124 (2018)

4th International Workshop on Natural Language Processing for Business Process Management (NLP4BPM 2025)

LLMs for BPM—From First-Wave Features to Process Understanding and Lasting Impact(?)

Adrian Rebmann(✉)

SAP Signavio, Berlin, Germany
adrian.rebmann@sap.com

Abstract. Inspired by recent advancements in applying Large Language Models for Business Process Management tasks, this keynote reflects on current developments in research and industry in this area. It highlights an evolution from first-wave text-extraction approaches to semantics-aware process analysis and in particular discusses the following directions: (1) moving beyond diverse text-extraction approaches that are hard to compare, by putting a growing emphasis on evaluation rigor (2) using LLMs to support data-driven process analysis by equipping them with a deeper understanding of processes, and (3) increasing the integration of LLMs as semantic connectors and coordinators for solving and supporting process analysis tasks. By focusing on these directions, the keynote aims to foster discussion on the next steps to ensure LLMs create a lasting and meaningful impact in the field of BPM.

1 Introduction

The rapid advancements of Large Language Models (LLMs) in the past couple of years have been affecting the field of Business Process Management (BPM) just like any other field. The BPM community has clearly taken notice of the potential of LLMs for tackling or supporting BPM tasks.

In this keynote article, I reflect on recently observed directions in research on applying LLMs for BPM tasks and provide an idea of what an approach that leverages existing research results could look like so that it creates impact in practice. First, after a wave of approaches that have been proposed for text-extraction tasks in BPM, such as extracting process models (e.g. BPMN diagrams) from textual process descriptions it becomes increasingly hard to compare their capabilities. To overcome the limitation of incomparable text-extraction methods, there is a growing emphasis on evaluation rigor, demanding the definition of precise benchmarking tasks and the development of novel assessment methods. Second, increasing attention is put on semantics-aware process analysis, where LLMs are equipped with a deeper understanding of how processes work (as compared to extracting process information from textual sources), enhancing process analysis capabilities such as anomaly detection and process discovery. From an

I. van de Weerd et al. (Eds.): BPM 2025 Workshops, LNBIP 569, pp. 405–411, 2026.
https://doi.org/10.1007/978-3-032-13426-4_29

industry perspective, our current take is that to realize the full value of applying LLMs in BPM, especially in data-driven process analysis and improvement, increasing the integration of LLMs with process analysis tools and content as semantic connectors and coordinators is required.

The provided directions and perspectives are naturally not exhaustive, but shaped by my experience as a PhD candidate researching semantics-aware process mining and the recent experiences in industry I gained thereafter. The goal is to foster a discussion on important next steps that our community may take to advance research and practice on the application of LLMs for BPM.

2 Extracting Process Specifications

Initial research on applying LLMs for BPM focused on translating textual descriptions into formal process specifications, such as Business Process Model and Notation (BPMN) [7,9]. An LLM generates a structured process model from a user's natural language description. To this end, the majority of approaches target intermediate representations, e.g., lists or graphs, that are subsequently turned into an established modeling notation such as BPMN. Beyond *text-to-model* capabilities, *text-to-query* approaches are proposed [1], where LLMs translate natural language questions into formal query languages like SQL to be executed on event logs, to compute specific metrics like cycle times, or on source data bases to extract event logs [16] that are then used for process mining, making data-driven process analysis more accessible.

However, the rapid development of diverse text-extraction approaches and product features raises questions about their comparability and differentiators. From the perspective of a vendor for process analysis software, curated data such as best-practice content as can be considered a differentiator. For instance, LLMs can be provided access to large collections of reference process models for various industries that can then help derive process models from text that are better tailored to the context of a user.

While this can provide a competitive edge in industry, from a research perspective, the development of such diverse approaches that pursue similar goals raises critical questions about their comparability and objective performance. This presents a hurdle for users of these approaches, as it is difficult to objectively assess which approach is most suitable for their specific context and needs. Thus, a considerable challenge is the rigorous evaluation of these LLM based approaches [6]. This has led to first proposals for benchmarks for Text-to-Model [4] and Text-to-Query [1], which clearly highlights the community's need for precise task definitions, comprehensive data, and consistent evaluation metrics. However, as of now, there is no alignment on such tasks and consequently there are no established task-specific benchmarking datasets such as those that the Natural Language Processing Community (NLP) has established for common tasks such as Question Answering [13] and Text Summarization [11]. Therefore, a promising direction could be to further promote the proposal of task definitions for NLP-powered BPM tasks and associated benchmarking data that can be used by the community.

To address the challenge of evaluating LLMs without ground-truth data, novel unsupervised methods are being developed. An example is *Round-Trip Correctness* (RTC) [10], which works in two steps: (1) an LLM converts an existing process model into a natural language description, and (2) the same LLM converts this description back into a process model. A similarity score is then derived by comparing the original and reconstructed models. A high score suggests the LLM understood the underlying process well. Findings show a strong correlation between high RTC scores and accuracy on traditional, human-annotated benchmarks, making it a cost-effective tool for assessing LLM performance [10].

3 Understanding Processes

Beyond text extraction, research is increasingly using LLMs for direct process analysis in a stream called *semantics-aware process mining*. The core idea is to leverage an LLM's understanding of the *meaning* (semantics) of activities and data to enhance analysis. This allows for the identification of logical flaws—such as a *Reject Order* followed by a *Create Invoice*—that traditional techniques might miss. This deeper understanding benefits tasks like anomaly detection [3, 5], next activity prediction [17], and process discovery [2,14].

To better understand the practical capabilities and limitations of LLMs in semantics-aware process mining, we conducted our own research to address two fundamental questions. First, we ask whether LLMs can effectively solve these semantics-aware tasks [14]. Second, and more challengingly, we investigate whether a single, flexible LLM can generalize its understanding across various and especially previously unseen process analysis tasks [12]. To answer these, we generated labeled evaluation datasets from a large public process model collection [15] for precisely defined tasks such as identifying semantically invalid activity sequences and generating structured process models based only on a set of possible activities.

We explored three primary adaptation strategies. *In-Context Learning (ICL)*, even with few-shot prompting, performed poorly. In contrast, *Fine-Tuning*, where a pretrained LLM is trained on a single task, yielded strong performance [14]. However, this approach is not scalable, as it requires creating an expensive, specialized model for each individual task. To address generalization, we turned to *Instruction-Tuning*, where an LLM is fine-tuned on a diverse mix of tasks and instructions, enabling it to handle new, unseen tasks.

The comparison reveals a critical trade-off. Fine-tuned models achieve the strongest performance on the specific task they were trained for. However, the key advantage of instruction-tuning is the ability to create a single, versatile model that can generalize, a crucial feature for a scalable process analysis tool. While smaller encoder models can match the performance of large fine-tuned models on simple classification tasks, the decoder architecture of LLMs is uniquely suited for the flexibility that instruction-tuning provides. Ultimately, the choice is between prioritizing specialized performance on a single task, using fine-tuning, or investing in a more flexible, general-purpose process analysis tool, using instruction-tuning.

There are many promising directions for additional research in this area, focusing, for instance, on extending the existing set of semantics-aware process mining tasks to investigate, but importantly also the integration of semantics-aware process analysis capabilities into existing process mining approaches.

4 Orchestrating Process Understanding and Analysis

Integrating LLMs into process modeling and analysis tools has the potential to create substantial impact in practice leading to business value. Text-extraction approaches and corresponding product features that generate BPMN diagrams from textual process descriptions, for instance, can considerably increase user efficiency by simplifying complex and time-consuming modeling tasks. Instead of starting from an empty canvas, a user can simply describe their process or leverage existing process documentation to get to a first version of their process model in seconds. Beyond extraction-oriented approaches, semantics-aware capabilities can provide a deeper level of process analysis. By taking the meaning behind process steps into account, such tools would allow organizations, among others, to more thoroughly identify and rectify logical flaws within process models and event data and to more reliably detect non-compliant or risky behavior based on semantic context. Such identification of semantic inconsistencies can help prevent costly operational errors and reduce rework in the future, ensuring the process executes logically as intended.

Given this potential, creating a single versatile LLM for solving any given process analysis task presents itself as an option. This would require embedding all possible knowledge directly into an LLM, though. From a practical point of view, such a strategy would be inefficient, inflexible, and not viable [12]. Therefore, a more modular and scalable architecture is required to leverage the power of LLMs effectively.

A more scalable solution may involve the creation and selection of specialists that are tailored to specific process analysis use cases. Crucially, these need to be provided with the right organizational context and analysis tooling to elicit informed answers to diverse process-related queries effectively. This aligns with the vision of a Large Process Model [8] and could be realized through an architecture where a central *Coordinator* LLM orchestrates a variety of task specialists, including, e.g., *Process Expert*, *Query Developer*, *Dashboard Retriever*, *Event Log Info Retriever*, *Metrics Expert*, etc. For example, the *Process Expert* is not a generic language model but an agent with access to context-specific information, including customer's content (specific process models, business rules, metric definitions, and more) and best practice content (a repository of established process models, rules, PPIs for end-to-end processes, process data models, common improvement opportunities, and industry benchmarks). The *Query Developer* would be an LLM specialized for Text-to-Query tasks. This division of labor ensures that each component of the analysis is handled by a specialist, grounded on data and process analysis tooling, while leveraging the semantic understanding of LLMs to link the relevant content.

While this vision of such a modular, orchestrated system is promising, its practical realization presents various challenges and thus directions for future research. One important research direction, for instance, is the governance of such a system and providing concepts for how to deal with the autonomy of the coordinating LLM as well as the individual specialists. Here, BPM research can play an important role, for instance, in providing guardrails for autonomous LLM agents when performing BPM tasks. For example, established BPM concepts like conformance checking and risk management frameworks can be adapted to define operational boundaries for these AI agents. This involves creating explicit process models for the LLM's decision-making, ensuring that the orchestrated system remains transparent and aligned with organizational goals.

5 Conclusion

In this keynote article, I discussed two recently observed directions in BPM research on applying LLMs for BPM tasks and provides an industry perspective on a promising approach to leverage LLMs for process analysis.

The advancement of research on NLP for BPM calls for increased evaluation rigor. This includes the development of novel evaluation approaches, such as round-trip correctness, to validate model understanding without constant reliance on vast amounts human-labeled data. Such validation is a prerequisite for building trust and ensuring the reliability of LLM-powered solutions for business process analysis. Furthermore, establishing precise tasks and comprehensive benchmarking data is crucial for measuring and comparing capabilities in a standardized way, which has already been addressed in various recent contributions.

Moreover, the ability of LLMs to understand process semantics can play a key role in developing the next generation of intelligent process analysis approaches and tools. However, attempting to embed and maintain all required specialized knowledge within an LLM, we currently consider neither viable nor scalable. Therefore, we rather focus on the strengths of LLMs as contextualizers and coordinators that can access existing process analysis tools and curated knowledge bases, which provide the essential data- and model-driven grounding. An LLM provides the necessary semantic understanding to link relevant content, interpret user intent, and orchestrate specialized functions. In this manner, we leverage the best of both worlds: the factual power of process analysis tools and the flexible, semantic understanding of LLMs.

Realizing such an architecture introduces substantial governance challenges, though, which the BPM field is uniquely equipped to address. Its mature toolkit of modeling and analysis approaches provides the methods that are needed to ensure the system operates in a robust and controlled manner. For instance, techniques such as process simulation can be used to test the behavior of LLM-driven systems in a controlled environment before deployment, while declarative process modeling and monitoring methods can ensure that their actions adhere to predefined business rules.

References

1. Berti, A., Kourani, H., van der Aalst, W.M.: PM-LLM-benchmark: evaluating large language models on process mining tasks. In: International Conference on Process Mining, pp. 610–623. Springer, Cham (2024)
2. Berti, A., Kourani, H., Häfke, H., Li, C.Y., Schuster, D.: Evaluating large language models in process mining: capabilities, benchmarks, and evaluation strategies. In: International Conference on Business Process Modeling, Development and Support, pp. 13–21. Springer, Cham (2024)
3. Busch, K., Kampik, T., Leopold, H.: xsemad: explainable semantic anomaly detection in event logs using sequence-to-sequence models. In: International Conference on Business Process Management, pp. 309–327. Springer, Cham (2024)
4. Busch, K., Leopold, H.: Towards a benchmark for large language models for business process management tasks. arXiv preprint arXiv:2410.03255 (2024)
5. Caspary, J., Rebmann, A., van der Aa, H.: Does this make sense? Machine learning-based detection of semantic anomalies in business processes. In: International Conference on Business Process Management, pp. 163–179. Springer, Cham (2023)
6. Estrada-Torres, B., del Río-Ortega, A., Resinas, M.: Mapping the landscape: exploring large language model applications in business process management. In: International Conference on Business Process Modeling, Development and Support, pp. 22–31. Springer, Cham (2024)
7. Grohs, M., Abb, L., Elsayed, N., Rehse, J.R.: Large language models can accomplish business process management tasks. In: International Conference on Business Process Management, pp. 453–465. Springer, Cham (2023)
8. Kampik, T., et al.: Large process models: a vision for business process management in the age of generative AI. KI-Künstliche Intelligenz 1–15 (2024)
9. Klievtsova, N., Benzin, J.V., Kampik, T., Mangler, J., Rinderle-Ma, S.: Conversational process modelling: state of the art, applications, and implications in practice. In: International Conference on Business Process Management, pp. 319–336. Springer, Cham (2023)
10. Klievtsova, N., Hadian, S., Kampik, T., Mangler, J., Engelns-Bauer, F., Rinderle-Ma, S.: Round-trip correctness: a new metric for generative AI-based process modeling (2025). https://community.sap.com/t5/technology-blog-posts-by-sap/round-trip-correctness-a-new-metric-for-generative-ai-based-process/ba-p/14091979. Accessed 15 Sept 2025
11. Narayan, S., Cohen, S.B., Lapata, M.: Don't give me the details, just the summary! topic-aware convolutional neural networks for extreme summarization. arXiv:1808.08745 (2018)
12. Pyrih, V., Rebmann, A., van der Aa, H.: LLMs that understand processes: instruction-tuning for semantics-aware process mining. In: International Conference on Process Mining (2025, accepted for publication)
13. Rajpurkar, P., Zhang, J., Lopyrev, K., Liang, P.: Squad: 100,000+ questions for machine comprehension of text. arXiv:1606.05250 (2016)
14. Rebmann, A., Schmidt, F.D., Glavaš, G., van der Aa, H.: On the potential of large language models to solve semantics-aware process mining tasks. Process Sci. **2**(1), 10 (2025)
15. Sola, D., Warmuth, C., Schäfer, B., Badakhshan, P., Rehse, J.R., Kampik, T.: Sap signavio academic models: a large process model dataset. In: International Conference on Process Mining, pp. 453–465. Springer, Cham (2022)

16. Stein Dani, V., et al.: Event log extraction for process mining using large language models. In: International Conference on Cooperative Information Systems, pp. 56–72. Springer, Cham (2024)
17. Yuan, J., Grigori, D., van der Aa, H.: Enhancing predictive process monitoring using semantic information. In: International Conference on Process Mining, pp. 293–305. Springer, Cham (2024)

Configuring Large Reasoning Models Using Process Mining: A Benchmark and a Case Study

Alessandro Berti[1,2(✉)], Humam Kourani[1,2], Gyunam Park[1,2], and Wil M. P. van der Aalst[1,2]

[1] Process and Data Science Chair, RWTH Aachen University, Aachen, Germany
{a.berti,wvdaalst}@pads.rwth-aachen.de
[2] Fraunhofer FIT, Sankt Augustin, Germany
{humam.kourani,gyunam.park}@fit.fraunhofer.de

Abstract. Large Reasoning Models (LRMs), a subset of Large Language Models (LLMs) trained to articulate their chain-of-thought, have shown promise in tackling complex scientific tasks. However, evaluating and configuring their reasoning processes remains underexplored. This paper leverages a process mining-specific LLM evaluation framework to propose a methodology for analyzing and configuring LRMs. We introduce an approach to extract and classify reasoning steps by type (e.g., Deductive Reasoning, or Hypothesis Generation) and effect (Positive, Indifferent, Negative) on the overall reasoning, enabling a detailed assessment of reasoning quality. From this, we derive a new benchmark, *PMLRM-Bench*, which evaluates not only the correctness of outputs but also the robustness of the reasoning process. A case study on the QwQ-32B LLM demonstrates how targeted adjustments to reasoning type frequencies can boost task-specific performance. Our results reveal distinct reasoning patterns across models and provide actionable insights for LRM configuration. This work bridges process mining and LLM evaluation, offering a scalable framework for reasoning analysis.

Keywords: Large Reasoning Models · Process Mining · Reasoning Analysis

1 Introduction

The rapid rise of Large Language Models (LLMs) has revolutionized natural language processing, excelling in tasks like text generation and question answering. Yet, for scientific reasoning—requiring transparent, logical, and verifiable processes—standard LLMs often falter. Large Reasoning Models (LRMs), a specialized LLM subset, address this by outputting their chain-of-thought, vital for scientific tasks where the reasoning process matters as much as the result. Still, evaluating and optimizing LRMs is insufficiently studied, lacking standard methods to enhance their reasoning abilities.

I. van de Weerd et al. (Eds.): BPM 2025 Workshops, LNBIP 569, pp. 412–424, 2026.
https://doi.org/10.1007/978-3-032-13426-4_30

Analyzing the reasoning traces—textual outputs of an LRM's step-by-step thought process—helps uncover the mechanisms driving LRMs, revealing patterns, strengths, and weaknesses in their reasoning. For instance, Fig. 1 illustrates the response of an LRM prompted to identify bottlenecks in a hypothetical event log, employing a diverse array of reasoning types, such as Pattern

```
<think>
Event log timestamps show Activity A takes 1 minute, B takes 1 minute, C
takes 5 minutes, D takes 1 minute across multiple cases, suggesting C is
significantly slower than others. Pattern Recognition - PE

C consistently takes 5 minutes while other activities take 1 minute, so C is
likely causing a delay in the process flow, as it exceeds the average
activity duration. Deductive Reasoning - PE

In process mining, an activity with consistently longer durations across
cases often indicates a bottleneck, as seen in similar logs where delays
cluster around a single activity. Inductive Reasoning - PE

Delay at C could result from insufficient resources, complex tasks, or
external dependencies, with resource scarcity being the most plausible given
uniform task complexity in the log. Abductive Reasoning - IND

Adding resources to activity C could reduce its duration and improve overall
process throughput, assuming resource constraints are the primary issue.
Hypothesis Generation - PE

Log shows C has fewer assigned resources (e.g., one worker vs. three for A,
B, D), supporting the resource bottleneck hypothesis. Validation - PE

If resource data is unavailable, the conclusion about C's bottleneck may be
premature, so reconsider if C's delay is due to task complexity rather than
resources. Backtracking - IND

Reallocating resources to C could disadvantage other activities or workers
(e.g., overburdening staff), raising ethical concerns about equitable
resource distribution. Ethical or Moral Reasoning - IND

If C had not been identified as the bottleneck, increasing resources for B
or D would likely not prevent delays, as their durations are already
minimal. Counterfactual Reasoning - IND

In process mining, prioritizing resource allocation to the slowest activity
often yields the fastest throughput improvement, so focus on optimizing C
first. Heuristic Reasoning - PE

Cases with high throughput show C with additional resources, reinforcing the
hypothesis that resource allocation mitigates the bottleneck. Validation - PE

If C's delay persists despite added resources, external factors (e.g.,
system downtime) may contribute, requiring further log analysis. Abductive
Reasoning - IND
</think>

Activity C is likely a bottleneck due to resource constraints, supported by
consistent delays and validated by resource allocation patterns. Further
analysis of external factors is recommended. Conclusion - C
```

Fig. 1. Example reasoning trace from an LRM analyzing an event log for bottlenecks, showcasing a diverse set of reasoning types (Sect. 2.2) classified using the LLMs-as-a-Judge evaluation strategy (the methodology and choice of the judge is explained in Sect. 2.3). Each step, as explained in Sect. 3.1, is labeled as PE (positive), IND (indifferent), or NE (negative) based on its effect on the overall reasoning correctness.

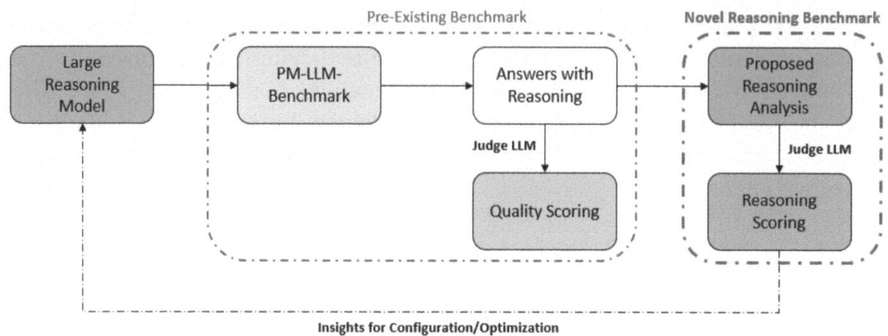

Fig. 2. Schematic overview of the reasoning analysis pipeline proposed in the paper.

Recognition, Deductive Reasoning, Hypothesis Generation, and Ethical Reasoning, each labeled with its effect on correctness (Positive, Indifferent, or Negative) of the overall reasoning.

This paper leverages the PM-LLM-Benchmark v2.0, a process mining-specific LLM evaluation framework providing a rich dataset of LLM responses to complex process mining prompts https://github.com/fit-alessandro-berti/pm-llm-benchmark [2], to propose a novel methodology for evaluating and enhancing Large Reasoning Models (LRMs).

We introduce a reasoning analysis pipeline, schematically overviewed in Fig. 2. This pipeline starts with the raw reasoning traces (textual outputs) collected from the PM-LLM-Benchmark v2.0 dataset as input. An extraction step then parses these unstructured traces, transforming them into structured objects. During this extraction, each identified reasoning step within a trace is classified by its type (e.g., Deductive Reasoning, Hypothesis Generation) and its effect on the overall correctness (Positive, Indifferent, or Negative), as demonstrated in Fig. 1. Subsequently, an analysis stage processes these structured JSON traces to compute various metrics and systematically evaluate the quality and patterns of the LRM's reasoning process, going beyond mere output accuracy.

Following the reasoning analysis pipeline, we propose two key contributions to advance the evaluation and configuration of LRMs for process mining tasks:

- *Benchmark Introduction*: We present *PMLRM-Bench*, an extension of the PM-LLM-Benchmark, designed to evaluate both the correctness of LRM outputs and the robustness of their reasoning processes, providing a comprehensive assessment of reasoning quality.
- *Case Study Insights*: A case study on the `qwen-qwq-32b` model illustrates how adjusting the frequency of specific reasoning types can address weaknesses, enhancing performance on process mining tasks and offering actionable strategies for optimizing LRMs for scientific applications.

The rest of the paper is organized as follows. Section 2 reviews related work. Section 3 presents our framework and the proposed benchmark. Section 4 evaluates LRM performance, while Sect. 5 showcases reasoning adjustments via a case study. Eventually, Sect. 6 summarizes findings and future steps.

2 Related Work

2.1 LLMs in Process Mining

Large Language Models (LLMs) have demonstrated potential in Business Process Management (BPM) and Process Mining (PM). Research shows LLMs can automate BPM tasks like process documentation, though challenges persist with complex structures [2,11,25]. Their application in process mining highlights the need for domain-specific fine-tuning [24]. Encoding process mining data into textual prompts is crucial due to LLMs' input limitations. Abstractions for representing event logs have been proposed, enabling tasks like conformance checking, though prompt engineering remains a hurdle [4]. Transforming logs into narratives for bottleneck detection emphasizes the role of structured prompts for accurate outputs [3].

Evaluation frameworks are vital for assessing LLMs in PM. Studies focusing on semantics-aware tasks find LLMs excel in contextual inference but struggle with complex tasks [24]. A benchmark for causal process reasoning notes LLMs' potential in decision-making but limitations in complex causal analysis [8]. Evaluations of LLMs on process modeling and querying show they generate correct models and answer queries effectively with structured prompts, though performance drops with ambiguous data [19,20]. The PM-LLM-Benchmark assesses LLMs across seven PM task categories, revealing strengths in pattern recognition but weaknesses in speculative reasoning [2].

This work builds on these efforts by introducing a reasoning analysis pipeline that classifies LRM reasoning steps by type and effect, extending the PM-LLM-Benchmark to optimize LRMs for scientific tasks through detailed evaluation.

2.2 Reasoning Types

A taxonomy of ten reasoning types is adopted to evaluate LRMs for scientific tasks like process mining: Pattern Recognition (PR), Deductive Reasoning (DR), Inductive Reasoning (IR), Abductive Reasoning (AR), Hypothesis Generation (HG), Validation (V), Backtracking (B), Ethical or Moral Reasoning (ER), Counterfactual Reasoning (CR), and Heuristic Reasoning (HR). These types draw from cognitive and computational theories, including deduction, induction, and abduction [7,12,22], meta-cognitive strategies like hypothesis generation and validation [15,23], and socio-technical considerations such as heuristics and ethical checks [5,10,21]. This taxonomy supports comprehensive analysis of LRM reasoning processes.

Each reasoning type is defined with its theoretical basis and relevance to process mining: PR detects patterns and anomalies [5]; DR derives logical conclusions [14]; IR generalizes from data [13]; AR infers plausible explanations [9]; HG formulates testable hypotheses [16]; V verifies reasoning steps [23]; B revises prior steps [17]; ER ensures ethical fairness [18]; CR explores causal scenarios [21]; and HR applies efficient rules [10]. This taxonomy enables the dissection of LRM reasoning traces, as shown in Fig. 1, where steps are classified by type and effect (Positive, Indifferent, or Negative) to assess reasoning quality.

2.3 LLMs-as-a-Judge Evaluation Strategy

The LLMs-as-a-Judge paradigm is employed to evaluate LRM reasoning processes, excelling in classifying reasoning traces by type and effect, surpassing traditional metrics. LLMs leverage their natural language understanding to assess response quality beyond correctness. Studies show LLMs align closely with human judgments in reasoning evaluation, enabling rapid processing of large datasets like the PM-LLM-Benchmark v2.0 [27]. Their ability to evaluate coherence and logical consistency is crucial for classifying reasoning types like Deductive Reasoning or Hypothesis Generation [26]. With appropriate prompting, LLMs handle domain-specific tasks effectively, achieving high-precision evaluations using detailed rubrics [6]. LLMs also outperform rule-based systems in evaluating multi-step reasoning [1].

3 Methodology

This section presents the core framework for analyzing and benchmarking Large Reasoning Models (LRMs) using the PM-LLM-Benchmark v2.0 dataset, culminating in the *PMLRM-Bench* benchmark available at https://github.com/fit-alessandro-berti/pmllmbench-lrms-reasoning-analysis. The approach leverages reasoning traces—textual outputs from LRMs that articulate their chain-of-thought—to assess not only the correctness of answers but also the quality and structure of the reasoning process. By extracting, classifying, and analyzing these traces, we establish a systematic method to evaluate and configure LRMs for scientific tasks, particularly within the process mining domain.

3.1 Reasoning Trace Extraction

The foundation of our framework lies in extracting structured data from the unstructured textual responses of LRMs, as provided by the PM-LLM-Benchmark v2.0 dataset (https://github.com/fit-alessandro-berti/pm-llm-benchmark/). This dataset contains a diverse set of process mining prompts spanning seven categories, such as contextual understanding and conformance checking, along with corresponding LRM outputs. Each response, referred to as a reasoning trace, is parsed into a sequence of individual reasoning steps, which are then stored as JSON objects. These steps are classified by *Gemini-2.5-Pro-Preview-03-25*, currently the latest model of the Google Gemini family, serving as the judge LLM to determine their reasoning type and effect. Every step is assigned a name that combines its reasoning type—such as PR, DR, IR, AR, HG, V, B, ER, CR, or HR—and its effect on correctness, labeled as **PE** for positive effect, **IND** for indifferent or neutral effect, or **NE** for negative effect. Alongside the name, each JSON object includes a text field containing the specific excerpt from the reasoning trace that corresponds to that step. At the end of each trace, a special conclusion entry is appended to indicate the overall correctness of the reasoning process, marked as Conclusion - **C** for correct, Conclusion - **PC** for partially correct, or Conclusion - **W** for wrong, also judged by *Gemini-2.5-Pro-Preview-03-25*. This conclusion entry does not include a text snippet, serving solely as a summary of the trace's outcome. Through this extraction process, we transform raw LRM outputs into a standardized format suitable for detailed analysis.

3.2 Metrics

The analysis pipeline processes structured JSON logs extracted in the previous subsection by aggregating reasoning steps and conclusions. The goal of the composite score S is to reward correct conclusions (**C**) and positive-effect steps (**PE**), which advance reasoning accuracy, while penalizing partially correct (**PC**) and wrong (**W**) conclusions, as well as indifferent (**IND**) and negative-effect (**NE**) steps, which either do not contribute to or detract from correctness.

The pipeline first counts conclusion outcomes (**C**, **PC**, **W**) to assess overall accuracy. It then aggregates step effects (**PE**, **IND**, **NE**) to evaluate reasoning quality. Frequencies of reasoning types (e.g., Pattern Recognition, Deductive Reasoning) are calculated, including the proportion of **PE** steps per type. The composite score is defined as:

$$S = (100 \cdot \mathbf{C} - 100 \cdot \mathbf{PC} - 200 \cdot \mathbf{W}) + (10 \cdot \mathbf{PE} - 1 \cdot \mathbf{IND} - 20 \cdot \mathbf{NE}),$$

Table 1. Model performance scores and reasoning step statistics for evaluated LRMs.

Model	S	C	PC	W	PE	IND	NE	PM-LLM-B. Score
Grok-3-thinking-20250221	**14459**	45	1	0	1039	131	10	**39.8**
qwen-qwq-32b-nostepbystep	**13281**	44	2	0	945	109	13	**36.9**
exaone-deep7.8b-fp16	**12381**	44	2	0	851	109	11	**30.2**
DeepSeek-R1-671B-HB	**12303**	45	1	0	830	97	15	**36.8**
Perplexity-R1-1776	**12095**	45	1	0	779	75	1	**32.1**
qwen-qwq-32b-stepbystep	**12027**	44	2	0	848	113	27	**35.8**
nvidia-nemotron-super-49b	**11856**	46	0	0	747	74	7	**36.4**
QwenQwQ-32B-Preview	**11725**	44	1	1	783	65	7	**28.9**
exaone-deep32b-fp16	**11187**	43	3	0	779	103	25	**31.6**
exaone-deep2.4b-fp16	**10481**	40	3	3	806	139	27	**23.5**
R1-Distill-Qwen-14B	**10433**	42	4	0	697	97	12	**27.8**
R1-Distill-Llama-70B	**10153**	40	5	1	717	57	13	**28.6**
R1-Distill-Qwen-32B	**9970**	42	4	0	650	50	14	**30.7**
DeepSeek-R1-Zero	**9765**	46	0	0	523	45	1	**29.9**
R1-Distill-Llama-8B	**7307**	33	10	3	726	153	75	**20.6**
R1-Distill-Qwen-7B	**3811**	26	16	4	578	149	101	**16.8**
R1-Distill-Qwen-1.5B	**-7724**	15	12	19	472	184	438	**9.9**

where weights reflect the relative impact of each component. Correct conclusions (**C**) receive a high positive weight (+100) to emphasize accurate outcomes. Wrong conclusions (**W**) are heavily penalized (-200) due to their detrimental effect on reliability. Partially correct conclusions (**PC**) receive a moderate penalty (-100) to account for partial accuracy. For steps, positive-effect steps (**PE**) are rewarded (+10) for advancing reasoning, negative-effect steps (**NE**) are penalized (-20) for introducing errors, and indifferent or redundant steps (**IND**) receive a small penalty (-1) for their neutral or inefficient contribution. These weights were tuned to balance the emphasis on correct outcomes and robust reasoning processes.

For example, consider the reasoning trace in Fig. 1 with 12 steps and a conclusion: 6 **PE** steps (PR, DR, IR, HG, V, HR), 5 **IND** steps (two AR, V, ER, CR), and no **NE** steps. The conclusion is $\mathbf{C} = 1$, $\mathbf{PC} = 0$, $\mathbf{W} = 0$. Limited to that answer, the score is:

$$S = (100 \cdot 1 - 100 \cdot 0 - 200 \cdot 0) + (10 \cdot 6 - 1 \cdot 5 - 20 \cdot 0) = 100 + (60 - 5) = 155.$$

4 Benchmark

This section proposes a benchmark evaluating Large Reasoning Models (LRMs) that do not artificially obscure their chain-of-thought. Models that obscure their reasoning process (such as OpenAI `o1-2024-12-17`) are excluded. The analysis, summarized in Tables 1, 2, 3 and 4, assesses model performance across overall scores, reasoning type distributions, correctness rates, and task-specific patterns.

Results: Table 1 reports composite scores (S) and reasoning step effects for the proposed *PMLRM-Bench*, alongside PM-LLM-Benchmark scores. Leading models achieve high S with predominantly positive-effect steps, excelling in structured reasoning tasks. Weaker models show more errors and negative-effect steps, reflecting challenges in logical coherence. Intermediate models balance accuracy and efficiency, indicating effective reasoning strategies. A strong positive correlation (Pearson's $r = 0.89$) between S and PM-LLM-Benchmark scores suggests that robust reasoning processes align closely with overall task performance.

Table 2 highlights how models allocate reasoning effort. Top performers favor deductive reasoning for structured tasks while balancing hypothesis generation and validation. Less effective models over-rely on speculative reasoning, often lacking sufficient validation, which impacts performance.

Correctness rates per reasoning type, shown in Table 3, reveal strengths in foundational reasoning like pattern recognition and deduction among strong models. Weaker models struggle across reasoning types, particularly in logical and exploratory tasks, reflecting inconsistent accuracy.

Category-Reasoning Correlation: Table 4 details reasoning steps by PM-LLM-Benchmark task category. DR and HG dominate, aligning with process mining challenges like contextual understanding and model generation. Fairness-related tasks show increased ER, while CR remains minimal, indicating limited "what-if" analysis.

Validation: To validate the robustness of reasoning step classifications by *Gemini-2.5-Pro-Preview-03-25*, we used *ChatGPT-4o-latest-2025-03-26* as a second judge to evaluate their correctness. This review assessed the alignment of each step's text with its assigned reasoning type and effect in the PM-LLM-Benchmark v2.0 dataset. Results showed 82.40% full agreement (Y), 13.01% partial agreement (P), and 4.59% no agreement (N), indicating high consistency in the primary classifications.

Table 2. Percentage distribution of reasoning types over total steps for each model.

Model	PR	DR	IR	AR	HG	V	B	ER	CR	HR
Grok-3-thinking-20250221	13.5	31.9	2.8	2.1	16.8	17.9	3.9	1.3	1.4	**8.5**
qwen-qwq-32b-nostepbystep	13.5	33.5	1.5	1.6	20.1	17.5	5.0	**2.2**	0.9	4.2
exaone-deep7.8b-fp16	14.8	33.2	**3.6**	2.9	19.4	14.4	5.3	0.8	0.9	4.7
DeepSeek-R1-671B-HB	13.0	32.0	2.2	**4.5**	16.9	**19.2**	2.1	1.0	1.1	8.2
Perplexity-R1-1776	16.5	28.2	2.9	2.7	20.4	16.6	3.6	1.3	1.5	6.3
qwen-qwq-32b-stepbystep	15.9	33.1	2.4	1.0	20.3	16.2	4.5	1.3	0.6	4.7
nvidia-nemotron-super-49b	16.2	35.4	1.0	1.9	17.4	18.1	2.9	1.0	0.7	5.4
QwenQwQ-32B-Preview	14.6	34.6	3.3	2.9	15.3	17.5	1.9	1.6	**1.8**	6.4
exaone-deep32b-fp16	12.8	32.1	2.5	2.6	17.3	17.9	5.6	1.4	0.8	6.9
exaone-deep2.4b-fp16	15.5	30.8	1.6	2.2	20.1	15.4	6.5	1.2	1.2	5.5
R1-Distill-Qwen-14B	18.6	30.5	2.6	1.6	19.7	15.9	3.3	0.7	0.7	6.2
R1-Distill-Llama-70B	16.1	31.4	1.9	2.9	21.6	14.2	3.3	0.9	0.9	6.7
R1-Distill-Qwen-32B	15.5	34.2	3.5	2.4	17.8	14.8	4.5	0.6	0.4	6.3
DeepSeek-R1-Zero	**18.8**	**40.1**	3.5	3.0	11.6	15.1	0.5	1.2	0.7	5.4
R1-Distill-Llama-8B	14.7	28.9	2.0	1.2	23.9	15.0	6.0	1.4	0.8	6.2
R1-Distill-Qwen-7B	15.8	27.1	2.5	0.6	21.1	18.7	5.6	1.1	1.0	6.5
R1-Distill-Qwen-1.5B	14.6	25.3	0.9	1.8	**29.2**	10.2	**9.5**	0.7	0.7	6.9

Table 3. Percentage of correctness per reasoning type for each model.

Model	PR	DR	IR	AR	HG	V	B	ER	CR	HR
Grok-3-thinking-20250221	97.5	96.3	90.9	68.0	72.2	94.3	76.1	**100.0**	47.1	75.0
qwen-qwq-32b-nostepbystep	95.1	96.9	**100.0**	88.2	77.2	89.3	60.4	**100.0**	60.0	82.2
exaone-deep7.8b-fp16	93.8	96.9	85.7	82.1	74.5	95.0	74.5	**100.0**	66.7	56.5
DeepSeek-R1-671B-HB	95.9	97.3	85.7	90.5	69.8	95.6	70.0	88.9	40.0	70.1
Perplexity-R1-1776	96.5	97.5	96.0	78.3	**88.5**	93.0	67.7	90.9	30.8	83.3
qwen-qwq-32b-stepbystep	93.6	93.6	**100.0**	60.0	66.7	91.9	52.3	**100.0**	**83.3**	**93.5**
nvidia-nemotron-super-49b	97.0	96.2	87.5	62.5	79.2	92.0	75.0	**100.0**	**83.3**	77.8
QwenQwQ-32B-Preview	97.6	97.6	**100.0**	76.0	85.5	90.7	87.5	92.9	40.0	80.0
exaone-deep32b-fp16	91.4	95.5	91.3	91.7	73.9	87.7	66.7	92.3	57.1	69.8
exaone-deep2.4b-fp16	91.4	91.6	**100.0**	76.2	68.7	88.7	69.8	**100.0**	25.0	67.9
R1-Distill-Qwen-14B	96.0	93.5	95.2	**100.0**	70.4	88.3	77.8	**100.0**	66.7	68.0
R1-Distill-Llama-70B	98.4	95.1	**100.0**	82.6	84.1	92.0	**88.5**	**100.0**	71.4	79.2
R1-Distill-Qwen-32B	96.4	95.9	96.0	82.4	87.4	**96.2**	50.0	**100.0**	66.7	80.0
DeepSeek-R1-Zero	**99.1**	**98.7**	**100.0**	88.2	78.8	83.7	0.0	**100.0**	25.0	80.6
R1-Distill-Llama-8B	92.9	88.8	**100.0**	81.8	61.0	77.6	42.1	**100.0**	12.5	59.3
R1-Distill-Qwen-7B	84.7	79.0	61.9	**100.0**	56.0	67.7	45.7	**100.0**	25.0	68.5
R1-Distill-Qwen-1.5B	72.5	46.6	60.0	65.0	21.6	50.0	34.6	87.5	25.0	50.0

Table 4. Percentage distribution of reasoning steps by category across all models.

PM-LLM-B. Category	PR	DR	IR	AR	HG	V	B	ER	CR	HR
cat01 (Context Understanding)	18.6	28.8	2.9	2.7	17.5	18.1	4.2	0.0	1.1	6.1
cat02 (Conformance Checking)	17.2	**38.1**	2.4	3.6	12.2	15.7	3.8	0.0	0.8	6.2
cat03 (Process Modeling)	12.7	30.1	2.2	1.0	**24.1**	15.9	7.6	0.0	0.4	6.0
cat04 (Process Querying)	8.3	32.9	1.7	2.9	20.4	19.9	4.1	0.0	1.5	**8.1**
cat05 (Hypotheses Generation)	18.0	28.9	1.6	0.7	**26.5**	15.2	2.2	0.1	0.3	6.6
cat06 (Fairness)	18.4	29.7	4.1	1.9	18.8	9.9	3.1	**9.5**	1.9	2.7

5 Case Study

In this case study, we explore how adjusting the frequency of specific reasoning types in Large Reasoning Models (LRMs) can enhance their performance, using the QwQ-32B model—a 32-billion parameter LRM from the Qwen Team at Alibaba Cloud, refined via reinforcement learning for complex problem-solving (https://huggingface.co/Qwen/QwQ-32B). We leverage the PM-LLM-Benchmark v2.0 benchmark to evaluate variants of the QwQ-32B model, modified through additional system prompts to emphasize or suppress reasoning types such as HG and ER The baseline model and its variants were assessed using the *PMLRM-Bench* framework, with the scores shown in Table 5.

As shown in Table 6, the baseline `qwq-32b` model exhibits a balanced reasoning profile, with notable strengths in DR and HG Adjustments to this baseline reveal varying impacts: increasing ER boosts the reasoning quality, particularly in fairness-related tasks, while enhancing HG aids exploratory reasoning. Conversely, reducing HG or ER can streamline reasoning but may compromise depth in specific contexts, as shown in Table 5.

To further validate these insights, we executed the PM-LLM-Benchmark on these custom variants, with results presented in Table 7. The benchmark evaluates performance across seven categories: Contextual Understanding, Conformance Checking, Process Modeling, Process Querying, Hypotheses Generation, and Fairness.

Key observations emerge from these results: the variant with more HG achieves the highest score in the PM-LLM-Benchmark (37.1), maintaining a high score in the Hypotheses Generation category (4.9), outperforming the baseline in Contextual Understanding (6.3) and Conformance Checking (7.1), suggesting broad benefits in exploratory tasks. However, the variant with less HG, displaying reduced performance in Hypotheses Generation (4.3), overall underperforms, indicating that limiting HG weakens performance on tasks requiring

Table 5. Performance scores and reasoning step statistics for QwQ-32B variants with adjusted system prompts.

Model	S	C	PC	W	PE	IND	NE	PM-LLM-B. Score
qwq-32b-moremoral	**14218**	44	2	0	1067	112	27	**35.4**
qwq-32b-morehypgen	**13372**	44	2	0	980	108	26	**37.1**
qwq-32b-lessvalidbacktr	**13310**	43	3	0	956	130	6	**36.4**
qwq-32b	**13281**	44	2	0	945	109	13	**36.9**
qwq-32b-lessmoral	**12584**	45	1	0	846	76	10	**35.7**
qwq-32b-lesshypgen	**11856**	39	6	0	913	94	24	**36.3**

Table 6. Percentage distribution of reasoning types over total steps for QwQ-32B variants, with percentage change relative to the baseline *qwq-32b* on the next line.

Model	PR	DR	IR	AR	HG	V	B	ER	CR	HR
-moremoral	13.3	34.0	1.5	1.6	18.0	18.2	3.9	3.2	0.4	6.0
	(−1.5%)	(+1.5%)	(0.0%)	(0.0%)	(−10.4%)	(+4.0%)	(−22.0%)	(+45.5%)	(−55.6%)	(+42.9%)
-morehypgen	14.7	32.1	1.1	1.4	23.8	15.7	5.4	1.5	0.5	3.7
	(+8.9%)	(−4.2%)	(−26.7%)	(−12.5%)	(+18.4%)	(−10.3%)	(+8.0%)	(−31.8%)	(−44.4%)	(−11.9%)
-lessvalidbacktr	14.7	33.1	2.3	1.6	21.5	16.6	3.8	0.8	1.1	4.5
	(+8.9%)	(−1.2%)	(+53.3%)	(0.0%)	(+7.0%)	(−5.1%)	(−24.0%)	(−63.6%)	(+22.2%)	(+7.1%)
qwq-32b	13.5	33.5	1.5	1.6	20.1	17.5	5.0	2.2	0.9	4.2
	(0.0%)	(0.0%)	(0.0%)	(0.0%)	(0.0%)	(0.0%)	(0.0%)	(0.0%)	(0.0%)	(0.0%)
-lessmoral	13.6	33.0	1.2	1.6	22.1	17.7	5.5	1.0	0.4	3.9
	(+0.7%)	(−1.5%)	(−20.0%)	(0.0%)	(+10.0%)	(+1.1%)	(+10.0%)	(−54.5%)	(−55.6%)	(−7.1%)
-lesshypgen	14.0	34.7	1.6	1.6	17.0	19.7	4.8	1.2	0.9	4.7
	(+3.7%)	(+3.6%)	(+6.7%)	(0.0%)	(−15.4%)	(+12.6%)	(−4.0%)	(−45.5%)	(0.0%)	(+11.9%)

Table 7. PM-LLM-Benchmark results for QwQ-32B variants, evaluated with 1-shot prompting.

Model	PM-LLM-B. Score	Contextual Underst.	Conf. Checking	Process Modeling	Process Querying	Hypotheses Generation	Fairness
qwq-32b-morehypgen	**37.1**	**6.3**	**7.1**	5.4	4.4	4.9	5.1
qwq-32b	36.9	5.7	6.4	**6.0**	4.5	4.9	5.7
qwq-32b-lessvalidbacktr	36.4	5.5	6.6	5.1	4.6	4.8	**6.0**
qwq-32b-lesshypgen	36.3	5.5	6.6	5.9	**4.8**	4.3	5.2
qwq-32b-lessmoral	35.7	5.9	6.7	5.0	4.3	**5.0**	5.1
qwq-32b-moremoral	35.4	5.0	6.5	5.7	**4.8**	4.3	5.3

creative exploration. Similarly, the variant with less ER fares worse than the baseline (5.1 versus 5.7) in Fairness, underscoring that suppressing ER diminishes effectiveness in fairness-related tasks. The variant with more ER also does not improve Fairness (5.3 versus 5.7) over the baseline, suggesting that excessive moral reasoning may introduce complexity without proportional gains.

These findings highlight trade-offs in LRM configuration. Enhancing HG improves performance, aligning with exploratory needs, while reducing it hampers performance. Adjusting ER shows mixed results: both variants fail to yield improvements in the PM-LLM-Benchmark score, possibly due to overcomplication in the variant with more ER.

This case study[1,2] demonstrates the *PMLRM-Bench* framework's ability to guide targeted LRM adjustments, optimizing performance for specific process mining challenges.

6 Conclusion

This paper introduced a novel framework for configuring and evaluating LRMs through a structured analysis of reasoning traces. While demonstrated using the PM-LLM-Benchmark v2.0 dataset, our proposed approach is generalizable and not inherently bound to this benchmark. The reasoning analysis pipeline can readily be initiated from any reasoning trace, facilitating applicability across various domains requiring structured and transparent reasoning evaluation.

Through a detailed analysis, distinct reasoning patterns emerged among different LRMs, emphasizing the importance of tailored configurations. The case study on `qwen-qwq-32b` variants further showcased the efficacy of targeted adjustments in reasoning types, such as boosting hypothesis generation to enhance exploratory reasoning or fine-tuning ethical considerations, highlighting both improvements and potential trade-offs.

[1] Results of the modified variants in *PMLRM-Bench*: https://github.com/fit-alessandro-berti/pmllmbench-lrms-reasoning-analysis/tree/ft-case-study.

[2] Results of the modified variants on the PM-LLM-Benchmark: https://github.com/fit-alessandro-berti/pm-llm-benchmark/tree/ft-case-study.

However, our methodology is subject to certain limitations. Primarily, its effectiveness depends significantly on the accuracy of the classification by the judge LLM, introducing potential biases or errors in the reasoning step categorization. Additionally, while the structured reasoning approach enhances transparency, it may not fully capture nuanced or implicit reasoning processes inherent in LLM processing (i.e., the latent space).

Future research could focus on refining the classification accuracy through ensemble methods or human-in-the-loop approaches and extending the pipeline's applicability to broader sets of reasoning-intensive tasks, beyond process mining, further validating its robustness and general utility.

Acknowledgment. The project on which this work is based upon was funded by the German Federal Ministry of Research, Technology and Space Travel (grant 01IS23065). The responsibility for the content of this publication lies with the authors.

References

1. Bai, Y., Ying, J., Cao, Y., Lv, X., et al.: Benchmarking foundation models with language-model-as-an-examiner. In: Advances in Neural Information Processing Systems, vol. 36, pp. 78142–78167 (2023)
2. Berti, A., Kourani, H., van der Aalst, W.: PM-LLM-Benchmark: evaluating large language models on process mining tasks. In: International Conference on Process Mining, pp. 610–623. Springer, Cham (2024)
3. Berti, A., Qafari, M.: Leveraging large language models (LLMs) for process mining (technical report). arXiv preprint arXiv:2307.12701 (2023)
4. Berti, A., Schuster, D., van der Aalst, W.: Abstractions, scenarios, and prompt definitions for process mining with LLMs: a case study. In: International Conference on Business Process Management, pp. 427–439. Springer, Cham (2023)
5. Bishop, C., Nasrabadi, N.: Pattern Recognition and Machine Learning, vol. 4. Springer, Cham (2006)
6. Chiang, C., Chen, W., Kuan, C., Yang, C., Lee, H.: Large language model as an assignment evaluator: insights, feedback, and challenges in a 1000+ student course. arXiv preprint arXiv:2407.05216 (2024)
7. Flach, P.: Abduction and induction: syllogistic and inferential perspectives. In: Abductive and Inductive Reasoning Workshop Notes, pp. 31–35. University of Bristol (1996)
8. Fournier, F., Limonad, L., Skarbovsky, I.: Towards a benchmark for causal business process reasoning with LLMs. In: International Conference on Business Process Management, pp. 233–246. Springer, Cham (2024)
9. Frankfurt, H.: Peirce's notion of abduction. J. Philos. **55**(14), 593–597 (1958)
10. Gigerenzer, G., Todd, P.: Fast and frugal heuristics: the adaptive toolbox. In: Simple Heuristics that Make Us Smart, pp. 3–34. Oxford University Press (1999)
11. Grohs, M., Abb, L., Elsayed, N., Rehse, J.: Large language models can accomplish business process management tasks. In: International Conference on Business Process Management, pp. 453–465. Springer, Cham (2023)
12. Holland, J.: Induction: Processes of Inference, Learning, and Discovery. MIT Press, Cambridge (1986)

13. Holland, P., Bowskill, I., Bailey, A.: Adaptors and innovators: selection versus induction. Psychol. Rep. **68**(3_suppl), 1283–1290 (1991)
14. Johnson-Laird, P.: Deductive reasoning. Annu. Rev. Psychol. **50**(1), 109–135 (1999)
15. Klahr, D., Dunbar, K.: Dual space search during scientific reasoning. Cogn. Sci. **12**(1), 1–48 (1988)
16. Klahr, D., Fay, A., Dunbar, K.: Heuristics for scientific experimentation: a developmental study. Cogn. Psychol. **25**(1), 111–146 (1993)
17. Knuth, D.: The Art of Computer Programming, vol. 3. Pearson Education (1997)
18. Kohlberg, L.: Stages of moral development as a basis for moral education. Center for Moral Education, Harvard University Cambridge (1971)
19. Kourani, H., et al.: Leveraging large language models for enhanced process model comprehension. arXiv preprint arXiv:2408.08892 (2024)
20. Kourani, H., Berti, A., Schuster, D., van der Aalst, W.: Evaluating large language models on business process modeling: framework, benchmark, and self-improvement analysis. arXiv preprint arXiv:2412.00023 (2024)
21. Pearl, J.: Causality. Cambridge University Press, Cambridge (2009)
22. Peirce, C.: The collected papers of Charles S. Peirce **8**, 1–6 (1931)
23. Prasad, A., Saha, S., Zhou, X., Bansal, M.: Receval: evaluating reasoning chains via correctness and informativeness. arXiv preprint arXiv:2304.10703 (2023)
24. Rebmann, A., Schmidt, F., Glavaš, G., van Der Aa, H.: Evaluating the ability of LLMs to solve semantics-aware process mining tasks. In: 2024 6th International Conference on Process Mining (ICPM), pp. 9–16. IEEE (2024)
25. Vidgof, M., Bachhofner, S., Mendling, J.: Large language models for business process management: opportunities and challenges. In: International Conference on Business Process Management, pp. 107–123. Springer, Cham (2023)
26. Wang, Z., Pang, Y., Lin, Y.: Large language models are zero-shot text classifiers. arXiv preprint arXiv:2312.01044 (2023)
27. Zheng, L., Chiang, W.L., Sheng, Y., Zhuang, S., et al.: Judging LLM-as-a-judge with MT-bench and chatbot arena. In: Advances in Neural Information Processing Systems, vol. 36, pp. 46595–46623 (2023)

Natural Language Processing for BPMN Model Generation with LLMs: A Systematic Literature Review

Alena Wimmer, Ana Costa(✉), and Luise Pufahl

School of Computation, Information and Technology, Technical University of Munich, Heilbronn, Germany
{alena.wimmer,a.costa,luise.pufahl}@tum.de

Abstract. Organizations increasingly rely on vast amounts of unstructured textual data to describe and manage their business processes. Recent advances in Natural Language Processing (NLP) and Large Language Model (LLM)s, demonstrate significant potential for automating the extraction of process information and generating Business Process Model and Notation (BPMN) models directly from text. However, a comprehensive assessment of the methods, tools, and evaluation outcomes related to this field is missing. We present a Systematic Literature Review (SLR) that synthesizes current research on NLP-based BPMN model generation. We show which NLP approaches have been used to extract process information before and after LLMs. Analyzing 17 primary studies, we extracted information on intermediate representations of models, on supported BPMN elements, generation methods, file types, and visualizations. We also reviewed how the selected publications evaluated model generation, and derived strengths, limitations, and future directions of the field. We found that integrating rule-based or LLM feedback loops could refine model generation accuracy, and establishing benchmarks and open datasets would increase reproducibility.

Keywords: Natural Language Processing · Business Process Model and Notation · Process Generation · Large Language Models

1 Introduction

Business Process Management (BPM) involves the analysis, design, and management of business operations within and across organizations [10] by using process models, an abstracted representation of a business operation with its activities and relations, as the main artifact for these tasks. BPMN is an industry standard for modeling business processes [32] with a defined syntax and semantics. Since organizations rely on textual documentation of their business processes, process experts constantly generate vast amounts of textual data [5,40]. Nevertheless, designing process models is time-consuming and complex, with only 18%

I. van de Weerd et al. (Eds.): BPM 2025 Workshops, LNBIP 569, pp. 425–437, 2026.
https://doi.org/10.1007/978-3-032-13426-4_31

of organizations relying on textual documents for business insights [17], while acquiring process models can consume up to 60% of a project's effort [18].

The potential of NLP-based techniques to support BPM tasks is substantial, especially in the context of generating BPMN models [22,40]. These techniques can be used for transforming textual descriptions into process models, translating model descriptions into a target language, text annotation and inference, verification of correctness and completeness, fine-tuning of semantic abstraction levels, process auto-completion, and others [5]. With the advent of LLMs, the capabilities these models have for process modeling tasks include improving process models through iterative exchange between domain experts and chatbots [28], mining imperative and declarative models from textual description [19], process querying [9], as well as various prompt engineering, error handling, and refining methods [29,30].

This research is necessary since it reviews NLP approaches to employing LLM-based frameworks for process model generation. In contrast to previous studies, we present a review of NLP methodologies, including but not limited to LLM, for extracting process information from unstructured text and generating BPMN process models, as well as their evaluation, analyzing the strengths and limitations. We focus on BPMN since the notation has emerged as the de facto industry standard for process modeling due to its ability to comprehensively communicate complex execution logic [36]. Previous literature reviews in the field do not focus specifically on BPMN model generation and do not explore the potential of traditional NLP techniques after LLMs became popular. With this research being conducted at the beginning of the year 2025, it is able to include recent publications that previous studies missed. With the aim to provide a comprehensive overview of the current state and trends in the research on generating BPMN models from textual process descriptions, this contribution employs a SLR [25] for covering the following research questions:

RQ1 Which NLP approaches can be used to extract process information from unstructured text?
RQ2 Which NLP approaches can be used to generate BPMN models from either unstructured text or intermediate representations?
RQ3 What evaluation techniques have been used to evaluate the extracted process information and generated BPMN models?
RQ4 What are the strengths and limitations of the proposed NLP approaches?

This article is organized as follows. Section 2 provides the background and an overview of earlier literature reviews in this field. Section 3 describes the search strategy, selection criteria, and data extraction. We present the results of the literature in Sect. 4, providing details on the extracted data of the selected publications. Finally, we discuss the strengths and challenges in Sect. 5, identify opportunities for future research in the field, and conclude in Sect. 6.

2 Background and Related Work

2.1 Background on NLP for BPMN Generation

In order to generate BPMN from text, it is necessary to first extract the process information from the text and then generate the model [39]. When extracting process information, NLP techniques are employed to label parts of the text and identify entities, and semantic roles [35]. These NLP approaches rely on tools for semantic similarity analysis, tokenization, part-of-speech tagging, entity recognition, and syntactic parsing [7]. More recently, LLMs have advanced the field since models like GPT-3, GPT-3.5, and GPT-4, apply in-context learning, multi-turn dialog strategies, and prompt engineering techniques for reasoning [13,30]. Considering this shift from NLP tools to employing unified LLM-based frameworks [1,2,8], we provide a review of NLP approaches for process extraction, including but not limited to LLMs.

The extracted process information is mapped to form a process model that captures control-flow or beyond elements, resulting in a BPMN diagram [3,33,39]. This is done either through a direct or two-step transformation [14]. While direct transformation maps a process model via an ad-hoc pipeline [6], a two-step transformation uses an intermediate representation to create the process model, transforming the text into a more structured format that captures the essential elements of a process [18,21]. This intermediate representation uses rules, lists, templates, trees, and syntactic analysis [14] that are not yet categorized in literature, but addressed in this review.

It is a common practice to limit the supported BPMN elements when generating process models [23]. Considering this, manual, hybrid, or automated generation methods are used, according to the level of user involvement [14]. While manual scenarios require a user to choose, correct, and validate the output data, in automated scenarios the user is not involved in the generation process. Furthermore, evaluation methods and metrics are used to assess the quality, performance, and applicability of the BPMN output artifact [14,40] to build trust among the users in the outputs. Thus, we aim at studying the applied methods and used data set for building trust in this review.

2.2 Related Work

We provide an overview of the related work that is addressing similar grounds[1]. Bellan et al. [14] further contributed in 2021 by reviewing NLP techniques used to extract process information from both structured and unstructured texts for model creation, and Klievtsova et al. [28] in 2023 conducted the discussion to include LLMs, using Generative Pre-trained Transformer (GPT) models within conversational process modeling. In 2022, Schüler and Alpers [37] conducted a general structured review on automating the generation of process models, while Weinzierl et al. [42] considered a broader range of Machine Learning (ML)

[1] An overview over related literature reviews in this research is provided at https://figshare.com/s/41ff58300680de3e6677.

applications within BPM beyond just NLP. In 2024, Hörner and Reichert [22] focus on transforming textual input into a process model and generating text from process models using chatbots and LLMs, while van Woensel and Motie [40] reviewed publications on NLP and ML methods for process extraction and the evaluation methods and datasets.

In contrast to previous studies, this review focuses specifically on BPMN model generation, emphasizing how NLP and LLMs facilitate the conversion of textual descriptions into BPMN and providing a more in-depth analysis of BPMN elements, generation methods, file types, visualizations, evaluation, datasets, and employed metrics. We deliver a comprehensive analysis of NLP-based BPMN model generation through a specific and detailed literature review.

3 Method

The method performed in this work follows Kitchenham [26,27]. Digital libraries in the field of information systems were selected for the literature search in order to cover the collection of publications: ACM Digital Library, IEEE Xplore, Springer Link, and Taylor & Francis. To ensure that relevant publications from other digital libraries are also covered, a forward and backward search was performed on the finally selected publications and the related literature reviews presented in Subsect. 2.2. The screening and extraction process was performed independently by one researcher and verified by another.

Table 1. Search keywords for extracting relevant literature from the digital libraries.

BPM	process extraction, process model, process modeling, BPMN, business process modeling notation, process discovery, process model generation
NLP	natural language processing, speech processing, unstructured data, large language models, language models, information extraction, chatbots, deep learning

For a systematic search of the digital libraries, a set of relevant keywords was defined on the intersection of BPM and NLP, as listed in Table 1. The keywords within the same category were combined in the plain keyword style, with an inclusive *OR* logic. The two categories were combined with an *AND* logic, requiring the studies to contain at least one keyword from the BPM field and one keyword from the NLP field. Furthermore, the search strategy is presented in Fig. 1. After screening the abstract, full papers were screened against the inclusion and exclusion criteria. Subsequently, to ensure that no papers from other databases were missed, a forward and backward search was performed and four additional relevant publications. Due to the different search capabilities of the libraries, the search string varied slightly for each library. Where possible, the search was also limited by publication type and year of publication, according to the exclusion criteria. The search was conducted in January 2025.

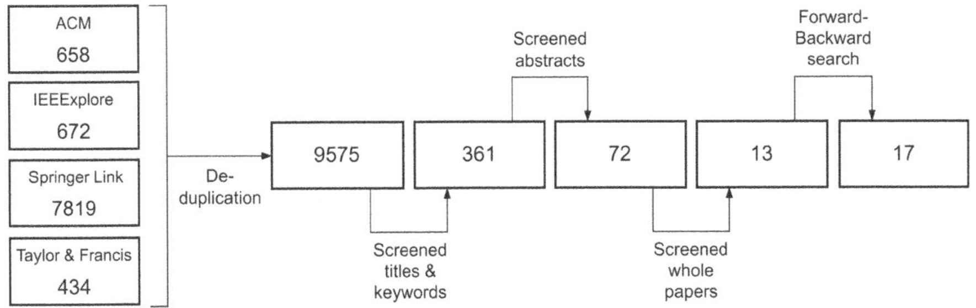

Fig. 1. Flow diagram of the results of the SLR.

Studies were included (IC1) if they focused on either extracting process information from unstructured text or speech with the aim of creating process models or (IC2) automatically generating BPMN models and if they employed NLP as an essential part of their methodology. Conversely, we excluded studies that (EC1) worked exclusively with structured input data, (EC2) did not evaluate the proposed approach or its application on a use case, (EC3) were published before 2017, (EC4) were not primary studies, (EC5) were not written in English, or (EC6) were not peer-reviewed scientific articles. The time limit of 2017 was chosen due to the publication of the paper *Attention is all you need* [41], which accelerated Deep Learning (DL) and NLP technologies.

3.1 Data Extraction

In order to systematically analyze the approaches of the relevant literature, we followed a structured inductive data extraction procedure covering key dimensions derived from the research questions. From each publication, we identified information on the NLP and LLM tools used in each publication to extract process information (***RQ1***), the BPMN transformation approach, supported elements, generation methods and output (***RQ2***), and the evaluation methodologies, metrics, and datasets (***RQ3***).

Table 2. Dimensions of the Concept Matrix.

Ref.	Basic information		Tools and approaches		Supported BPMN elements					Generation methods and output				Evaluation		Datasets				
	Year	Publication type	NLP/ LLM Tool	Transformation approach	Task	Events	Gateways	Roles	Data	Automation degree	Generation method	Output file types	Visualisation library	Evaluation method	Evaluation metrics	Origin	Synthetic or Real	Number of processes	Domain	Availability

A concept matrix provides an overview of these results[2] and the dimensions of the matrix is provided in Table 2. For tools and approaches, the *NLP and LLM tools* for extraction of process information are listed, and the *transformation approach* can be a direct, list-based, graph-based, or partial order-based. The captured *supported BPMN elements* are tasks, events, gateways, roles, and data. For generation methods and output, we capture the *automation degree* that can be manual, hybrid, or automated, the *generation method*, *output files*, and *visualization library*. For evaluation, we analyze the *evaluation method* such as case study, test dataset, and expert evaluation, and the *evaluation metrics* such as precision, recall, and F1-Score. Finally, we captured the datasets providing their *origin*, *synthetic or real* data, *number of processes* included, *domain*, and *availability*.

4 Results

This section presents the results of analyzing the 17 identified studies. Our review shows a clear increase in publications over recent years, a trend also noted in previous literature reviews (Subsect. 2.2). This growing interest aligns with advancements in LLM, which have significantly improved methods for information extraction and model generation. Most of the selected publications are conference papers. Three of the publications have been published in scientific journals. An overview of the results showing the number of publications per dimension is provided in Fig. 2. Since recent publications are included, there are more LLM tools used than traditional NLP for process extraction. Transformation approaches are mostly list-based, automated, and generated using rule-based methods. Furthermore, the datasets are predominantly self-created, synthetic, and publicly available.

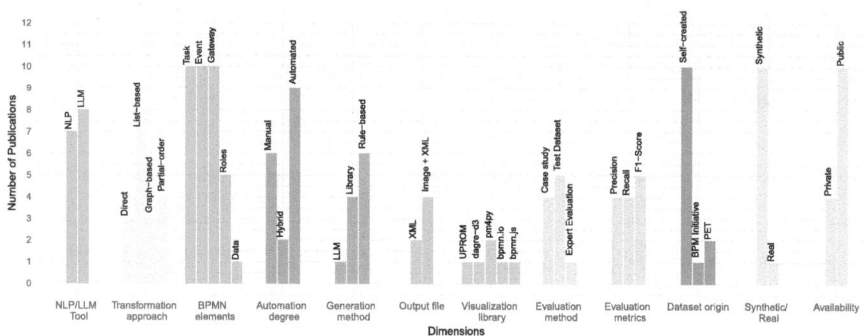

Fig. 2. Number of publications per dimension.

[2] Due to limitations in length, we provide the entire results of the concept matrix, overview of tables, and bibliography in a separate document online https://figshare.com/s/41ff58300680de3e6677.

The following sections answer the respective research questions, focusing on the approaches that can be used to extract process information (Subsect. 4.1) and to generate BPMN models from unstructured text or intermediate representations (Subsect. 4.2), evaluation techniques (Subsect. 4.3), and the strengths and limitations of proposed approaches (Sect. 5).

4.1 NLP Approaches

The objective of this subsection is to answer ***RQ1*** by analyzing which NLP approaches have been used to extract process information from unstructured text. An overview of the NLP tools used in the reviewed publications highlights a diverse range of tools, most of which focus on a specific part of NLP [7,20,21,35,39]. Some tools were combined with other tools to facilitate an information extraction pipeline, e.g., GloVe and Word2Vec for semantic similarity analysis [7]. A few tools, such as the Stanford CoreNLP and spaCy, are comprehensive NLP suites that offer multiple functionalities such as tokenization, Part-of-Speech tagging, Named Entity Recognition, and syntactic parsing [7,20,21,39].

Compared to these methods, NLP approaches with LLMs can support not only information extraction but also BPMN model generation. Starting in 2022, we observe first approaches that use LLMs for the information extraction task [12]. Table 3 provides an overview of the LLMs used by the reviewed publications. The other models are multimodal LLMs. Gemini being the only model from Google, most of the models used by the publications were OpenAI's GPT models, GPT-3 [15] and its successors GPT-3.5 and GPT-4, which represent significant advances in language modeling.

Table 3. LLMs leveraged in the publications.

LLM	Publications
Gemini	[29,43]
GPT-3 [15]	[12,13]
GPT-3.5	[34,43]
GPT-4	[16,29,30,43]

Bellan et al. [12] use in-context learning on GPT-3 for their information extraction. A consequent study [13] uses the same approach in a multi-turn dialog strategy. Nivon and Salaün [34] use the GPT-3.5 model. Kourani et al. [29,30] use multiple prompt engineering methods and asked the LLM to extract information and generate the `python` code to create the respective model. The authors have also shown that feedback loops with self-improvement, asking the LLM to improve its own output, increase the quality of the generated models. Daclin et al. [16] use GPT-4 for information extraction and Wenger et al. [43] test multiple LLM, as well as zero-shot, few-shot, and chain-of-thought prompting.

4.2 BPMN Generation

This subsection aims to answer ***RQ2*** by analyzing how BPMN models can be generated from unstructured text: first by looking at the intermediate representations, second by inspecting the BPMN elements, and lastly by analyzing the generation methodology, file types, and visualization.

List-based representations: These representations are easy to read and useful for manual process modeling when automation isn't possible [12]. Honkisz et al. [21] list BPMN activities, conditions, and actors. Bellan et al. [12,13] focus on activities and actors. Sholiq et al. [38] extract elements from text analysis without mapping to BPMN. Similarly, Quishpi et al. [35] and Ackermann et al. [7] produce annotated textual process descriptions, while Daclin et al. [16] create a list of elements, which they call formalized process data.

Graph/tree-based representations: Graph/tree-based representations capture the flow between process nodes. Sonbol et al. [39] generate concept maps linking concepts, while Gürbüz and Demirörs [20] build ontologies with entities, relationships, rules, and instances. Nivon and Salaün [34] create abstract syntax trees representing activities and decisions, transform them into directed cyclic graphs to model loops, and then back into trees as the basis for BPMN models.

Partial order-based representations: Partial order-based representations focus on graphs with a hierarchical structure, extended with control flow operators for representing choices and loop structures [31], or declarative constraints [4,6]. One way to use partially ordered representation is declarative constraints, focusing on the relations between activities and allowing multiple valid execution paths [4,6]. The `ProMoAI` artifact was developed using leveraging Partially Ordered Workflow Language (POWL), as first proposed by Kourani and van Zelst [31], as an intermediate representation [29,30].

Supported BPMN Elements. Of the 17 publications identified, eleven include the generation of BPMN models. For the sake of artifact development, it is common practice to limit the subset of supported BPMN elements. The generic BPMN task is supported by all eleven publications. In addition, Ivanchikj et al. [23,24] support the specification of the different task types. None of the publications claim to support sub-processes. Regarding events, most publications only support start and end events. Only three publications support other events [23,24,38], with only two of them also including the specific types for intermediate events, namely time, error, send, receive, escalate, and terminate, or signal such as notify and publish [23,24]. All publications support exclusive gateways. The parallel gateway is supported by seven publications [16,23,24,30,34,38,43]. The inclusive gateway is only supported by three publications [16,34,38]. The least commonly supported gateway is the event-based gateway [23,24]. Pools and lanes are supported by half of the publications [23,24,38,39,43]. Sholiq et al. [38] are the only publication that support data objects and data stores.

BPMN Generation Methodology, File Types, and Visualization. Six of the 17 publications do not provide any BPMN modeling, requiring the user to transform the process information extracted from the text in its intermediate representation into the corresponding BPMN model (i.e., *manual generation*).

In *hybrid generation*, a tool assists in the modeling process, but the user is also involved to some degree. *Automated generation* either uses a custom rule-based approach where sometimes also process mining techniques are applied, or, rarely, leverages LLMs directly for XML generation. Honkisz et al. [21] use the `bpmn_python` library to convert their list into XML. BPMN Sketch Miner [23,24] applies rule-based steps to define elements, while Sonbol et al. [39] transform concept maps into BPMN. `ProMoAI` uses `pm4py` for BPMN model creation and visualization [29,30]. Daclin et al. [16] and Nivon and Salaün [34] also follow rule-based approaches, mapping tree patterns to BPMN flows and rendering with bpmn.io. Wenger et al. [43] introduce the only method that has the LLM directly generate the BPMN XML file, which its displayed using `bpmn-js`.

4.3 Evaluation Methods, Metrics, and Datasets

This subsection answers ***RQ3*** by analyzing the different evaluation methods, datasets, metrics, and results.

Methodologies and Metrics. Case studies, expert evaluation, and experimental testing with datasets are used as evaluation methodologies. Some authors follow an experimental testing approach for their information extraction solution, calculating metrics such as precision, recall, and the F1-score for their results [6,7,12,13,35]. In this review, we do not differentiate between micro and macro F1 score. Sonbol et al. [39] employ multiple evaluation methods, including Graph Edit Distance (GED), comparing their output against a dataset of process descriptions and manually created models. Furthermore, when dealing with text annotation, there are different matching strategies to decide if a partial match of the token span to annotate is considered valid or invalid, but in this review we don't differentiate between them. Wenger et al. [43] compute F1-scores for text-to-BPMN creation but provide limited details on their evaluation. Other authors use a case study to demonstrate both the information extraction and the BPMN creation of the artifact [16,21,38]. Kourani et al. [29,30] evaluate their artifact by doing a benchmark on case studies. Expert evaluation is a common technique that focuses on the usability of the artifact, e.g., calculating the System Usability Scale (SUS) score [4,23]. Furthermore, van der Aa et al. [4] uses interviews with experts as the source for the evaluation.

Datasets. Of the 17 publications, three publications do not use any dataset for their evaluation, because their evaluation is based solely on expert evaluation of the methodology [4,23,24]. Most studies rely on self-created datasets. Some of them integrate existing datasets in their datasets [34,39], and others integrate with self-created data or through benchmark [11,18]. While some publications rely on datasets with only a few models for their case study evaluation [16,30], the largest dataset is created and evaluated by Nivon and Salaün [34], containing 200 process descriptions. Most of the datasets are domain-agnostic, with only a few, especially the smaller-sized ones, focusing on a specific industry. However, some studies' evaluations are based on private datasets, which limits the possibility of reproducing their results, since the data is not publicly accessible.

Overall, a wide range of datasets is used in these studies, indicating that no standard dataset for evaluation exists in the field.

5 Discussion

In this section, ***RQ4*** will be answered and the challenges and potential for future research in this field will be discussed.

Many different NLP tools and methods have been used for information extraction and approaches using intermediate representations have the advantage that both steps can be visualized, understood, and evaluated separately. However, the heavy reliance on different NLP tools, such as GloVe, Word2Vec, Stanford CoreNLP, or spaCy, is a limitation since each tool handles only a fragment of the process information extraction pipeline. This often requires building and maintaining complex pipelines that are difficult to generalize specific use cases. It was observed that approaches with LLMs have their pipelines leaner and do not rely on rule-based techniques for the BPMN model generation.

Although there is a gap in the quantitative evaluation of the BPMN model output, the studies have evaluated the usability with experts and demonstrated their output with process examples in case studies. However, the reliance on subjective or qualitative feedback limits comparability and reproducibility. Another factor contributing to this limitation is the lack of a large-scale, publicly available dataset against which to evaluate the solutions.

Most of the reviewed approaches support only a basic and limited set of BPMN elements. Only two solutions support intermediate events [23,24], only one solution supports data objects [38], and only half of the solutions support pools and lanes. This restriction reduces the representational character of the resulting models, resulting in incomplete or oversimplified process diagrams.

Future research directions could focus on building robust, end-to-end automated solutions. The capabilities of new, more powerful LLM for advancing automated BPMN model generation should be explored. This subsequently leads to the exploration of prompting strategies to allow models to understand and generate more complex and realistic process models including more BPMN elements. Due to the complexity of this task, the inclusion of rule-based or LLM feedback loops to improve BPMN models based on the textual input as part of the model generation could be leveraged. Furthermore, the concept matrix could be extended with techniques that are able to match mentions of the same entity in order to generate only one BPMN element instead of multiple. The creation of common benchmarks and open datasets would promote the reproducibility and comparability of different approaches to the task. Such benchmarks should include, especially, a diversity of domains, different process complexity levels, and annotation guidelines.

Threats to validity of this study include the search terms and criteria. However, by incorporating a forward-backward search and adding works through prior knowledge, we reduced the influence of this threat. Furthermore, the recent and rapid development in the field of LLMs threatens the validity since publications after this work are not included. Inductive coding inherently relies on subjective judgments and constitutes, therefore, a further threat. We addressed this by following a systematic protocol and by clarifying uncertainties through discussions.

6 Conclusion

A systematic literature review on NLP for BPMN model generation is presented, analyzing studies from 2017 upwards, including studies from 2024 since the advent of LLMs. We observed a shift in techniques used from traditional NLP pipelines to direct or two-step XML generation with the use of LLMs, which inherently are not dependent on rule-based processing. Despite the diversity of intermediate representations and methodologies for generation, traditional approaches rely on a combination of NLP tools and present an incomplete support for BPMN elements. Consequently, future research should prioritize generating fully automated models with the support of LLM-driven methods, integrate systematic feedback loops to improve accuracy, and address explainability concerns to increase reliability. Additionally, the establishment of open datasets and standardized evaluation benchmarks is essential for reproducibility and comparative assessment.

References

1. A Decomposed Hybrid Approach to Business Process Modeling with LLMs, pp. 243–260. Springer, Cham
2. Efficient LLM-Based Conversational Process Modeling, pp. 259–270. Springer, Cham
3. Nala2BPMN: Automating BPMN Model Generation with Large Language Models, pp. 398–404. Springer, Cham
4. van der Aa, H., Balder, K.J., Maggi, F.M., Nolte, A.: Say it in your own words: defining declarative process models using speech recognition. In: Fahland, D., Ghidini, C., Becker, J., Dumas, M. (eds.) BPM 2020. LNBIP, vol. 392, pp. 51–67. Springer, Cham (2020). https://doi.org/10.1007/978-3-030-58638-6_4
5. van der Aa, H., Carmona Vargas, J., Leopold, H., Mendling, J., Padró, L.: Challenges and opportunities of applying natural language processing in business process management. In: COLING, Santa Fe, New Mexico, USA, pp. 2791–2801. Association for Computational Linguistics (2018)
6. van der Aa, H., Di Ciccio, C., Leopold, H., Reijers, H.A.: Extracting declarative process models from natural language. In: Giorgini, P., Weber, B. (eds.) CAiSE 2019. LNCS, vol. 11483, pp. 365–382. Springer, Cham (2019). https://doi.org/10.1007/978-3-030-21290-2_23
7. Ackermann, L., Neuberger, J., Jablonski, S.: Data-driven annotation of textual process descriptions based on formal meaning representations. In: CAiSE, pp. 75–90. Springer, Cham (2021)
8. Ajmal, F., Wijekoon, P., Dhanamina, H., Ravishan, Y., Nawinna, D., Attanayaka, B.: Automated BPMN diagram generation. In: 2024 6th International Conference on Advancements in Computing (ICAC), pp. 7–12. IEEE (2024)

9. Berti, A., Schuster, D., van der Aalst, W.M.: Abstractions, scenarios, and prompt definitions for process mining with LLMs: a case study. In: BPM, pp. 427–439. Springer, Cham (2023)
10. Beerepoot, I., et al.: The biggest business process management problems to solve before we die. Comput. Ind. **146**, 14 (2023)
11. Bellan, P., van der Aa, H., Dragoni, M., Ghidini, C., Ponzetto, S.P.: Pet: an annotated dataset for process extraction from natural language text tasks. In: BPM, pp. 315–321. Springer, Cham (2022)
12. Bellan, P., Dragoni, M., Ghidini, C.: Extracting business process entities and relations from text using pre-trained language models and in-context learning. In: EDOC, pp. 182–199. Springer, Cham (2022)
13. Bellan, P., Dragoni, M., Ghidini, C.: Process knowledge extraction and knowledge graph construction through prompting: a quantitative analysis. In: Proceedings of the 39th ACM/SIGAPP Symposium on Applied Computing, pp. 1634–1641 (2024)
14. Bellan, P., Dragoni, M., Ghidini, C., van der Aa, H., Ponzetto, S.P.: Process extraction from text: benchmarking the state of the art and paving the way for future challenges. preprint arXiv:2110.03754 (2021)
15. Brown, T., et al.: Language models are few-shot learners. In: NIPS, vol. 33, pp. 1877–1901 (2020)
16. Daclin, N., Mallek-Daclin, S., Zacharewicz, G.: Generative AI for business model generation (GAI4BM): from textual description to business process model. In: The 10th International Food Operations and Processing Simulation Workshop. CAL-TEK srl (2024)
17. Davenport, T.H., Guszcza, J., Smith, T., Stiller, B.: Insight-driven organization. Deloitte Insights (2019)
18. Friedrich, F., Mendling, J., Puhlmann, F.: Process model generation from natural language text. In: Mouratidis, H., Rolland, C. (eds.) CAiSE 2011. LNCS, vol. 6741, pp. 482–496. Springer, Heidelberg (2011). https://doi.org/10.1007/978-3-642-21640-4_36
19. Grohs, M., Abb, L., Elsayed, N., Rehse, J.R.: Large language models can accomplish business process management tasks. In: BPM, pp. 453–465. Springer, Cham (2023)
20. Gürbüz, Ö., Demirörs, O.: From organizational guidelines to business process models: exploratory case for an ontology based methodology. In: 2017 IEEE 19th Conference on Business Informatics (CBI), vol. 1, pp. 320–329. IEEE (2017)
21. Honkisz, K., Kluza, K., Wiśniewski, P.: A concept for generating business process models from natural language description. In: KSEM, Changchun, China, Proceedings, Part I 11, pp. 91–103. Springer, Cham (2018)
22. Hörner, L.F., Reichert, M.: Generating process models by interacting with chatbots–a literature review. Future Internet **16**(10) (2024)
23. Ivanchikj, A., Serbout, S., Pautasso, C.: From text to visual BPMN process models: design and evaluation. In: Proceedings of the 23rd ACM/IEEE International Conference on Model Driven Engineering Languages and Systems, pp. 229–239 (2020)
24. Ivanchikj, A., Serbout, S., Pautasso, C.: Live process modeling with the BPMN sketch miner. Softw. Syst. Model. **21**(5), 1877–1906 (2022)
25. Keele, S., et al.: Guidelines for performing systematic literature reviews in software engineering. Technical report, ver. 2.3 EBSE technical report. EBSE (2007)
26. Kitchenham, B., Madeyski, L., Budgen, D.: Segress: software engineering guidelines for reporting secondary studies. IEEE Trans. Softw. Eng. **49**(3), 1273–1298 (2022)

27. Kitchenham, B.A., Charters, S.: Guidelines for performing systematic literature reviews in software engineering. EBSE, University Joint Report (2007)
28. Klievtsova, N., Benzin, J.V., Kampik, T., Mangler, J., Rinderle-Ma, S.: Conversational process modelling: state of the art, applications, and implications in practice. In: BPM, pp. 319–336. Springer, Cham (2023)
29. Kourani, H., Berti, A., Schuster, D., van der Aalst, W.M.: Process modeling with large language models. In: BPMDS, pp. 229–244. Springer, Cham (2024)
30. Kourani, H., Berti, A., Schuster, D., van der Aalst, W.M.: Promoai: process modeling with generative AI. IJCAI (2024)
31. Kourani, H., van Zelst, S.J.: Powl: partially ordered workflow language. In: BPM, pp. 92–108. Springer, Cham (2023)
32. Licardo, J.T., Tanković, N., Etinger, D.: A method for extracting BPMN models from textual descriptions using natural language processing. Procedia Comput. Sci. **239**, 483–490 (2024)
33. Neuberger, J., Ackermann, L., van der Aa, H., Jablonski, S.: A universal prompting strategy for extracting process model information from natural language text using large language models
34. Nivon, Q., Salaün, G.: Automated generation of BPMN processes from textual requirements. In: ICSOC, pp. 185–201. Springer, Cham (2024)
35. Quishpi, L., Carmona, J., Padró, L.: Extracting annotations from textual descriptions of processes. In: BPM, Proceedings 18, pp. 184–201. Springer, Cham (2020)
36. Recker, J.: Opportunities and constraints: the current struggle with BPMN. Bus. Process. Manag. J. **16**(1), 181–201 (2010)
37. Schüler, S., Alpers, S.: State of the art: automatic generation of business process models. In: BPM, pp. 161–173. Springer, Cham (2024)
38. Sholiq, S., Sarno, R., Astuti, E.S.: Generating BPMN diagram from textual requirements. J. King Saud Univ.-Comput. Inf. Sci. **34**(10), 10079–10093 (2022)
39. Sonbol, R., Rebdawi, G., Ghneim, N.: A machine translation like approach to generate business process model from textual description. SN Comput. Sci. **4**(3), 291 (2023)
40. Van Woensel, W., Motie, S.: NLP4BPM: a systematic review on process extraction using natural language processing with rule-based, machine and deep learning methods. Enterprise Inf. Syst. 2417404 (2024)
41. Vaswani, A.: Attention is all you need. In: Advances in Neural Information Processing Systems (2017)
42. Weinzierl, S., Zilker, S., Dunzer, S., Matzner, M.: Machine learning in business process management: a SLR. Expert Syst. Appl. 124181 (2024)
43. Wenger, S., Spahic-Bogdanovic, M., Martin, A.: Large language models for democratizing business process modeling: BPMN model generation and style guide adherence. In: SACAIR, pp. 372–389. Springer, Cham (2024)

Large Language Models for Business Process Management: A Practice Overview

Cielo González Moyano[1,2](✉), Rachmadita Andreswari[1,2,4], Kristina Sahling[1,2], Jennifer Haase[1,2], Kate Revoredo[1], and Jan Mendling[1,2,3]

[1] Humboldt-Universität zu Berlin, Berlin, Germany
{c.gonzalez.moyano,rachmadita.andre.swari,kristina.sahling, jennifer.haase,kate.revoredo,jan.mendling}@hu-berlin.de
[2] Weizenbaum Institute, Berlin, Germany
[3] Vienna University of Economics and Business, Vienna, Austria
[4] Telkom University, Bandung, Indonesia

Abstract. Large Language Models (LLMs) are transforming how organizations manage and understand their processes. Recent conceptual studies have outlined opportunities for integrating LLMs throughout the BPM lifecycle. Prior structured reviews offer initial insights into practical application, but the rapidly evolving nature of the field requires continuous reassessment to maintain clarity on existing solutions, encountered challenges, and opportunities within each BPM lifecycle phase. Through a structured review of recent studies, we analyze how LLMs are applied across all BPM lifecycle phases. We specifically address three aspects per phase: contribution, implementation, and evaluation. Based on this, research and practical opportunities are identified. Our analysis shows that LLMs can integrate heterogeneous process documentation, generate process models from natural language, support process automation through executable outputs, and enable more accessible analysis and monitoring. Common technical approaches and recurring challenges, notably prompt sensitivity and scalability constraints, are identified. By connecting theoretical opportunities with practical applications, we offer a synthesized view of LLMs role in BPM and outline implications for future research and system development.

Keywords: Large Language Models · Business Process Management · Lifecycle

The authors' research was partly supported by the Federal Ministry of Research, Technology and Space under the grant 16DII133, founded by the German Federal Ministry of Education and Research in 2017. Kate Revoredo is funded by the Berliner Chancengleichheitsprogramm (BCP) as part of the DiGiTal Graduate Program. Rachmadita Andreswari is funded by Elsa Neumann Stipendium (H78027).

I. van de Weerd et al. (Eds.): BPM 2025 Workshops, LNBIP 569, pp. 438–450, 2026.
https://doi.org/10.1007/978-3-032-13426-4_32

1 Introduction

Large Language Models (LLMs) are being explored across various domains, including Business Process Management (BPM), due to their ability to interpret natural language, generate context-aware responses, retrieve and summarize information, and transform unstructured inputs into structured formats. In BPM, previous efforts [2,7,25] have identified opportunities for LLM integration throughout the tasks of the BPM lifecycle [6], and highlighted key research directions to guide future implementations. However, actual demonstrations of LLM-enabled BPM applications remain scattered and primarily confined to individual lifecycle phases such as discovery and analysis [9,13] or are centered around the possibilities of what might be accomplished with LLMs [25]. This understanding is essential for both researchers seeking to build upon existing work and practitioners evaluating the maturity of LLM applications in BPM. We like to advance this picture, by adressing the research question: *How are the opportunities of LLMs across the BPM lifecycle actualized by researchers so far?* We present a curated synthesis of exemplary studies that demonstrate how LLMs have been applied across different phases of the BPM lifecycle. We adopt a structured case-based approach, selecting representative implementations that demonstrate technical feasibility and also engage with previously identified research challenges. Our analysis reveals that LLMs are supporting BPM by converting unstructured information into process models, enhancing analysis accessibility, democratizing BPM tasks through natural language interfaces, supporting automation, and improving monitoring comprehensibility. We identify variations in technical approaches and evaluation methods while highlighting common challenges, including prompt dependency and complexity limitations. By connecting conceptual opportunities with practical implementations, we provide an integrated view of LLMs impact on BPM for both researchers and practitioners, concluding with implications for future development.

The remainder of this paper is structured as follows. Section 2 reviews related work and positions our contribution. Section 3 outlines our methodology. Section 4 presents lifecycle-spanning cases. Section 5 discusses our findings, and Sect. 6 concludes the paper with implications for future research and system design.

2 Related Work

In this section, we review prior literature that examines how LLMs have been applied across the phases of the BPM lifecycle, which traditionally includes identification, discovery, analysis, redesign, implementation, and monitoring [6]. We focus on structured reviews that organize LLM-related research along these phases, as they form the foundation for our own contribution.

An early structured overview was published in 2023 by Vidgof et al. [25], who outline potential applications of LLMs in tasks of the BPM lifecycle. While primarily visionary, their work provides a valuable starting point by proposing a broad conceptual landscape and identifying research directions. A key insight from this paper is that LLMs could play a role across all lifecycle phases, but particularly in the discovery phase. Building on similar motivations, papers from 2024, such as Bennoit et al. [2], begin to review early engineering work. Their study conducted a literature review to identify potential use cases, and also included concrete examples from published studies that describe actual applications. They show that the use cases are most concentrated in the discovery and implementation phases, particularly in activities such as the extraction of process knowledge.

Estrada-Torres et al. [7] present a literature review to assess the coverage of LLM applications in BPM lifecycle phases. Their study identifies common research trends and categorizes the types of evaluation used in existing work. They find that most LLM applications to date focus on the discovery and analysis phases. Additionally, the authors observe that the majority of studies rely heavily on GPT-based models, with limited exploration of other alternatives.

Collectively, these reviews indicate a growing interest in systematizing knowledge about LLMs in BPM, yet they reflect an early and fast-evolving landscape. We aim to build on this work by providing an updated understanding of how LLMs have been operationalized in each phase of the BPM lifecycle.

3 Method

We adopt a representative review approach following [16,19] that focuses on identifying and analyzing exemplary implementations to exemplify the actualization of the opportunities of LLMs in BPM.

We searched Google Scholar for primary studies from 2023–2025 using "LLM" combined with "Business Process Management" and BPM lifecycle terms. This timeframe captures the emergence of LLM applications in BPM following the widespread availability of advanced language models [7]. Papers were included if they: (1) demonstrated concrete LLM implementations in BPM contexts, (2) were written in English, and (3) addressed BPM lifecycle phases. We excluded purely theoretical discussions and traditional NLP approaches without LLM integration.

For each BPM lifecycle phase, we selected exemplary studies that demonstrate novel LLM applications, and provide implementation evidence. Each study was analyzed regarding its BPM lifecycle phase, LLM application approach, technical contribution, and evaluation method.

4 Results

We identified 20 studies that present novel applications of LLMs to at least one task within the BPM lifecycle. Table 1 provides an overview of these studies, indicating the BPM lifecycle phase they belong to, the specific LLMs used, and the nature of their contributions. In the following subsections, we discuss these works in more detail, structured according to the phases of the BPM lifecycle.

Table 1. Overview of LLM use across BPM lifecycle phases

Paper	BPM Phase	LLM	Approach	Key Contribution of the LLM
Franzoi et al. [8]	Identification	GPT-4	Prompting techniques, RAG, Flowise, Prototype	Enabling knowledge integration
Ayad and Alsayoud [1]	Discovery	GPT-3.5	Prompting techniques	Supporting model quality
Grohs et al. [9]	Discovery	GPT-4	Prompting techniques	Supporting knowledge integration
Koepke and Safan [11]	Discovery	GPT-4	Prompting techniques, Prototype	Supporting conversational modeling
Kourani et al. [13]	Discovery	GPT-4, Gemini-1.5, Claude-3.5, O1, Codestral, Llama3, Mistral, WizardLM, Qwen2.5	Prompting techniques, Prototype	Supporting model quality
Kourani et al. [12]	Discovery	GPT-4, Gemini	Prompting techniques	Supporting knowledge representation transformation
Norouzifar et al. [21]	Discovery	GPT-4o	Prompting techniques	Supporting model quality
Ziche and Apruzzese [26]	Discovery	GPT-3.5 Turbo	Prompting techniques, RAG, Prototype	Supporting conversational modeling
Nour Eldin et al. [22]	Discovery	GPT-4o	Prompting techniques, Prototype	Supporting knowledge representation transformation, supporting model quality
Buss et al. [4]	Analysis	LLaMA-2	Fine-tuning, Prompting techniques, Prototype	Making accessible process analysis
Dolha et al. [5]	Analysis	GPT-4	Prompting techniques	Supporting semantic analysis
De Nicola et al. [20]	Analysis	Gemini, GPT-3.5, Claude-2	Prompting techniques	Extracting analyzable process elements
Michele et al. [17]	Analysis, Redesign	GPT-3.5 Turbo	Prompting techniques	Enabling qualitative analysis, supporting process optimization decisions
Klievtsova et al. [10]	Redesign	GPT-4o, Gemini-1.5-pro, Mistral	Prompting techniques	Supporting conversational modeling
Lashkevich et al. [15]	Redesign	GPT-4 Turbo	Fine-tuning, Prompting techniques	Recommending redesign options
Toxtli and Li [24]	Implementation	GPT-4o	Prompting techniques	Generating executable process model
Monti et al. [18]	Implementation	GPT-4o	Prompting techniques, RAG, LangChain	Generating executable code
Schnepf [23]	Implementation	GPT-3.5 Turbo, GPT-4 , GPT-4 Turbo, LLaMA2, Mistral	AutoGen (Multi-agent LLM), Prompting techniques	Automating enterprise processes
Kubrak et al. [14]	Monitoring	ChatGPT	Prompting techniques, Prototype	Supporting understanding of recommendations
Berti et al. [3]	Monitoring	GPT-4	Prompting techniques	Enabling analysis of process execution data

4.1 Identification

The BPM lifecycle begins with the identification phase [6], during which the set of business processes within an organization is defined, along with criteria to select specific processes for improvement. At this stage, process analysts typically face a large volume of documentation, often heterogeneous, such as textual descriptions, slide decks, or BPMN models, and with limited structure, that must be compiled and analyzed to identify and evaluate the set of processes. LLMs can support this phase by enabling *heterogeneous process knowledge integration.* Franzoi et al. [8] developed a prototypical solution in which an LLM is used not just to access or summarize individual documents, but to integrate the contents of multiple heterogeneous sources into a unified internal representation. The LLM is then able to serve as a single point of access for querying the entire body of process knowledge. By instructing the LLM to answer only based on the pre-processed input documents, the approach minimizes hallucination and turns fragmented process documentation into coherent, actionable insights within the organization.

The essential architectural design for integrating LLMs into process identification relies on creating a uniform textual representation of heterogeneous process knowledge. This involves converting various source formats into a standardized textual format that the LLM can process. Franzoi et al. [8] implemented this strategy through an automated pipeline built with Microsoft Power Automate. The preprocessed textual data is then chunked and embedded using OpenAI's API, and stored in a vector database (Pinecone) to enable Retrieval-Augmented Generation (RAG). The authors also build a functional chatbot that integrates GPT-4 which handles query answering, context tracking, and document linking. This architecture not only enables long-term memory and domain-specific reasoning, but also supports representation-agnostic knowledge integration, allowing the system to relate process knowledge across formats, such as linking knowledge in a slide deck with knowledge in a process model. Moreover, the system can adapt its output to the user, making the delivery of process knowledge more user-centric and improving overall process affinity within the organization.

Franzoi et al. [8] evaluate their LLM-based chatbot using 29 questions, covering single-choice, multiple-choice, open-ended, and trick questions to detect hallucinations. Responses were manually compared against reference answers on seven metrics: factuality, completeness, relevance, coherence, conciseness, consistency, and grammatical correctness. The system passed 28 of 29 questions, suggesting strong performance in a controlled setting. However, limitations include loss of visual information in text conversion, text-only responses, privacy concerns from broad knowledge access, and limited generalizability from testing in a single organization. Future work should consider multimodal inputs to incorporate visual elements, varied output formats, role-based access controls, and broader evaluations, as well as studying context-aware representations and long-term organizational impacts on BPM.

4.2 Discovery

The Discovery phase in the BPM lifecycle focuses on constructing an accurate as-is process model [6], traditionally derived from interviews, process documentation, and execution logs. This task demands a significant manual effort, especially in data preparation and in translating unstructured information into formal process models. Recent developments highlight the potential of LLMs to assist in this task [9]. They bridge the gap between informal textual descriptions and formal modeling representations, making process modeling more accessible and scalable [9,11,22]. More specifically, based on the studies presented in Table 1, four main contributions are identified. First, they enable *knowledge representation transformation* and *knowledge integration* by converting domain-specific textual inputs into formal modeling constraints [21]. Grohs et al. [9] also highlight how LLMs can generate models that reflect domain-specific knowledge embedded in textual descriptions, even without training on BPM-specific corpora. Second, LLMs support *conversational modeling* through tools such as PRODIGY [26] or BPMN-Chatbot [11], which allow users to iteratively create or refine process models through natural language interaction. Finally, they assist on *model quality* by enhancing clarity, completeness, and coherence of the generated models compared to user input [1,11–13,22].

LLMs have been integrated into process discovery through several architectural strategies. One common approach is to use LLMs to generate process models from textual descriptions via *intermediate representations*. For instance, Kourani et al. [12] employ prompt-engineered LLMs to create partially ordered workflow models (POWL), which are then converted into BPMN or Petri nets. Another strategy involves *interactive assistants*, which often rely on RAG to include relevant documentation and use few-shot prompting to guide outputs [26]. A third approach centers on *refining models using textual feedback*. Norouzifar et al. [21], for example, extract declarative rules from expert-provided textual descriptions. Then, these rules guide the construction of process models that are aligned with both domain knowledge and recorded event logs.

Across the reviewed studies, several evaluation methods are commonly used. These include *manual assessments of model quality*, where experts rate the clarity, completeness, and correctness of generated process models [11,13]; *quantitative metrics* such as fitness, precision, and behavioral appropriateness [13]; *comparative benchmarks* across prompt variants (e.g., zero-shot vs. few-shot vs. chain-of-thought) [1]; *and user studies* in enterprise settings, where LLM-based tools like PRODIGY are tested with business analysts to gather qualitative feedback on usability and usefulness [26]. Besides the contributions, evaluation also shows common limitations emerge across the reviewed studies. One major challenge is the over-reliance on prompt quality. The effectiveness of LLM outputs is often highly sensitive to prompt formulation, which can limit reproducibility and scalability [1,21]. Additionally, some models suffer from reduced precision or completeness, especially in complex processes, which undermines their reliability in real-world applications [9,21]. In addition, many studies base their evaluations on simplified or small-scale test settings, such as controlled experiments or limited user involvement. This reduces the strength and applicability of the conclusions drawn from those studies [12]. It is also frequently highlighted that meaningful process modeling requires iterative human interaction to ensure relevance, completeness, and clarity of the outputs [1,12]. Future opportunities include the expansion of modeling perspectives beyond control-flow to include data, resource, and operational dimensions, as well as the extension of meta-models to support richer process constructs [11,12,21]. Another shared opportunity involves improving evaluation rigor through broader user studies, formal benchmarking, and sensitivity analysis, which are seen as critical for establishing generalizability and robustness [1,9,11]. Finally, technical improvements in generation methods, including the direct production of BPMN models without intermediate representations and the development of new prompt strategies and rule templates, are also seen as promising paths forward [1].

4.3 Analysis

The process analysis phase in the BPM lifecycle [6] concerns the identification, documentation and quantification of issues in the process. Traditional methods, such as value-added analysis or root-cause analysis, often require significant manual effort and expert involvement. Additionally, techniques may have specific requirements, such as flow analysis requiring a block-structured process model, which may demand manual effort to accommodate and can be time-consuming and error-prone. Recent developments highlight the potential of LLMs on minimizing the manual tasks required for process analysis. More specifically, LLMs enable the automatic *extraction of analyzable process elements* from documents and interviews, and support both objective and subjective analysis tasks [17,20]. They also *enhance the interpretation of BPMN models* and *enable semantic analysis*, particularly when leveraging structured representations like RDF graphs [5]. Domain-specific models like ProcessLLM [4] *automate and make accessible process analysis* for both experts and non-experts.

Most current designs integrate LLMs through structured prompts and the input of process documentation or model files, such as BPMN diagrams in XML or RDF formats. For instance, approaches by Dolha et al. [5] and De Nicola et al. [20] utilize advanced models like GPT-4, Gemini, or Claude-2, which are accessed via APIs or platforms that support prompt engineering. Some studies go further by fine-tuning LLMs on business process data, such as the ProcessLLM model introduced by Buss et al. [4], which is specifically trained on BPMN-related data to improve understanding and output quality for both expert and non-expert users.

The common evaluation method used is a comparison between manual and automatic analysis. For example, De Nicola et al. [20] assess extraction accuracy by comparing LLM outputs against expert annotations from interview transcripts, showing that LLMs can achieve better results than traditional NLP pipelines with significantly less manual configuration. The ProcessLLM framework [4] is evaluated on multiple BPMN analysis tasks and demonstrates improved accuracy and usability. Future research should focus on refining these approaches by developing more robust and adaptive prompting strategies. This would address the sensitivity of LLMs to prompt formulation and the handling of complex and domain specific scenarios [4,5]. Key opportunities also include leveraging reinforcement learning for automated prompt optimization, integrating business process event logs for more comprehensive and predictive analysis, and creating smart assistant agents that can support business users throughout the analysis process [17,20]. These advances aim to make process analysis more efficient, reliable, and accessible for a broader range of users and organizations.

4.4 Redesign

Process Redesign represents the fourth phase of the BPM lifecycle [6], where process improvement suggestions are developed to create a to-be model addressing shortcomings discovered in earlier phases. This phase traditionally requires specialized expertise in both domain knowledge and modeling techniques, creating a gap between business experts and technical modelers. LLMs offer capabilities to bridge this gap by supporting *conversational modeling redesign* and *recommending design options.*

For *conversational modeling redesign*, Klievtsova et al. [10] developed a conversational redesign pipeline that interprets natural language requests through a multi-step architecture, mapping user intent to 14 predefined change patterns for controlled model modifications. *Recommending design options* is explored by Lashkevich et al. [15]. In their work, they created a structured prompting system using GPT-4 Turbo to analyze process mining data, identify waiting time causes, and generate redesign recommendations based on established patterns. Additionally, Michele et al. [17] built a framework that uses GPT-4 to extract process objectives and stakeholder concerns from texts, providing structured evaluations to inform redesign decisions by identifying value misalignments.

Evaluations demonstrate promising results across these approaches. Klievtsova et al. [10] successfully implemented complex model changes through natural language instructions. Lashkevich et al. [15] found that pattern-based prompting significantly outperformed zero-shot approaches in generating useful recommendations. Michele et al. [17] framework showed high accuracy in extracting process objectives from unstructured texts. Despite these advances, limitations persist in complex pattern matching, prompt dependency, and the need for human oversight. Future opportunities include integration with mining tools, domain-specific prompting, enhanced explainability, and multi-modal modeling environments combining LLMs with process simulators.

4.5 Implementation

The implementation phase [6] focuses on realizing the designed process improvements. It encompasses both organizational change, which involves adapting the way of working for those participating in the process, and automation, which refers to the development and deployment of IT systems. This phase requires detailed technical specifications, knowledge of available tools, and technical skills to implement and operate process solutions. LLMs contribute to this phase in several ways. They can support with *tool selection*. Monti et al. [18] used an LLM to identify the most suitable tool for a given task based on its textual description. LLMs also support *executable code generation*. Monti et al. [18] proposed a method where LLM generates Python code for deployment in a process execution engine using textual process descriptions, the process model, and a list of tools along with their operations. In addition, LLMs support *executable process model generation*. Toxtli and Li [24] used GPT-4o to produce BPMN XML diagrams compatible with the Camunda platform. Their approach incorporated background information on Camunda's XML format and included detailed instructions to ensure correct tagging and object placement. LLMs can also contribute to *automating enterprise processes*. Schnepf et al. [23] explored how LLMs can support automation of the procure-to-pay process within SAP ERP systems, specifically using SAP ECC 6.0 configured with the IDES model company.

LLMs have been integrated into process implementation through different architectural strategies. A common approach involves the use of interactive assistants that incorporate RAG to ground responses in relevant documentation and apply few-shot prompting to steer outputs [18]. AutoGen, an open-source framework developed by Microsoft that enables the creation of LLM-based applications composed of multiple agents working collaboratively to accomplish tasks was used by Schnepf et al. [23]. In this setting, distinct agent roles were defined, such as Purchaser and Purchasing Manager, each equipped with functions to interact with SAP systems and execute transactions. The agents used a range of LLMs, including GPT-3.5 Turbo, GPT-4, GPT-4 Turbo, LLaMA2, and Mistral, all of which required knowledge of the process being automated. Another architectural approach was presented by Monti et al. [18], who employed the LangChain framework to orchestrate interactions between LLMs and the process data. This design makes the solution independent of any specific LLM provider, allowing GPT-4, the model used, to be substituted with other current LLM, such as like LLaMA2 or future LLMs without requiring changes to the overall workflow.

Different levels of process complexity were considered in the evaluation. GPT-4o was able to generate structurally sound BPMN diagrams that could be rendered correctly in standard viewers, making them suitable as a starting point for process automation. It also showed strong performance in distinguishing between tasks that should be assigned to humans and those that could be automated, supporting effective task delegation. However, the approaches present several limitations. Monti et al. [18] note the sensitivity of tool selection to the specific repository used and the reliance on natural language descriptions for both processes and services. Toxtli and Li [24] report difficulties in handling highly complex processes, especially in ensuring diagram completeness and correct sequencing, suggesting that human validation may still be necessary. Schnepf et al. [23] identify input size constraints and token limitations as technical challenges, and emphasize that LLM costs vary significantly, which is relevant for deployment decisions. The studies also suggest concrete directions for future research. One possibility is to extract tool descriptions directly from their source code where available. Another is to combine natural language-based deployment scripts with statistical simulation parameters obtained from event logs. A third direction involves fine-tuning LLMs using datasets of complex BPMN diagrams and corresponding textual descriptions. Finally, interactive model generation approaches, where LLMs provide initial models and users iteratively refine them, could enhance both quality and usability.

4.6 Monitoring

The monitoring phase [6] of the BPM lifecycle begins once a (re) designed process is deployed and operational. During this phase, executions are observed to identify recurring issues, deviations, or inefficiencies. Based on the insights gathered, corrective actions can be taken. Recent studies show that LLMs can support this phase by making monitoring insights more accessible, interpretable, and actionable, particularly for non-technical users.

Kubarek et al. [14] explore how LLMs can improve the *understandability of recommendations* in Prescriptive Process Monitoring by providing interactive explanations via a chatbot interface. The authors designed a chatbot that interacts with users to provide natural language explanations of monitoring recommendations. Berti et al. [3] explore how LLMs can be guided through prompt engineering to *enabling natural language querying and analysis* of a real-world healthcare event log. The paper highlights that LLMs can be beneficial in the monitoring phase by identifying deviations and anomalies, analyzing and explaining performance issues, and recommending potential process improvements based on log patterns.

These studies used both user-based and system-based evaluation methods. Kubrak et al. [14] conducted interviews with 12 process analysts and found that natural language explanations from LLMs enhanced understanding and trust in recommendations. Berti et al. [3] assessed GPT-4 using four real-world event logs, with domain experts rating its responses as useful for identifying deviations and suggesting process improvements. Despite promising results, limitations remain in prompt sensitivity, domain-specific reasoning, and output reliability. Future work should focus on improved prompting, domain adaptation, and integration with causal or visual analysis tools to enhance robustness and interpretability.

5 Discussion

LLMs are contributing to three major shifts in BPM. They democratize process work by enabling non-technical users to interact with and shape processes through natural language [3,4,10,11,26]. They enhance interpretation by structuring diverse inputs, integrating them, and generating insights that support both technical and strategic decision-making [5,8,9,14,20]. Finally, LLMs contribute to automation by generating executable models, deployment scripts, and even tool configurations, reducing the manual effort required to implement process changes [15,18,23,24].

Despite their potential, current research reveals important limitations in the use of LLMs for BPM. Many approaches are highly sensitive to prompt design, which affects the reliability and reproducibility of results. Several solutions are tightly coupled to a specific LLM provider with GPT based models dominating 18 out of the 20 studies, which is a trend also observed in the prior study by Estrada-Torres et al. [7], limiting flexibility and long-term sustainability. Only Monti et al. [18] and Franzoi et al. [8] adopted a provider independent architectures, ensuring future applicability without requiring changes to the overall workflow. Furthermore, while LLMs can generate process improvements, most studies do not evaluate whether these improvements lead to measurable gains in actual process performance. Addressing these gaps requires developing more robust prompting techniques, encouraging provider agnostic solutions, and conducting empirical studies that assess the real world impact of LLM generated process changes. Notably, several LLM application scenarios proposed by Vidgof et al. [25] remain unrealized, particularly in the BPM phases of monitoring (e.g., process dashboards chatbots) and analysis (e.g., issue spotting), highlighting key opportunities for future research.

This study has typical literature review limitations, including potential reviewer bias and limited search scope. Future work should improve validation, broaden database coverage, and refine inclusion criteria.

6 Conclusion

This study set out to examine how LLMs are shaping BPM by mapping their actual implementation across the BPM lifecycle. We found out that LLMs have been effectively used in all phases. In most of the cases the power of LLM to interpret natural language and generate textual output is used to leverage a BPM task, such as integrating heterogeneous process documentation and explaining process artifacts. These advancements support broader participation, including non technical participants, and offer more efficient and accessible BPM practices. However, most studies are still limited by factors such as prompt sensitivity, scalability constraints, and the need for robust human oversight.

Our findings suggest that while LLMs hold great promise for transforming BPM practice and research, further work is needed to address current gaps. The main ones are the use of alternatives such as LangChain to enable long-standing solutions and evaluating them in real-world settings.

References

1. Ayad, S., Alsayoud, F.: Prompt engineering techniques for semantic enhancement in business process models. Bus. Process. Manag. J. **30**(7), 2611–2641 (2024)
2. Bennoit, C., Greff, T., Baum, D., Bajwa, I.A.: Identifying use cases for large language models in the business process management lifecycle. In: 26th International Conference on Business Informatics, CBI 2024, Vienna, Austria, 9–13 September 2024, pp. 256–263. IEEE (2024)
3. Berti, A., Schuster, D., van der Aalst, W.M.P.: Abstractions, scenarios, and prompt definitions for process mining with LLMs: a case study. In: Business Process Management Workshops, vol. 492, pp. 427–439. Springer, Cham (2023)
4. Buss, A., Kratsch, W., Schmid, S.J., Wang, H.: Processllm: a large language model specialized in the interpretation, analysis, and optimization of business processes. In: Business Process Management Workshops. LNBIP, vol. 534, pp. 221–232. Springer, Cham (2024)
5. Dolha, D., Ghirana, A.M., Buchmann, R.A.: Revisiting business process analysis through the lens of large language models. IOS Press Journal (2025)
6. Dumas, M., Rosa, M.L., Mendling, J., Reijers, H.A.: Fundamentals of Business Process Management, 2nd edn. Springer, Cham (2018)
7. Estrada-Torres, B., del-Río-Ortega, A., Resinas, M.: Mapping the landscape: exploring large language model applications in business process management. In: BPMDS/EMMSAD@CAiSE, vol. 511, pp. 22–31. Springer, Cham (2024)
8. Franzoi, S., Delwaulle, M., Dyong, J., Schaffner, J., Burger, M., vom Brocke, J.: Using large language models to generate process knowledge from enterprise content. In: Business Process Management Workshops, vol. 534, pp. 247–258. Springer, Cham (2024)
9. Grohs, M., Abb, L., Elsayed, N., Rehse, J.: Large language models can accomplish business process management tasks. In: Business Process Management Workshops, vol. 492, pp. 453–465. Springer, Cham (2023)
10. Klievtsova, N., Kampik, T., Mangler, J., Rinderle-Ma, S.: Conversational Process Model Redesign (2025)

11. Köpke, J., Safan, A.: Efficient LLM-based conversational process modeling. In: Business Process Management Workshops, vol. 534, pp. 259–270. Springer, Cham (2024)
12. Kourani, H., Berti, A., Schuster, D., van der Aalst, W.M.P.: Process modeling with large language models. In: BPMDS/EMMSAD@CAiSE, vol. 511, pp. 229–244. Springer, Cham (2024)
13. Kourani, H., Berti, A., Schuster, D., van der Aalst, W.M.: Evaluating large language models on business process modeling: framework, benchmark, and self-improvement analysis. arXiv preprint arXiv:2412.00023 (2024)
14. Kubrak, K., Botchorishvili, L., Milani, F., Nolte, A., Dumas, M.: Explanatory capabilities of large language models in prescriptive process monitoring. In: Marrella, A., Resinas, M., Jans, M., Rosemann, M. (eds.) Business Process Management, pp. 403–420. Springer, Cham
15. Lashkevich, K., Milani, F., Avramenko, M., Dumas, M.: LLM-assisted optimization of waiting time in business processes: a prompting method. In: Marrella, A., Resinas, M., Jans, M., Rosemann, M. (eds.) Business Process Management, pp. 474–492. Springer, Cham (2024)
16. Lecy, J.D., Beatty, K.E.: Representative Literature Reviews Using Constrained Snowball Sampling and Citation Network Analysis (2012)
17. Michele, W.D., Cervantes, A.A., Frermann, L.: Automated business process analysis: an LLM-based approach to value assessment. arXiv preprint arXiv:2504.06600 (2025)
18. Monti, F., Leotta, F., Mangler, J., Mecella, M., Rinderle-Ma, S.: Nl2processops: towards LLM-guided code generation for process execution. In: BPM (Forum), vol. 526, pp. 127–143. Springer, Cham (2024)
19. Munn, Z., Peters, M.D.J., Stern, C., Tufanaru, C., McArthur, A., Aromataris, E.: Systematic review or scoping review? Guidance for authors when choosing between a systematic or scoping review approach. BMC Med. Res. Methodol. **18**(1), 143 (2018)
20. Nicola, A.D., Formica, A., Mele, I., Missikoff, M., Taglino, F.: A comparative study of LLMs and NLP approaches for supporting business process analysis. Enterprise Inf. Syst. (2024)
21. Norouzifar, A., Kourani, H., Dees, M., van der Aalst, W.M.: Bridging domain knowledge and process discovery using large language models. In: International Conference on Business Process Management, pp. 44–56. Springer, Cham (2024)
22. Nour Eldin, A., Assy, N., Anesini, O., Dalmas, B., Gaaloul, W.: A decomposed hybrid approach to business process modeling with LLMs. In: CoopIS, pp. 243–260. Springer, Cham (2024)
23. Schnepf, J., Engin, T., Anderer, S., Scheuermann, B.: Studies on the use of large language models for the automation of business processes in enterprise resource planning systems. In: NLDB (1). LNCS, vol. 14762, pp. 16–31. Springer, Cham (2024)
24. Toxtli, C., Li, W.: Automating automation: using LLMs to generate BPMN workflows for robotic process automation. In: Arabnia, H.R., Deligiannidis, L., Amirian, S., Shenavarmasouleh, F., Ghareh Mohammadi, F., de la Fuente, D. (eds.) Artificial Intelligence and Applications, pp. 221–229. Springer, Cham (2025)

25. Vidgof, M., Bachhofner, S., Mendling, J.: Large language models for business process management: opportunities and challenges. In: BPM (Forum). LNBIP, vol. 490, pp. 107–123. Springer, Cham (2023)
26. Ziche, C., Apruzzese, G.: Llm4pm: a case study on using large language models for process modeling in enterprise organizations. In: International Conference on Business Process Management, pp. 472–483. Springer, Cham (2024)

An LLM Pipeline for Automatic Extraction and Evaluation of Care Pathways from Clinical Guidelines

Alireza Houshidari[1(✉)], William Van Woensel[2], Daniel Amyot[1], and El Mostafa Bouattane[3]

[1] School of EECS, University of Ottawa, Ottawa, Canada
{a.houshidari,damyot}@uottawa.ca
[2] Telfer School of Management, University of Ottawa, Ottawa, Canada
wvanwoen@uottawa.ca
[3] Montfort Hospital, Ottawa, Canada
mostafabouattane@montfort.on.ca

Abstract. Clinical Practice Guidelines (CPGs) are continually updated, yet translating such narrative recommendations into formal Care Pathway (CPW) processes remains labor-intensive and prone to inconsistency. We introduce a modular, end-to-end extraction pipeline that leverages Large Language Model (LLM) frameworks to automatically generate and evaluate BPMN models of CPWs from CPG text. Our system standardizes different output formats, applies LLM-based label alignment to harmonize terminology, and evaluates models against reference models using node- and structural-similarity metrics. Experiments on four stroke-related CPGs, using two state-of-the-art LLM frameworks—ProMoAI and a multi-agent orchestration approach (MAO)—shows the feasibility of automated CPW process extraction. We further observe that the multi-agent framework (MAO) demonstrates markedly higher fidelity. A web-based UI supports experiment configuration and result inspection. We released all code, prompts, and datasets as open-source to promote reproducibility and future enhancements.

Keywords: Process extraction · LLM · BPMN · Process modeling · Clinical practice guidelines

1 Introduction

Clinical Pathways (CPWs) operationalize evidence-based guidelines, such as Clinical Practice Guidelines (CPGs), into step-by-step protocols that standardize care and reduce unwarranted practice variation; and, by doing so, cut in-hospital complications, shorten length of stay, lower costs, and improve documentation [6,21]. However, free-text guidelines, even in the form of CPWs, typically lack clear control-flow semantics, making them difficult to interpret [6].

I. van de Weerd et al. (Eds.): BPM 2025 Workshops, LNBIP 569, pp. 451–463, 2026.
https://doi.org/10.1007/978-3-032-13426-4_33

By translating CPWs into formal, graphical process models, such as in the Business Process Model and Notation (BPMN) [16], these semantics become explicit, improving clarity, consistency, and machine readability. Graphical models provide quick, intuitive visual overviews, facilitating the understanding of complex clinical pathways. They further enable integration into Clinical Decision Support Systems and compliance checking with real-world care trajectories [11,20].

However, there are some pain points in manually creating and maintaining CPW process models. Just in 2023, over 26,000 cancer-related papers were published on PubMed. As a result, CPGs are continually updated to incorporate the latest evidence. In turn, CPW processes should be continuously revised to align with current CPGs. However, the manual extraction of CPWs from narrative guidelines is complex and susceptible to interpretation bias; these difficulties are compounded by the need to keep pace with the volume of new research [6].

Large Language Models (LLMs), pre-trained on extensive text corpora, have demonstrated remarkable potential across various NLP tasks [26]. They are generally effective for extracting information from text, and have the potential to automate the process of CPW extraction form CPGs. LLMs can parse natural language and embed general knowledge with high accuracy. Earlier research highlighted that LLMs struggled with process extraction from clinical guidelines due to ambiguity and domain specificity [6]. Nevertheless, recent architectural advances, including multi-agent frameworks (MAO [15]) and improved error handling (ProMoAI [13]), can be used to address these issues.

Given these developments, we believe it is timely to present a modular pipeline to evaluate novel LLM approaches for BPMN process extraction from clinical guidelines. This paper contributes an automated pipeline that integrates:

1. Existing LLM frameworks tailored to extract processes from text. Currently, these include MAO and ProMoAI, running over GPT-4.1 [17]. Other LLM frameworks can be plugged into our pipeline as they are developed, as well as other foundational models.
2. A new unified conversion layer that translates heterogeneous LLM outputs (processes) into canonical BPMN models with auto-layout.
3. A new automated evaluation of generated processes against reference process models using standard node- and structural-similarity metrics [4], for repeatable and scalable performance measurement;
4. A new GPT-based label-alignment component that harmonizes LLM-generated activity labels with the reference terminology. This ensures that semantically correct but differently phrased labels can still be matched;
5. A new web-based tool for launching experiments and inspecting results.

We compare empirically MAO and ProMoAI, both running on GPT-4.1, using four stroke-related Quality-Based Procedures (Ontario, Canada [7]). The LLM frameworks use different techniques for process extraction from CPGs, enabling an evaluation of how modern LLM architectures perform on this challenging task. Our results demonstrate that automated process extraction from CPGs is feasible with current LLM technology, with the agentic MAO framework offering the best performance at this time. Looking beyond the current study, we envision the integration of Knowledge-Graph-Enhanced LLMs to inject domain facts and constraints, as well as behavioral model comparison and visual diff tools to support human evaluation. Our ultimate goal is rapid, cost-effective CPW updates that ensure pathways stay current without manual rework.

In a prior paper [23], we embedded our pipeline within a broader compliance-checking workflow, which used the extracted CPW to assess real-world care trajectories. While that work treated the pipeline as a black box, this work details its components and significantly elaborates on the experiment results.

Section 2 situates our work within the process extraction literature. Sections 3 and 4 detail the LLM pipeline and experiment design, respectively. Section 5 presents the results. Section 6 analyses threats to validity. Section 7 discusses future work directions. Section 8 concludes the paper.

2 Background and Related Work

2.1 Process Extraction

Care Pathways (CPWs) translate clinical guidelines into step-by-step sequences for clinical practice, offering more detailed and actionable guidance. Converting CPWs into formal process models, such as BPMN, further supports control-flow clarity, machine readability, and integration into clinical decision support systems [11,20]. An automated process extraction framework can hereby parse narrative CPGs and convert them into CPW process models, without the need for labor-intensive and error-prone manual updates.

Over the past decade, automated process extraction methods have evolved significantly [24]. While early approaches relied on manually encoded linguistic patterns, works from around 2016 onward increasingly relied on statistical classifiers that offered greater adaptability at the cost of extensive feature engineering [24]. With the introduction of pre-trained transformers (e.g., BERT) and recurrent architectures (LSTM, ON-LSTM) in 2018, deep learning pipelines emerged that outperformed prior approaches in entity recognition (ER) and relation extraction (RE) tasks [24]. Only recently have a handful of studies explored few-shot, in-context prompting of LLMs for generating process models from narrative descriptions [1,6]. While early results are encouraging, accurately capturing control-flow constraints and ensuring output stability remain open challenges [1,6,24]. To address these challenges, recent work has introduced multi-agent architectures [15] and error handling [13]. We chose ProMoAI and MAO because they (a) exemplify these two novel architectural approaches, and (b) have demonstrated better outcomes than previous frameworks. This choice thus allows for the evaluation of different paradigms in LLM frameworks.

2.2 ProMoAI and MAO

The ProMoAI and MAO frameworks both utilize LLMs to convert natural-language process descriptions into structured process models with minimal user intervention. However, they follow different approaches:

ProMoAI [13] has an architecture that follows a sequential pipeline of modules: initially, a *prompt-generation module* transforms user input into a structured instruction prompt. This prompt embeds Partially Ordered Workflow Language (POWL) semantics, expert-role framing, least-to-most decomposition strategies, and few-shot examples to guide the LLM in generating Python code based on a custom POWL function library. Next, an *LLM invocation layer* generates the POWL code using this prompt, and forwards it to a *sandboxed execution environment*, where validation checks are performed, and the scripts are safely executed to produce POWL models. If execution errors are detected there, an *automated error-handling module* triggers self-refinement prompts to iteratively debug and regenerate the code. Ultimately, validated models are output in standardized notations, such as BPMN and Petri nets. An *interactive feedback loop* module enables user input to be incorporated into future prompt iterations for continual model enhancement.

MAO (Multi-Agent Orchestration) [15] is a novel agentic framework for generating process models in an XML "BPMN text" representation. MAO's architecture orchestrates a specialized *team* of LLM agents-Team Leader (instructor), Process Design Expert (executor), and Process Reviewer-through four phases: (1) Generation, where the initial BPMN text is produced via knowledge-injection, few-shot exemplars, and chain-of-thought prompting; (2) Refinement, which decomposes and enriches activities and gateways; (3) Reviewing, where semantic hallucinations are autonomously detected and corrected through multi-round agent dialogue; and (4) Testing, in which external validation tools are invoked to locate and repair format errors in the BPMN text. Hence, whereas ProMoAI depends on user intervention to resolve semantic and logical hallucinations, MAO's multi-agent workflow automates those corrections end to end.

3 Pipeline

3.1 LLM Pipeline Overview

Our pipeline includes four modular components-(1) LLM Execution, (2) Output Standardization, (3) Automated Evaluation, and (4) User Interface-each with clearly defined inputs, processing steps, and outputs. The pipeline accepts any type of text that narratively describes a process as input, however, our primary focus is on CPW[1].

Figure 1 shows an overview of the pipeline components. The implementation is freely available online with instructions [9].

Given a CPW text and a configuration, the *LLM Execution layer* invokes the selected LLM framework, which will produce a process model in a particular format (e.g., POWL script or BPMN-Text). These intermediate outputs are passed to the *Output Standardization* module, which transforms them into canonical BPMN diagrams and applies auto-layout for readability. The *Automated Evaluation* module accepts the resulting BPMN models, together with a

[1] Accordingly, current prompt templates are specifically designed for this purpose.

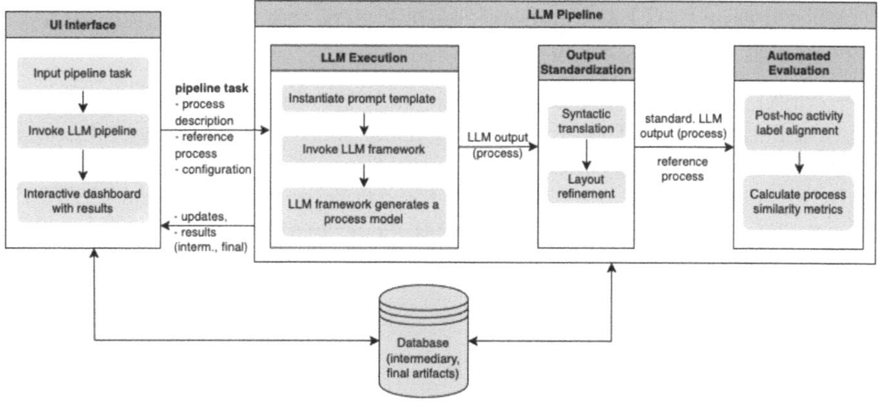

Fig. 1. Overview of the LLM pipeline.

gold-standard reference BPMN, and outputs a comparison of the two in terms of similarity metrics. The pipeline is accessible via a web-based UI for experiment configuration, running, and dashboarding the results. All artifacts (logs, model files, evaluation scores) are persisted to a relational database.

3.2 LLM Execution

A pipeline *task* bundles two elements: process description (e.g., CWP document) and a configuration, including the LLM framework (currently, ProMoAI or MAO), the underlying LLM model to use (e.g., `gpt-4.1` [17]), prompt-template settings (i.e., predefined setup to use), number of runs, and project/job identifier.

When a *task* is submitted, this component injects the process description into the framework-specific prompt template, and then dispatches the filled prompt to the chosen LLM framework via its pipeline adapter. During execution, each framework emits structured events-such as “request sent”, “partial response”, “retry attempt”, and “final response”-to a (framework-agnostic) pipeline listener. An LLM framework will have internal retry logic to perform error recovery (e.g., ProMoAI's self-refinement loop, MAO's multi-agent review). The listener captures and persists these events, together with metadata (timestamps, input/output paths, retry counts). Note that the “final response” event encapsulates the generated process model as this component's output.

Our modular design means new LLM frameworks can be easily plugged in, by adding the provider's SDK and implementing an adapter and listener mapping.

3.3 Output Standardization

Next, this component accepts the generated process models and converts them into standardized BPMN 2.0. This allows for their automated evaluation using the same component and similarity metrics (Sect. 3.4), and their visual interpretation by clinicians and process analysts with knowledge of BPMN.

Depending on the LLM framework output, steps may include *syntactic translation* as well as *layout refinement*:

- ProMoAI. For *syntactic translation*, we translate the generated POWL script into a Petri net and then into BPMN using the PM4Py library [19]. *Layout refinement* was already performed by PM4Py in the former step.
- MAO. For *syntactic translation*, a custom script parses its generated BPMN-Text and emits standard BPMN XML. For *layout refinement*, we call an external auto-layout library [2] for node coordinates and improving readability.

3.4 Automated Evaluation

The *Automated Evaluation* component takes as inputs (**a**) the generated BPMN model, as the standardized output of an LLM framework, and (**b**) an expert-validated, gold-standard reference standard, and calculates similarity scores between (a) and (b). This component involves the following steps:

Post-hoc activity label alignment. In our experience, the LLM-generated activity labels are often semantically similar to the reference labels, however, they are too far apart syntactically for existing similarity metrics (e.g., using string edit distance). We thus first attempt to align the labels from models (a) and (b). Specifically, we extract the list of activity names from both models and invoke an LLM model (currently, GPT-4.1) with a structured prompt that specifies the alignment task and desired output format. The first API call asks for a mapping from generated labels to reference labels; the second call asks to verify and refine each match. We then apply this mapping to update the activity labels in the generated model to match the reference terminology. Our initial experiments demonstrated that a single LLM invocation for activity alignment often produces imperfect label mappings; however, issuing a second, refinement-focused call more reliably yielded the correct alignments.

Calculate process similarity metrics. We compare the aligned process models by calculating node-similarity, structural-similarity, and graph edit distance (GED) using Dijkman's method [4]. We selected Dijkman's method over alternatives (EGED [25], BPMN-Sim [5]) because it natively incorporates label matching, captures gateway types in its soft-cost GED, and has an open-source implementation [3]. Nevertheless, the pipeline's modular design allows plugging in other evaluation metrics.

3.5 User Interface

Users interact with the system via a web-based UI (Fig. 2) that features (1) an experiment form, for configuring and launching pipeline tasks, and (2) a results dashboard for analyzing the results of completed tasks.

In the *experiment form*, users supply their OpenAI API key, choose the LLM framework upload a narrative process description and reference BPMN file, and specify configuration parameters. Any relevant pipeline output will be persisted in a database. The *results dashboard* then reads from this database to present interactive charts of evaluation metrics and descriptive statistics. The entire application is containerized, and a publicly available image allows users to easily deploy the system [9].

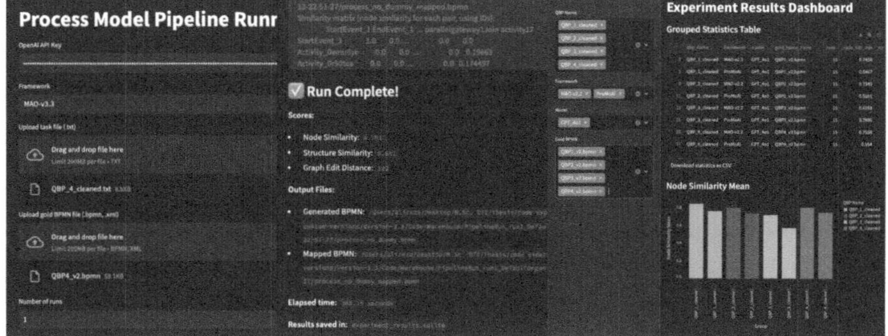

Fig. 2. UI overview

4 Experimental Setup

4.1 Datasets

As input CPGs, our evaluation uses 4 stroke-related Quality-Based Procedures (QBPs) from Health Quality Ontario's public repository [8]. We selected the December 2016 Clinical Handbook for Stroke (Acute and Postacute), considering its different modules as separate QBPs each spanning approximately 2–3 pages. For each guideline, we removed noise text related to acknowledgements and references.

4.2 Framework Configuration and Execution Protocol

We evaluated two state-of-the-art LLM frameworks, namely ProMoAI and MAO (Sect. 2.2), using GPT-4.1 as the underlying LLM model. Each framework uses template-based prompts with few-shot examples; we adapted these templates to signal that inputs are clinical pathways rather than business processes. Network or API failures trigger up to five automatic retries (exponential backoff); failures after these retries are recorded and excluded from downstream analysis. Hyperparameters are fixed (temperature=0.2, top_p=1.0, max_tokens=2000–2048, frequency_penalty=0.0, presence_penalty=0.0). Hyperparameters were selected to prioritize accuracy and consistency: temperature=0.2 ensures highly deterministic and consistent outputs with minimal randomness, while max_tokens limit aligns with token limits commonly used in state-of-the-art process extraction frameworks [13,15]. The entire stack (Python 3.12/3.9; PM4Py 2.7.12.4; OpenAI SDK 1.79.0/1.63.0) is containerized with Docker for consistency [9]. Experiments were executed on a MacBook Pro 2020 (Intel i5, 8 GB RAM) without GPU acceleration.

4.3 Evaluation Methods

We follow 2 major types of evaluation from the process extraction literature [24]:

- **Expert Evaluation:** A healthcare specialist conducted a comprehensive review of the standardized (BPMN) LLM output[2]. For each process, the expert, who is the paper's 4th author, (a) scored the process' fidelity to the corresponding QBP on a 5-point Likert scale, and (b) provided free-text comments on missing activities, incorrect branch labels, sequencing errors, and unclear layouts. We report the mean of the overall ratings and a qualitative summary of the expert's observations.
- **Systematic (Graph-Based) Evaluation:** Using our *Automated Evaluation* component, we quantitatively compared each standardized LLM output process against an expert-validated reference process. Each guideline underwent 15 pipeline runs; we report the mean results. To evaluate performance differences between MAO and ProMoAI, we applied Welch's t-test (as it is robust to unequal variances) and calculated Cohen's d to quantify effect sizes.

5 Results

5.1 Expert Evaluation

As shown in Table 1, the healthcare expert rated the MAO-generated models slightly higher. Among the evaluated QBPs, QBP2 achieved the highest rating at 5/5, while QBP3 received the lowest at 3.5/5. In their feedback, the expert noted that, although the LLM-generated models generally captured the essential clinical tasks, their accuracy was limited by the lack of contextual and background information within the source guidelines. Clinical guidelines are typically intended for expert audiences and often omit details considered common knowledge among practitioners. To increase fidelity, the expert highlighted the importance of providing the LLM with additional contextual information, such as institutional constraints and standard emergency department workflows.

5.2 Systematic Similarity Analysis

As shown in Table 2, MAO demonstrated superior performance, achieving the highest average node-level similarity (0.78) and structural similarity (0.63). ProMoAI exhibited greater variability in performance, with the highest run-to-run

[2] We omitted the activity alignment step so as to review the original LLM outputs.

Table 1. Expert Ratings of LLM-Generated Process Models

Model	Mean Score	Highest QBP Rating	Lowest QBP Rating
MAO	4.25	5.0 (QBP 2, QBP 4)	3.0 (QBP 3)
ProMoAI	4.00	5.0 (QBP 2)	3.0 (QBP 4)

Table 2. Comparison of MAO vs. ProMoAI on similarity metrics.

Statistic	Node Similarity	Structure Similarity
Mean (MAO)	0.782	0.630
Mean (ProMoAI)	0.696	0.585
CV (MAO)	0.058	0.046
CV (ProMoAI)	0.158	0.090
t (df)	5.29 (91)	5.16 (113)
p	<0.001	<0.001
Cohen's d	0.97	0.94

variability in node similarity (Coefficient of Variation = CV = 0.158). We note that the two similarity measures showed very strong correlation (r = 0.89; not in the table), indicating that LLM frameworks performing well on node-level matching also tend to excel at structural alignment. Statistical analysis confirms that MAO's superior performance is statistically significant. Welch's t-tests revealed significant differences for both metrics: node similarity (MAO: 0.781 vs. ProMoAI: 0.696; $t(\approx 91) = 5.294$, $p < 0.001$, Cohen's $d = 0.967$) and structural similarity (MAO: 0.630 vs. ProMoAI: 0.585; $t(\approx 113) = 5.159$, $p < 0.001$, Cohen's $d = 0.942$). Both comparisons yielded large effect sizes and p-values well below the 0.05 significance threshold. Hence, we observe that MAO has significantly superior performance in automated process extraction from clinical guidelines.

5.3 Discussion

We observe that MAO's agent-based workflow-where dedicated agents take turns drafting, critiquing, and polishing segments of the process-leads to a superior fidelity with the reference input text and models, according to healthcare experts and process similarity metrics. By delegating responsibilities such as label harmonization, error checking, and validation to distinct LLM agents, MAO reduces sequencing and branching errors, and yields process models that experts find more coherent and comprehensive. We note that this is in line with general observations on agentic LLM frameworks [22]. Nevertheless, the expert's observations on implicitly understood clinical steps suggests that integrating domain-specific knowledge could further improve LLM performance.

6 Threats to Validity

Regarding *construct validity*, Dijkman's similarity metrics emphasize structural matching and may overlook critical details embedded in labels. This focus on structural isomorphism also penalizes logically equivalent refactorings; incorporating behavioral conformance (Sect. 7) will give a fuller picture. LLM output is sensitive to prompt wording. We kept prompt templates consistent across all experiments to ensure fair comparison, though we did not optimize these templates for maximum performance. Although each guideline was processed 15 times, a larger run count or different seeds could shift means and variances.

For *internal validity*, the models were rated by a single domain expert who is also a co-author, potentially introducing bias. Inter-rater reliability is thus also unknown. Additional expert-based verifications are planned. We publicly released the prompts and logs [9] to support replication and future complementary behavioral or semantic metrics.

In terms of *external validity*, we only evaluated 4 QBPs, each having 2–3 pages, in the stroke domain; other specialties and longer guidelines may lead to different results. The results also reflect GPT-4.1's capabilities and may not hold for open-source or future LLM models.

7 Future Directions

Knowledge-Graph Injection. Knowledge graphs (KGs) provide structured, unambiguous, domain-specific facts that can represent biomedical knowledge, clinical standards, and institutional protocols. Integrating KGs with LLMs has been shown to improve reasoning, reduce hallucinations, and enhance performance in healthcare settings [18]. To address the lack of contextual constraints noted by our expert (Sect. 5.1), based on the state-of-the-art, we will develop a KG-enhanced LLM framework that retrieves relevant KG subgraphs at inference time to dynamically augment prompts with relevant clinical knowledge.

Conversational Process Modeling. A complementary way of injecting knowledge is to support interactive conversations with the LLM. In particular, we will explore the integration of Klievtsova's framework [12] for extracting BPMN models from text and conversations.

Behavioural Compliance Metrics. To check whether extracted process models capture the same clinical logic as the reference model, rather than just graph topology, we plan to augment our evaluation with behavioural-similarity metrics as defined by Dijkman et al. [4]. These metrics also compare the causal, concurrent, and conflicting relations encoded in each model.

Visual BPMN Diff and Expert Validation Tools. There are several tools available [10,14] that facilitate visual comparisons of BPMN models, by highlighting differences including additions, removals, or modifications of activities. By incorporating these visual diff methods into our pipeline, we can directly support expert-based evaluation in addition to automated evaluation, allowing them to interactively examine disparities between extracted and reference processes.

8 Conclusion and Future Work

This work presents a modular LLM pipeline for the automated extraction and evaluation of care pathways from clinical guidelines. The pipeline currently features i) two state-of-the-art LLM frameworks-ProMoAI and MAO-on GPT-4.1; ii) a layer to convert LLM output to canonical BPMN with auto-layout; iii) an automated evaluation that computes relevant metrics; iv) a GPT-based label-alignment component to help ensure semantically consistent comparisons; and v) a web-based UI and dashboard for seamlessly running experiments and analyzing their results. In doing so, the LLM pipeline enables accurate, scalable and repeatable extraction and evaluation of structured process models.

Prior work had indicated that the automated use of LLM's for process extraction from clinical guidelines was unrealistic at the time [6]. Our empirical results on 4 stroke-related QBPs demonstrate the feasibility of LLM-driven CPW extraction, using novel LLM architectures. We also found that MAO outperforms ProMoAI in both node- and structural-similarity metrics, and receives higher expert quality ratings. This observation points towards the effectiveness of multi-agent refinement for this task.

Note that our experiments utilized QBPs, which are more constrained than full CPGs-typically featuring text-only narratives describing a single process, without interspersed tables or images. As such, the demonstrated feasibility may not directly extend to more complex CPGs with multimodal content or multiple processes; future work could explore preprocessing techniques to handle such elements.

Looking ahead, integrating domain-specific KGs to ground LLM reasoning, conversational modeling, behavioral conformance metrics, and visual diff tools for expert validation, will drive us toward our goal of rapid, cost-effective, and contextually accurate CPW updates. We aim for this pipeline to lay the foundation for scalable, automated maintenance of clinical pathways, ensuring that care protocols remain timely and evidence-based with minimal manual effort.

Acknowledgements. This work is supported by the Discovery Grant program of NSERC (Canada).

References

1. Bellan, P., Dragoni, M., Ghidini, C.: Extracting business process entities and relations from text using pre-trained language models and in-context learning. In: Almeida, J.P.A. (ed.) EDOC 2022. LNCS, vol. 13585, pp. 182–199. Springer, Heidelberg (2022). https://doi.org/10.1007/978-3-031-17604-3_11
2. BPMN-auto-layout (2025). https://github.com/bpmn-io/bpmn-auto-layout
3. BPMN-python: Comparing the Similarity of Two BPMN Graphs (2025). https://github.com/KrzyHonk/bpmn-python/pull/38
4. Dijkman, R., Dumas, M., van Dongen, B., et al.: Similarity of business process models: metrics and evaluation. Inf. Syst. **36**(2), 498–516 (2011). https://doi.org/10.1016/j.is.2010.09.006

5. Garcia, M.T., Nunes, M.M., Fantinato, M., et al.: BPMN-Sim: a multilevel structural similarity technique for BPMN process models. Inf. Syst. **116**, 102211 (2023). https://doi.org/10.1016/j.is.2023.102211
6. Grathwol, D., van der Aa, H., López, H.A.: Automating pathway extraction from clinical guidelines: a conceptual model, datasets and initial experiments. In: Cooperative Information Systems, pp. 296–312 (2025). https://doi.org/10.1007/978-3-031-81375-7_17
7. Health Quality Ontario & Ministry of Health and Long-Term Care, Quality-Based Procedures: Clinical Handbook for Heart Failure (Acute and Postacute) (2023). https://www.ontario.ca/files/2023-12/moh-qbp-clinical-handbook-heartfailure-en-2023-12-11.pdf
8. Health Quality Ontario and Ministry of Health and Long-Term Care, Quality-Based Procedures: Clinical Handbook for Stroke (Acute and Postacute). Technical report (2016). https://www.ontario.ca/page/quality-based-procedures. Health Quality Ontario
9. Housidari, A.: LLM4QBP (2025). https://github.com/alireza-hsi/LLM4QBP
10. Ivanov, S., Kalenkova, A.A., van der Aalst, W.M.P.: BPMNDiffViz: a tool for BPMN models comparison. In: BPM Demo Session 2015. CEUR Workshop Proceedings, pp. 35–39. CEUR-WS.org (2015). https://ceur-ws.org/Vol-1418/paper8.pdf
11. Kassim, S.A., Gartner, J.-B., Labbé, L., et al.: Benefits and limitations of business process model notation in modelling patient healthcare trajectory: a scoping review protocol. BMJ Open **12**(6), e060357 (2022). https://doi.org/10.1136/bmjopen-2021-060357
12. Klievtsova, N., Kampik, T., Mangler, J., et al.: Conversational process model redesign (2025). arXiv: 2505.05453 [cs.AI]
13. Kourani, H., Berti, A., Schuster, D., et al.: ProMoAI: process modeling with generative AI. In: Thirty-Third International Joint Conference on Artificial Intelligence, IJCAI 2024 (2024). https://doi.org/10.24963/ijcai.2024/1014
14. La Rosa, M., Dumas, M., Uba, R., et al.: Business process model merging: an approach to business process consolidation. ACM Trans. Softw. Eng. Methodol. **22**(2) (2013). https://doi.org/10.1145/2430545.2430547
15. Lin, L., Jin, Y., Zhou, Y., et al.: MAO: a framework for process model generation with multi-agent orchestration (2024). https://arxiv.org/abs/2408.01916
16. OMG. Business Process Model and Notation (BPMN), version 2.0.2 (2014). https://www.omg.org/spec/BPMN/2.0.2
17. OpenAI, GPT 4.1 (2025). https://platform.openai.com/docs/models/gpt-4.1
18. Pan, S., Luo, L., Wang, Y., et al.: Unifying large language models and knowledge graphs: a roadmap. IEEE Trans. Knowl. Data Eng. **36**(7), 3580–3599 (2024). https://doi.org/10.1109/TKDE.2024.3352100
19. Process Intelligence Solutions, PM4Py - Process Mining for Python (2025). https://processintelligence.solutions/pm4py
20. Rodríguez-Loya, S., Aziz, A., Chatwin, C.: A service oriented approach for guidelines-based clinical decision support using BPMN. In: Studies in Health Technology and Informatics, pp. 107–113. IOS Press (2014). https://doi.org/10.3233/978-1-61499-432-9-43
21. Rotter, T., Kinsman, L., James, E., et al.: Clinical pathways: effects on professional practice, patient outcomes, length of stay and hospital costs. Cochrane Database Syst. Rev. (2010). https://doi.org/10.1002/14651858.CD006632.pub2
22. Sypherd, C., Belle, V.: Practical considerations for agentic LLM systems (2024). arXiv: 2412.04093 [cs.AI]

23. Van Woensel, W., Houshidari, A., Amyot, D.: Towards automated compliance checking for care trajectories: process extraction using large language models. In: 2nd International Workshop on Process Mining Applications for Healthcare (PM4H 2025). CCIS6. Springer, Cham (2025)
24. Van Woensel, W., Motie, S.: NLP4PBM: a systematic review on process extraction using natural language processing with rule-based, machine and deep learning methods. Enterprise Inf. Syst. **18**(11), 2417404 (2024). https://doi.org/10.1080/17517575.2024.2417404
25. Waspada, I., Sarno, R.: An improved method of graph edit distance for business process model similarity measurement. In: 4th International Conference on Informatics and Computational Sciences (ICICoS), pp. 1–6. IEEE (2020). https://doi.org/10.1109/ICICoS51170.2020.9299037
26. Yang, J., Jin, H., Tang, R., et al.: Harnessing the power of LLMs in practice: a survey on ChatGPT and beyond. ACM Trans. Knowl. Discov. Data **18**(6) (2024). https://doi.org/10.1145/3649506

3rd International Workshop on Object-centric processes from A to Z (OBJECTS 2025)

Transforming Football Data into Object-Centric Event Logs with Spatial Context Information

Vito Chan[1,2](✉), Lennart Ebert[1], Paul-Julius Hillmann[1], Christoffer Rubensson[1,2], Stephan A. Fahrenkrog-Petersen[1,2], and Jan Mendling[1,2,3]

[1] Humboldt-Universität zu Berlin, Berlin, Germany
{vito.chan,lennart.ebert,paul.hillmann,christoffer.rubensson, stephan.fahrenkrog-petersen,jan.mendling}@hu-berlin.de
[2] Weizenbaum Institute, Berlin, Germany
[3] Wirtschaftsuniversität Wien, Vienna, Austria

Abstract. Object-centric event logs expand the conventional single-case notion event log by considering multiple objects, allowing for the analysis of more complex and realistic process behavior. However, the number of real-world object-centric event logs remains limited, and further studies are needed to test their usefulness. The increasing availability of data from team sports can facilitate object-centric process mining, leveraging both real-world data and suitable use cases. In this paper, we present a framework for transforming football (soccer) data into an object-centric event log, further enhanced with a spatial dimension. We demonstrate the effectiveness of our framework by generating object-centric event logs based on real-world football data and discuss the results for varying process representations. With our paper, we provide the first example for object-centric event logs in football analytics. Future work should consider variant analysis and filtering techniques to better handle variability.

Keywords: Event Log Generation · Football Analytics · Object-centric Process Mining

1 Introduction

Object-centric process mining [1] is focussed on analyzing complex systems with multiple objects that interact with each other through their behavior. So far, real-world data of this type is scarce due to confidentiality and privacy concerns [4]. In the past, alternative data sources have been proposed to address these issues. For example, Liss et al. [8] utilized data from the strategy game *Age of Empires 2* to generate object-centric event logs. However, there is still a lack of object-centric event data and studies that evaluate its usefulness.

Team sports offer an excellent setting for object-centric process mining. Not only because of its sequential nature [6], which involves multiple objects to con-

I. van de Weerd et al. (Eds.): BPM 2025 Workshops, LNBIP 569, pp. 467–478, 2026.
https://doi.org/10.1007/978-3-032-13426-4_34

sider, such as teams, players, and game commodities, but also due to the relatively high number of publicly available football (soccer) data. Data-driven methods for analyzing sports data are gaining popularity (cf., [6,12]) in fields such as visual computing and visual analytics [6,9]. In process mining, work that considered football data shows the benefits of applying process-centric techniques to analyze football tactics [3,7]. Still, these works only consider conventional event logs with a single case notion, where the ball possession of a team was modeled as a specific case. Limiting analysis to on-ball actions ignores other behaviors that could be important to understand game performance, such as those of an idle player. In addition, the object-centric notion could better reflect the complexity of football games, while also addressing issues such as convergence and divergence (cf., [1]). However, work that considers object-centric event logs is lacking.

In this paper, we present a framework to transform football data into object-centric event logs. By considering multiple objects, such as teams, players, and the ball, we enable the modeling of more comprehensive behaviors in football games using process mining. We also consider spatial information, as this can further support analysis, such as investigating behaviors at different positions on a football field. We evaluate the framework by generating an object-centric event log from a real-world dataset and qualitatively comparing how changing the number of objects impacts the analysis at both the process and instance levels of the data. Future work could consider combining object-centric process mining with variant analysis and filtering techniques to handle the high complexity and variability of such logs.

The remainder of this paper is structured as follows. Section 2 discusses the theoretical foundations. Section 3 presents our framework. Section 4 validates our framework with real-world data. Section 5 discusses the findings, and Sect. 6 concludes this paper.

2 Background

In this section, we first describe object-centric process mining in Sect. 2.1. Then, in Sect. 2.2, we discuss previous work on football analytics and process mining, as well as provide an overview of football data. We conclude with a problem statement in Sect. 2.3.

2.1 From Case-Centric to Object-Centric Process Mining

Process mining techniques derive process-centric insights from event data [2]. Event data are records of events of a process, partially ordered in an event log. Each event is associated with at least an *event id*, an *event type* (activity), a *timestamp*, and a *case id*. Typically, other attributes specific to the process are included, such as information about where an activity was executed and by whom. A conventional event log refers only to a single case notion[1], i.e., all cases

[1] We will use the terms *case notion* and *object type* interchangeably.

are of the same type to which all events apply. For example, in an order-to-cash process, all cases could be referred to orders. A single order is then a sequence of events that describes the activities executed from order placement to payment and delivery.

Real-world processes are complex, and events can be associated with multiple case notions. For example, the events of an order-to-cash process could be associated with one or more object types, such as an order, item, package, and/or route [1]. Enforcing events to be associated with only one of these notions can lead to missing events (deficiency), unintentional duplications of events (convergence), or unclear causal dependencies between events related to multiple case notions (divergence) [2, p. 20]. Hence, instead of referring to a single case notion, as in conventional event logs, an object-centric event log allows events to be associated with multiple case notions. In this way, object-centric process mining can provide a more comprehensive view of the process while mitigating some of the issues associated with traditional process mining based on conventional event logs. For instance, returning to the earlier example, instead of treating each order as completely separate, object-centric process mining can capture their interrelations and connections to other objects and object types—such as a shipping event and a truck fulfilling a delivery on a certain route, which could be related to multiple orders.

2.2 Football Analysis

Football analysis research is an emerging field that is receiving increasing attention, with multiple studies already summarizing the current state of knowledge. Sarmento et al. [10,11] conducted two systematic reviews to identify the most common topics in match analysis research up to and including 2016. In [11], they grouped work based on the type of analysis: *descriptive*, *comparative*, and *predictive*. They found that most studies investigate performance by describing player behavior while ignoring situational or socio-contextual characteristics [11, p. 9]. In [10], they investigated studies in the analytical topics *set plays*, *activity profiles*, and *group behavior*. They found an increasing use of spatiotemporal data to explore behavioral patterns in groups [10, p. 833]. In more recent surveys, Goes et al. [5] summarized studies on tactical behaviors that employed position-tracking data. They identified methodological differences between sports science and computer science, which could present opportunities for future work through interdisciplinary work. Moreover, Wakelam et al. [12] focused specifically on studies that analyze player attributes. They found that the majority of the studies applied statistical techniques to analyze player traits, rather than, for example, machine learning techniques [12, p. 62].

In recent years, there has also been an increase in data-driven sports analysis (cf., [6,12])—utilizing either event data or trajectory data [6]. This opens up opportunities for applying data mining techniques such as those in process mining. In the following subsections, we provide an overview of football logs and then discuss works that have applied process mining techniques to such data.

Table 1. An overview of football datasets.

Event log	# of Games	Ball actions	Non-ball actions (fouls, cards etc.)	Player movements	Availability
StatsBomb open data	>1000	Yes	Yes	No	Public[a]
OPTA Sports *(England-Iceland Euro 2016)*	1	Yes	Yes	No	Private
Wyscout dataset	>1000	Yes	Yes	No	Public [b]
DFL dataset	7	Yes	Yes	Yes (25 Hz)	Public [c]
Metrica Sports sample data	3	Yes	Yes	Yes (25 Hz)	Public [d]

[a] https://github.com/statsbomb/open-data/ (Accessed: 2025-06-10).
[b] https://figshare.com/collections/Soccer_match_event_dataset/4415000/2 (Accessed: 2025-06-10).
[c] https://springernature.figshare.com/articles/dataset/An_integrated_dataset_of_spatiotemporal_and_event_data_in_elite_soccer/28196177 (Accessed: 2025-06-10).
[d] https://github.com/metrica-sports/sample-data (Accessed: 2025-06-10).

Football Logs. Table 1 provides an overview of football datasets. Multiple football event logs have been used by previous research, some of which are publicly available (cf., Table 1). The most comprehensive datasets are provided by professional data providers Statsbomb and Wyscout, each including more than 1,000 games. These event logs consist of discrete ball actions (e.g., passes, shots, and free kicks) as well as events not directly related to the ball (e.g., fouls, and cards).

Furthermore, two recently released datasets, DFL and Metrica Sports, also include player movement data. By automated visual player tracking, these datasets report all player positions at a rate of 25 Hz (i.e., 25 recorded player positions per second). The Metrica Sports dataset encodes the positions of all players as (x, y) coordinates in a vertically flipped Cartesian coordinate system, with $(0, 0)$ indicating the origin in the top-left corner, whereas $(1, 1)$ is located in the bottom-right corner.

Football Analysis in Process Mining. Only a couple of works have considered football logs in process mining. Kröckel and Bodendorf [7] were the first to demonstrate how process mining techniques, in combination with visual analytics, can be applied to football logs to support better decision-making. By applying multiple process mining techniques such as discovery and social network analysis on the OPTA Sports dataset (see Table 1), they found that process mining methods can provide analysts with user-friendly options to derive a wide range of insights about game success and game tactics from different perspectives. Furthermore, Caparrós [3] proposed a process discovery methodology to analyze team behavior. The methodology employed a *purpose-oriented* trace filtering technique that reduces variability, thereby making the analysis more tailored for such data while handling some of its complexity. They demonstrated their methodology using the StatsBomb dataset (see Table 1).

2.3 Problem Statement

Current work on process mining for football analysis is limited in that it focuses on players directly involved in on-ball actions and does not account for the impact of other players on game performance. However, all players, including those who are idle, may also play a significant role in the game's success. Moreover, the traditional event log for football data also suffers from the problems of divergence and convergence when attempting to capture the complexity of the game under a single case notion. Hence, this study aims to address these issues by applying the notion of object-centric process mining.

3 Object-Centric Framework for Football Event Data

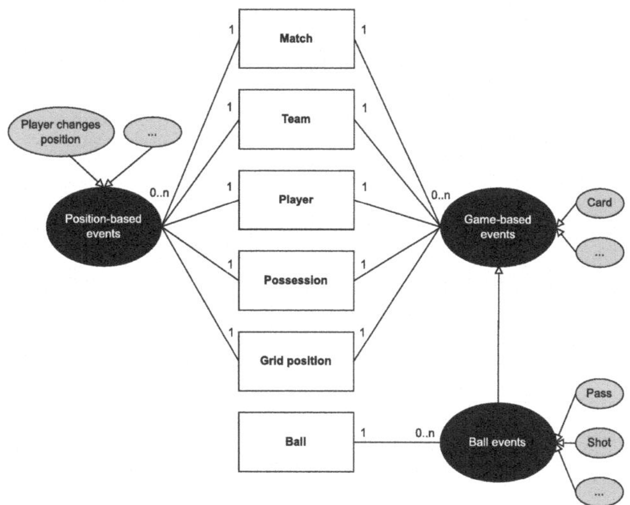

Fig. 1. Object-Centric Framework for Football Event Data.

In this section, we propose a novel object-centric framework for representing football match data. This framework includes football-specific objects, events and object-event relationships that enable multi-variate process mining analysis.

Figure 1 depicts the proposed object-centric framework. It defines three event classes: *game-based events*, *ball events*, and *position-based events* (shown as black ellipses). Light gray ellipses illustrate concrete examples of activities that belong to a corresponding event class. The six object types are: *match*, *team*, *possession*, *player*, *grid position* and *ball* (shown as squares). *Ball events* can inherit all object types from game-based events, illustrated by an arrow. The cardinalities indicate that each event must involve all object types to which it is connected. In the following, we discuss the individual event classes and object types.

3.1 Event Classes

The framework defines three event classes that each contain related event types. Example event types are given in Fig. 1. The actual event types depend on the source data. The first event class is *game-based events.* These include referee events, such as yellow cards, as well as tackles. The second event class is *ball events*, which are specialized game-based events that involve a ball. Passes, shots, and free kicks are examples of ball actions in football. The third event class is *position-based events.* These include all types of events related to player positions. Our concrete implementation of the framework includes the "Player changes position" activity as part of position-based events. Other implementations may include all player positions at all times.

3.2 Object Types

In the following, we present each object type in detail, describe how they relate to the different event classes, and provide example analytical questions for each object. Although each question is associated with a single object, they can be adapted or combined to investigate intra- or inter-related object behaviors, such as interactions between players or between player and ball.

Match. Matches represent separate games. An example game involves two teams competing against each other at a specific date, such as VfL Wolfsburg playing against Bayern Munich on August 25, 2024. The match object provides an overview of the process of an entire game, hence can answer questions such as:

1. How many goal shots occurred in a specific match?
2. How many matches did a particular player play in?
3. What tactical movement patterns show after a goal is scored against a team?

Team. Teams compete with each other, either during a specific match, in a league or in a tournament. Examples for teams are Bayern Munich, the German national team or a university's football club. With teams as objects, we can answer team-level questions such as:

1. How did team tactics evolve across multiple games?
2. What was the interaction pattern between two teams during a match (e.g., how did one team typically react to another team's movement)?
3. How much did a team's players move during a match?

Player. Players represent the individual actors who participate in various events, including passes (ball events), card assignments (game-based events) or positional movements (position-based events). The *player* object type enables analysis of dependencies between players and player behavior:

1. Which player did one specific other player typically pass to?
2. How much did a player move during a match?
3. What was the running path of a player before intercepting the possession of the other team?

Possession. A possession starts when a team gains control over the ball and ends when the opposing team gains control. Thereafter, the next possession starts. During a possession, one team is attacking, while the other is defending the ball. E.g., at the very start of a football game, the first possession begins with the kickoff. If the team that kicked off loses the ball to the other team, the first possession ends, and the second possession begins. Possessions can be used to identify offensive and defensive plays and allow for analysis such as:

1. What activity variants led to possessions that resulted in a goal being scored?
2. How did the average running distance per possession vary between teams?
3. What was the average number of passes per possession?

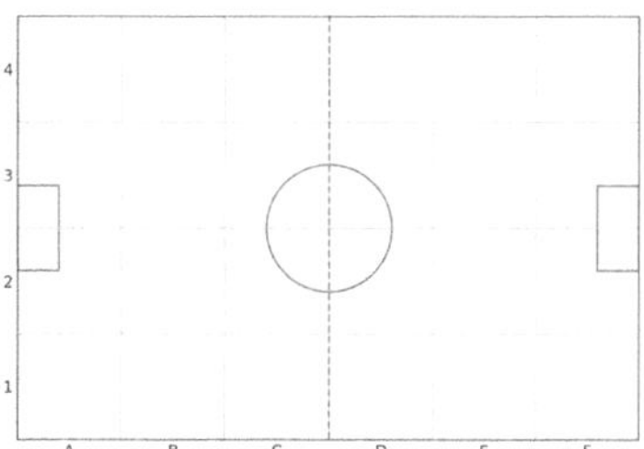

Fig. 2. Extracted grid positions (6 by 4).

Grid Position. The football field can be divided into a grid with individual grid positions, simplifying spatial analysis. For our purposes, we consider a six-field-wide and four-field-long grid, as this greatly reduces the spatial complexity while still maintaining basic positional information. Figure 2 illustrates such a grid. The six-by-four grid results in 24 grid positions numbered A1 (bottom left) to F4 (top right). Grid positions are recorded for all events, denoting the location where each event occurred. Modeling grid positions as objects instead of attributes allows for queries such as:

1. How many goal shots occurred from a specific grid position?
2. Which is the player that spends the most time on a specific grid position?
3. How long are players in specific grid positions?

Ball. The ball is the central object that moves across the field during a football match. It is contained in all ball events (e.g., passes). By modeling the ball as a separate object type, we can answer questions such as:

1. What activities happened to the ball before a goal was scored?
2. Which players played the ball most often?
3. How frequent are ball passes vs. shots?

4 Evaluation

In this section, we validate our framework. Specifically, we first generate an object-centric event log using real-world data. Then, we qualitatively analyze the data by comparing a single-object type version with a multi-object type version of the log from a process perspective using a directly-follows graph, as well as from an instance perspective, with instances represented as graphs on a spatial map. Section 4.1 describes the applied dataset and log generation process, whereas Sects. 4.2 and 4.3 discuss evaluation results.

4.1 Event Log Generation

We applied the data of two football matches from the Metrica Sports sample data (see Table 1) to generate an object-centric event log using our framework in the following steps. First, we recognized meaningful player movement events by reprojecting the player movement traces onto the grid coordinate system and identifying movements across grids. We used Pandas[2] to process and transform the raw data. Second, we performed event engineering by decomposing aggregated events to improve interpretability and clarify the association between specific objects and events. We then merged the movement and game-based event logs based on temporal order and propagated the contextual information to enrich the movement events. Finally, we further enriched the event log with derived attributes such as travel distance, durations, and the current score. The final processed *DataFrame* was converted into an object-centric event log using PM4Py[3]. The resulting log comprises 37,358 events, 813 objects, and 747 possessions, capturing both game-based events and position-based events. The source code to generate the event logs and perform subsequent visualization is publicly available on GitHub.[4]

4.2 Perspective 1: Process Model

Figures 3a and 3b present directly-follows graphs discovered from a single-object type event log and a multi-object type event log, respectively. To reduce their complexity, both graphs are filtered to the four possessions of the home team

[2] https://pandas.pydata.org (Accessed: 2025-06-10).
[3] https://processintelligence.solutions (Accessed: 2025-06-10).
[4] https://github.com/VitoChan01/Soccer.

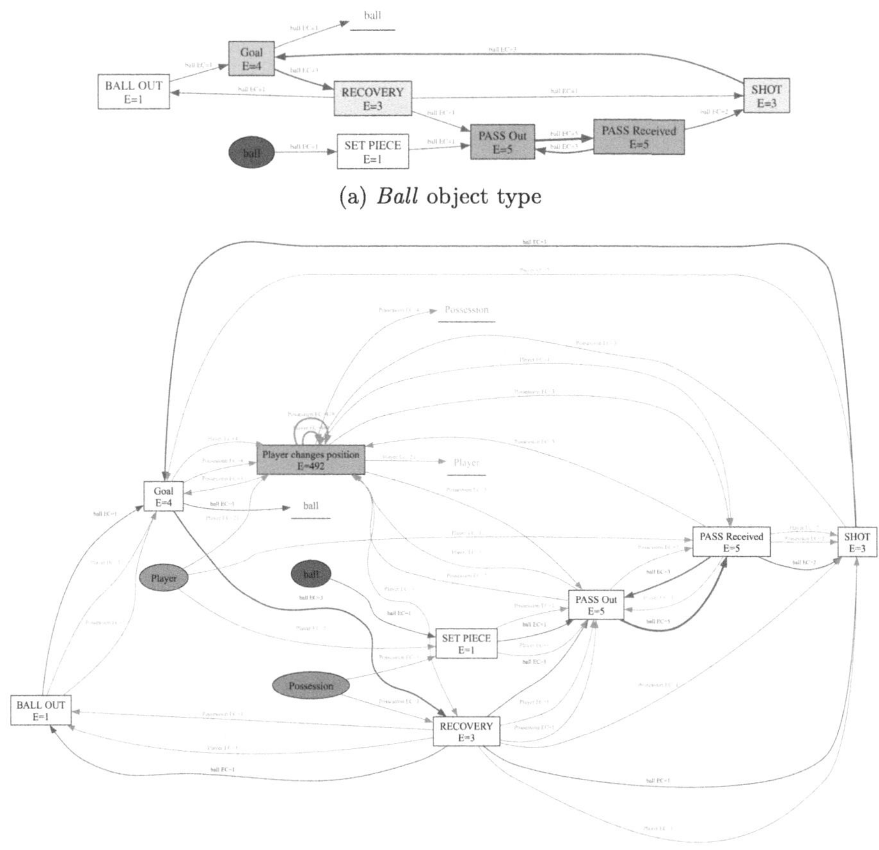

(a) *Ball* object type

(b) *Ball*, *possession* and *player* object types

Fig. 3. Discovered directly-follows graphs from the object-centric event log.

that led to a goal. The first graph discovered from the single-object type event log (Fig. 3a) depicts the sequences of actions related to the *ball* object type, i.e., all on-ball actions such as passes. The graph shows, for instance, that *set piece* activities (e.g., kick-offs, free-kicks, and throw-ins) are always followed by playing a pass. After one or multiple passes, there is a shot. For the possessions in this scenario, all shots led to a goal. The data also shows a recovery activity leading to an out ball and, subsequently, a goal. However, this behavior is likely caused by erroneous data. Furthermore, note that as we depict the *ball* object type, there are also goals followed by a recovery, since the ball remains the same throughout the entire game.

The multi-object type process graph (Fig. 3a) additionally shows *player* and *possession* objects. Further object types were omitted to avoid visual complexity. This graph provides additional information not visible in the previous graph, such as new directly-follows relations for the different object types, like *player*.

Also, an additional activity, "Player changes position", is now visible, as it is associated with these two object types. This activity shows a high count of self-loops, as many players might move one or multiple positions between other activities.

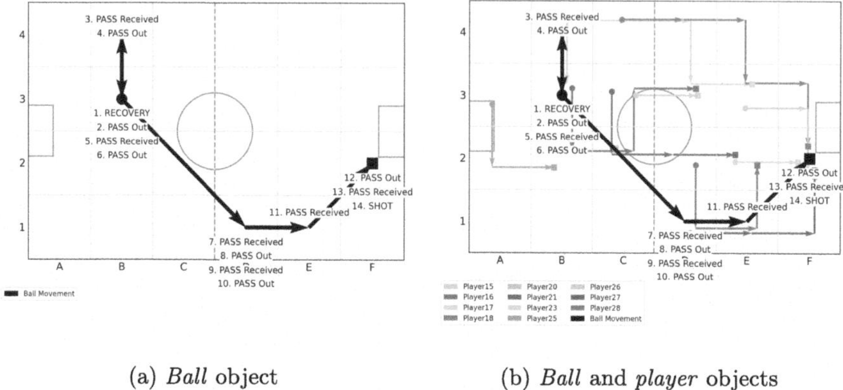

(a) *Ball* object

(b) *Ball* and *player* objects

Fig. 4. Process instances, visualized as directed graphs on a spatial map.

4.3 Perspective 2: Process Instances on Spatial Map

Based on the grid notion described in Sect. 3, we created a custom visualization to display the spatial positions of events on the football field. Specifically, we visualized all events associated with a team for a single process instance of a possession that resulted in a shot on the opponent's goal (possession id: AA156). The first visualization (Fig. 4a) illustrates the process instance from the perspective of a single object (*ball*). Whereas the second visualization (Fig. 4b) is based on multiple objects (*ball* and *player*).

In Fig. 4a, depicting a single *ball* object, we can observe where the possession of the ball started, and how the ball moves across the grid cells of the field until the possession ends. Here, the possession begins with a ball recovery in the middle of the field, located in cell $B3$. It is then passed to $B4$, where it is received and passed back to $B3$. Then, the ball is passed out again and received on the right side in the opponent's half of the field. Here, the ball is first passed within the grid cell and then passed out to $E1$ where the pass is received, moving closer to the opponent's goal. The next on-ball action happens in $F2$, meaning that the player who received the ball in $E1$ moved to $F2$ before the ball is passed within that grid cell and then shot toward the opponent's goal.

In Fig. 4b, the same on-ball behavior can be observed. However, as this includes the addition of *player* objects, the figure also provides information on the movement of individual players, allowing for a more detailed analysis. For instance, the visualization shows that *Player15* moved only from grid cell $C3$ to $D3$ during the entire possession and therefore stayed relatively stable in the center of the field. In contrast, *Player18* moved all the way from grid cell C4 in the left midfield to grid cell $F2$ where the shot on the opponent's goal was taken, highlighting a higher involvement in the offense. In addition to single-player insights, an overall forward movement of all players in the direction of the ball is also visible during the possession.

5 Discussion

This section discusses the findings from the evaluation and the limitations of our work. By generating an object-centric event log and analyzing it from two different perspectives, we could demonstrate the effectiveness of our framework. Compared to a conventional event log, modeling multiple object types for football data provides a more comprehensive and realistic view of a football game, supporting a better understanding of tactics and game behaviors. The explicit modeling of spatial information further extends the analytical possibilities, as it enriches the control-flow perspective with important contextual cues for examining idle players (cf., Sect. 4.3), which are essential for understanding tactical decisions.

We highlight two limitations as motivations for future work. First, football games are, from a process perspective, complex and highly variable. Object-centric models can better capture this complexity; however, techniques for reducing variability and extracting outcome-centric patterns are necessary to enhance understanding. Future work could consider incorporating variant analysis techniques, filtering methods, or interactive visualization. Complementing the spatial perspective with *time* could also improve analysis by examining specific temporal behavior, such as episodes of a game.

Finally, we have only considered football games and a single dataset in this paper. Although our framework is general enough to be applied to other team sports that involve a ball, adaptations may be necessary to facilitate a more specific analysis of different sports types. The effectiveness of object-centric process mining for football analysis and other team sports also needs to be tested using various real-world event datasets in future work.

6 Conclusion

In this paper, we introduced the first study concerned with transforming football data into an object-centric event log. The proposed framework considers object types essential for analyzing the performance of football games, including matches, teams, possessions, players, the ball, and grid positions. We validated our framework using a real-world football log, combined with a qualitative analysis of different process visualizations of that log with varying amounts of object types, to demonstrate its effectiveness. In this way, we demonstrated that object-centric process mining of football data provides a more complete and detailed analysis of football games. Still, analyzing football games is challenging due to their high variability. Hence, future work should consider reducing variability with variant analysis and filtering techniques.

Acknowledgments. The research of the authors was supported by the Einstein Foundation Berlin under grant EPP-2019-524, by the German Federal Ministry of Research, Technology and Space under grant 16DII133, and by the Deutsche Forschungsgemeinschaft under grants 496119880 (VisualMine), 531115272 (ProImpact), and 414984028 (FONDA).

Disclosure of Interests. The authors have no competing interests to declare that are relevant to the content of this article.

References

1. van der Aalst, W.M.P.: Object-centric process mining: dealing with divergence and convergence in event data. In: SEFM. Lecture Notes in Computer Science, vol. 11724, pp. 3–25. Springer (2019)
2. van der Aalst, W.M.P.: Process mining: a 360 degree overview. In: Process Mining Handbook, Lecture Notes in Business Information Processing, vol. 448, pp. 3–34. Springer (2022)
3. Caparrós, M.G.: Leveraging team traces to optimize process-aware tactical style discovery. StatsBomb Conference (2023). https://statsbomb.com/wp-content/uploads/2023/10/Leveraging-Team-Traces-to-Optimise-Process-Aware-Tactical-Style-Discovery.pdf. Accessed 10 June 2025
4. Elkoumy, G., et al.: Privacy and confidentiality in process mining: threats and research challenges. ACM Trans. Manag. Inf. Syst. **13**(1), 11:1–11:17 (2022)
5. Goes, F.R., et al.: Unlocking the potential of big data to support tactical performance analysis in professional soccer: a systematic review. Eur. J. Sport Sci. **21**(4), 481–496 (2021)
6. Gudmundsson, J., Horton, M.: Spatio-temporal analysis of team sports. ACM Comput. Surv. **50**(2), 22:1–22:34 (2017)
7. Kröckel, P., Bodendorf, F.: Process mining of football event data: a novel approach for tactical insights into the game. Front. Artif. Intell. **3**, 47 (2020)
8. Liss, L., Elbert, N., Flath, C.M., van der Aalst, W.M.P.: Framework for extracting real-world object-centric event logs from game data. In: ICPM Workshops. Lecture Notes in Business Information Processing, vol. 533, pp. 363–375. Springer (2024)
9. Naik, B.T., Hashmi, M.F., Bokde, N.D.: A comprehensive review of computer vision in sports: open issues, future trends and research directions. Appl. Sci. **12**(9), 4429 (2022)
10. Sarmento, H., Clemente, F.M., Araújo, D., Davids, K., McRobert, A., Figueiredo, A.: What performance analysts need to know about research trends in association football (2012–2016): a systematic review. Sports Med. **48**, 799–836 (2018)
11. Sarmento, H., Marcelino, R., Anguera, M.T., Campaniço, J., Matos, N., Leitão, J.C.: Match analysis in football: a systematic review. J. Sports Sci. **32**(20), 1831–1843 (2014)
12. Wakelam, E., Steuber, V., Wakelam, J.: The collection, analysis and exploitation of footballer attributes: a systematic review. J. Sports Anal. **8**(1), 31–67 (2022)

An Object-Centric Approach to Inferring and Analyzing Queues

Sander van Gansewinkel[1,2(✉)], Vadim Denisov[1], and Dirk Fahland[2]

[1] ServiceNow, Santa Clara, USA
{sander.vangansewinkel,vadim.denisov}@servicenow.com
[2] Process Analytics, Eindhoven University of Technology, Eindhoven, Netherlands
d.fahland@tue.nl

Abstract. Processes rely on queues to hold and prioritize cases and objects being passed between workers and teams. Consequently, analyzing queue behavior provides insights into process performance. As queue behavior is not explicitly recorded in event logs, missing information has to be restored. Existing queue mining techniques leverage queue models to restore abstractions of a queue. In this paper, we show that by treating queues and workers as objects, we can use an object-centric approach to infer missing queue information and to analyze queue behavior and performance. Evaluation on an industrial incident management process demonstrates the feasibility of the approach.

Keywords: queue mining · data quality · object-centric event logs

1 Introduction

Executing a process usually involves passing work between different people or teams. The passed *work item* (a case, document, or object) then typically has to wait for the receiving person or team to be available to pick up the work. A *queue* that collects and prioritizes work items waiting for resources can be defined per activity (viz. station) as well as per worker or team [1]. A worker may take an item to be worked on from the queue or re-assign it to a different worker (thereby re-assigning it to a different queue). Consequently, the time a work item spends in queues due to queueing policies or reassignment substantially impacts the overall throughput time of a case and is a relevant aspect of process performance analysis, e.g., estimating waiting times [2] or identifying deviations from ideal schedules [3]. For instance, in an industrial context of improving performance of IT support processes, the following queue-related Analysis Questions (AQs) arise:

AQ.1 Which teams and resources are responsible for Time to Case Completion (TCC) outliers during each process activity, and what likely caused the corresponding delays?

I. van de Weerd et al. (Eds.): BPM 2025 Workshops, LNBIP 569, pp. 479–491, 2026.
https://doi.org/10.1007/978-3-032-13426-4_35

AQ.2 How does the performance of a team or resource differ from the performance of another team or resource?

AQ.3 How does workload variation impact queue handling time for a specific team or resource?

AQ.4 To what extent are tasks handled in a fair manner based on First-Come, First-Served (FCFS) or priority policies within a team or resource?

However, answering these AQs requires information about queueing behavior, often lacking in regular logs [4]. Queue mining [5] aims at reconstructing the missing information as well as estimating queue states. Established queue mining methods leverage models from queueing theory to infer missing queue information [2,3,6,7]. However, the reliance on queueing models imparts assumptions or expected knowledge on queues that is not always applicable or available, such as (known) distributions of activity durations.

We note that queue models aim to build an abstraction of inter-case dependencies between cases traversing a shared network of queues and resources. In [8] it was shown that such dependencies can also be studied directly using an *object-centric event data model* where cases, queues, and resources (agents) are modeled as explicit entities synchronizing in shared events. On this object-centric model, missing information can be reconstructed without assumptions from queueing theory. However, these techniques are limited to reconstructing time-stamps when activity and agent queues are known and synonymous.

In this paper, we study a more general setting of *parallel queues of multiple agents and teams holding work items for multiple activities*, see Sect. 2. The available event log records the case perspective and resource perspective, but lacks reliable information on whether the case is actively being worked on or in which of the queues it is currently waiting. The objective is to reconstruct this missing information and use it to answer AQ.1–AQ.4.

Analysis of existing queue mining and object-centric techniques (Sect. 3) suggests using a rule-based approach to infer missing queue information. We present such a rule-based approach for our setting that makes minimal assumptions on the general life-cycle of cases passing through queues in Sect. 4. The technique is implemented in an open-source tool that was validated for correctness using simulated logs. Further, we evaluated feasibility of the approach by reconstructing queue information of an industrial incident management process; we specifically show in Sect. 5 that the reconstructed information allows answering AQ.1–AQ.4 in an industrial setting.

2 Problem Definition

We address the challenge of enhancing queue information in incomplete process data. A running example is used to illustrate typical issues encountered in real-world scenarios and to motivate the need for reconstructing missing queueing information. We then define the subclass of processes targeted in our study, those in which tasks are transferred between teams and resources, and where waiting times are implied but not explicitly recorded. This is followed by a discussion

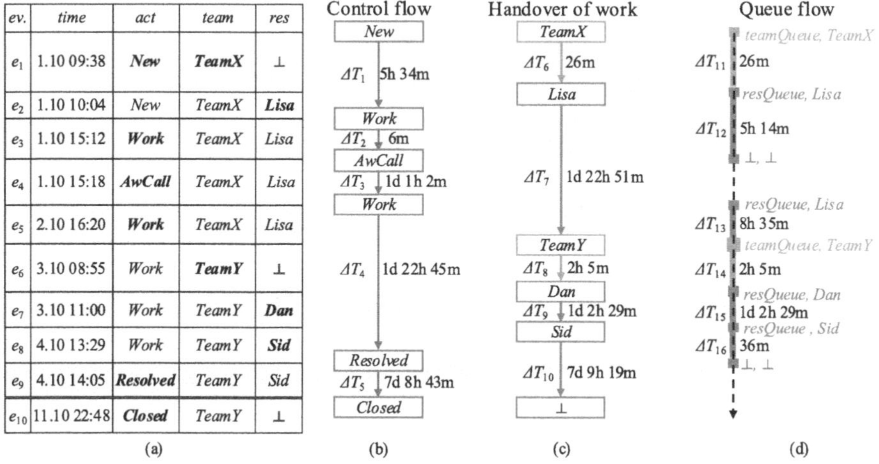

ev.	*time*	*act*	*team*	*res*
e_1	1.10 09:38	***New***	***TeamX***	⊥
e_2	1.10 10:04	*New*	*TeamX*	***Lisa***
e_3	1.10 15:12	***Work***	*TeamX*	*Lisa*
e_4	1.10 15:18	***AwCall***	*TeamX*	*Lisa*
e_5	2.10 16:20	***Work***	*TeamX*	*Lisa*
e_6	3.10 08:55	*Work*	***TeamY***	⊥
e_7	3.10 11:00	*Work*	*TeamY*	***Dan***
e_8	4.10 13:29	*Work*	*TeamY*	***Sid***
e_9	4.10 14:05	***Resolved***	*TeamY*	*Sid*
e_{10}	11.10 22:48	***Closed***	*TeamY*	⊥

Fig. 1. Recorded events of a trace (a), the corresponding activity sequence (b), handover of work (c), and the queue flow (d).

of common data quality issues that undermine the reliability of performance analysis. We conclude the section by stating the problem addressed in this paper.

Notation on Event Data. We write *Val* for the attribute value universe, including the set *Act* of activity names, set *Time* of timestamps, and set *ID* of identifiers, $Act, Time, ID \subset Val$, and $Act \cap Time \cap ID = \emptyset$. *Time* is totally ordered by $\leq$.

An event table $T = (E, ent, AN, \#)$ consists of events E, entity identifier *ent* (i.e. the attribute to track an object or a case), event attribute names $\{ent, time, act, team, res\} \subseteq AN$, and a partial attribute function $\# : E \times AN \nrightarrow Val$ that assigns an event $e \in E$ and attribute name $an \in AN$ a value $\#_{an}(e) = v$ with always defined $\#_{ent}(e) \in ID$, $\#_{time}(e) \in Time$, and $\#_{act}(e) \in Act$. Function $\#$ returns $\perp$ if attribute *an* is undefined for *e*. In the following, we use the terms event table and event log interchangeably.

Attribute *ent* holds the entity identifier, allowing us to track an entity in a trace as follows. The instances of type *ent* are $ent(T) = \{n \mid n \in \#_{ent}(e), e \in E\} \subseteq ID$. For an entity instance $id \in ent(T)$, a trace of *id* is a trace of entity *id* is a sequence $\pi = \langle e_1, \ldots, e_k \rangle$ of events $\{e_1, \ldots, e_k\} = \{e \in E \mid id = \#_{ent}(e)\}$ ordered by time $\#_{time}(e_i) \leq \#_{time}(e_j)$ for $1 \leq i < j \leq k$.

Running Example. We investigate an anonymized trace from a large company's *IT Service Management* (ITSM) process, in which multiple teams of agents (resources) collaborate to resolve incidents. The real-life trace depicted in Fig. 1(a) includes each event with an event ID, a timestamp, incident activity, currently assigned team, and currently assigned agent, and the incident ID (omitted here for brevity). For each event, each attribute that changes relative to the previous event is highlighted in bold.

Each incident is initiated by two roles: a *Service Requester* (SR), who submits or needs an issue, and a *service provider*, who is responsible for addressing it. Together, these roles define the division of *responsibilities* in resolving the case.

At the creation of the incident in event e_1, the incident is put to activity *New* and assigned to team *TeamX*. Shortly after, resource *Lisa* is assigned to the incident (e_2), and it transitions to the *Work* activity (e_3). When additional input from the SR is required, the incident is moved to *AwCall* (e_4), indicating that the case is "parked" and waits for more information. Upon receiving a response, the incident returns to *Work* (e_5), where *Lisa* determines that the issue requires a more specialized team and reassigns the incident to team *TeamY* (e_6). The incident is then sequentially assigned to *Dan* (e_7) and *Sid* (e_8), who eventually proposed a resolution to the customer (e_9). The incident is eventually closed one week later (e_{10}).

Figure 1(b) and Fig. 1(c) visualize information that can be derived from this log directly by projection: Fig. 1(b) visualizes control-flow activity changes, Fig. 1(c) visualizes Handover of Work (HoW) along the trace as activity changes in the *Team* and *Res* columns. Both views also summarize waiting times between state changes. We explain the dynamics of this incident next and highlight in which sense the queue perspective of the incident is missing and how a queue flow representation (as shown in Fig. 1(d)) would help answering AQ.1–AQ.4.

With a classical process mining approach, we analyze the extended throughput time of the case, the TCC, as defined in (AQ.1), the durations in the control-flow (Fig. 1(b)) and HoW (Fig. 1(c)), which together constitute the same TCC. As illustrated in Fig. 1(b), longer durations are observed in *New* (duration ΔT_1), *AwCall* (ΔT_3) and the second occurrence of *Work* (ΔT_4). Additionally, delays are apparent in the *sojourn time* of resources *Lisa* (ΔT_7), *Dan* (ΔT_9), and most notably, *Sid* (ΔT_{10}). Based on the HoW flow, one might conclude that the extended TCC is primarily caused by *Sid*, followed by *Lisa*, and then *Dan*.

However, we argue that the above insights are misleading and a correct analysis requires describing for which entity (resource, team, SR) the incident was waiting, i.e., in which *queue* it resided. To understand if a case was in a team or resource queue, it is insufficient to consider the control-flow or HoW in isolation. Moreover, it must be known whether the activity happened under the *Service Provider's Responsibility* (SPR), i.e., the assigned team or resource was responsible for the case progress, or if it happened outside the SPR, i.e., no team or resource could handle the case. That is, a combination of attributes *act*, *team*, *res*, and some domain knowledge, usually missing in logs, is required for deriving queue information. As a result, such recorded logs, which we call in the following *incomplete*, cannot be used directly to answer the AQs introduced in Sect. 1. Specifically, AQ.1 and AQ.2 require accurate information of team handling time, and agent sojourn time; AQ.3 depends on knowing the queue size for a team or resource at any point in time; and AQ.4 requires insight into the queue ordering.

Figure 1(d) visualizes how the case *flowed through the different queues.* While in Sect. 4 we present a method to reconstruct this information, observe for now in Fig. 1(d) that the case traverses through several team queues and resource queues but also is outside queues (with the SR) during e_4-e_5 and e_9-e_{10}. Consequently, the insights into where time is spent changes. For instance, the time the incident remained in the queue of *Sid* is now measured as 36 min (ΔT_{16}), substantially shorter than previously inferred. Similarly, the time attributed to *Lisa* is now split into two distinct intervals ($\Delta T_{12}, \Delta T_{13}$). This comes to a total of 13 h, which is, again, significantly less than the initial estimate. By removing the SR time from the queues of *Lisa* and *Sid*, we observe the time the incident was waiting for them, instead of the time the incident was assigned to them.

Thus, the queue flow reveals a different perspective; the incident spent the longest time waiting in the queue of resource *Dan* (ΔT_{15}), changing our conclusion on AQ.1.

Problem Statement. We focus on a specific subclass of processes characterized by their suitability for reconstructing queueing information, while also covering many widely used and operationally significant workflows, i.e., ITSM, Customer Service Management (CSM). We consider processes with the following properties: (P1) the process consists of clearly defined activities, each identified by an activity label that reflects the state of the case; (P2) at most one team can be assigned to a process instance at any given time; (P3) each resource is part of one team; (P4) at most one resource can be assigned to a process instance at any given time; (P5) a process instance may be assigned to a team without being assigned to an individual resource; (P6) a process activity can be executed either by assigned resources or completed by external entities, such as SRs or external processes; (P7) a non-empty subset $Act_{\text{res}} \subseteq Act \neq \emptyset$ of activities is exclusively executed by resources; (P8) process activities are executed in a sequential order, i.e. no activities are executed in parallel; (P9) the process records event logs that capture the control flow perspective via logging activities (attribute *act*), and HoW via logging assigned teams and resources (*team* and *res*).

However, the log for processes with P1-P9 is *incomplete* wrt. the information in which *queue* the case was waiting to be worked on (i.e., who is responsible). And we illustrated above that this information is not derivable as a combination control-flow (*act*) and resource attributes (*team*, *res*) alone.

The objective of this paper is to reconstruct *complete* event logs from *incomplete* ones by enriching each event with attributes describing in which queue a case was in at the time the event occurred.

3 Related Work

Queue mining [5] is a class of mining tasks to describe and analyze queues from event data. In [2], the notion of a queue log is introduced which essentially matches the *complete event log* of Sect. 2 we aim to reconstruct, where we additionally distinguish *agent* from *team queues.* On such logs, queue parameters and waiting times in individual queues can be estimated.

Data quality issues of queue logs can be classified [4] as missing case identifiers and missing start and/or completion times. Our setting has known case identifiers and start times (indicated by control-flow state changes in the case), but *lack time-stamps for suspending, resuming, and completing an activity*. We face an additional data quality issue: as the queue is not determined by the activity but by the agent and team, corresponding *queue identifiers are missing* for reliable analysis.

Missing life-cycle information can be estimated using known queueing (network) models and assumptions about distributions of activity durations [6] or by training a queue inference engine (QIE) model on complete training data and subsequently inferring the missing information [7]. When complete (or inferred) queue information is available, queue logs allow estimating (states of) resource queues and waiting times of cases in entire processes (treated then as queueing networks) [6] and checking conformance to desired schedules [3] providing insights for adapting scheduling policies for performance improvement. However, in our setting neither complete training data for a QIE is available nor are other queue characteristics known.

By treating agent and queue identifiers in our partial and complete event logs as dedicated objects our data becomes *object-centric*. Object-centric approaches have been used to reconstruct timestamps in a setting where queues are already known [8]. Object-centric approaches have also been successful for inferring missing object identifiers using a rule-based approach [9] and in improving case performance analysis by modeling agent behavior across parallel cases [10]. We build on these ideas by also developing a rule-based approach to infer queue identifiers from an (incomplete) object-centric event log, the enriched log then provides more fine-granular activity labeling that in turn provides the missing life-cycle information for cases across all queues. Our work thus can be seen as a complementary, object-centric approach for information inference in a descriptive setting where other techniques are inapplicable.

4 Approach

We can reformulate the problem of reconstructing queue information from Sect. 2 as a problem to infer missing queue identifiers in an object-centric data model: given an event table $T = (E, ent, AN, \#)$ with $ent, time, act, team, res \subseteq AN$ as defined in Sect. 2, extend T with attributes *queueID* and *queueType*, identifying queue objects and their type (team or resource), and infer missing values such that for each event $e \in E$ attributes $\#_{queueID}(e)$ and $\#_{queueType}(e)$ state in which queue the entity $\#_{ent}(e)$ waited.

In the following, we propose a rule-based inference approach, which we call **QRec**, to infer the values for *queueID* and *queueType* from the other attributes in T and relying on the process characteristics P1-P9 stated in Sect. 2. Thereby, P6 allows the entity to be under the responsibility of an external actor, i.e., outside a queue controlled by the process. As such information is not logged, we have to rely on domain knowledge - here formalized as an oracle *isProv* :

$E \rightarrow Bool$ - to inform whether event e occurred when the service provider was responsible, i.e., $isProv(e) = true$, or not. For example, when a service provider is only responsible for a specific subset Act_{Res} of activities, e.g., $isProv(e) = true$ iff $\#_{act}(e) \in Act_{\text{Res}} \subseteq Act$.

The rules of **QRec** for inferring queue information are summarized in Table 1. In this table, the first four columns contain the rule number, the assigned team and resource identifiers, and the result provided by oracle *isProv*, respectively. A cell is blank if its value is ignored. Let $QueueType \subset Val$ containing queue types $\{teamQueue, resQueue\}$ be the set of queue types, corresponding to the team and resource queues, respectively; $\#_{queueType}(e) \in QueueType$. Let $QueueID \subset ID$ be the set of queue identifiers. The remaining two columns $\#_{queueType}(e) \in QueueType$ and $\#_{queueID}(e) \in QueueID$ contain the values of the queue type and identifier being reconstructed. The rows of Table 1 describe rules for inferring these attributes depending on the presence of the team and resource identifiers (i.e., depending on whether they are defined or undefined) under and outside the SPR.

Table 1. Rules for inferring queue information.

Rule number	$\#_{team}(e)$	$\#_{res}(e)$	$isProv(e)$	$\#_{queueType}(e)$	$\#_{queueID}(e)$
1	$\neq\perp$	$\perp$	*true*	*teamQueue*	$\#_{team}(e)$
2		$\neq\perp$	*true*	*resQueue*	$\#_{res}(e)$
3	$\perp$	$\perp$	*true*	$\perp$	$\perp$
4			*false*	$\perp$	$\perp$

Thus, Rules 1–3 correspond to events that occur under the SPR. Rule 1 applies when a team is assigned while the resource is still undefined, i.e., a case is waiting for assigning a resource of team $\#_{team}(e)$ to be able to progress. That is, the case is in the corresponding team queue, i.e., $\#_{queueType}(e) = teamQueue, \#_{queueID}(e) = \#_{team}(e)$. Table 2 shows an example where the incident was assigned to team $\#_{team}(e_1) = TeamX$ at event e_1 while $\#_{res}(e_1) = \perp$. As a result, $\#_{queueType}(e_1) = teamQueue$ and $\#_{queueID}(e_1) = TeamX$.

Rule 2 applies when a resource is assigned to a case. It does not matter if a team is assigned or not (the cell in column $\#_{team}(e)$ is blank). That is, the case is in the queue of resource $\#_{res}(e)$. As a result, $\#_{queueType}(e) = resQueue, \#_{queueID}(e) = \#_{res}(e)$. For example, the incident was assigned to team $\#_{team}(e_2) = TeamX$ and resource $\#_{res}(e_2) = Lisa$ at e_2 in Table 2. As a result, $\#_{queueType}(e_2) = resQueue$ and $\#_{queueID}(e_2) = Lisa$.

Rule 3 applies when neither team nor resource is assigned to a case. As a result, the case cannot be in a team or resource queue, so both queue type and identifier are undefined, i.e., $\#_{queueType}(e) = \#_{queueID}(e) = \perp$.

Finally, Rule 4 applies when an event occurs outside the SPR, and the case is not in a team or resource queue, i.e., $\#_{queueType}(e) = \#_{queueID}(e) = \perp$. For example, despite the incident was assigned to team $\#_{team}(e_4) = TeamX$ and resource

Table 2. Trace of a complete log reconstructed from the trace shown in Fig. 1(a).

eventID	*time*	*act*	*team*	*res*	*queueType*	*queueID*
e_1	1.10 09:38	*New*	*TeamX*	⊥	***teamQueue***	***TeamX***
e_2	1.10 10:04	*New*	*TeamX*	*Lisa*	***resQueue***	***Lisa***
e_3	1.10 15:12	*Work*	*TeamX*	*Lisa*	*resQueue*	*Lisa*
e_4	1.10 15:18	*AwCall*	*TeamX*	*Lisa*	⊥	⊥
e_5	2.10 16:20	*Work*	*TeamX*	*Lisa*	***resQueue***	***Lisa***
e_6	3.10 08:55	*Work*	*TeamY*	⊥	***teamQueue***	***TeamY***
e_7	3.10 11:00	*Work*	*TeamY*	*Dan*	***resQueue***	***Dan***
e_8	4.10 13:29	*Work*	*TeamY*	*Sid*	***resQueue***	***Sid***
e_9	4.10 14:05	*Resolved*	*TeamY*	*Sid*	⊥	⊥
e_{10}	11.10 22:48	*Closed*	*TeamY*	⊥	⊥	⊥

$\#_{res}(e_4) = \mathit{Lisa}$ at event e_4 in Table 2, $\#_{queueType}(e_4) = \#_{queueID}(e_4) = \perp$ because the incident was outside the SPR.

In terms of our event data notation, a materialization of these rules requires defining a different attribute function $\#^q$ mapping events in E, and attributes *queueType* and *queueID*, onto the queue types and identifiers, respectively, in addition to the existing mapping of #. In the following, we define auxiliary functions to determine the values of *queueType* and *queueID*, and use them for defining $\#^q$.

Let a queue type partial function $\mathit{getQueueType} : E \nrightarrow \mathit{QueueType}$, defined as follows.

$$\mathit{getQueueType}(e) = \begin{cases} \mathit{teamQueue} : \mathit{isProv}(e) = \mathit{true}, \#_{res}(e) = \perp, \#_{team}(e) \neq \perp \\ \mathit{resQueue} \quad : \mathit{isProv}(e) = \mathit{true}, \#_{res}(e) \neq \perp, \text{and} \\ \perp \qquad\qquad : \text{otherwise.} \end{cases}$$

In the equation above, the first and second lines correspond to Rule 1 and Rule 2 respectively of Table 1, while the last line corresponds to Rule 3 and Rule 4.

Let a queue identifier partial function $\mathit{getQueueID} : E \nrightarrow \mathit{QueueID}$, defined as follows.

$$\mathit{getQueueID}(e) = \begin{cases} \#_{team}(e) : \mathit{isProv}(e) = \mathit{true}, \#_{res}(e) = \perp, \\ \#_{res}(e) \quad : \mathit{isProv}(e) = \mathit{true}, \#_{res}(e) \neq \perp, \text{and} \\ \perp \qquad\quad : \text{otherwise.} \end{cases}$$

In this equation, similarly to *getQueueType*, the first and second lines correspond to Rule 1 and Rule 2 of Table 1, while the last line corresponds to the other rules.

Finally, we define the attribute function $\#^q$ as follows.

$$\#^q_{an}(e) = \begin{cases} \mathit{getQueueType}(e) : an = \mathit{queueType}, \\ \mathit{getQueueID}(e) \quad : an = \mathit{queueID}, \text{and} \\ \#_{an}(e) \qquad\quad : \text{otherwise.} \end{cases}$$

The next section describes the evaluation of this approach.

5 Evaluation

To evaluate the proposed approach, we measured its errors on a synthetic dataset where ground truth was available, and answered the AQs, stated in Sect. 1, in industrial settings.

Validation on Synthetic Logs. We developed an open-source tool[1] implementing **QRec**, and a simplified ITSM process simulation model for generating synthetic logs. To enable experimenting with publicly available datasets, we supported import of the incident process log,[2] and export of reconstructed queue information in the form of the performance spectrum [11] to be explored in the performance spectrum miner [12].

We generated incomplete $L_{\mathrm{In}}^{\mathrm{Syn}}$ and complete $L_{\mathrm{GT}}^{\mathrm{Syn}}$ event logs containing 100.000 incident traces representing various sequences of activities, and different combinations of team and resource assignments, where the trace length varied from 4 to 200 events. We used our tool to reconstruct log $L_{\mathrm{R}}^{\mathrm{Syn}}$ from $L_{\mathrm{In}}^{\mathrm{Syn}}$. To estimate reconstruction errors, we used log $L_{\mathrm{GT}}^{\mathrm{Syn}}$ as the ground truth and reported the number of events where the queue type and/or identifiers were wrongly reconstructed, which was zero. It allowed us to conclude that $L_{\mathrm{R}}^{\mathrm{Syn}}$ was correctly reconstructed, i.e., each event in $L_{\mathrm{R}}^{\mathrm{Syn}}$ had the same attributes as in $L_{\mathrm{GT}}^{\mathrm{Syn}}$.

Queue-Based Analysis in Industrial Setting. We demonstrated the feasibility of queue-based process analysis by reconstructing queue information from a large company's ITSM process log L_{In}, containing 60 000 traces, and answering the AQs of Sect. 1. We reconstructed a complete log L_{R} from L_{In}, using **QRec** implemented in the tool described above. We also reconstructed log $L_{\mathrm{R}}^{\mathrm{B}}$ using a baseline approach **Bsl** assuming the equality of team/resource assignment and team/resource en-queueing, to compare **QRec** with the classical HoW-based approach. We computed the team queue waiting time t^{team}, resource sojourn time t^{res}, the time outside the SPR $t_{\mathrm{total}}^{\mathrm{nonSPR}}$, and various metrics over them from L_{R} and $L_{\mathrm{R}}^{\mathrm{B}}$, using a proprietary software tool. Although ground truth was unavailable for L_{In}, we assumed **QRec** provided accurate results based on the evaluation on synthetic logs above. Analysis of a trace in L_{R} (AQ.1), shown in Table 2, is already discussed in Sect. 2. In the following, we first consider various performance measures for the entire logs, and then investigate team and resource performance.

Overall Performance Analysis. Descriptive statistics over queue times is shown in Table 3, where some metrics drastically differ for **Bsl** and **QRec**. Thus, $t_{\mathrm{total}}^{\mathrm{res}}$ and $t_{\mathrm{total}}^{\mathrm{nonSPR}}$ computed by **QRec** are much smaller and larger, respectively,

[1] https://github.com/ServiceNow/queue-reconstruction-tool.

[2] https://doi.org/10.4121/uuid:500573e6-accc-4b0c-9576-aa5468b10cee.

with the difference of 84.9% and 85.9%, compared to **Bsl**, while the difference in $t^{\text{team}}_{\text{total}}$ is insignificant (1%). Further, both team and resource average and Standard Deviation (SD) metrics $t^{\text{team}}_{\text{avg}}$, $t^{\text{team}}_{\text{SD}}$, $t^{\text{res}}_{\text{avg}}$, and $t^{\text{res}}_{\text{SD}}$ computed by **QRec** are significantly smaller than those computed by **Bsl**, especially for $t^{\text{res}}_{\text{avg}}$, where the difference is five days.

Table 3. Metrics computed by **Bsl** and **QRec** approaches.

Metric	Notation	**Bsl**	**QRec**
Total team queue waiting time, %	$t^{\text{team}}_{\text{total}}$	6.4	5.4
Total resource sojourn time, %	$t^{\text{res}}_{\text{total}}$	93.5	**8.6**
Total non-service provider's resp. time, %	$t^{\text{nonSPR}}_{\text{total}}$	0.1	**86.0**
Mean team queue waiting time	$t^{\text{team}}_{\text{avg}}$	12 h 35 m	**9 h 6 m**
Standard deviation of team queue waiting time	$t^{\text{team}}_{\text{SD}}$	1 d 13 h 43 m	**1 d 26 m**
Mean resource sojourn time	$t^{\text{res}}_{\text{avg}}$	5 d 16 h 40 m	**15 h 19 m**
Standard deviation of resource sojourn time	$t^{\text{res}}_{\text{SD}}$	4 d 6 h 46 m	**1 d 6 h 17 m**

We also computed average t^{res} observed for various resource queue lengths (AQ.3), and determined that the dependency between queue length and average t^{res} was invariant when computed from L^{B}_{R} (**Bsl**) but displayed a linear trend when computed from L_{R} (**QRec**).

We concluded **Bsl** tended to overestimate $t^{\text{res}}_{\text{total}}$ due to not considering whether assignment time spans intersected periods of the SPR. For example, it wrongly considered the resource time spent during activities like *AwCall*, *Resolved*, i.e., outside the SPR, as t^{res}. Consequently, $t^{\text{nonSPR}}_{\text{total}}$ was underestimated. For the same reasons, $t^{\text{team}}_{\text{avg}}$, $t^{\text{team}}_{\text{SD}}$, $t^{\text{res}}_{\text{avg}}$, and $t^{\text{res}}_{\text{SD}}$ were much longer when computed by **Bsl**. Similarly, **QRec** revealed that t^{res} tended to be longer on average when the queue length increased. As a result, using **Bsl**, the analyst might have wrongly concluded that the largest part of incident handling time was t^{res}, which had a large absolute average value $t^{\text{res}}_{\text{avg}}$ and spread $t^{\text{res}}_{\text{SD}}$, but did not depend on the length of resource queues. In this case, the process improvements could be related to increasing the resource performance and making it more predictable by minimizing $t^{\text{res}}_{\text{avg}}$ and $t^{\text{res}}_{\text{SD}}$, respectively.

In contrast, results obtained from **QRec** showed a similar percentage of $t^{\text{team}}_{\text{total}}$ and $t^{\text{res}}_{\text{total}}$. The analyst would have decided to minimize unnecessary waiting time in team queues ($t^{\text{team}}_{\text{total}}$) through better incident dispatching on teams, to improve the process performance. Thus, we showed how overall process performance, derived due to answering AQ.1, could be estimated differently when analyzed from logs reconstructed using **QRec** and **Bsl**, and how the inferred process improvements could be opposite. Next, we show how accurate queue information allowed for fine-grained team and resource comparative analysis.

Team Comparative Analysis. We address AQ.2–AQ.4 by comparing the performance of *Team1*-*Team3*, handling the same types of incidents at different locations. We compared their performance by analyzing average t^{team} and t^{res}, and inferred possible reasons considering their SD, and behaviors in queues. For the latter, we plotted the dependency between queue length and t^{res}, and computed *fairness* to estimate (1) whether the teams and their resources observed the FCFS control policy, and (2) whether they observed incident priorities. Thus, metric F_{FCFS} showed the percentage of cases that were not *overtaken* by cases that came to the queue later, while F_{Pr} showed the percentage of cases that were not overtaken by cases with *lower* priorities.

We write $t_{\text{avg}}^{\text{res},\,TeamN}$ and $t_{\text{SD}}^{\text{res},\,TeamN}$ for the average and SD resource sojourn time of team *TeamN*'s resources. Table 4 shows that t_{avg}^{Team1}, t_{SD}^{Team1}, $t_{\text{avg}}^{\text{res},\,Team1}$, and $t_{\text{SD}}^{\text{res},\,Team1}$, were longer than those of *Team3*, while the values of t_{avg}^{Team2} and t_{SD}^{Team2} were in between. However, $t_{\text{avg}}^{\text{res},\,Team2}$ and $t_{\text{SD}}^{\text{res},\,Team2}$ were significantly shorter than those of *Team1* and *Team3*. F_{FCFS} and F_{Pr} were higher for *team* queues of *Team2* and *Team3* compared to *Team1*, while F_{FCFS} and F_{Pr} were higher for *resource* queues of *Team2* compared to *Team1* and *Team3*. Finally, Fig. 2 demonstrates that t^{res} exhibited a positive correlation with load for *Team1* and *Team2*, but a negative correlation for *Team3*.

Table 4. Performance metrics of *Team1*-*Team3* and their resources.

Metric	*Team1*	*Team1* res.	*Team2*	*Team2* res.	*Team3*	*Team3* res.
$t_{\text{avg}}^{\text{team}}$ or $t_{\text{avg}}^{\text{res}}$	6 h 24 m	**12 h 49 m**	7 h 48 m	4 h 28 m	9 h 45 m	**13 h 40 m**
$t_{\text{SD}}^{\text{team}}$ or $t_{\text{SD}}^{\text{res}}$	13 h 10 m	24 h 10 m	15 h 1 m	12 h 15 m	17 h 14 m	26 h 25 m
F_{FCFS}	22.7%	12.1%	51.0%	44.9%	49.6%	23.2%
F_{Pr}	44.7%	15.3%	73.0%	65.6%	74.2%	39.2%

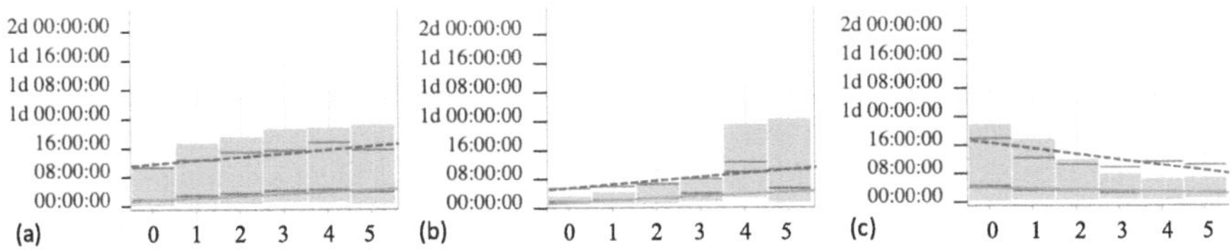

Fig. 2. Dependency between resource queue length (x-axis) and sojourn time: average (dotted violet) and median (solid green) for *Team1* (a), *Team2* (b), and *Team3* (c). (Color figure online)

The average t^{team} of *Team1*-*Team3* could be considered roughly equal, indicating similar incident dispatching performance. However, the average t^{res} of

Team1 and *Team3* were significantly larger than that of *Team2*. The larger $t_{\text{avg}}^{\text{res},\,Team1}$ compared to $t_{\text{avg}}^{\text{res},\,Team2}$ could be explained by much lower FCFS and priority fairness in the resource queues of *Team1*. The poor FCFS fairness could cause longer waiting times, while poor priority fairness showed that the FCFS discipline was not violated due to the need for observing the priorities. At the same time, the larger $t_{\text{avg}}^{\text{res},\,Team3}$ could not be explained by the FCFS fairness since it was higher than that of *Team1*. However, the counter-intuitive trend in Fig. 2(c) suggested *Team3* resources tended to accumulate incidents (in a batch) before handling them, causing unnecessarily longer t^{res}.

6 Conclusion and Future Work

In this paper, we studied the problem of inferring missing queueing information in event logs that contain data on the activity, assigned team, and assigned resource of each incident. We showed that this problem can be addressed using a rule-based approach that injects domain knowledge into the interpretation of an incident activity, allowing us to derive queue identifiers where they are not explicitly recorded. This approach enables more accurate analysis of resource sojourn times, responsibility division, and workload distribution across teams and resources. Our approach offers a powerful way to enhance an incomplete event log with queueing data, without requiring changes to system logging or the use of advanced process models. This enables the analyst to answer questions that would otherwise remain inaccessible, such as identifying bottlenecks caused by queues rather than processing delays. The approach relies on specific assumptions about process structure and domain semantics, such as the availability of consistent team and resource assignments. In future work, we plan to evaluate it on CSM, HR, and in settings where agents are shared among multiple processes.

Acknowledgment. The research leading to these results was done by Process Intelligence & Optimization, ServiceNow, in collaboration with Process Analytics, TU/e.

References

1. Dumas, M., Rosa, M.L., Mendling, J., Reijers, H.A.: Fundamentals of Business Process Management, 2nd edn. Springer (2018)
2. Senderovich, A., Weidlich, M., Gal, A., Mandelbaum, A.: Queue mining - predicting delays in service processes. In: CAiSE 2014. LNCS, vol. 8484. Springer (2014)
3. Senderovich, A., et al.: Conformance checking and performance improvement in scheduled processes: a queueing-network perspective. Inf. Syst. **62**, 185–206 (2016)
4. Gal, A., Senderovich, A., Weidlich, M.: Challenge paper: data quality issues in queue mining. ACM J. Data Inf. Qual. **9**(4), 18:1–18:5 (2018)
5. Senderovich, A.: Queue mining. In Sakr, S., Zomaya, A.Y. (eds.) Encyclopedia of Big Data Technologies. Springer (2019)
6. Senderovich, A., Leemans, S.J.J., Harel, S., Gal, A., Mandelbaum, A., van der Aalst, W.M.P.: Discovering queues from event logs with varying levels of information. In: BPM 2015 Workshops. LNBIP, vol. 256, pp. 154–166. Springer (2015)

7. Berkenstadt, G., Gal, A., Senderovich, A., Shraga, R., Weidlich, M.: Queueing inference for process performance analysis with missing life-cycle data. In: ICPM 2020, pp. 57–64. IEEE (2020)
8. Fahland, D., Denisov, V., van der Aalst, W.M.P.: Inferring unobserved events in systems with shared resources and queues. Fundam. Informaticae **183**(3–4) (2021)
9. Swevels, A., Dijkman, R.M., Fahland, D.: Inferring missing entity identifiers from context using event knowledge graphs. In: BPM 2023. LNCS, vol. 14159, pp. 180–197. Springer (2023)
10. Klijn, E.L., Tentina, I., Fahland, D., Mannhardt, F.: Decomposing process performance based on actor behavior. In: ICPM 2024, pp. 129–136. IEEE (2024)
11. Denisov, V., Fahland, D., van der Aalst, W.M.P.: Unbiased, fine-grained description of processes performance from event data. In: BPM 2018. LNCS, vol. 11080, pp. 139–157. Springer (2018)
12. Denisov, V., Belkina, E., Fahland, D., van der Aalst, W.M.: The performance spectrum miner: visual analytics for fine-grained performance analysis of processes. In: BPM 2018 Demos, pp. 96–100. CEUR-WS org (2018)

Object-Based Process Model Generation

Selina Schüler[1(✉)] and Sascha Alpers[2]

[1] Institute of Applied Informatics and Formal Description Methods (AIFB), Karlsruhe Institute of Technology (KIT), Kaiserstr. 89, 76133 Karlsruhe, Germany
selina.schueler@kit.edu

[2] Heilbronn University, Max-Planck-Straße 39, 74081 Heilbronn, Germany
sascha.alpers@hs-heilbronn.de

Abstract. Despite the recognized importance of business process models, many processes remain unmodeled or inadequately modeled due to the time-consuming nature of manual modeling and the lack of expertise in this field. This paper proposes a novel approach for the automated process model generation, based on object analysis. It utilizes object instances, which are represented in documents and data entities, and which activities create, read, modify and consume during process execution. In contradistinction to conventional approaches that rely on event logs, our object-based approach encompasses both automated and manual activities by analyzing these tangible artifacts such as orders, invoices, and delivery notes that are already documented. In contrast, activities frequently require supplementary tracking mechanisms. The approach extracts process knowledge by identifying object types, assigning object instances to process instances, and deriving activity types from object relationships. The resulting process models are represented as high-level Petri nets, where places represent object types, transitions represent activity types, and arcs capture control and object flow while preserving object structures. Evaluation results show that this method produces more compact models than conventional discovery algorithms and identifies activities and business rules often missed by purely temporal analyses. It enables process discovery even in environments with limited system visibility or significant manual work.

Keywords: Model Generation · Business Process Model · Petri Nets

1 Introduction

Business process modeling enables systematic documentation, analysis, and monitoring of organizational workflows [24]. Despite its importance, organizations struggle with creating accurate models due to manual modeling requirements, specialized expertise needs, and cross-departmental complexity [11]. Business process modeling traditionally follows a structured approach of defining purpose, collecting information, mapping to model constructs, and evaluating the resulting model. Traditional manual approaches are time-intensive and error-prone, creating opportunities for automated approaches that derive structured

I. van de Weerd et al. (Eds.): BPM 2025 Workshops, LNBIP 569, pp. 492–504, 2026.
https://doi.org/10.1007/978-3-032-13426-4_36

representations from various information sources, reducing costs while improving consistency. Existing automated approaches rely on event logs or textual descriptions, which primarily capture temporal relationships while facing significant limitations: event logs miss manual activities, textual descriptions contain ambiguities, and both typically fail to integrate object and control flow perspectives [22].

This paper presents a novel approach to automated process modeling based on analyzing object instances (documents and database entities) that naturally exist within organizations. Business processes continuously interact with objects like orders, invoices, and delivery notes, which serve as indirect witnesses to process execution, capturing both system-supported and manual activities, and implicit business rules. Our method extracts process knowledge by identifying object types and their relationships, then deriving activity types and ordering relationships from content-based and temporal correlations. The method transforms this information into object-aware high-level Petri nets, where places represent object types, transitions represent activities, and arcs capture control and object flow, while preserving object structures and manipulations [8,12].

We demonstrate our approach's practical applicability through a software prototype and evaluation with synthetic datasets representing common control flow patterns [2]. With regulations increasingly mandating digital availability of process-related objects (e.g., electronic invoicing), our approach leverages these digital assets to create accurate process models without requiring specialized system knowledge.

The remainder of this paper is structured as follows: Sect. 2 reviews business process model generation fundamentals and examines existing automated approaches. Section 3 presents our object-based method. Section 4 describes the prototype implementation. Section 5 provides empirical evaluation results. Section 6 summarizes our contributions and future research directions.

2 Background and Related Work

Business process models capture temporal-logical ordering relationships between activities: **sequential relationships** reflecting causal dependencies (e.g., a letter can only be sent after being printed) or organizational policies (e.g., shipping products only after payment verification), **concurrent relationships** for activities with no prerequisite dependencies (e.g. shipping products and sending digital product manual), and **alternative relationships** representing mutually exclusive execution paths, resulting from inherent exclusivity (e.g., a product is either picked up or delivered) or organizational policies (e.g., sending an invoice by email or mail).

Petri nets provide a formal mathematical notation for representing these relationships as a bipartite directed graph with places (P), transitions (T) and directed arcs ($F \subseteq (P \times T) \cup (T \times P)$). Places represent states or conditions, while transitions represent activities that can change the system's state. The state of a Petri net is defined by its marking, which is represented by tokens distributed across places. The dynamic behavior of a system is modeled through the firing of transitions, which move tokens between places according to the network structure [19].

Automated process modeling approaches leverage diverse data sources including event logs from IT systems [1], textual process descriptions [7,23], enterprise artifacts including policy documents and data models [9,13], and communication data such as emails [4,10]. Object-centric and artifact-centric process discovery techniques have established sophisticated methods for extracting process models from object instance information. [17] present automated discovery of artifact-centric process models from flat collections of event records, decomposing the problem to enable reuse of existing process discovery methods while focusing on business artifacts as key entities driving company operations. Their approach particularly addresses processes with one-to-many or many-to-many relations between entities. Complementing this work, [14] extract separate process models for each data object notion in data-centric systems like ERP systems, extracting event information and case identifiers from relational databases and decomposing data sources into multiple logs describing individual object lifecycles. [18] address variable-sized synchronization conditions, such as purchasing decisions requiring multiple quotes from an undetermined set of suppliers, specifically targeting artifact-centric processes with collections of interacting artifacts. [3] generate hierarchical BPMN models with subprocesses, boundary events, and activity markers by analyzing dependencies between data attributes attached to events. [15] address the challenges of ERP systems operating on multiple interrelated business objects, presenting semi-automatic approaches for analyzing event data to identify artifact-centric process models while preventing data convergence and divergence issues. These established methods demonstrate comprehensive frameworks for object-centric process discovery, typically operating with structured event logs from information systems, predefined database schemas with explicit activity-object relationships, and clear temporal-causal relationships captured in system logs. However, they assume the availability of structured process execution data where object types, relationships, and activities are explicitly recorded or can be systematically extracted from relational databases. Our object-based approach extends this paradigm by reconstructing process models from unstructured business documents without requiring structured logs or predefined schemas, using 'indirect witnesses' that result from process execution.

3 Method for Object-Based Process Model Generation

Activities within business processes often interact with objects—creating, modifying, and consuming documents and database entities during execution. Objects serve as both inputs and outputs for activities while carrying valuable information. When an order leads to a delivery note then to an invoice, these relationships reveal the underlying process structure through shared attributes, transferred values, or temporal sequences. By analyzing content-based and temporal relationships, we infer activities that manipulate objects and their ordering relationships.

Our approach transforms object instances into comprehensive process models through four integrated phases (see Fig. 1)[1]: object type classification, relationship identification, activity derivation, and model transformation into high-level Petri nets that capture both control flow and data perspectives.

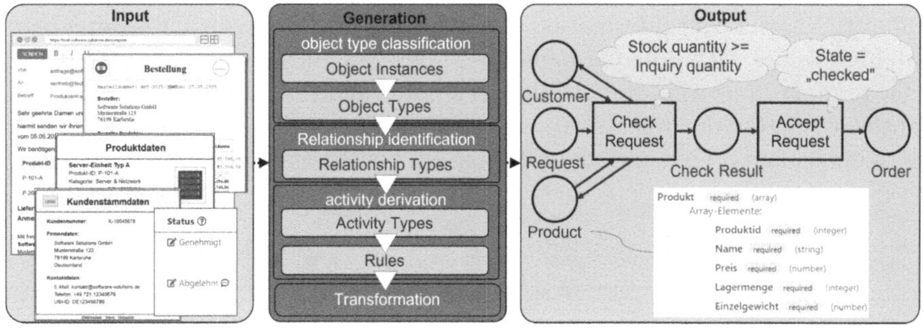

Fig. 1. Approach for object-based process model generation.

3.1 Object Type and Process Instance Assignment

The first challenge is correctly assigning object instances of various object types across multiple process instances to their respective object types and process instances (see Fig. 2; top). This assignment is fundamental to extracting meaningful process information from object data.

We distinguish between *process instance dependent* objects tied to single process instances (e.g., specific orders) and *process instance independent* objects used across multiple processes (e.g., product catalogs). We identify correlating elements linking objects through matching identifiers such as order numbers, extending Engels's correlation technique [6] in a two-step approach: first establishing correlations among process-instance-dependent objects using unique identifiers, then incorporating process-instance-independent objects by identifying shared reference values that appear across multiple process instances. This extension recognizes that certain data elements may not serve as correlators due to repeated values or their information being unrelated to individual process instances. For object type classification, we employ unsupervised clustering based on structural similarities. After preprocessing (tokenization, normalization, stopword elimination), we apply K-Means clustering [16] with cluster optimization through Silhouette scores and Sum of Squared Errors analysis. After classification, the data structures of object types are defined from the aggregation of states of different classified object instances. Language models generate

[1] The method is described in detail in [21].

descriptive names for each type based on structural patterns. Data quality significantly impacts generation, necessitating thorough cleansing to address errors, outliers, and missing values.

3.2 Identifying Object Relationships Types

We identify relationships types between objects types using complementary content-based and temporal analysis. Content-based analysis examines attribute similarities to discover information flow patterns: identical attribute-value pairs, matching values with different names, and derived calculations. For example, an order number appearing in both delivery notes and invoices, or product details transferred across documents. Temporal analysis examines chronological ordering to determine precedence and information flow direction (see Fig. 2; bottom).

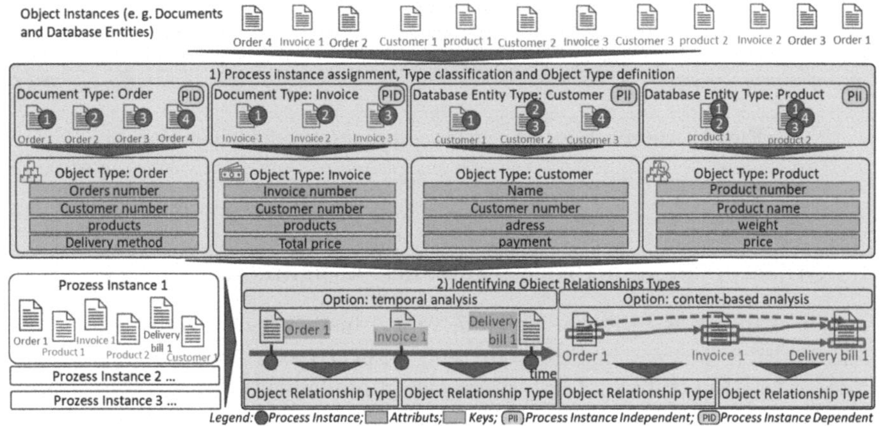

Fig. 2. Step 1 and 2 of the process model generation approach.

To ensure statistical significance, relationships must exceed thresholds SW_P and SW_O (typically 90%) for process instance coverage and object pair frequency, respectively. We validate relationships through frequency analysis and consistency checking across process instances. The result is a set of verified object relationship types that capture both data dependencies and temporal ordering, forming the foundation for activity derivation.

3.3 Deriving Activity Types

Activity types are inferred from object relationship types by determining which activities create, read, modify, or consume objects. For each identified relationship, we determine input and output roles by evaluating multiple factors: temporal sequence (earlier object instance: input [−1.0], later object: output [+1.0]), process instance independence classification (reference data typically serves as input [−1.0] unless values change across process instances), and calculation patterns (source of calculation: input, result: output). We calculate aggregate scores for each object type, with scores below −0.2 indicating input objects and above 0.2 indicating output objects. Values in between (−0.2 to 0.2) trigger additional analysis using already defined activity types, with adjustments of ±0.15 based on prior classifications.

To identify the most relevant activity types and avoid redundancy, we employ a weighted multi-criteria assessment that considers:

1. **Structural positioning:** Activity types occurring early in business processes receive positive weighting (*early_position_bonus* = 1.5), while later activities receive reduction factors (*late_position_penalty* = 0.5), based on the assumption that objects should be processed as early as possible.
2. **Integration of process-independent object types:** The processing of process-independent object types is governed by a base weight (*reference_weight* = 2.0) enhanced by position factors (*reference_position_factor* = 2.0), since this information can be used regardless of process instance state and should be incorporated early.
3. **Relationship properties:** This evaluation considers frequency of activity instances (*sequence_weight* = 1.5), significance of transferred attributes (*attribute_weight* = 1.2), and temporal proximity between object instances (*temporal_weight* = 4.0).

The weighting factors and thresholds are pre-configured with empirically determined default values but can be adjusted by domain experts to optimize results for specific contexts. Additional factors influence evaluation, including penalties for inverse relationships (*inverse_object_penalty* = 3.0, reduces rating when inverse ordering relationships occur between involved object types) and loop structures (*loop_weight* = 0.5), while version factors (*version_weight* = 0.5) increase ratings for activity types involving disjoint object versions.

Based on this assessment, activity types undergo a three-phase selection process to ensure comprehensive process coverage:

Phase 1: Identify activity types involving process-independent objects and those addressing new object types or attributes not yet covered by previously selected activities.

Phase 2: Add activity types involving process-independent objects that address new attributes, ensuring all reference data is appropriately integrated.

Phase 3: Incorporate activity types whose instances involve new object instances as input or output that have not been covered by existing selections. We verify that each object instance can be represented through the selected activity types, ensuring complete process coverage while checking temporal positioning constraints.

The process coverage verification works by tracking which object instances and their state transitions are addressed by selected activity types. If object instances appear for the first time as input (or output) in an activity instance, we verify they are temporally positioned as the first (or last) object instance of a process instance, preventing logical inconsistencies. The result is a comprehensive yet smaller set of activity types covering all object types and relationships. By specifying a minimum score ($Min\_AT\_score = 2.0$), we can control whether all activity types must be considered, preventing modeling of outliers. The attribute analysis can be performed either per object type or for the entire business process type, depending on whether we need to check attribute coverage at the object level or process level.

To generate concise process representations, we merge similar activity types using a case-based approach. Activity types are first grouped by their input and output object types, then analyzed based on object instance usage:

1. Different process instances: Activities representing alternative paths are not merged.
2. Same process instances: (a) If activities affect the same object instances at the same time, they are merged by combining input/output objects and rules. (b) If they affect different object instances or the same ones at different times, they remain separate and are further analyzed during transformation.
3. Partial overlap of process instances: Merging occurs only if activities impact the same object instances simultaneously.

The detailed examination for complex cases occurs during the transformation phase, where ordering relationships between activity types must be considered. For example, if object types Order and Invoice are defined as input and output in two activity types, and a process instance contains order $b1$ and invoices $r1\_1$ and $r1\_2$, then activity type "Create Invoice" produces $r1\_1$ and activity type "Correct Invoice" produces $r1\_2$ (both based on $b1$). Although both activity types have the same input and output object types, they represent different activities. Therefore, we must verify whether both activity types can be executed within a process instance given the discovered ordering relationships, and whether they should be merged based on temporal constraints and process logic.

For merging decisions, we apply threshold-based analysis (default 90% overlap) to determine similarity sufficiency, verify absence of contradictory temporal relationships, and consolidate rules while eliminating redundancies. This systematic approach ensures that resulting activity types accurately capture observed process behavior while minimizing redundancy and preserving distinct process variants.

3.4 Transformation to Process Model

The final phase transforms identified objects, relationships, and activities into an integrated process model using high-level Petri nets, that integrate control flow and data perspectives. We define object-based generated business process models as:

Definition 1 (Object-based generated Business Process Model). *An object-based generated business process model is a tuple BPM = (P, T, F, PL, TL, TI) where:*

- *P and T are finite sets of places and transitions with* $P \cap T = \emptyset$, $P \cup T \neq \emptyset$. *Places represent object types and transitions represent activity types.*
- $F \subseteq (P \times T) \cup (T \times P)$ *is the flow relation.*
- *The place labeling* $PL : P \rightarrow OT$ *assigns each place an object type, the transition labeling*$TL : T \rightarrow AT$ *assigns each transition an activity type*
- *The transition inscriptions* TI *assigns to each transition execution conditions* $EC(t) \subseteq EXPR(\{PL(p)|p \in \bullet t\})$ *and object manipulations* $OM(t) \subseteq EXPR(\{PL(p)|p \in \bullet t \cup t\bullet\})$.

The transformation process operates in three steps:

Step 1: Structure Creation - We create a place for each object type and a transition for each activity type. Input object types of activities connect to transitions via incoming arcs, while output object types connect via outgoing arcs. For each activity type, we define transformation rules that specify how object instances are manipulated during execution, capturing the creation, modification, reading, and consumption patterns observed in object relationships.

Step 2: Control Flow Integration - We implement ordering relationships discovered from temporal and content analysis: sequential relationships appear as connected transitions through intermediate places, alternative paths as XOR-splits with multiple outgoing arcs from a place, and concurrent execution as AND-splits enabling parallel firing. If needed, additional places and transitions are added when content-based or temporal analysis reveals alternative or independent ordering relationships.

Step 3: Enhancement with Execution Logic - We incorporate execution conditions by analyzing process instance variations at decision points. Using classification methods (e.g., decision trees [20]), we identify patterns that correlate with specific execution paths (e.g., orders above certain values following different approval routes). These conditions are formalized as transition inscriptions that specify both when transitions can fire and how they manipulate object states.

The resulting model extends Petri nets by incorporating object manipulation information, enabling richer representation of business process semantics while maintaining formal analysis capabilities. The integrated approach ensures models accurately reflect underlying business logic and preserve the connection between control flow and object transformations.

4 Implementation

We implemented our object-based process model generation approach as a Python-based software prototype[2] that analyzes heterogeneous document col-

[2] Code and Testfiles available at https://gitlab.kit.edu/kit/aifb/BIS/kit-bis/objektbasiertemodellgenerierung under MIT license.

lections through a modular pipeline architecture. The implementation follows a Model-View-Controller (MVC) pattern with three specialized components:

Data Preprocessing: Structures document data in standardized dataframes using the DeepDive framework [5], with consistent date formatting for reliable temporal analysis. Supports JSON and XML formats, with extensible preprocessing for OCR-based document processing.

Information Extraction: Employs clustering algorithms from scikit-learn [16] for object type identification, using Silhouette Score and Sum of Squared Errors metrics to determine optimal clusters. Relationship detection performs pairwise recursive comparisons identifying three overlap types: identical key-value pairs, matching values with different keys, and common standard values. Utilizes NetworkX to create weighted directed graphs where nodes represent object types and edges represent activity types. Edge weights combine sequence properties, attribute significance, and temporal proximity: $w = \alpha \cdot AttributeWeight + \beta \cdot SequenceWeight + \gamma \cdot NormalizedDistance$. For discovering inverse ordering relationships, we apply Footprint Discovery algorithms to object instances, creating traces where events correspond to object types and timestamps represent average input/output times. The prototype implements also an iterative approach, allowing users to review and validate results after each phase before proceeding to the next step.

Model Generation: The prototype provides comprehensive visualization through Graphviz integration, exports models in PNML standard format, and maintains detailed logging for process traceability.

The modular design effectively handles complex scenarios including nested data structures, multiple object instances within documents, heterogeneous formats, implicit relationships, and process-instance-independent data, adapting to the inherent complexity of business document collections. Key technical dependencies include Pandas for data processing, NetworkX for graph analysis, PM4Py for process mining functionality, and scikit-learn for machine learning operations. The configurable architecture supports extension with additional data formats and analysis techniques while preserving system modularity.

5 Evaluation

We evaluated our object-based process model generation method through both a systematic assessment of the method against defined requirements and empirical testing with controlled datasets representing common business process patterns by using the software prototype.

We developed a structured test suite with five distinct datasets representing specific control flow patterns [2]: sequential, concurrent, alternative, loop, and iteration. Each dataset contained JSON documents representing object instances from multiple process executions with temporal sequencing, while process-independent data (like product catalogs) contained no timestamps to test our approach's handling of reference data. Table 1 summarizes these datasets.

Table 1. Test Data Overview

Pattern	Files	PI	OT
Sequence (Linear process flows: Order$rightarrow$Delivery$rightarrow$Invoice)	16	5	4
Concurrency (Parallel activities: logistics vs. payment)	30	4	9
Alternative (Exclusive paths: approval vs. rejection)	50	9	11
Loop (Repeated activities: document revisions)	16/18	4	6
Iteration (Process restarts: order modifications)	33	4	8

PI: Process Instances, OT: Object Types

For model generation, we used configurable weighting factors prioritizing temporal relationships (weight 4.0) while applying conservative weights (0.5) to loop detection to minimize false positives. Our evaluation assessed: (1) correct object classification and process instance identification, (2) recognition of control flow patterns, and (3) comparative analysis between content-based and purely temporal approaches.

The prototype successfully identified correct object types and process instances across all test cases, distinguishing between process-dependent and process-independent objects without requiring explicit variant labels. All fundamental control flow patterns were correctly recognized and modeled: sequential patterns through temporal ordering, concurrent patterns via AND-splits/joins, alternative patterns through XOR-splits/joins, and loop/iteration patterns through repeated activity detection. The comparative analysis revealed four significant advantages of content-based over purely temporal approaches: (1) incorporation of process-independent objects excluded by temporal analysis due to missing timestamps, (2) more accurate input/output relationship identification through multi-stage analysis, (3) more compact model generation (e.g., 7 places/5 transitions vs. 7 places/9 transitions for loop patterns), and (4) discovery of business rules embedded in object relationships that temporal analysis cannot detect (Fig. 3).

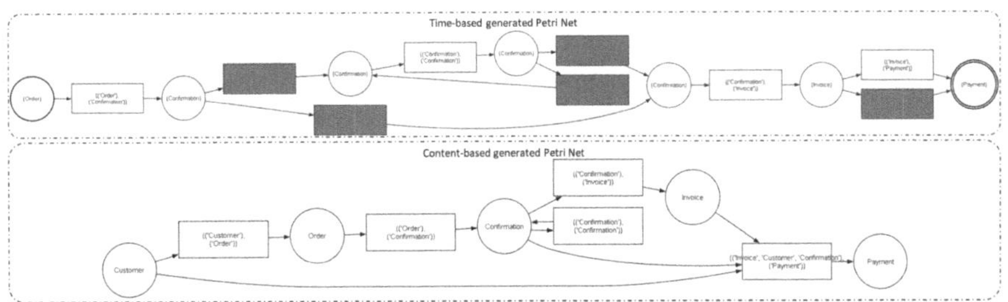

Fig. 3. Comparison of process models generated through temporal analysis (top) versus content-based analysis (bottom) for the loop pattern, demonstrating the structural compactness achieved through object-based modeling.

Our evaluation demonstrates effectiveness under controlled conditions including distinguishable object structures, representative timestamps, sufficient attribute overlaps, and appropriate process-independent object identification. Key limitations include small-scale test processes, controlled rather than real-world data with irregularities, format restrictions (JSON/XML), and evaluation of individual patterns rather than complex combinations. While not systematically evaluated, the prototype handles the tested datasets efficiently. However, scalability concerns exist due to pairwise object comparisons and configurable weighting factors that require domain expertise for optimization. The object-based approach successfully models fundamental control flow patterns while providing enhanced understanding of data dependencies and business rules embedded in processes through integration of temporal and content-based analysis perspectives.

6 Conclusion and Outlook

This paper presented a novel approach for fully automated business process model generation based on the analysis of object instances from operational documents. By shifting focus from event logs to objects, our method overcomes key limitations of existing approaches, transforming object knowledge into business process models, specifically in high-level Petri nets via a four-stage approach.

Our approach leverages existing organizational documents without requiring specialized event logs or system access, enabling process discovery where traditional process mining would fail due to limited system visibility or manual activities. The generated models are more compact yet information-rich, representing control flow patterns with fewer elements while maintaining comprehensive process semantics. This object-oriented perspective aligns with how business stakeholders conceptualize processes, providing an intuitive representation that bridges the gap between technical models and business understanding. Our object-based method offers complementary strengths—discovering process structures directly from organizational artifacts and capturing both explicit and implicit process knowledge embedded in objects, providing empirical grounding that probabilistic approaches (e.g. LLM-based) cannot match.

Future research could extend this work by: (1) expanding beyond direct attribute-value matches to identify more complex semantic relationships through advanced machine learning techniques; (2) empirically validating the configurable weighting factors across different application contexts; and (3) exploring hybrid approaches that combine our evidence-based structural discovery with LLMs' knowledge synthesis capabilities.

The generated models support simulation, verification, and automation initiatives. They formally specify both process logic and data manipulations, making Robotic Process Automation especially suitable because the rule-based operations from object analysis align well with RPA functions. This work contributes to automated business process modeling by pioneering the systematic use of objects as primary data sources, integrating control flow and object perspectives while addressing key gaps of traditional approaches and enabling deeper process understanding and automation.

References

1. van der Aalst, W.M.P.: Process mining: a 360 degree overview. In: Process Mining Handbook. Lecture Notes in Business Information Processing, vol. 448, pp. 3–34. Springer, Cham (2022)
2. van der Aalst, W., et al.: Workflow patterns. Distrib. Parallel Databases **14**(1), 5–51 (2003)
3. Conforti, R., et al.: Beyond tasks and gateways: discovering BPMN models with subprocesses, boundary events and activity markers. In: Business Process Management, vol. 8659, pp. 101–117. Springer, Cham (2014)
4. Di Ciccio, C., Mecella, M.: A two-step fast algorithm for the automated discovery of declarative workflows. In: Symposium on Computational Intelligence and Data Mining (CIDM), pp. 135–142. IEEE, Singapore (2013)
5. Elwany, E., et al.: DeeperDive: The Unreasonable Effectiveness of Weak Supervision in Document Understanding A Case Study in Collaboration with UiPath Inc (2022). https://doi.org/10.48550/arXiv.2208.08000
6. Engel, R., et al.: Mining Inter-organizational Business Process Models from EDI Messages: A Case Study from the Automotive Sector. Lecture Notes in Computer Science, vol. 7328. Springer, Cham (2012)
7. Forell, M., Schüler, S.: Modeling meets Large Language Models. In: Modellierung 2024 Satellite Events. Gesellschaft f r Informatik e.V., Potsdam (2024)
8. Fritsch, A., Schüler, S., Forell, M., Oberweis, A.: Modelling and execution of data-driven processes with JSON-nets. In: Enterprise, Business-Process and Information Systems Modeling. Lecture Notes in Business Information Processing, vol. 479, pp. 29–43. Springer, Cham (2023)
9. González López de Murillas, E., et al.: Connecting databases with process mining: a meta model and toolset. Softw. Syst. Model. **18**(2), 1209–1247 (2019)
10. Kecht, C., et al.: Event log construction from customer service conversations using natural language inference. In: International Conference on Process Mining (ICPM), pp. 144–151. IEEE, Eindhoven, Netherlands (2021)
11. La Rosa, M., et al.: Fundamentals of Business Process Management. Springer, New York (2018)
12. Lenz, K., Oberweis, A.: Inter-organizational business process management with XML nets. In: Petri Net Technology for Communication-Based Systems, pp. 243–263. Springer, Heidelberg (2003)
13. Li, J., et al.: A policy-based process mining framework: mining business policy texts for discovering process models. Inf. Syst. e-Bus. Manag. **8**(2), 169–188 (2010)
14. Lu, X., et al.: Discovering interacting artifacts from ERP systems. IEEE Trans. Serv. Comput. **8**(6), 861–873 (2015)
15. Nooijen, E.H.J., et al.: Automatic discovery of data-centric and artifact-centric processes. In: Business Process Management Workshops, vol. 132, pp. 316–327. Springer, Heidelberg (2013)
16. Pedregosa, F., et al: Scikit-learn: machine learning in python. J. Mach. Learn. Res. **12**(85), 2825–2830 (2011)
17. Popova, V., et al.: Artifact lifecycle discovery. Int. J. Coop. Inf. Syst. **24**(01), 1550001 (2015)

18. Popova, V., Dumas, M.: Discovering unbounded synchronization conditions in artifact-centric process models. In: Business Process Management Workshops, vol. 171, pp. 28–40. Springer, Cham (2014)
19. Reisig, W.: Understanding Petri Nets: Modeling Techniques, Analysis Methods, Case Studies. Springer, Heidelberg (2013)
20. Rozinat, A., Van Der Aalst, W.M.P.: Decision mining in ProM. In: Business Process Management. Lecture Notes in Computer Science, vol. 4102, pp. 420–425. Springer, Heidelberg (2006)
21. Schüler, S.: Objektbasierte Generierung von Gesch ftsprozessmodellen. Dissertation, Karlsruher Institut f r Technologie (KIT) (2025). https://doi.org/10.5445/IR/1000183000
22. Schüler, S., Alpers, S.: State of the art: automatic generation of business process models. In: Business Process Management Workshops, vol. 492, pp. 161–173. Springer, Cham (2024)
23. Sonbol, R., et al.: A machine translation like approach to generate business process model from textual description. SN Comput. Sci. **4**(3), 291 (2023)
24. Weske, M.: Business Process Management: Concepts, Languages, Architectures, 3 edn. Springer, Berlin (2019)

2nd International Workshop on Processes, Laws, and Compliance (PLC 2025)

Towards Holistic Business Process Compliance: Leveraging Logs, Models and Textual Data

Karolin Winter(✉)

Department of Industrial Engineering and Innovation Sciences ,Eindhoven University of Technology, Eindhoven, The Netherlands
k.m.winter@tue.nl

Abstract. Ensuring that business processes adhere to the rules imposed on them is the goal of business process compliance (BPC). The source for those rules are mainly laws, guidelines, or regulations, and consequently, BPC bridges the gap between the legal and the process domain. BPC can be structured into three phases: design-time, run-time and auditing. During each of those phases different data sources, ranging from process models to event logs, event streams and natural language texts such as process descriptions or regulatory documents, are of interest. This diversity of data sources and BPC phases requires a broad range of methods and techniques. In this keynote paper, selected approaches addressing the research vision of working towards holistic BPC are presented. Furthermore, current limitations and directions for future work are outlined, for example, how to ensure compliance of processes under changing laws and how to mitigate effects of changes to restore compliance.

Keywords: Business Process Compliance · Regulatory Documents · Data-Driven Compliance Management · Large Language Models

1 Introduction

Business process compliance (BPC) has the objective of ensuring that business processes adhere to the rules imposed on them, with those rules stemming from, e.g., laws, guidelines, or regulations [7,9]. Consequently, BPC bridges the gap between the legal and process domain [7]. Considering, for example, that 560 basic legal acts were adopted by the European Union in 2024[1] and the tremendous fines which can be imposed in case of compliance violations, e.g., for the General Data Protection Regulation (GDPR) "20 000 000 EUR, or in the case of an undertaking, up to 4 % of the total worldwide annual turnover of the preceding financial year, whichever is higher" [4] the significance of BPC becomes evident. In literature, BPC is often divided into design-time, run-time, and auditing [7] and for each of those phases different data sources become relevant. During

[1] https://eur-lex.europa.eu/statistics/2024/legislative-acts-statistics.html.

I. van de Weerd et al. (Eds.): BPM 2025 Workshops, LNBIP 569, pp. 507–515, 2026.
https://doi.org/10.1007/978-3-032-13426-4_37

design-time, typically *process models* represented in form of, e.g., Business Process Model and Notation (BPMN) [13] or Declare [14] are crucial. Process models can be developed through conducting interviews or, if *textual descriptions of processes* are available, process models can be extracted using Natural Language Processing (NLP) techniques. For the latter, most recently the potential of Large Language Models (LLMs) has been explored, e.g., [6,12]. Process models must be checked for compliance, i.e., contrasted against the rules described in *regulatory documents*[2]. LLMs can be used to formalize rules, e.g., in Metric Temporal Logic [2], or as goal models, e.g., Legal Goal-oriented Requirements Language [8]. In addition, LLMs open up new possibilities to enable direct compliance assessment between rules given in natural language and process models or event logs [10,11]. Moving to run-time compliance monitoring, i.e., keeping track of compliance while processes are executed [9] *event streams* constitute one relevant data source. During process execution, *event logs* can be produced, allowing for auditing, i.e., analyzing if the process was executed according to compliance rules in an ex-post manner [7]. Besides the traditional three phases of BPC, predictive compliance monitoring (PCM) [15] recently gained attention. Thereby, predictive process monitoring techniques can be used to enable forecasting of compliance violations of running instances. Such timely detections of violations could help to take actions in order to prevent compliance breaches, and again *event logs and event streams* constitute relevant data sources for this task. In summary, BPC is a complex task, requiring to be addressed in a holistic manner, as summarized in the following research vision statement.

My aim is to work towards holistic business process compliance through analysis of heterogeneous data originating from diverse data sources.

The term holistic is to be understood from two angles: i) covering all phases of BPC from design-time, to run-time, auditing and recently prediction, ii) considering data not in isolation. The diversity of data sources relevant for BPC requires knowledge on a broad set of methods ranging from process and data mining to process modeling but more increasingly important NLP. Section 2 of this keynote paper reports on a selection of approaches aiming to address the described research vision. Section 3 discusses limitations and outlines future work before the paper concludes in Sect. 4.

2 Towards Holistic Business Process Compliance

This section reports on selected research contributing to holistic BPC structured along three topics. Section 2.1 covers analysis of regulatory documents [16,17,22–24,26], Sect. 2.2 modeling of regulatory documents [2,8,25] and Sect. 2.3 compliance analysis [1,10,11,18,21].

[2] In the remainder of this paper we consider regulatory documents as an overarching term for legislative texts up to internal regulations, e.g., on how to implement the General Data Protection Regulation (GDPR), within a particular company [18].

2.1 Facilitating Analysis of Regulatory Documents

This section centers around the question

How to facilitate analysis of regulatory documents?

Considering the vast amount of regulatory documents companies have to cope with, it is evident that automated support in analyzing those is crucial. Moreover, analysis of regulatory documents is often the first step in ensuring BPC laying the foundation for following BPC tasks [9]. While doing so, several challenges relating to the nature of regulatory documents must be considered. For example, regulatory documents are often lengthy and can address multiple stakeholders at the same time, like in the case of the GDPR companies but also member states. This makes it difficult to properly delineate which requirement is relevant for which stakeholder. Moreover, complex terminology and several legal definitions which can be specific to the regulatory document under consideration must be taken into account [17]. To address this variety of challenges, we developed the following approaches employing NLP and data mining techniques.

Document Length and Variety of Stakeholders. By means of text fragmentation [26], grouping and comparing compliance requirements [23], we could demonstrate that the number of compliance requirements users have to read can potentially be reduced, e.g., for the GDPR by up to roughly 20% depending on the target group considered [24]. In [23] we not only presented how to group requirements based on target groups but also how to identify redundant, subsuming, or conflicting requirements. Such an automated analysis can again reduce the reading effort. Consider, for example, two redundant constraints with one being mentioned on page 2 the other on page 72. When reading through the document in a chronological order, it is likely that this relationship is overlooked. Furthermore, if a process has already proven to be compliant for certain requirements, there is no need to check compliance again for redundant requirements. Another use case of [23] is related to changing regulatory documents. In particular, when comparing two sets of requirements, one before the change one after a change, quite a lot of redundant requirements are expected, which can be flagged accordingly, and, more importantly, conflicts between requirements might be discovered. As an example, consider a requirement stating "This check must be performed within 2 weeks." being changed to "This check must be performed within 1 week.". Such a change induces a conflict in terms of a shortened time period for performing the check. Based on discussions with stakeholders from the financial domain, a prototype [22] was developed. Thereby we recognized different preferences among user groups. For example, persons with a legal background suggested to not only display extracted requirements in isolation in form of a graph but to also provide the paragraph this requirements stems from. These insights were incorporated into subsequent works by providing annotations on top of the original regulatory documents as described in the following.

Complexity of Terminology and Legal Definitions. To address the challenges of complexity of terminology and legal definitions, we developed approaches capable of identifying legal definitions and their relations as well as implicit actors from regulatory documents [16,17]. A legal definition consists of a term plus an explanation [16], e.g., " 'personal data' means any information relating to an identified or identifiable natural person ('data subject'); ..." [4]. As can be seen in this example an explanation of a definition can again contain a legal definition, here "data subject". Consequently, relations between definitions are possible and must be captured accordingly. To do so, in [16] we elicit semantic relations including hyponyms, meronyms, and synonyms and use a knowledge graph to visualize those relations. The approach was tested on European regulations and the developed prototype takes as input a CELEX number (an identifier for European regulations) and provides users with a list of definitions, the knowledge graph capturing the semantic relations and an annotated version of the regulatory document which, when hovering over a definition in the text, displays the explanation. In [17] we extended this work and the prototype by including an approach to determine and resolve implicit mentions of actors. As example, consider Article 7, paragraph 3 of the GDPR "Conditions of Consent" stating: "Prior to giving consent, the data subject shall be informed thereof.". In this sentence it is unclear of what the data subject shall be informed of but more importantly, who needs to be the informant, i.e., the actor is not explicitly mentioned. Only when considering the context, "controller" can be identified as actor. Our approach makes this knowledge explicit and the prototype displays an annotated version of the regulatory document with implicit actor suggestions.

2.2 Modeling Compliance Requirements

This section centers around the question

How to model compliance requirements from regulatory documents?

A large variety of formalisms for modeling legal and compliance requirements has been presented in literature [7]. Each of these has their own advantages and disadvantages. In the following, two examples of formalizations are described.
Formalized Rules. One line of research extracts formalized rules, e.g., in the form of Linear Temporal Logic. In [2] we presented a structured literature survey combined with an approach using LLMs to extract and formalize temporal requirements from natural language texts in Metric Temporal Logic (MTL). Our approach, NL2MTL, addresses five out of ten findings elicited in the structured literature survey. NL2MTL can handle process descriptions, system specifications and legal texts as input. It provides users with the formalized rules as well as additional information, e.g., if the LLM was imposing assumptions to generate the MTL expression. This additional information can help users judge the reliability of the automatic formalization. Although formalized rules have advantages, such as avoiding ambiguities, they might not be suitable for all application scenarios and user groups due to their rather mathematical nature [3].
(Goal) Models. Extracting models, for example, Legal Goal-oriented Requirements Language (Legal GRL) models [5] can be considered a suitable alternative to formalized rules. In [8] we explored the capabilities of LLMs to extract Legal

GRL models from regulatory documents. For prompting the LLM we relied on prompt patterns [20], e.g., the persona and context manager patterns. As mentioned in Sect. 2.1, regulatory documents can address multiple stakeholders. In addition, multiple topics can be present, making it necessary to be able to pull a certain actor or topic into focus. Although in [8] we did not explicitly test whether those two patterns have an influence on the final results when including them into our prompts, we could still recognize improvements of results while designing our prompts. Since [12] found that these patterns seemed to not significantly influence their results, we require more experiments to objectively confirm our observations. In contrast to Legal GRL models, extracting BPMN models directly from regulatory documents is challenging because of their inherently different levels of granularity. Therefore, in [25], we extract process model fragments constituting an intermediate representation based on which a process model can be developed. By connecting this extraction with the approach presented in [23], we could demonstrate that process model fragments are not only useful by themselves but also help to pinpoint which model parts can be reused from other, as redundantly flagged process model fragments.

2.3 Compliance Analysis with Heterogeneous Data

This section centers around the question

How to enable compliance analysis with heterogeneous data?

Considering the large variety of data sources ranging from event logs, to event streams, to process models, formalized rules, and natural language texts, compliance analysis becomes increasingly complex since, i.a., consistency of results must be ensured. To achieve this, in theory, all data sources should be checked against each other. To work towards this goal, we presented several approaches in which natural language texts are either paired with event logs, allowing for ex-post compliance verification (auditing) [1,10,11], or process models and other natural language texts, allowing for design-time compliance checking [18,21].

Compliance Verification and Auditing. Event logs capture how processes have been executed and can therefore be used to verify if compliance rules have been adhered to [7]. In contrast to existing work, we do not require that rules have already been formalized, instead we consider rules in their original form, i.e., natural language text. In particular, we focused on verification of quantitative temporal [1] and resource constraints [10,11], respectively.

Design-time Compliance Checking. In [21] we presented an approach allowing to assess compliance between a regulatory document and a set of process models. We consider the regulatory document as its set of paragraphs and define a fitness score measuring the likelihood that a process model reflects a particular paragraph. In addition, we provide a cost score measuring three types of compliance violations between paragraph and process model pairs: missing obligatory activities, strict order violations and resource responsibility violations. We envision two application scenarios: 1) paragraph model pairs are not known in advance. Then the fitness score can help to determine potential matches first before compliance violations can be identified via the cost score in more detail. 2) paragraph model pairs are known in advance. In this case the cost score again assesses potential compliance violations in detail, while the fitness score serves now as sanity check in the sense that high fitness between the model and another paragraph could point out compliance constraints that are currently not considered but still match with the model. In [18], we followed a similar idea but with two differences. First, we consider two natural language texts as input, i.e., a regulatory document and its internal realization, which can comprise company policies or handbooks. For example, we assess compliance between the GDPR and an internal document describing how a particular company is implementing the GDPR. Another difference to [21] is that we consider more types of compliance violations, including execution style, negation, resource responsibility and data deviations. The evaluation showed promising results, however, due to, for example, ambiguities or implicit knowledge [17] which often require human interpretation, fully automated compliance assessment between two natural language texts remains challenging [18].

3 Limitations and Future Research Directions

Limitations and directions for future work arising from those are outlined below.
Extension to Run-Time. The selection of approaches as presented in Sect. 2 mainly covered the design-time and auditing phases of BPC. To address also the run-time phase of BPC some approaches could be either directly used or be extended. For example, the MTL expressions as extracted by [2] could serve as input for existing run-time compliance monitoring approaches [9]. Moreover, future research could investigate how [1,10], which are currently taking event logs as input, could be extended to allow for considering event streams instead.
Predictive Compliance Monitoring. The presented approaches have not yet focused on predicting compliance violations. However, given the substantial amount of fines companies face when violating compliance, paired with the increasing amount of regulatory documents, predicting compliance breaches becomes essential. Predictive Compliance Monitoring (PCM) [15] combines predictive process and compliance monitoring to do so.
Handling Change. Another limitation of the presented approaches is that they only implicitly consider non-static scenarios. However, the underlying rules or the processes can change over time. This problem has already been identified in, e.g., [7] and the TRPro project[3] is one example of a research project looking at this particular problem. Thereby, not only detecting changes and potential compliance violations caused by changes, but also investigating feasible mitigation actions to restore compliance and how to implement them, are relevant tasks.
Alignment Between Data Sources. Considering changes and the large variety of data sources relevant for BPC it becomes evident that inconsistencies

[3] https://gepris.dfg.de/gepris/projekt/514769482?language=en.

could be introduced. Consider a process that is described in natural language and modeled as BPMN. If the BPMN model changes, the description must be updated accordingly to avoid inconsistencies. Building upon process trees, in [19] we demonstrate how to update process descriptions. Thereby, we opt for the least invasive adaptations possible to preserve as much original text as possible.

4 Conclusion

Business process compliance is a challenging but at the same time crucial task for companies. Challenges arise due to the broad range of phases constituting BPC (run-time, design time, auditing) but also due to the large variety of data sources required during the different BPC phases. Consequently, BPC must be addressed in a holistic manner. In this keynote paper, a selection of approaches working towards holistic BPC has been presented covering analysis and modeling of regulatory documents, as well as compliance analysis. Limitations and future research directions have been outlined, including BPC change management and alignment between different data sources.

Acknowledgement. I would like to sincerely thank my co-authors for their valuable contributions.

References

1. Barrientos, M., Winter, K., Mangler, J., Rinderle-Ma, S.: Verification of quantitative temporal compliance requirements in process descriptions over event logs. In: Advanced Information Systems Engineering - 35th International Conference, CAiSE 2023, Zaragoza, Spain, 12–16 June 2023, Proceedings. LNCS, vol. 13901, pp. 417–433. Springer (2023). https://doi.org/10.1007/978-3-031-34560-9_25
2. Barrientos, M., Winter, K., Rinderle-Ma, S.: Automatic extraction and formalization of temporal requirements from text: a survey. In: Enterprise Design, Operations, and Computing - 28th International Conference, EDOC 2024, Vienna, Austria, 10–13 September 2024, Revised Selected Papers. LNCS, vol. 15409, pp. 259–278. Springer (2024). https://doi.org/10.1007/978-3-031-78338-8_14
3. Brunello, A., Montanari, A., Reynolds, M.: Synthesis of LTL formulas from natural language texts: state of the art and research directions. In: 26th International Symposium on Temporal Representation and Reasoning, TIME 2019, 16–19 October 2019, Málaga, Spain. LIPIcs, vol. 147, pp. 1–19. Schloss Dagstuhl - Leibniz-Zentrum für Informatik (2019). https://doi.org/10.4230/LIPICS.TIME.2019.17
4. European Parl., Council of the EU: Regulation (EU) 2016/679 of the European Parliament and of the Council. https://data.europa.eu/eli/reg/2016/679/oj
5. Ghanavati, S., Amyot, D., Rifaut, A.: Legal goal-oriented requirement language (legal GRL) for modeling regulations. In: 6th International Workshop on Modeling in Software Engineering, MiSE 2014, Hyderabad, India, 2–3 June 2014. pp. 1–6. ACM (2014). https://doi.org/10.1145/2593770.2593780

6. Grohs, M., Abb, L., Elsayed, N., Rehse, J.: Large language models can accomplish business process management tasks. In: Business Process Management Workshops - BPM 2023 International Workshops, Utrecht, The Netherlands, 11–15 September 2023, Revised Selected Papers. LNBIP, vol. 492, pp. 453–465. Springer (2023). https://doi.org/10.1007/978-3-031-50974-2_34
7. Hashmi, M., Governatori, G., Lam, H.-P., Wynn, M.T.: Are we done with business process compliance: state of the art and challenges ahead. Knowl. Inf. Syst. **57**(1), 79–133 (2018). https://doi.org/10.1007/s10115-017-1142-1
8. de Kinderen, S., Winter, K.: Towards taming large language models with prompt templates for legal GRL modeling. In: Enterprise, Business-Process and Information Systems Modeling - 25th International Conference, BPMDS 2024, and 29th International Conference, EMMSAD 2024, Limassol, Cyprus, 3–4 June 2024, Proceedings. LNBIP, vol. 511, pp. 213–228. Springer (2024). https://doi.org/10.1007/978-3-031-61007-3_17
9. Ly, L.T., Maggi, F.M., Montali, M., Rinderle-Ma, S., van der Aalst, W.M.P.: Compliance monitoring in business processes: functionalities, application, and tool-support. Inf. Syst. **54**, 209–234 (2015). https://doi.org/10.1016/J.IS.2015.02.007
10. Mustroph, H., Barrientos, M., Winter, K., Rinderle-Ma, S.: Verifying resource compliance requirements from natural language text over event logs. In: Business Process Management - 21st International Conference, BPM 2023, Utrecht, The Netherlands, 11–15 September 2023, Proceedings. LNCS, vol. 14159, pp. 249–265. Springer (2023). https://doi.org/10.1007/978-3-031-41620-0_15
11. Mustroph, H., Winter, K., Rinderle-Ma, S.: Social network mining from natural language text and event logs for compliance deviation detection. In: Cooperative Information Systems - 29th International Conference, CoopIS 2023, Groningen, The Netherlands, October 30–November 3, 2023, Proceedings. LNCS, vol. 14353, pp. 347–365. Springer (2023). https://doi.org/10.1007/978-3-031-46846-9_19
12. Neuberger, J., Ackermann, L., van der Aa, H., Jablonski, S.: A universal prompting strategy for extracting process model information from natural language text using large language models. In: Conceptual Modeling - 43rd International Conference, ER 2024, Pittsburgh, PA, USA, 28–31 October 2024, Proceedings. LNCS, vol. 15238, pp. 38–55. Springer (2024). https://doi.org/10.1007/978-3-031-75872-0_3
13. Omg, O., Parida, R., Mahapatra, S.: Business process model and notation (BPMN) version 2.0. Object Management Group (2011)
14. Pesic, M., Schonenberg, H., van der Aalst, W.M.P.: DECLARE: full support for loosely-structured processes. In: 11th IEEE International Enterprise Distributed Object Computing Conference (EDOC 2007), 15–19 October 2007, Annapolis, Maryland, USA, pp. 287–300. IEEE Computer Society (2007). https://doi.org/10.1109/EDOC.2007.14
15. Rinderle-Ma, S., Winter, K., Benzin, J.: Predictive compliance monitoring in process-aware information systems: state of the art, functionalities, research directions. Inf. Syst. **115**, 102210 (2023). https://doi.org/10.1016/J.IS.2023.102210
16. Sai, C., Damaratskaya, A., Winter, K., Rinderle-Ma, S.: Identification and visualization of legal definitions and legal term relations. In: Advances in Conceptual Modeling - ER 2023 Workshops, CMLS, CMOMM4FAIR, EmpER, JUSMOD, OntoCom, QUAMES, and SmartFood, Lisbon, Portugal, 6–9 November 2023, Proceedings. LNCS, vol. 14319, pp. 151–161. Springer (2023). https://doi.org/10.1007/978-3-031-47112-4_14

17. Sai, C., Rossi, L., Damaratskaya, A., Winter, K., Rinderle-Ma, S.: Identification and visual representation of explicit legal definitions, their relations and implicit actors in regulatory documents. Comput. Law Secur. Rev. **58**, 106174 (2025). https://doi.org/10.1016/j.clsr.2025.106174
18. Sai, C., Winter, K., Fernanda, E., Rinderle-Ma, S.: Detecting deviations between external and internal regulatory requirements for improved process compliance assessment. In: Advanced Information Systems Engineering - 35th International Conference, CAiSE 2023, Zaragoza, Spain, 12–16 June 2023, Proceedings. LNCS, vol. 13901, pp. 401–416. Springer (2023). https://doi.org/10.1007/978-3-031-34560-9_24
19. Sai, N., Winter, K., Dijkman, R.M.: Repairing process descriptions by discovering deviations from process models. In: Enterprise, Business-Process and Information Systems Modeling - 26th International Conference, BPMDS 2025, and 30th International Conference, EMMSAD 2025, Vienna, Austria, 16–17 June 2025, Proceedings. LNBIP, vol. 558, pp. 71–86. Springer (2025). https://doi.org/10.1007/978-3-031-95397-2_5
20. White, J., et al.: A prompt pattern catalog to enhance prompt engineering with ChatGPT. CoRR abs/2302.11382 (2023). https://doi.org/10.48550/ARXIV.2302.11382
21. Winter, K., van der Aa, H., Rinderle-Ma, S., Weidlich, M.: Assessing the compliance of business process models with regulatory documents. In: Dobbie, G., Frank, U., Kappel, G., Liddle, S.W., Mayr, H.C. (eds.) ER 2020. LNCS, vol. 12400, pp. 189–203. Springer, Cham (2020). https://doi.org/10.1007/978-3-030-62522-1_14
22. Winter, K., Gall, M., Rinderle-Ma, S.: RegMiner: taming the complexity of regulatory documents for digitalized compliance management. In: Proceedings of the Best Dissertation Award, Doctoral Consortium, and Demonstration & Resources Track at BPM 2020 co-located with the 18th International Conference on Business Process Management (BPM 2020), Sevilla, Spain, 13–18 September 2020. CEUR Workshop Proceedings, vol. 2673, pp. 112–116 (2020). https://ceur-ws.org/
23. Winter, K., Rinderle-Ma, S.: Detecting constraints and their relations from regulatory documents using NLP techniques. In: On the Move to Meaningful Internet Systems. OTM 2018 Conferences - Confederated International Conferences: CoopIS, C&TC, and ODBASE 2018, Valletta, Malta, 22–26 October 2018, Proceedings, Part I. LNCS, vol. 11229, pp. 261–278. Springer (2018). https://doi.org/10.1007/978-3-030-02610-3_15
24. Winter, K., Rinderle-Ma, S.: Untangling the GDPR using conrelminer. CoRR abs/1811.03399 (2018)
25. Winter, K., Rinderle-Ma, S.: Deriving and combining mixed graphs from regulatory documents based on constraint relations. In: Advanced Information Systems Engineering - 31st International Conference, CAiSE 2019, Rome, Italy, 3–7 June 2019, Proceedings. LNCS, vol. 11483, pp. 430–445. Springer (2019). https://doi.org/10.1007/978-3-030-21290-2_27
26. Winter, K., Rinderle-Ma, S., Grossmann, W., Feinerer, I., Ma, Z.: Characterizing regulatory documents and guidelines based on text mining. In: On the Move to Meaningful Internet Systems. OTM 2017 Conferences - Confederated International Conferences: CoopIS, C&TC, and ODBASE 2017, Rhodes, Greece, 23–27 October 2017, Proceedings, Part I. LNCS, vol. 10573, pp. 3–20. Springer (2017). https://doi.org/10.1007/978-3-319-69462-7_1

From Text to Process: Leveraging LLMs to Unveil Italian Lawmaking

Matilde Contestabile[1(✉)], Chiara Ferrara[1], Alberto Giovannetti[1], Giovanni Parrillo[1], and Andrea Vandin[1,2]

[1] Sant'Anna School of Advanced Studies, Pisa, Italy
matilde.contestabile@santannapisa.it
[2] DTU Technical University of Denmark, Kongens Lyngby, Denmark

Abstract. The Italian lawmaking process involves a complex interplay of institutions, actors, and procedural stages. Despite the existence of previous research, systematic process-oriented studies remain scarce, largely due to the absence of structured data detailing its procedural steps. We introduce ProLiFIC (Procedural Lawmaking Flow in Italian Chambers), a machine-accessible dataset of Italian legislative preparatory works from 1985 to the present. These texts are available in unstructured form on the Normattiva portal. By leveraging large language models for event extraction, we transform this data into structured event logs suitable for analyses in process-oriented Data Science and Process Mining (PM). Our approach promotes transparency in process studies and paves the way for analyses of procedural dynamics, temporal patterns, and inefficiencies in the Italian lawmaking process. Preliminary exploratory data analyses and PM tasks demonstrate the dataset's potential for supporting inquiries in political and legal studies.

Keywords: Normattiva · Lawmaking process · Process mining · LLMs

1 Introduction

The Italian lawmaking process, characterized by a complex interplay of institutions, actors and procedural stages, offers fertile ground for empirical analyses across multiple disciplines, including political science, law, and public administration (see, e.g., [1–3]). Nevertheless, systematic studies of this process remain constrained by the lack of structured data capturing the detailed progression of lawmaking procedures. While previous research has examined aspects such as party coalitions, party switches, legislative output, raw performance, and policy agendas (see, e.g., [2–4]), there is a lack of studies with a process-oriented approach to track the concrete procedural steps that laws undergo during their lifecycle. In this paper, we apply to this domain process-oriented techniques from the field of Process Mining (PM). PM is an interdisciplinary research area that aims at extracting insights and knowledge from execution traces of a process, bridging the gap between data science and process science [5].

I. van de Weerd et al. (Eds.): BPM 2025 Workshops, LNBIP 569, pp. 516–530, 2026.
https://doi.org/10.1007/978-3-032-13426-4_38

The Italian Parliament is bicameral, composed of two chambers with equal powers: the *Camera dei Deputati* (Chamber of Deputies) and the *Senato della Repubblica* (Senate of the Republic). Laws can originate in either chamber and follow a legislative process that requires approval by both. Alongside ordinary laws, the system also includes *decree-laws* (*decreti-legge*), urgent government measures that must be converted into law within 60 days. The procedural history of each law is recorded in unstructured textual documents known as *preparatory works* (it. *lavori preparatori*), official records of the parliamentary events and institutional actions leading to the law's approval. In Italy, these are available starting from 1985 via the Normattiva portal [6] managed by the Presidency of the Council of Ministers. The portal provides a rich but unstructured source of information, covering all laws passed by the Italian Parliament.

We leverage this massive source of information by constructing `ProLiFIC` (*Procedural Lawmaking Flow in Italian Chambers*), a machine-accessible dataset containing Normattiva's preparatory works. These have been first curated, and then encoded as an event log. `ProLiFIC` covers the Italian lawmaking process from 1985 to March 2025, the timeframe available in Normattiva, for overall 5208 laws. By systematically converting the textual content of preparatory works into a structured event log, we offer a detailed representation of legislative activities and procedural steps suitable for automated PM analyses.

Extracting legislative events from natural language, however, poses significant challenges. Preparatory works are written in discursive, often ambiguous, language. As such, manual retrieval and analysis are time-consuming and impractical for large-scale studies. At the same time, rigorous approaches based, e.g., on parsers may be problematic. Preparatory works may, in fact, contain inconsistent formatting over the years, or factual errors (e.g., typos, see Sect. 4).

To overcome these limitations, we designed a multi-stage pipeline consisting of: (i) web scraping of preparatory texts from Normattiva; (ii) event extraction from the downloaded corpora using large language models (LLMs); and (iii) post-processing and validation to ensure data quality.

The process of Italian lawmaking has been already studied, in part. The authors of [3] use the ILMA dataset [7] to study the temporal dimension of lawmaking. This is a very thorough dataset, with a wider scope than `ProLiFIC`. For example, it also includes information on parliamentary votes, parties, etc. However, these studies use less fine-grained data on procedural aspects, do not use process mining techniques, and consider only a limited time period (19872008)[1].

`ProLiFIC` may support rich and diverse types of inquiries in political and legal studies, in part discussed in Sects. 5 and 6. These studies complement a growing body of work in European legislative studies, where procedural data is increasingly valued (e.g., [8]). Most notably, `ProLiFIC` allows the application of the rich PM toolbox to legislative data, offering the ability to discover procedural dynamics, compare different lawmaking instances, uncover temporal patterns, and detect inefficiencies in the Italian lawmaking process.

[1] Notably, as of this writing the project appears to be discontinued and unavailable https://159.149.130.120/ilma/sito/.

By providing a structured, scalable, and reproducible approach to modeling legislative processes, our work also contributes to the field of legal informatics, demonstrating how natural language processing (NLP), large language models (LLMs), and data science can enhance the transparency and efficiency of legal systems by introducing *structure* into otherwise unstructured legislative texts [9, 10].

Our aim is therefore dual. First, we present a new dataset. Then, we demonstrate its potential by performing preliminary exploratory data analyses and PM tasks (Sects. 5 and 6, resp.). Our analyses focus on the last four Italian legislatures, from 2008 to the present (legislatures XVI to XIX), which we us as a testbed to obtain preliminary empirical insights from real parliamentary data. Exploratory data analysis is done using Python (libraries Pandas and PM4py [11]), while PM analyses with Fluxicon Disco [12]. Thanks to these analyses we can study the following two research questions: **(RQ1)** How do legislative trajectories differ between ordinary laws and the conversion of government decrees? **(RQ2)** How do procedural patterns vary between the two chambers?

2 Related Work and Research Context

2.1 Prior Domain-Specific Datasets

Though no longer publicly accessible, the Italian Law-Making Archive (ILMA) [7] is a fundamental effort in the study of the Italian lawmaking process. Designed for political science research, ILMA provided a relational database that integrated data on laws, legislative initiatives, parliamentary actors, and party positions from the X to the XV legislature (19872008).

While our work is inspired by ILMA, it diverges significantly in both scope and methodology. Unlike ILMA, which aimed to provide a comprehensive and centralized overview based on structured institutional metadata, our goal is to construct a fine-grained event log tailored for PM tasks. For this reason, we rely on a different data source (unstructured narrative documents, namely the preparatory works available in Normattiva) and introduce a novel data extraction approach exploiting LLMs (see Sect. 4). We also broadened the temporal scope, covering a larger and more current view of Italian legislative activity.

2.2 LLMs and NLP for (Legal) Process Mining

In recent years, the PM community has shown growing interest in the intersection with NLP and generative AI, leading to several dedicated initiatives including workshops on NLP for BPM[2]. The need to automatically translate natural language texts into structured representations suitable for business process management (BPM) tools has been recognized for some time. In response, several NLP-based frameworks have been proposed (see, e.g., [13]). Among the most significant contributions in this area, the capabilities of LLMs across a variety of PM

[2] sites.google.com/view/nlp4bpm2025 , www.genai4pm2024.info.

tasks, including process querying, model generation, and the interpretation of complex procedural logic have been explored by [14] and further extended in [15], which provides the most recent benchmarks on the subject. These demonstrate that LLMs are highly proficient in understanding process structures, showcasing their potential as general-purpose tools for the domain.

With regard to event log generation specifically, [16] introduces CSV-PM-LLM-Parsing, a Python library that uses LLMs to automatically transform CSV files containing unstructured events into PM event logs. This work shows how LLMs can support data cleaning and standardization.

This literature review highlights a further contribution of our work to this area. We propose a novel use of LLMs in PM: constructing structured event logs from unstructured (and unannotated) legal texts. Rather than using LLMs to clean or standardize already partially structured data (e.g., CSV files), we employ them as semantic extractors capable of identifying and isolating discrete events from raw legislative texts written in natural language, a task that poses significant challenges to legal process discovery [17].

3 On the Italian Legislative Process: Structure, Executive Influence, and European Integration

The Italian lawmaking process reflects an evolving system shaped by both constitutional heritage and modern institutional demands. This process has progressively adapted to the operational needs of a legal framework increasingly influenced by executive exigencies arising from European integration [18].

Central to the Italian legislative model is the notion of perfect bicameralism. As prescribed by Article 70 of the Constitution, legislative authority is exercised collectively by both the Chamber of Deputies and the Senate. Consequently, no bill may become law unless it is approved in identical form by both chambers. This requirement sets in motion a procedural cycle that begins with the submission of a legislative proposal, followed by detailed scrutiny and potential approval in the originating chamber. The text is then passed to the second chamber, which undertakes its own review. It is common for the text to undergo revisions, prompting a back and forth between the two chambers, a process colloquially referred to as the *navetta* (*shuttle*)

Legislative initiative in Italy may originate from multiple institutional actors. Once presented, a bill is assigned to a parliamentary committee, which plays a central and substantive role in the legislative process. It is within these committees that the bulk of the legislative work takes place. Committees are responsible not only for the in-depth examination of the bill, but also for coordinating multiple revisions, consolidating similar proposals, collecting expert opinions, and discussing amendments. After successful passage in one chamber, the bill advances to the other, where a parallel examination occurs. When an identical version is approved by both chambers, the proposal proceed to the President of the Republic for promulgation. The President may return the bill with comments for reconsideration, but once reapproved, promulgation becomes obligatory. The law is then published in the *Gazzetta Ufficiale* (with a unique identifier) and, unless otherwise specified, enters into force 15 days after publication.

In addition to the ordinary legislative process, Article 77 authorizes the issuance of *decreti-legge*, or decree laws, which are temporary legislative acts with immediate legal force. These measures must be ratified by Parliament within 60 days of issuance, or they become null and void retroactively. Originally conceived as instruments for emergency use, decree laws have become a recurring tool in legislative practice. Their widespread use has prompted debate regarding the balance of power between the executive and legislative branches [19]. Nevertheless, decree laws remain a central feature of legislative output and are frequently employed also to expedite politically sensitive measures. This mechanism also contributes to broader structural issues within the Italian legislative system. One such issue is the tendency toward *de facto* unicameralism: the urgency of decree conversion and tight timelines often shift the balance of deliberation in favour of a single chamber, marginalising the role of the other in practice [20].

In addition to the increasing use of decree laws, European integration has also significantly influenced the development of Italy's lawmaking. The country's membership in the EU requires it to transpose directives into national law and to ensure domestic systems are compatible with European regulations and case law [21]. The primary instrument used for transposing directives is the annual *legge di delegazione europea* (European delegation law), which delegates authority to the government to adopt legislative decrees in line with European obligations.

To sum up, the Italian legislative process exhibits a dual character: it is over-bureaucratic and procedurally complex, yet increasingly shaped by executive decisions and supranational commitments. The coexistence of multiple legislative routes (ordinary laws, decree laws, and integration of European directives) offers a unique field for legal analysis, which can significantly leverage on process-oriented data science techniques, and in particular process mining ones.

4 Dataset Construction and Description

Here we provide a detailed description of the pipeline to build `ProLiFIC`. We discuss the specific challenges posed by the semi-structured nature of the source data, explaining how these challenges informed our methodological choices (Sect. 4.1). A concrete example is provided using the case of Law No. 41/1987 (Sect. 4.2). Finally, we present the structure of the resulting dataset, which consists of two interlinked components: a *metadata table* and an *event log* that captures the procedural trajectory of each law (Sect. 4.3).

4.1 From Raw Text to Structured Data

`ProLiFIC` has been constructed in three steps: (i) data collection by web scraping Normattiva for preparatory works, (ii) LLM-based event extraction, (iii) post-processing and validation. A visual overview of the pipeline is given in Fig. 1.

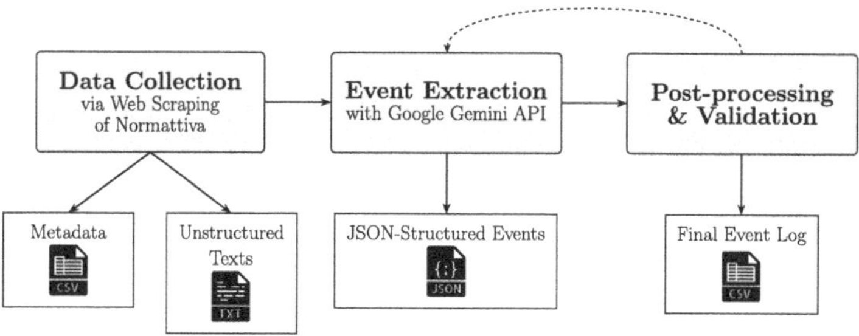

Fig. 1. Dataset construction pipeline.

Data Collection: Scraping Normattiva. As introduced earlier, we began by scraping the Normattiva portal. This provided centralized access to all preparatory works published in the *Gazzetta Ufficiale* since 1985, allowing for comprehensive coverage of the legislative process. For each law, we collected: (i) the full text of the preparatory works, and (ii) a set of metadata fields including the title, description, publication date, and other attributes. Section 4.3 discusses in greater detail the metadata fields. We currently do not make available the dataset, as it is subject to further extensions. We will make it available in an extended version of this work.

Event Extraction via LLMs. The main challenge in transforming the collected data into a processable event log lay in the semi-structured nature of the texts. While some recurring phrasing and formatting conventions exist, they are neither consistent nor sufficient for reliable rule-based parsing. In our initial attempt, we sought to leverage these patterns using traditional parsing techniques such as regular expressions and custom rule-based parsers, supplemented by basic NLP pre-processing steps (e.g., abbreviation expansion, text normalization). However, this method proved inadequate due to the high heterogeneity of the corpus resulting from *ambiguously grouped dates* (e.g., "Esaminato in Aula il 10 giugno 2014; il 3, 4 e 8 luglio 2014 e approvato il 9 luglio 2014."), *inconsistent labels for commissions and chambers* (e.g., "VIII Comm." vs. "8ª Commissione"), and *typographical errors* both in texts and dates, to name just a few.

These factors rendered deterministic and exact approaches unreliable, motivating the shift to LLMs for semantic parsing and event extraction. We used the python APIs of Google's Gemini 2.5 Flash (and Gemini 1.5 Pro for longer texts exceeding the maximum tokens allowed by 2.5 Flash). Thanks to a tailored prompt, we parsed each narrative paragraph into a chronological sequence of standardized procedural events namely, presentation (*presentazione*), commission assignment (*assegnazione a commissione*), request for opinion (*richiesta di parere*), commission examination (*esame in commissione*), report to the assembly (*relazione all'aula*), plenary discussion (*esame in aula*), and approval (*approvazione*). Extracted event logs were returned in JSON format. Moreover, to facilitate reproducibility and enable future corrections, each extracted event in the dataset was linked to the corresponding excerpt (`chunk`) from the original legal source. This design choice ensures that all procedural inferences remain fully traceable to their textual origin, thereby allowing for manual verification. Given the volume and complexity of the corpus, this is an essential feature.

Post-processing and Validation. Following the LLM-based extraction, we conducted a rigorous post-processing phase to ensure the accuracy and internal consistency of the event log. We found several errors. Notably, the vast majority of traced errors could not be attributed directly to the LLM's output. Instead, almost all detected anomalies originated from irregularities in the source material, such as typographical errors or formatting inconsistencies in the official legal texts. The post-processing activities included the *normalization of timestamps to minute-level resolution*, *validation of event labels against a fixed taxonomy*, and *correction of start and end markers* using PM techniques (via the pm4py library [11]), to name just a few. We also performed manual reviews to adjust for typographical errors in the original texts, and flagged any procedural trajectories that could not be reconstructed reliably. These records were excluded from the final dataset to preserve overall data quality.

4.2 A Case Study: Law No. 41/1987

As a concrete illustration of our pipeline, we examine Law No. 41/1987, which established the Sant'Anna School of Advanced Studies. This case demonstrates how complex legislative records can be converted into a structured event log.

Step 1: Raw Preparatory Works. We begin showing the preparatory works associated with the law, which we have crawled from Normattiva. In particular, we show a simplified and translated excerpt from these documents, which serves as the input to our extraction pipeline:

Chamber of Deputies (Bill No. 3780):
Presented by the Minister of Public Education (FALCUCCI) on May 21, 1986.
Assigned to the 8th Commission (Education), in a legislative session, on September 17, 1986, with opinions requested from the 1st and 5th Commissions.
Examined by the 8th Commission on December 11, 1986. Approved on December 18, 1986.

Senate of the Republic (Bill No. 2115):
Assigned to the 7th Commission (Public Education), in a deliberative session, on January 20, 1987, with opinions requested from the 1st and 5th Commissions.
Examined and approved by the 7th Commission on January 29, 1987.

Step 2: Extracted Event Log. Using our LLM-based extraction approach, we then convert the narrative text into a structured event log. We performed a number of iterations of prompt engineering trying to capture the essential procedural events such as presentations, commission assignments, discussions and approvals, along with associated metadata like dates, institutional actors, and commissions involved. For presentation reasons, we omit the actual prompt. The results obtained are shown in Table 1. We can see that each basic activity of the process has indeed been transformed into an actual event in the log.

Table 1. Extracted event log for Law No. 41/1987. Translated in English for presentation reasons

Date	Chamber	Activity	Commission	Actor
21/05/1986	Chamber of Deputies	Presentation	–	Minister Falcucci
17/09/1986	Chamber of Deputies	Assignment	8th Commission	–
17/09/1986	Chamber of Deputies	Request for Opinion	1st, 5th Commissions	–
11/12/1986	Chamber of Deputies	Examination	8th Commission	–
18/12/1986	Chamber of Deputies	Approval	8th Commission	–
20/01/1987	Senate	Assignment	7th Commission	–
20/01/1987	Senate	Request for Opinion	1st, 5th Commissions	–
29/01/1987	Senate	Examination	7th Commission	–
29/01/1987	Senate	Approval	7th Commission	–

Step 3: Process Visualization. Finally, we visualize the extracted sequence in a simplified process diagram (Fig. 2). Such visualizations can be obtained with virtually any PM tool, like e.g., pm4py or Disco. These graphical representations not only enhance interpretability for human analysts but also serves as a basis for downstream PM tasks such comparative analysis across legislative cases.

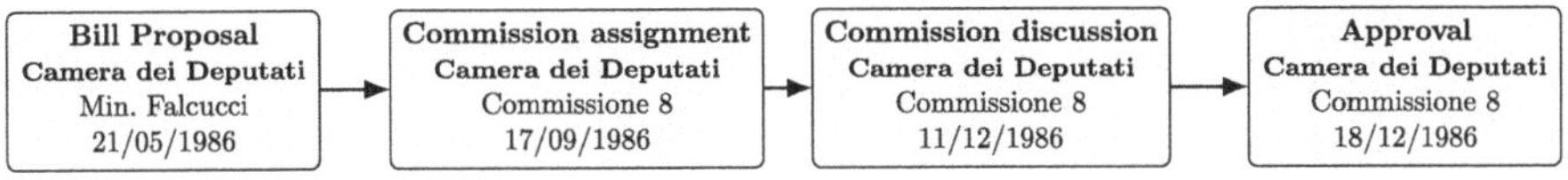

Fig. 2. Simplified process of Law No. 41/1987 establishing Sant'Anna School.

4.3 Dataset Description

The output of our pipeline is a structured dataset that captures both the substantive content (the metadata part of `ProLiFIC`) and the procedural history (the actual event log). It consists of two complementary components that can be linked via a shared identifier, `case_id`, which corresponds to the *codice redazionale* assigned to the law upon publication in the *Gazzetta Ufficiale*. Together, these components offer a rich foundation for both descriptive statistics and process mining analyses of lawmaking in the Italian Parliament, enabling researchers to trace legislative lifecycles, identify bottlenecks, and explore institutional dynamics across changing political configurations.

Metadata Part of ProLiFIC. Table 2 shows the attributes stored in the metadata. They include general information on each law, such as formal characteristics and dates. Notably, the straightforward structure of this component also allows for future extensions to include additional informative dimensions.

Table 2. Metadata attributes for each law. One row per law.

Attribute	Description
`case_id`	Unique identifier for the law
`title`	Official title of the law
`publishing_date`	Date of publication in the *Gazzetta Ufficiale*
`implementation_date`	Date the law takes effect
`decree_conversion`	Indicates if it's a decree-law conversion
`description`	Short summary of the law's purpose
`articles`	Number of articles in the law
`full_text_url`	Link to full legal text on Normattiva

Event Log part of `ProLiFIC`. Table 3 illustrates the information contained in this component, which captures the procedural trajectory of each law as a sequence of time-stamped events, all sharing the same case id, allowing for detailed reconstruction and analysis of the lawmaking process.

Table 3. Event log with all events of all laws. One row per event.

Attribute	Description
`case_id`	Unique identifier for the law
`activity`	Type of legislative action (e.g., proposal, approval)
`time`	Timestamp of the activity, with granularity given in days
`commission`	Commission involved in the event (if applicable)
`person`	Sponsor, speaker, or institutional actor
`chunk`	Extract of legal text or speech related to the activity
`chamber`	*Camera* or *Senato*
`legislature`	Legislative session number (XVIIXIX)
`government`	Executive in office at the time

5 Exploratory Data Analysis on Recent Legislatures

Here we shed further light on `ProLiFIC` by providing a picture of the data contained in four reference legislatures. In particular, we focus only on the most recent ones, namely XVI (2008–2013), XVII (20132018), XVIII (20182022), and XIX (2022March 2025), for a total of 1244 laws (both decree-laws and ordinary laws). We remark that, at the time of writing, legislature XIX has not concluded yet. Therefore, we have data for around 50% of its overall length.

Table 4. Legislative activity: counts and median duration by legislature. Median duration is shown separately for ordinary and decree laws.

Legislature	Laws *(total)*	% Decrees	Median Duration *(days)*	
			Ordinary	Decrees
XVI	373	30%	159	53
XVII	367	23%	375	54
XVIII	312	33%	413	54
XIX *(ongoing)*	192	38%	251	53

Table 4 shows, for each legislature, the total number of enacted laws (including the percentage of decree-laws) and the median duration of the legislative process, calculated as the number of days elapsed between the first and last recorded event in the law's procedural history.

These numbers reveal some meaningful patterns. While the total number of laws passed remains relatively stable across the four legislatures, their durations vary considerably. In particular, Legislature XVIII stands out for ordinary laws: while enacting a slightly lower, yet comparable number of laws, it shows a notably higher median duration for ordinary laws (413 days), nearly double that of Legislatures XVI and XIX. This pronounced delay raises important questions about potential procedural or political factors that may have contributed to the slowdown during that term, possibly related to the COVID-19 pandemic and the instability of parliamentary majorities.

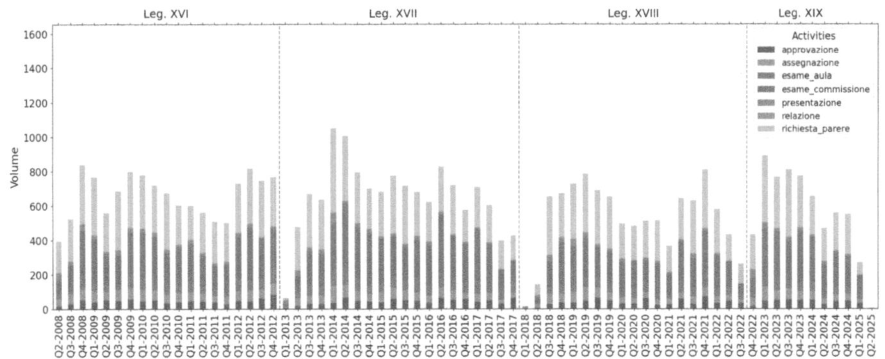

Fig. 3. Frequencies of events. Dashed lines separate the different legislatures.

This is further illustrated from a different perspective in Fig. 3. We analyze a disaggregated view of parliamentary activity, focusing on the volume of activities indicating "hops" between committees and chambers. The figure shows strong fluctuations in legislative intensity over time. While a comprehensive explanation of these trends lies beyond the scope of this paper, we highlight a few notable examples. The longer median durations observed during the COVID-19 period appear to coincide with a marked decline in legislative output. However, this may not be the primary factor explaining the most visible peaks. Similar slowdowns in other legislatures suggest that the heterogeneity of governing majorities and the fragmentation of the parties might offer another plausible explanation. E.g., a sharp increase is observed between the fourth quarter of 2013 and the first one of 2014, coinciding with the establishment of a strong and cohesive government majority. Conversely, the first two quarters of 2018 show a significant drop, reflecting a period of political instability.

Returning to Table 4, some notable insights emerge regarding decree-laws. First, there is a clear trend of increasing reliance on this legislative instrument, as evidenced by the growing percentage of decree-laws over time. Second, and perhaps more striking, is the remarkable consistency in their median duration across legislatures. In contrast to ordinary laws, the duration of decree-laws remains in fact consistent across legislatures. However, this is not surprising, as decree laws must be ratified by Parliament within 60 days of issuance, otherwise they become null. This reinforces the notion that different legislative issues follow distinct procedural path and highlights the value of examining not just how many laws are passed, but how they are processed. In the next section, we turn to PM techniques to investigate these procedural dynamics in greater depth, analyzing the structure and frequency of legislative activities.

6 Process Mining with Fluxicon Disco

To demonstrate the analytical potential of structuring legislative data as event logs, we used *Fluxicon Disco* [12], a leading PM tool. We reconstruct and compare the procedural paths of two major categories of legislation: ordinary legislative proposals and decree conversion laws.

Table 5. Comparison of ordinary laws and decree conversions by number.

Category	Variants	Median Duration
Ordinary laws	579	9.6 months
Decree conversions	370	54 days

Disco allows us to identify variants, i.e., process instances with the same events (ignoring timings), to measure durations, and to detect structural patterns. This is reported in Table 5. We see that ordinary laws follow a greater number of variants and exhibit significantly longer durations compared to decree conversions. This is consistent with what we expected, i.e., ordinary laws involve more iterative steps, suggesting a less streamlined and more deliberative process, while conversions of decrees are prioritised (indeed, they are required to be approved by Parliament within 60 days). Most interestingly, although the timelines differ significantly, the processes remain largely the same: the same activities are carried out, but at completely different paces. This is shown in the process maps obtained with Disco shown in Fig. 4. Disco allows setting *importance filters* to focus on more or less frequent/important activities (the boxes) and paths (actually, edges). In order to preserve all activities while focusing on only the most important relations, we have set 100% and 0% for activities and paths, respectively.

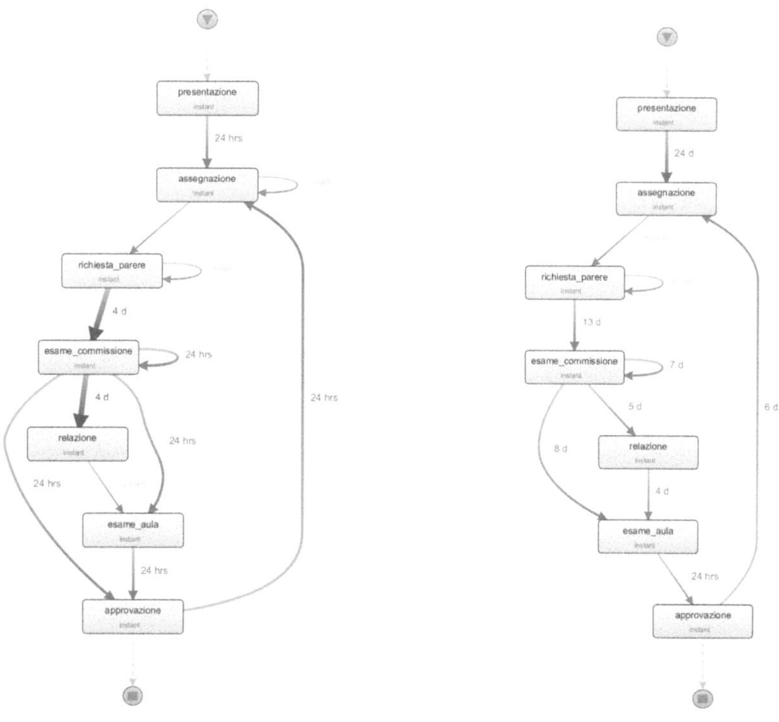

(a) Maps for decree conversion laws (b) Map for ordinary laws

Fig. 4. Disco's process maps showing median durations. We have set 100% and 0% as importance zoom for activities and paths, respectively.

Furthermore, we can visualize the differences in the work of the two chambers with the diagram in Fig. 5, where we have refined the first activity of laws (presentazione) by denoting whether it has been initiated by the Senate (Senato) or by the Chamber of Deputies (Camera). Then, using Disco's filters, we filtered for laws initiated in one of the two chambers only (not shown in the figure). We find out that there is no relevant divergence in the process of laws initiated in either chamber. Instead, it is important to note that, as shown in Fig. 5, the Senate is

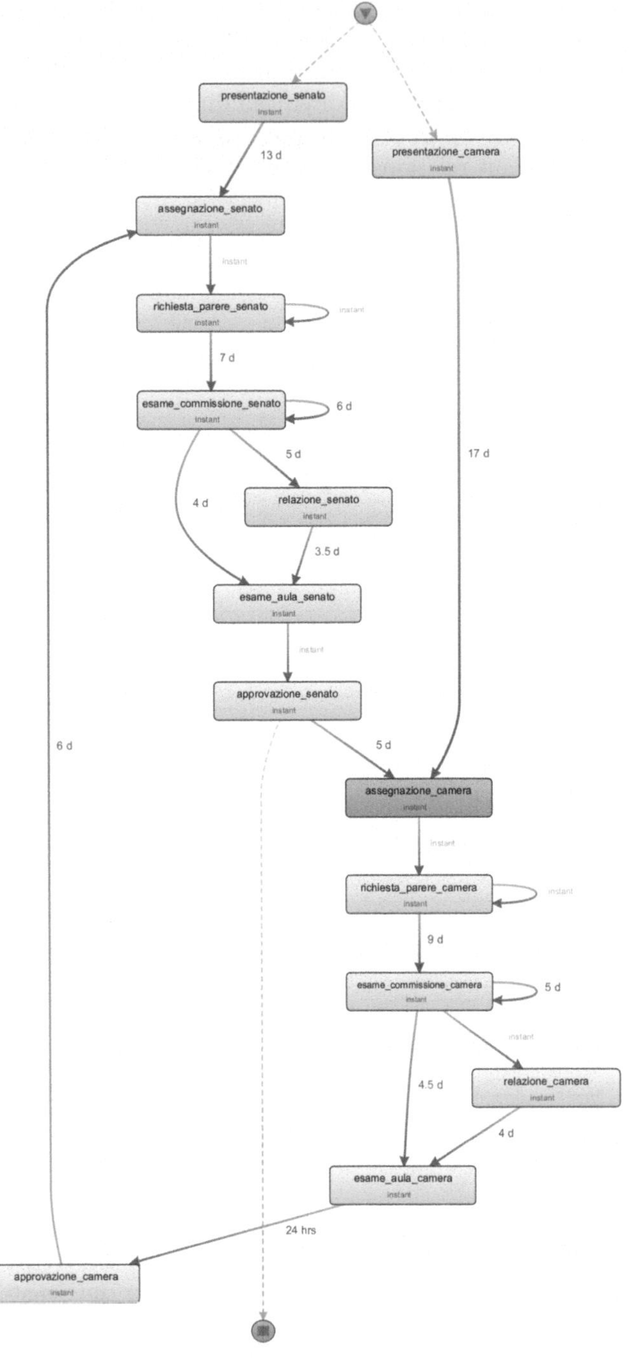

Fig. 5. Disco's process maps with median times and chamber-specific events. We have set 100% and 0% as importance zoom for activities and paths, respectively.

consistently more expedite than the Chamber in every step of the *iter legis* independently of the starting chamber. Studying the reasons of these asymmetries is beyond the scope of this work. Here we remark that, despite under perfect bicameralism the two organs have the same functions and prerogatives, they do differ in: Internal Rules of Procedures; Active and passive electorate (minimum 25 and 40 years old to be elected in the Chamber and Senate, respectively – until 2021, minimum 25 years old to vote for the Senate, now uniformed to the minimum voting age of 18); Numbers, 200 Senators (315 before 2020) and 400 Honourables (630 before 2020). Further analyses on such divergence could be carried out using ProLiFIC. We plan to do it in future works.

7 Conclusions

We presented ProLiFIC (*Procedural Lawmaking Flow in Italian Chambers*), an event log of preparatory works of Italian laws, together with preliminary exploratory data and Process Mining analyses. We built and applied an LLM-based pipeline to unstructured texts from the Normattiva portal, extracting structured event logs capturing the Italian lawmaking process for 1985–2025. We discussed the methodological challenges in the creation and curation of the dataset.

The preliminary analyses allowed us to address two research questions of interest to the Law and Political Science: **(RQ1)** *How does the legislative process differ between ordinary laws and decree conversions?* and **(RQ2)** *How do procedural trajectories vary between the Chamber of Deputies and the Senate?* Although preliminary, our findings reveal meaningful patterns in both cases, demonstrating that this type of data can support substantive empirical research.

Beyond these initial insights, the dataset establishes a foundation for more comprehensive investigations into legislative behavior, institutional dynamics, and the temporal structure of lawmaking.

Future Work. On the dataset side, we plan to extend its coverage and enhance its richness by incorporating additional dimensions from complementary sources. E.g., we aim to explore the feasibility of linking each law to its corresponding policy domain, enabling domain-specific analyses. We will also improve and systematize the validation of the dataset. A revised version of the dataset is presented here [22]. We may also consider a wider domain, e.g., European Laws. On the analysis side, we plan to extend our PM analyses using conformance checking techniques (e.g., [23]), moving beyond the visual exploration enabled by Discos maps. To support this, we will integrate the PM4Py library into our analytical workflow. More in general, we will deepen the presented analyses, e.g., by explaining the reasons behind the discovered asymmetries in the performance of the two chambers, and by further analysing the impact of COVID.

Acknowledgments. The work has been partially supported by project SMaRT COnSTRUCT (CUP J53C24001460006), in the context of FAIR (PE0000013, CUP B53C22003630006) under the National Recovery and Resilience Plan (Mission 4, Component 2, Line of Investment 1.3) funded by EU - NextGenerationEU.

References

1. Capano, G., Giuliani, M.: Governing without surviving? An Italian paradox: law-making in Italy, 1987–2001. J. Legislative Stud. **7**(4), 13–36 (2001)
2. Kreppel, A.: The impact of parties in government on legislative output in Italy. Eur J Polit Res **31**(3), 327–349 (1997)
3. Borghetto, E., Giuliani, M.: A long way to Tipperary: time in the Italian legislative process 1987–2008. South Eur. Soc. Polit. **17**(1), 23–44 (2012)
4. Meneghetti, N., et al.: Predicting party switching through machine learning and open data. iScience **26**(7), 107098 (2023)
5. van der Aalst, W.: Process Mining: Data Science in Action (2016)
6. Presidenza del Consiglio dei Ministri: Normattiva. https://www.normattiva.it/
7. Borghetto, E., Curini, L., Giuliani, M., Pellegata, A., Zucchini, F.: Italian law-making archive (ILMA): a new tool for the analysis of the Italian legislative process. Rivista Italiana di Scienza Politica **3** (2012)
8. Reh, C., Héritier, A., Bressanelli, E., Koop, C.: The informal politics of legislation: explaining secluded decision making in the European union. Comp. Polit. Stud. **46**(9), 1112–1142 (2013)
9. Caponecchia, V., D'Agostino, B., Comandè, G., Licari, D., Vandin, A.: Towards visualizing and analysing legal proceedings with process mining. In: Proceedings of PLC 2024, co-located with ICPM 2024. Volume 3850 of CEUR, 46–57 (2024)
10. Caponecchia, V., D'Agostino, B.S.A.S., Comandè, G., Licari, D., Vandin, A.: Process mining for legal courts: visualising, analysing and comparing Italian divorce proceedings. Comput. Law Secur. Rev. (2025)
11. Berti, A., van Zelst, S.J., van der Aalst, W.M.P.: Process mining for python (PM4Py): bridging the gap between process- and data science. CoRR (2019)
12. Günther, C.W., Rozinat, A.: Disco: discover your processes. In: BPM Demo (2012)
13. Sànchez-Ferreres, J., Burattin, A., Carmona, J., Montali, M., Padró, L., Quishpi Betun, L: Unleashing textual descriptions of business processes. Softw. Syst. Model. **20** (2021)
14. Berti, A., Schuster, D., van der Aalst, W.M.P.: Abstractions, scenarios, and prompt definitions for process mining with LLMs: a case study (2023)
15. Berti, A., Kourani, H., van der Aalst, W.M.P.: PM-LLM-benchmark: evaluating large language models on process mining tasks. In: PM Workshops (2025)
16. Berti, A., van der Aalst, W.M.P.: CSV-PM-LLM-parsing: automatic ingestion of CSV event logs for process mining using LLMs. In: BPM Demo (2024)
17. López, H.: Challenges in legal process discovery. In: ITBPM, pp. 68–73. CEUR (2021)
18. Bartole, S., Bin, R., Pitruzzella, G.: Diritto costituzionale: profili teorici ed evoluzione giurisprudenziale. Giappichelli, Torino (2022)
19. Redi, C.: Il decreto-legge: strumento di legislazione "straordinariamente ordinaria". In: Osservatorio sulle fonti – Speciale Decreto-Legge (2014)
20. Lolli, I., et al.: Decreti-legge e disegni di legge: il governo e la'sua'maggioranza. Osservatorio sulle fonti (3), 1–59 (2016)
21. Morosini, M.: L'attuazione del diritto dell'eu nel più recente periodo: legge di delegazione europea e legge europea alla luce della prassi applicativa. Osservatorio sulle fonti – The Implementation of EU Law in Member States 2 (2017)
22. Contestabile, M., Ferrara, C., Giovannetti, A., Parrillo, G., Vandin, A.: The ProLiFIC dataset: leveraging LLMs to UNVEIL the Italian lawmaking process (2025)
23. Incerto, E., Vandin, A., Ahrabi, S.S.: Stochastic conformance checking based on variable-length Markov chains. Inf. Syst. **133**, 102561 (2025)

Understanding Feature Contributions to Remaining Time Prediction in Judicial Processes

Musa Salamov[1(✉)], Marlon Dumas[2], and Barbara Pernici[1]

[1] Politecnico di Milano, Milan, Italy
{musa.salamov,barbara.pernici}@polimi.it
[2] University of Tartu, Tartu, Estonia
marlon.dumas@ut.ee

Abstract. Providing accurate estimates of time-to-resolution of legal cases contributes to building trust in judicial systems. However, this task is challenging due to the temporal variability of legal proceedings and the multitude of factors influencing the time to resolution. While machine learning methods for remaining-time prediction have been extensively studied in the context of business processes, their application to judicial processes remains underexplored. A key component of remaining time prediction methods is the set of features used to train the machine learning models. In this study, we investigate the predictive power of different feature sets for estimating the time-to-resolution of legal cases in the specific context of Italian courts. We conduct an ablation study to evaluate the contribution of five categories of features: control-flow (activity sequences), temporal context, case attributes, global process state, and judge workload. The results show that, while case attributes alone perform poorly, combining them with state and temporal context significantly enhances the predictive performance. This combination achieves a mean absolute error (MAE) within an acceptable range for practical use, underscoring the value of integrating procedural and contextual information in predictive models for judicial processes.

Keywords: process mining · judicial processes · remaining time predictions

1 Introduction

The efficiency of judicial systems is essential, as it ensures the delivery of justice and plays a vital role in maintaining individual rights and trust in public institutions. The European Union (EU) emphasizes the importance of timely case resolution, the quality and independence of the judiciary, and the effectiveness of judicial systems. These factors are considered crucial for the proper enforcement of EU law [8]. In this context, the CEPEJ Evaluation Report [5] provides a comprehensive analysis of judicial systems across Europe. The report highlights

I. van de Weerd et al. (Eds.): BPM 2025 Workshops, LNBIP 569, pp. 531–546, 2026.
https://doi.org/10.1007/978-3-032-13426-4_39

substantial differences among member states in terms of institutional budgets, the number of justice professionals, and case resolution performance. Although Italy has shown measurable improvements in judicial efficiency between 2020 and 2022 [8], it still ranks among the slowest systems in Europe in terms of the estimated time needed to resolve cases. These delays particularly appear in civil proceedings. Furthermore, Italy has one of the highest shares of second-instance cases pending for over two years, underscoring challenges in its appellate courts.
In the context of addressing inefficiencies, Process Mining (PM) is a promising data-driven approach for analyzing end-to-end processes and extracting meaningful insights about their execution and performance [1]. While originally developed for business applications, where processes are often well-structured and temporally consistent, PM has since been applied in different fields such as healthcare, logistics, and manufacturing [9,17]. In contrast, judicial processes, especially in civil domains, are often associated with far greater temporal and procedural variability. For instance, in the banking sector, workflows like loan origination (as in the BPIC 2017 dataset [6]) are typically completed within 30 to 60 days. Procurement processes such as Purchase-to-Pay (e.g., BPIC 2019 [7]) show slightly higher variability but still resolve the vast majority of cases within six months. However, judicial proceedings, such as those from the Brazilian Court system, frequently extend well beyond a year, with only around 30% of cases resolved within six months [23]. The situation is even more severe in Italian courts, where case durations can be significantly prolonged, resulting in highly unpredictable timelines. Moreover, although judicial processes are under legal frameworks that are intended to standardize procedures, they often demonstrate high control-flow variability, with complex, non-linear execution paths. This is due to case-specific factors, difficult judicial decisions, and interactions among multiple actors [18]. Interactions with external stakeholders usually require more time, and decisions that require additional documents or information also demand more time and effort. These characteristics make judicial processes substantially more complex to analyze and predict compared to workflows in more structured domains.
Considering the high temporal and control-flow variability observed in judicial processes, there is a clear need to identify the key factors that influence the time required to resolve a case. Understanding these factors is also essential for court stakeholders, who can leverage such insights to make more informed decisions about resource allocation and procedural adjustments. In the context of predictive process monitoring, several studies have examined prediction methods in the judicial domain [15,24]. In contrast to prior work, we conduct an ablation study by systematically training a model on different subsets of features to assess their individual and combined contributions to the predictive performance.
This work is structured as follows. Section 2 reviews related work in the field. Section 3 provides background on the data, organizational context, domain-specific knowledge, and data preprocessing steps. A methodology, including the sets of features explored and the rationale behind the chosen approach, is given

in Sect. 4, which is followed by the evaluation and results in Sect. 5. Finally, Sect. 6 summarizes the key findings and outlines directions for future research.

2 Related Work

Efficient time-to-resolution is one of the main concerns in the judiciary. There have been several efforts aimed at addressing different aspects of judicial proceedings [18,20,24]. A novel deep learning-based approach [20] shows that predictions for law articles can potentially help to reduce the workload of judges. Pernici et al. [18] utilize data mining techniques and highlight the potential to improve inefficiencies in the court by enabling better management of judge distribution. The study on lawsuit process duration in Brazil [24] application of machine learning and process mining techniques to judiciary and highlights the importance of clustering features for predicting case durations. Oliveira et al. [15] discuss machine learning techniques for predicting the number of days in court cases and reveal that AdaBoost outperforms other methods for this task. These studies collectively demonstrate how AI-based and data-driven approaches can support and enhance legal processes.

Predictive process monitoring [4] primarily focuses on three prediction targets: process outcomes, the next activity, and time-related aspects such as the timestamp of the next event or the remaining duration of the case. In this paper, we focus on exploring the feature sets that can be used in the context of predicting remaining time in the judiciary. Although there has been previous work [25,27] that focuses on comparing the performance of different machine learning algorithms, our aim is to analyze which features contribute most significantly to predictive performance.

We acknowledge that there is a substantial body of related work in this area. Models like CatBoost and LSTM have previously been utilized to predict remaining time or similar process outcomes [3]. State of the art consistently finds that ensemble methods, particularly those derived from XGBoost (including CatBoost), tend to outperform traditional models such as SVMs [21,22], and often achieve performance comparable to neural network-based approaches like LSTMs. Vercose et al. [24] compare DART and SVMs in the context of lawsuit process duration; however, our aim is not to conduct a comparative evaluation of machine learning models. Instead, we assume a reasonably effective learning method (CatBoost) is in place and focus on evaluating which types of features can meaningfully enhance model performance. In our work, we aim to expand on the current state-of-the-art by exploring the importance of different types of features and their relevance in the remaining time predictions in the judiciary context.

3 Organizational Context and Data Description

In this section, we provide an overview of the organizational context, the data source, and the high-level pre-processing activities undertaken, in order to contextualize the case study.

3.1 Metadata About Trials

The dataset used in this case study was obtained from SICID, the District Information System on Civil Litigation. The dataset comprises records of judicial cases from the Milan Court of Appeal, including detailed information such as the sequence of procedural steps, the (anonymized) assigned judge, event dates, and categorical attributes such as case category and legal section. All historical records contained in the system are confidential and are not intended for public disclosure.

An *event* in the dataset represents procedural steps—discrete actions taken during the course of each case. Alongside these events, cases are also described by distinct phases, referred to as states in this context. A *state* is particularly useful for assessing the advancement of a case and estimating its proximity to resolution. The acquired records store all events, states, and cases with uniquely assigned identifiers, accompanied by descriptive metadata. These descriptions are examined during data analysis to provide contextual understanding.

3.2 Data Cleaning

Cases with missing data or inconsistent timestamps were excluded from the dataset, as the remaining number of cases was sufficient for training and testing purposes. All filtering steps were applied after joining different tables based on the case, event, state identifiers. Given that the number of recorded events and the average case duration were significantly lower toward the end of the dataset, these later cases were excluded from the analysis, in line with the recommendations provided by Weytjens et al. [26].

Context-Aware Data Cleaning: Since the focus of this study is on civil trials, the cases were selected from the five court sections relevant to civil jurisdiction. Trials were selected based on the procedural classification assigned by the system, specifically those marked with the code 4O, as it represents the general procedure for the Court of Appeal cases.
Identifying completed cases was essential for evaluating the predictive performance of the machine learning models. For incomplete cases, assessing the prediction error is not feasible due to the unavailability of actual outcome values. Drawing on domain knowledge, ten distinct states were identified as indicators of case resolution. Consequently, only events occurring up to these states were retained in the dataset. Additionally, events occurring after the final states were examined and found not to have an impact on the actual verdict , often involving minor updates or supplementary notes. Therefore, events following the first event of the final state were excluded from the dataset.
Finally, cases containing only a single recorded event—whether a final event or a supplementary note—were also excluded from the dataset, as they did not accurately represent the complete historical sequence of events within the case. These single-event cases typically represented instances where the case had already

been closed before the start of the logging period, and an annotation was added afterward either to reflect updates or to document missing information.

Table 1. Summary of data statistics after cleaning

Statistic	Value
Number of cases	23,549
Number of events	471,182
Number of unique events	236
Average case duration (days)	412.34
Maximum case duration (days)	1,827
Number of unique judges	104
Number of unique states	58

Table 1 summarizes the dataset statistics after the data cleaning steps described above. The final dataset comprises 23,549 cases, which provides a sufficient volume for training predictive models. However, the presence of 236 unique events (activities) indicates a high level of process variability. Additionally, the average case duration of 412.34 days, with a maximum duration of 1,827 days, underscores the importance of developing predictive models for estimating remaining time in Italian civil trials. The cleaned dataset spans cases recorded between February 1, 2015, and March 31, 2023. During this period, a total of 104 unique judges were assigned to active cases, while 58 unique states of the process were available. It is worth noting that some of these judges may have retired, moved to other court sections, or otherwise discontinued their service during the observed period of time.

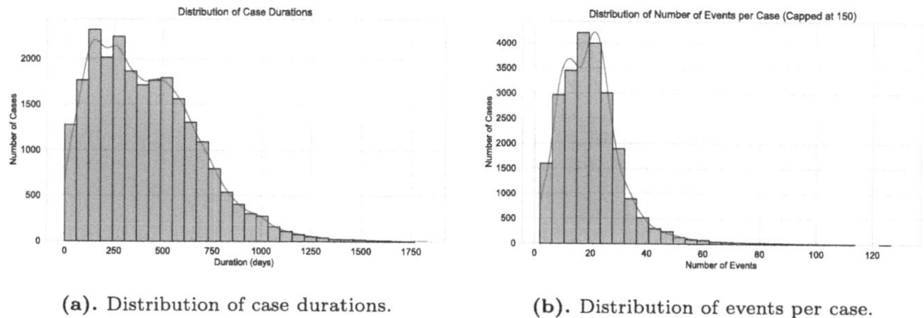

(a). Distribution of case durations. **(b).** Distribution of events per case.

Fig. 1. Descriptive statistics for trial cases.

Figure 1a shows the distribution of case durations, revealing a substantial number of cases that extended beyond 750 days. This visualization illustrates the significant temporal variability within the dataset effectively, with the median case duration exceeding six months. Similarly, Fig. 1b captures the procedural complexity of the cases, as indicated by the number of events recorded per case.

4 Approach

This section outlines and justifies the approach used to construct machine learning models for predicting remaining time.

In line with previous work [25], we train a regressor that, given a prefix of a case, returns an estimated remaining time. To train this regressor from a training set consisting of completed traces of a process, we extract all the strict prefixes from these traces, and we map each strict prefix into a feature vector.

We then train a regression model, using CatBoost, a high-performing state-of-the-art ensemble method [21]. It is particularly well-suited for handling categorical features and achieves competitive performance, often comparable to deep learning models, while retaining greater interpretability.

To construct the feature vectors, we selected a list of feature sets based on two criteria: the availability of information in judicial event logs, and the inclusion of commonly used feature types that are applicable across domains in process mining. The main goal was to determine what is the relative accuracy that each of these feature sets brings to the predictions.

Table 2. Feature Sets

Feature Set	Description
Control flow	Frequency or clustering-based encoding of events in a case
Case attributes	Category of a case and section of the court
State features	Aggregated number of events in a given common state
Inter-case features	Work-in-progress features aggregated by state and section of the court
Judge workload	Workload of a judge on a given date of a trace
Temporal features	Weekday, week number, month number, time since the last event, elapsed time

Table 2 describes which set of features have been chosen for the model training and comparison of results.

- **Control Flow:** To construct this feature set, the total number of occurrences in each sub-trace was aggregated for the 50 most frequent events. Although this representation does not preserve the order of events, it provides a compact summary of event frequency. Given the high number of unique events in the dataset (see Table 1), limiting the features to the top 50 ensures a manageable and efficient input size for the model. Additionally, we experimented with encoding based on the last two events and clusters, which represent events that tend to appear in similar positions within traces. The encoding of last two events was simply added as two additional features to the trace vector.

For clustering, we created a co-occurrence matrix of activities based on how frequently they appear next to each other. Then, K-Means was applied to identify clusters of activities with similar co-occurrence patterns, dividing them into 10 groups. In the trace vector, this introduced 10 additional features that capture control flow.

- **Case attributes:** Each case is associated with a specific court section and categorized accordingly. Additionally, a judge is assigned to oversee the case. Therefore, these three features—court section, case category, and judge ID are selected as the case-level attributes.
- **State features:** One of the key differences that makes the justice dataset unique is the inclusion of *states* that represent the status of a case. Due to the large number of distinct events, event-level frequency encoding is not suitable. Instead, this feature set includes frequency-based encodings of the most common and legally significant states relevant to judicial proceedings, ensuring a more manageable and meaningful representation, which also aligns with the advantages of the stage-based approach [14].
- **Inter-case features:** Given that the judicial process is structured into states, we adopt a state-based approach to represent inter-case variables. The number of active cases as per the most common states was computed for each trace in the trace vector. This reflects work in progress (WIP), aligning with the recommendation by Senderovich et al. [19], who emphasize the importance of WIP to capture the load and resource constraints. However, unlike their activity level encoding, we decided to calculate WIP, the number of active cases, at state level, as well as based on the sections of the court. This choice reduces feature dimensionality while still preserving essential information.
- **Judge workload:** The workload of judges was frequently highlighted by court officials as a key factor potentially influencing case duration. Although this constitutes an inter-case feature, since it was already expected to have an impact by the officials, we treated it as a distinct category due to its specific relevance.
- **Temporal features:** Oyamada et al. [16] propose a set of time-related features which enhance the performance of predictive process monitoring models. We selected a subset which are relevant to the context of the court trials in Italy, such as weekday, week number, and month number. These are considered to be especially relevant because of the holidays in Italy (e.g., extended holidays in August).

5 Evaluation

We assessed the impact of individual feature sets through an ablation-inspired methodology, drawing on the concept of ablation [13], where components of a neural network are systematically removed to evaluate their contribution. In contrast, our approach follows a bottom-up strategy: instead of removing features, we begin with a minimal baseline set and incrementally add additional feature sets. At each step, we evaluate the predictive performance of the model, allowing us to observe how different combinations of features influence the accuracy of remaining time predictions.

Hyperparameter Ranges. Table 3 shows the main details of the model and hyperparameter optimization. We applied Tree-Structured Parzen Estimator (TPE) variant of Bayesian optimization via Hyperopt [2] library.

Table 3. CatBoost Model Parameters

Parameter	Default Value	Optimization Range
`iterations`	1000	{100, 300, 500}
`learning_rate`	0.1	[0.01, 0.3] (uniform)
`depth`	6	{4, 6, 8, 10}
`l2_leaf_reg`	3.0	[1, 10] (uniform)

Data Split. To construct the training and test datasets, we applied a strict temporal split [26], including only cases completed before the split timestamp in the training set, which comprised 80% of the data. This approach ensures the model is trained only on past information, preventing data leakage. It also simulates a real-world scenario, where the predictions have to be made for unseen cases.

Goodness Measure. As we predict the remaining time for each sub-trace at a given event date, Mean Absolute Error (MAE) is used, because it provides intuitive interpretability in terms of prediction error in days. It is both relevant and readily understandable for stakeholders within the judiciary. Throughout the paper, MAE values are presented in days.

Baselines. The main evaluation is conducted using a baseline model incorporating only case attributes. The model trained with case attributes is selected as a baseline because it serves as a more meaningful and domain-relevant baseline, considering that it conveys organizational context with domain-specific categorical values. It is particularly important in the judiciary, as the section of the court, the judge of the case, category of the case can influence the trial outcome and have a potential impact on the predictions. Additionally, we also adopted a random regressor as a naive benchmark, making predictions by sampling from the empirical distribution of remaining time values observed in the training data. This provides a reference point for understanding how well more informed models perform in comparison to purely random guessing.

Results. Table 4 reports the Mean Absolute Error (MAE) of predicted remaining times by predictive models trained on different sets of features.

Table 4. MAE comparison of feature sets for remaining time prediction.

Feature Set	Approach	MAE
Control Flow	Events	103.92
	Clusters	112.09
	Last Two Events	110.10
Case Attributes (baseline)	–	140.56
State Features	–	116.28
Inter-case	–	138.63
Judge Workload	–	135.27
Temporal Features	–	117.99
All Features	–	**110.41**

The results of experimenting with three different encodings for the control flow feature set show that using frequency encoding for the most common 50 events yields the best result at 103.92 days. While the difference between clustering and the last two events encoding is lower by comparison. Despite providing arguably the most important domain knowledge for the cases, case attributes (e.g., category of the case) perform the worst, with a MAE of 140.56 days.

Figure 2 shows how much each feature in the feature sets contributed to the prediction in terms of SHAP[1] values [12]. Despite their low standalone performance, categorical case attributes such as case category and judge ID exhibit high SHAP impact. Mainly because they lack contextual signals provided by temporal and control flow features, the overall performance of this feature set is relatively low.

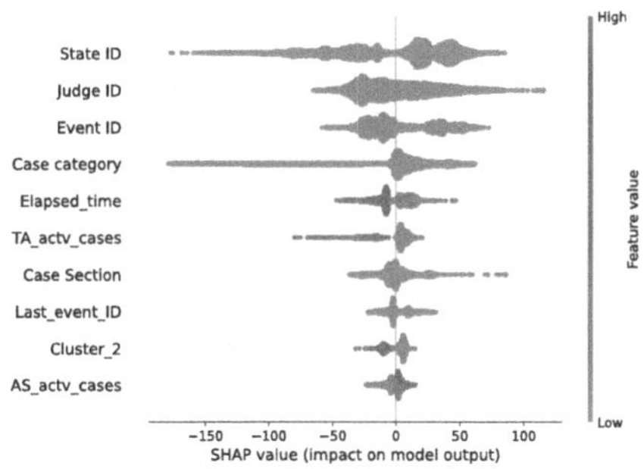

Fig. 2. SHAP values in the model with all features

It is worth mentioning that the number of features in this set is lower than in all other feature sets, with the exception of judge workload. The judge workload feature set, despite having the fewest features, outperforms the case attributes feature set. State features and temporal features both seem to have similar performance. Overall, training the predictive model with features from all feature sets performs reasonably well, however, it does not provide the best predictions. [1]

Considering the result of the random regressor is 205.64 days, training the model with all features performs approximately 46% better, while the best control flow feature set produces approximately 49% better performance. Furthermore, both the model with all features and the best control flow feature set outperform the baseline trained only on case attributes, with improvements of approximately 21.5% and 26.0% respectively.

According to our bottom-up ablation study strategy, we add one different feature set to our baseline model at a time and evaluate the impact. Figure 3 reports each step executed and the respective results.

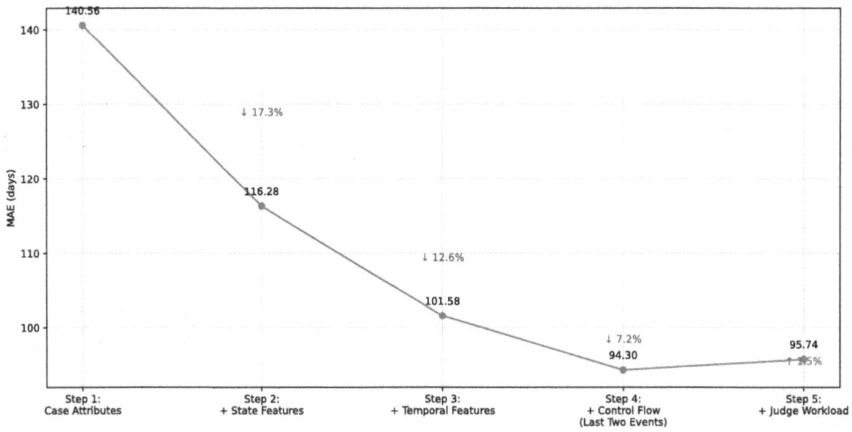

Fig. 3. Steps in the ablation study.

Step 1. As mentioned, in the first step, we started with the baseline model trained with only case attributes, at 140.56 days of MAE.

[1] SHAP (SHapley Additive exPlanations) is a method for interpreting model outputs by quantifying the contribution of each feature to the prediction.

Step 2. States in the judicial process in the Court of Appeal of Milan are another substantial piece of information that gives stakeholders an understanding of the status of the case. Thus, we added state features in the second step. It essentially improved the performance of the predictive model; however, it did not top either the model with all features or the one with control flow features, despite improving the predictions by 17.3%. This is quite expected, considering the input of domain knowledge and the importance of states in the Court of Appeal of Milan.

Step 3. In the next step, temporal and inter-case features were incorporated. Temporal features contributed to a performance improvement of 12.8%, whereas the addition of inter-case features increased the prediction error, resulting in an MAE of 123.22 days. Thus, we selected to utilize only the combination of case attributes, state, and temporal features, which produced an MAE of 101.58 days and already outperformed both the models with all features and with control flow features. One can notice that while the performance of models with these three feature sets separately was not exactly promising, the combination of these feature sets can outperform the initially best-performing models.

Step 4. The addition of the control flow feature set, based on the top 50 most frequent events, clustering, and the last two event encoding, resulted in errors of 99.04, 98.69, and 94.3 days, respectively. Although the frequency-based encoding of the most common events performs well separately, it did not help improve the predictions; on the contrary, it worsened them. Furthermore, it shows that the performance gap between using 50 features and 10 clusters which represent the same control flow in similar ways, becomes less obvious once more features are introduced into the CatBoost regressor. Additionally, noticeable improvement of performance while only introducing two new features of the last two events (one feature for last, another for second last event), shows the importance of maintaining the optimal number of features to be trained, while keeping enough contextual information. Furthermore, it shows that the difference between using 50 features and 10 clusters, which both represent the same control flow in similar ways, becomes less significant once more features are introduced into the CatBoost regressor. Additionally, the noticeable improvement in performance from introducing only two new features based on the last event encoding highlights the importance of maintaining an optimal number of features.

Step 5. Last but not least, the workload of judges is another factor that is interesting to the Court of Appeal of Milan. Considering that the decision authority in legal cases lies with the judges and the volume of incoming cases, the impact is anticipated by the court. However, adding the workload of judges to the model made the predictions slightly worse, with an MAE of 95.74 days. This suggests that the number of cases does not represent the workload of a judge solely, as, depending on the case complexity, the duration needed for resolution might be longer even when the number of active cases assigned to a judge is limited. With that being said, we should not overlook the possibility that the information may already be captured by the algorithm through other feature sets.

Figure 4 shows the MAE in days for each event position based on predictions from the best predictive model obtained in step 4.

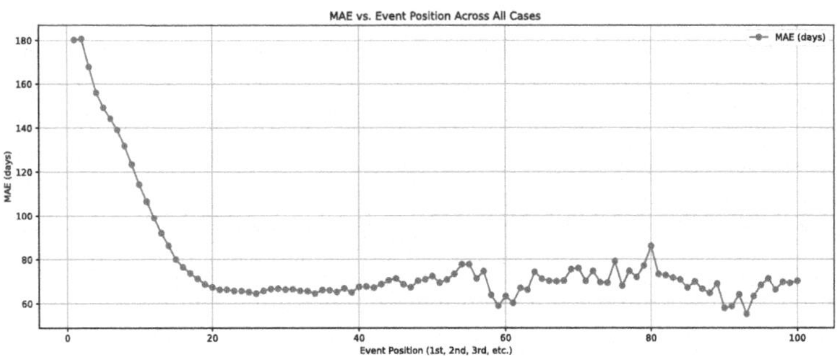

Fig. 4. MAE by Event Position in Case Timeline.

One can notice that the predictions are much less accurate during the first several events within a case. It also shows that prediction accuracy fluctuates after a certain number of events and becomes less reliable. This can be explained by the high temporal variability of judicial processes and the fact that a greater number of events in a case may also indicate increased case complexity. Furthermore, the MAE fluctuation at higher event positions is likely to be influenced by the number of cases with a high number of events, because the cases that have more than 40 events represent only about 4.2% of the total cases in the predictions.

Threats to Validity. We acknowledge that the findings of this study potentially suffer from the limitations that are common to case studies. First, the results are based on data from a single organization, and therefore may not be generalizable to other organizations or settings. Second, for predictive model, we only use CatBoost, which is widely recognized and high-performing ensemble algorithm. The relative predictive power of the feature sets might be different when using other models such as LSTM or XGBoost. Moreover, the relatively narrow search space used for hyperparameter optimization might have prevented the discovery of optimal settings. Lastly, although some effort was made to validate the relevance of selected features in consultation with domain experts, the detailed design and selection of features was primarily driven by an analysis of the data by the researchers of this study.

6 Conclusion

This study systematically evaluated the importance of feature sets on the predictive models to predict remaining time for judicial processes, where the temporal variability is notably high. With the main focus on the cases from a Court of Appeal in Italy, and through a series of ablation experiments, we found that no single feature group was sufficient on its own. However, the combination of case attributes, state and temporal features, and control flow (last two events) yielded a substantial reduction in prediction error, achieving the best overall MAE of 94.3 days. Essentially, although the error is relatively high, it is still useful and acceptable in the court, since the main planning is done based on semesters. Thus, errors below six months are somewhat acceptable for certain decisions, like planning activities and assigning judges. While a set of case attributes performed poorly on its own, it provided valuable input when combined with contextual information from other feature sets. State and temporal features notably improved the predictions for the remaining time, aligning with the domain knowledge about procedural stages and timelines in legal processes. The results of this work suggest that designing feature sets aligned with domain knowledge is potentially more valuable than relying on individual features selected purely through statistical methods without contextual understanding. Furthermore, we found that some domain-driven hypotheses did not influence the results as expected. For example, we had hypothesized that the workload of the judge (measured by the number of cases handled) has impact, but this was not supported by the results.

Future work. In this study, we found that the feature capturing the workload of the judge (number of active cases handled by the judge) did not add accuracy to the final predictive model. A promising direction for future work is to investigate more fine-grained encoding of the workload of judges, for example, by distinguishing between different types of cases. For example, incorporating the number of cases a judge handles by category (e.g., type A, type B, etc.) could provide more contextual information. If simpler cases take less time and lead to a higher number of active cases, then a larger workload does not necessarily imply more remaining time, as a few complex cases may require more time than several simple ones. Another direction could be to study the applicability of techniques for encoding resource experience (in this case, previous experience of the current judge), using, for example, the techniques proposed in the study by Kim et al. [11].

Existing methods for remaining time prediction in business processes focus on providing point estimates, e.g. "the case will be resolved in 60 days". Recent studies in the field of customer service have shown that users prefer range estimates. e.g. "the case will be resolved in 50 to 75 days" [10]. Accordingly, another avenue for future work is to extend the evaluation methods for producing range estimates of time-to-resolution and to empirically evaluate if stakeholders in judicial processes would find such range estimates more useful than point estimates. Additionally, in future work, we aim to explore different starting points for feature set selection, as well as adaptations of proposed approach to other legal systems.

Source code. All the source code required to replicating this study on other datasets is available at https://github.com/musaslmv/judiciary-ppm-feature-contributions.git. The dataset used in this study cannot be made publicly available due to confidentiality requirements imposed by data protection laws.

Acknowledgments. Research supported by a PhD scholarship funded under the Italian National Recovery and Resilience Plan (PNRR), I.4.1–ublic Administration.

References

1. van der Aalst, W.: Process mining: overview and opportunities. ACM Trans. Manage. Inf. Syst. **3**(2) (2012). https://doi.org/10.1145/2229156.2229157
2. Bergstra, J., Yamins, D., Cox, D.: Making a science of model search: Hyperparameter optimization in hundreds of dimensions for vision architectures. In: Dasgupta, S., McAllester, D. (eds.) Proceedings of the 30th International Conference on Machine Learning. Proceedings of Machine Learning Research, vol. 28, pp. 115–123. PMLR, Atlanta, Georgia, USA (2013). https://proceedings.mlr.press/v28/bergstra13.html
3. Cao, R., et al.: Business process remaining time prediction using explainable reachability graph from gated RNNs. Appl. Intell. **53**(11), 13178–13191 (2022). https://doi.org/10.1007/s10489-022-04192-x
4. Ceravolo, P., Comuzzi, M., De Weerdt, J., Di Francescomarino, C., Maggi, F.M.: Predictive process monitoring: concepts, challenges, and future research directions. Process Sci. **1**(2) (2024). https://doi.org/10.1007/s44311-024-00002-4. Accessed 27 Sept 2024
5. Council of Europe: European Judicial Systems CEPEJ Evaluation Report. Council of Europe (2024). printed at the Council of Europe
6. van Dongen, B.: BPI challenge 2017 (2017). https://doi.org/10.4121/uuid:5f3067df-f10b-45da-b98b-86ae4c7a310b
7. van Dongen, B.: BPI challenge 2019 (2019). https://doi.org/10.4121/uuid:d06aff4b-79f0-45e6-8ec8-e19730c248f1. dataset
8. European Commission: Eu justice scoreboard (2024). https://commission.europa.eu/strategy-and-policy/policies/justice-and-fundamental-rights/upholding-rule-law/eu-justice-scoreboard_en. Accessed 06 June 2024
9. Garcia, C.D.S., et al.: Process mining techniques and applications a systematic mapping study. Expert Syst. Appl. **133**, 260–295 (2019). https://doi.org/10.1016/j.eswa.2019.05.003
10. Hu, B., Gaertig, C., Dietvorst, B.J.: How should time estimates be structured to increase customer satisfaction? Manag. Sci. (2024). https://doi.org/10.1287/mnsc.2023.00137. Online First
11. Kim, J., Comuzzi, M., Dumas, M., Maggi, F.M., Teinemaa, I.: Encoding resource experience for predictive process monitoring. Decision Support Systems **153**, 113669 (2022)
12. Marc Lio, W.E., Eler, D.M.: From explanations to feature selection: assessing SHAP values as feature selection mechanism. In: 2020 33rd SIBGRAPI Conference on Graphics, Patterns and Images (SIBGRAPI), pp. 340–347 (2020). https://doi.org/10.1109/SIBGRAPI51738.2020.00053

13. Meyes, R., Lu, M., Waubert de Puiseau, C., Meisen, T.: Ablation studies in artificial neural networks. arXiv preprint arXiv:1901.08644 (2019), https://arxiv.org/abs/1901.08644
14. Nguyen, H., Dumas, M., ter Hofstede, A.H.M., Rosa, M.L., Maggi, F.M.: Business process performance mining with staged process flows. In: Nurcan, S., Soffer, P., Bajec, M., Eder, J. (eds.) Advanced Information Systems Engineering (CAiSE 2016). Lecture Notes in Computer Science, vol. 9694, pp. 100–116. Springer, Cham (2016). https://doi.org/10.1007/978-3-319-39696-5_11
15. de Oliveira, R.S., Reis Jr., A.S., Sperandio Nascimento, E.G.: Predicting the number of days in court cases using artificial intelligence. PLOS ONE **17**(5), e0269008 (2022). https://doi.org/10.1371/journal.pone.0269008
16. Oyamada, R.S., Tavares, G.M., Junior, S.B., Ceravolo, P.: Enhancing predictive process monitoring with time-related feature engineering. In: Guizzardi, G., Santoro, F., Mouratidis, H., Soffer, P. (eds.) Advanced Information Systems Engineering (CAiSE 2024). Lecture Notes in Computer Science, vol. 14663, pp. 80–96. Springer, Cham (2024). https://doi.org/10.1007/978-3-031-61057-8_5
17. Partington, A., Wynn, M.T., Suriadi, S., Ouyang, C., ter Hofstede, A.H.M.: Process mining for clinical processes: a comparative analysis of four Australian hospitals. ACM Trans. Manag. Inf. Syst. (TMIS) **5**(4), 19 (2015). https://doi.org/10.1145/2676971
18. Pernici, B., Bono, C.A., Piro, L., Del Treste, M., Vecchi, G.: Improving the analysis of the judiciary performance the use of data mining techniques to assess the timeliness of civil trials. Int. J. Publ. Sect. Manag. **37**(1), 59–76 (2024). https://doi.org/10.1108/IJPSM-02-2023-0058
19. Senderovich, A., Di Francescomarino, C., Ghidini, C., Jorbina, K., Maggi, F.: Intra and inter-case features in predictive process monitoring: a tale of two dimensions, pp. 306–323 (2017). https://doi.org/10.1007/978-3-319-65000-5_18
20. Tagarelli, A., Simeri, A.: Unsupervised law article mining based on deep pre-trained language representation models with application to the Italian civil code. Artif. Intell. Law **30**(4), 417–473 (2022). https://doi.org/10.1007/s10506-021-09301-8. accepted 18 August 2021, Published 15 September 2021, Issue Date September 2022
21. Tama, B.A., Comuzzi, M., Ko, J.: An empirical investigation of different classifiers, encoding and ensemble schemes for next event prediction using business process event logs (2020). https://arxiv.org/abs/2008.10748
22. Teinemaa, I., Dumas, M., Rosa, M.L., Maggi, F.M.: Outcome-oriented predictive process monitoring: review and benchmark (2018). https://arxiv.org/abs/1707.06766
23. Unger, A., dos Santos Neto, J., Fantinato, M., Peres, S., Trecenti, J., Hirota, R.: Event log belonging to the publication: process mining-enabled jurimetrics: analysis of a Brazilian court's judicial performance in the business law processing (2021). https://doi.org/10.4121/14593857.v1
24. Vercosa, L., Silva, V., Cruz, J., Freire, J., Figueiredo, D.: Investigation of lawsuit process duration using machine learning and process mining. Discov. Analytics **2**(9) (2024). https://doi.org/10.1007/s44257-024-00015-0
25. Verenich, I., Dumas, M., Rosa, M.L., Maggi, F.M., Teinemaa, I.: Survey and cross-benchmark comparison of remaining time prediction methods in business process monitoring. ACM Trans. Intell. Syst. Technol. **10**(4) (2019). https://doi.org/10.1145/3331449

26. Weytjens, H., De Weerdt, J.: Creating unbiased public benchmark datasets with data leakage prevention for predictive process monitoring. In: International Conference on Business Process Management, pp. 18–29. Springer (2021)
27. Weytjens, H., Weerdt, J.D.: Learning uncertainty with artificial neural networks for improved remaining time prediction of business processes (2021). https://arxiv.org/abs/2105.05559

2nd International Workshop on Visual Process Analytics (VIPRA 2025)

VESPA: Visual Event-Stream Progressive Analytics

Andrea Burattin[1(✉)], Silvia Miksch[2], Shazia Sadiq[3], Hans-Jörg Schulz[4], and Katerina Vrotsou[5]

[1] Technical University of Denmark, Kgs. Lyngby, Denmark
andbur@dtu.dk
[2] TU Wien, Vienna, Austria
silvia.miksch@tuwien.ac.at
[3] The University of Queensland, Brisbane, Australia
shazia@eecs.uq.edu.au
[4] Aarhus University, Aarhus, Denmark
hjschulz@cs.au.dk
[5] Linköping University, Campus Norrköping, Linköping, Sweden
katerina.vrotsou@liu.se

Abstract. This paper introduces VESPA (Visual Event-Stream Progressive Analytics), a framework that integrates Streaming Process Mining (SPM) with Progressive Visual Analytics (PVA) to support timely, informed decisions using partial, evolving data. VESPA addresses the challenges of analyzing transient, multifaceted event-streams by coupling process mining with progressive visualizations. Our framework is structured around key dimensions (context, task, data, algorithm, user roles, and interaction modalities). Two central research questions guide our work: identifying optimal timing for progressive visualizations and determining their effectiveness and appropriateness in streaming contexts. A prototype with ward-centric and patient-centric views was conceptualized, based on a simulated real-world scenario in the context of an emergency department (ER). These views support user roles from passive monitoring to active exploration, enabling dynamic prioritization and resource allocation. Preliminary results demonstrate the potential of VESPA to enhance situational awareness and decision-making.

Keywords: Streaming Process Mining · Progressive Visual Analytics

1 Introduction

In dynamic, high-stakes environments, such as emergency response (ER) departments, decision-makers must act based on incomplete and continuously evolving data. Traditional process mining techniques, which rely on static, retrospective data, fall short in such contexts. Streaming Process Mining (SPM) addresses this limitation, but often lacks the interpretability needed for decision-making.

I. van de Weerd et al. (Eds.): BPM 2025 Workshops, LNBIP 569, pp. 549–556, 2026.
https://doi.org/10.1007/978-3-032-13426-4_40

This paper proposes the integration of SPM with Progressive Visual Analytics (PVA), which supports sensemaking through incremental visual feedback and interaction, even when data or computations are incomplete. Together, SPM and PVA form a unified framework—VESPA (Visual Event-Stream Progressive Analytics)—that empowers users to monitor, explore, and act on streaming data in real-time. By coupling algorithmic insights with visualization, VESPA supports various user roles and tasks, from passive observation to active exploration.

Consider the real-time decision-making needed when managing a busy ER. Patients undergo a sequence of diagnosis and possibly treatment steps that can be conceptually captured as a process model, which may change depending on the time of day (working hours vs. after hours) and case load (business as usual vs. state of emergency). The head of the ER needs to monitor the current intake, throughput, and related KPIs, like the length of stay (LOS) or ward load (WL), to decide in real-time whether to allocate additional resources (activate on-call doctors), to fast-track certain patients (increase their urgencies), explicitly switch from the usual procedures to the streamlined emergency procedures or back, etc.

To support such time-critical decisions in real-time scenarios, we propose to combine SPM with PVA. Our key contributions include: **(1)** A conceptual framework for integrating SPM and PVA in time-critical decision-making contexts; **(2)** Definition of a multi-dimensional problem space; **(3)** VESPA-VIS: a prototype visualization system showcasing views in a high-stakes real-time environment.

2 Related Work

Streaming Process Mining (SPM). SPM [4] techniques have emerged to handle the processing of constantly updating, real-time information. In a streaming setting, events are processed, immediately after they are generated, by a SPM pipeline, yielding intermediate. SPM algorithms can be used to handle the control-flow discovery, where the control-flow is expected to represent the process *currently* being executed [6]. Another problem that can be tackled is streaming conformance checking [4], where the conformity of each event is verified against a corresponding reference model. Despite these benefits of SPM, in a real-time scenario as described above, the effectiveness of SPM cannot be fully realized without providing effective intermediate insights.

Progressive Visual Analytics (PVA). PVA refers to iterative or incremental approaches for the visual analysis of large amounts of data that could not be processed, visualized, or interacted with in a traditional, whole-dataset-at-once manner [7]. PVA produces partial results, which are usually the outcome of some technical process—e.g., a running computation that refines over time or a complex data query yielding more and more data over time. These intermediate results are then utilized for making time-critical decisions—e.g., in disaster recovery and emergency response scenarios [7, ch.7.6]. Hence, PVA focuses mainly on displaying the progression of intermediate results to allow such decisions, but less on providing insight into the progressive process itself. This is where the combination with SPM comes into the picture.

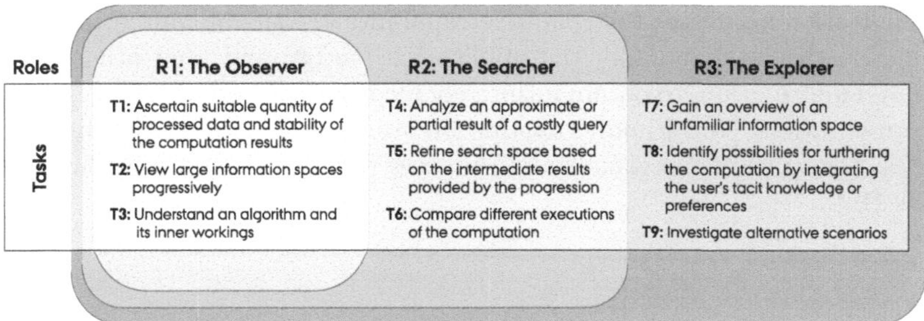

Fig. 1. Common user roles and tasks in PVA. Ranging from observers with limited involvement and interaction possibilities to explorers directly wrangling with one or more running processes in parallel. (adapted from [7, ch.7] under CC-BY 4.0).

3 Our Approach: VESPA

In developing our approach for VESPA, we first outline the the problem space, from which we derive two key research questions. We then present the VESPA architecture followed by a demonstration of preliminary results.

Aspects of the Problem Space. VESPA requires consideration of the following aspects: **(1)** Context, i.e. business process; **(2)** Task, e.g., conformance checking or process enhancement; **(3)** Data space assumes at least an event log but it could be augmented with other facets relevant to the problem; **(4)** Algorithm space, i.e. the specific algorithm relevant to the task; **(5)** Guards/Rules [9] that signal potential attention triggers for users; **(6)** Users include full spectrum from monitoring scenario all the way to a fully explorative scenario following the categorization into Observers, Searchers, Explorers [11] (see Fig. 1); **(7)** Visualization and Interaction space, e.g., interactive visualizations of event sequences [2] and dynamic networks [3,8].

Research Questions. We defined two research questions (RQs) posed by such an SPM setting with a continuous flow of events:

RQ1 What are the required time points for progressive visualization for streaming process mining? Identification of time points is related to the needs of the analytical intention of the user. We identified three needs that may arise at different time points and refer to them as scheduled, triggered, and on demand: *(i)* Scheduled (e.g., results are ready); *(ii)* Triggered (e.g., a guard/rule fires when a conformance score is falling below threshold); *(iii)* On demand (e.g., an explorer wants to probe on a particular facet, such as the trend in urgency levels). These time points in turn influence the suitability of the visualization and interaction which leads us to our second research question.

RQ2 What are the effective, efficient, and appropriate progressive visualizations and interactions for streaming process mining? *Expressiveness* refers to the requirement of visualizing exactly the information contained in the data; nothing more and nothing less [10]. *Effectiveness* considers the degree to which the visualization addresses the cognitive capabilities of the human visual system, but also the task at hand, the application background, and other context-related information, to obtain intuitively recognizable and interpretable visual representations [10]. Finally, *appropriateness* involves a cost-benefit ratio to assess the value of the visualization process with respect to achieving a given task [15].

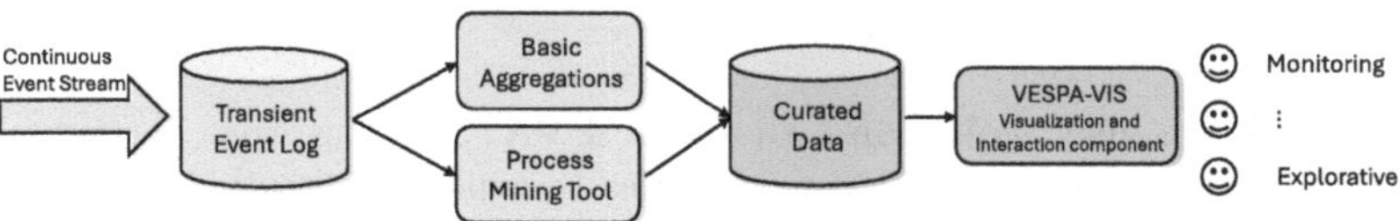

Fig. 2. VESPA's Architecture: The proposed software architecture for PVA in SPM.

VESPA's Architecture. The overall approach is proposed to be embedded in a software architecture as provided in Fig. 2. The continuous event-stream is a key feature of the problem space. Depending on the velocity of the event-stream, there may or may not be a persistent storage and hence the system architecture presents it as a 'transient' event log. A process mining tool is selected based on the task e.g. conformance checking. In addition to the discovered process, the proposed system architecture also produces a process mining results dataset. This includes details such as conformance scores and multi-faceted event data [14]. When needed, the transient event log may also be used to produce basic aggregations such as patient load over a period of time. Together the aggregations and the process mining results constitute a curated dataset that forms the input to the visualization. The results from the visualization component are expected to empower users to perform a range of tasks from monitoring all the way to interactive exploration to support timely (or even real-time) decision making.

Preliminary Results. We outline a user story expressed in two levels of detail to frame and guide our VESPA approach.

- **Patient-centric:** An ER administrator wants to know if the LOS for one ER patient is too high requiring to prioritize them in the waiting queue.
- **Ward-centric:** An ER administrator wants to know if the LOS for a cohort of ER patients is too high / too low to adjust the allocation of resources.

This user story manifests in the problem dimensions: **(1)** Context: Healthcare; **(2)** Task: Primarily we will focus on conformance checking, but this is intended to be augmented with relevant facets; **(3)** Data space: Ideally, data should come from the information system of the ER; **(4)** Algorithm space: We can use behavioral conformance checking (BCC) [4]; **(5)** Progressive Guards [9]: Three guards are considered: conformance falling below threshold; a load of an urgent category (critical/high) increasing over a threshold; and the LOS of a given patient increasing over a threshold; **(6)** Users: Interchangeable roles of

Observers, Searchers, Explorers; and **(7)** Visualization and Interaction space is aligned with the patient-centric and ward-centric user stories. We assume that the processes happening in the ER are not stationary and can change according to different criteria. For example, we can assume that a typical ER process changes during off-peak (with fewer doctors available) or during an intense scenario (with many patients checked at once and doctors coming from other wards).

A SPM pipeline can be implemented using pyBeamline [5]. The pipeline processes each event and computes the following: **(1)** The DFG model [1,5] updated up to the given point in time; **(2)** The conformance value of the stream against the ER's operational models (off-peak vs intense).

VESPA-VIS's Prototypical Mock-Up. Based on the use case and outlined problem dimensions, we designed a prototype mock-up, VESPA-VIS. VESPA-VIS comprises two main views, the *Ward view* (cf. Fig. 3) and the *Patient view* (cf. Fig. 4), designed to address the two outlined levels of detail of our ward-centric and patient-centric use cases.

The *Ward view* is split into a *Patient Flow* view (cf. Fig. 3A) and a *Temporal Facet* view (cf. Fig. 3B). The *Patient Flow* displays the event-streams flowing into the ER ward. A node-link diagram representing the currently active reference model is shown as a backdrop in the view. As the events stream into the ward model, the current patient load is mapped to node sizes and edge widths. Deviations to the model (i.e., "unexpected" events not included in the reference model) are drawn in a dashed style. The *Patient Flow* displays the flow of patients over a given expert-user defined time-interval preceding the current time point (e.g., 10 min). A time slider allows exploration of past intervals. Hovering over a node or edge pops up a tool-tip displaying the number of patients belonging to the corresponding event or transition over time.

The *Temporal Facet* view displays a selection of graphs showing the temporal distribution of relevant facets (cf. Fig. 3B). These facet graphs complement the *Patient Flow* view and allow an expert to inspect surrounding factors and reason about the processing state of the ward. On the top, the *conformance score* over time is displayed. Conformance w.r.t. the currently explored model is displayed by default (e.g., regular operations), and on hover, conformance w.r.t. two complementary model variations is also shown (e.g., off-peak, intense). This graph allows the expert to monitor the conformance of the process over time, detect fluctuations from the expected behavior, and assess whether the correct model is used as a reference or whether another model should be used. If the conformance score falls below a certain threshold over a certain period of time, a guard is triggered, calling for the attention of the expert. The second graph displays the *ward load* over time, i.e. the total number of patients being processed, allowing the expert to monitor the overall stress on the ward over time. Third, the average *LOS* of patients being processed is displayed over time, providing an additional cue to the load on the ward. The fourth graph gives a summary overview of the urgency of the patients being processed over time. The distribution of the urgency classes (e.g., low, medium, high) is displayed as a

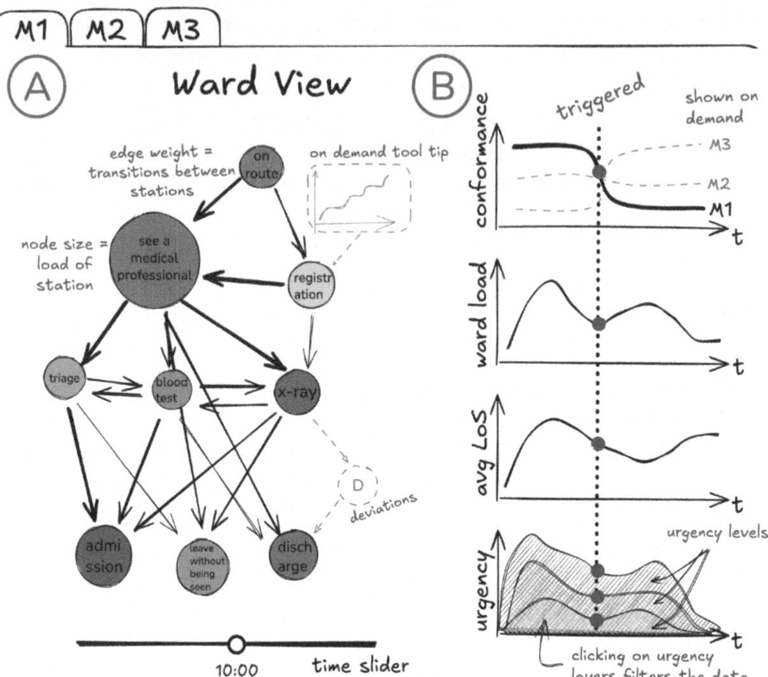

Fig. 3. **VESPA-VIS** ***Ward View*** comprising (A) the *Patient Flow* view displaying the event-streams flowing into the ER ward, and (B) the *Temporal Facet* view displaying the temporal distribution of relevant facets.

stacked area graph, allowing an expert to reason about the characteristics of the patients currently putting load on the ward. Additional facets could be displayed in a similar manner in the view, if deemed appropriate for the task at hand.

The *Patient Flow* and *Temporal Facet* views are updated according to three timing strategies: **(1)** at regular pre-defined intervals (e.g., every 10 min or 100 events) by default (scheduled), **(2)** if a guard/trigger is activated (triggered), **(3)** upon request of the user (on-demand). The *Ward view* is displayed for all of the available reference models in different tabs. A user can switch between exploring the event-streams against these at any time.

The *Patient View* (cf. Fig. 4) is designed to drill-down into the individual patient event-streams when a need arises. In the *Patient View*, the individual patient streams are displayed as event sequences. Time is displayed on the horizontal axis and the user can toggle relative and absolute time. Patient sequences are sorted along the vertical axis by an *urgency score*. If the computed *urgency score* of a patient exceeds a predefined threshold, a guard triggers, calling attention to the need to prioritize individual patients. The *urgency score* is computed as a distance from a benchmark sequence. We consider three alternative benchmark sequences in VESPA-VIS: **(1)** The "Golden standard" pre-defined by an expert as an ideal path through the process both in terms of sequence of events and timing. Different ideal sequences can be defined for different times of day or days of the week. **(2)** The "Current average" as a typical patient sequence reflecting the current ordering and average duration of events. **(3)** A "User adjusted" patient sequence where an expert (e.g., ER manager) makes online decisions regarding the target duration of events. The ability to choose between benchmarks to compare against allows the expert user of VESPA-VIS (e.g., ER manager) to flexibly adjust the notion of urgency and control prioritization of patients according to the current situation, their domain knowledge and previous experience.

Together, the *Ward* and *Patient views* allow users to transition smoothly between user roles: monitoring the current situation, reacting on evolving changes, reasoning about possible explanations, and potentially anticipating outcomes.

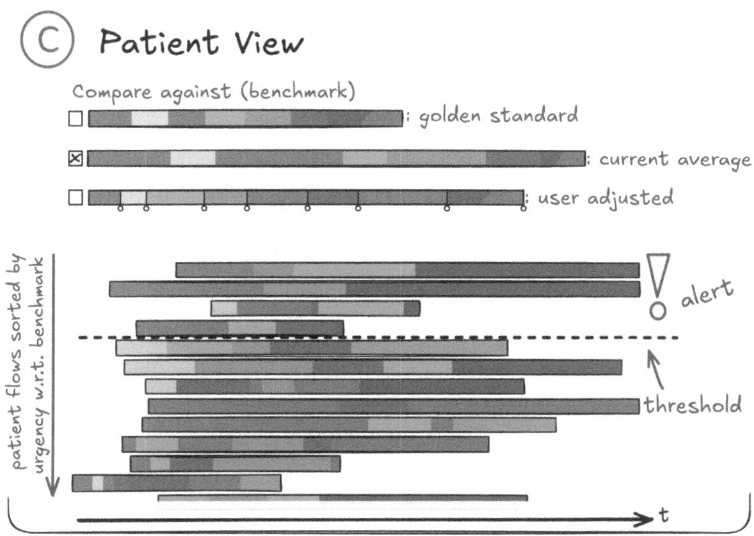

Fig. 4. VESPA-VIS *Patient View* displaying individual patient streams as sequences of events sorted along the vertical axis by an *urgency score*.

4 Conclusion and Future Work

The presented VESPA-VIS's mockups provide an initial illustration of our research questions. That is, when and how PVA can best support real-time decision-making in a SPM context. The illustration of the approach through the use case indicates fertile ground for further developing the approach, however, there remain a number of further considerations for the approach to be fully realized.

A robust evaluation with carefully planned user studies with representative participant groups will help to assess the effectiveness of PVA for (real-time) decision support. Given the continuous nature of the event-stream, it is natural to expect a need to 'forget' previous event-streams when they are no longer relevant for the current decision making. For example, the straightforward way of simply 'forgetting' patients who have exited the ER through discharge or transferal to another ward, prevents the head of the ER department from comparing the currently observed situation with previously observed situations such as processes occurring on a current New Years holiday day to the processes on the same day in previous years, to identify best practices or simply "what has worked in the past". Identification of 'forgetfulness' thresholds is in itself a complex and multi-faceted problem that requires further work, although prior literature gives hints (e.g., [12,13]). Although the focus of the approach is to support real-time decision making, the insights gained from the proposed approach present an opportunity to inform process enhancement.

Acknowledgements. This paper resulted from discussions at Dagstuhl Seminar 25152 "Multi-Faceted Visual Process Mining and Analytics".

References

1. van der Aalst, W.M.P.: Process Mining - Data Science in Action, 2nd edn. Springer, Cham (2016)
2. Aigner, W., Miksch, S., Schumann, H., Tominski, C.: Visualization of Time-Oriented Data, 2nd edn. Springer, Cham (2023)
3. Beck, F., Burch, M., Diehl, S., Weiskopf, D.: A taxonomy and survey of dynamic graph visualization. CGF **36**(1), 133–159 (2017)
4. Burattin, A.: Streaming process mining. In: van der Aalst, W.M.P., Carmona, J. (eds.) Process Mining Handbook, LNBIP, vol. 448, pp. 349–372. Springer (2022)
5. Burattin, A.: Beamline: a comprehensive toolkit for research and development of streaming process mining. Softw. Impacts **17**, 100551 (2023)
6. Burattin, A., Sperduti, A., van der Aalst, W.M.P.: Control-flow discovery from event streams. In: Proc. of the IEEE CEC, pp. 2420–2427. IEEE (2014)
7. Fekete, J.D., Fisher, D., Sedlmair, M. (eds.): Progressive Data Analysis – Roadmap and Research Agenda. Eurographics Press (2024)
8. Hadlak, S., Schumann, H., Schulz, H.J.: A survey of multi-faceted graph visualization. In: Eurographics Conference on Visualization. The EA (2015)
9. Jo, J., L Yi, S., Lee, B., Seo, J.: ProReveal: progressive visual analytics with safeguards. IEEE TVCG **27**(7), 3109–3122 (2021)
10. Mackinlay, J.: Automating the design of graphical presentations of relational information. ACM Trans. Graph. **5**(2), 110–141 (1986)
11. Micallef, L., et al.: The human user in progressive visual analytics. In: Short Paper Proceedings of EuroVis'19, pp. 19–23. Eurographics Association (2019)
12. Pavan, A., Chakraborty, S., Vinodchandran, N.V., Meel, K.S.: On the feasibility of forgetting in data streams. Proc. ACM Manag. Data **2**(2) (2024)
13. Schulz, H.J., Weaver, C.: Transient visual analytics. In: Proc. of EuroVA. Eurographics (2024)
14. van den Elzen, S., et al.: Towards multi-faceted visual process analytics. Inf. Syst. **133**, 102560 (2025)
15. Van Wijk, J.J.: Views on visualization. IEEE TVCG **12**(4), 421–432 (2006)

Milana: Bridging Process Mining and Visual Analytics Through Task Classification

Lisa Zimmermann[1(✉)], Katerina Vrotsou[2], Pnina Soffer[3], Philipp Koytek[4], Barbara Weber[1], and Shazia Sadiq[5]

[1] University of St. Gallen, St. Gallen, Switzerland
lisa.zimmermann@unisg.ch
[2] Linköping University, Campus Norrköping, Norrköping, Sweden
[3] University of Haifa, Haifa, Israel
[4] Celonis Labs GmbH, Munich, Germany
[5] The University of Queensland, Brisbane, Australia

Abstract. Process mining is a powerful approach for analyzing event data, benefiting greatly from human-in-the-loop methods due to its reliance on human interpretation and decision-making. However, current tools do not fully exploit the potential of integrating process mining with interactive visual support. To address this gap, we adopt a design science research approach to systematically connect task concepts from both domains. As a result, we introduce Milana, a method that links process mining tasks, expressed as analysis questions, to established visual analytics requirements. Milana fosters a shared vocabulary, improves communication between the communities, and offers practical guidance for designing effective visualizations tailored to process mining.

Keywords: process mining · visual analytics · analysis tasks · visualization design

1 Introduction

Effective visualization is critical for empowering process analysts to derive meaningful insights from complex process data [3]. Over the last two decades, process mining (PM) has developed into an established research field and offers a collection of techniques and tools that provide immense value for the analysis of processes, enabling diverse analyses such as process discovery, conformance checking, performance analysis, or prediction [4]. While techniques in these areas are constantly advancing, human-centered aspects of PM, including the use of existing tools and the perception of artifacts produced by these techniques, have received less attention [10,19]. As analysts often face complex decision-making tasks, providing appropriate and intuitive visual support is essential for facilitating insight generation and ensuring that conclusions drawn from PM analyses lead to meaningful impact in practice [17].

I. van de Weerd et al. (Eds.): BPM 2025 Workshops, LNBIP 569, pp. 557–572, 2026.
https://doi.org/10.1007/978-3-032-13426-4_41

Concurrently, the field of visual analytics (VA) [15] offers an extensive body of knowledge about how visualizations can support analytical reasoning and decision making [22]. Established VA taxonomies describe tasks, intents, and visualization techniques across diverse domains [7,9,24] and can help guide visualization design. However, the application of these taxonomies to domain-specific needs of PM remains underexplored [19,28]. One key obstacle is a missing shared vocabulary. For example, what VA defines as comparison or correlation analysis may manifest as conformance checking or performance benchmarking in PM. So far, there is a lack of systematic mapping, and without a common language, it remains difficult to translate PM needs into visual solutions and vice versa.

In this paper, we take a step toward bridging this gap. Rather than defining a new taxonomy of PM tasks, we build on an established VA task typology [9] and existing categorization schemes in PM [8,31]. We consider PM tasks as analytical activities that are often driven by concrete questions. In their projects, analysts aim to answer these questions based on process data [12]. Accordingly, our approach starts from a set of PM analysis questions, which we use as a practical entry point to abstract task types. This in turn provides the basis for abstracting the set of operations and data types required for making decisions on appropriate visual encodings [21]. The result is a structured mapping that helps to describe PM tasks in terms that are meaningful within the VA community. Our goal is to support the selection, design, and evaluation of visualizations tailored to the actual analytical needs of PM users.

In particular, we introduce *Milana*[1], a method developed through a design science approach that serves as a conceptual bridge between these two domains. Milana reuses and connects well-established categories from VA and PM and enables analysts, visualization designers, and researchers to systematically reflect on what kind of visual analytic support is appropriate for specific PM tasks.

2 Related Work

This section reviews existing classification systems for analytical tasks and visualization needs. We focus on established schemes from VA and PM, which form the conceptual basis for our work.

2.1 Tasks and Task Definitions in Visual Analytics

In the existing VA literature, the concept of "task" is used in varying ways, with taxonomies reflecting different levels of abstraction and granularity. For example, they might be reflected as low-level operations of analytic activity [6], users' interactions intents [29] or visualization usage [9,13]. Munzner [21] especially highlighted that a task can be described at different levels, i.e., from domain-specific problems to abstract operations.

[1] Milana is an Urdu word that means "compound" or "to unite" (see https://www.urdupoint.com/dictionary/urdu-to-english/milana-meaning-in-english/19252.html, accessed 12.06.2025).

Rind et al. [24] extended this idea by formalizing task definitions within a conceptual space called TaskCube, consisting of three orthogonal dimensions: abstraction, composition, and perspective. *Abstraction* spans from generic analytical tasks to those specific to a data type (e.g., network or temporal data), a domain, or a specific tool. *Composition* refers to the granularity, ranging from concise low-level to broader high-level tasks. *Perspective* distinguishes the user's objective (why a task is done) from the action taken (how it is done). An *objective* is "a question on data [...] to solve a problem [...]" while an *action* is "a discrete step towards addressing an objective".

Moving to concrete classification schemes for tasks, one of the most recognized frameworks is the typology by Brehmer and Munzner [9]. It structures tasks along three dimensions—*why*, *how*, and *what*—capturing the user's intent, the means of execution, and the data involved. The *why* dimension is especially relevant to our work, as it clarifies the intentions of users rather than describing the execution methods, which tend to be more specific to the domain and tools used [9]. Depending on the user's knowledge of the tasks' target and its location, the *why* dimension describes high-level goals (e.g. consume vs. produce), mid-level search behaviors (e.g. look up or explore) and low-level queries (e.g. identify or compare). This typology serves as a strong foundation for translating domain-specific problems into abstract tasks [24] and can inform visualization design. We therefore use it as a basis for abstracting relevant aspects of PM tasks in order to clarify their visualization requirements.

2.2 Tasks in Process Mining

While task taxonomies in VA are well-established, PM lacks a shared understanding of tasks. As Klinkmüller et al. [16] note, little is known about the types of questions practitioners address in practice. Still, some studies have categorized PM tasks from various perspectives. We review key developments below.

The Process Mining Manifesto [1] outlines a widely cited classification of three core PM techniques: process discovery, conformance checking, and process enhancement. While useful, these categories cover diverse use cases. To provide more detail, van der Aalst [4] later introduced six types: process discovery, conformance checking, performance analysis, comparative PM, predictive PM, and action-oriented PM, each reflecting distinct purposes and tool capabilities.

A growing body of research complements this classification of PM techniques with categorizations derived from case studies. For example, Klinkmüller et al. [16] revealed a list of common domain problems and Milani et al. [20] examined business questions driving PM projects. The latter identified twelve use cases grouped under five business objectives: transparency, efficiency, quality, compliance, and agility. Based on our knowledge, these works offer the most comprehensive overviews of PM use cases derived from case studies.

Additionally, Barbieri et al. [8] proposed a multi-dimensional taxonomy to categorize questions answerable via their natural language interface. Though focused on interface evaluation rather than task modeling, the taxonomy describes PM tasks along multiple dimensions (e.g., task perspective, filtering, context, composition). Similarly, Zimmermann [31] highlighted the need to classify PM analysis questions along a well-developed taxonomy or classification scheme to structure the analysis phase and ensure a common understanding of the analysis goals. Their tool is built on a six-dimensional classification scheme, including the main use case, process perspective, and data level needed to answer a question.

This work does not propose a new task taxonomy or definition of PM tasks. Instead, we build on existing literature and, following recent work advocating a question or goal-driven analysis approach [26,30,31], treat analysis questions as the starting point for PM. Our aim is to derive and frame visualization requirements from these questions.

3 Design Science Approach

To develop *Milana*, we adopt a Design Science Research (DSR) [23] approach as outlined in Fig. 1. In particular, in this paper, we focus on the problem motivation, the objectives of our solution, the design and development steps, and the demonstration of Milana. While our demonstration already reveals its value, a complete evaluation remains for future work.

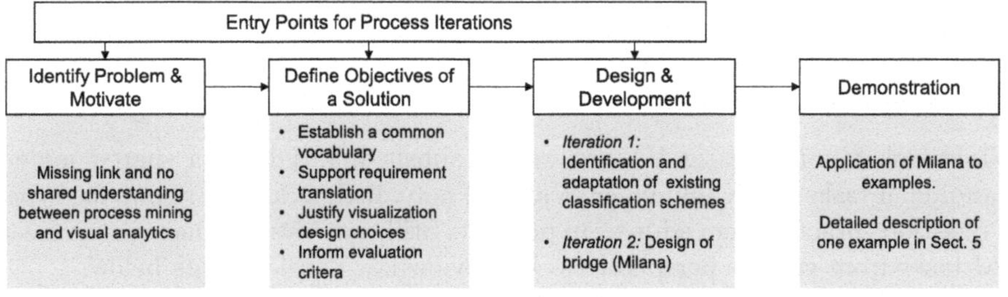

Fig. 1. Overview of our method, adapted from the DSR Process [23].

3.1 Identify Problem and Motivate

PM relies on human-centered analysis processes in which analysts engage with process data iteratively, formulate questions, interpret results, and derive insights given their domain and context [26]. However, during an analysis, individual analysts struggle with diverse aspects, including the interpretations of visualizations produced by PM algorithms [32].

Overall, the application of VA principles in PM remains underdeveloped. As noted in Sect. 1, a key reason is the lack of a shared conceptual foundation. PM and VA rely on different task models, terminologies, and design rationales, making it difficult to translate requirements across domains [28]. Current process analysis tools offer little structured support to align human analytical tasks with appropriate visual interfaces, essential for understanding, exploring, and decision-making. This gap is especially problematic in collaborative settings or for tool development, where process analysts define high-level goals while visualization experts must decide how to support them visually. Without a shared vocabulary or task-to-visualization mapping, communication suffers and design potential is lost. Therefore, our goal is to enable a structured translation of requirements from PM use cases into visualization solutions that are cognitively appropriate and analytically meaningful to respective VA experts.

3.2 Define Objectives of a Solution

Having identified the gap between PM and VA, we define the following objectives for the proposed solution.

- **Establish a common vocabulary across domains.** Our first objective is to provide a conceptual foundation that aligns key concepts, tasks, and terminology across PM and VA. To achieve this, we abstract from specific tasks, typically expressed in PM terms, to ensure a broader, shared understanding.
- **Translate PM requirements into the Visual Design Space.** We aim to support the structured translation of analytical goals and user needs in PM into actionable visualization requirements. This includes mapping abstract tasks (e.g., discovering deviations, profiling behaviors) to suitable operations and visual encodings, enabling VA experts to design effective solutions without deep PM expertise.
- **Support the justification of visualization design choices.** By connecting process tasks to visual design options, our mapping should serve as a reference framework to justify why specific visualizations are appropriate for given tasks. This might facilitate design rationale documentation and enhance interpretability of VA components in PM tools.
- **Inform evaluation criteria for process visualizations.** Our mapping should also form a basis for the development of evaluation protocols by making explicit the expected support for a given PM task. This enables researchers and practitioners to assess not only correctness but also usability and task fit of visualizations based on explicit requirements.

3.3 Design and Development

After identifying the problem and defining clear objectives, we initiated the design and development phase of Milana. Following the principles of DSR, our target artifact can be understood as a method [14] that offers a structured approach to clarify tasks and guide visualization design. Its development was iterative, with ongoing refinement and validation. We grounded our work in empirical observations, analyzing PM analysis questions from [8] and [31], which stem from real-world and educational use cases. These questions helped us understand analysts' intentions and cognitive demands. We sought to characterize what information is essential for visualization experts to meaningfully support these tasks.

These empirically grounded basis helped to ensure that Milana remains rooted in realistic analysis settings and not only theoretical assumptions. The result of our iterative refinement is presented in Sect. 4 and can be summarized in the following main development components:

1. **Identification and adaption of existing typologies and classification schemes.** We identified foundational classification schemes to describe PM tasks in terms of visualization and data requirements, and developed guiding questions to clarify additional key aspects in a less formal structure.
2. **Design of Milana.** We combined the elements of the first component into meaningful statements to finalize our artifact.

3.4 Demonstration

After its development, we performed a demonstration of how Milana can be used to guide VA experts in making informed choices for effective visualizations relative to the PM task (cf. Sect. 5). The demonstration indicates the capability of Milana to establish a common vocabulary across the two domains and enable the translation of PM requirements into the visual design space. It also informs the evaluation criteria for process visualizations which we aim to further develop towards a more detailed and empirical evaluation in future work.

4 Result: Milana

In this section, we present the outcome of our DSR approach outlining the results of the design and development phases.

4.1 Identification and Adaptation of Existing Typologies

Identification of Base Typology. As pointed out in Sect. 2, in comparison to PM, VA provides a more cohesive understanding of visualization and analysis tasks. We chose the well-known and widely accepted typology of Brehmer and Munzner [9] as a starting point for our method due to its flexibility and expressiveness. It defines tasks in three dimensions, indicating *why* it is performed, *how* it is performed, and *what* kind of input and output (data) is produced. Focusing on the *why* dimension provides us with a path to abstract a given PM question into a visualization task objective which can then inform the design of a visualization solution supporting the underlying intention of the task.

Applying the *why* dimension to PM tasks, i.e., a set of analysis questions, revealed certain interpretative challenges. In particular, the notions of *target* and *location*, which are central to the mid-level (search) part of the dimension, required further contextualization. We, therefore, developed refinements tailored to the PM domain:

- **Target**, in PM, refers to the condition an analyst is trying to isolate or investigate. We consider it *known* when this condition can be directly specified and evaluated on the data (e.g., "identify cases longer than 5 days"). The target is *unknown* when solving the task requires first evaluating a comparative or abstract criterion (e.g., "cases that take the most time"), where the benchmark or reference emerges from the data.
- **Location** defines where in the process data the target is expected to be found. In PM, this includes the levels of log, trace, and event. The location is *known* when the task explicitly constrains the data subset (e.g., "cases processed by department B and lasting longer than 5 days"). It is *unknown* when no such reference is made, requiring broader exploration (e.g., "which cases take longer than 5 days?").

The resulting PM tailored version of the typology which we adopt for Milana is presented in Fig. 2A.

Classification of PM Tasks. Next, we focused on identifying further relevant categories of PM tasks to specify the nature of the required PM analysis in more detail. To this end, we built on top of existing question classification approaches described in Sect. 2. After testing different combinations of classification schemes on our set of questions, we identified three dimensions inspired by the classification scheme used by Zimmermann [31] as both analytically relevant and practically useful for building our translation bridge (cf. Fig. 2B):

- **Use Case** refers to the underlying purpose or motivation for analysis. Rooted in common PM objectives, we distinguish four primary use cases: transparency, performance, compliance, and automation. These are aligned with established PM categories [4,20] and tool functionalities.
- **Perspective** denotes the angle from which the process is analyzed. Following the definitions by van der Aalst [2], we include perspectives such as *control-flow*, *time*, *resources*, *data*, and identified a need for an *"other"* category, allowing to describe tasks that require the consideration of multiple perspectives or perspectives not part of the previous list. The perspective of a task describes what aspect of the process is foregrounded in an analysis.
- **Data Level**, inspired by the XES standard [5], reflects the granularity of the data involved: *log*, *trace*, *event*, or *other*. It indicates the scope of data that is required to answer a question, helping visualization experts assess the necessary resolution and abstraction level.

Clarification of Key Aspects. Throughout the development iterations of Milana, it became evident that even questions with similar surface structure could differ substantially in their analytic implications. Therefore, beyond classification, we introduced two clarifications of finer-grained aspects of task formulation (cf. Fig. 2C):

A — Visualization Task Typology

Consume Intention of performing a task	present	communicate information, storytelling, guide audience.
	discover	find patterns or insights that are not yet known.
	enjoy	cencounter visualizations without a specific purpose.
Search Finding elements of interest	lookup	search target known, location known.
	browse	search target unknown, location known.
	locate	search target known, location unknown.
	explore	search target unknown, location unknown.
Query User action to complete the task	identify	determine the identity of a presented element.
	compare	examine similarities or differences between two or more elements.
	summarize	provide an overview or aggregation of the data.

B — Process Mining Task Classification

Use Case Underlying purpose for analysis	transparency	gain transparency regarding a particular perspective of the process.
	performance	measure or improve a performance aspect of the process.
	compliance	reveal divergence between as-is process and prescribed or expected behavior.
	automation	measure or improve the automation level of the process.
Perspective Primary angle and data attributes relevant for analysis	control-flow	ordering or existence of events, transitions, traces, and their execution.
	time	timing of events or traces or their execution duration.
	resources	resources involved in the process (e.g., actors, organizational units) and their attributes (e.g., role).
	data	data attributes (e.g., their value or distributions) and their interrelations.
	other	no clear predominant perspective or does not contain any specific concept.
Data Level Data scope required to answer	log	refers to the event log as a whole and not to specific traces or events.
	trace	refers to (a set of) specific traces (cases, instances) that satisfy a given characteristic. Can be considered in full (start-end) or as subsequences (Activity X to Activity Y).
	event	refers to (a set of) events or event attributes.
	other	focus on a specific data level cannot be inferred.

C — Clarification Questions

C1: What is expected from the answer, i.e., is a definite value (binary/numeric) expected or a qualitative description/explanation? If latter applies, what perspective constitutes the relevant context for the qualitative analysis?

C2: How are the specific concepts that are referred to by the questions defined (e.g., bottleneck, "working as agreed upon,..")? In case these concepts require knowledge/information (e.g., a threshold, a normative model), specify it!

D — MILANA

1. The visualization should support the ______ (CONSUME) for a ______ (USE CASE) analysis.
2. To find an answer to the question, users need to ______ (SEARCH) ______ (PERSPECTIVE) aspects of ______ (DATA LEVEL).
3. It must be possible to ______ (QUERY) ______ (C1) ______ (C2).

Fig. 2. Overview of the different parts of the Milana method. (A) The "why" perspective of Brehmer and Munzner's visualization task typology [9]. (B) Classification of PM Tasks inspired from [31]. (C) Additional clarifications of key aspects. (D) Milana bridge, which makes use of all three parts to translate PM analysis tasks into actionable design guidance for VA experts.

- **C1:** What is expected from the answer, i.e., is a definite value (binary/numeric) expected or a qualitative description/explanation? If latter applies, what perspective constitutes a relevant context for the qualitative analysis?
- **C2:** How are the specific concepts are referred to by the questions defined (e.g., bottleneck, "working as agreed upon,..")? In case these concepts require knowledge/information (e.g., a threshold, a normative model), specify it!

4.2 Design of Milana

After completion of the iterations on the identification and adaptation of existing typologies, the second main component of the development phase was to operationalize the connection between PM tasks and VA methods. Therefore, we formulated a structured bridge that translates PM analysis tasks into actionable design guidance for VA experts. After testing several versions of it on our set of empirical analysis questions and discussing among the authors, Milana emerged as the composition of the following three sentences. They act as the final translation layer informing a task-oriented design of visualizations in PM (cf. Fig. 2D):

1. **"The visualization should support the *[Consume]* for a *[Use Case]* analysis."**
   This sentence sets the analytical objective by expressing the user's intention ("why" dimension) and grounding it in a concrete PM use case (e.g., compliance, performance). This framing aligns the visualization with the underlying motivation for analysis.
2. **"To find an answer to the question, users need to *[Search]* *[Perspective]* aspects of *[Data Level]*.**
   This sentence links the analytical objective to the required user actions and the relevant process characteristics. It draws from the "how" and "what" dimensions of the visualization task typology, connecting them to PM perspectives (e.g., time, control-flow) and the data granularity (log, trace, event).
3. **"It must be possible to *[Query]* *[C1]* *[C2]*".**
   This sentence provides technical design implications by specifying how users must be able to interact with the data. The placeholders [C1] and [C2] denote task-specific contextual constraints, such as comparison operators, filtering techniques, or temporal relationships that must be supported to accomplish the task (cf. Sect. 4.1).

5 Demonstration

To illustrate Milana's use, consider the following scenario: a PM expert prepares the bridge specifications for a PM task. A VA expert then takes these specifications and proposes a suitable VA interface design. Our overall vision is that in a realistic setting applying Milana to a collection of relevant PM tasks for

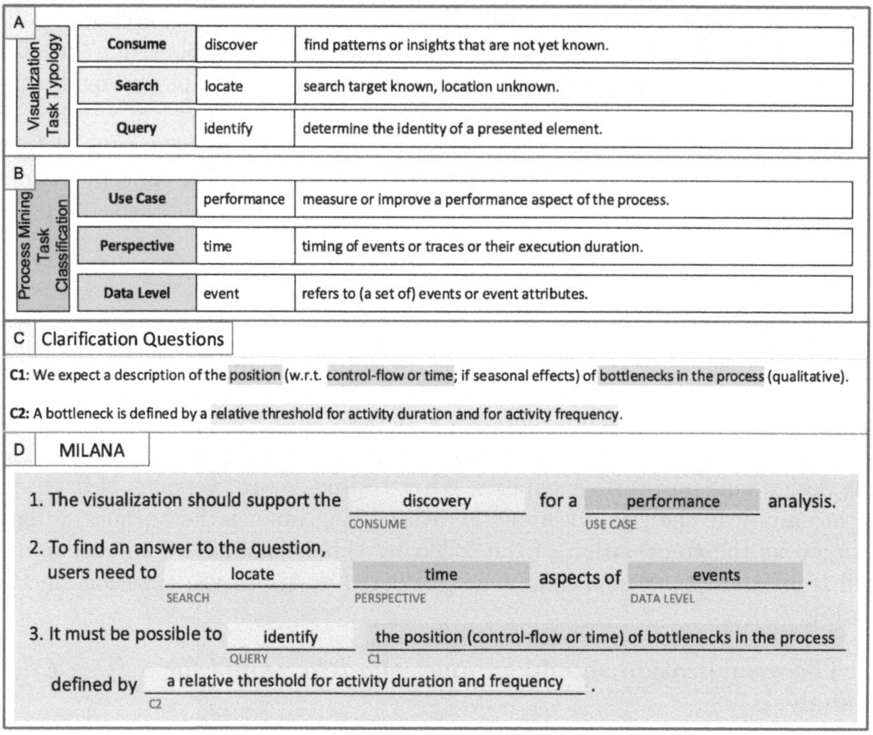

A Visualization Task Typology

Consume	discover	find patterns or insights that are not yet known.
Search	locate	search target known, location unknown.
Query	identify	determine the identity of a presented element.

B Process Mining Task Classification

Use Case	performance	measure or improve a performance aspect of the process.
Perspective	time	timing of events or traces or their execution duration.
Data Level	event	refers to (a set of) events or event attributes.

C Clarification Questions

C1: We expect a description of the position (w.r.t. control-flow or time; if seasonal effects) of bottlenecks in the process (qualitative).

C2: A bottleneck is defined by a relative threshold for activity duration and for activity frequency.

D MILANA

1. The visualization should support the discovery (CONSUME) for a performance (USE CASE) analysis.
2. To find an answer to the question, users need to locate (SEARCH) time (PERSPECTIVE) aspects of events (DATA LEVEL).
3. It must be possible to identify (QUERY) the position (control-flow or time) of bottlenecks in the process (C1) defined by a relative threshold for activity duration and frequency (C2).

Fig. 3. (A)–(C) Classifications made by the PM expert as input to Milana. (D) Application of Mialna to the demonstration example.

a given (business) process will help identify the common analytical needs and functionality requirements to guide the design of a tailored (interactive) visual interface for analysis.

For this demonstration, we choose a common and recurring task in PM projects: ***"Where are the bottlenecks in the process?"***. Identifying bottlenecks is relevant for uncovering concrete inefficiencies and has been identified as a commonly raised question in projects [18]. Several techniques, which can be attributed to the broader category of performance analysis [4], have been proposed and applied to support the analysis of bottlenecks. The relevance of this question has also been highlighted in the context of the Business Process Intelligence Challenge (BPIC) 2020, where it was among the questions posed by the process owners.

The classifications that were established by the PM expert for the task at hand are provided in Fig. 3A-C and form the input for Milana, which is provided in Fig. 3D. Based on the Milana bridge, the following visualization-related interpretations are made by the VA expert. The visualization interface should support *discovery* for performance analysis; this implies that the interface should enable *interactive exploration* of the process and its relevant performance aspects (in this case *temporal aspects*). Specifically, the interface needs to enable a user to *identify* where in the process (i.e. the control flow) bottleneck *events* occur. Bottleneck events are defined by a threshold for frequency and duration (*time aspects*) which is set interactively by the analyst.

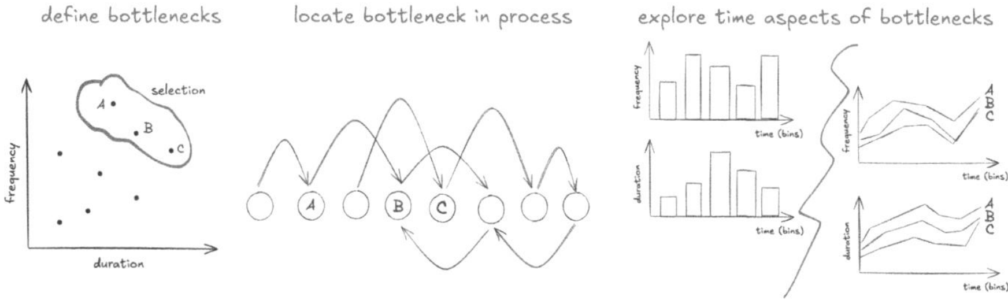

Fig. 4. Concept mockups of potential complementary views for bottleneck analysis

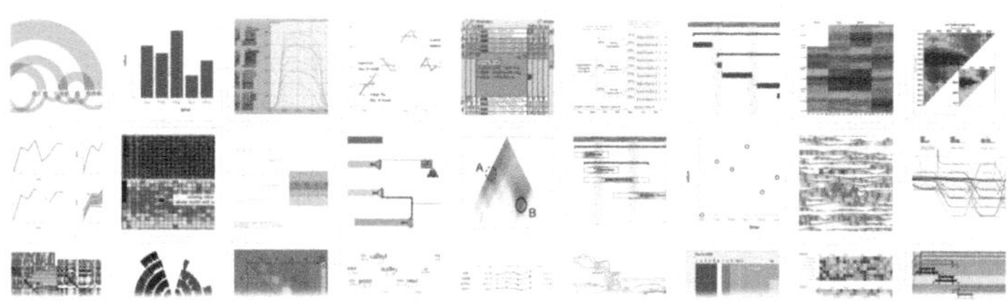

Fig. 5. Visualization techniques for time-oriented data from the TimeViz Browser [27].

This interpretation of the Milana bridge outlines the requirements for the visual interface enabling the VA expert to sketch initial mockup views, as provided in Fig. 4. To set the bottleneck threshold a representation is needed that shows an overview of the duration and frequency of events in which a user can make selections (qualitative identification). A representation for displaying continuous 2-dimensional data is the scatter plot (Fig. 4 left). A scatter plot mapping the average frequency vs average duration of events would reveal common events with long durations which could be selected as (potential) bottlenecks for further exploration. To locate these events in the context of the process and explore their temporal characteristics, a set of temporal views are needed. There are several alternatives that can be equivalently valid and the selection could be guided by surveys of visualization techniques for different data types (e.g., the survey of visualization techniques for time-oriented data [27]) as presented in Fig. 5). For displaying the process in a simplified manner a directional arc diagram was sketched (Fig. 4 middle) displaying the transitions between events with the bottlenecks highlighted. Temporal aspects such as average frequency and duration of events over time can with advantage be explored in well-established temporal representations such as histograms or line plots (Fig. 4 right).

Based on the sketched representation alternatives, a mockup of a prototype interface was created to experiment with the proposed views (cf. Fig. 6) based on the BPIC dataset 2020 [11]. The proposed interface comprises a scatter plot representation (Fig. 6, top left) showing the relationship between frequency and average duration, enabling a user to define the conditions (thresholds) for the bottleneck exploration by interactively selecting suspicious event types. Selecting events will highlight them by rendering the remaining semi-transparent.

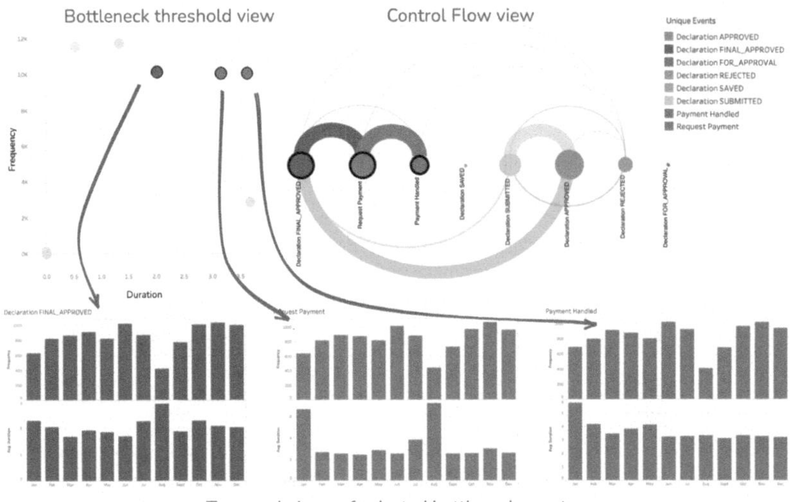

Fig. 6. Visualization interface mockup for bottleneck exploration elicited from Milana.

The control-flow is captured through an arc diagram showing the process overview (Fig. 6, top right). Nodes are drawn along a horizontal axis with connecting arcs marking transitions between events, enabling the quick identification of order and positioning the events of interest. Nodes are drawn proportional to their frequency and arcs are weighted by the number of transitions. "Forward" transitions are drawn above the nodes and "backward" transitions below. The nodes are by default sorted to reduce edge crossings but can be sorted according to different criteria such as a benchmark event order. Upon selection of bottleneck events in the scatter plot, they are highlighted in the arc diagram by a thicker stroke around the nodes and arcs starting from these are drawn opaque. In addition, corresponding histogram views are created for each selected bottleneck at the bottom of the interface (Fig. 6, bottom) revealing temporal aspects (duration and frequency over time) and providing additional context for analysis (e.g., the identification of seasonal bottlenecks).

Exploring the domestic travel declarations dataset from the BPIC 2020[2] in the proposed interface reveals that events with a high average duration and relevant frequencies are: `Payment Handled`, `Request Payment`, and `Declaration FINAL_APPROVED`. The arc diagram shows how these are connected to the other process events. The frequency distribution of all three is similar showing a notable drop in August. The distribution of durations varies between the selected events. `Declaration FINAL_APPROVED` peeks in August and shows a notable increase in January, July, October ($>$ 2 days). `Request Payment` displays large peeks in January and August while `Payment Handled` takes longest in January.

6 Discussion and Future Work

In this paper, we proposed a novel method for bridging PM tasks to visualization requirements. In particular, Milana serves as a conceptual bridge between domain-specific questions and VA design considerations, offering a shared foundation for PM analysts and visualization experts. To develop Milana, we reviewed existing task classifications from both VA and PM, and applied them to practical PM tasks until we converged to a version that could be applied to our selected subset of PM questions and successfully informed visualization design decisions, as demonstrated in Sect. 5. Thereby, our objectives when developing Milana were fourfold: (1) to establish a common vocabulary; (2) to translate PM-specific requirements into the visual design space; (3) to justify design decisions for visualization interfaces; and (4) to inform evaluation criteria. Milana addresses each of these goals by offering a structured format for articulating analysis needs by abstracting from concrete tasks, mapping them to actionable design elements, and fostering traceable rationales for interface decisions.

While Milana contributes a decisive step towards closer cooperation between the communities there is substantial room for further research. For example, we observed that the final translation of the Milana sentences by VA experts is not deterministic. Users may arrive at different, yet equally valid, design solutions for the same analytical question. This flexibility reflects the creative nature of design and the diversity of visualization strategies. Still, future work could investigate whether specific combinations of task characteristics tend to correlate with certain visualization patterns being more effective, thereby enabling more prescriptive guidance.

Additionally, a comprehensive evaluation needs be conducted to determine if Milana leads to *good* visualizations as well as to assess the overall utility of the bridge mechanism. The evaluation should follow an experimental design involving two groups: (1) a control group tasked with designing visualizations without structured guidance; and (2) a treatment group receiving guidance through Milana. This comparative approach will help isolate the impact of the bridge on users' ability to identify, interpret and utilize suitable visualizations effectively.

---

[2] Before analysis, we preprocessed the events and removed role names from the activity names.

To ensure the successful application of Milana, we plan to develop structured guidelines of use. At the moment, it is essential to involve a domain or PM expert to accurately categorize the analytical question. Their expertise is crucial in interpreting the context and ensuring that the question is framed correctly. However, we expect additional guidance will be needed to support the use of Milana, especially when not only applied by experts. This may include common classification patterns, examples of common question types and corresponding visualizations, or navigation support through existing surveys of visualization techniques, such as provided by [25,27], to guide users in selecting the right visualization based on Milana.

Acknowledgements. This paper resulted from discussions at Dagstuhl Seminar 23271. The authors thank the input of all participants on this topic. Further, this work was supported by the SNF (Grant No. 200021_197032), ISF (Grant No. 2005/21), and ARC Training Centre for Information Resilience IC200100022.

References

1. van der Aalst, W., et al.: Process mining manifesto. In: Daniel, F., Barkaoui, K., Dustdar, S. (eds.) BPM 2011. LNBIP, vol. 99, pp. 169–194. Springer, Heidelberg (2012). https://doi.org/10.1007/978-3-642-28108-2_19
2. van der Aalst, W.M.: Process discovery from event data: relating models and logs through abstractions. Wiley Interdiscip. Rev.: Data Min. Knowl. Discov. **8**(3) (2018)
3. van der Aalst, W.M., de Leoni, M., ter Hofstede, A.: Process mining and visual analytics: breathing life into business process models. BPM Center Report BPM-11-15, BPMcenter. org **17**, 699–730 (2011)
4. van der Aalst, W.: Process mining: a 360 degree overview. In: van der Aalst, W., Carmona, J. (eds.) Process Mining Handbook, pp. 3–34. Springer, Cham (2022). https://doi.org/10.1007/978-3-031-08848-3_1
5. Acampora, G., Vitiello, A., Di Stefano, B., van der Aalst, W., Günther, C., Verbeek, E.: IEEE 1849: the XES standard. IEEE Computational Intelligence Magazine, pp. 4–8 (2017)
6. Amar, R., Eagan, J., Stasko, J.: Low-level components of analytic activity in information visualization. In: IEEE Symposium on Information Visualization, pp. 111–117. IEEE (2005)
7. Andrienko, N., Andrienko, G.: Exploratory Analysis of Spatial and Temporal Data. Springer, Cham (2006)
8. Barbieri, L., Madeira, E., Stroeh, K., van der Aalst, W.: A natural language querying interface for process mining. J. Intell. Inf. Syst. **61**(1), 113–142 (2023)
9. Brehmer, M., Munzner, T.: A multi-level typology of abstract visualization tasks. IEEE Trans. Vis. Comput. Graph. **19**(12), 2376–2385 (2013)
10. vom Brocke, J., Jans, M., Mendling, J., Reijers, H.A.: A five-level framework for research on process mining. Bus. Inf. Syst. Eng. **63**(5), 483–490 (2021). https://doi.org/10.1007/s12599-021-00718-8

11. van Dongen, B.: BPI challenge 2020 (2020). https://doi.org/10.4121/uuid:52fb97d4-4588-43c9-9d04-3604d4613b51. 4TU.ResearchData collection
12. van Eck, M.L., Lu, X., Leemans, S.J.J., van der Aalst, W.M.P.: PM^2: a process mining project methodology. In: Zdravkovic, J., Kirikova, M., Johannesson, P. (eds.) CAiSE 2015. LNCS, vol. 9097, pp. 297–313. Springer, Cham (2015). https://doi.org/10.1007/978-3-319-19069-3_19
13. Heer, J., Shneiderman, B.: Interactive dynamics for visual analysis: a taxonomy of tools that support the fluent and flexible use of visualizations. Queue **10**(2), 30–55 (2012)
14. Hevner, A.R., March, S.T., Park, J., Ram, S.: Design science in information systems research. MIS Q. 75–105 (2004)
15. Keim, D., Andrienko, G., Fekete, J.-D., Görg, C., Kohlhammer, J., Melançon, G.: Visual analytics: definition, process, and challenges. In: Kerren, A., Stasko, J.T., Fekete, J.-D., North, C. (eds.) Information Visualization. LNCS, vol. 4950, pp. 154–175. Springer, Heidelberg (2008). https://doi.org/10.1007/978-3-540-70956-5_7
16. Klinkmüller, C., Müller, R., Weber, I.: Mining process mining practices: an exploratory characterization of information needs in process analytics. In: Hildebrandt, T., van Dongen, B.F., Röglinger, M., Mendling, J. (eds.) BPM 2019. LNCS, vol. 11675, pp. 322–337. Springer, Cham (2019). https://doi.org/10.1007/978-3-030-26619-6_21
17. Kubrak, K., Milani, F., Nolte, A.: A visual approach to support process analysts in working with process improvement opportunities. Bus. Process. Manag. J. **29**(8), 101–132 (2023)
18. Mans, R.S., van der Aalst, W.M.P., Vanwersch, R.J.B., Moleman, A.J.: Process mining in healthcare: data challenges when answering frequently posed questions. In: Lenz, R., Miksch, S., Peleg, M., Reichert, M., Riaño, D., ten Teije, A. (eds.) KR4HC/ProHealth -2012. LNCS (LNAI), vol. 7738, pp. 140–153. Springer, Heidelberg (2013). https://doi.org/10.1007/978-3-642-36438-9_10
19. Miksch, S., Di Ciccio, C., Soffer, P., Weber, B.: Visual analytics meets process mining: challenges and opportunities. IEEE Comput. Graph. Appl. **44**(6), 132–141 (2024). https://doi.org/10.1109/MCG.2024.3456916
20. Milani, F., Lashkevich, K., Maggi, F., Di Francescomarino, C.: Process mining: a guide for practitioners. In: In: Guizzardi, R., Ralyté, J., Franch, X. (eds.) RCIS 2022. LNBIP, vol. 446, pp. 265–282. Springer, Cham (2022). https://doi.org/10.1007/978-3-031-05760-1_16
21. Munzner, T.: A nested model for visualization design and validation. IEEE Trans Vis. Comput. Graphics **15**(6), 921–928 (2009)
22. Oral, E., Chawla, R., Wijkstra, M., Mahyar, N., Dimara, E.: From information to choice: a critical inquiry into visualization tools for decision making. IEEE Trans Vis. Comput. Graphics **30**(01), 359–369 (2024). https://doi.org/10.1109/TVCG.2023.3326593
23. Peffers, K., Tuunanen, T., Rothenberger, M.A., Chatterjee, S.: A design science research methodology for information systems research. J. Manag. Inf. Syst. **24**(3), 45–77 (2007)
24. Rind, A., Aigner, W., Wagner, M., Miksch, S., Lammarsch, T.: Task cube: a three-dimensional conceptual space of user tasks in visualization design and evaluation. Inf. Vis. **15**(4), 288–300 (2016). https://doi.org/10.1177/1473871615621602
25. Schulz, H.J.: Treevis.net: a tree visualization reference. IEEE Comput. Graphics Appl. **31**(6), 11–15 (2011). https://doi.org/10.1109/MCG.2011.103

26. Sorokina, E., Soffer, P., Hadar, I., Leron, U., Zerbato, F., Weber, B.: PEM4PPM: a cognitive perspective on the process of process mining. In: Di Francescomarino, C., Burattin, A., Janiesch, C., Sadiq, S. (eds.) BPM 2023. LNCS, vol. 14159, pp. 465–481. Springer, Cham (2023). https://doi.org/10.1007/978-3-031-41620-0_27
27. Tominski, C., Aigner, W.: The TimeViz browser – a visual survey of visualization techniques for time-oriented data (2023). https://browser.timeviz.net
28. Yeshchenko, A., Mendling, J.: A survey of approaches for event sequence analysis and visualization. Inf. Syst. **120**, 102283 (2024)
29. Yi, J.S., ah Kang, Y., Stasko, J., Jacko, J.A.: Toward a deeper understanding of the role of interaction in information visualization. IEEE Trans Vis. Comput. Graphics **13**(6), 1224–1231 (2007)
30. Zerbato, F., Koorn, J., Beerepoot, I., Weber, B., Reijers, H.: On the origin of questions in process mining projects. In: Almeida, J.P.A., Karastoyanova, D., Guizzardi, G., Montali, M., Maggi, F.M., Fonseca, C.M. (eds.) EDOC 2022. LNCS, vol. 13585, pp. 165–181. Springer, Cham (2022). https://doi.org/10.1007/978-3-031-17604-3_10
31. Zimmermann, L.: The process mining question forge. In: Proceedings of the Best Dissertation Award, Doctoral Consortium, and Demonstration and Resources Forum at BPM 2024 (2024)
32. Zimmermann, L., Zerbato, F., Weber, B.: What makes life for process mining analysts difficult? A reflection of challenges. Softw. Syst. Model. **23**(6), 1345–1373 (2024). https://doi.org/10.1007/s10270-023-01134-0

Addressing Directly-Follows Graphs Limitations with Visualization of Event Sequences

Luis Montana[1], Manuel Resinas[2], and Maria-Cruz Villa-Uriol[1,3](✉)

[1] School of Computer Science, University of Sheffield, Sheffield, UK
{l.montanagonzalez,m.villa-uriol}@sheffield.ac.uk
[2] Universidad de Sevilla, Seville, Spain
resinas@us.es
[3] INSIGNEO Institute for in silico Medicine, University of Sheffield, Sheffield, UK

Abstract. Visual Process Analytics (VPA) is emerging as a discipline where Process Mining (PM) and Visual Analytics (VA) experts collaborate to simplify the analysis and enhance the understanding of complex processes. In this work, we focus on Directly-Follow Graphs (DFGs), a common visualization technique used in PM, and identify how some of its limitations can be overcome by complementing DFGs with a timeline-based visualization strategy used in VA systems analyzing event sequences obtained from event logs. To illustrate this, we have chosen the Road Traffic Management Process dataset, a well-known dataset to the PM community. We have identified four cases where DFGs struggle to easily convey the exact nature of the underlying processes and show how timeline-based visualization strategies help disambiguate findings.

Keywords: Visual process analytics · Directly-Follows Graph · Event sequence visualization

1 Introduction

Data visualization plays a crucial role in analyzing datasets and uncovering meaningful insights. In process mining (PM), visualization techniques are essential to understand the execution of processes [4,8]. The Directly-Follows Graph (DFG) is a common visualization used in PM to represent control-flow behavior based on event logs. DFGs are simple to compute and generally easy to understand, though they can sometimes be misinterpreted [1].

Despite their advantages, DFGs also have limitations [1]. First, they become too complex with a high number of variants. The more variants, the larger the number of edges in the DFG, leading to Spaghetti-like DFGs difficult to interpret (**L1**). To simplify them, frequency-based thresholds are typically used, often leading to misinterpretations [1]. Second, concurrent activities may appear in varying orders across traces in the event log, leading to DFGs with loops,

I. van de Weerd et al. (Eds.): BPM 2025 Workshops, LNBIP 569, pp. 573–581, 2026.
https://doi.org/10.1007/978-3-032-13426-4_42

even when each activity occurs only once per case [1] (**L2**). Unlike more expressive modeling notations like Petri nets, DFGs often misrepresent concurrency as cyclic behavior. Third, DFGs usually have a low precision, i.e., they allow behaviors that are not observed in the event log (**L3**). Figure 1(a) shows the traces in an event log and its corresponding DFG in (c). This DFG allows traces like a → b → c → f → g (path in *red*), even though this behavior is not present in the event log. To address this problem, analysts use a range of manual and time-consuming strategies, such as exploring the process variants one by one, or filtering the event log to determine if a certain behavior is present or not. This task is, in some cases, unmanageable for large numbers of variants. Finally, DFGs represent repetitions of activities as loops. In Fig. 1(d), the repetition of activity c in a → b → c → c → c → g is shown as a self-transition in node c (arrow in *black*). However, it is not possible to obtain the number of repetitions in the DFG, i.e., whether c repeats three times or, for instance, eight times (**L4**). This also happens with loops involving several activities.

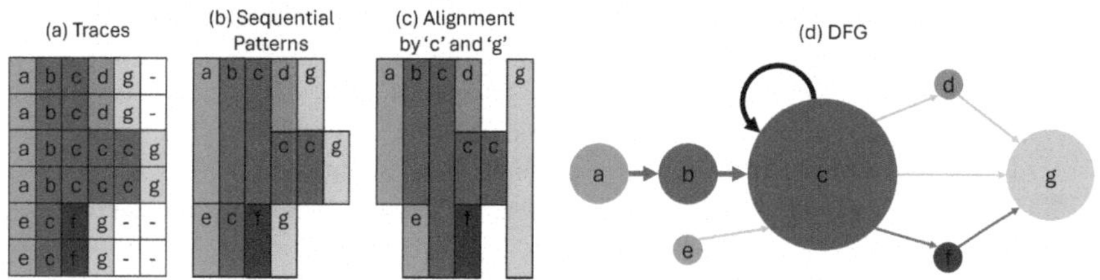

Fig. 1. (a) Event log with six traces represented as (b) sequential patterns, (c) sequential patterns with aligned activities, and (d) the corresponding DFG.

In recent years, visual process analytics has emerged to emphasize the role of interactive visualizations and the multifaceted nature of the data involved in process analysis [12,14]. Visual process analytics aims to make complex process data more accessible and actionable for analysts by combining the strengths of PM with principles from visual analytics (VA). This approach goes beyond static diagrams by integrating dynamic, user-driven visual tools that support exploration, comparison, and interpretation of process behavior. In this paper, we adopt this perspective to overcome these limitations of DFG-based analysis. We argue that they can be addressed by complementing the DFGs with a timeline-based visualization technique [11,17] that uses hierarchical clustering [11] and sequence alignment [6]. Figure 1 illustrates how, for the event log in (a), the sequential patterns representation in (b) is enhanced in (c) by using alignment by activities 'c' and 'g'. First, we provide an overview of the related work. Then, we describe the four scenarios analyzed, and we finally present the conclusions.

2 Related Work

Process mining and visual analytics, particularly the literature on VA of event sequences, differ in the terminology used for core concepts in the analysis of sequential event data. In PM, *activity* refers to a categorical action within a process, and is analogous to the *event type* in VA. A single *event* in PM, an instance of an activity with a timestamp and case ID, corresponds to an *event occurrence* (or *event*) in VA. *Traces* or *cases* are sequences of events associated with a single process instance in PM, being referred to as *individual sequences* in VA. *Variants* or *unique traces*, meaning distinct observed sequences across different cases, are *unique sequences* in VA. Finally, a *process model* in PM, which provides a high-level model of the process flow, serves a similar role to *sequential patterns* in VA, which provides an abstraction of frequent or representative event sequences across a dataset.

Visualization of Event Sequences. In PM, variant diagrams [14] are commonly used to visualize process variants, which represent unique sequences of activities. These diagrams arrange the variants vertically, and aligned to the left for consistency. Each activity within a variant is encoded using rectangles or horizontal chevrons, using distinct colors to enhance differentiation and readability. One limitation is that processes tend to have hundreds of variants, complicating the extraction of relevant insights. To address this, [2] proposed the use of sampling to select a representative set of variants, removing visual noise by coloring only the top 5 activities, and by ordering the traces by similarity to facilitate their reading. [13] also focus on visualizing variants using variant diagrams. However, in this case, they focus on event logs with partially ordered event data and heterogeneous temporal information per event (time intervals and time points).

In VA, existing techniques for visualizing event sequences primarily focus on encoding common pathways or sequential patterns [7,15]. In this context, van der Linden et al. [15] identified as still open challenges in the comparison of event sequences the definition of similarity metrics, the granularity of comparisons, the representation of temporal attributes, the integration of sequence attributes, and scalability. Recent surveys [7,18] provide an overview of these techniques, being particularly relevant timeline-based visualizations [5,10,16].

Table 1. Road traffic fines dataset. Acronyms representing activities and descriptions.

ID	Description	ID	Description
AP	Add Penalty	PAY	Payment
AJ	Appeal to Judge	RRA	Receive Result Appeal from prefecture
CF	Create Fine	SAP	Send Appeal to Prefecture
IDA	Insert Date Appeal to prefecture	SF	Send Fine
IFN	Insert Fine Notification	SFC	Send For Credit collection
NRA	Notify Result Appeal to offender		

3 Selected Scenarios

We have selected four scenarios where event sequence visualizations can complement DFGs to address some of their limitations in representing general structure, parallelism, repetitions, and precision. We use the Road Traffic Fines dataset [9], which spans 13 years of road traffic fine management by a police force in Italy, comprising 150,370 cases and 561,480 events (Table 1).

Screenshots for the timeline-based event sequence visualizations have been obtained using Sequen-C [11], a visual analytics system for the analysis of event sequences that uses hierarchical agglomerative clustering to identify clusters of similar sequences. This strategy facilitates the simplification of complex datasets and enables the breakdown of the complexity of the processes under study [3]. DFGs have been created in Python, using `Dash`, `Cytoscape` and `distinctipy`.

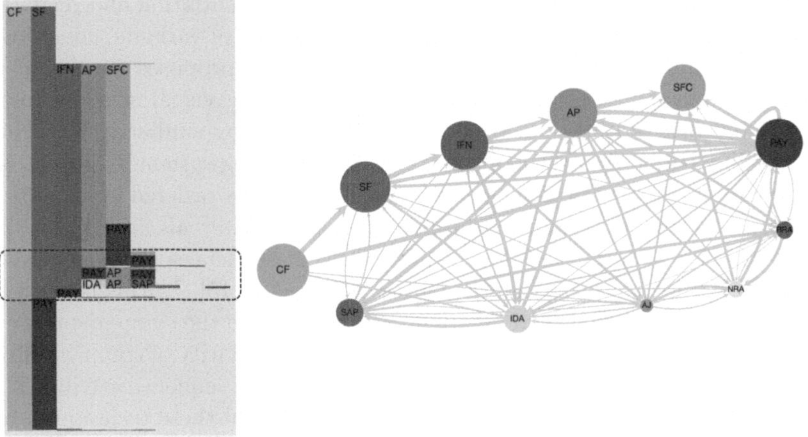

Fig. 2. Timeline-based event sequence visualization (*left*) vs. DFG (*right*) for the Road Traffic Fines dataset [9], highlighting the less frequent traces (dashed line).

General Structure (L1). Event sequence visualizations and DFGs use a different visual encoding to reveal the general structure and dominant patterns in a dataset. Figure 2 (*left*) shows the complete road fine dataset, with height encoding frequency. This visualization allows for an easy identification of recurrent structures and frequent and infrequent sequences. The vertically aligned bars and stacked events reveal the key activities (CF, SF, IFN, AP, SFC). The most commonly repeated patterns are exposed (e.g., CF → SF; CF → SF → IFN → AP → SFC; CF → SF → IFN → AP → PAY; and CF → PAY), also revealing the proportion of infrequent sequences and their complexity. This allows the quick identification of those sequences that deviate the most from the most common patterns. In contrast, the corresponding DFG representation Fig. 2 (*right*), despite encoding the frequency of occurrence of activities and transitions, is complex to interpret. The high connectivity and visually dense network obscure the identification of how sequences progress. While the DFG effectively captures all possible transitions between events, its capacity to reveal high-level structure is limited.

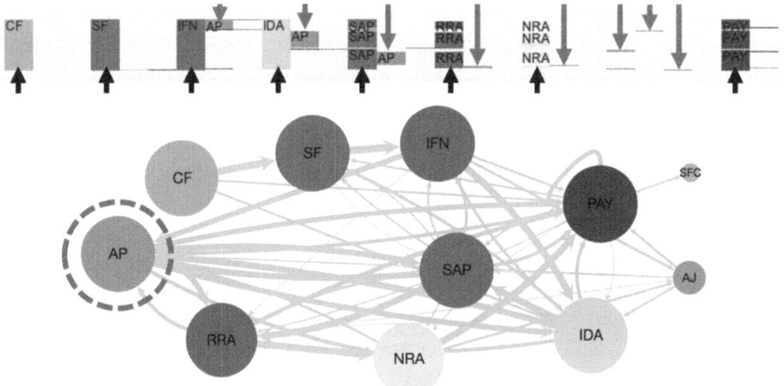

Fig. 3. Timeline-based event sequence visualization (*top*) vs. DFG (*bottom*) for 516 traces in the road traffic fines dataset [9]. The activity of interest AP is highlighted using *red arrows and circle*, and the alignment events using *black arrows.*

Parallelism (L2). Event sequence visualizations and DFGs represent differently concurrent activities, i.e., activities that can be run in parallel and may appear in varying orders across traces in the event log. Figure 3 shows an example where the activity AP occurs repeatedly over time (*red* arrows), and is not always preceded by the same activity. AP follows activities as distinct as IFN, IDA, SAT, RRA, and NRA. This suggests that AP does not exhibit a strong dependency on specific prior events and can be interleaved with a wide range of other activities. This representation is particularly effective in revealing this positional variability. In this case, AP might have been triggered after a pre-established period and after checking that a fine has not yet been paid in full. To obtain the visualization in Fig. 3, event alignment (*black* arrows) has been used to align and group the activities of interest that have been identified as precursors of AP, namely, IFN, IDA, SAT, RRA and NRA. Alignment is often used in event sequence visualization as a means to explore temporal order. To achieve alignment, additional spaces are inserted between the events of interest selected as alignment events. In this case, we chose IFN, IDA, SAT, RRA and NRA to explore their relationship with AP. While alignment maintains the order of activities, it introduces visual gaps that do not represent real time. These gaps support alignment and visual comparison, but they may reduce the visibility of the broader process context by spacing activities apart.

The corresponding DFG representation in Fig. 3(*bottom*) abstracts away temporal ordering in favor of aggregated transition relations. While the AP node has incoming edges from nearly all other activities, except for CF, SF, and SFC, indicating high in-degree, the graph structure cannot communicate when and how frequently AP occurs in different contexts. As a result, the DFG lacks the expressiveness needed to assess the degree to which AP is executed concurrently with other activities in the process.

Precision (L3). Event sequence visualizations visualize behaviours that occurred in the event log, whereas DFGs allow for behaviors that may have never occurred in the event log (see Sect. 1). This forces the analyst to use strategies to confirm whether a certain behavior in the DFG has occurred or not. Next, we show how event sequence visualizations can support the analyst in this task.

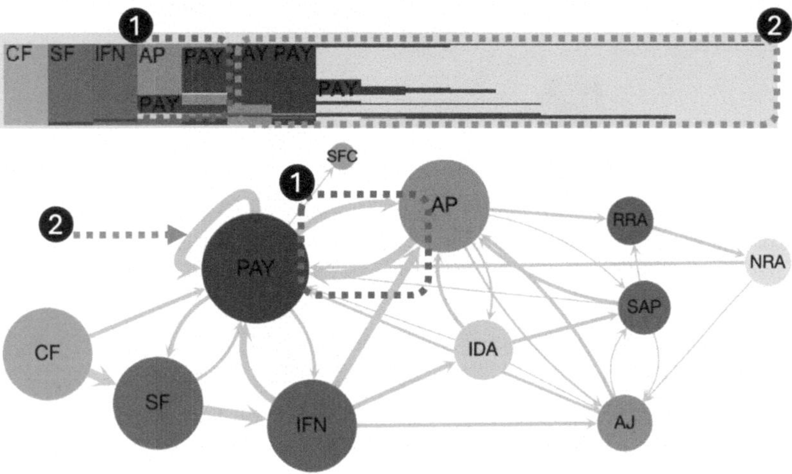

Fig. 4. Timeline-based event sequence visualization (*top*) vs. DFG (*bottom*) for 170 traces in the road traffic fines dataset [9].

Cycles vs Order. The area highlighted (*red rectangle*) in the DFG in Fig. 4 illustrates a typical example of a cycle between two activities: PAY and AP. However, simply looking at the DFG does not reveal whether this is a true cycle, i.e., whether traces exist that include multiple alternating occurrences of penalties and payments, such as ... → AP → PAY → AP → PAY. In contrast, the event sequence visualization provides a clearer picture of the actual behavior recorded in the event log and makes it clear that such a cycle does occur. The highlighted area (*red rectangle*) in the event sequence visualization shows that multiple payments (PAY) can occur within the same case, while penalties (AP) are applied only once.

Focus on a Single Activity. When analyzing process data, a typical scenario involves characterizing the sequence of activities that lead to the execution of a particular activity. For instance, in our case, we might be interested in identifying which activity sequences typically precede or avoid the activity Send for Credit Collection (SFC), which indicates that a case has been forwarded to a credit collection agency due to non-payment of a fine. This kind of analysis is difficult to perform directly using a Directly-Follows Graph (DFG), which aggregates control-flow relations without preserving trace-level detail. For instance, the DFG in Fig. 2 shows that SFC is most commonly preceded by AP and PAY, and occasionally by NRA, RRA, AJ, or SAP. However, due to the limited support of DFGs for path disambiguation, it is not possible to reconstruct the full context or differentiate between alternative sequences that converge on SFC. In contrast, the event sequence visualization in the same figure keeps the temporal ordering of individual traces. This allows analysts to visually identify common and exceptional paths that lead to SFC. For example, it becomes apparent that SFC frequently follows the path CF → SF → IFN → AP → SFC, and less commonly, CF → SF → IFN → AP → PAY → SFC. It also becomes clear that certain paths—such as CF → PAY (without SF) or CF → SF → PAY (without IFN)—systematically avoid SFC. Such insights are possible because the event sequence visualization preserves trace-level granularity and visually encodes sequence variation.

Repetitions (L4). One key distinction between event sequence visualizations and DFGs lies in their ability to represent consecutive repetitions of events. In the event sequence visualization of Fig. 4(*top*), the area highlighted (*blue rectangle*) shows clearly that the event PAY occurs repeatedly and in immediate succession. The visual encoding of sequential order along the horizontal axis facilitates the identification of repetitions but also their exact frequency and position within the temporal sequence. In contrast, the DFG representation (*bottom*) abstracts away the temporal order. The presence of a self-loop on the node PAY (*blue arrow*) indicates that PAY can transition to itself, but this fails to convey how frequently or when this transition occurs within the cases containing this activity. While the graph effectively summarizes possible transitions, it omits critical information about the temporal ordering of events.

Combining DFGs and Timeline-Based Visualizations. Both offer complementary insights for process analysis. DFGs provide a high-level overview of all possible transitions, highlighting activities with high connectivity, identifying self-transitions and potential repetitions. Timeline-based visualizations reveal dominant patterns, highlighting frequency of events, and exposing the main paths leading to or avoiding key activities. Together, these views enable a more nuanced and complete understanding of processes.

4 Conclusions

This work contributes to the emerging field of visual process analytics. We examined four limitations of DFGs, commonly used in PM, and illustrated them through some examples in the Road Traffic Fines Management dataset. We have shown how a timeline-based visualization, commonly used in VA for event sequence analysis, offers more interpretable insights by preserving trace-level detail and highlighting patterns that are otherwise obscured by the aggregated structure of DFGs. However, these visualizations can be difficult to interpret with increasing number of sequences and events, often suffering from visual clutter.

Our paper highlights how this type of visualizations can address DFGs limitations, but they are not a replacement. DFGs can reveal infrequent yet important behaviors that may be overlooked in timeline-based visualizations due to frequency-based scaling. Both approaches are complementary. As future work, we aim to develop interactive mechanisms to support their seamless coordination.

Acknowledgments. This work started at Schloss Dagstuhl (Leibniz-Zentrum für Informatik), seminars 23271 "Human in the (Process) Mines" and 25152 "Multi-Faceted Visual Process Mining" and was partially supported by the European Union's Sano project (No. 857533), PID2021-126227NB-C21/AEI/10.13039/501100011033/FEDER, EU; TED2021-131023B-C22/AEI/10.13039/501100011033/Unión Europea NextGenerationEU/PRTR, and PID2024-156482NB-I00/AEI/10.13039/501100011033/ESF+.

Disclosure of Interests. The authors have no competing interests to declare that are relevant to the content of this article.

References

1. van der Aalst, W.M.P.: A practitioner s guide to process mining: limitations of the directly-follows graph. Procedia Comput. Sci. **164**, 321–328 (2019)
2. Bernard, G., Andritsos, P.: VisuELs: visualization of event logs (extended abstract). In: ICPM Conference (2021)
3. Bose, R.P.J.C., van der Aalst, W.M.P.: Trace clustering based on conserved patterns: towards achieving better process models. In: Rinderle-Ma, S., Sadiq, S., Leymann, F. (eds.) BPM 2009. LNBIP, vol. 43, pp. 170–181. Springer, Heidelberg (2010). https://doi.org/10.1007/978-3-642-12186-9_16
4. Capitán-Agudo, C., Salas-Urbano, M., Cabanillas, C., Resinas, M.: Analyzing how process mining reports answer time performance questions. In: Di Ciccio, C., Dijkman, R., del Río Ortega, A., Rinderle-Ma, S. (eds.) BPM 2022. LNCS, vol. 13420, pp. 234–250. Springer, Cham (2022). https://doi.org/10.1007/978-3-031-16103-2_17
5. Chen, Y., Xu, P., Ren, L.: Sequence synopsis: optimize visual summary of temporal event data. IEEE Trans. Vis. Comput. Graph. **24**(1), 45–55 (2018)
6. Du, F., Shneiderman, B., Plaisant, C., Malik, S., Perer, A.: Coping with volume and variety in temporal event sequences: strategies for sharpening analytic focus. IEEE Trans. Vis. Comput. Graph. **23**(6), 1636–1649 (2016)
7. Guo, Y., Guo, S., Jin, Z., Kaul, S., Gotz, D., Cao, N.: Survey on visual analysis of event sequence data. IEEE Trans. Vis. Comput. Graph (2022)
8. Jalali, A., et al.: dfgcompare: a library to support process variant analysis through Markov models. BMC Med. Inform. Decis. Mak. **21**(1), 356 (2021)
9. de Leoni, M., Mannhardt, F.: Road traffic fine management process (2015). https://doi.org/10.4121/uuid:270fd440-1057-4fb9-89a9-b699b47990f5

10. Liu, Z., Kerr, B., Dontcheva, M., Grover, J., Hoffman, M., Wilson, A.: CoreFlow: extracting and visualizing branching patterns from event sequences. Comput. Graph. Forum **36**(3), 527–538 (2017)
11. Magallanes, J., Stone, T., Morris, P.D., Mason, S., Wood, S., Villa-Uriol, M.C.: Sequen-C: a multilevel overview of temporal event sequences. IEEE Trans. Vis. Comput. Graph. **28**(1), 901–911 (2022)
12. Miksch, S., Di Ciccio, C., Soffer, P., Weber, B.: Visual analytics meets process mining: challenges and opportunities. IEEE Comput. Graph. **44**, 132–141 (2024)
13. Schuster, D., Zerbato, F., van Zelst, S.J., van der Aalst, W.M.P.: Defining and visualizing process execution variants from partially ordered event data. Inf. Sci. **657**, 119958 (2024)
14. van den Elzen, S., Jans, M., Martin, N., Pieters, F., Tominski, C., Villa-Uriol, M.C., van Zelst, S.J.: Towards multi-faceted visual process analytics. Inf. Syst. **133**, 102560 (2025)
15. van der Linden, S., de Fouw, E., van den Elzen, S., et al.: A survey of visualization techniques for comparing event sequences. Comput. Graph. (2023)
16. Vrotsou, K., Nordman, A.: Exploratory visual sequence mining based on pattern-growth. IEEE Trans. Vis. Comput. Graph. **25**(8), 2597–2610 (2019)
17. Wongsuphasawat, K., Guerra Gómez, J.A., Plaisant, C., Wang, T.D., Taieb-Maimon, M., Shneiderman, B.: LifeFlow: visualizing an overview of event sequences. In: SIGCHI, pp. 1747–1756. ACM (2011)
18. Yeshchenko, A., Mendling, J.: A survey of approaches for event sequence analysis and visualization. Inf. Syst. **120**, 102283 (2024)

Visualizing Object-Centric Petri Nets

Tobias Brachmann[1](✉), István Koren[2,3], Lukas Liss[2], and Wil M. P. van der Aalst[2]

[1] RWTH Aachen University, Aachen, Germany
tobias.brachmann@rwth-aachen.de
[2] Chair of Process and Data Science, RWTH Aachen University, Aachen, Germany
[3] Department of Data Science and Engineering, ELTE University, Budapest, Hungary

Abstract. Object-centric process mining (OCPM) is gaining traction in both academia and industry due to its ability to model real-world processes more accurately than traditional case-centric approaches. By considering multiple interacting objects, object-centric Petri nets (OCPNs) offer a richer process representation, but this also introduces unique challenges for visualization. The presence of multiple object types, variable arcs, and complex interactions complicates the creation of clear and interpretable layouts. In this paper, we address these challenges by presenting a dedicated layout algorithm tailored to the structural characteristics of OCPNs. Inspired by the Sugiyama framework, the algorithm balances aesthetic and functional criteria, guided by a set of domain-specific quality metrics. We implemented our approach in an open-source web-based tool, OCPN Visualizer, and a reusable JavaScript library for integration into third-party applications. A user study confirms the practical relevance of our approach and highlights its effectiveness in improving the interpretability of object-centric process visualizations.

Keywords: Object-Centric Petri Net · Process Visualization · Layout Algorithm · Sugiyama

1 Introduction

The rise of object-centric process mining (OCPM) reflects a shift in how organizations analyze and understand processes. Traditional process mining approaches typically rely on a case-centric perspective, modeling a process in terms of a single entity, such as an order. Real-world processes involve interactions among entities (e.g., orders, customers, products) that case-centric models cannot adequately capture. This disconnect has motivated the development of OCPM, which provides a more realistic and comprehensive representation of complex business processes [32].

Object-centric Petri nets, an extension of classical Petri nets with typed places representing different object types, have emerged as a key modeling formalism for OCPM. OCPNs support richer modeling but pose new visualization

I. van de Weerd et al. (Eds.): BPM 2025 Workshops, LNBIP 569, pp. 582–597, 2026.
https://doi.org/10.1007/978-3-032-13426-4_43

challenges. The structural complexity arising from multiple object types, variable arcs, and inter-object dependencies makes it difficult to generate intuitive layouts. Traditional visualization approaches for Petri nets are often insufficient, as they do not account for the semantics introduced by object-centricity.

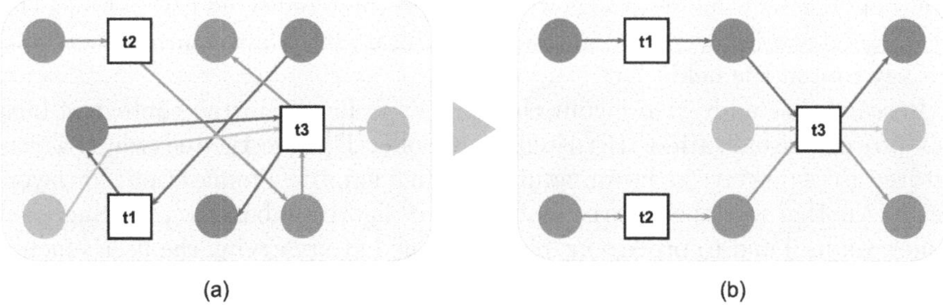

Fig. 1. Two visualizations of the same OCPN, where (a) represents a poorly organized layout and (b) illustrates an improved, more structured layout

Larger OCPNs, especially those mined from real data, make clear visualization increasingly difficult. Poorly structured layouts can lead to visual clutter and obscure the underlying relationships between entities, complicating interpretation. Figure 1 illustrates the impact of layout quality: while the left-hand side displays a disorganized structure with overlapping edges and weak object separation (objects distinguished by colors), the right-hand side demonstrates how a layout tailored to object-centric properties improves readability and interpretability by grouping related elements and emphasizing structural flow.

Despite the growing interest in OCPM, existing tools offer limited support for visualizing OCPNs. We address this gap by proposing a layout algorithm tailored to OCPNs, extending the Sugiyama framework [28] to incorporate object-type grouping, flow direction, and edge clarity. Our contributions are threefold: (1) quality metrics that combine graph aesthetics with object-centric criteria, (2) the layout algorithm itself, and (3) an open-source implementation available both as a web-based visualizer and a JavaScript library. We evaluate our approach through runtime analysis and a user study.

The remainder of this paper is structured as follows. Section 2 reviews related work in process mining and graph drawing. Section 3 introduces key concepts and definitions. Section 5 presents our layout algorithm and quality metrics. Section 6 describes the implementation. Section 7 reports the evaluation results, including a comparison with existing tools and a user study. Finally, Sect. 8 concludes the paper and outlines directions for future work.

2 Related Work

This section reviews prior work on process mining techniques and graph drawing methods relevant to the visualization of object-centric process models.

2.1 Object-Centric Process Mining

Traditional process mining focuses on analyzing event logs under a single case notion [31]. However, many real-life processes involve interactions between multiple entities, which led to the development of *object-centric process mining*. This paradigm shift addresses the limitations of single-case models by enabling the discovery of OCPNs from event logs with multiple interconnected case notions [33]. The method was implemented in the *pm4py* library [8], which continues to evolve as a key tool in the field.

Research has addressed layout challenges specifically in the context of business process visualization. Bernstein and Soffer [7] investigated which layout features users perceive as meaningful, providing empirical foundations for layout design. Another work proposes a stable layout algorithm based on the Sugiyama framework, tailored to process graphs and aimed at preserving the user's mental map during interactive filtering [22]. Gschwind et al. [20] introduced a linear-time layout algorithm for business process models that emphasizes readability through structural simplification. Sonke et al. [26] focused on optimal algorithms for compact linear layouts, which are particularly relevant for minimizing space while retaining clarity in flow-based visualizations.

Despite these advances, tools for visualizing OCPNs remain limited. *Celonis* is a commercial tool supporting object-centric visualizations. *OC*π [1] offers sequence-based visualizations and filtering capabilities for OCPNs, relying on the *Graphviz* library. Meanwhile, *pm4py* supports object-centric discovery and visualization within a Python environment. General-purpose graph layout libraries (e.g., Graphviz) do not consider domain semantics like object grouping, making their output hard to interpret in OCPN contexts. This motivates the need for specialized visualization approaches.

2.2 Graph Drawing

Graph drawing aims to represent relational data visually using algorithms that produce readable, structured layouts [5,13]. One prominent approach is the already mentioned Sugiyama method [28], a framework for drawing directed graphs by organizing vertices into hierarchical layers. The method is composed of multiple steps (i.a., cycle breaking, layering, vertex ordering), and has inspired extensive research into optimizing each step (e.g., [16,29].

Force-directed algorithms such as Fruchterman-Reingold [18] use the physical analogies of vertices repelling each other and edges acting as springs to achieve visually balanced layouts. These methods are intuitive and flexible but computationally intensive for larger graphs. Magnetic-field-based techniques [27] introduce directional forces to emphasize hierarchies or flows, especially useful in layered or directed graphs. Hybrid approaches aim to combine the strengths of these techniques [12].

Aesthetic principles play a vital role in enhancing graph readability. Studies emphasize minimizing edge crossings, maintaining consistent edge lengths, and maximizing symmetry [24]. These criteria improve user comprehension and reduce cognitive load when interpreting complex graphs [6].

3 Preliminaries

In this section, we provide an overview of key concepts in process mining and graph drawing.

3.1 Process Mining

OCPM extends classical process mining by modeling interactions between multiple object types, such as orders, products, and customers. While traditional Petri nets rely on a single-case notion, OCPNs support multiple interacting lifecycles. For example, the transition "ship product" may involve both an order and a product. This complexity complicates visualization and motivates our graph-based layout approach. We assume universes of activity names ($\mathbb{U}_{act}$) and object types ($\mathbb{U}_{ot}$) as given.

Definition 1 (Labeled Petri Net [33]). *A labeled Petri net is a tuple* $N = (P, T, F, l)$ *where:*

- P*: Set of places*
- T*: Set of transitions, with* $P \cap T = \varnothing$
- $F \subseteq (P \times T) \cup (T \times P)$*: Flow relation between places and transitions*
- $l \in T \nrightarrow \mathbb{U}_{act}$*: Labeling function that maps transitions to activity names*

While the underlying graph structure of Petri nets is bipartite, we formally define relevant graph-theoretic concepts in Sect. 3.2.

Definition 2 (Object-Centric Petri Net [33]). *An object-centric Petri net is a tuple* $ON = (N, pt, F_{var})$*, where:*

- $N = (P, T, F, l)$*: Labeled Petri net*
- $pt \in P \to \mathbb{U}_{ot}$*: Mapping function that assigns object types to places*
- $F_{var} \subseteq F$*: Subset of variable arcs*

In an OCPN, places represent typed objects and transitions represent activities involving them. Arcs define token flow (i.e., object references) between places and transitions. *Variable arcs*, rendered as double lines, indicate that the number of involved objects is not fixed (e.g., "assemble order" may consume multiple products).

3.2 Graphs

To support our layout algorithm, we now formalize the underlying graph structures derived from OCPNs.

Definition 3 (Directed Graph [3]). *A directed graph* $G = (V, E)$ *consists of a set of vertices* V *and a set of ordered pairs* $E \subseteq V \times V$ *called edges.*

For an edge (u, v), often denoted $u \to v$, u is the *head*, v the *tail*. Vertices u, v are *adjacent* if $(u, v) \in E$, and each is a *neighbor* of the other. A vertex is *incident* to an edge if it is either head or tail. A sequence $\langle u_1, \ldots, u_k \rangle$ is a *path* if $(u_i, u_{i+1}) \in E$ for all $i < k$; it is a *cycle* if also $(u_k, u_1) \in E$. A digraph is *acyclic* if it contains no cycles.

Definition 4 (DAG [30]). *A DAG is a directed acyclic graph.*

The *outdegree* and *indegree* of a vertex u are denoted $d_G^+(u)$ and $d_G^-(u)$, respectively. A vertex with zero outdegree is a *sink*; with zero indegree, a *source* [14]. A graph $G = (V, E)$ is *bipartite* if V can be partitioned into $V_1 \cup V_2$ such that no two vertices within the same set are adjacent [2]. OCPNs can be modeled as bipartite graphs with places P and transitions T as vertex sets, and flow relation F as edges.

A key step in layered layout is converting cyclic graphs into DAGs. Since OCPNs derived from real-world data may contain cycles, these must be removed as a preprocessing step for layout computation.

Definition 5 (Feedback Arc Set (FAS) [11]). *A feedback arc set in a digraph $G = (V, E)$ is a subset $F \subseteq E$ such that $(V, E \setminus F)$ is acyclic.*

Finding a minimal FAS is NP-hard [9,25] and underpins the preprocessing for layer assignment.

Layer Assignment. Given a DAG $G = (V, E)$, a *layering* is a partition $\mathcal{L} = \{L_0, \ldots, L_h\}$ of V, where $(u, v) \in E$ implies $u \in L_j, v \in L_i, i < j$. We define:

Definition 6 (Layer Assignment Problem [17,21]). *Given a DAG, find a layering $\mathcal{L}$ such that all edges point from lower to higher layers.*

The *rank* of a vertex u is the index i such that $u \in L_i$, denoted $\text{rank}(u, \mathcal{L})$. The *span* of edge (u, v) is $\text{rank}(u) - \text{rank}(v) \geq 1$. If span $= 1$, the edge is *tight*; otherwise, *long*. We convert long edges to tight ones by inserting *dummy vertices* at intermediate layers.

The *height* of a layering is $h + 1$, its *width* is the maximum layer size, and its *area* is the product of both [14,21,30].

Barycenter Heuristic. Vertex ordering within layers plays a crucial role in reducing edge crossings and preserving structural clarity. A common technique for this is the barycenter heuristic, which reorders vertices based on the average positions of their neighbors in adjacent layers.

Definition 7 (Barycenter [14,28]). *For a vertex u in a layer, let $N(u)$ denote the adjacent vertices of u in the layer above (or below). The barycenter $b(u)$ is defined as:*

$$b(u) = \frac{1}{\mid N(u) \mid} \sum_{v \in N(u)} pos(v)$$

where $pos(v)$ is the position of the vertex v in the adjacent layer.

Having established the key graph-theoretic foundations, the next section defines the quality metrics that guide and evaluate our layout algorithm. These metrics combine classical aesthetic criteria from graph drawing with domain-specific considerations relevant to object-centric process models.

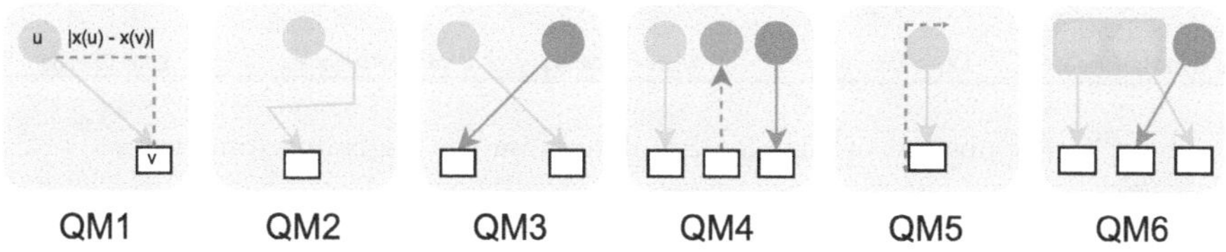

Fig. 2. The six quality metrics used in the layout algorithm

4 Quality Metrics

Our layout algorithm is driven by the following six quality metrics, which can be categorized into two groups. The first five metrics (**QM1**–**QM5**) are derived from principles in the graph drawing literature [24] and aim to promote general readability. The final metric (**QM6**) is specific to the object-centric nature of OCPNs, capturing structural aspects that are unique to this modeling formalism.

QM1 *Total edge length.* Measures the sum of edge lengths across the layout. While longer edges are not inherently problematic, reducing total length often leads to more compact visualizations and helps avoid excessive whitespace.

QM2 *Edge bends.* Counts the number of bends along edges. Layouts with fewer bends tend to produce simpler and more coherent visual connections.

QM3 *Edge crossings.* Counts the number of edge intersections. Minimizing crossings is a well-known heuristic to support visual clarity and reduce ambiguity in complex graphs.

QM4 *Flow consistency.* Identifies edges that run counter to the dominant flow direction (e.g., from bottom to top in a top-down layout). While not all reversed edges hinder interpretation, a consistent flow direction can support the mental map of users and improve navigation through the process structure.

QM5 *Aspect ratio balance.* Assesses the ratio between the width and height of the layout. Extremely wide or tall layouts can lead to inefficient use of space and fragmented views when visualized in scrolling interfaces.

QM6 *Object-type grouping.* Measures the spatial variance of places with the same object type across the layout. A lower variance indicates stronger grouping, which can help users identify object-level structure and interpret inter-object dependencies.

Figure 2 illustrates the six quality metrics using synthetic examples. These metrics are used throughout the layouting pipeline and also inform the evaluation described in Sect. 7.

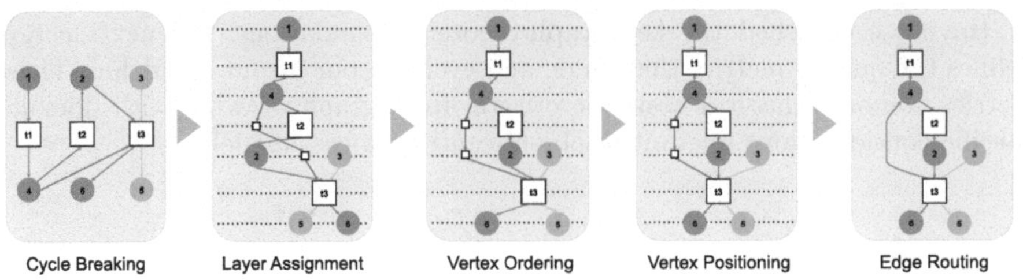

Fig. 3. Substeps of our algorithm based on the Sugiyama framework

5 Layout Algorithm

In this section, we present the design of our layout algorithm, based on the Sugiyama framework [28]. The general pipeline of our algorithm consists of five steps, shown in Fig. 3.

In the first step, **Cycle Breaking**, the possibly cyclic graph is transformed into an acyclic graph by reversing the minimum number of edges whose reversal makes the graph acyclic. This is necessary for the following step, **Layer Assignment**, where each vertex of the graph is assigned a rank so that for each edge of the graph, the tail has a lower rank than the head. For edges where the head and tail vertices are not on adjacent layers, so-called dummy vertices are inserted in every layer between the layers of the head and tail. After each vertex has been assigned a rank, the **Vertex Ordering** step minimizes the number of edge crossings and groups related vertices together by determining a relative order within the layers. Now, every vertex has a relative position determined by its rank and index in its layer. The next step, **Vertex Positioning**, computes the actual X and Y coordinates for the vertices based on their rank and index in their layer. In the last step, **Edge Routing**, the edges between adjacent vertices are drawn with their original direction. For edges where dummy vertices had been introduced in the Layer Assignment step, the positions of the dummy vertices are used as path points to draw the edge.

Input. The inputs of our layout algorithm are the OCPN $ON = (N, pt, F_{var})$ where $N = (P, T, F, l)$, and the user settings *Config*, including various parameters and preferences that influence the layout, such as flow direction, included object types, distances, and vertex sizes.

Cycle Breaking. To build a layered visualization using the Sugiyama framework, the input graph must be acyclic. However, the input graph, $G = (V, E)$, derived from the OCPN may contain cycles. To address this issue, our algorithm includes a cycle-breaking step, which reverses a set of edges to make the graph acyclic. Following QM4 (flow direction), we aim to find the smallest possible set that satisfies the condition of making the graph acyclic upon reversal. In our implementation, we adapt and modify an algorithm, known as Greedy Cycle Removal, proposed by Eades et al. [15]. This algorithm provides a good, though not necessarily optimal, solution to the minimum FAS problem and runs in linear time. The greedy FAS algorithm computes a linear ordering of vertices and solves the FAS problem by taking the set of edges with direction against the ordering as a solution (Fig. 4).

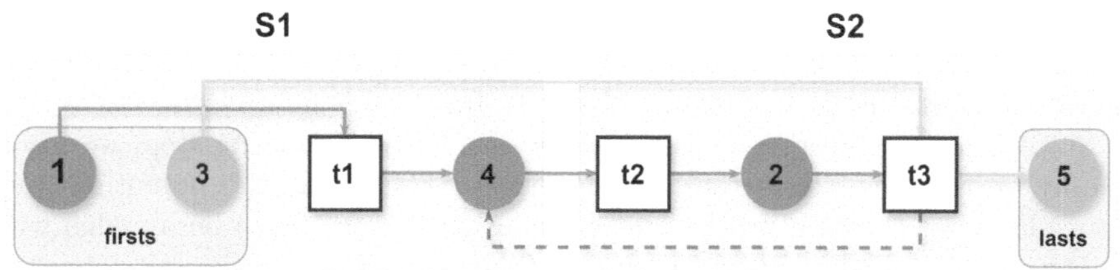

Fig. 4. The modified Greedy Cycle Removal algorithm. For this example, the user has selected $firsts = [1, 3]$ and $lasts = [5]$. The edge $e = (t3, 4)$ will be reversed because $ind_s(t3) = 6 > 3 = ind_s(4)$. Note that reversing the edge $e = (t3, 4)$ results in a DAG.

We modified the algorithm by incorporating two sets of vertices: *firsts* and *lasts*. The vertices in *firsts* are placed at the beginning of the ordering and the vertices in *lasts* are placed at the end. This modification enables users to control the assignment of vertices to the horizontal layers, assigned during the Layer Assignment.

Layer Assignment. The objective for the layer assignment step is to obtain a proper layered DAG G' by solving the layer assignment problem for the DAG G^*. That means we assign each vertex of the DAG to a specific layer, ensuring that every edge flows from a higher layer (head) to a lower layer (tail) while inserting dummy vertices for edges spanning multiple layers. This process provides a clear directional flow for all edges, addressing QM4. Furthermore, a compact layering is crucial, as it directly impacts the quality of the layout. Fewer layers result in fewer dummy vertices, which can shorten edge lengths (QM1), reduce edge bends (QM2), and positively influence the number of edge crossings (QM3). Additionally, a good layer assignment improves the proportion between the width and height of the visualization (QM5).

To achieve an optimal layering, $\mathcal{L} = \{L_0, L_1, \ldots, L_h\}$, of G^*, we employ an ILP approach, first introduced by Gansner and Emden [19]. This method minimizes h, the number of layers required, and thus the amount of dummy vertices, while respecting the graph's structural constraints. The ILP formulation is as follows:

$$\text{minimize} \sum_{e \in E^*} span(e, \mathcal{L}) \qquad \text{(Objective Function)}$$

Subject to:

$$rank(u, \mathcal{L}) - rank(v, \mathcal{L}) \geq 1, \forall (u, v) \in E^* \quad \text{(Edge Constraint)}$$
$$rank(u, \mathcal{L}) \geq 0, \forall u \in V \quad \text{(Positive Constraint)}$$
$$rank(u, \mathcal{L}) \in \mathbb{N}, \forall u \in V \quad \text{(Integer Constraint)}$$

To solve the above ILP formulation, we utilize a library that implements a simplex method [23] that returns a layering $\mathcal{L}$ of G^*. That is, for every vertex u we obtain a $rank(u, \mathcal{L})$ so that the objective function is minimized.

Since a proper layering is essential for the Vertex Ordering step, we insert dummy vertices for edges that are not tight. This turns the potentially not proper layering $\mathcal{L}$ into a proper one. Formally, let $e = (u, v)$ be an edge with $rank(u, \mathcal{L}) = j$ and $rank(v, \mathcal{L}) = i$ and $span(e, \mathcal{L}) = j - i > 1$. Then we add dummy vertices d_e^{i+1}, $d_e^{i+2}, \ldots, d_e^{j-1}$ to the layers $L_{i+1}, L_{i+2}, \ldots, L_{j-1}$ and replace edge e by the path $(u,\ d_e^{j-1}, \ldots,\ d_e^{i+1},\ v)$ [21].

Vertex Ordering. The Vertex Ordering step aims to minimize edge crossings and promote the clustering of places with the same object type, addressing layout quality metrics such as edge crossings (QM3), total edge length (QM1), edge bends (QM2), and object type grouping (QM6). The output is a reordered layering $\mathcal{L}$ of the graph G' with the lowest observed layout score.

Layer-by-Layer Sweep. Our algorithm applies a layer-by-layer sweep based on a modified barycenter heuristic, alternating between two directions: a *downward sweep*, where layers L_{h-1} to L_0 are reordered based on the positions of vertices in the layer below (L_{i+1}); and an *upward sweep*, where layers L_1 to L_h are reordered based on the positions of vertices in the layer above (L_{i-1}).

An optional presorting step may precede the sweeps, where object types are ordered according to a user-defined mapping and places are sorted accordingly to promote initial clustering.

Barycenter Computation for Places. Each place vertex $p \in L_i$ receives a barycenter value $b_p(p)$ combining neighbor-alignment and object type grouping. The value is computed as:

$$b_p(p) = (1 - \alpha) \cdot b(p) + \alpha \cdot b_{\text{object}}(p),$$

where $\alpha \in [0, 1]$ is a user-defined weight, $b(p)$ is the average position of p's neighbors in $L_{i\pm1}$ (depending on sweep direction), and

$$b_{\text{object}}(p) = \frac{1}{\mid N_{\text{object}}(p) \mid} \sum_{u \in N_{\text{object}}(p)} pos(u),$$

with $N_{\text{object}}(p)$ being the set of places with the same object type as p in a user-defined range of layers above or below the current layer.

Barycenter Computation for Other Vertex Types. For *transitions*, the barycenter $b(t)$ is computed using only adjacent vertices in the neighboring layer; clustering is not applied. For *dummy vertices*, which connect to exactly one neighbor in the adjacent layer, the barycenter equals the position of that neighbor.

Reordering Based on Barycenters. Once barycenter values are computed for all vertices in layer L_i, the layer is reordered from left to right by sorting vertices in ascending order of these values. In case of ties, the previous order is preserved to maintain stability.

Termination Conditions. The sweep process alternates downward and upward passes across the layered graph. After each *complete sweep* (i.e., one downward and one upward pass), the current vertex layering $\mathcal{L}$ is evaluated using the layout score:

$$score(\mathcal{L}, G') = |\text{Edge Crossings}| + \alpha \cdot \text{Object Attraction Quality},$$

where the first term counts edge crossings and the second quantifies how well places of the same type are grouped. The process continues until either (i) no score improvement is observed after k consecutive sweeps (with k from the configuration), or (ii) the vertex ordering matches a previous sweep. The final output is the layering $\mathcal{L}$ with the lowest score, minimizing edge crossings and promoting object-type clustering.

Vertex Positioning. Given the reordered layering $\mathcal{L}$ from the vertex ordering step, the graph G', and user configurations $Config$, the goal is to assign X and Y coordinates to all vertices, while respecting the layer structure.

Our algorithm supports both top-down (vertical) and left-right (horizontal) layouts, aligning with the flow semantics in QM4. We describe the top-down case: X coordinates are computed based on the within-layer order, while Y coordinates are uniform across each layer. Since Y positioning is straightforward, we focus on the more complex task of X coordinate computation. In the horizontal layout, this logic is mirrored.

To compute horizontal positions while preserving edge straightness and vertex order, we adapt the heuristic by Brandes and Köpf [10], which addresses layout quality via QM1 and QM2. The algorithm consists of three phases: **Vertical Alignment**, **Horizontal Compaction**, and **Balancing**. The first two are repeated across four alignment variants (upper/lower, leftmost/rightmost medians), and the final layout is obtained by averaging the results to ensure a well-balanced visual structure.

Edge Routing. With the X and Y coordinates for all vertices in the graph G' determined, the next step is to finalize the layout by routing the edges. Edge routing ensures that edges are drawn clearly and do not overlap with other elements of the graph, such as places or transitions, while preserving the structure and flow of the graph. Any edges that were reversed during the cycle-breaking step are restored to their original direction during this phase.

We begin by adjusting the positions of the outer dummy vertices, ensuring that they are aligned at the top or bottom of their respective layers. For an edge e, which had been replaced by the path $(u, d_e^{j-1}, \ldots, d_e^{i+1}, v)$, the outer dummies are d_e^{j-1} and d_e^{i+1}. After adjusting the positions of the outer dummies the edges are routed to the center of the respective vertices. Finally, the outer dummy vertices are used as path points to guide the edges. The inner dummy vertices, if any, are ignored for routing, as the horizontal alignment guarantees that long edges will follow a straight path along the X-axis. This simple approach results in a clear, well-organized layout where edges are routed to the appropriate connection points of vertices and avoid overlap.

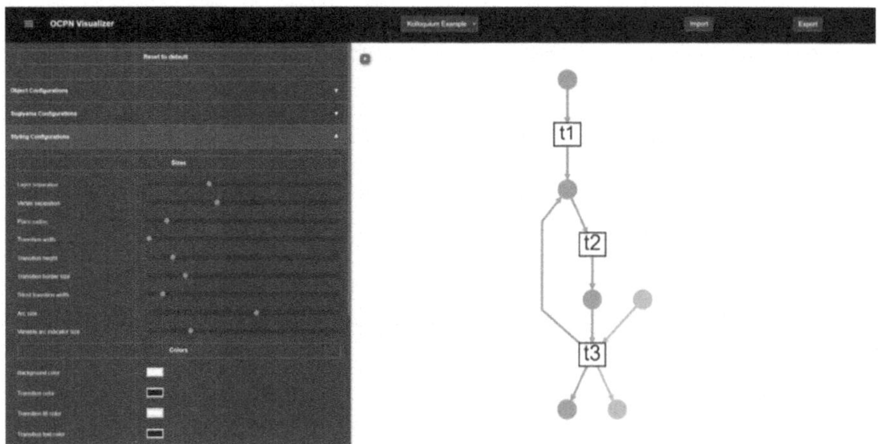

Fig. 5. GUI of the OCPN Visualizer with layout configuration options on the left (not intended to be readable here)

6 Implementation

The OCPN Visualizer is a web-based tool that integrates our layout algorithm[1]. It is developed using a state-of-the-art technology stack, consisting of a React and Next.js frontend and a TypeScript backend. Our implementation utilizes several libraries: `GLPK.js` is employed to solve the layer assignment problem, and `D3.js` supports the creation of interactive and visually expressive SVG-based graphics. The core layouting logic is available as the reusable npm package `ocpn-viz`.

Figure 5 shows the GUI of the OCPN Visualizer with the configuration options on the left. To support flexible exploration, our tool includes a configuration panel that allows users to adjust visual parameters, such as node width, arc curvature, and label padding, and see the layout update in real time. This

[1] Source code and app: https://github.com/rwth-pads/ocpn-visualizer.

helps users adapt the visualization to specific model characteristics or preferences (e.g., focusing on arc routing or text readability). Additionally, hovering and clicking on transitions or places reveals further details, aiding the interpretation of densely connected models. While we do not yet support filtering or collapsing parts of the net, these interactive adjustments already improve navigability and comprehension, especially for large models.

7 Evaluation

To evaluate the performance of our approach, we used a set of OCPNs of varying sizes and structural complexities. These included both small, synthetic models and larger, more complex instances designed to reflect real-world characteristics. All benchmarks were run on a modern consumer-grade laptop using Chrome. For each OCPN, the metrics recorded included the number of places ($|P|$), transitions ($|T|$), edges ($|F|$), variable arcs ($|F_{var}|$), dummies introduced during layer assignment ($|D|$), and object types ($|OT|$). *Layout time* refers to the time required to compute the coordinates for all vertices in the OCPN, while *visualization time* is the time taken to draw the output SVG. Table 1 summarizes the performance results across OCPNs of varying complexities.

Table 1. Run times in ms for OCPNs of increasing sizes

$\mid P\mid$	$\mid T\mid$	$\mid F\mid$	$\mid F_{var}\mid$	$\mid D\mid$	$\mid OT\mid$	Layout (ms)	Visualization (ms)
1	1	2	0	0	1	25.81	18.24
17	9	28	9	0	3	28.61	163.41
25	9	40	20	2	5	37.14	173.81
23	17	46	10	4	3	28.27	318.13
17	22	50	4	34	3	44.18	449.44
37	23	74	6	48	7	66.7	440.39
48	44	116	10	86	7	85.87	828.29
38	62	140	4	210	2	149.2	1222.7

Using the profiler within Chrome DevTools, we measured the memory usage of the *OCPN Visualizer* across OCPNs of varying complexity. The memory usage grew proportionally with the size of the OCPNs, starting at 746 kB for a small OCPN with two vertices and reaching 1.5 MB for a larger OCPN with 310 vertices. This trend indicates good scalability, as the memory usage remains manageable even for more complex OCPNs.

7.1 PM4Py vs OCPN Visualizer

We compared visualizations generated by the *OCPN Visualizer* and *pm4py* [8] using three OCPNs of varying sizes to highlight their respective strengths.

For small and medium models, the *OCPN Visualizer* offers faster run times, interactive features, and clearer layouts, thanks to object-type grouping, variable arc support, and styling options. In contrast, *pm4py* produces aesthetically polished, compact layouts with curved edges and clear source/sink labeling, but lacks interactivity and customization. For larger models, *pm4py* outperforms in runtime and visual metrics such as edge length, bends, and crossings, though its layouts vary across executions. The *OCPN Visualizer*, while slower on large inputs, delivers consistent, interpretable results. Overall, *pm4py* suits large-scale visualization, while the *OCPN Visualizer* excels in usability and clarity for smaller models. Further improving its layout algorithm could extend its competitiveness to larger OCPNs.

7.2 User Study

To evaluate the user experience of our tool *OCPN Visualizer* we conducted a user study employing the System Usability Scale (SUS) [4]. The 20 participants that had varying levels of expertise were given two tasks: First, they had to follow a set of guided instructions to visualize a provided OCPN. Then, they were asked to achieve a target visualization by utilizing the available user configurations. After completing both tasks, participants submitted the SUS questionnaire, consisting of ten standardized questions, and open feedback. The SUS score averaged 78.6, indicating good usability. While most users found the tool highly usable, a few experienced moderate difficulties. Informal feedback indicated that the live configuration options and responsive layout adjustments improved the comprehensibility and usability of the tool. To further assess the practical value of our approach, we plan to conduct additional user studies using models discovered from real event logs to evaluate effectiveness in realistic process analytics scenarios, and to directly compare our visualizations with those produced by commercial tools such as Celonis.

8 Conclusion

This paper addressed the challenge of visualizing OCPNs, a task complicated by the lack of specialized tools and evaluation methods. To bridge this gap, we developed the *OCPN Visualizer*, a web-based tool featuring a dedicated layout algorithm and user configuration options, along with *ocpn-viz*, a reusable NPM package. Our work was guided by three objectives focusing on layout strategies, user interaction features, and quality metrics for visualization evaluation.

We defined six quality metrics tailored to OCPNs, combining established graph aesthetics with domain-specific needs such as object-type clustering. These informed the development of our layout algorithm. A two-part evaluation comparing our tool with *pm4py* and conducting a user study demonstrated strong performance in usability, interpretability, and scalability. The algorithm produced clear layouts for small and medium models, while offering improvements in clarity and interactivity over existing tools.

The findings validate our approach while highlighting areas for future improvement, including layout refinements, more advanced edge routing, and empirical validation of the proposed metrics. The defined quality metrics may also serve as a foundation for replicable comparisons of alternative layout algorithms in future work. Overall, this research provides a solid foundation for advancing OCPN visualization in both academic and practical contexts.

Acknowledgements. Funded by the Deutsche Forschungsgemeinschaft (DFG, German Research Foundation) under Germany's Excellence Strategy - EXC-2023 Internet of Production - 390621612.

References

1. Adams, J.N., van der Aalst, W.M.P.: OCπ: object-centric process insights. In: Bernardinello, L., Petrucci, L. (eds.) PETRI NETS 2022. LNCS, vol. 13288, pp. 139–150. Springer, Cham (2022). https://doi.org/10.1007/978-3-031-06653-5_8
2. Asratian, A.S., Denley, T.M.J., Häggkvist, R.: Bipartite Graphs and Their Applications, 1 edn. Cambridge University Press (1998). https://doi.org/10.1017/CBO9780511984068
3. Bang-Jensen, J., Gutin, G.Z.: Digraphs - Theory, Algorithms and Applications. Springer Monographs in Mathematics, 2nd edn. Springer (2009)
4. Bangor, A., Kortum, P.T., Miller, J.T.: An empirical evaluation of the system usability scale. Int. J. Hum. Comput. Interact. **24**(6), 574–594 (2008). https://doi.org/10.1080/10447310802205776
5. Battista, G.D., Eades, P., Tamassia, R., Tollis, I.G.: Algorithms for drawing graphs: an annotated bibliography. Comput. Geom. **4**(5), 235–282 (1994). https://doi.org/10.1016/0925-7721(94)00014-X
6. Bennett, C., Ryall, J., Spalteholz, L., Gooch, A.: The aesthetics of graph visualization. In: Cunningham, D.W., et al. (eds.) 3rd International Symposium on Computational Aesthetics in Graphics, Visualization, and Imaging, Banff, AB, Canada, 20–22 June 2007, pp. 57–64. Eurographics Association (2007). https://doi.org/10.2312/COMPAESTH/COMPAESTH07/057-064
7. Bernstein, V., Soffer, P.: How does it look? Exploring meaningful layout features of process models. In: Persson, A., Stirna, J. (eds.) Advanced Information Systems Engineering Workshops, vol. 215, pp. 81–86. Springer, Cham (2015). https://doi.org/10.1007/978-3-319-19243-7_7
8. Berti, A., van Zelst, S., Schuster, D.: PM4Py: a process mining library for Python. Softw. Impacts **17**, 100–556 (2023). https://doi.org/10.1016/j.simpa.2023.100556
9. Brandenburg, F.J., Hanauer, K.: Sorting heuristics for the feedback arc set problem (2011)
10. Brandes, U., Köpf, B.: Fast and simple horizontal coordinate assignment. In: Mutzel, P., Jünger, M., Leipert, S. (eds.) GD 2001. LNCS, vol. 2265, pp. 31–44. Springer, Heidelberg (2002). https://doi.org/10.1007/3-540-45848-4_3
11. Charbit, P., Thomassé, S., Yeo, A.: The minimum feedback arc set problem is NP-hard for tournaments. Comb. Probab. Comput. **16**(1), 1–4 (2007). https://doi.org/10.1017/S0963548306007887
12. Chimani, M., Gutwenger, C., Jünger, M., Klau, G.W., Klein, K., Mutzel, P.: The open graph drawing framework (OGDF). In: Tamassia, R. (ed.) Handbook on Graph Drawing and Visualization, pp. 543–569. Chapman and Hall/CRC (2013)

13. Eades, P., Hong, S.H.: Symmetric graph drawing. In: Tamassia, R. (ed.) Handbook on Graph Drawing and Visualization, pp. 87–113. Chapman and Hall/CRC (2013)
14. Eades, P., Lin, X.: How to draw a directed graph. In: IEEE Workshop on Visual Languages, VL 1989, Rome, Italy, 4–6 October 1989, pp. 13–17. IEEE Computer Society (1989). https://doi.org/10.1109/WVL.1989.77035
15. Eades, P., Lin, X., Smyth, W.F.: A fast and effective heuristic for the feedback arc set problem. Inf. Process. Lett. **47**(6), 319–323 (1993). https://doi.org/10.1016/0020-0190(93)90079-O
16. Eades, P., Wormald, N.C.: Edge crossings in drawings of bipartite graphs. Algorithmica **11**(4), 379–403 (1994). https://doi.org/10.1007/BF01187020
17. Eiglsperger, M., Siebenhaller, M., Kaufmann, M.: An efficient implementation of Sugiyama's algorithm for layered graph drawing. J. Graph Algorithms Appl. **9**(3), 305–325 (2005). https://doi.org/10.7155/JGAA.00111
18. Fruchterman, T.M.J., Reingold, E.M.: Graph drawing by force-directed placement. Softw. Pract. Exp. **21**(11), 1129–1164 (1991). https://doi.org/10.1002/SPE.4380211102
19. Gansner, E.R., Koutsofios, E., North, S.C., Vo, K.P.: A technique for drawing directed graphs. IEEE Trans. Software Eng. **19**(3), 214–230 (1993). https://doi.org/10.1109/32.221135
20. Gschwind, T., Pinggera, J., Zugal, S., Reijers, H.A., Weber, B.: A linear time layout algorithm for business process models. J. Visual Lang. Comput. **25**(2), 117–132 (2014). https://doi.org/10.1016/j.jvlc.2013.11.002
21. Healy, P., Nikolov, N.S.: Hierarchical drawing algorithms. In: Tamassia, R. (ed.) Handbook on Graph Drawing and Visualization, pp. 409–453. Chapman and Hall/CRC (2013)
22. Mennens, R.J., Scheepens, R., Westenberg, M.A.: A stable graph layout algorithm for processes. Comput. Graphics Forum **38**(3), 725–737 (2019). https://doi.org/10.1111/cgf.13723
23. Nelder, J.A., Mead, R.: A simplex method for function minimization. Comput. J. **7**(4), 308–313 (1965). https://doi.org/10.1093/COMJNL/7.4.308
24. Purchase, H.C.: Metrics for graph drawing aesthetics. J. Vis. Lang. Comput. **13**(5), 501–516 (2002). https://doi.org/10.1006/JVLC.2002.0232
25. Simpson, M., Srinivasan, V., Thomo, A.: Efficient computation of feedback arc set at web-scale. Proc. VLDB Endow. **10**(3), 133–144 (2016). https://doi.org/10.14778/3021924.3021930
26. Sonke, W., Verbeek, K., Meulemans, W., Verbeek, E., Speckmann, B.: Optimal algorithms for compact linear layouts. In: 2018 IEEE Pacific Visualization Symposium (PacificVis), pp. 1–10. IEEE, Kobe (2018). https://doi.org/10.1109/PacificVis.2018.00010
27. Sugiyama, K., Misue, K.: Graph drawing by the magnetic spring model. J. Vis. Lang. Comput. **6**(3), 217–231 (1995). https://doi.org/10.1006/JVLC.1995.1013
28. Sugiyama, K., Tagawa, S., Toda, M.: Methods for visual understanding of hierarchical system structures. IEEE Trans. Syst. Man Cybern. **11**(2), 109–125 (1981). https://doi.org/10.1109/TSMC.1981.4308636
29. Tamassia, R.: On embedding a graph in the grid with the minimum number of bends. SIAM J. Comput. **16**(3), 421–444 (1987). https://doi.org/10.1137/0216030
30. Tang, H., Hu, Z.: Network simplex algorithm for DAG layering. In: 2013 International Conference on Computational and Information Sciences, pp. 1525–1528. IEEE, Shiyang (2013). https://doi.org/10.1109/ICCIS.2013.401
31. van der Aalst, W.M.P.: Process Mining - Data Science in Action, 2nd edn. Springer, Cham (2016)

32. Aalst, W.M.P.: Object-centric process mining: dealing with divergence and convergence in event data. In: Ölveczky, P.C., Salaün, G. (eds.) SEFM 2019. LNCS, vol. 11724, pp. 3–25. Springer, Cham (2019). https://doi.org/10.1007/978-3-030-30446-1_1
33. van der Aalst, W.M.P., Berti, A.: Discovering object-centric petri nets. Fundam. Inform. **175**(1–4), 1–40 (2020). https://doi.org/10.3233/FI-2020-1946

What BPM Researchers Should Know About Visual Analytics

Maria-Cruz Villa-Uriol[1,2,3(✉)]

[1] School of Computer Science, University of Sheffield, Sheffield, UK
m.villa-uriol@sheffield.ac.uk
[2] INSIGNEO Institute for in silico Medicine, Sheffield, UK
[3] Healthy Lifespan Institute (HELSI), Sheffield, UK

Abstract. Visual Process Analytics (VPA) is an emerging discipline at the intersection of Process Mining (PM) and Visual Analytics (VA), aiming to facilitate the analysis and enhance the understanding of complex processes. In this keynote, the speaker reflected on her research journey in the visual analysis of temporal event sequences, commonly referred to as cases or traces within the PM community, and situated this work within the broader context of process mining and VPA. To illustrate this trajectory, she used two systems developed in her VA research group, Sequen-C Explorer and EventBox, as case studies for examining both the benefits and challenges of applying visual analytics to process data, while also pointing to future opportunities for advancing the field.

Keywords: Visual process analytics · Visual analytics · Process mining

1 Introduction

Process Mining (PM) seeks to generate insights into the execution of complex processes by analyzing event data recorded in event logs [1]. Visual Analytics (VA), more broadly, develops interactive visual methods to support human understanding of multifaceted data. At their intersection, Visual Process Analytics (VPA) has emerged as a research opportunity that unites the goals of both communities: advancing methods to make complex processes and phenomena more comprehensible [7,12]. This convergence has been further stimulated by dedicated forums such as the Schloss Dagstuhl seminars 23271 Human in the (Process) Mines and 25152 Multi-Faceted Visual Process Mining.

Traditionally, PM has focused on discovering, analyzing, and improving process models derived from event logs, with particular attention on temporal aspects and contextual attributes [1]. Its methods are largely algorithmic and strongly oriented toward delivering actionable insights for organizations. In contrast, VA is grounded in the integration of data, analytical tasks, and the characteristics of the end-users posing those tasks. VA systems combine visualization, computation, and interactivity to support human sense-making across diverse

I. van de Weerd et al. (Eds.): BPM 2025 Workshops, LNBIP 569, pp. 598–602, 2026.
https://doi.org/10.1007/978-3-032-13426-4_44

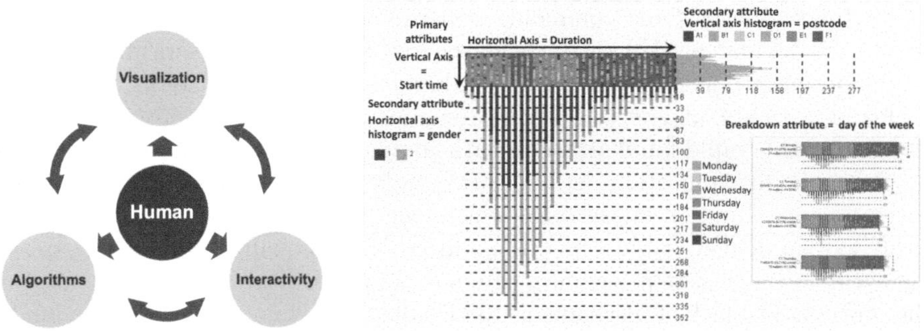

Fig. 1. Human-centered VA.

Fig. 2. Example of VA comparisons [8].

types of data (see Fig. 1). Authors such as Munzner [9] have highlighted the foundational dimensions of data, representation, and interaction design, while Tominski et al. [11] have stressed the pivotal role of interactivity (Fig. 2).

Despite clear synergies, the two fields retain distinct emphases: PM tools have a focus on established visualizations and user-driven exploration strategies, while VA research, although methodologically rich, lacks the strong links to companies interested in improving their internal operations. As noted by Yeshchenko et al. [14], PM tends to prioritize algorithmic discovery, whereas VA emphasizes exploration, interpretation and evaluation of the proposed visualizations.

This disciplinary gap exists in the use of terminology. Concepts central to PM have direct analogues in VA, albeit under different names. Activities in PM correspond to event types in VA; individual events (activity instances with a timestamp and case ID) to event occurrences; traces or cases to individual sequences; variants to unique sequences; and process models to sequential patterns.

The VA community has already developed extensive resources on time-oriented data visualization [2], visual data analytics [3], and interactive techniques [11], alongside the formalization proposed by Munzner in terms of data abstractions, tasks abstraction, visual representations and validation [9]. Recent work has also identified open challenges in the analysis of event sequences [5,13,14], which includes the development of a multilevel task framework [15]. Interactive online tools such as the Event Sequences Viz Browser [4] and the TimeVis Browser 2.0 [10] provide valuable entry points for exploring this body of knowledge.

2 Risks and Benefits of VA for PM

The use of VA in PM applications offers substantial benefits. However, each benefit entails potential risks, especially when data quality, uncertainty, heterogeneity and scalability challenges are not adequately addressed. Some of these are illustrated below.

Overviews. VA systems commonly generate visual summaries that present event logs at a high level of abstraction (see Fig. 3). These overviews give analysts a valuable entry point to quickly identify dominant temporal patterns, frequently occurring variants, and overall process dynamics. As such, they provide orientation and enable rapid familiarization with complex datasets. However, overviews may also obscure important details, particularly in large or noisy datasets. Rare variants, anomalies, or exceptions—which can carry high diagnostic value—are easily hidden in aggregated views. In addition, if data quality is poor (e.g., missing events or inconsistent logging), summaries may present distorted pictures of the process. The lack of mechanisms to visualize uncertainty further compounds this risk, creating a misleading sense of precision.

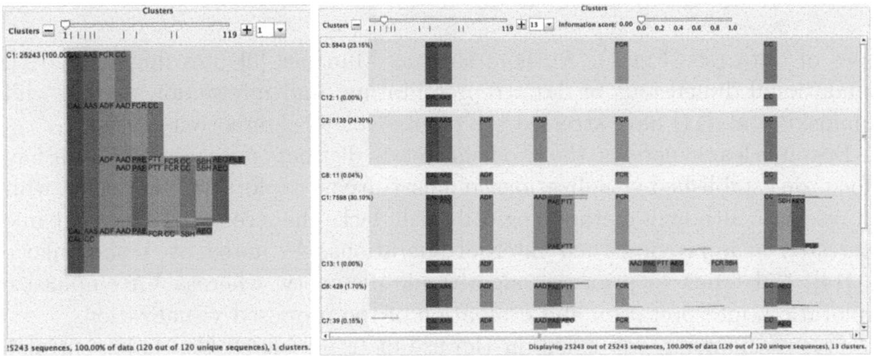

Fig. 3. Two examples of overviews (*left*) a single overview, and (*right*) an overview containing 13 clusters [6].

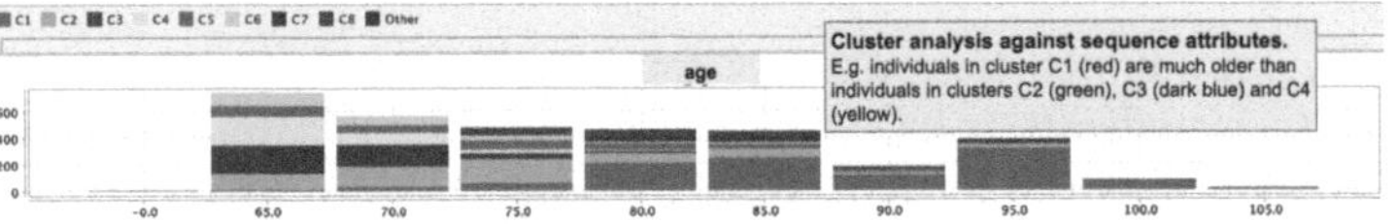

Fig. 4. Example of relationships exploration [6].

Relationships. Another benefit of VA lies in uncovering relationships among multiple attributes of the data (see Fig. 4). Through interactivity and specialized visual encodings, analysts can investigate dependencies, correlations, or temporal interactions between activities and cases. This exploratory capability supports hypothesis generation and can point to areas where algorithmic methods should be applied more systematically. The main risk is that heterogeneous and noisy datasets often contain coincidental or weak correlations. Without explicit representation of uncertainty or rigorous statistical grounding, analysts may over-interpret patterns that are in fact artifacts of the data. Misleading relationship visualizations may thus lead to premature or unsupported conclusions.

Comparisons. VA excels in supporting side-by-side comparisons of processes, subgroups, or variants (see Fig. 3(*right*). Coordinated and aligned visual views allow analysts to identify differences, and to investigate how these differences relate to multivariate attributes. Interactivity empowers analysts to choose what to compare, making the analysis flexible and user-driven. Yet comparisons can be difficult to sustain as data complexity grows. Large datasets with many cases and attributes often overwhelm visual interfaces, leading to clutter and loss of interpretability. In addition, if the provenance of analytical steps is not captured, comparisons may be difficult to reproduce or validate, raising concerns about transparency. Finally, failing to communicate uncertainty may lead to over- or underestimation of differences between subgroups.

Serendipity. VA encourages serendipitous discovery by supporting multiple perspectives and open-ended exploration. This capability is particularly valuable in PM, where rare or anomalous cases can reveal critical inefficiencies, compliance issues, or opportunities for process improvement. Analysts may identify unexpected behaviors that would remain hidden in more rigid, hypothesis-driven analyses. However, serendipity can also introduce risks. Noise in the data may be mistaken for insight, and open exploration can reinforce confirmation bias if findings are not critically validated. Without systematic provenance tracking, it may also be difficult to explain or replicate how a particular discovery was made.

Transparency and Interpretability. A key benefit of VA is its potential to enhance transparency and interpretability. By providing interactive visualizations, VA can make algorithmic analyses more accessible, empowering analysts. This human-centered approach aligns with PM's goal of actionable organizational insight. Nonetheless, transparency is not guaranteed. Complex visual encodings, scalability limitations, or poor design may reduce interpretability, especially for non-expert users. Misinterpretations of visual patterns may lead to misguided process interventions. Moreover, if user interactions are not systematically recorded, the exploration process lacks reproducibility, limiting both scientific validity and practical accountability.

3 Conclusions

VA strengthens PM by enhancing exploration, interpretation, and discovery, highlighting the promise of Visual Process Analytics (VPA) as a discipline. However, challenges remain, particularly regarding data quality, uncertainty, scalability, and heterogeneity. *Provenance* tracking and systematic *evaluation* are open research problems, complicating validation, reproducibility, and assessment of usability and insight generation. Addressing these challenges is crucial for realizing the full potential of VPA in both research and practice.

Acknowledgments. The author would like to thank the participants in Schloss Dagstuhl (Leibniz-Zentrum für Informatik), seminars 23271 "Human in the (Process) Mines" and 25152 "Multi-Faceted Visual Process Mining".

Disclosure of Interests. The author has no competing interests to declare that are relevant to the content of this article.

References

1. van der Aalst, W.M.P.: A practitioner s guide to process mining: limitations of the directly-follows graph. Procedia Comput. Sci. **164**, 321–328 (2019)
2. Aigner, W., Miksch, S., Schumann, H., Tominski, C.: Visualization of Time-Oriented Data, 2nd edn. Springer (2023). https://doi.org/10.1007/978-1-4471-7527-8
3. Andrienko, N., Andrienko, G., Fuchs, G., Slingsby, A., Turkay, C., Wrobel, S.: Visual Analytics for Data Scientists. Springer (2020). https://doi.org/10.1007/978-3-030-56146-8
4. Guo, Y., Guo, S., Jin, Z., Kaul, S., Gotz, D., Cao, N.: Event sequences viz browser (2020). http://eventvis.idvxlab.com/
5. Guo, Y., Guo, S., Jin, Z., Kaul, S., Gotz, D., Cao, N.: Survey on visual analysis of event sequence data. IEEE Trans. Vis. Comput. Graph. **28**(12), 5091–5112 (2022)
6. Magallanes, J., Stone, T., Morris, P.D., Mason, S., Wood, S., Villa-Uriol, M.C.: Sequen-C: a multilevel overview of temporal event sequences. IEEE Trans. Vis. Comput. Graph. **28**(1), 901–911 (2022)
7. Miksch, S., Di Ciccio, C., Soffer, P., Weber, B.: Visual analytics meets process mining: challenges and opportunities. IEEE Comput. Graph. **44**, 132–141 (2024)
8. Montana, L., et al.: EventBox: a novel visual encoding for interactive analysis of temporal and multivariate attributes in event sequences. IEEE Trans. Vis. Comput. Graph. (2025). https://doi.org/10.48550/arXiv.2507.14685. In press
9. Munzner, T.: Visualization Analysis and Design. CRC Press (2014)
10. Tominski, C., Aigner, W.: The TimeViz browser – a visual survey of visualization techniques for time-oriented data (2023). https://browser.timeviz.net. Version 2.0
11. Tominski, C., Schumann, H.: Interactive Visual Data Analysis. CRC Press (2020)
12. van den Elzen, S., et al.: Towards multi-faceted visual process analytics. Inf. Syst. **133**, 102560 (2025)
13. van der Linden, S., de Fouw, E., van den Elzen, S., et al.: A survey of visualization techniques for comparing event sequences. Comput. Graphics (2023)
14. Yeshchenko, A., Mendling, J.: A survey of approaches for event sequence analysis and visualization. Inf. Syst. **120**, 102283 (2024)
15. Zinat, K.T., Sakhamuri, S.N., Chen, A.S., Liu, Z.: A multi-level task framework for event sequence analysis. IEEE Trans. Visual Comput. Graphics **31**(1), 842–852 (2025). https://doi.org/10.1109/TVCG.2024.3456510

BP-Meet-IoT: a Look Back at the Past, the Present, and the Future

Estefanía Serral[1(✉)], Agnes Koschmider[2], and Victoria Torres[3]

[1] KU Leuven, Leuven, Belgium
estefania.serralasensio@kuleuven.be
[2] University of Bayreuth, Bayreuth, Germany
agnes.koschmider@uni-bayreuth.de
[3] Universitat Politècnica de València, Valencia, Spain
vtorres@upv.es

The Business Process Management and the Internet of Things (BP-Meet-IoT) workshop series established itself approximately ten years ago as a platform for exploring the intersection of Business Process Management (BPM) and the Internet of Things (IoT). The workshop idea originated in a Dagstuhl seminar in 2016 and since then, the workshop has grown into a format bringing an audience to discuss a wide range of topics at the intersection of BPM and IoT. The founding of the BP-Meet-IoT workshop evolved at a time when the IoT and BPM domains themselves were mature, but its intersection remained largely unexplored. The workshop aimed to bring together the community to discuss the challenges and opportunities presented by this new paradigm. From its inception, the focus was on integrating process modeling, analysis, and automation with the specific requirements and possibilities of IoT environments. The increasing use of IoT devices, the growing complexity of interconnected systems, and the need for efficient process automation called for related research. The BPM IoT manifest [17] has become a frequently cited reference. Within the manifest that summarizes the key concepts, challenges, and future directions for combining BPM and IoT, the focus was on leveraging data from connected devices to automate, monitor, and optimize business processes.

An advantage of integrating BPM with IoT lies in the mutual relationship between data acquisition and process control. IoT devices generate a high volume of (real-time) data reflecting the execution of underlying business processes. This data provides opportunities to automate process activities and proactively identify and address bottlenecks. Furthermore, the data provided by IoT is suited for process mining (PM) allowing efficient process discovery, conformance checking and analysis of activities that may not have been explicitly modeled. In contrast, BPM provides the foundation for controlling the flow of data generated by IoT devices. By applying BPM principles such as process modeling, workflow automation, and performance monitoring organizations can ensure the compliance of IoT-driven processes, transforming raw data into efficient decision making.

During the last 9 workshop editions, the following topics have been discussed, offering a good overview of the status and evolution of the research performed at the intersection of BPM and IoT:

I. van de Weerd et al. (Eds.): BPM 2025 Workshops, LNBIP 569, pp. 603–606, 2026.
https://doi.org/10.1007/978-3-032-13426-4_45

- **Mining Daily Living Activities:** Among the earliest workshop threads, researchers leveraged IoT datasets on daily routines in smart spaces to apply PM techniques [1,2]. Having datasets collected by IoT was, and unfortunately still is, an issue [12]. However, back in 2017 when the workshop started, there were already a few IoT datasets collecting data on daily habits in smart spaces, which enabled early investigations. The BPM community leveraged therefore this opportunity applying PM techniques to mine daily living activities from these datasets [1,2,18]. Although different challenges needed to be addressed before applying standard PM techniques (e.g., lack of a Case ID, abstraction gap between IoT sensor data and BP data, ...), several works successfully extracted meaningful activities, including recent advances on human routines and habit discovery and consolidated research challenges [9,12] while explicitly addressing abstraction issues discussed in the broader PM literature [22,26].
- **Bridging Abstraction Levels:** The difference in conceptual abstraction between IoT events and process events is a well-known challenge for the IoT-BP community [22,26]. Several authors have proposed different data models to conceptualize the issue, converting many of them into data formats capable of storing IoT BP event logs [7,16,19]. Led by Prof. Serral and Prof. Bertrand, the different groups working on this topic joined forces to create a core IoT-centric log format to enable reusability and standardization [15]. Also, many authors have tried to bridge the abstraction level gap by using different techniques, starting with rule/CEP-style approaches [22] and moving to more advanced ones such as motif-based methods [7] and, more recently, LLM-based methods [8]. Industrial-strength extraction pipelines for turning raw sensor streams into event logs further operationalize this bridge [9].
- **Process contextualization:** Incorporating the execution context perspective into the BP view has also been a topic of discussion. Several conceptualizations have been presented at the workshop [2,9] and different techniques have been implemented to mine process models that are context-dependent, such as contextualized process discovery with activity hierarchies [11].
- **IoT Process Modelling, Simulation, Execution and Evolution.** Besides IoT BP mining, other phases of the BPM cycle have been addressed in the workshop editions and beyond; several modelling languages have been proposed, using standard languages such as BPMN 2.0, extending standard languages, or proposing new languages [4,23,24]. Some of these languages have also been extended offer IoT BP simulation and execution [4,23–25], or even their evolution at runtime [5,21].
- **IoT Scenarios:** Many different scenarios have been used to showcase the research done at the intersection of BPM and IoT, starting with smart spaces such as smart homes, smart offices or smart universities [2,12]; moving towards smart industry cases and construction [4,8]; and other innovative and surprising cases such as the study of pigs or bees' behaviour [10,20], alongside sectoral applications like cattle farming and manual process discovery [3].
- **IoT Process Visualization and Object-centric logs** have also been touched upon in the workshop, reflecting the new research directions. Recent

work includes methods to identify process activities by visualizing sensor events [6], as well as novel object-centric approaches for handling concurrency in IoT-aware processes [7]. Additionally, a core metamodel for IoT-enhanced event logs has been introduced to support interoperability and scalability across domains [36].
- **Advanced PM Approaches:** in the last years, different advanced approaches have been developed dealing with the inherent challenges of IoT event logs or their combination with process event logs. These approaches consider the challenges posed by such processes using the latest technological advances, such as a multi-perspective trace clustering technique for IoT-enhanced processes in smart manufacturing [13], real-time PM across the edge-cloud continuum [9], or predictive process monitoring for IoT processes [14].

In this keynote, we reflected on the evolution and consolidation of the BP-Meet-IoT community, which for almost a decade has served as a reference forum to discuss the challenges and opportunities at the intersection of BPM and IoT. The session provided an overview of the main achievements reached so far, while also highlighting open challenges related to the topics discussed above.

As a natural continuation of these reflections, we also introduced a new collaborative initiative aimed at identifying and prioritizing the key research challenges that will shape the BP-Meet-IoT agenda in the coming years. This initiative is structured in several phases: first, the collection of challenges and problem proposals from community members, followed by a community voting process to select the most relevant ones. For each selected challenge, a dedicated working group will be created with the goal of preparing short joint contributions. These contributions will then be integrated into a collective publication that will serve as a shared reference point for the field.

The timeline foresees clear milestones: challenge submission in October 2025, community voting and challenge selection in early November, the creation of working groups by mid-November, and the submission of short papers in April 2026. Subsequently, during the next edition of the workshop in Toronto (September 2026), a dedicated session will be held to discuss the results, whose synthesis will feed into a joint journal article. To further stimulate engagement, the initiative will also include a system of recognition through "badges", rewarding groups for their activity and achievements. Through this initiative, our aim is not only to continue the conversation started during the workshop, but also to structure a sustained collaborative effort that enhances both the visibility and the impact of research at the crossroads of BPM and IoT.

References

1. 1st International Workshop on Business Process Management and the Internet of Things (BP-Meet-IoT). BPM 2017 (2017)
2. 2nd International Workshop on BP-Meet-IoT. BPM 2018 (2018)
3. 3rd International Workshop on BP-Meet-IoT. BPM 2019 (2019)

4. 4th International Workshop on BP-Meet-IoT. BPM 2020 (2020)
5. 5th International Workshop on BP-Meet-IoT. BPM 2021 (2021)
6. 6th International Workshop on BP-Meet-IoT. BPM 2022 (2022)
7. 7th International Workshop on BP-Meet-IoT. BPM 2023 (2023)
8. 8th International Workshop on BP-Meet-IoT. BPM 2024 (2024)
9. 9th International Workshop on BP-Meet-IoT. BPM 2025 (2025)
10. Ahmadi, Z., Bertrand, Y.: Pozo Romero, M.I., Serral, E.: Analysing the foraging behaviour of bees using process mining: a case study. In: ICPM Workshops 2023. LNBIP, vol. 503, pp. 5–18. Springer, Cham (2024)
11. Ahmadi, Z., De Weerdt, J., Serral Asensio, E.: Context-driven process discovery: enhancing process flow interpretability with contextualized activity hierarchies. Softw. Syst. Model. (SoSyM) (2025)
12. Bertrand, Y., Van den Abbeele, B., Veneruso, S., Leotta, F., Mecella, M., Serral, E.: A survey on the application of process discovery techniques to smart spaces data. Eng. Appl. Artif. Intell. **126**, 106748 (2023)
13. Bertrand, Y., De Weerdt, J., Serral, E.: A novel multi-perspective trace clustering technique for IoT-enhanced processes: a case study in smart manufacturing. In: BPM (2023)
14. Bertrand, Y., Stevens, A., Deforce, B., De Smedt, J., De Weerdt, J., Serral, E.: Approaches for IoT-enhanced predictive process monitoring. Process Sci. (2025)
15. Bertrand, Y., et al.: An object-centric core metamodel for IoT-enhanced event logs. arXiv preprint (2025)
16. Bertrand, Y., Veneruso, S., Leotta, F., Mecella, M., Serral, E.: NICE: The native IoT-centric event log model for process mining. In: ICPM Workshops 2023. LNBIP, vol. 503, pp. 32–44. Springer, Cham (2024)
17. Janiesch, C., et al.: The internet of things meets business process management: a manifesto. IEEE Syst. Man Cybern. Mag. **6**(4), 34–44 (2020)
18. Janssen, D., Mannhardt, F., Koschmider, A., van Zelst, S.J.: Process model discovery from sensor event data. In: Leemans, S., Leopold, H. (eds.) ICPM 2020. LNBIP, vol. 406, pp. 69–81. Springer, Cham (2021). https://doi.org/10.1007/978-3-030-72693-5_6
19. Mangler, J., et al.: DataStream XES extension: embedding IoT sensor data into extensible event stream logs. Future Internet **15**(3), 109 (2023)
20. Melfsen, A., Lepsien, A., Bosselmann, J., Koschmider, A., Hartung, E.: Describing behavior sequences of fattening pigs using process mining on video data and automated pig behavior recognition. Agriculture **13**(8), 1639 (2023)
21. Serral Asensio, E.: Automating routine tasks in smart environments: a context-aware model-driven approach. Ph.D. thesis, UPV (2011)
22. Soffer, P., et al.: From event streams to process models and back: challenges and opportunities. Inf. Syst. **81**, 181–200 (2019)
23. Torres, V., Serral, E., Valderas, P., Pelechano, V., Grefen, P.: Modeling of IoT devices in business processes: a systematic mapping study. In: 22nd IEEE Conference on Business Informatics (CBI 2020), pp. 221–230. IEEE (2020)
24. Valderas, P., Torres, V., Serral, E.: Modelling and executing IoT-enhanced business processes through BPMN and microservices. J. Syst. Softw. **184**, 111139 (2022)
25. Veneruso, S., Bertrand, Y., Leotta, F., Serral, E., Mecella, M.: A model-based simulator for smart homes: enabling reproducibility and standardization. J. Ambient Intell. Smart Environ. (2023)
26. van Zelst, S.J., Mannhardt, F., de Leoni, M., Koschmider, A.: Event abstraction in process mining: literature review and taxonomy. Granular Comput. **6**(3), 719–736 (2021)

Author Index

A
Alpers, Sascha 492
Amyot, Daniel 82, 451
Andreswari, Rachmadita 438
Atwi, Hassan 311

B
Bala, Saimir 28
Berti, Alessandro 412
Bertrand, Yannis 199
Bouattane, El Mostafa 451
Bozorgi, Zahra Dasht 274
Brachmann, Tobias 582
Brekke, Kristoffer Alves 374
Brissard, Alexis 55
Broucke, Seppe vanden 41
Brurok, Lasse 374
Brzychczy, Edyta 232
Burattin, Andrea 549

C
Calegari, Daniel 139
Ceravolo, Paolo 94
Chan, Vito 467
Chapela-Campa, David 3
Ciftci, Seyyid A. 109
Contestabile, Matilde 516
Costa, Ana 425
Cuppens, Frédéric 55

D
Damiani, Ernesto 94
De Smedt, Johannes 274
De Weerdt, Jochen 274
Delgado, Andrea 139
Denisov, Vadim 479
Donadello, Ivan 249
Dumas, Marlon 3, 531

E
Ebert, Lennart 467
Elhami, Erfan 82
Enríquez, J. G. 127

F
Fahland, Dirk 479
Fahrenkrog-Petersen, Stephan A. 467
Fernandes, Ricardo M. F. 345
Fernández, Antonio M. Gutiérrez 345
Ferrara, Chiara 516
Flisikowski, Karol 360

G
Gerolami, Emilio 139
Giaccio, Romina 139
Giovannetti, Alberto 516
Grigore, Iuliana Malina 15
Grzesiak, Marzena 360

H
Haase, Jennifer 438
Halvorsrud, Ragnhild 374
Hasselbring, Wilhelm 217
He, Xiaomeng 41
Hillmann, Paul-Julius 467
Houshidari, Alireza 451

I
Imenkamp, Christian 217

J
Janiesch, Christian 109
Jans, Mieke 187
Jarijch, Dries 187
Jessen, Urszula 232
Jiménez-Ramírez, A. 127
Johnson, Ethan 69
Junior, Sylvio Barbon 15

I. van de Weerd et al. (Eds.): BPM 2025 Workshops, LNBIP 569, pp. 607–609, 2026.
https://doi.org/10.1007/978-3-032-13426-4

K
Kalenkova, Anna 69
Kluza, Krzysztof 232
Köpke, Julius 303
Koren, István 582
Koschmider, Agnes 603
Kourani, Humam 412
Koytek, Philipp 557
Kurowski, Kelly 155

L
Landsiedel, Olaf 217
Leribaux, Aurélie 274
Liss, Lukas 582
Löhr, Bernd 288
Lu, Xixi 155

M
Maggi, Fabrizio Maria 249
Mahendrawathi, E. R. 387
Maldonado, Andrea 217
Mannhardt, Felix 374
Meironas, Otas 374
Mendling, Jan 187, 438, 467
Miksch, Silvia 549
Milani, Fredrik 3
Mitchell, Lewis 69
Montana, Luis 573
Moszyński, Marek 360
Moyano, Cielo González 438

N
Nettelnstroth, Manuel Vargas 232

O
Oukharijane, Jamila 249
Ouyang, Chun 199
Oyamada, Rafael 274

P
Park, Gyunam 412
Parrillo, Giovanni 516
Parschew, Nastasja Stephanie 28
Pasquadibisceglie, Vincenzo 15
Pautasso, Cesare 311
Pernici, Barbara 531
Polyvyanyy, Artem 274
Pufahl, Luise 425

R
Rathje, Patrick 217
Rebmann, Adrian 405
Reijers, Hajo A. 155, 262
Reiter, Hendrik 217
Resinas, Manuel 573
Revoredo, Kate 438
Rodríguez-Ruiz, A. 127
Rubensson, Christoffer 467
Ruhsam, Christoph 345

S
Sadiq, Shazia 549, 557
Sahling, Kristina 438
Salamov, Musa 531
Schüler, Selina 492
Schulz, Hans-Jörg 549
Senkus, Piotr 360
Serral, Estefanía 603
Shabira, Rinda Faiz 387
Skolik, Alexander 171, 288
Sliż, Piotr 360
Smedt, Johannes De 41
Soffer, Pnina 557
Sriram, Sridhar 232
Stiehle, Fabian 327
Syahputra, Muhammad Febrilian Dwi 387
Szelągowski, Marek 345, 360

T
Tavares, Gabriel Marques 15
Torres, Victoria 603

V
van der Aalst, Wil M. P. 412, 582
van der Waal, Wouter 262
van Gansewinkel, Sander 479
Van Woensel, William 82, 451
Vandin, Andrea 516
Villa-Uriol, Maria-Cruz 573, 598
Vrotsou, Katerina 549, 557

W
Wang, Fang 94
Weber, Barbara 557
Weber, Ingo 327
Weerdt, Jochen De 41
Wei, Jia 199

Weytjens, Hans 327
Wimmer, Alena 425
Winter, Karolin 507

Z
Zimmermann, Lisa 557
Zouaq, Amal 55

The manufacturer's authorised representative in the EU is Springer Nature Customer Service Centre GmbH, Europaplatz 3, 69115 Heidelberg, Germany. If you have any concerns regarding our products, please contact ProductSafety@springernature.com

Printed and bound by CPI Group (UK) Ltd, Croydon, CR0 4YY

07/07/2026

02160906-0020